ADVANCE PRAISE FOR *FIDELITY & CONSTRAINT*

"Yet another liberal originalist has come out of the closet and I say: Welcome to the club! But Larry Lessig is a liberal originalist with a twist. Make that many twists. In this provocative and panoramic book he serves up a veritable smorgasbord of original ideas about originalism. This is definitely not your father's originalism—not Originalism 1.0 or even 2.0 or 3.0. More like Originalism $\pi^2$. Actually, it's not fair to pigeonhole Lessig as a mere liberal. A cultural hero of today's Left who once clerked for Justice Right (Antonin Scalia), Lessig is rightly renowned for his intellectual independence, range, and iconoclasm, all of which are on full display here, as is his extraordinary intellectual generosity: He paints strikingly sympathetic portraits of justices across the spectrum and across the centuries."

—**Akhil Reed Amar**, Sterling Professor of Law and Political Science, Yale University

"Lessig's examination of Supreme Court Constitutional interpretation is a tour de force. While nearly every Supreme Court Justice has appreciated the importance of fidelity to the Constitution, Lessig observes, Constitutional adjudication is a product of two competing fidelities: fidelity to meaning and fidelity to judicial role. Further, every text including the Constitution is written and interpreted against a background that is inevitably and appropriately determined by history. In each period Justices responded not only to their understanding of the Constitutional document, but also to their own social, economic and philosophical world views. This makes universal theories of interpretation impossible. There is no holy grail. This book is a novel approach to understanding the meaning of the United States Constitution across the history of Supreme Court interpretation. People of every political stripe who take Constitutional interpretation seriously should read it."

—**Herbert Hovenkamp**, James G. Dinan University Professor, University of Pennsylvania School of Law and The Wharton School

Fidelity & Constraint

LAWRENCE
LESSIG

# Fidelity & Constraint

*How the Supreme Court Has*
*Read the American Constitution*

OXFORD
UNIVERSITY PRESS

# OXFORD
UNIVERSITY PRESS

Oxford University Press is a department of the University of Oxford.
It furthers the University's objective of excellence in research, scholarship,
and education by publishing worldwide. Oxford is a registered trade mark of
Oxford University Press in the UK and certain other countries.

Published in the United States of America by Oxford University Press
198 Madison Avenue, New York, NY 10016, United States of America.

Library of Congress Cataloging-in-Publication Data

Names: Lessig, Lawrence, author.
Title: Fidelity & constraint : how the Supreme Court has read the
    American constitution / Lawrence Lessig.
Other titles: Fidelity and constraint
Description: New York, NY : Oxford University Press, 2019.
Identifiers: LCCN 2018059943 | ISBN 9780190945664 (hardback) |
    ISBN 9780190932572 (electronic publication)
Subjects: LCSH: Constitutional law—United States. | Law—United States—
    Interpretation and construction. | United States. Supreme Court. |
    BISAC: LAW / General. | LAW / Constitutional. | LAW / Government / Federal.
Classification: LCC KF4550 .L44 2019 | DDC 342.73—dc23 LC record available at
    https://lccn.loc.gov/2018059943

9 8 7 6 5 4 3 2 1

Printed by Sheridan Books, Inc., United States of America

*To Patricia West Lessig*

# CONTENTS

Fidelity & Constraint

# Introduction

WHEN I WAS AT COLLEGE, I worked for an econometrician. Then a professor at the University of Pennsylvania, Yacov Sheinin had been hired by Nobel Prize–winning economist Lawrence Klein to build a mini growth model of the United States economy. I had been Sheinin's student in macroeconomics. I was a good student. He asked me to work for Klein's firm, Wharton Econometrics Forecasting Associates (WEFA).

The job of econometrics is to use data to build more robust and testable theories of economic behavior. Econometricians collect a massive amount of data and then run regressions to discover connections between one variable and another. Does a rise in the money supply explain a rise in inflation? Does an increase in government spending explain a fall in unemployment? There are a million theories about how one part of the economy might relate to another. The job of econometrics is to test those theories to see just how much they might actually explain.

But the theory part is important. Once I had learned how to run the software that ran the regressions, I spent a whole day running all the regressions I could think of. WEFA had a massive database of every economic variable one could imagine. It was trivially simple to type an equation into the terminal and see how well one thing linked with something else. Did the number of votes for Republicans link with the growth of GDP? Did the number of Democrats in Congress link to a rise or fall in unemployment? I had a million questions I wanted to test. And on the Monday after my regression marathon, I presented a bunch of "equations" that "proved" various crazy theories that I wanted to prove.

Working in the same team were two graduate students getting their PhDs in economics. I presented my findings to one, John Greene. Greene laughed and told me, "Look, what you've got here are correlations. But a correlation is nothing without a theory to explain why it might also suggest causation. Numbers without theory are just junk." (And expensive junk, I learned: I hadn't realized that the firm was charged per regression run!) The correlations were fun. (Indeed, there's a great website that collects spurious correlations.)[1] But alone, they showed nothing.

Over the next three years I worked for WEFA on and off. After I graduated, I worked for Sheinin after he returned to Tel Aviv University in Israel. That experience—of building and testing economic models—gave me a kind of intuition. It was my practice—a million times over—to take a massive amount of data and test a theory by building equations that aimed to explain the underlying behavior. With each estimate, the question was the same— how much of the variation could the model explain? And though there were many statistics we used to answer that question, the crudest (and coolest) was R-squared. If we could produce a high R-squared, say 95, then we could say that 95 percent of the variance in the dependent variable was explained by the equation we'd developed. Again, that wasn't enough to say anything interesting. The equation needed to fit within a theory. But if you had a theory and an equation that tested it, and that equation was populated with variables, each considered significant, then a high R-squared was gold.

It has been more than a generation since I have estimated an equation in economics, or tried to build, or even understand, an econometric model. But this book is a kind of econometrics brought to constitutional theory. Not literally—there are no equations or statistics anywhere in these pages—but figuratively. My aim here is to understand the history of constitutional interpretation by the United States Supreme Court in the way an econometrician would try to model an economy. Following the approach of the late Ronald Dworkin, who himself followed the philosophy of Donald Davidson, my aim is to provide an account that fits the data—the decisions by the U.S. Supreme Court—while justifying the practice these data reveal. I want a model that describes the moving parts of American constitutional interpretation. And I want to test that model by asking whether it fits the history, and then if it does, whether it can be justified normatively, given at least the explicit commitments of our constitutional tradition.

This is a very particular kind of interpretive practice, and I mean to approach it in a very particular way. In the course of this book, reviewing broad swaths of American constitutional history, I introduce a model that I believe fits the practice of the Supreme Court as it has interpreted our Constitution.

That model is relatively simple, and I apply it in a range of different contexts. Not in every context—I leave many important domains of constitutional law untouched. But at least for the fields I do review (and also, I believe, for the domains I do not review) there is a pattern we can capture through this model.

Once that survey is complete, I then shift to the justification. What does this model say about the work of the Supreme Court? Would the drafters of a constitution actually choose this practice as their own? Would we? Can, in other words, a practice so understood be justified?

It will be no surprise that I believe it can.[2] One doesn't publish a book about a theory one thinks is unjustified. But I do believe that the model I describe here is one we should be happy to embrace, given two critical facts about our Constitution—first, that it is old, and second, that it is practically unamendable. Those two conditions mean I am talking about our Constitution now and saying nothing about whether this model makes sense of, or for, other constitutions with other constraints.

In the (way too many) years that I have been thinking and talking about this theory, I have come to recognize many common strategies for resisting it. For example: In articulating the model, I introduce new variables (new moving parts) along the way. With each introduction, some may be tempted to charge, "This is merely a just-so theory." But of course, every empirical (in the broad sense that I mean) theory is a just-so theory. The question is whether there's a better theory, with fewer moving parts, that can explain the data better and still remain justified.

Likewise, as you work through my account, it may strike you as a kind of "originalism," meaning a theory or an approach to constitutional law that gives special weight to the words or meaning (or, for some originalists, the intent) of the drafters of a constitution or amendments to a constitution.[3] That's true—the model is, in an important sense, originalist. But my claim is that it is originalist in precisely the way necessary to explain a wide range of actual decisions by the Supreme Court. And while one may (with good reason) reject originalism, my claim, if I'm correct, is that you can't simultaneously reject originalism and explain what the Supreme Court has actually done.

Finally, you might be driven to ask (if you're like the majority of the people to whom I've sketched out this theory) whether the theory is falsifiable. Is there a way in which it could be proven wrong? Or is it, by definition, always going to be right?

Again, if you understand the approach, the answer to that question is obvious as well. Conceptually, the data I'm trying to explain is the evolution of the Supreme Court's interpretation of the provisions of our Constitution.

Though that data is not like the history of interest rates or the money supply (and that second group of data is not like the history of temperatures in Key West or sunset times in Juneau, Alaska), I am assuming there's an understanding of that evolution that I am trying to fit. Looking backward, the ideal would be an account that would fit everything. Of course, that's not possible (and I don't pretend to get close here), but that's the ideal. And even if we achieved that ideal, then certainly, going forward, one might see decisions by the Supreme Court that are inconsistent with what the theory would predict.

That inconsistency, in turn, will demonstrate either that the theory is incomplete or that the Court is changing its practice—not in a single case or a single term, but across a range of cases over time. Nothing that I'm describing here should be understood to be forever. At most, I'm offering a "here's the game we've been playing so far" account of our Court's past. But of course, the Court is perfectly free (or at least free enough now) to change that game.

Throughout, however, there is a framing norm to the enterprise of this sort of theory building—the norm that Davidson called a principle of charity. It is critically important to understand what that norm is and is not.

The principle of charity here says that when we try to understand what the Supreme Court has done, we assume the very best of the justices on that Court. (As the philosopher Simon Blackburn defines the principle, in contexts of doubt it requires interpretations that "maximize the truth or rationality in the subject's sayings.")[4] That is, we assume they are doing their best as judges, and we assume they are not compromising their work with inappropriate or improper considerations. That's not to assume they are Hercules.[5] Justices of the Supreme Court are quintessentially human. And by assuming the very best, I am not asserting that the justices actually were behaving in the very best way possible. The principle of charity, in other words, is not a representation about the world. It is a frame for understanding a different people.

There are other accounts of the Court's history that don't embrace this principle. Empirical legal and political historians, for example, have built elaborate models that try to predict the decisions of the Court based only upon the political views of the justices or the politics of the cases.[6] Those accounts are similarly holistic. They are more authentically econometric.

Yet in the end, I believe they miss something in the dynamic of how legal doctrine evolves. They certainly miss something in the lived experience of justices and the people working with them. The very best, most self-respecting judges don't approach their work as though they were party hacks. Nor must we assume that they are in order to understand what they've done.

So here, then, is the simple requirement that I insist you embrace as we work through this story of American constitutional law: Put your politics in a box and lock it away. Don't approach this story from the Left or the Right; approach it as an enlightened anthropologist would, and listen, engage, and try to understand it as the work of judges trying to do the best they can do at the time in which they work.

When you listen like this, you will hear a story that is at once more interesting and more edifying. And you will see something of the potential for constitutionalism, at least in the place America's Constitution now finds itself.

## Plan of the Book

I begin in Part I with an understanding of interpretive fidelity. How is meaning made? How does it change? These are questions asked not before the altar of philosophy or political science but through a practice that our Supreme Court has engaged.

That practice is at its core a kind of translation. It is the effort to preserve a foundational value across contexts that change in ways no Framer ever imagined. In Part II, I describe that practice, both on the Right (Section 1) and on the Left (Section 3). I describe as well a set of cases that don't read easily on either the Right or the Left (Section 2).

In each case, that practice will reveal a dance between two very different conceptions of fidelity: fidelity to meaning and fidelity to role. Doctrine on the Right, on the Left, and in the middle moves as these two fidelities dance sometimes with and sometimes against each other.

To make this account understandable, I must go deep in some places, while I can remain near the surface in others. To see the translation on the Right takes extra work. That part is therefore longer than I wish it had to be. To see the constraint of role on the Left takes a great deal of extra work. That part must work extra hard to recover an understanding of the critical history after the Civil War. But there are parts that move much more quickly—and, given the extraordinary scholarship that marks this field, probably too quickly, as too much is passed over without notice or even a note. The repetitions of translation on the Right are easy to see once the first pattern is set. And the evolution of equality through sex and sexual orientation is easy to discern once the pattern is seen clearly in the context of race.

Part III then turns to the challenges of justification. The practice this book reveals is not obvious. It was not planned. It requires a justification if it is to sustain its vitality, especially within the highly partisan moment we find ourselves in now. That justification as well moves too quickly, and too impressionistically. My aim, however, is not to prove; it is to suggest what a proof would look like. So I begin by mapping the strongest competing theory for a normative account of the history of our legal tradition, which is Bruce Ackerman's. I then draw the contrast between the account offered here and his, to the end of offering an alternative to the most difficult parts of his that is more consistent with the history of our Supreme Court, especially the more recent history.

I end the book not confident that the dynamic within the Supreme Court I have described will survive. This is an edifying account; yet that is no guarantee that the practice it describes *can* survive. My money is against it. My hope is that I am wrong—wrong, that is, about the future, not about our past.

PART ONE | Elements

CHAPTER ONE | Text and Context

T HE AMERICAN CONSTITUTION is seven articles and twenty-seven
    amendments long. Article V describes the process by which the Consti-
tution gets amended:

> The Congress, whenever two thirds of both Houses shall deem it
> necessary, shall propose Amendments to this Constitution, or, on the
> Application of the Legislature of two thirds of the several States, shall
> call a Convention for proposing Amendments, which, in either Case,
> shall be valid to all Intents and Purposes, as Part of this Constitution,
> when ratified by the Legislatures of three fourths of the several States, or
> by Conventions in three fourths thereof, as the one or the other Mode
> of Ratification may be proposed by the Congress.

Pretty dense stuff, at least on first read. Yet if you tease the bits apart, the
paths are pretty clear.

Amendments come in two steps—first a proposal, then a ratification. The
proposal is made either by Congress or by a convention. The ratification is
made either by state legislatures or by state conventions. All the amendments
to our Constitution have been proposed by Congress. All but one have been
ratified by state legislatures. (The Twenty-first Amendment, repealing prohibition, was ratified by state conventions—giving state legislators an easy
escape from the anger of the prohibitionists.)

So imagine that frustration with the way political campaigns are financed
in America reaches a boiling point (finally). The people want change.
Decisions by the United States Supreme Court have limited the scope of

possible change. Leaders of reform movements advance an amendment to overcome those limits. That amendment provides as follows:

1. Congress shall fund federal elections publicly, in a manner and at a level determined by a Federal Elections Board.

2. Nothing in this Constitution shall be construed to restrict the power of the Federal Elections Board or the states to limit, in a viewpoint-neutral way, (a) the period of campaigning for any elective office, (b) the size of contributions to any campaign, or (c) the size of contributions to any independent political action committee.

3. The Federal Elections Board shall consist of five members, appointed by the president for seven-year terms. Appointees must have served as federal judges for at least five years and shall be compensated at the level of a justice on the Supreme Court. The board shall also specify levels of public funding to ensure an adequate opportunity for candidates to be competitive in federal elections. The board shall recommend rules to govern federal elections, which shall be considered law unless Congress rejects such rules within 180 days of their proposal.

Organizers backing this amendment succeed in getting it on the ballot in fifty states—in some states through referendum procedures, in others by a special act of the state legislature allowing voters to vote on the referendum. Imagine finally that the amendment receives overwhelming popular support—80 percent of those voting (in the nation as a whole, but not necessarily 80 percent in each state) vote to support the amendment.

Is this amendment—which more than three-fourths of American voters support—part of the Constitution?

Students of American constitutional law will recognize this as a version of my teacher Akhil Amar's puzzle.[1] Let's consider what this puzzle teaches.

Applying the text of the Constitution, the answer seems pretty easy. The amendment was not proposed by either Congress or a convention. Neither was it ratified by either state legislatures or state conventions. And though at least three-fourths of voters supported it, it's not clear from the facts that a majority in each of thirty-eight states (three-fourths of the fifty states) supported it—it could have won big in some states but not in others. In just about every possible way, this amendment fails the requirements of the text of Article V. Thus, according to the Article V police, this amendment would not be part of our Constitution.

Yet my question was not whether the amendment complied with the rules of Article V. My question was whether it is part of the Constitution. Could it become part of the Constitution even though it fails to follow the rule specified in Article V?

The very question is likely to annoy. "Obviously," the annoyed sorts repl "an 'amendment' that fails to satisfy the rules of the Constitution is not part of the Constitution. That's why there are *rules*: to help us see which bits are included and which bits are not. This bit, however sensible, however popularly supported, has not satisfied the requirements of those rules. Therefore, this bit is not part of the Constitution."

It's a perfectly understandable response. But hold that happy certainty for a second and consider a bit of our Constitution's history.

In 1787, America had a constitution. It was just not the Constitution that we have today. America then was governed by the Articles of Confederation. Adopted by all thirteen colonies in 1781, the Articles of Confederation and Perpetual Union erected a government—basically a Congress—charged with regulating to America's mutual benefit.

But in 1787, that government was dying. The nation that had four years earlier beaten the British, the most powerful empire in the world, was quickly falling apart. As law professor Calvin Johnson recounts, "In the wording of the time, the federal government was 'imbecilic' and 'impotent.'"[2] Its orders were ignored. Its treasury was empty. In 1786, Congress's requisition to the states (basically its bill for services rendered) required the states to contribute $3.8 million to the United States treasury. Of that, $663 was paid.[3]

Many thought the only remedy for this failing republic was to amend the Articles of Confederation. One of those articles specified the procedure for amendment—a procedure much simpler than the one specified in our own Constitution. As it stated:

> And the Articles of this confederation shall be inviolably observed by every state, and the union shall be perpetual; nor shall any alteration at any time hereafter be made in any of them; unless such alteration be agreed to in a congress of the united states and be afterwards confirmed by the legislatures of every state.

Thus, the rules as of 1787: "any alteration" (that is, an amendment) had to "be agreed to in a congress of the united states." And then once agreed to by that "congress," it must be "confirmed by the legislatures of every state."

Again: "every state," not three-fourths of the states. "By the legislatures" of "every state," not by state conventions. Proposed by "a congress" only, not by either "a congress" or "a convention." And finally, according to the plain language of this very clear text, unless unanimity was achieved, the articles would remain as they were, "perpetual[ly]."

By 1786, every sane soul was beginning to recognize that the young nation was falling apart. Virginia recommended that states send delegates to a meeting in Annapolis, Maryland, to "Consider and Recommend a Federal Plan for Regulating Commerce"—just one of the unresolved problems facing the new nation.[4] Five states showed up at that meeting, which was not enough for a quorum. And after hanging about for less than a week, the delegates from those states decided they would adjourn rather than waste more time.[5]

But before they left, the delegates decided to make a statement. Without any real authority—again, a quorum hadn't shown up—they told Congress that they thought there should be a new convention, with a broader mandate, to address the question of how best to save the union. They proposed that convention be held in May 1787, in Philadelphia.

That was September 14, 1786. Six months later, and long after the project was in motion, Congress endorsed the idea of a convention "to devise such further provisions as shall appear to them necessary to render the constitution of the Federal Government adequate to the exigencies of the Union."[6]

When the convention met in Philadelphia, among its the first decisions was to make the proceedings of the convention secret. The delegates then proceeded to exceed the terms of their charge—willfully and intentionally. Rather than propose amendments to the old constitution, they decided to draft something brand-new. This new constitution conflicted with the Articles of Confederation. To adopt it was, in effect, to "alter" or "amend" (in the sense of reject) the Articles of Confederation.

So how did the convention purport to bring about this amendment? What procedure did it propose to follow?

Our Constitution may be unclear on many points. On this point, however, it is crystal clear. Article VII of the Constitution states: "The Ratification of the Conventions of nine States, shall be sufficient for the Establishment of this Constitution between the States so ratifying the Same." If your math is a bit fuzzy or if you're not up on early American history, in 1787 "nine states" was not "every state." The "conventions of nine states" was not "the legislature of every state." Finally, and obviously, the Philadelphia convention was not "a congress of the united states." At every point, the new constitution violated the terms of the old.[7] Which then prompts the obvious question: is the Constitution constitutional?

If you were impatient before, you are likely even more impatient now. "Come on," you'll insist, "you're not saying the Constitution is unconstitutional, are you? And anyway, the Articles of Confederation had failed. Why would you think that the Constitution would need to be justified in terms of the Articles of Confederation?"

I'm not arguing that the Constitution is unconstitutional. It isn't, and certainly it wasn't. My point is very different. My aim is to get you to reflect on exactly *why* our illegally ratified Constitution is nonetheless legally our Constitution.

The reason is exactly the reason offered by those defending the new Constitution against the charge of those who said it violated the Articles of Confederation.[8] That reason drew its inspiration from the words of the Declaration of Independence. As Thomas Jefferson had famously penned:

> We hold these truths to be self-evident, that all men are created equal, that they are endowed by their Creator with certain unalienable Rights, that among these are Life, Liberty and the pursuit of Happiness,—That to secure these rights, Governments are instituted among Men, deriving their just powers from the consent of the governed,—That whenever any Form of Government becomes destructive of these ends, it is the Right of the People to alter or to abolish it, and to institute new Government, laying its foundation on such principles and organizing its powers in such form, as to them shall seem most likely to effect their Safety and Happiness.[9]

Jefferson was pointing to a "right," one that he characterized as "unalienable." (In correspondence with John Cartright, Jefferson wrote, "Nothing then is unchangeable but the inherent and unalienable rights of man.")[10] That right is for the people to alter a form of government whenever that form becomes "destructive" of the proper ends of government. Certainly, the Framers believed the Articles of Confederation had become destructive in that sense. Thus, this rule, if valid, would entitle the Framers to abolish the Articles of Confederation and move on. According to this rule, Article XIII, despite sounding exclusive, was not to be read as exclusive.[11] As Federalist historian David Ramsay wrote in 1791:

> It is true, from the infancy of political knowledge in the United States, there were many defects in their [state] forms of government; but in one thing they were all perfect. They left the people in the power of altering and amending them, whenever they pleased.[12]

This was the rule—or precedent "recognized . . . in practice," as Roger Sherman, one of the Framers, called it—that governed constitutional government in the framing context.[13] This rule meant that the Framers could ignore the Articles of Confederation and enact a new constitution despite its requirements.[14]

Yet who made this rule? Where is it written down, beyond the parchment of the Declaration? What made it a valid rule for them? And if it was valid for them, is it still valid for us? Could fifty-five white men meet in secret in Philadelphia today and propose a new constitution that could then be ratified outside the terms of Article V?

The answer to that question points to the fundamental question of this book. This rule was valid not because it was found in some authoritative rule book, but because it had become *taken for granted* by the Framers' generation. Not by everybody, but by enough. Its validity was in the background, part of the furniture of constitutional law, an element of the context within which the Constitution was drafted. And because it was in the background—because it wasn't one of the many things the Framers were arguing about and trying to frame—it could be pointed to, and relied upon, by those advocating the ratification of the Constitution, just as certainly as those advocating the liberty of man could rely upon the idea that man should be free of the divine right of kings, as Thomas Paine had insisted in *Common Sense* (1776).

Reframed in these terms, the rule says just this: that no constitution can specify the exclusive means of its own amendment. Even if the Constitution says "this is the only way," "this" is not the only way. According to this rule, always standing behind any specification is a Jeffersonian injunction: that the people can alter or abolish the constitution. That right was unalienable, as Jefferson had said, and this was something the nation had gone to war to defend.

So let's go back, then, to the hypothetical that began this chapter. If the Constitution is constitutional—meaning if it is valid even though it failed to follow the explicit rules laid down in the Articles of Confederation—is our hypothetical campaign financing amendment also (hypothetically) constitutional? Would it be possible for proponents of that amendment to argue that the corruption of money in politics has rendered the U.S. government destructive of the ends of government? That the people therefore have the unalienable right to alter that government?

Well, anyone can argue anything, of course. And being able to argue that the Framers were of the same mind as some group of citizens today is usually a smart move, at least within our constitutional tradition.

Yet even if you could convince someone that this idea did stand in the background of the minds of everyone who was anyone in 1787, I take it that most people (or most lawyers, at least) would think it just nuts that our hypothetical amendment could be part of our Constitution today. Whatever the Framers would have said, Article V has become for us the exclusive means by which the Constitution gets amended.[15] Whatever rule stood in the background in 1787, that rule no longer stands in the background today.[16] For us, the natural or proper way to read Article V is to presume it sets out the only mode by which the Constitution can be amended. Anything beyond Article V is beyond the Constitution. That, if anything, is conventional wisdom among lawyers and Congress alike.

This is not to say this is how things should be or that things couldn't be different. Amar is plainly correct when he writes, "Perhaps it remains possible for this right to be exhumed and exercised by some future generation, in a world where a majority of Americans actually finds the idea of amendment outside Article V plausible, principled and necessary."[17] Given the profound problems that our Constitution now faces and the practically impossible burden of amending it, this is indeed a possible and hopeful thought. Yet as Amar recognizes, "that future world ... remains very far from the general sentiment today."[18] Today the rules requires that Article V be read as exclusive.

Or to be precise, at least today the unreflective judge or lawyer would conclude that the rules require that Article V be read as exclusive. As we'll see in Chapter 21, another Yale law professor, Bruce Ackerman, has a powerful and completely convincing argument about why we cannot interpret our Constitution faithfully without recognizing that Article V is in fact not exclusive. But my point here is not about how best to read Article V. My point is to get you to reflect upon the constraints that would confront any judge tempted to read Article V as not exclusive.

Let's say you were a judge charged with deciding whether the campaign finance amendment is part of our constitution. To answer that question, you seek to interpret Article V faithfully. You believe your job is to read the Constitution with fidelity. You aspire to become an Antonin Scalia, committed to the views of the Framers of our Constitution. To you, that means giving Article V the meaning the Framers would have given it. Let's assume you are convinced by the Amars and Ackermans of the world that for the Framers, there was a rule standing as background to the Constitution's text that permitted, at least in theory, amendments beyond the text of the Constitution. And finally, let's assume you believe that today there is no such rule standing as background to the Constitution. That is, you believe that today most people aren't in this sense Jeffersonian.

What do you do? Should you read the Constitution as the Framers would have read it, and thus ratify the campaign finance amendment? Or should you read the Constitution as if it had been written today, without any such background understanding or rule, and thus reject the campaign finance amendment?

Does fidelity mean doing what the Framers would have done, by giving Article V the meaning the Framers would have given it? Or does fidelity mean giving Article V the meaning it plainly has for us today—the exclusive means by which the Constitution gets amended?

In this single example, I suggest, lies the core of the problem of constitutional interpretation within the American tradition.

A constitution is a text. Any text gets written against a background. Call that background its context. That context includes a host of assumptions that inform any reading of the text. Those assumptions are the stuff against which the text has meaning.[19]

Those assumptions change. And the one truly difficult problem of constitutional interpretation is to figure out what to do when they change. Do you read the text as it would have been read originally, imagining yourself back in the original context of interpretation? Or do you read the text as it would be read today, ignoring the changes in these background assumptions? Or do you ignore some of the changes but recognize others? And if you're selective, what rule determines the criteria of selectivity?

These are questions of interpretive fidelity. In this book, I argue, they can be divided into two types. The first is the question of *fidelity to meaning*. It asks: How does a judge preserve the meaning of the Constitution's text within the current interpretive context? If the judge believes that the background understanding has changed, what strategy should she adopt? Should she ignore the changes, or incorporate them? And if she incorporates them, does that mean she is changing the meaning of the Constitution? Or is there a way of incorporating those changes without changing the meaning of the Constitution?

But in answering that first question, the judge is confronted with a second: How does she do this, given the constraints of her role? How she behaves will be understood against the background of who she is and what she has done. Put most crudely, that fact forces the judge to ask: "How much of a nut do I want to be seen to be? Sure, the Framers might well have thought Article V was not exclusive. But that was a particular group of people at a particular time and place. Today that idea is for most people crazy. So, is 'crazy' what I want to be known as?" (Compare Scalia: "I am an originalist, but I am not a nut.")[20]

The problem could be even more difficult. Return to our hypothetical campaign finance reform amendment. Imagine a judge who had been a prominent politician before becoming a judge, and who, as a politician, had fought hard to get the campaign finance amendment passed. Imagine further that she reads Article V as Amar argues the Framers would have read it. Imagine she believes Amar is right—that a framing assumption was the right of the people to alter or abolish a constitution. If the judge followed that understanding and allowed this amendment to be recognized as part of the Constitution, would her decision be read by others—by the press, by us—as one faithful to the Constitution, or as one driven by her own political values rather than the Constitution?

The point is quite general. Whatever the judge does, and for whatever reason she does it, her actions will be perceived in ways that she just cannot control. Think of the Republican justices on the Supreme Court who voted in *Bush v. Gore* (2000) to stop the recount in Florida: whatever those justices believed in their heart of hearts, there was no way they could control the fact that their actions would be *perceived to be* political, whether they were or not. In a case like that, even the most powerful court in the history of the world just cannot control how its actions will be read.

To go back to our hypothetical campaign finance amendment: where the premise to the argument is pulled from left field (or from law reviews discussing political theory circa 1787, which for many people amounts to the same thing), a judge also couldn't avoid the charge that the result was political (at least if the judge decided it in a way that coincided with her politics). The argument, even if true, would be rendered in a way that the judge can't perfectly control. And that fact might well matter to the judge in deciding how she would decide the case. The reasonable *perception* that the judge's decision is based not upon law but instead upon politics (or craziness) might matter to the judge's conception of her fidelity not to the meaning of the Constitution but *to her role as a judge.* That is, a fidelity to role might constrain the judge in his pursuit of fidelity to meaning. *Fidelity to role,* then, is thus a second question of interpretive fidelity, often as central as the first.

This idea, however—that judges might decide a case based not solely upon the law but upon how the decision might seem to the public—might shock you. Isn't a judge supposed to do justice, regardless of how things might seem?

Of course she is—in principle. But, as I'll argue throughout the balance of this book, across a wide range of cases judges on both the Left and the Right have acted as if they are constrained not just by a fidelity to meaning but also by a fidelity to role. The decision of a court must be, and must seem to be, judicial, meaning (very roughly) a decision that follows consistently from the law and not from the particular politics of an individual judge. And where a particular decision would plainly seem not to be judicial in this sense—where the rule it invoked couldn't be applied consistently, or where the result, in light of the reasons given, seems driven more by politics than by reason—then I suggest that a second kind of fidelity, fidelity to role, has in fact operated throughout our history to constrain the outcome the court would otherwise adopt. As Jack Balkin puts it, "The first is the question of what the Constitution means and how to be faithful to it. The second asks how a person in a particular institutional setting—like an unelected judge with life tenure—should interpret the Constitution and implement it through doctrinal constructions and applications. The first is the question of fidelity; the second is the question of institutional responsibility."[21]

Thus, however strongly our judge in the campaign finance hypothetical might argue, her upholding an amendment that she plainly favors politically, in the face of "what everyone knows to be true" (namely, that Article V is exclusive, even if, on balance, what everyone knows just happens to be false), on the basis of an unwritten rule that has lain dormant for more than 225 years can't help but seem to be something beyond the law. That fact may or may not matter to a particular judge. But as I'll argue, fidelity to role has mattered to many across the thousands of cases decided by our highest court.

Putting it all together, then, my claim is this: There are two fidelities within our tradition that compete for the attention of a court—fidelity to meaning and fidelity to role. These two fidelities sometimes complement each other. An interpretation of the Constitution that says Alaska gets two senators is both consistent with the meaning of the Constitution and consistent with the judicial role. At other times those two fidelities conflict with each other, as in the hypothetical that began this chapter. And the difficult choice for a court is how best to accommodate these two kinds of fidelity when they conflict. Judges must ask themselves: "What does it mean to be faithful to the Constitution's meaning? How do I keep faith with the judicial role?"

In the balance of this book, my objective is to show you how our tradition has in fact accommodated these two fidelities. Relative to current debates about fidelity and constitutional interpretation, my claim will strike you as extreme: that throughout the history of American constitutional law, we can see courts on both the Right and the Left following the same practice of interpretive fidelity, a practice that is the product of these two separate fidelities. This practice will explain many of the most important shifts in American constitutional law. And in the end, I believe, this history will provide a normative justification for this mix of fidelities. Put differently, and in a more directly Dworkinian sense, this practice will explain how the U.S. Supreme Court has arrived at its current position. Once we see that, we can then decide whether the practice that got it there is justified as well.

CHAPTER TWO | Framing Readings

T HE STORY OF THIS BOOK is a practice of fidelity. It is a practice our Supreme Court has developed and engaged, wittingly or not, for at least the last century.

We can see the origins of this practice in the earliest cases of the constitutional law canon. *Marbury v. Madison* (1803) and *McCulloch v. Maryland* (1819) introduce the idea of fidelity to role. In *Gibbons v. Ogden* (1824) we can see elements of the practice of fidelity to meaning.[1]

## *Fidelity to Role:* Marbury

Soon after I started teaching, in the early 1990s, I was invited to visit the former Soviet Republic of Georgia. Georgians were just beginning the process of drafting a new constitution. They were eager for insight wherever they could find it.

On my second day in that extraordinary country, I met its president, Eduard Shevardnadze. It was a totally boring and predictable meeting. Shevardnadze had been a politician for more than forty years. He had mastered the art of saying nothing.

But just before I entered that meeting, I had about ten minutes with the foreign secretary, Aleksandr Davidovich Chikvaidze. *He* was an interesting man—curious, knowledgeable, extremely well-read. And as if to test me, two minutes into our conversation he asked, "What was the most important moment in the history of the United States?"

I struggled through some obvious dates. July 4, 1776: the signing of the Declaration of Independence? September 3, 1783, the end of the Revolutionary War? April 9, 1865, the end of the Civil War? November 4, 1980, the date Ronald Reagan was elected?

"Wrong, wrong, wrong, wrong," he said.

Clearly, I'd failed his test. "Okay," I said. "So, what's the right answer?"

Chikvaidze smiled like a precocious ten-year-old and said, "March 4, 1801."

It took me a few seconds to remember what had happened on that date. And yet even when I realized that was when Thomas Jefferson had taken the oath of office as America's third president, I still didn't quite see why this was the most important date in American constitutional history. But as I thought about that history, Chikvaidze's insight made a great deal of sense.

Jefferson had had an unexpectedly difficult struggle to get to that historically critical place in March 1801. He had run against his friend John Adams (though at this time in their lives both of them seemed to have forgotten that they were in fact friends). He had beaten Adams handily, winning more than 61 percent of the popular vote (though most states didn't yet select presidential electors through popular vote).[2] But though he had won the popular vote overwhelmingly, the vote in the Electoral College was tied. And under the rules of the Constitution as they then stood, that tie would have to be resolved in the House of Representatives—where John Adams's party, the Federalists, was still in power.

This conflict, however, between the popular vote and the Electoral College vote was not the conflict of Trump against Clinton in 2016 or Bush against Gore in 2000. This was much more bizarre. The tie was not between Jefferson and his opponent, John Adams. The tie was between Jefferson and the man meant to be Jefferson's vice president—the devious soon-to-be assassin of Alexander Hamilton and later a traitor to the nation, Aaron Burr.[3]

The people who established the rules for electing the president never imagined that candidates would run on a ticket, one for president and another for vice president. The theory of the original Constitution was that the president would be the man (and yes, a man) getting the most votes in the Electoral College, so long as he won a majority. The vice president would be the runner-up ("No hard feelings, okay?"). According to the Constitution, each elector had two votes and had to vote for two people, one of whom had to be from a state other than the elector's own. The president was the candidate who got the most votes (if a majority); the vice president was the candidate for president who came in second.

This system worked fine in the first three elections. In the first two, George Washington received one vote from every elector. The electors' second vote was divided among many candidates, but among the others John Adams received the most votes in each of the two contests. When Washington decided not to run for a third term (even though his first term had been less than four years), the nation's first real contest for the presidency was born. Jefferson challenged Adams and came within one state of beating him. Under the rules at the time, Jefferson became vice president, the only time in our history that the vice president had run against the president from a different party.

The discomfort between Adams and Jefferson led pragmatic politicians of the day to craft a clever hack to the Constitution's scheme for electing a president. Rather than wind up with a vice president who might be an opponent to the president, the politicos invented the idea of what would eventually be called the "running mate"—someone running to be vice president rather than president.[4] And the mechanism for securing that result would be a simple convention: one state, presumably the home state of the running mate, would hold back one vote for the running mate. Thus the president would "beat" the vice president by a single vote yet have a partner who was an ally rather than an opponent.

So, for example, imagine there are 138 electoral votes. And imagine 65 are pledged to candidate A for president and 73 to candidate J. Under this scheme, all but one of the 65 electors would also vote for A's vice president, giving that person 64 votes. And all but one of the 73 electors would vote for J's vice president, giving him 72. Seventy-three is a majority, so J would become president. And J's VP, with 72, would be number two, and become vice president.

That was exactly the plan for 1800, and it worked perfectly well—among the Federalists. Adams was the Federalist candidate for president. Charles Pinckney was his running mate. Adams received 65 Electoral College votes. Pinckney received 64. The remaining vote from South Carolina went to John Jay, another Federalist.

But the scheme didn't work as planned for the other party—then known (confusingly to us) as the Democratic-Republican Party. Jefferson received 73 votes. His running mate, Aaron Burr, also received 73 votes. Burr's delegation (New York) apparently "forgot" the deal, so no New Yorker held back his vote. Thus the tie that threw the election into the House was not a tie between Adams and Jefferson, the two candidates for president. It was between Jefferson and his running mate. Burr had double-crossed Jefferson.[5] Jefferson, understandably, was furious.

Immediately after the tie was officially reported, the House began balloting to choose which of the two men who had received 73 votes, Jefferson or

Burr, would become the next president. But the House was the previous House, still controlled by the party that had just lost the presidency, and thus held by people who hated Jefferson. Whether or not Burr had misbehaved, the congressmen were free to vote as they wished. And many loved the idea of denying Jefferson his victory, even if that meant handing the presidency to the "scoundrel" Aaron Burr.[6]

Balloting continued for seven days. A bed was brought in for one ailing congressman. After twenty-seven ballots, the House took a break. The next day, February 17, a deal was struck: James A. Bayard, a congressman from Delaware, changed his vote to let Jefferson become president.[7]

I rehearse this history to suggest the impression you should have about this very early moment in our Constitution's life. All was not safe or set at the start. The outcome in 1800 could easily have gone the other way. That was my Georgian friend's point. A certain anarchy could have overwhelmed the Constitution's scheme. The smell of the story is the reality of the time: America, a banana republic (without the bananas) just waiting to happen.

And then the story only got worse.

As I said, the Federalists took a beating in the 1800 election. Jefferson had defined the election as a chance to rediscover the Revolution. Indeed, he saw his victory as just as significant as the Revolution, which he had helped launch in 1776. As he wrote: "[It was] as real a revolution in the principles of our government as that of 1776 was in its form; not effected indeed by the sword . . . but by the rational and peaceful instrument of reform, the suffrage of the people."[8] The Federalists had become too remote, too undemocratic, at least in Jefferson's view; too much like the monarchy the Revolution was supposed to end. And that message resonated with the people. After the dust settled, his party had won a two-vote majority in the Senate and a thirty-vote majority in the House.

But under the rules at the time, the new Congress would not meet until the day Jefferson was to be sworn into office, March 4, 1801. That meant that after Jefferson was finally selected, the old, and defeated, Congress still had fifteen days to cause as much trouble as it could.

And trouble it caused—by grabbing control of the judicial branch before handing the democratic branches over to the Jeffersonians.

First, the lame duck Congress confirmed President Adams's appointment of John Marshall (then the secretary of state and a key Federalist) to be the chief justice of the Supreme Court.

Second, the same Congress passed the Judiciary Act of 1801, which increased the number of federal circuit courts from three to six and increased the number of federal judges by sixteen, while reducing the number on the

Supreme Court from six to five.[9] The obvious aim was to deny the Republicans a chance to appoint a new Supreme Court justice, while increasing the number of Federalist circuit court judges.

Third, the lame duck Congress passed a new statute to regulate the District of Columbia, including the creation of a large number of new magistrate judges for the District—magistrates, again, who would be Federalists.[10]

And finally, President Adams nominated judges to fill these newly created offices as quickly as he could. Congress confirmed the nominations—often literally overnight.

All this was designed to ensconce the Federalists into the woodwork of American government—after the public had essentially told them to go home. As Larry Kramer describes it:

> By this none-too-subtle means, the Federalists rewarded themselves with numerous appointments to the inferior courts—not just the judges, but also marshals, clerks, federal attorneys, and all the other supporting personnel attached to a court—while simultaneously requiring the incoming Republican Administration to wait for two vacancies on the Supreme Court before it could make its first appointment there.[11]

It was a brilliant if anti-democratic plan, executed almost flawlessly.

One of these intended District of Columbia magistrates was a man named William Marbury. Nominated by Adams on March 2, 1801, Marbury was confirmed by the Senate on the next day.[12] After that vote, all that was needed was for the president to sign the commission, for the secretary of state to record it, and for the commission to be delivered to the appointee. (This last bit wasn't so much to make it effective in theory as in practice: people needed to see a signed commission to recognize a person as a commissioner. As of 1804, Google didn't yet list that information within its index.)

President Adams signed Marbury's commission, and the commissions of forty-one other judges, on March 3. Secretary of State John Marshall applied the seal of the United States to each of them. And then John Marshall's brother, James Marshall, himself a judge in a D.C. circuit court, picked up the commissions at the White House so he could deliver them before the new president came into office. But finding it too difficult to carry all forty-two commissions, James Marshall left four to be collected and delivered later. Those four were promptly forgotten and remained in the desk of the secretary of state as Marshall and Adams left the White House. Two days later, Jefferson discovered them. Among the four was William Marbury's commission.[13]

Upon coming into office, Jefferson could do little about the judges who had already taken their seats. But there was something obvious that he could do about those who had not yet received their commissions: he could hold on to those commissions. And so he did. The Federalists had behaved badly, so he would behave badly too. Tit for tat.

This decision triggered a fight that threatened a constitutional crisis. That fight would proceed along two separate but connected tracks.

The first track follows the undelivered commissions: the Federalists would go to the Supreme Court to demand that the president's agent, James Madison, deliver the undelivered commissions to the judges who had been nominated, confirmed, and appointed.

The second track follows the last-minute judges: the Republican Congress repealed the act that created the new judges, and the Federalists insisted that under the Constitution, the Republicans had no such power.

Both tracks would set the power of the democratic branches against the power of the judicial branch. No one had a clue about which branch would win.

## TRACK I: DEMANDING THE COMMISSIONS

In December 1801, William Marbury and three others, William Harper, Robert Home, and Dennis Ramsay, filed suit in the United States Supreme Court against Jefferson's secretary of state, James Madison. They demanded that Madison deliver their commissions, and they asked the Court to issue an order to that effect. (Thirteen other justices of the peace also hadn't received their commissions, but they didn't file suit.)

Four months later, the Jeffersonians in Congress responded to this demand. In March 1802, Congress repealed the Judiciary Act of 1801, abolishing the courts created by the Federalists and returning the judiciary to the structure established in 1789.[14] One month later, Congress enacted the Judiciary Act of 1802, which, among other things, canceled the two existing terms of the Supreme Court (June and December) and replaced it with a single term in February. The motive, political scientist Justin Crowe believes, was to deny the Supreme Court a chance to rule on the repeal of the Judiciary Act until at least a year after it had gone into effect—thereby making repeal of the repeal less likely.[15] Regardless of the motive, the Federalists were furious. Yet with the Supreme Court's term canceled, there was no forum for them to make their complaints.

The Supreme Court couldn't be sent home forever. So, after a year's break, Congress let the Court get back to work. And at the top of its docket in 1803 were the challenges to the two actions taken by the Republicans after they had come to power—first, the complaint of William Marbury that the secretary of state, James Madison, had not delivered his commission, and second, though raised only indirectly, the complaint of the wrongly removed federal judges that, under the Constitution, Congress had no power to fire them during their "good behavior."

These lawsuits were a serious threat to the newly empowered government—and they may well have marked an even more important date in our history than the one identified by my friend the Georgian foreign minister. Because if March 4, 1801, was the Appomattox of that first American civil war, the new Supreme Court term in 1803 could well have been the first Bloody Sunday. The newly assembled Supreme Court could easily have declared its defiance of the Republicans and Jefferson. It could have ordered Madison to deliver the commissions. It could have told Congress that the judges it had fired still had their jobs.

Yet John Marshall was much smarter than that. And in his very different response, he gives us the first clear example of the Court practicing fidelity to role rather than fidelity to meaning.[16]

———

Marbury's case asked the Supreme Court to order an agent of the president to obey the law. Today we take it for granted that a court would have such a power. It was not obvious in 1803. Indeed, some believed that courts had no such authority over a coordinate branch—the president—any more than the president had power to order the clerk of the Supreme Court to refuse Marbury's petition. The challenge for Chief Justice Marshall was how to establish that power, in the Supreme Court at least, and not just for this case but for all cases going forward.

This was not, however, the only power that Marshall wanted. As well as the power to tell the president's agents to obey the law, John Marshall also wanted the power to tell Congress to obey the law that governed it—namely, the Constitution. In Marshall's view, the judiciary should be a check on both the executive and legislative powers. It was the Court's job, in his view, to ensure that neither exceeded the bounds the Constitution set.

Marshall's view was not unheard of at the time of the Founding; it was just not taken for granted. It was an idea that some embraced and others rejected. Marshall's challenge, therefore, was to move it from a contested idea to an assumed premise—from an argument to a bit of the furniture of constitutional law.

How was he going to do that? Neither Congress nor the president had any patience for what John Marshall had to say. Indeed, if there was one enemy of the people that the Revolution had clearly recognized, it was the judges. Moreover, Congress and the president had a recent democratic landslide on their side. Not only were judges not elected, but these judges in particular had been appointed by the party that had just lost power. There could have been no entity with less political capital in the capital of the United States just then. The challenge for Marshall was how to build the political capital that the judiciary needed. The question was how he could establish the authority of the Court.

———

Shortly after my Georgia trip in 1993, the newly formed Russian Constitutional Court gave a pretty clear example of how not to do what Marshall needed to do—that is, how not to use power to establish power.

Valery Zorkin, a former law professor (which perhaps should have fore-shadowed that he would be trouble), became a judge on the Russian Constitutional Court in October 1991. In November he was elected as the court's first chairman. He then took it to be his job to teach the new democracy how a constitution was to be respected. In a series of decisions, Zorkin's court aggressively defended its view of the Russian constitution against a powerful new president, Boris Yeltsin. In January 1992, the court declared that a presidential decree unifying the state security ministry with the ordinary police was unconstitutional. The members of the court received death threats, but its chairman was not going to back down:

> My manner seems mild after years of teaching.... But I know I am tough inside. Toughness is essential. How can you afford to be mild when you are told that there is one law for the rich and another for the poor, that might goes before right? ... [T]he President who won the general election has his mandate, but not an indulgence.[17]

Later, the court declared unconstitutional a referendum declaring independence for Tatarstan. When the state proceeded to impose the result of the referendum, Zorkin called a news conference "to warn Tatarstan not to ignore the Constitution."[18]

Then, in a most extraordinary move, three days after Yeltsin appeared on television to declare a state of emergency, the court issued an opinion declaring that the television broadcast—yes, *the television broadcast*—violated the Constitution. That led fellow justice Ernest Ametistov to write publicly that the court had no authority to rule on a television broadcast, or to make public statements on a case before it was decided. That evidence of division among the justices encouraged Yeltsin to join the attack against the court. "The Constitutional Court has gone into politics," Yeltsin's justice minister insisted. Prominent politicians called for the abolition of the court. And on October 3, 1993, Yeltsin did the next best thing: he sent tanks to surround the Constitutional Court's building and shut it down. Zorkin's crusade had failed. He had taken on the most powerful man in Russia—and lost.

What Zorkin apparently missed was that in politics, power is not simply declared. It is earned. If the Russian Constitutional Court wished to gain authority, it would have to take authority from other, more powerful institutions. No one, and especially no one in government, likes to give up power voluntarily. Thus, what Zorkin needed was a way to establish authority without challenging directly those whose power he sought to diminish.

That's not an easy task. But Zorkin could have learned lots had he paid a bit more attention to how John Marshall had done the same thing 190 years before. For the manner by which Marshall resolved the question of *Marbury v. Madison* and then the question of fired federal judges stands as one of the most brilliant strategic decisions in American political history.

———

When the Supreme Court was finally permitted to hear the case of *Marbury v. Madison*, Jefferson was still so angry he refused even to send a lawyer to defend the president's position.[19] This, Jefferson thought, was a show trial, and he would not dignify it with the presence of his own representative.[20]

That didn't stop Chief Justice Marshall. After all, why did he need a lawyer from the administration? He knew everything there was to know about this case. He literally had been in the room when everything had happened (except for the failed delivery, which had been botched by his brother). And he wasn't going to let Jefferson stop him from deciding what would prove to be perhaps the most important case of his tenure. Even if Jefferson couldn't see it, Marshall believed that something much more important was at stake than their petty political disputes.

The civics book story about *Marbury v. Madison* focuses on just one part of that important decision—the part that declares that the Supreme Court has the power to strike down laws of Congress. But that focus obscures the brilliance of the opinion by ignoring an embarrassment. For the reasoning that gets Marshall to the conclusion that the Court can declare laws unconstitutional is extremely weak. From the perspective of fidelity to meaning, it is a C– at best. The brilliance of the opinion is in the way he effectively declares this power without giving anyone a meaningful chance to challenge it. That part, from the perspective of fidelity to role, is a clear A+.

## Marshall's C–: Fidelity to Meaning

The only important question presented to the Court was whether the Supreme Court should order Madison to turn over Marbury's commission. The answer the Supreme Court would ultimately give to that question was that it had no jurisdiction over the matter—meaning there was no valid law that gave the Supreme Court the power to compel Madison to turn over the commission.

The puzzle, however, is how long it took the Supreme Court to reach that conclusion—not in the sense that they sat on the case for a long time (the Court issued its opinion less than two weeks after argument) but in the sense that the opinion of Chief Justice Marshall wandered through an array of legal issues he never needed to consider just to reach the conclusion that the Supreme Court didn't have the power to order Madison to do anything. Supreme Court opinions are not (intended to be) stream-of-consciousness novels. And if the Court concludes there is no jurisdiction, ordinarily it simply writes an opinion that shows why that's true and then it shuts up.

Marshall didn't do that. Instead, he set for himself three separate questions on the way to answering the only important question. First: "Has the applicant a right to the commission he demands?" Second: "If he has a right, and that right has been violated, do the laws of his country afford him a remedy?" And the punch-line question: "If they do afford him a remedy, is it a mandamus [mandate or order] issuing from this court?" Given his answer to question three, questions one and two were unnecessary. So why did Marshall trek across a whole field of law when answering just one simple question ("Does this Court have the power to issue the remedy asked of it?") would have finished his work?

Marshall's first question ("Has the applicant a right to the commission he demands?") is the least important for our purposes. Though many have questioned the steps he took, he concludes quite firmly that Marbury was entitled to his commission. The time for decision had passed. All that was left was the president's duty to give Marbury the evidence that he needed to perform his duties—literally, the piece of paper declaring he was a justice of the peace.

It is the second question ("If he has a right, and that right has been violated, do the laws of his country afford him a remedy?") that begins to get interesting. From Jefferson's perspective, the whole issue was whether the Court would have the power to tell Jefferson's officers what to do. Jefferson thought the very idea was monstrous. The officers of the executive branch worked for the president, not for Chief Justice Marshall. Marshall could no more order the president's staff to do something than the president could order Marshall's staff to copy opinions and deliver them to the White House.[21]

But in what may be the most important part of Marshall's opinion, the chief justice drew a distinction upon which the whole of administrative law rests. While of course Jefferson was right that no court would ever have the power to question what an agent of the president does when that agent is exercising the president's "political power," as Marshall described it, a very different rule applies when the agent is acting not as the "officer of the president," but as an "officer of the law." When an agent is an "officer of the law," it is perfectly possible for a court to determine whether the agent is obeying the law. The rule of law requires as much, and ours is a nation founded upon the rule of law. It is the Court's job, in Marshall's view, to ensure that an officer of the law is obeying the law, even if that officer of the law is also, in different contexts, performing different tasks as an officer of the president.

With this single innovation, Marshall had succeeded in establishing the first of two critically important claims: that the Court has the power to control at least part of the executive branch, at least when that part of the executive branch is exercising authority vested in it by a law rather than by a president.

Under this reasoning, the obligation that bound Madison came not from the president but from a statute. It was a statute that directed the secretary of state to apply the seal to a signed commission, and to record it.[22] Thus in principle, under the rules that Marshall had set, the Court should have been able to order Madison to obey the law, at least so long as Madison refused to do what the statute plainly required.

Yet after declaring this important power, Marshall recognized a very real practical constraint: Jefferson was *never* going to obey an order from John Marshall. Had Marshall ordered Madison to do what he said the law required, Marshall's power to issue such an order would immediately have been challenged and, in practice, proven wrong, for Madison would have followed Jefferson's commands. The precedent Marshall wanted would have been reversed: rather than a clear understanding that the courts get to order executive officers (below the president, at least) to obey the law, history would have taught that it was the president who gets to decide whether and when his officers obey the law.

The important point here was precedent. We forget today just how important precedent was to lawyers in the early republic—and not just, or even especially, judicial precedent, but precedent within government more generally. When something was done and was not challenged, that it was done provided a foundation for doing it in a similar way later. This was the basis of British constitutional law. In America too, everyone recognized that if an act was left unchallenged, it had force even if it was not affirmed.[23]

Now hold this problem—of how Marshall can establish the precedent with a president who he knows will defy him—in your head for moment while we move on to Marshall's final question: assuming Marbury has a right, and assuming that right can be enforced by some court, is the Supreme Court the court to enforce this law?

That might strike you as an odd question—what is the purpose of the Supreme Court if not to enforce the law when it sees that the law has been violated? But no court can act unless it has been given jurisdiction to act.

And so the issue that Marshall had to resolve first was whether the Supreme Court had been given the jurisdiction to order Madison to hand over the commission.

"Jurisdiction" in a judicial sense simply means the power of a court to say what the law is and to apply it—in the words of the Supreme Court, the "power to declare the law."[24] Federal courts have jurisdiction over U.S. citizens violating Lyle Lovett's copyrights in Nashville, Tennessee. French courts do not.

Under our Constitution, jurisdiction comes in two flavors—original and appellate. "Original jurisdiction" means the jurisdiction to hear a cause initially. If you want to sue your neighbor for trespass, you go to a trial court and file your claim. That court has original jurisdiction over the matter. It hears evidence, and it makes the initial ruling.

Once that court is finished, the parties may have the right to appeal. If they do, then the court that hears the appeal exercises "appellate jurisdiction." Ordinarily, an appellate court will not re-decide all the issues decided in the lower court, instead limiting its review to matters of law, not fact.

The Supreme Court has both appellate and original jurisdiction. The Constitution names four classes of cases in which the Court has original jurisdiction. "In all other cases," the Constitution states, the Court has appellate jurisdiction only.

Marbury had filed his case in the Supreme Court. That means he was trying to invoke the Court's original jurisdiction—and in that he could be successful only if the Court had the power to hear his claim as a matter of original jurisdiction.

Yet it is here that the great chief justice's opinion begins to get funky.

Marbury's lawsuit relied upon Section 13 of the nation's Judiciary Act of 1789. That section, Marshall said, purported to give the Supreme Court original jurisdiction to issue a mandamus. But a jurisdiction to issue a mandamus to Marbury was not one of the four classes of original jurisdiction that the Constitution had specified. So as Marshall framed the question, the issue was whether a statute could give to the Supreme Court an original jurisdiction where the Constitution did not.

The answer to this question is the famous bit of *Marbury v. Madison*: the part where Marshall establishes the Court's power of "judicial review." Marshall waxes eloquent about how it must be the case that the Supreme Court has the power to declare unconstitutional a law that is inconsistent with the Constitution. What else would a written constitution mean if Congress could evade it without recourse? Surely a Court sworn to uphold the law must uphold all the law, including the Constitution. And if a law is inconsistent with the Constitution, then that law must be rejected.

There is a long history of quibbling with Marshall's logic about the necessity that the Constitution includes the power of judicial review.[25] But let's put that debate aside. For our purposes, there are two critical facts.

First, Marshall is asserting against Congress the same power that he had just claimed against the president. The Court, he says, has the power to order Congress, indirectly at least, to obey the law; it has the power to order the president, or his agents at least, to obey the law. The "law" in the two cases is different—one is statutory and the other constitutional. But the effect is the same: the courts were to be the law police within the Constitution's domain. Or so Marshall believed.

Second, Marshall is asserting this power over Congress in the most abstemious way possible. On his reading of the Judiciary Act, Congress had given the Supreme Court a power that Marshall says the Supreme Court can't take. He is thus declaring a power (the power to strike down a law of Congress) by denying his Court a power (the power of original jurisdiction to issue a mandamus). "Thank you for your gift," Marshall in effect tells Congress, "but there's no way I could possibly accept it."

Yet here's the problem with Marshall's mock restraint: everything hangs upon believing that Congress in Section 13 of the Judiciary Act actually meant to give the Supreme Court original jurisdiction to issue a mandamus against Madison.

Did it?

When I present this material to my law students, it takes them just a minute to see Marshall's mistake, and then a good two or three minutes more before they let themselves believe they have actually recognized a mistake by the great chief justice. For the Judiciary Act plainly grants the Supreme Court the power of mandamus. But the statute also makes it plain that it is giving the Court mandamus power *only where the Supreme Court otherwise has jurisdiction.*[26] Put differently, the Judiciary Act didn't say, "You have jurisdiction and you can issue a mandamus"; instead, it essentially said, "Where you have jurisdiction, you also have the power of mandamus."

Yet the Supreme Court plainly did not have jurisdiction to hear Marbury's claim. It obviously didn't have appellate jurisdiction, as Marshall noted, because that "revises and corrects the proceedings in a cause already instituted." And it didn't have original jurisdiction, because Madison was not a state. Nor was he an ambassador, other public minister, or consul, as those terms were understood. Thus Marbury had no right to ask the Supreme Court to help him secure his job—and the Supreme Court had no right to oblige Marbury by hearing his case.

So the mistake in *Marbury* was not by Congress. The mistake was by Marbury's lawyer. Marbury had asked for a mandamus. The Court should have said, "I'm sorry, but we have no original jurisdiction in this case, so we can't issue a mandamus." The Court, in other words, should simply have dismissed the case for want of jurisdiction, rather than declare a law of Congress unconstitutional on the bogus grounds that Congress had purported to force upon the Court an unconstitutional jurisdiction. Marbury should not have filed his case in the Supreme Court. He should have filed his claim in another court and then taken the appeal to the Supreme Court if needed.[27]

At this point the students are stunned. The case seems like a no-brainer. Yet our most respected chief justice to date missed this obvious point. What could possibly explain his mistake?

## Marshall's A+: Fidelity to Role

Let's recap: Marshall concludes that Marbury is entitled to his commission. He concludes that a court, in the right case, would have the power to order the secretary of state to deliver the commission. But he reasons that this isn't the right case because Congress has tried to give the Supreme Court a power that the Constitution forbids it. That effort by Congress is therefore unconstitutional, Marshall declares. So Marshall strikes down the law that Congress had enacted and leaves poor Marbury empty-handed.

All that sounds fine until you realize the gaping hole smack dab in the middle of Marshall's reasoning: the Judiciary Act didn't give the Supreme Court the power that Marshall strikes down. Marshall has simply misread the statute. So what explains this obvious mistake by America's greatest chief justice?

The clue is eminently practical. For what is the consequence of the Court's decision? Just as with Jefferson, Marshall knows that if he declares a precedent and Congress acts against it, the precedent is defeated. So he needed to declare unconstitutional a law that Congress would never pass again. No law could better fit that description than a law that gives the (Federalist) courts power over executive officers. If Marshall knew anything, he knew Congress was not going to contradict his precedent by passing another law to give him the power of mandamus.

Thus, the brilliance: against the president, the Court asserts the power to order the executive to obey the law. Yet it issues no order, and thus there is nothing for the president to disobey.

And against Congress, the Court asserts the power to strike down an unconstitutional law. Yet it does so with a law that Congress is not going to reinstate.

The result is a precedent that establishes the ultimate authority of the courts in a manner that can't easily be denied by those from whom power is being taken away. The case plants a seed that grows for almost a generation before it is invoked against the president again (*Kendall v. U.S.* (1838)) and for almost three generations before it is invoked against Congress (*Dred Scott v. Sanford* (1857)).

So there is a genius in the case. Yet the brilliance has nothing to do with the exposition of the law. The brilliance is strategic.[28] Marshall bends the meaning of Section 13 of the Judiciary Act to create an opportunity to build a judicial branch. His interpretive sin was real, but history hardly even noticed it, because the consequence of his sin is the blessing we call judicial review. We have a Congress constrained by the Constitution because of Marshall's sin. And we have an executive (in part) constrained by the Constitution because of Marshall's sin.

For John Marshall's job was much bigger than William Marbury's commission. His job, or the job of a court more fundamentally, is to establish and sustain an institution that stands in the most precarious position of any within a democratic government—the judiciary. The courts have no army; they have no power to tax. Any authority they have is given to them by the very people the Court purports to control. Coercion is not a tool in the tool box of a judiciary just starting out. The power to coerce—whether it is to coerce presidents, Congress, or citizens—must be earned.

Thus do we see the first clear conflict between a fidelity to role and a fidelity to meaning. Meaning says Marbury filed his suit in the wrong court. The consequence of that decision would have done nothing to establish the power of the Supreme Court. But by bending the meaning of Section 13, Marshall creates a powerful precedent that would, over time, establish the institution of the courts. It was a sin. It was a beautiful sin.

## TRACK 2: MARSHALL'S MUMBLE

This left the second track still to be resolved: could the Jeffersonians simply fire the Federalist judges by abolishing the courts they were hired to serve on? The Constitution says that judges have life tenure (or serve during "good behavior"). Can Congress evade that protection, not directly but indirectly?

The answer is not obvious, and here Hamilton may have had the most sensible view. Writing just before the repeal, Hamilton called the question "nice" (in the sense of calling for great precision). As he observed:

> On the one head it is not easy to maintain that Congress cannot abolish Courts, which having been once instituted, are found in practice to be inconvenient and unnecessary: On the other, if it may be done, so as to

include the annihilation of existing Judges, it is evident that the measure may be used to defeat that clause of the Constitution which renders the duration and emoluments of the judicial office coextensive with the good behavior of the officer; an object essential to the independence of the Judges, and the security of the citizen and the preservation of the government.[29]

The solution, Hamilton suggested, was to allow Congress to abolish a court but to protect the judges themselves from removal.

*How* to establish that principle, however, was not obvious at the time. Congress considered a resolution to declare that it was not constitutional to fire the judges. The resolution was debated but defeated, leading a Federalist paper to write: "The memorial of the Circuit Judges has been dismissed without much ceremony by those who, in feeling power, appear to forget there are such principles as right and wrong."[30]

Having lost in Congress, at least some sought victory before the courts. The case that finally presented the question to John Marshall was *Stuart v. Laird* (1803)—and for Marshall's purposes, the case was brilliantly obscure and hopelessly complex.

In January 1801, John Laird had filed suit against Hugh Stuart for breach of contract. The case was filed in one district, tried in a second, and then finally returned to the original district in which it had been filed.

The reason it bounced around was Congress. The Judiciary Act of 1789 had established the court in which it was originally filed. The Judiciary Act of 1801 (the law passed by the Federalists in the waning days of their power) created the second court (as well as five others). And then the Repeal Act of 1802 (the law passed by the Republicans) eliminated those new courts and transferred the cases in those courts to the federal courts that were still remaining.[31]

Hugh Stuart complained about the second transfer, because in the view of his lawyers, Congress had no power to eliminate courts. If it did, Stuart's lawyer (refreshingly) conceded, "there is no error . . . because, in that case, the courts ceased to exist." But if Congress didn't have the power to eliminate the courts (and the judges that went with them), "then [the second court] still exists, the judges were not removed, and the transfer of jurisdiction did not take place."[32]

Laird's lawyers wisely ducked the constitutional question. Whether or not Congress can abolish courts, they argued, Congress can still transfer a case from one court to another. The Supreme Court should thus ignore the abolition question, Laird's lawyers argued, and stay focused on the much simpler transfer question.

Stuart's contract claim was weak, but the constitutional question was quite strong.[33] As the case went up to the Supreme Court for review, some feared that the Court that would eventually lecture both Congress and the president in *Marbury v. Madison* would go on to insist that its brother judges had not been fired, or at least not constitutionally.

But then Marshall blinked. Presented with two critical questions—whether Congress had transferred the case properly, and whether Congress can abolish courts—the Supreme Court ignored the second and decided just the first. Stuart's argument hadn't been rejected. Stuart's argument had been ignored. Whether or not Congress could fire the judges, Congress was free to transfer their cases to another court. End of story. Next case.

Commentators have no good account of the Court's omission.[34] This was the same Court that just the week before had just gone out of its way to declare that Marbury was entitled to his commission, only to also declare that the Court could not issue it. Why did it now all of a sudden discover humility? Why did it ignore the (sexy) constitutional question in order to decide the (boring) transfer question?

Yet from the perspective that I've been sketching, the account is fairly obvious. *Stuart* is, as Bruce Ackerman puts it, a "moment of judicial accommodation," in contrast to Marbury's "moment of conservative resistance." But it accommodates because Marshall recognizes he has no other choice. If he declared that judges couldn't be fired, what then? What was he to do? Marshall couldn't pay the judges. He couldn't direct that courthouses give them chambers. As Justin Crowe describes, "Since Marshall did not lecture or dictate orders to Jefferson, as Federalists had hoped, Jefferson could not defy, punish, or humble Marshall, as Democrat-Republicans had planned."[35] Once again, Marshall's act makes sense in light of the tiny power he actually has. And he bends his jurisdiction in light of that practical recognition.

It is an "accommodating style," Ackerman writes, "of judicial statesmanship ... that enabled the Court to emerge from the presidential revolution of 1800 without sacrificing its claim as a privileged interpreter" of the Constitution.[36] As Kramer quotes Dean Alfange describing it:

> *Stuart v. Laird* was manifestly not an example of nonpartisan fairness, but of craven unwillingness on the part of the Court even to admit the existence of the principal constitutional issue presented by the case. The Court refused to consider the constitutional question even though the author of its opinion had earlier categorically written that he believed the law to be invalid for precisely the reasons that he here chose not even to mention. The Court acted out of a fully justified fear of

the political consequences of doing otherwise, not out of an overriding compulsion to reach the correct legal result at whatever sacrifice of their own political preferences.[37]

Both *Marbury* and *Stuart* thus display the institutional awareness and sensitivity that I call fidelity to role. In both cases, the Court bends meaning so as to support the judicial role. As with Zorkin and the Russian Constitutional Court, here the threat to the U.S. Supreme Court was as crass as it could be: Had Marshall ordered the president to obey the law, the president would have ignored him. Had he ordered Congress to pay the wrongly fired judges, Congress would have ignored him. Had he issued orders, in other words, based on what the law actually required, he faced a threat to the very survival of the institution of the Supreme Court. So Marshall, unlike Zorkin, responded with a brilliant political (as in institutional) response. In time, that response would secure his institution so that it could grow to be the most powerful court in history.[38]

Yet modern lawyers resist this account. It feels dirty, beneath the stature of the great chief justice. But I suspect it feels dirty because most of us have forgotten just how contingent the Court's authority at the Founding was. And not just at the Founding. Throughout the early history of the Supreme Court, it struggled with institutions that resisted it—the states most flagrantly.[39] Throughout history, it was shown that its existence was not foreordained. It thus understood that it needed to insinuate its way into the structures of the American republic, not through simple declarations of right and wrong, but through a wisdom impossible to hide.

## *Fidelity to Role II:* McCulloch

Marshall understood that an institution could not simply presume the power it needed. Neither could it simply demand that power. Instead, if the Supreme Court was to secure the authority to hold Congress to the Constitution, and the president to the law and Constitution, it would have to earn that authority. To earn it, it would need to lay precedents that could not be easily dislodged and that would secure its power, at least over time. This was fidelity to role—to the institution Marshall administered, and to a protected and effective future for that institution.

That same recognition helps us understand a second foundational case, *McCulloch v. Maryland* (1819). This time, however, the pressure comes not from the other branches, but from within—from the limits of judicial capacity itself.

The Constitution doesn't expressly say that Congress has the power to establish a bank. Yet just after the Founding, Alexander Hamilton pushed Washington to support the idea as a way to manage the nation's finances and spur confidence that America had a financial future.

Hamilton's idea was deeply controversial. Jefferson opposed it, strongly. But after a forceful debate (both orally and in writing) between Hamilton and Jefferson, Washington sided with Hamilton.[40] The First Bank of the United States was chartered in 1791.[41] It was authorized to live for twenty years. In 1811, the Senate was tied on the question of whether to renew the charter. Vice President George Clinton voted against its renewal, and the bank expired.

For opponents of the bank, however, this was very bad timing. For when the United States was drawn into its second war with Britain, in 1812, the absence of any federal mechanism for paying troops and buying supplies was disastrous for the nation. Recognizing that weakness, four years later, in 1816, Congress established the Second Bank of the United States—once again over strong opposition from both the intellectual heirs of Jefferson and the many states not eager to see a new (and federal) competitor.

Some of these state opponents continued that opposition even after they had lost the vote in Congress. In 1818, Maryland passed a law requiring that any bank that operated in Maryland but was not chartered by Maryland (i.e., the Second Bank of the United States) purchase special stamps to be affixed to any circulating banknote. The cost of those stamps was designed to cripple the competing bank, as would the fine that would be levied against a bank for any notes circulating without the stamp. When the Second Bank of the United States circulated a note without the proper stamp, a fine was levied against the cashier, James W. McCulloch. McCulloch refused to pay the fine, declaring Maryland's law unconstitutional. The Maryland Court of Appeals upheld the law. The United States then appealed that judgment to the Supreme Court.[42]

The struggle over the assets of the Second Bank of the United States would eventually become quite dramatic. In a later case, the government of Ohio tried to seize the assets of the bank after it refused to pay a tax Ohio had imposed upon banks.[43] And no doubt, the question of whether a state can tax the federal government is itself quite interesting.

But the question that is important for our purposes here is the more fundamental question that Jefferson and Hamilton had debated: whether the Constitution granted Congress the power to establish a bank of the United States. The government of the United States was to be a government of "enumerated powers." The power to establish a bank was not among those powers. So how was it that Congress could exercise a power that was not enumerated?

Marshall (stealing part of his argument directly from Hamilton's text) would show the world how.[44] Though the Constitution had no specifically enumerated power to establish a bank, that power, the Court held, could be implied. And even without implication, it could be found in this case because the Constitution explicitly enumerated a power to act beyond powers expressly granted—the so-called necessary-and-proper clause.

The Constitution's necessary-and-proper clause states that Congress has the power

> to make all Laws which shall be necessary and proper for carrying into Execution the foregoing Powers, and all other Powers vested by this Constitution in the Government of the United States, or in any Department or Officer thereof.

There are four components to the power articulated in this clause:

1. laws
2. "necessary and proper"
3. to the execution
4. of some power

The clause gives Congress (not the courts, not the executive) the power to set the rules by which all of the government's other powers get executed. Those rules are specified by laws and relate to, or support, how a power gets executed.

Think, for example, about the Department of Defense. There's no express power in the Constitution to establish a Department of Defense. Can Congress do it? Simple answer: yes. The necessary-and-proper clause says Congress can pass a law necessary and proper to the execution of a power. So a bill to establish a department would be a law; that law would help the president execute the power granted to him as commander in chief. And the only question then is whether such a department was necessary and proper. It would be hard to find anyone, then or now, who would argue it was not.

The question about the bank would be answered in a similar way. Was a law establishing a federal bank necessary and proper to the execution of some federal power? Marshall concluded it was. There were many federal powers that might be better executed if there were a federal bank: most prominent was the power to raise and support an army, as the War of 1812 had just demonstrated. Thus requirements 1, 3, and 4 were satisfied. The only question was requirement 2: whether the bank was "necessary and proper."

Yet here Marshall's opinion begins to feel a bit funky.

We all have a pretty clear sense of what the word "necessary" means. The *Oxford English Dictionary* doesn't suggest it was very different in 1819.[45] In its most natural sense, the word suggests a restriction: "Take only what's necessary," "Don't make unnecessary noise," "Is that tapping really necessary?" And indeed, when conjoined with the word "proper," the sense of restriction is even stronger. The aim of the second requirement seems plainly to be to restrict the range of laws that Congress might otherwise pass to help some federal entity execute its powers—restricted, that is, to just those that are necessary and proper, where "necessary" means only those means that are direct and simple.

Yet this is not how Marshall read the clause. As he wrote:

Is it true, that this is the sense in which the word "necessary" is always used? Does it always import an absolute physical necessity, so strong, that one thing to which another may be termed necessary, cannot exist without that other? We think it does not. If reference be had to its use, in the common affairs of the world, or in approved authors, we find that it frequently imports no more than that one thing is convenient, or useful, or essential to another. To employ the means necessary to an end, is generally understood as employing any means calculated to produce the end, and not as being confined to those single means, without which the end would be entirely unattainable. Such is the character of human language, that no word conveys to the mind, in all situations, one single definite idea; and nothing is more common than to use words in a figurative sense. Almost all compositions contain words, which, taken in their rigorous sense, would convey a meaning different from that which is obviously intended. It is essential to just construction, that many words which import something excessive, should be understood in a more mitigated sense—in that sense which common usage justifies. The word "necessary" is of this description. It has not a fixed character, peculiar to itself. It admits of all degrees of comparison; and is often connected with other words, which increase or diminish the impression the mind receives of the urgency it imports. A thing may be necessary, very necessary, absolutely or indispensably necessary. To no mind would the same idea be conveyed by these several phrases. The comment on the word is well illustrated by the passage cited at the bar, from the 10th section of the 1st article of the constitution. It is, we think, impossible to compare the sentence which prohibits a state from laying "imposts, or duties on imports or exports, except what may be absolutely necessary for executing its inspection laws," with that which authorizes congress "to make all laws which shall be necessary and proper for carrying into execution" the powers of the general government, without feeling a conviction, that the convention understood itself to change materially the meaning of the word "necessary," by prefixing the word "absolutely." This word, then, like others, is used in various senses; and, in its construction, the subject, the context, the intention of the person using them, are all to be taken into view.[46]

It is a common reaction that when you read something strange by someone well respected, you think maybe the strangeness is your fault. None of us is John Marshall. Who are we to question his interpretation of the Constitution? But feel entitled for just a moment and question Chief Justice Marshall. Because in that question we'll find a clue to exactly what Marshall was doing.

The effect of Marshall's reading is to essentially give Congress a free pass under the necessary-and-proper clause. Or put differently: if you can dream it, Congress can pass it. There's almost nothing Congress can't assert is necessary to some legitimate end, if "necessary" means nothing more than "convenient."

Why would Marshall stretch the language of the Constitution like this? Why not give the words their ordinary meaning, to which we may be deferential but which nonetheless would still require the Court to draw lines?

Once again, the clue is in the practical. Imagine the practice of drawing that line. What would the Court have to do? What abilities would it have to possess?

For example, imagine Congress passed a law that said, "All dogs in the United States must be vaccinated against rabies." Is that law constitutional? At first you might think, "Obviously not. There's no federal power to regulate dogs. And what federal power would be better executed if dogs were vaccinated?"

But Article I, Section 8, Clause 7 gives Congress the power "to establish Post Offices and Post Roads." Dogs may be man's best friend, but not the postal worker's. Avoiding the risk of rabies would improve the lot of the postal worker at least marginally. So, under Marshall's method for reading the necessary-and-proper clause, this particular law looks just fine.

Imagine, however, you didn't think this law was fine. Imagine you wanted to argue it exceeded Congress's power. That whatever "necessary" means, this just goes too far. What kind of argument would you have to make?

Well, you might say the cost of this law was far greater than any possible benefit—most dog owners would immunize their dogs anyway; if dog owners don't, they're not likely to do so because of this law; yet to avoid prosecution, dog owners would need to keep records; and so on.

These are all fine arguments. They try to answer the question of whether, on balance, the law would do more good than harm. That's a great question, no doubt not asked by lawmakers often enough.

Yet how would a court answer such a question? How would a court make that evaluation? Think about the tools a court has. What sort of opinion would it write? Would it commission economic studies? Would it review those studies and then conclude the law was unconstitutional? What if different judges looked at different studies? Could some judges conclude that, given their studies, the law was constitutional, even if in light of other studies it was not?

Indeed, just such a conflict happened around the Supreme Court's decision to ban segregation in public schools. We'll see much more about this case later on in this book, but in 1954, the Supreme Court famously held that the Constitution forbids state-sponsored segregation in schools on the basis of race. Part of the opinion made it sound as if the decision was grounded on a factual finding: that African American children had negative attitudes about themselves caused, in part, because of the practice of segregation. The Court cited psychological data to support that conclusion. On the basis of that citation, a district court in Georgia decided to evaluate whether segregation had the same effect on African Americans in that state. The judge found that it did not, and thus upheld state-sponsored segregation in Georgia.[47] "Whatever psychological injury may be sustained by a Negro child out of his sense of rejection by white children," the district court held, "is increased rather than abated by forced intermixture, and this increase is in direct proportion to the number and extent of his contacts with white children."[48] It took but eleven days for that decision to be effectively reversed by the Court of Appeals.[49]

The point is the institutional capacity of courts. Is it within their ken to evaluate which means are "really necessary"? I'm not saying it's not possible. But whether possible or not, the process would be very weird. It would be very hard for different courts to follow the precedent set by any of these opinions. And over time that would mean that the same issue could be decided inconsistently by different courts. The courts, in exercising their role as supervisors of "necessity," would produce a range of opinions that would inevitably be inconsistent even if all were written in good faith. That inevitable, predictable—indeed, almost certain—inconsistency is a reason to avoid any reading of the Constitution that produces it. Such a reading, in other words, would be inconsistent not with a fidelity to meaning but with a fidelity to role.[50]

The fidelity to role that I am describing here is a different facet from the fidelity to role I described in *Marbury*. There the concern was external and foundational. The aim and practice of Marshall in *Marbury* was to establish a certain kind of court. Here the concern is more internal and pragmatic: What is the consequence of a certain jurisdiction—the jurisdiction to say whether a selected means is "necessary"? And can the institution thrive when burdened with that jurisdiction? *McCulloch* rightly avoids this jurisdiction, because Marshall rightly recognized that these lines could not be drawn by a court. He thus steers the interpretation of the Constitution to a path that helps build a sustainable jurisdiction for the court over time.

So again, from the perspective of fidelity to meaning, there's lots lacking in *McCulloch*. From the perspective of fidelity to role, the decision makes perfect sense. Marshall keeps the Court out of the business of evaluating whether a law is really necessary or not. The Court thus limits itself to those things it can do and avoids those things it can't do. Weighing the costs and benefits of a law thought by Congress to be "necessary" is held beyond the ken of a court.

Notice, however, one important consequence of this interpretation: just because it isn't appropriate for the Supreme Court to say whether a law is really "necessary," it doesn't follow that members of Congress can't argue about whether a law is "necessary."

Imagine the Supreme Court reviewed our Postal Worker Rabies Protection Act. And imagine the Supreme Court said the law was "necessary and proper." But you, as a member of Congress, believe the law is an unfair burden on dog owners. If you introduced a bill into Congress to repeal the law, it would be inappropriate for another member of Congress to say, "Wait, that law has already been held to be necessary and proper." You should be able to say, "Whether or not the Supreme Court is in a position to say whether the law is necessary, we, as political actors, plainly are in a position to say."

The reason is the obvious difference between how a court functions and how Congress functions. A court is to decide cases and in those decisions issue opinions that give reasons for their outcomes. Presumptively, those decisions ought to be consistent. If a court decides a case one way on day one and a different way on day two, it erodes confidence in the court as an institution applying the law in a proper manner.

Congress, on the other hand, doesn't live under any such constraint. If Congress votes for the Postal Worker Rabies Protection Act on day one, it doesn't need to give reasons. The votes are the reasons. And it's free on the next day to repeal the law it has just passed. Change, responding to preferences and political pressure, is just what Congress as an institution is supposed to do, while change, responding to preferences and political pressure, is just what courts are not supposed to do.

Thus, there's no institutional reason why Congress should feel shy about deciding what it believes is really necessary. Indeed, the point should be made more strongly: just because the Supreme Court feels free to ignore the restrictive sense of the word "necessary" in the necessary-and-proper clause, it doesn't follow that Congress should be free to ignore that sense. The scope of Congress's duty under the Constitution is different from the Court's. In some places, odd as this might sound, Congress has to be more careful than the Supreme Court in interpreting the Constitution.

———

We can now put these two foundational cases together and draw the lesson I believe they teach.

From the very beginning of our tradition, the Supreme Court has been focused not just on the abstract questions of the Constitution's meaning. It has also been focused on very practical questions about its own appropriate role. That practical question is not answered in a formula. There's no way anyone could have understood its contours in 1787 fully. And most importantly, as we'll see through the balance of this book, the particulars of its contours change.

But what stays constant, I want to suggest, is a normative principle—or, in the sense philosopher Robert Nozick gave us, a normative side constraint—that conditions the Court's work.[51] The Court seeks to apply the law subject to the constraint of fidelity to role. Or again, the Court seeks a fidelity to meaning subject to the constraint of fidelity to role.

That sensitivity is not something that has been grafted onto the Court's practice recently by anti-activist judges, whether liberal or conservative. My claim is that it has been foundational from the very beginning of the Supreme Court's practice. The most interesting part of these early cases is not their exposition of the meaning of the Constitution's words. The most interesting part is the dissembling—to the end of building a viable and plausible judicial branch.

## *Fidelity to Meaning:* Gibbons

Aaron Ogden was an entrepreneur who, like many entrepreneurs, got a little help from his government. In 1813 (and no doubt simply coincidentally), just as he was elected its governor, New Jersey granted him a monopoly to operate steamboats from most New Jersey ports to New York. That monopoly clashed with one given by the state of New York to Robert Livingston and Robert Fulton, widely recognized as the inventor of the first commercially successful steamboat. Robert Livingston's brother John acquired the Livingston/Fulton monopoly, got Ogden's monopoly revoked, and then licensed his boat to Ogden for $600 a year. Relying upon the exclusive right granted by Livingston, Ogden started providing steamboat service on the Hudson.[52] (Who said life was simple in the old days?)

Thomas Gibbons was a Georgia native and a former mayor of Savannah. In 1817 he acquired a boat named the *Stoudinger* and started competing with Ogden. Competitors don't like government-granted exclusive rights (aka monopolies), at least when the incumbent has them. Beneficiaries of government-granted monopolies don't like competitors. Ogden went to state court to get Gibbons excluded from the market. Gibbons went to federal court to get the state-granted monopoly ruled invalid.[53]

Gibbons claimed, through his lawyers, that New York did not have the power to issue exclusive rights (because that was a federal power under Article I, Section 8, Clause 8 of the Constitution: Congress may "promote the progress of science and useful arts, by securing for limited times to authors and inventors the exclusive right to their respective writings and discoveries"—the "progress clause"), or alternatively that New York didn't have the power to issue this exclusive right (because Congress had granted Gibbons a license to sail on intracoastal waterways, and the laws of Congress trump the laws of the states).

If you read the arguments made in the Supreme Court, it's pretty clear the lawyers thought the Court would decide the case on the basis of the first question. And no doubt that was a really significant matter: Did the states have the power to grant monopolies? Or did the Constitution's progress clause mean that only the federal government could issue monopolies and only for the enumerated reasons?

The Court, however, avoided that question completely. Instead, it decided a second, more particular question, yet in a profoundly important way.

A law of Congress had granted Gibbons the license to operate his boat. Thus, the first question Marshall addressed was whether Congress had the power to pass such a law. If it did, that power would likely come from the commerce clause. The commerce clause states that Congress has the power "to regulate Commerce with foreign Nations, and among the several States, and with the Indian Tribes." The relevant part of the clause was the power "to regulate Commerce . . . among the several States." What was this power? asked Marshall.

He answered his own question in two parts. First, he asked, what does it mean for Congress to have the power "to regulate Commerce"? And second, whatever that power is, how broadly does it extend?

It is the second question that is important for our purposes here.[54] The Constitution specifies that Congress's power is to regulate commerce "among the several States." The easiest example of this power would be commerce that travels between two states—interstate commerce. If it reaches anything, the Commerce Power must reach interstate commerce.

But Marshall didn't see the power stopping there. In addition to commerce that travels between two states, the word "among," Marshall reasoned, must also mean "intermingled with." "Commerce among the States," Marshall wrote, "cannot stop at the external boundary line of each State but may be introduced into the interior." It does not refer to all commerce interior to a state, however; it doesn't mean "commerce, which is completely internal, which is carried on between man and man in a State, or between different parts of the same State, and which does not extend to or affect other States." Instead, the commerce that is "interior" to the state but nonetheless within the scope of the commerce clause must "be restricted to that commerce which concerns more States than one." As the Court would describe in 1995, "The 'affecting commerce' test was developed . . . to define the extent of Congress's power over *purely intrastate commerce activities* that nonetheless have substantial interstate effects."[55] Commerce that is "completely internal, which is carried on between man and man in a State, or between different parts of the same State, and which does not extend to or affect other States," is not "commerce among the states."

Thus, there are three categories of commerce in Marshall's universe: (1) interstate commerce, (2) intrastate commerce "which concerns more States than one," and (3) intrastate commerce "which does not extend to or affect other States." The commerce power gives Congress authority over the first two. Does that mean Congress has no authority over the third category?

The answer, for Marshall, was plainly no. Congress's power is not limited to the power of the commerce clause. It includes as well the power of the necessary-and-proper clause. So while some bits of commerce may "not extend to or affect other States," it may still be the case that regulating such commerce is necessary and proper to "carrying into execution" Congress's other powers. So, in addition to these first two horns of power growing from the commerce clause, Marshall is also careful to include concerns "with which it is . . . necessary to interfere, for the purpose of executing some of the general powers of the government."[56]

Congress's power relating to commerce thus includes (1) interstate commerce, (2) intrastate commerce that concerns more than one state—that "extend[s] to or affect[s] other States"—and (3) intrastate commerce "with which it is necessary to interfere for the purpose of executing" either the power under the commerce clause or any of the other general powers of the government.

On this reading of Congress's power, the licensing statute governing interstate waterways was plainly constitutional. The license granted to Gibbons was therefore valid. To the extent New York law purported to restrict that federal license, the supremacy clause (which establishes explicitly what was pretty clearly implicit in the federal design: that federal law is supreme) meant the New York law would fail.

*Gibbons* demonstrates two features of the practice of American constitutional interpretation. First is what we might call, following Akhil Amar, the "intertextuality" of constitutional interpretation—the way in which one bit must be read in conjunction with another. The question of the commerce clause's power is not determined on its own. It is instead read along with the necessary-and-proper clause (or "sweeping clause") in light of a more general principle about implied limits on the scope of an "enumerated constitution."

Second, and critically, the opinion shows quite plainly how the text of the Constitution does not live in a world of its own. It is instead *contingent* upon facts in this world. The power of Congress—here, the reach of its power under the commerce clause—turns upon patterns of actual economic activity. The power has its roots in reality. It is driven (or restricted) based on that reality.

Specifically here, two of the three heads of commerce clause jurisdiction hang upon some fact in the world—or more accurately, a set of facts in the world. Not just particular facts, such as whether some item of commerce moves between two states, but more general facts about how integrated the economy as a whole is. The more integrated the economy is, the wider the authority of Congress to regulate it. The less integrated the economy is, the narrower the authority of Congress to regulate it.

Consider a simple example to make the point clear: the dairy industry. In 1787, milk production was local. A century before pasteurization would be applied to milk, and more than sixty years before refrigerated railroad cars could carry milk from one market to another, the production and distribution of milk was the sort of stuff done only in one town or perhaps the next one over.

"Local," in this context, means that what happens to milk production in one area doesn't significantly affect the price of milk somewhere else, at least in the short term. As Adam Smith would put it, the activity is local when the "extent of the market" doesn't include it. A flood in the Shenandoah Valley in 1787 that drowned all the milk cows from Harrisonburg to Staunton (poor cows!) would not affect the price of milk in Atlanta.

On Marshall's reading, then, Congress should have no general power to regulate milk production—in 1787. Sure, some milk produced in Trenton might make its way to nearby Philadelphia, and that interstate commerce would be within the reach of Congress's regulatory power. But milk production generally would not. There is no national market for milk such that Congress's regulation of local production could be said to be a regulation that affects interstate commerce.

Now consider the same question in 1887—after pasteurization comes to milk and refrigerated railroad cars are the norm. Milk can now be produced and shipped great distances. The supply in one area thus affects the price somewhere else. The dynamic of the industry changes, simply because the technology of the infrastructure of distribution has changed. Stupid farm policies in Pennsylvania could reasonably hurt New York consumers. The concerns of a Delaware congressman about New Hampshire practices are no longer, necessarily, officious intermeddling. There really is an effect in one part of the nation plausibly tied to an action somewhere else. The "extent of the market" has thus changed. And as it changes, under Marshall's formula at least, Congress's legitimate claim to regulate this industry changes as well.

"Legitimate," of course, does not mean sensible. That Congress has the power to regulate something doesn't mean it makes sense for Congress to regulate it. It means only that it is within Congress's power to regulate. Congress could no doubt choose to regulate unwisely. (Imagine that!) But the question of power is different from the question of wisdom. And the line Marshall was drawing was the line around authority, not insight.

Now, consider this point generalized. Consider the consequences of an ever-increasing scope for congressional power, caused by the ever-tightening integration of the national economy. As the economy becomes more integrated, with more cases in which activity in one state plausibly affects other states—should the reach of Congress's power grow as well? Under Marshall's formulation, it is clear that it does grow. But whether it *should* grow—whether that growth is consistent with the intent of the Framers—depends upon what we think they expected about the scope of federal authority. Certainly the Framers believed that federal authority would be limited—in 1791. Certainly they believed the dominant locus of regulatory power would be the states— in 1791. But did they mean that balance to remain the same throughout time? Did they expect that their Constitution would keep the division roughly the same? Or did they expect that as the nation became more of a nation, the scope of federal power would grow?

There are strong advocates for each side of this fundamental divide.[57] Some say the Framers intended federal power to grow as the nation became more integrated and that the plain consequence of that growth would be the displacement of state authority. Some say the Framers intended federal power to be perpetually checked by vigorous state authority—that the balance struck in 1791 was to be preserved across time, by whatever means, to ensure that the federal government would never be the exclusive, or even dominant, source of legislative authority.

We don't need to determine which of these two sides is right as a matter of historical fact. For now, I want you to imagine you're a justice of the Supreme Court who believes that fidelity requires you to check the expansion of federal authority. That the *meaning* of the Constitution, in other words, is that the Framers constitutionalized a balance between federal and state authority in which the federal government certainly had a legitimate and important domain of authority, touching at least those important federal matters that one or a few states alone couldn't, but the state governments would retain a perpetual predominance in regulatory authority over their citizens.

If you were such a justice, what should you do as an ever-increasing economy brings more and more within the reach of federal power? How should you respond to this conflict between the apparently plain meaning of the constitutional text (which, as reasonably interpreted by Chief Justice Marshall, gives Congress an ever-expanding scope for federal authority) and your view about what the Framers meant? Between text and meaning, which should prevail? And even if you're convinced that, on balance, meaning should prevail, how could it? What could you do? If you can't get the actual words of the Constitution changed, how can you preserve what you view as its meaning?

The answer comes from a metaphor drawn from a technique that we're all familiar with but that doesn't immediately or obviously suggest itself when we think about the work of a Court. That metaphor I call *translation*. The core of fidelity to meaning—at least for an old text, interpreted across time— is a practice of translation. But to introduce that practice, we need to think a bit more about what translation is. That's the objective of Chapter 3.

| Translation

E VERYONE KNOWS WHAT translation is. Every one of us has seen an interpreter's work many times: with a headphone and a mic, the interpreter listens to a speech in one language and reproduces the speech in another language almost immediately. It is a craft that inspires. So too with texts: the translator starts with a text written in one language and works to reproduce that text in a second language. The two texts are different—indeed, the script could even be different, with one in the Latin alphabet, the other in the Cyrillic alphabet—but if the translation work is done well, the meaning of the two different texts is the same. The task of translation may seem almost automatic, and the results may seem either right or wrong, like when a fifth-grade teacher grades a math exam. Translation, on this view, is the process of finding an equivalence in the meaning of texts, differences in language notwithstanding.

But this process is not easy, either between languages or even within a single language across time. Consider three stories that reveal something of the complexity in the search for equivalence in meaning, even within a single language, even across a relatively brief period of time.

In 2007, the American Movie Channel launched a new series by Matthew Weiner: *Mad Men*, set in the 1960s and based on Madison Avenue advertising firms. The production was beautiful, the characters were compelling, and the story (for a certain generation at least) utterly fascinating. But after obsessively watching the first season, I found myself hating just about everyone in the show. And then I found myself hating the period—the early 1960s.

At first I couldn't quite understand why. But then I recognized that some of the hatred must have been intended.[1] The show seemed designed to get us to hate our parents. Episodes are punctuated with behavior that we today find completely reprehensible. There isn't a moment when someone isn't smoking in places where today it is a crime. There isn't a woman in any position of power (in the first season at least) or a woman who isn't in some way affected by the sexism of the age. Alcohol is consumed throughout the day; people drive while drunk all the time. And in one particularly egregious example, a kid comes into a room with a plastic dry-cleaning bag over his head. The audience's reaction is terror—at the possibility that the bag will suffocate the child. The mother's reaction is terror—at the thought that the dress that had been in the bag was lying somewhere crumpled on the floor.

Once you notice this strategy of hatred-by-design, you can recognize something about other films or television shows made today depicting the same period. While they too have smoking and drinking and what we'd call sexual harassment within the story, those elements are often muted. They're made more subtle than they actually were, almost to the point of making them invisible. At least where they are not central to the story, they're downplayed. Relative to how things actually were, they are distorted.

So how could a director defend a decision to distort the reality of the world she was depicting? What could ever justify it?

One justification for such distortion could, paradoxically, be fidelity.

If it is a love story you're telling, with the aim of making compelling or attractive one or both characters in the telling, that story is distorted if it gets burdened by behaviors that today we would find repulsive and which are not central to that love. If the main characters are not evil, stupid, or weak, portraying them as harassers (because of the way a man deals with a woman), or oblivious (the kid with a plastic bag), or pathological drinkers (driving with an open fifth of whiskey) distracts from the story. The director wants the interaction of the characters to be the story, not our moralisms about their society or ours. And so she downplays elements from the past when they would distract us today—unless, of course, her purpose is precisely to reveal the moralism of today by the contrast with the past.

Or put differently, the director might well *translate* the story she is telling, by changing parts of the original in order to preserve the meaning of the original in a different context.

A second example: We all know the story of the Good Samaritan. Here's the account as it appears in the King James Bible:

But he, willing to justify himself, said unto Jesus, and who is my neighbor?

And Jesus answering said, A certain *man* went down from Jerusalem to Jericho, and fell among thieves, which stripped him of his raiment, and wounded him, and departed, leaving him half dead.

And by chance there came down a certain priest that way: and when he saw him, he passed by on the other side.

And likewise, a Levite, when he was at the place, came on and looked on him, and passed by on the other side.

But a certain Samaritan, as he journeyed, came where he was: and when he saw him, he had compassion on him, and went to him, and bound up his wounds, pouring in oil and wine, and set him on his own breast, and brought him to an inn, and took care of him.

And on the morrow when he departed he took out two pence and gave them to the host, and said unto him, Take care of him; and whatsoever thou spendest more, when I come again, I will repay thee.

Which now of these three, thinkest thou, was neighbor unto him that fell among the thieves?

And he said, He that shewed mercy on him.

More than forty years ago, thinking the meaning of this story was obscure to modern audiences, Clarence Jordan offered a different "translation" of the story in his *Cotton Patch Version of Luke and Acts*:[2]

But the Sunday school teacher, trying to save face, asked, "But...er... but...who *is* my neighbor?"

Then Jesus laid into him and said, "A man was going from Atlanta to Albany and some gangsters held him up. When they had robbed him of his wallet and brand-new suit, they beat him up and drove off in his car, leaving him unconscious on the shoulder of the highway.

"Now it just so happened that a white preacher was going down that same highway. When he saw the fellow, he stepped on the gas and went scooting by.

"Shortly afterwards a white Gospel song leader came down the road, and when he saw what had happened, he too stepped on the gas.

"Then a black man traveling that way came upon the fellow, and what he saw moved him to tears. He stopped and bound up his wounds as best he could, drew some water from his water-jug to wipe away the blood and then laid him on the back seat. He drove on into Albany and took him to the hospital and said to the nurse, 'You all take good care of this white man I found on the highway. Here's the only two dollars I got, but you all keep account of what he owes, and if he can't pay it, I'll settle up with you when I make a pay-day.'

"Now if you had been the man held up by the gangsters, which of these three... would you consider to have been your neighbor?"

The teacher of the adult Bible class said, "Why, of course, the nig— I mean, er... well, er... the one who treated me kindly."[3]

Jordan's text is different from the text in the King James Bible. But in an important sense, to us, today, it is more faithful to the original meaning than the original text would be. As Jordan explained his revision:

> Why a "cotton patch" version? While there have been many excellent translations of the Scriptures into modern English, they still have left us stranded in some faraway land in the long-distant past. We need to have the good news come to us not only in our own tongue but in our own time. We want to be participants in the faith, not merely spectators.... So, the "cotton patch" version is an attempt to translate not only the words but the events. We change the setting from first-century Palestine to twentieth-century America. We ask our brethren of long ago to cross the time-space barrier and talk to us not only in modern English but about modern problems, feelings, frustrations, hopes and assurances.[4]

Jordan, as a translator, changed the words that had lost their meaning—for example, "Samaritan," which for most people today is a positive descriptor because of the story, but in Jesus's day it referred to a native of Samaria, people who at the time had a reputation for being insensitive. That change, he believed, was a change of fidelity, at least if the consequence was that the original meaning was better conveyed to his intended audience.

Among translation theorists, some might question whether Jordan's work should be called "translation" rather than a creative paraphrase. But translations of the Bible raise precisely the most important current theoretical struggle among translation theorists. Should a translator "domesticate" the text she is translating, or should she leave the feeling that the text is foreign?

This is the question at the core of Lawrence Venuti's powerful and important work *The Translator's Invisibility: A History of Translation* (2008). Venuti laments practices of translation that render the translator invisible. In the pursuit of fluency, the translator devalues his own work. That leads to fewer great translators, and to fewer translations that preserve the values of the source culture. Hegemonic translation bleeds original difference from the text; "deforming tendencies," as Antoine Berman calls them, render the original culture invisible.[5]

Yet the reason for this deformation, of course, is quite practical. The most common aim of biblical translation is conversion. Venuti reviews the work of Eugene Nida, a founding member of the Wycliffe Bible Translators. That group's aim, Venuti reports, is to translate the Bible into every currently spoken language. In that process, Nida distinguishes between "formal equivalence" and "dynamic equivalence." Formal equivalence focuses upon the form and content of a message. Its aim is to reproduce the grammatical units of the original. By contrast, dynamic equivalence is concerned with naturalness of expression or fluency. Its aim, as with the *Cotton Patch* versions of the Gospels, is to replicate the reader's response across languages rather than replicating the semantic content across languages.

Which method is appropriate, of course, cannot be determined in the abstract. If you're saving souls, it's a fair argument that you should focus on the most efficient tool for soul saving. (Wrote literary critic George Steiner: "No man must be kept from salvation by mere barriers of language.")[6] But if your focus is the preservation of a practice of knowledge or an understanding of a culture, the readers' responses are not the only end to be kept in view. The truth, understanding, or reflection might also be relevant.

Bibles are important to the story this book will tell. Our Constitution is our civic bible. How the religious carry their meaning forward has plenty to teach us here.

The third example: A 1985 federal law said that a veteran could pay an attorney no more than $10 for services related to a veterans' benefit suit.[7] The effect of that limit, of course, was to make it all but impossible to retain an attorney to advocate for a veterans' benefit. The puzzle was why the government was so keen to keep lawyers away.

In *Walters v. National Association of Radiation Survivors* (1985), the Supreme Court upheld this limitation against a challenge based in due process.[8] According to the Court, the government had an interest in keeping the benefits proceedings simple and cheap. That interest would be defeated if attorneys were allowed to muck up the process. Effectively barring attorneys thus served a rational end. The statute was constitutional.

So far, so good—for a statute written in 1985. But the limit in the statute interpreted in *Walters* was not written in 1985. It was written in 1865. And when it was written in 1865, its meaning (or purpose or intent or function or aim or effect or whatever else you want to say) was simply to limit the fees attorneys could charge, not to exclude lawyers from veterans' benefits proceedings altogether. As Justice John Paul Stevens (in dissent) pointed out, in 1865 $10 was the equivalent of $580 in 1986, and $580 in 1986 was certainly adequate for the services an attorney would render (as $10 was in 1868).

When enacted, therefore, the statute was a price ceiling, and like all meaningful ceilings, it was a ceiling because it was well above the price floor. But given how the statute was read by the Court in 1986, because of inflation the ceiling had fallen to the floor. The failure to change the $10 figure was thus, as Stevens argued, a failure to interpret the statute faithfully.[9] Fidelity, Stevens insisted, would require a change; not changing the statute, by contrast, was infidelity.[10]

———

All three stories circle the same fundamental point. In each, an interpreter must decide how best to carry over something from the past. (The early Renaissance historian Leonardo Bruni's use of the word *traductio* rather than the previously used Latin words for "translation," *interpretare, vertere,* and *convertere,* is suggestive here. *Traductio* is a spatial metaphor—carrying a text from a foreign land, as either the spoils of war or a gift.)[11] In each, she must decide how "to preserve the force of the original utterance—not only the overall meaning of what has been said but the meaning that the saying of it has."[12] In each, that decision is not obvious. A simple or direct rendering of the original text in the new context could well obscure the original meaning. To avoid that obscuring, the person rendering the old text in the new context must make choices about which bits to carry over and which bits to leave alone. In a very literal sense, that person *changes* the original text, no doubt. Her justification, if indeed that change is justified, is that those changes *preserve* an original meaning in a new or different context.

These stories force into the foreground an assumption about the relationship between fidelity and change—an assumption that is common among lawyers but which obviously fails. That assumption is this: that fidelity means no change. Or conversely, that change means infidelity.

Justice Hugo Black (serving on the Court from 1937 to 1971) was the high priest of this canonical view. His scoldings produced a generation of lawyers who believed there was a badge of infidelity affixed to those who desired to keep the Constitution "in tune with the times."[13] And cowering before the tower of Justice Black's righteousness have been generations of constitutional "tuners," defending their "tunings" on grounds of necessity while attacking Black's refusal to "tune" with the claim that not "tuning" is just impossible.[14]

Yet just think for a second about the image that Black's metaphor evokes: "tuning." Is "tuning" really unfaithful?

A concert pianist plays a series of outdoor concerts. On the third night, the temperature falls dramatically, causing the piano to fall out of tune. Is it more faithful to Beethoven to leave the piano out of tune? Would tuning the piano be the same kind of infidelity as adding a couple of bars to the end of the first movement? Is there no difference between tuning so that the music sounds the same at each performance and changing the tempo or cutting some particularly dark passages so the music sounds "better"?

The point that Justice Black apparently missed, but which the translator relies upon, is that meaning is contextual.[15] Words are written in a context. If they have meaning, they have meaning because of that context. "Political actions...that happen in and through the use of language," as political scientist Terence Ball puts it, "presuppose shared understandings among political actors, understandings that are deeply embedded in social and political practices."[16] Meaning depends on context: how a context *is* affects what a text will mean.

Likewise, how the context changes affects how the meaning can change. Think about it like this: If meaning is what these words do, then it is as if these words pull certain levers, or press certain buttons, or tap certain keys on a keyboard; these levers or buttons or keys are the context, and what this pulling or pressing or tapping does depend upon how these levers or buttons or keys are structured. If they are structured one way, then they have one meaning; another way, another meaning. Any author choosing her meaning, then, must be aware of, and depend upon, how the context is structured.

It follows that if meaning depends on context, then the very same text written in two different contexts can mean quite different things ("Meet me in Cambridge" written in England can mean something very different from "Meet me in Cambridge" written in Massachusetts).[17] Likewise, a different text written in two different contexts can mean the same thing ("Meet me in Cambridge, Massachusetts" written in England can mean the same thing as "Meet me in Cambridge" written in Massachusetts). Whether the meaning changes from one context to another depends not just on whether the text remains the same, but also on whether the contexts have remained relevantly similar as well. If the text is the same but the contexts are different, then the meanings may be different; if both the texts and the contexts are different, it is possible that the texts may have the same meaning. As professor and translator David Bellos puts it, describing translators who change the words they translate, "They are not trying to change anything—whereas when we repeat something without translating it, we usually intend to make some small or large difference to it."[18]

This point is as true about writing as about reading, for words are read in context no less than they are written in context. Just as differences in meaning can follow from differences in the context of writing (X means A here but B there), so too may differences in meaning follow from differences in the context of reading, or, more important, from the gap between the context of reading and the context of writing (X means A when read here but B when read there).[19] "Richard Branson was a public school dropout" written and read in America would mean that Branson attended and dropped out of a state-funded school; the same text written and read in England would mean that Branson attended and dropped out of a private school; but the same text written in America and read in England would either confuse or simply raise questions.[20] What its meaning was—or what its author intended its meaning to be, or what "those words would mean in the mouth of a normal speaker of English, using them in the circumstances in which they were used"—depends upon a judgment about the context against which we will read the text.[21] Obviously, at times this judgment can be critical.

Between the context of writing and the context of reading, then, there can arise an interpretive gap. It is this gap that suggests the general problem that gives rise to the subject of this book. When the gap is small—when the context of writing is very close to the context of reading—then any confusion caused by differences in context can also be small. Reading can proceed as if context did not matter; judges can say "interpretation begins as always with the text read" as if interpretation really did involve just a text that is read.[22] Or again, where contexts remain close, they may also remain invisible.

But when the gap is not small—when the differences in context grow quite large—then reading cannot proceed as if context did not matter.[23] Or at least it cannot so proceed if the aim is fidelity. For by ignoring the change in context, the reader may well rewrite original meaning. A reading of fidelity must take responsibility for the context of interpretation. She must make sure that context doesn't render the meaning different.

"Translation" in this sense is a heuristic for reckoning differences in context. It is a device for rendering a text in a target context that preserves the meaning of the source text in the source context. As applied to the law, it is a device for rendering a reading of a text in the target context (usually a judicial opinion) that preserves the meaning of the source text (a statute, or in the context we'll consider most carefully, a constitution). The reading aims to achieve the same meaning in the target context that a faithful reading in the source context would have produced. It aims to neutralize, to the extent that is possible, the changes that would undermine an original meaning.

We can represent the relationship as shown in Figure 1.

Obviously, I mean this heuristic as a metaphor for a linguistic practice typically carried out elsewhere. That practice, too, is often described as "a special, heightened case of the process of communication and reception in any act of human speech."[24] As George Steiner puts it:

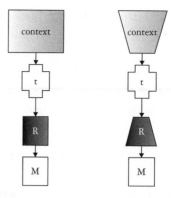

"Translation," properly understood, is a special case of the arc of communication which every successful speech-act closes within a given language.... The model 'sender to receiver' which represents any semiological and semantic process is ontologically equivalent to the model 'source-language to receptor-language' used in the theory of translation.... [T]he motions of spirit, to use Dante's phrase, are rigorously analogous. So, as we shall see, are the most frequent causes of misunderstanding or, what is the same, of failure to translate correctly. In short: inside or between languages, human communication equals translation.

———

As I've studied the theory and practice of linguistic translation, I've been struck by the similarities in the challenges faced by the linguistic translator and the judge.[25] Those similarities have inspired the theory I am building here.

Like the judge, the linguistic translator aims to preserve meaning across context. How that is done, whether it can be done, and whether it can be done well are questions, not givens. But the stated objective of both orients the work of each: to find an equivalence between two contexts. In a legal context, this is in the reading the judge gives of a text written much earlier; in the literary context, this is the translation a translator gives of a text written in a different context.

As is also the case for the judge, the linguistic translator's job is made more difficult by the passing of time. As George Steiner writes:

As Dilthey was probably the first to emphasize, every act of understanding is itself involved in history, in a relativity of perspective. This is the reason for the commonplace observation that each age translates anew, that interpretation, except in the first momentary instance, is always reinterpretation, both of the original and of the intervening body of commentary.[26]

The same is true for the law: "each age translates anew," not necessarily to improve or update the original text, but even just to preserve the original meaning in a new interpretive context.

Like the judge, the linguistic translator recognizes the difficulty in her work but rejects the idea that the work is impossible. Again, Steiner: "To dismiss the validity of translation because it is not always possible and never perfect is absurd."[27] He continues:

> Not everything can be translated.... Not everything can be translated now. Contexts can be lost, bodies of reference which in the past made it possible to interpret a piece of writing which now eludes us.... There are texts which we cannot yet translate but which may... become translatable in the future. The source language and the language of the translator are in dual motion.... The argument against translatability is, therefore, often no more than an argument based on local, temporary myopia.[28]

Like the judge, the linguistic translator must decide how he will respect the original text. Should he improve the text translated, making it the best it could be? Or is his job to carry over the warts as well as the gems?

This question points to a strong conflict within both the law and the theory of linguistic translation. One side in both fields rejects the idea that the translator should improve the text being translated. No doubt the translation work must be creative, but creativity must not cover up illicit change.[29]

> "A translator is to be like his author," wrote Dr. Johnson in reference to Dryden, "it is not his business to excel him." Where he does so, the original is subtly injured. And the reader is robbed of a just view.[30]

This resistance to improvement is for many an ethic. Consider how one commentator describes it:

> The ethos of the translator is a perfect blend of humility and pride. His two greatest virtues... are the reverence he feels toward the author or work he translates, and the sense of his own integrity as an interpreter, which is based on both modesty and self-respect.... There is no literary worker more respectful of the property of his fellow artist, none less willing to infringe on what takes the legal name of copyright. The translator always gives full credit, sometimes even more credit than is due, to the maker of a blueprint that he could not use without considerably changing and adapting. All these characteristics indicate that the translator is perhaps the only modern artist who acts and

behaves as if he were only an artisan . . . serving with simple and single-minded devotion a beauty to which he cannot give his name, and yet not unaware of the nobility of his calling, of the dignity of his task.[31]

Or as the writer and academic Reuben Brower put it, "Faithful ugliness and faithless beauty."[32] "The aim of the good translator," writes the Italian comparative literature scholar Renato Poggioli, "is to sacrifice himself so completely to the work that his personality completely disappears."[33]

These same sentiments are the party line in the law as well. The judge's duty, or so fidelitists insist, is not to improve the text she interprets. The duty of fidelity is fidelity to the strengths and weaknesses in the source text. It is democracy that crafts the source text, not the judges. And if there is a failing in the source, it is democracy's task to fix it.

Finally, like the practice of a judge, the practice of translation must embody an ethic of charity. It involves, as George Steiner puts it, an "initiative trust":

All understanding, and the demonstrative statement of understanding which is translation, starts with an act of trust. This confiding will, ordinarily, be instantaneous and unexamined, but it has a complex base. It is an operative convention which derives from a sequence of phenomenological assumptions about the coherence of the world, about the presence of meaning in very different, perhaps formally antithetical semantic systems, about the validity of analogy and parallel. The radical generosity of the translator ("I grant beforehand that there must be something there"), his trust in the "other," as yet untried, unmapped alternity of statement, concentrates to a philosophically dramatic degree the human bias towards seeing the world as symbolic, as constituted of relations in which "this" can stand for "that," and must in fact be able to do so if there are to be meanings and structures. . . . As he sets out, the translator must gamble on the coherence, on the symbolic plenitude of the world.[34]

The translator, as Leonardo Bruni notes, like the judge, must "turn his whole mind, heart, and will to his author, and in a sense transform him."[35] It is an ultimate act of humility; the translator's practice is essentially one of self-effacement, as Venuti has described it. But in that self-effacement, the translator, like the judge, credits the author. She yields to the author's judgment, and aims not to question or critique, but to carry the work across a cultural and hence linguistic distance, rendering it as beautiful as it can be. This is an obligation of the translator, like the judge. It is an ethic that links both interpretive practices.

And not just a link in ethics. Even more compelling are the parallels in the details of the practice. The translator, we are told, must "have a perfect grasp of 'the sense and spirit' of his author. He must possess knowledge in depth of the language of the original as well as of his own tongue."[36] The text must be "related to [its] own world view before we can accurately assess what timeless truths [it] may convey to us."[37] And to understand it effectively, "we learn to listen... we must discipline our own attention.... The need for self-effacement, for submissive scruple, is imaged in 'understand.' The more receptive our listening inward, the better the chance that we shall hear a force and logic of expression more central than 'meaning.'"[38]

Likewise with the judge. As Thomas Jefferson put it in personal correspondence, "On every question of construction, [we should] carry ourselves back to the time when the Constitution was adopted, recollect the spirit manifested in the debates, and instead of trying [to find] what meaning may be squeezed out of the text, or invented against it, conform to the probable one in which it was [passed]."[39] Noted Justice Joseph Story: "The first and fundamental rule in the interpretation of all instruments is, to construe them according to the sense of the terms, and the intention of the parties."[40] That is only done by the judge "immers[ing] herself in the world of the adopters to try to understand constitutional concepts and values from their perspective."[41] Wrote the founding jurist of American law (though he himself was not American), William Blackstone:

> The fairest and most rational method to interpret the will of the legislator, is by exploring his intentions at a time when the law was made, by signs, the most natural and probable. And these *signs* are either the words, the context, the subject matter, the effects and consequence, or the spirit and reason of the law.[42]

For judge and translator both, this common ethic and common method yield common challenges. For example, both confront the problem of the underdetermined source. The translator who needs to translate "Gorbachev went to New York" into certain dialects of Zapotec needs to know whether he had ever been to New York before.[43] To translate "I hired a worker" into Russian, he must know whether the worker was male or female.[44] In both cases, the source text is incomplete; with both, the context must be interrogated. For the judge, a statute that provides for the shifting of "attorney's fees as part of costs" is ambiguous, because the law has changed about whether such words include the shifting of expert witness fees. To resolve that ambiguity, the date of the statute must be included as well.[45]

Both may also confront the problem of an overdetermined source. For the translator, if an English text includes the sex of a worker, the sex is likely significant to the story. If the sex is not significant, it isn't indicated. But in Russian, sex is always indicated. So the translator of a Russian reference to a "worker" must decide whether carrying the sex of the worker over into English is required. Whether that is indeed required cannot be determined from the text alone; it derives from the text in context. In the judicial context, consider the issue of whether the Constitution permits Congress to establish an air force. The text explicitly grants Congress the power "to raise and support armies" (but only for two years), and also the power "to provide and maintain a Navy" (not so limited). But it nowhere speaks of an air force. Does that mean an air force is not permitted?[46] If the Constitution were so drafted today, that would be a strong argument. But because it was drafted in 1787, long before any air force was technologically possible, the argument makes no sense. So to resolve the question one need look beyond the text; alone, the text is overdetermined.

Oliver Wendell Holmes Jr., long before he was a justice on the United States Supreme Court, confronted a similar example in 1901, while he was chief justice of the Massachusetts Supreme Judicial Court. The state constitution provided that voting was to be accomplished by "written vote." Did that rule exclude voting machines? If a law were passed today requiring voting by "written vote," that would most likely be read to exclude voting machines, since voting machines are now present, and are apparently excluded by a clause requiring "written votes." But given that the clause in the Massachusetts constitution was written in 1780, when there were no voting machines, Holmes read the provision not to exclude voting machines. Reading the clause restrictively in this way would be to read it anachronistically.[47] But to know whether it is anachronistic is to know something more than the text.

Translators and judges may also encounter the problem of transformed significance. Legal and literature scholar James Boyd White notes, for example, that "the German 'Wald' is different from the English 'forest,' or the American 'woods,' not only linguistically but physically: the trees are different."[48] Because of such differences in significance, the translator may have to pick a wholly different term, or construct a wholly different phrase, to capture the sense of the source term in the target context. Translator Gregory Rabassa describes a source text that was important for the very fact that it had coined the phrase being translated, but the translated text would lose that significance.[49] Bellos describes translating a crime novel that had a "comically grandiloquent passage of direct speech that recycled a famous line from Victor Hugo." To recreate the effect of "misplaced hyperbole," Bellos substituted "a barely altered quotation from a speech by Winston Churchill."[50]

In the legal realm, it is completely clear that the Framers envisioned the death penalty as part of the new nation's legal practice. The due process clause of the Fifth Amendment explicitly contemplates someone being "deprived of life," so the idea that the Eighth Amendment (prohibiting "cruel and unusual punishments") banned the death penalty would be odd, at least in the original context. But as American constitutional law scholar Paul Brest has argued, "Was death the same event for inhabitants of the American colonies in the late eighteenth century as it is two centuries later? Death was not only a much more routine and public phenomenon then, but the fear of death was more effectively contained within a system of religious belief."[51] That difference may justify asking whether death as a penalty should be deemed "cruel."

For both judge and translator, there is a decision to be made about the level of generality that will guide the translation. Cicero famously distinguished between translating "as an interpreter" and translating "as an orator." The orator "keeps the same ideas and the forms, or as one might say, the 'figures' of thought, but in language which conforms to our usage." The interpreter "render[s] word for word." He defended his own practice, arguing, "I did not think I ought to count [words] out to the reader like coins, but to pay them by weight, as it were."[52] And Supreme Court justices Antonin Scalia and John Marshall Harlan II have weighed in on the seemingly endless debate about the "level of generality" at which our legal "tradition" gets rendered, with Scalia arguing for the most specific and Harlan rejecting the limits of specific traditions.[53]

Finally, both the judge and the translator face a particular challenge with texts that are old. In translation, as Brower puts it, "translating is necessitated not only by differences in the national language of speakers or writers, but also by distance in space and time within a single language."[54] That's because "when we read, we read from a particular point in space and time."[55] A given time embeds understandings that may be invisible later on. George Steiner describes the difficulty for us in reading Jane Austen:

> A thorough gloss on Miss Dashwood's thoughts would engage not only problems of contemporary diction, but an awareness of the manifold ways in which Jane Austen enlists two previous bodies of linguistic convention: that of Restoration comedy, and that of post-Richardsonian sentimental fiction. The task is the more difficult because many of the decisive words have a "timeless," immediately accessible mien. In fact, they are firmly localized in a transitional, partially artificial code of consciousness.[56]

In law, Francis Lieber, a nineteenth-century legal theorist whose theory of interpretation comes the closest to the idea of translation I am using here (his word was "construction"), writes,

> The farther removed the time of the origin of any text may be from us, the more we are at times authorized or bound, as the case may be, to resort to extensive construction. For times and the relations of things change, and if the laws, &c., do not change accordingly, to effect which is rarely in the power of the construer, they must be applied according to the altered circumstances if they shall continue to mean sense or to remain beneficial.[57]

"The older a law," Lieber writes, "or any text containing regulations of our actions... the more extensive the construction must be."[58]

———

These parallels suggest that the metaphor of translation might illustrate the practice of judicial interpretation of our Constitution. They show how, for example, readings of the Supreme Court that are nominally different might nonetheless be readings of fidelity—not necessarily, of course, but possibly. Put differently, translation offers one possible way to read "change" charitably. No doubt the doctrine of the Court has, in one sense, changed. With the metaphor of translation, we could then ask whether that change was real or merely nominal. Did the change, in other words, actually alter the meaning? Or was the change a way to preserve the meaning? The challenge is to understand how much of the change that we've seen across the history of Supreme Court doctrine might be charitably interpreted.[59]

My own work has not tried to develop a complete map of the translation metaphor. Others have, and their work is rewarding for a theoretical inquiry.[60] My work instead has embraced this general tool to a particular end: If translation is a kind of fidelity, then how much of the changes in the readings of the Supreme Court can be understood as, in effect, translations to the end of fidelity?

The answer is surprising. As I argue in the chapters that follow, the most important so-called innovations in Supreme Court doctrine—both from the Right and from the Left—are best understood as translations. They reflect, in other words, not infidelity, but fidelity given a particular conception of the original meaning.

Translation also gives us a clear way to understand two kinds of originalism—what I will call "one-step originalism" and "two-step originalism." Translation itself is a two-step process. In the first step, the translator understands the text in its original context. In the second step, the translator then carries that first step meaning into the present or target context. This is two-step originalism. By contrast, one-step originalism stops at the first step, asking, "What would the Framers have done?" and then doing just that. Thus, Justice Scalia, ordinarily a one-step originalist, famously struggled about whether he could accept the one-step conclusion that the Eighth Amendment should not prohibit flogging. In that context at least, Scalia believed originalism requires just one step—asking how the Framers would have answered the question in 1791.[61] In the balance of this book, two-step originalism will explain the most important innovations that originalists will practice.

That's not the end of the story. It is just the beginning. Translation alone leaves many twists in the history of Supreme Court doctrine unexplained. But for now, let's focus on the sense in which these important doctrinal innovations are understandable as translations of an earlier constitutional commitment. Once that point is clear, we will then consider how those twists should best be understood.

## *Simple Starts:* Classic

My aim is to reveal a common pattern among judicial interpreters on the Left and the Right across the history of the Court's interpretation of our Constitution. Yet before we frame this move in a ideological way, let's begin with an example that none of us would see in a ideological way today: *United States v. Classic* (1941).[62] In many ways, this case—practically forgotten today because the conclusion is so obvious—illustrates precisely the practice of the Court as translator.

The issue in *Classic* was whether federal election law applied in a primary to select candidates who would run for Congress. Specifically, did federal law protecting the right of voters to have their votes counted fairly apply to the votes in a primary as well as to the votes in a general election?

The premise for the claim that such law did apply was Article I, Section 2:

The House of Representatives shall be composed of Members chosen every second Year by the People of the several States, and the Electors in each State shall have the Qualifications requisite for Electors of the most numerous Branch of the State Legislature.

That choosing is done, as Section 4 of the same article describes, through elections, with the "Times, Places and Manner of holding [such] Elections...prescribed in each State by the Legislature thereof." The people entitled to vote in such elections (that is, the electors) are the same as the people entitled to vote in the election for the "most numerous Branch of the State Legislature." So if you are allowed to vote for candidates in the Texas state house of representatives, you are allowed to vote for members of Congress in the election where they are chosen.

But is the primary such an "election"? The consequence of an election is that someone is elected. Yet the thing about a primary is that no one is elected to anything at all; instead, all a primary does is determine who gets to run in the actual (or "general") election. So if it's clear (and it is) that federal law governing elections applies to a general election, can it also apply to a primary?

This is a puzzle because for most of the history of the United States before *Classic*, there were no such things as primaries. Candidates were selected at party conventions by party members or party bosses. The ordinary public had no right to participate in those selections. They only had a right to vote for the candidate selected—or not.

But once states began to select candidates through primaries, voters had a wider role. Now it wasn't just the bosses who selected the candidates, it was also the public. Thus, the question the Supreme Court had to resolve was whether this change meant that the primary was also now an election subject to the (indirect) control of Congress.

The Court, through Justice Harlan Fiske Stone, held that it was. Its reasoning began with a point that was quite practical: it was effectively impossible to be elected to anything in Louisiana if you did not run in the primary. The loser in a primary was forbidden from running in the general election. So, apart from winning a primary, the only way to appear on the general election ballot (or to have a vote for you counted if your name was written in) was to decide not to run in the primary election and then qualify as an "independent" for the general election or indicate to the state your willingness to have write-in votes for you counted. These restrictions meant that, practically speaking, the primary was a part of the process by which candidates ultimately get elected.

Yet did that mean that the primary is subject to federal law? As Stone wrote:

> We may assume that the framers of the Constitution in adopting that section, did not have specifically in mind the selection and elimination of candidates for Congress by the direct primary any more than they contemplated the application of the commerce clause to interstate telephone, telegraph and wireless communication which are concededly within it. But in determining whether a provision of the Constitution applies to a new subject matter, it is of little significance

that it is one with which the framers were not familiar. For in setting up an enduring framework of government they undertook to carry out for the indefinite future and in all the vicissitudes of the changing affairs of men, those fundamental purposes which the instrument itself discloses. Hence, we read its words, not as we read legislative codes which are subject to continuous revision with the changing course of events, but as the revelation of the great purposes which were intended to be achieved by the Constitution as a continuing instrument of government.[63]

The words of our Constitution do more than speak—they "reve[al]...the great purposes which were intended to be achieved." And it is by "reading" the Constitution's words in this particular way that the Court would determine whether a primary counts as an election. As Stone continued:

We turn to the words of the Constitution read in their historical setting as revealing the purpose of its framers, and in search for admissible meanings of its words which, in the circumstances of their application, will effectuate those purposes....

Long before the adoption of the Constitution the form and mode of that expression had changed from time to time. There is no historical warrant for supposing that the framers were under the illusion that the method of effecting the choice of the electors would never change or that if it did, the change was for that reason to be permitted to defeat the right of the people to choose representatives for Congress which the Constitution had guaranteed.... Where the state law has made the primary an integral part of the procedure of choice, or where in fact the primary effectively controls the choice, the right of the elector to have his ballot counted at the primary, is likewise included in the right protected by Article I, § 2.... [W]e cannot close our eyes to the fact already mentioned that the practical influence of the choice of candidates at the primary may be so great as to affect profoundly the choice at the general election even though there is no effective legal prohibition upon the rejection at the election of the choice made at the primary and may thus operate to deprive the voter of his constitutional right of choice.[64]

Looking to the framing context, the Court finds an original meaning. Here a one-step originalist would stop. But a two-step originalist takes one step more: looking to the context within which it decides the case, the Court takes account of changes in context that would defeat that original meaning.

Within the constraint of the Constitution's words, the Court seeks to avoid that defeat by a "search for admissible meanings of its words which, in the circumstances of their application, will effectuate those purposes." That search yielded the conclusion that a primary was indeed an election—even though it was an election that elected no one. The "great purposes" were secured by reading the Constitution to reach a practice that would not have been reached in 1789; any other reading would have defeated those "great purposes" by allowing the states to escape federal control (if desired) over the election of federal officers—that is, members of Congress.

This is translation. In Parts II and III, we'll consider how much in our tradition follows this pattern. But before we do that, to orient at least the scholars, it is important to distinguish what I'm describing from other related accounts.

## *What Translation Is Not*

There is an extraordinary diversity of interpretive theories about our Constitution, few of which try to fit themselves into clear categories. But among the most prominent, we can distinguish which are within the family of translation and which are not.

The best and most prominent example that seems to come close, but which is not, on my understanding, "translation" is David Strauss's account of "common law constitutionalism." In a series of articles and an extraordinary book, Strauss, a professor at the University of Chicago, maps a practice of interpretation that sees the results of cases changing over time.[65] And he links that change, both descriptively and normatively, to the idea of common-law lawmaking.

To any American lawyer, that idea will be familiar. But because I hope that at least a few non-lawyers might find themselves in these pages, let me introduce the idea in a few paragraphs.

Unlike many continental systems, the Anglo-American tradition of law has always held a prominent place for judges. Partly because, especially in the American context, judges are appointed late in their career, judges hold an esteem within the system of law that career judges in the Continental system just can't quite match. That prominence has allowed them to play a more creative or constructive role in crafting the law. Legislatures have been willing to effectively delegate to judges policymaking authority, at least interstitially (and in some cases not just interstitially—for example, federal courts have played an extraordinary role in defining the nature and development of antitrust law, and state courts have had a powerful role defining the evolution of contract law and tort law).

Critically, in this process judges are not asking what someone else meant or intended or wanted. In the best of the common-law tradition, they're simply asking, "What makes sense?" That question might be bent in particular cases, with judges asking not "What makes sense?" but "What makes sense for liberals [or conservatives] like us?" But the balance of these many different questions asked by many different judges is a common law that evolves, as some have insisted, to produce an efficient set of legal norms.[66]

Strauss has taken this idea and applied it to the Constitution itself. He invites us to understand the evolution in constitutional doctrine in the same way as we understand the evolution of tort law or antitrust law: not as an effort to make sense of what happened before, but as an effort to simply make sense of the law. On this understanding, the Constitution evolves—not without constraint and not without reason—to take on the character of the time, both its values and its facts. And once we understand that dynamic, it liberates us from the task of understanding what the Framers thought about any particular issue.

Strauss's theory is beautifully framed and largely compelling. What it misses is the dynamic of fidelity to role that the next two parts of this book will describe, as well as a sufficiently convincing (to some at least) justification for judges playing this role at all. The difference between justifying the creativity of judges as translators and justifying their creativity as common-law lawyers is small, no doubt. But conceptually it is important. "I'm working as hard as I can to make sense of your choices here and now" is different from "I'm working hard to make sense of the law." The translator empowers and respects authorship differently than the common-law judge does.

The common-law judge also has difficulty explaining reversals. As we'll see later in this book, the dynamic of our jurisprudence has often taken one step forward and then two steps back. That is the dynamic that fidelity to role explains; that dynamic requires a continuing attention to framing values, even when the context will require they be suppressed.

Strauss's approach still demands a certain restraint. There's only so far a court can (or should) go, regardless of what it believes is right. By contrast, the most famous bogeyman of the conservatives—especially for the late Chief Justice William Rehnquist—is the "living constitutionalist," the judge (or more likely law professor) who wants to minimize the constraint of the Constitution and maximize the opportunity for courts to "do justice." At the extreme, the living constitutionalist simply fits her desires into the constraints of a text abstracted from any particular original context or meaning. As Attorney General Edwin Meese once described it, interpretation in this sense is "like a picnic to which the framers bring the words and the judges the meaning."[67]

It's fair to say that there are no true living constitutionalists on the Supreme Court today—and maybe never have been. But the invocation of the term certainly points in the direction of the most masterful translator in American law just now, Jack Balkin.

In his book *Living Originalism* (2011), Balkin tries to cut the knot that blocks understanding between those who believe the Constitution needs to be "updated" (so-called living constitutionalists) and those who believe we are constrained by the meaning of the text the Framers gave us (so-called originalists). Balkin rejects the distinction. Instead, in a manner that I will parallel here, he emphasizes the contingency of meaning upon understandings within the culture. That contingency means that the application of the Constitution will change, consistent with the very best ideals of fidelity. Balkin points to my own earlier work that described this as "translation." That "metaphor," Balkin agrees, "is powerful and evocative."[68] But whereas my work, Balkin insists, applies the idea vertically, telling judges what "judges *should* do," Balkin uses the idea horizontally, as a way to understand the resources available to the constitutional culture broadly to explain how meaning properly gets articulated. Translation, Balkin insists, is "something judges *actually* do, whether they intend to or not."[69]

As will become clear over the course of this book, I don't accept Balkin's distinction between his work and mine. Indeed, in my view, the "should" of constitutional law follows after the recognition of the right theory of constitutional law. Translation—or fidelity of meaning through translation—is only one part of that theory. And as I'll describe in the balance of this book, the influence of the background is certainly something that judges are not free to ignore. In this, Balkin's work is extraordinarily powerful.

If there's a difference to insist upon between our work, it is the explicit part that fidelity to role plays; there are also significant differences in how each of us accounts for particular cases or periods. I will note those differences later in this book. For now, it is enough that Balkin is a principal practitioner of the method that I endorse here, even if there are places where I will quibble about how he practices that method.

———

In the end, the translator accepts the normative authority of texts written long ago. She insists that we practice that authority through a kind of translation— horizontal *and* vertical. But if the translator is practicing the theory of fidelity this book will sketch, that effort at fidelity to meaning is inherently incomplete. Yes, changes can be faithful. But fidelity is more than fidelity to meaning.

PART TWO | Translations

THE AIM OF A COURT interpreting a constitution, at least according to the ideals of interpretive fidelity, should be to preserve that constitution's meaning across time. Translation is a metaphor for understanding how such preservation might work. A court preserves meaning by translating a text into the current context. Its aim is to produce a reading of the original text in the current context that has the same meaning as an original reading of that text in its original context.

My claim is that our Supreme Court has engaged in such translations, in cases that the Right celebrates, and in cases that the Left celebrates. That's not to say the Court has done so perfectly. It's not to say every twist in the history of constitutional law can be explained by translation alone. But it is to say that the best account of the interpretive practice of our Supreme Court over the past century puts translation at the core—at least for the range of issues I've covered here.

Yet not just translation: fidelity to meaning, it turns out, is not the only master that the Supreme Court serves. As the cases will demonstrate, the Court also practices a fidelity to role. And building upon the model of fidelity to role sketched by both *Marbury* and *McCulloch*, we can understand the evolution of Supreme Court doctrine as the product of the interaction between these two fidelities.

In the chapters that follow, I track examples of this dynamic that seem to come from the Right, and from the Left. In the middle are examples that are more (politically) ambiguous. Some of these examples will be pure instances of translation. Some will be an interaction between translation and fidelity to role. In either case, my aim is to demonstrate the centrality of both dynamics to the history of constitutional interpretation in America. Once that fit is established, a justification for both will be the subject of Chapters 20 and 21.

SECTION ONE | Fidelity on the Right

| Federalism I

O UR CONSTITUTION ESTABLISHED a government of enumerated power. That means that the federal government, unlike state governments, has only the powers that are delegated to it by the Constitution. The Framers made this idea explicitly clear in Article I, where they wrote, "Congress has the powers herein granted." *"Herein granted"*—not any power you might imagine a government to have; just those powers specified in the Constitution.

From the beginning, many constitutional lawyers have assumed that the fact of enumerated powers means that the power of the federal government must be limited. As Marshall said in *Gibbons,* "The enumeration presupposes something not enumerated."[1] Why specify particular powers if the intent was to grant power generally?

For more than a century, conservatives have tried to breathe life into this claim. In the name of federalism, they have sought ways to cabin the scope of the federal government's power, so as to preserve the balance that they believe the Framers intended between federal and state authority.

My claim is that this effort to limit the scope of federal power can best be understood as an act of fidelity—if fidelity, that is, is understood as translation. Those translations have been many. In this chapter, I sketch the first round.

## The Infidelity from Following the Text

As I described in Chapter 2, in *Gibbons v. Ogden* (1824), Chief Justice Marshall read the Constitution to grant a federal power contingent upon economic facts. Congress's commerce authority could reach (1) interstate commerce, (2) intrastate commerce that affected interstate commerce, or (3) any activity that it was necessary to regulate in order to better regulate interstate commerce. The first two heads of this authority Marshall drew from the commerce clause directly. The last most likely came from the necessary-and-proper clause.

As I've argued, this way of defining the federal commerce authority produces an obvious yield: as the national economy grows more integrated, the scope of federal authority would grow as well. If the question is whether an activity affects interstate commerce, then as technology weaves more and more commerce together, more and more would affect interstate commerce. Thus, activities not plausibly within the reach of the federal government in 1787 can, as technology and the economy change, come within the scope of federal authority in 2018.

This reading of the commerce power was not compelled. There were obvious alternatives, some pressed by the attorneys in *Gibbons* itself. Daniel Webster, representing Gibbons, advanced an even broader conception of "commerce":

> Nothing was more complex than commerce; and in such an age as this, no words embraced a wider field than commercial regulation. Almost all the business and intercourse of life may be connected, incidentally, more or less, with commercial regulations.[2]

Thomas Addis Emmet, arguing for Ogden, insisted that the Framers intended the power to regulate commerce to be concurrent—as evinced, he maintained, by the draft text of the commerce clause being changed from "shall have the power" to "shall have power."[3]

But given Marshall's reading, a good-faith interpretation of the scope of federal power circa 1825 would have yielded a federal government with a relatively small reach of commerce authority—no doubt complete and important in national matters, but incomplete where the national interest was not pronounced. As Justice Sandra Day O'Connor would put it much later, "Because virtually every *state* activity, like virtually every activity of a private individual, arguably 'affects' interstate commerce, Congress can now supplant the States from the significant sphere of activities envisioned for them by the Framers."[4] Put more directly: circa 1825, there was plenty that only the states could legitimately regulate. For much of our history, their authority was exclusive.

Over the course of the nineteenth century, as economic integration grew, the predicate for this restrictive reading on the scope of Congress's authority changed. Especially after the Civil War, as the nation's economy exploded, the plausible reach of federal authority began to explode as well. Internal improvements and changing technologies meant the "extent of the market," as Adam Smith would put it, increased.[5] Canals, railroads, refrigerated rail cars, and grain elevators all combined to integrate the economy nationally in a way that few originally had imagined. If Congress could regulate anything that affected interstate commerce, then Congress could regulate much more in the late nineteenth century than it could in the late eighteenth century. Franklin D. Roosevelt would make the case directly and effectively just after his efforts at federal regulation were struck down by the Court (more on that later):

> The whole tendency over these years has been to view the interstate commerce clause in the light of present-day civilization. The country was in the horse-and-buggy age when that clause was written and if you go back to the debates on the Federal Constitution you will find in 1787 that one of the impelling motives for putting in that clause was this: There wasn't much interstate commerce at all—probably 80 or 90 percent of the human beings in the thirteen original States were completely self-supporting within their own communities.
>
> They got their own food, their own clothes; they swapped or bought with any old kind of currency, because we had thirteen different kinds of currency. They bought from their neighbors and sold to their neighbors. However, there was quite a fear that each of the thirteen States could impose tariff barriers against each other and they ruled that out.... [T]he interstate commerce clause was put into the Constitution with the general objective of preventing discrimination by one of these Sovereign States against another Sovereign State.
>
> They had in those days no problems relating to employment. They had no problems relating to the earning capacity of people—what the man in Massachusetts earned, what his buying power was. Nobody had ever thought of what the wages were or the buying capacity in the slave-holding States of the South. There were no social questions in those days. The question of health on a national basis had never been discussed. The question of fair business practices had never been discussed. The word was unknown in the vocabulary of the Founding Fathers. The ethics of the period were very different from what they are today. If one man could skin a fellow and get away with it, why, that was all right.
>
> . . .
>
> The prosperity of the farmer does have an effect today on the manufacturer in Pittsburgh. The prosperity of the clothing worker in the city of New York has an effect on the prosperity of the farmer in

Wisconsin, and so it goes. We are interdependent—we are tied in together. And the hope has been that we could, through a period of years, interpret the interstate commerce clause of the Constitution in the light of these new things that have come to the country. It has been our hope that under the interstate commerce clause we could recognize by legislation and by judicial decision that a harmful practice in one section of the country could be prevented on the theory that it was doing harm to another section of the country.[6]

At first, as the predicate for commerce authority changed, the Court anticipated FDR's formula. As governments regulated more and more, the Court was deferential, even inviting. As Chief Justice Morrison Waite, in *Pensacola Tel. Co. v. Western Union Tel. Co.* (1877), recounts:

> The powers thus granted are not confined to the instrumentalities of commerce, or the postal service known or in use when the Constitution was adopted, but they keep pace with the progress of the country and adapt themselves to the new developments of time and circumstances. They extend from the horse with its rider to the stage-coach, from the sailing-vessel to the steamboat, from the coach and the steamboat to the railroad, and from the railroad to the telegraph, as these new agencies are successively brought into use to meet the demands of increasing population and wealth. They were intended for the government of the business to which they relate, at all times and under all circumstances.[7]

Waite's view was not uncommon. It is classic one-step originalism: throughout this period, the Court simply applied Marshall's test to the new circumstances of commerce, with the predictable consequence that the scope of potential federal power increased. Obviously, potential doesn't mean actual. Just because Congress had the power didn't mean it would exercise that power. But as Congress did exercise more and more power, the Court accepted that change. As the Court said (in an otherwise infamous case):

> Up to a recent date commerce, both interstate and international, was chiefly by water, and it is not strange that both the legislation of Congress and the cases in the courts have been principally concerned therewith. The fact that in recent years interstate commerce has come to be carried on mainly by railroads and over artificial highways has in no manner narrowed the scope of the constitutional provision, or abridged the power of Congress over such commerce. On the contrary,

the same fullness of control exists in the one case as in the other, and the same power to remove obstructions from the one as from the other.[8]

On this view, the power of Congress extends further than before not because the power had changed, but because the empirical predicate to the power's reach had changed. As one commentator put it near the turn of the century: "If the power of Congress has a wider incidence in 1918 than it could have had in 1789, this is merely because production is more dependent now than then on extra-state markets. No state liveth to itself alone to any such extent as was true a century ago. What is changing is not our system of government, but our economic organization."[9] The expanded commerce authority "was the result of the natural development of interstate commerce under modern conditions," wrote the Court in 1922. "It was the inevitable recognition of the great and central fact that such streams of commerce from one part of the country to another...are in their very essence the commerce among the states...."[10] The fact "that Congress is now legislating on matters that were left a century ago to state action does not mean that the constitutional scheme has been changed from its original design," Justice William O. Douglas wrote.[11] It meant instead that the predicate to federal power had changed as "an integrated national economy" developed.[12]

Yet if the Court permitted the reach of federal power to expand whenever the economy became more integrated, wasn't there a point at which the whole idea of limited federal authority would be erased? Or put differently, at some point, even if it was just the economic organization of the nation that was changing, didn't that change also begin to affect the system of government itself? If Congress could regulate anything that affected interstate commerce, wouldn't Congress's power extend far beyond the limits originally envisioned by our Framers? This is the question that two-step originalism asks: Is there a translation that might better preserve an original meaning?

## The Fidelity by Ignoring the Text: First Moves

The answer to these questions was obviously yes. A federal power whose scope was harnessed to the economic integration of the nation is a federal power whose limits would become increasingly invisible. The consequence would be—and was—a growing gap between federal power as the Framers imagined it (at least according to conservatives) and federal power as it was actually practiced. "The inevitable tendency of Marshall's doctrines," wrote political scientist Edward Corwin in 1920, summarizing James Madison's views, "was to expose even the most uncontroverted and best established powers of the states to overthrow by the National Government."[13]

As the recognition of this "overthrow" grew, lawyers and political theorists grappled with how it might be resisted. Their solution would become a model for the type of translation we will see in this book. And their practice became a pattern that we'll see in other contexts.

In this pattern, an ordinary, typically text-based interpretation of the Constitution grows increasingly out of tune with an ordinary understanding of the Framers' purpose. Let's call this stage "originalist dissonance." Originalist dissonance then presents the Court with a choice: either the Court can ignore the dissonance and permit the Constitution as then-currently interpreted to grow even more "out of tune" with the Framers' design, or the Court can respond to that dissonance by finding a way to bring the interpretation back in tune with the Framers' meaning.

The second option is two-step originalism: fidelity through translation. Courts recognize the originalist dissonance and respond by crafting an alternative interpretive strategy. That alternative changes the way the Constitution is read. But that change is not infidelity (or at least is not meant as infidelity). That change restores (or at least is said to restore) the Constitution's meaning to the Framers' design.

This dynamic doesn't happen all at once. Instead, it typically begins in the dissent of justices describing the originalist dissonance; then, over time, if those arguments in dissent are compelling, the Court evolves a response that effects a translation. Usually such dissents are by justices who see the dissonance and want to correct it. Yet in this first example of federalism translation, it was a dissent that recognized the dissonance, but the author of that dissent had no desire that the dissonance be corrected.

In 1892, the American Sugar Refining Company, a New Jersey holding company that controlled all but five sugar refining operations in the United States, bought out four of its Pennsylvania competitors. That gave the company control over 98 percent of sugar refining in the United States. That combination was challenged by government under the Sherman Act, which forbids "every contract, combination in the form of trust or otherwise, or conspiracy, in restraint of trade or commerce among the several states." The government claimed, plausibly enough, that this "combination" of sugar manufacturers effected a monopoly, which would inevitably restrain trade.

Yet in *United States v. E. C. Knight Co.* (1895), Chief Justice Melville Fuller, for the Court, rejected the government's argument.[14] The Sherman Act may well reach "commerce among the several states," Fuller wrote. But "commerce," the Court held, did not include "manufacturing." Drawing upon a case that had interpreted the constitutional authority of the states to regulate economic activity, the federal commerce clause notwithstanding—what constitutional lawyers call the "negative commerce clause" or "dormant commerce clause"— the Sherman Act was read to exclude a monopoly of manufacturers, despite the obvious effect on interstate commerce.[15]

Fuller's opinion did not affect Congress's commerce authority. The issue was not the constitutionality of the Sherman Act. The issue was, instead, simply whether the Sherman Act reached manufacturing. And as the Sherman Act had no "necessary and proper"–like clause attached to its jurisdictional grant, it may well have been proper to read the criminal jurisdiction of that statute narrowly. That was certainly how many commentators understood the case at the time.[16]

But the dissent of Justice John Marshall Harlan had the unintended consequence of rendering the majority opinion a strong statement about the potential limits on constitutional authority. For Harlan read the Sherman Act to reach the boundaries of congressional authority. Even though there was no "necessary and proper"–like language in the statute, he read it as if Congress had tried to reach every bit of commerce it could reach.[17] Based on this interpretation, Harlan chided the Court for ignoring the method of reasoning that Marshall had adopted in *McCulloch* and *Gibbons*. For him, the question wasn't just whether manufacturing was commerce. Even if it wasn't, Congress had the power to regulate manufacturing under the necessary-and-proper clause if the goal of the regulation was, citing *McCulloch*, "legitimate." The purpose of the Sherman Act, Harlan insisted—to "protect trade and commerce among the states against lawful restraints"—was clearly a legitimate objective for a national government.[18]

Encouraged by Harlan's suggestion that the case was really a case about constitutional power, and not just about the jurisdictional limits of a statute, *Knight* gave birth to a new industry of litigation. That industry of lawyers challenged Congress's power by using the categories developed in negative commerce clause cases to cabin the reach of the positive commerce clause.[19] Once the link to the negative commerce clause was made, it provided a treasure trove of ready-made justifications for cabining Congress's authority— and limitations that reflected the legal culture of the time: formal, absolute, and insensitive to matters of degree.[20]

This innovation, however, did not yield an immediate return on investment. Indeed, initially, *Knight* seemed an anomaly. For twenty-five years after the Court decided *Knight*, the Court continued, in the main, to take an organic view of the economy ("primitive conditions have passed; business is now transacted on a national scale") and to recognize expanded congressional authority.[21] As well as upholding bans on particular flavors of interstate commerce (lottery tickets, for example), regardless of the motive of Congress and whether or not the commerce was commercial (the Mann Act banned the moving of women across state lines for "immoral purposes"), the Court throughout this period took a pragmatic view about the effect of intrastate transaction on interstate commerce and recognized federal authority where intrastate effects reached beyond local activity.[22]

*Swift & Co. v. United States* is perhaps the paradigm case among these.[23] *Swift* was the product of Theodore Roosevelt's first foray into "trust busting." The nation's six largest meatpackers were alleged to have been engaged in price fixing and a division of the meatpacking market. In response to threats of antitrust actions against them, the six merged into a single company, the National Packing Company, so that they could continue their conspiracy, but now under the protection of the "beef trust."

The meatpackers resisted federal regulation on the same ground the sugar makers had done—the monopoly they were alleged to have created was not over "commerce." The Supreme Court, however, through Justice Holmes, rejected the argument. Said the Court in *Swift*, again interpreting the Sherman Act (and thus effectively overruling *Knight*), "Commerce among the states is not a technical legal conception, but a practical one drawn from the course of business."[24] Similar conclusions were reached in *Southern Railway*, where the Court held that the power reached the regulation of intrastate railroad cars; a year later in *Interstate Commerce Commission v. Goodrich Transit*, where it wrote that the power included the power to regulate accounting practices; in the following term, when it held the power reached wholly internal railroad rates; five years after that, when the power was held to reach the regulation of bills of lading; and then most expansively in 1922, when it included the power to regulate "whatever amounts to more or less constant practice, and threatens to obstruct or unduly to burden the freedom of interstate commerce," whether wholly internal or not.[25] On the whole, this was not a Framers-focused Court. It had little problem in recognizing growing federal authority and the potential for "overthrow" that lay therein.

But throughout this period, there was a consistent dissent—and this time by justices who, like Harlan, recognized the originalist dissonance, but who, unlike Harlan, wanted to remedy it. Chief Justice Fuller most prominently, but Justices David Brewer, George Shiras, and Rufus Wheeler Peckham as well, continued to emphasize the logical implication of the interpretive method that the Court was adopting—namely, that federal power, if so interpreted, would be unlimited.

In the 1902 *Lottery Cases*, which upheld Congress's power to prohibit the importation of and interstate and intrastate trade in lottery tickets and lottery advertisements, Fuller made this point powerfully (though again in dissent):

> An invitation to dine, or to take a drive, or a note of introduction, all become articles of commerce under the ruling in this case, by being deposited with an express company for transportation. This in effect breaks down all the differences between that which is, and that which is not, an article of commerce, and the necessary consequence is to take from the States all jurisdiction over the subject so far as interstate communication is concerned. It is a long step in the direction of wiping out all traces of state lines, and the creation of a centralized Government.[26]

The conservatives lost again in the *Shreveport Rate Case*.[27] The Interstate Commerce Commission, the Court held, had the power to regulate rates for rail shipments on purely intrastate routes of an interstate railroad carrier. Congressional power included the ability to regulate "operations in all matters having such a close and substantial relation to interstate traffic."[28] Two justices, Horace H. Lurton and Mahlon Pitney, dissented without opinion.

*Hammer v. Dagenhart* (1918) finally gave *Knight* its second wind.[29] The issue was child labor. Many states permitted children to be employed as laborers. Some states wanted that practice to end. So, following the pattern that had been upheld in the *Lottery Cases*, Congress banned not child labor, but the interstate transport of items made with child labor.

The lawyers challenging the statute drew upon *Knight*. As they argued to the Supreme Court:

> There is practically involved in this case the right of Congress to regulate, under the guise of a commerce regulation, every relation of life.... If the views of those who assert the constitutionality of this method are sound, there is no practical necessity, nor reason, for State legislatures, and certainly none for constitutional amendments.[30]

To the surprise of many, the Supreme Court took the lawyers' bait:

> The far-reaching result of upholding the act cannot be more plainly indicated than by pointing out that if Congress can thus regulate matters entrusted to local authority by prohibition of the movement of commodities in interstate commerce, all freedom of commerce will be at an end, and the power of the states over local matters may be eliminated, and thus our system of government be practically destroyed.[31]

The view of the Court was plain: if the Court didn't draw the line here, then there would be no line left to draw.[32]

This recognition is the second step of a very common motivation for translation that we will see in this book: the *reductio ad absurdum*. Confronted by originalist dissonance, the Court declares that unless that dissonance is remedied, a fundamental principle of the Constitution will be violated. Here, the fundamental principle is the limit on federal authority: that essential postulate of the Framers' design is rendered useless, the Court holds, if Congress has the power at issue in this case. The Court must then find a way to avoid the *reductio*. It must, that is, adopt a reading of the text that seems to preserve its original meaning.

This *reductio* justifies the third step of the constitutional translator: crafting what I will call "tools" to enable the Court to effect limits on federal power in this case. *Hammer* engages this third step by drawing upon the tools left lying around from the negative commerce clause cases.

The first tool was drawn directly from *Knight* (which, again, had drawn it from negative commerce clause jurisprudence). The target of the child labor regulation was "production." Even though it was the transportation of certain goods that triggered the regulation, production (like manufacturing) is not commerce:

> Over interstate transportation, or its incidents, the regulatory power of Congress is ample, but the production of articles, intended for interstate commerce, is a matter of local regulation.[33]

The second tool was a type of pretext analysis, first and most famously suggested in *McCulloch*. The aim, said the Court, of this child labor regulation was to invade the state regulatory domain. That intent was improper, and it rendered the statute invalid.[34] As the Court wrote:

> The act in its effect does not regulate transportation among the states, but aims to standardize the ages at which children may be employed in mining and manufacturing within the states.[35]

Standardizing a rule that was within the sovereign domain of the states is not a proper purpose of the federal government, the Court held. Thus, even though the activity regulated—the transportation of goods across state lines—was at the core of the interstate commerce authority, an improper motive rendered the act invalid.

*Hammer* was an extreme—the most aggressive two-step originalism in the history of the commerce clause. No other case in the history of the Court invalidates Congress's power to regulate goods traveling interstate. But the case can also be understood as an act of fidelity if we view it as an instance of translation. The commerce clause text, as read by Marshall, had yielded a constitutional meaning that conflicted with the meaning intended by the Framers. The Court couldn't change that constitutional text. But it could adopt techniques for reading that text differently—translations. Those translations are justified to the extent they restore an original meaning. To the extent one believes the Framers intended the Constitution to protect extensive and exclusive state authority, *Hammer* is translation.

If *Hammer* was extreme, it still did not mark a radical change in the Court's actual commerce clause jurisprudence. In the very next term, for example, the Court permitted Congress to regulate the transportation of narcotics, despite the true target being "a moral end...in view."[36] (Indeed, this case stands in a crowd of "morality" cases, where even the conservatives allowed Congress to regulate. We'll return to this dissonant crowd later in Chapter 5.)

If *Hammer* was extreme, did, however, provide the model for the eventual federalist translations to limit commerce clause authority. That model was not deployed consistently or extensively at first. But it was available to the conservatives, just waiting to be summoned into service. That call would be a few years in coming. And when it came, the model was deployed repeatedly to effect federalist ends.

## *The Fidelity in Ignoring the Text:* Hammer *to Scale*

The inspiration for this first consistent string of cases affirming the limits on federal commerce authority was a president, Franklin D. Roosevelt, and his program of reform, the New Deal. But I don't mean the programs we are most likely to associate with FDR—social security, the national minimum wage, the Wagner Act. Instead, as many have noted before, there were at least two "new deals," and it was the first to which the Court was most allergic. And it is a good thing too—for the First New Deal was, and still is, a terrifying conception of federal power, which literally no one today would defend.

The story here is familiar to constitutional scholars, but not familiar enough to most Americans. In the wake of the Depression, and after four years of doing-nothing-ism by President Herbert Hoover, the nation was politically and economically frustrated. That frustration begat a significant flirtation with very foreign ideas.

Even before the Depression, many in America were looking fondly upon Italian fascism as an alternative to the rampant competition of unregulated free markets. In 1927, social scientist Horace Kallen wrote that "the fascist revolution...should have the freest opportunity once it has made a start of demonstrating whether it be an exploitation of men by special interests or a fruitful endeavor after the good life."[37] That same year, Herbert Croly, the prominent progressive editor and founder of the *New Republic*, wrote that "whatever the dangers of fascism, it has at any rate substituted movement for stagnation, purposive behavior for drifting, and visions of a great future for collective pettiness and discouragement."[38]

Of course, by "fascism," Kallen and Croly were not talking about the racism that would eventually produce the Holocaust. Fascism at this stage was Italian, not German. The two would not forge a formal link until 1936. At the start of the 1930s, the word referred simply to an idea about the relationship between the state and economic organization—in a word, corporatism. Hitler's Nazism would eventually destroy the market for the ideal (just as he destroyed the market for the name "Adolf"). But years before anyone even knew of a particular German named Adolf, many were focused upon the "great promise" of fascism.

The Depression fed this fascistic fervor. As Roosevelt was coming into office, Donald Richberg—a former Bull Moose, a Progressive cohort of Robert La Follette Jr., a labor lawyer, and one of the drafters of the National Industrial Recovery Act (NIRA) of 1933—testified before the Senate Finance Committee, "We have reached a stage in the development of human affairs where it has become intolerable to have our primitive capitalistic system operated by selfish individuals engaged in ruthless competition.... A planned control of the great essential industries is essential."[39] Five months later, Roosevelt's "brain trust" advisor Rexford G. Tugwell wrote similarly: "Competition in most of its forms is wasteful and costly.... Unrestricted individual competition is the death, not the life, of trade."[40]

Roosevelt stumped for the presidency upon similar ideas. As described by legal scholar Peter Irons:

> The ideology of recovery embodied in Roosevelt's campaign speeches... represented a plan for government by trade association. At its heart was the conviction that the Depression proved that the laissez-faire ideology of unbridled competition was anachronistic and unworkable. In its place, the industrial leaders who supported Roosevelt proposed a plan of political-economic corporatism based on relaxation of the antitrust laws and a system of business-government collaboration in the regulation of production and prices.[41]

Following these ideas, the first important legislation drafted after FDR came into power, the National Industrial Recovery Act, was, as its name and lightning-bolt iconography suggested, little more than an American version of European fascism. As FDR "brain trust" member Raymond Moely described it, the NIRA was a "thorough hodge-podge of recovery plans designed to 'lay the groundwork for permanent business-government partnership and planning.'"[42] "The entire experiment," as historian Alan Brinkley puts it, "raised uncomfortable images of the corporatist economic policies of fascist Italy, which in 1933 had many American admirers."[43]

Yet despite the urgency of the economic malaise, and despite Roosevelt's incredible popularity, not everyone was enamored of American fascism. As Peter Irons describes, "With varying degrees of intensity, the antitrust flame still burned among those who deplored the increasing growth of monopoly and industrial concentration."[44] That flame burned bright, even among FDR's strongest allies.

The most famous of these allies was Louis Brandeis.[45] Brandeis, of course, was not just an "elder statesman," as Irons describes him, at the time FDR was elected. He was also a justice of the Supreme Court. And when the Court finally got its chance to rule on FDR's fascism, the rest of the Court sided with Brandeis and against Roosevelt—unanimously. As the lawyer Thurman Arnold wrote at the time, the Supreme Court

> dramatized the fear that a government which assumed responsibility for gaps left by the failures of an industrial feudalism was gradually pushing on toward a Russian or a German Culture. The word-symbols for this idea—regimentation, bureaucracy, fascism, and communism— were what the Court was credited with saving us from.[46]

The occasion for this defeat (for FDR, at least) was a series of cases that challenged the NIRA. These challengers acknowledged that the economy was integrated, and that this integrated economy had just suffered an incredible collapse, bringing down with it every single region of the nation and throwing millions onto the streets. But they rejected the notion that these economic consequences had repealed federalism. So long as a federalist system remained, those challenging the NIRA insisted, there had to be a limit to how far the federal government could reach. The NIRA, they claimed, violated that limit. It crossed the line.

In an extraordinary trilogy of cases decided on what would become known as Black Monday, May 27, 1935, the Court agreed with the challengers. Twenty-six months after Roosevelt had come to power, the Supreme Court sent the president a very clear message: the First New Deal was doomed.

Indeed, Justice Brandeis was so keen that the message not be misunderstood that he pulled aside a key Roosevelt aide, Tommy Corcoran, and gave him clear instructions for how the unanimous decisions of the Supreme Court were to be read.[47] As Irons recounts:

> Before Tommy Corcoran could depart, a Supreme Court page tapped him on the shoulder and said that Justice Brandeis would like to see him in the justices' robing room. Brandeis wanted Corcoran to convey a message to the White House: "This is the end of this business of centralization, and I want you to go back and tell the President that we're not going to let this government centralize everything. It's come to an end."[48]

The constitutional resistance to the NIRA came in two parts. One attacked the way the law delegated federal power. The other attacked the substantive reach of the law. The NIRA had effectively delegated the power to make law to private actors—representatives from labor and business. But the power to make law, the Court held, had to be executed by democratically accountable representatives:

> If § 9(c) [of the NIRA] were held valid, it would be idle to pretend that anything would be left of limitations upon the power of the Congress to delegate its lawmaking function. The reasoning of the many decisions we have reviewed would be made vacuous, and their distinctions nugatory. Instead of performing its lawmaking function, the Congress could, at will and as to such subjects as it chooses, transfer that function to the President or other officer or to an administrative body. The question is not of the intrinsic importance of the particular statute before us, but of the constitutional processes of legislation which are an essential part of our system of government.[49]

*Panama Refining* (1935) was the first case in the history of the Court to invalidate a federal law on delegation grounds, even though there was no explicit constitutional text that supported this almost unanimous decision. But plainly, framing values informed it—values that every justice believed still resonated within the Constitution.[50]

The second part of the resistance was more substantive and links more directly to the model that *Hammer* had built. Congress, the Court held, had tried to regulate beyond its delegated powers. In *Schechter Poultry*, the NIRA purported to establish codes to regulate the conditions under which chickens were to be slaughtered. These codes, the Court held, were invalid for the same reasons the codes in *Panama Refining* (1935) were invalid—they were the product of improper delegation. But even if the codes had been constitutionally ratified, they would still be unconstitutional: Congress, the Court held—for the first time since *Hammer*—had no power under the commerce clause to reach this bit of commerce.

The commerce at issue here was chickens. The codes that Schechter had violated purported to regulate the quality of Schechter's chickens. The government had argued that Schechter's chickens were within "a flow of commerce," since they moved from one part of the country to another. The government's regulation was therefore at the core of the commerce power: a regulation of interstate commerce.

That argument built upon a string of earlier decisions upholding regulations of the flow of commerce.[51] And the government supported the factual predicate for this flow in a classically Brandeisian manner, by pointing to extensive economic data establishing conclusively that these chickens moved across state borders.[52]

But the Court was not buying it. Even if these chickens had flowed across state boundaries, at the point at which the NIRA codes applied they were done with their flowing. The chickens were in Brooklyn for the balance of their sorry existence. This was not like *Swift & Co. v. United States, Lemke v. Farmers' Grain Co., Stafford v. Wallace, Board of Trade of City of Chicago v. Olsen*, or *Tagg Bros. & Moorhead v. United States*, where the meat, grain, livestock, grain futures, or livestock, respectively, "come to rest within a state temporarily and are later to go forward in interstate commerce."[53] These birds were dead—in their interstate-related movement as well as their own physical life.

Nor, the Court held, did these carcasses "affect" interstate commerce. But to hold this, the Court needed to revive a distinction first made in *Hammer*—a distinction between direct and indirect effects on interstate commerce. "There is a necessary and well-established distinction," the Court instructed the New Dealers, "between direct and indirect effects."[54] The chickens fell on the wrong side of that line. The effect on interstate commerce alleged here was indirect only. And if the "why" wasn't clear from the logic, it was compelled, the Court suggested, by the logical consequence:

> If the commerce clause were construed to reach all enterprises and transactions which could be said to have an indirect effect upon interstate commerce, the federal authority would embrace practically all the activities of the people, and the authority of the state over its domestic concerns would exist only by sufferance of the federal government.[55]

The aim of this legislation, the Court rightly surmised, was to centralize economic rationalization within a single regulated structure. That strategy (again, the essence of pre-Hitler fascism) may or may not have been good economics, the Court conceded. (It wasn't, but put that aside.) But "it is not the province of the Court to consider the economic advantages or disadvantages of such a centralized system. It is sufficient to say that the Federal Constitution does not provide for it."[56]

Justice Benjamin Cardozo concurred in the judgment but wrote separately. Cardozo was not willing to allow such an obviously empirical question of the effects of some commerce upon interstate commerce to be decided by formalisms—direct versus indirect. But he did credit the logical consequence that animated the Court's decision. As he wrote: "To find immediacy or directness here is to find it almost everywhere. If centripetal forces are to be isolated to the exclusion of the forces that oppose and counteract them, there will be an end to our federal system."[57] This was step two in the translator's formula, the *reductio*. Step two thus justified the striking down of this keystone of the First New Deal.

And it was not just the NIRA. With similar motivation, and very similar reasoning, the Court decided the other commerce clause case from Black Monday: *Railroad Retirement Board v. Alton Railroad Company* (1935).[58]

*Railroad Retirement* addressed a compulsory retirement system for employees of railroads and certain other common carriers. Writing for a 5–4 majority, Justice Roberts engaged in an extensive factual review of the alleged effects on interstate commerce. The Court simply discounted most of the economic effects claimed to justify the statute. And the one clear effect left remaining—inducing a "contented mind" in common-carrier employees—was insufficient, the Court held, to ground federal commerce authority. As Roberts wrote,

> The question at once presents itself whether the fostering of a contented mind on the part of an employee by legislation of this type is in any just sense a regulation of interstate transportation. If that question be answered in the affirmative, obviously there is no limit to the field of so-called regulation. The catalogue of means and actions which might be imposed upon an employer in any business, tending to the satisfaction and comfort of his employees, seems endless.[59]

Here again is the *reductio*. Practicing its two-step originalism again, the Court engages in a kind of heightened review of the factual predicate to the statute, on the way to rejecting the truth of those factual claims.

One year later, in *Carter v. Carter Coal Co.* (1936), the court addressed a similarly invasive market regulation, this time a law conferring the power to set a price for bituminous coal and regulate labor conditions in the industry.[60]

This time, just five justices voted to limit Congress's power. But the tools those five deployed were becoming increasingly familiar.

Mining, the Court held, like manufacturing, is not commerce. Neither does mining directly affect interstate commerce. George Sutherland, writing for the Court, knew this not because he had measured the economic consequences of coal mining on the economy. He knew this because he knew the logic, as he saw it, of direct versus indirect. As he wrote,

> The distinction between a direct and an indirect effect turns, not upon the magnitude of either the cause or the effect, but entirely upon the manner in which the effect has been brought about.[61]

And again:

> The matter of degree has no bearing upon the question here, since that question is not—What is the extent of the local activity or condition, or the extent of the effect produced upon interstate commerce? but— What is the relation between the activity or condition and the effect?[62]

Because of the *meaning* of "indirect," in other words, coal did not affect commerce.

There are at least two ways to understand Sutherland's point. One would affirm that he is an idiot: Degree doesn't matter? Of course degree matters! Of course "the distinction between a direct and indirect effect turns...upon the magnitude of either." To miss this is to betray a mind-numbing obliviousness that is almost impossible to fathom.

But this understanding of Sutherland's opinion is not mine. He is not reporting a fact of nature. He is deploying a strategic device to a constitutional end. As Corwin put it, "The distinction is one of *kind,* not of *degree...because the purpose of this distinction is to maintain the states in exclusive possession of the power to regulate productive industry.*"[63] The formalism is thus a strategy. And here it is deployed, Sutherland would argue (and I certainly agree), for the purpose of achieving a kind of fidelity. The aim is, as Justice Clarence Thomas would describe it almost sixty years later, to "construct[] a standard that reflects the text and history of the Commerce Clause."[64] A "construction," no doubt, but one justified by interpretive fidelity.

Chief Justice Hughes wrote separately in *Carter Coal*. He agreed that

> Congress may not use this protective authority as a pretext for the exertion of power to regulate activities and relations within the States which affect interstate commerce only indirectly. Otherwise, in view of the multitude of indirect effect, Congress in its discretion could

assume control of virtually all the activities of the people to the subversion of the fundamental principle of the Constitution.[65]

But Hughes drew a distinction between the provisions of the statute that governed labor conditions and those that regulated prices. Prices of goods in interstate commerce could certainly be regulated under the interstate commerce clause, Hughes believed.

Cardozo dissented. While he had joined the Court in *Schechter*, finding that the flow of chickens didn't affect interstate commerce, in this case he thought the price of coal undoubtedly did. He thus rejected expressly the method of the majority, with perhaps the most memorable quip against legal formalism of the age: "A great principle of constitutional law is not susceptible of comprehensive statement in an adjective." As he continued:

> The holding is not directed at prices or wages considered in the abstract, but at prices or wages in particular conditions. The relation may be tenuous or the opposite according to the facts. Always the setting of the facts is to be viewed if one would know the closeness of the tie.[66]

The vote was close, 5–4, but the meaning clear. Probably by the end of June 1935, and certainly a year later, after *Carter Coal,* "the corporatist ideology of the First New Deal" was dead.[67] By the October 1936 term, FDR could well believe that without substantial change, the federal government's power to deal with the economic crisis would be severely constrained.

We will get to the rest of this story in Chapter 6. For now, it is important only to link these separate cases and give them a frame within which they can be understood.

From the perspective of *fidelity to meaning*, each case is a translation. Whether rightly or wrongly, through the lens of two-step originalism, the majority in each case viewed the effectively unlimited power of the federal government as inconsistent with the Framers' design. They adopted an interpretive strategy to correct for that inconsistency—translation.

To effect these translations, the Court had to craft limits on government power that were not anywhere expressed in the constitutional text. No doubt, the commerce clause speaks of "commerce" and not manufacturing or mining. But Article I also grants Congress the power to pass laws "Necessary and Proper for carrying into Execution the foregoing Powers, and all other Powers vested by this Constitution in the Government of the United States or in any Department or Officer thereof." And were that clause read in the manner Marshall read it, it would plainly have reached each of the activities the Court struck down.

Likewise with the distinction between direct and indirect effects. The commerce clause doesn't say anything about "indirect" or "direct." Neither does the necessary-and-proper clause. But here again, the Court crafted them (or for a critic, it "made them up") for the purpose of limiting a power that the government otherwise would have. As Edward Corwin put it in 1936,

> The term "indirect" in this context is a mere *device*, a *formula* pulled out of the judicial hat, for the purpose of "shooing" away what the Court itself appears to recognize as an altogether natural and logical extension of the national commercial power.[68]

But the Court is entitled to shoo away Congress only if the constraint it applies has sanction in the Constitution's original meaning. That is the claim of the translator: that even though the constraints that are "pulled out of the judicial hat," as Corwin puts it, are not express in the Constitution's text, they were expressed in the Constitution's meaning.

How do the justices know that this much federal power is inconsistent with the Framers' design? For the purposes of this book, I don't care. In the range of examples that we will cover, on the Right and the Left, one could be more or less skeptical about the fidelity in the translator's claim. At the end, I will say something about how to think about that fidelity. But for now, the conditional is sufficient: assuming there is fidelity in the translation, watch the tools that get used to effect it.

Throughout this period of federalism translations—indeed, as we will see, throughout the whole period of federalism translation—the *reductio* is the most consistent and common move.[69] *Knight* begins the story: "Slight reflection will show that if the national power extends to all contracts and combinations in manufacture, agriculture, mining, and other productive industries, whose ultimate result may affect external commerce, comparatively little of business operations and affairs would be left for state control."[70] Its refrain gets repeated in *Dooley*, in *Kidd*, in *Hooper v. California*, in *Keisler v. Thomas Colliery*, and in *Schechter Poultry*.[71]

The *reductio* is also, I suspect, the most compelling motivation. The "textual strategy [of the Constitution] would have been pointless," as Bruce Ackerman summarizes the argument, "if one of the enumerated powers . . . was read so expansively as to embrace the whole."[72] For those who sought to carry into effect the Framers' design, the *reductio* was a powerful move.

Throughout this period, there were justices on the Court who believed in this claim. By the end of this period, a majority was willing to stand by it. The *reductio ad absurdum* invoked in each case—that unless a line is drawn here, there is no line—pushed this majority to act, even against a strong and popular president.

The means for this translation were a set of formalist tools: the distinction between commerce and manufacturing/production/mining/agriculture, the distinction between direct and indirect, the logical device of the *reductio*. Each tool found its origin elsewhere. The distinction between manufacturing and commerce first arose in a dormant commerce case. Likewise with the distinction between direct and indirect effects.[73] Both tools were originally crafted for different reasons. But both were handy for the purpose of limiting the scope of federal authority.

One could well quibble with the strategy—was this the best way to effect the translation? One could question the ultimate motive—was this really fidelity to the Constitution, or was it just fancy politics? These are fair questions, but put them aside for the moment. My claim is that the best way to understand the effort is as an attempt to reclaim a lost reality of federalism. As Felix Frankfurter put it, what was "submerged" in these distinctions was the view that "local affairs are subject to national control when that affect interstate commerce."[74] But that view was submerged by the Court because essentially all local affairs were now potentially subject to national control—contrary, the conservatives believed, to the Framers' design. The Court was attempting to reconstruct an "initial fact of division," an effort not made any easier by the fact that these two fields were now "overlapping" in their reach.[75]

The product of this evolution was a translation of federal power. That translation follows a pattern we will see again and again: The government exercises some sort of power. A majority of justices come to view that exercise of power as inconsistent with framing values. That majority then crafts affirmative, non-textual limits to the government's power as a way to restore that initial balance. The pattern will be universal, though the particular instances of claimed governmental overreaching will be different. Some are concerns of the Left; some are concerns of the Right. But both Left and Right use the very same techniques to remedy the infidelity they view the Constitution as having fallen into.

CHAPTER FIVE | Due Process

T HE RIGHT DIDN'T stop with limiting the power of the federal government. Much more famous (or infamous, perhaps) were efforts to limit the
power of government generally. In a string of decisions intertwined with the
federalism decisions we've just seen, the conservatives on the Court articulated an increasingly rigid set of limits on the scope of both the state and the
federal government. These limits were said to flow from a single clause that's
repeated twice in our Constitution: the requirement that persons not be
"deprive[d] of life, liberty, or property, without due process of law."

These limits apply to the federal government via the Fifth Amendment.
They apply to state and local governments because of the Fourteenth
Amendment. The constraint both limits imposed, however, was not against
deprivation. They were against deprivation without due process of law.
Beginning late in the nineteenth century and flourishing through the first
third of the twentieth, courts, including the Supreme Court, struck down
hundreds of regulations said to deprive persons of life, liberty, or property
without due process of law.

In principle, the simplest of these cases are about process. What process is
due might be a hard question to resolve, but at least the cases signal that a
denial of what's due violates the Constitution.[1]

Process, however, is not the focus of this chapter. Substance is. For in addition to the cases invalidating state (meaning governmental) action involving
process, courts also invalidated state action because it crossed a substantive
line. It wasn't the *way* the state did what it did. It was *what* the state did. And
as courts from the beginning of the republic have indicated, if you got a wildly
wrong answer, that's pretty good evidence you followed the wrong procedure.

These cases are among the most reviled in the Supreme Court's history, coming in for attack today from jurists on both the Left and the Right. But in my view, that condemnation comes too quickly and too cheaply. There is a fidelity to meaning in what the Court did, even if (as we'll see in Chapter 6) there was a fidelity to role in the Court's eventual retreat.

To see these two fidelities, first we have to frame these cases correctly. That a law violates due process is a conclusion, not an argument. The reasons a law might violate due process are multiple. And to understand the character of the reasons the Court relied upon in these cases, we need to say a bit more about the nature of state power and the limits thought to inhere in that power.

## Beginnings

It is common ground that the federal government is a government of enumerated powers. As I have described, that means it has only the powers that the Constitution gives it. These powers, in turn, are constrained by express limits written into the Constitution. No government in the United States can take private property without compensation—both because of the federal constitution and because every state constitution forbids it.[2] The federal government can't grant a title of nobility, impose a duty on goods exported from a state, or pass an ex post facto law.

Yet in addition to those express constraints, there has always been (in theory at least) an implied limit that comes from the very nature of enumerated powers itself. One must always ask both "Is this within the scope of a power granted to Congress?" and "Is the exercise of this power limited by some express constitutional constraint?"

So, for example, if Congress passes a statute banning all Republican blogs, we could first ask whether Congress has any power to regulate blogs. (Are blogs interstate commerce? Do they affect interstate commerce? Is the regulation of blogs necessary and proper to regulating interstate commerce?) But even if we conclude Congress has the power to regulate blogs, that power would be limited by the restrictions of the First Amendment. Whatever else the First Amendment means, it certainly means that Congress can't silence one side in a political debate.

State governments, however, are not governments of enumerated powers. They have all the power of government except where a constitution limits it. For states, those constitutional limits may come from the state constitution or the federal Constitution. Either way, the limit conditions what would otherwise be a valid exercise of state power.

Yet as with the federal government, in the view of some at least, not every exercise of state power is valid. To say that a state has all the powers of a government is not to say the state has all power. The power the state exercises can have an internal limit, just as the commerce power exercised by Congress has its own internal limit.

The core power that a state exercises is the power of police. This power, however, has nothing to do with uniformed officers driving around in cars with sirens. Instead, the "police power" is the power of the state to regulate, as Justice Robert Cooper Grier put it, "for the restraint and punishment of crime, for the preservation of the health and morals of her citizens, and of the public peace."[3] The nineteenth-century jurist Thomas Cooley described it like this:

> The police of a State, in a comprehensive sense, embraces its system of internal regulation, by which [the State seeks] not only to preserve the public order and to prevent offenses against the State, but also to establish for the intercourse of citizens with citizens those rules of good manners and good neighborhood which are calculated to prevent a conflict of rights, and to insure to each the uninterrupted enjoyment of his own so far as is reasonably consistent with a like enjoyment of rights by others.[4]

Notice the logical structure of this power: If your behavior affects more than you—if your behavior is, in this sense, "public"—then the police power says the state can regulate you, or at least your behavior. If your behavior does not affect more than you—if your behavior is, in this sense, "private"—then the police power does not give the state the power to regulate you or your behavior.

Whether your behavior affects more than you is, in an important and obvious sense, contingent, or potentially contingent. If I live on a farm, miles from anyone else, in theory the state would have no power to regulate the loudness of the music at my birthday party. No matter how loud my music or my guests get, no one else could possibly hear it. But if I live in a suburb, the state would have plenty of power to regulate how loud the music at my party was, since the noise from my party can now affect other people. The difference in the two cases is in the context. In one, my behavior affects others. In the other, it doesn't.

If the state's power is in this sense contingent upon where I live, it is also contingent upon how where I live changes. I may have a house on a farm. Imagine that every year, I have a large and loud birthday party. But imagine that, partly to pay for those parties, every year I sell off plots of land on my farm. And imagine that eventually all I have is my house, surrounded by lots of other houses. That change may have restricted the freedom that I formerly had. But that's because my freedom—or, in other words, the stuff I do that's private—is contingent upon others.

It is also contingent upon technology. If my party causes noise that disturbs my neighbors, the state has the power to tell me to stop. But if a technology would block the noise that disturbs my neighbor, the justification for the state's regulating me may change. Technology can make private what was once public; it can make public what was once private. So in this sense, the state's power can also turn upon the contingency of technology.

I've belabored this point to make sure that a particular parallel is unavoidably obvious: that in the logic of the police power, like the logic of the commerce power as interpreted by Marshall, the power is contingent upon facts in the world. And that, as with the commerce power, over time those facts change. As the integration of a society increases over time, the presumptive reach of police regulation increases, so over time what was once a liberty could be lost as the reach of state power increases.

So just as I argued that a state might have had exclusive jurisdiction over milk in 1790, since milk in 1790 was not within interstate commerce, but then lose that exclusive jurisdiction in 1890, because by 1890 technology enabled milk to be transported within interstate commerce safely, so too might an individual enjoy a liberty at one time that, because of changes in technology, he loses at another. In both cases, government power changes because the context or technology of social life changes. In both cases, that change may well raise questions, at least for someone focused on the liberty (in the context of the police power) or exclusive state authority (in the context of the commerce power) that was enjoyed before.

Thus, a state statute might be invalid either because it exceeds the police power (just as a federal statute might be invalid because it exceeds the commerce power) or because even though it is within the police power, another constitutional interest is held to restrict that otherwise valid exercise of police power (as, for example, the First Amendment would constrain the regulation of Republican blogs).

The due process cases in this period revolve around both kinds of limits. Some of the cases are best understood as cases in the first category: instances where the law exceeds the logic of the power. Some are best understood as cases in the second category: instances where the law is within the logic of the power but another constitutional interest limits that otherwise legitimate exercise of power.

Among cases in the second category, some are easy and some are not. If a state passes a law banning "indecent" speech in newspapers, that's certainly within the police power, but it violates the First Amendment. The express limit of the First Amendment makes this easy in this sense (even if figuring out what violates the First Amendment is hard). But in the cases that I will consider here, there is not an express constitutional text that can make the case easy. Like federalism in commerce clause cases, the limits derive from a presumption drawn from the framing context that drives the Court to constrain otherwise legitimate governmental power.

In the federalism cases, that presumption was simple to describe. In these cases, it will take more work. The two principles that animate these substantive due process cases are alien to us today, yet were alive at the time of the Civil War, and are latent in the constitutional text. One is easy enough to understand but seems hopeless to pursue. The other may not even be understandable anymore.

## Latent Values: Neutrality

Implicit in the idea of the police power is a strong conception of a "common good." The police power within the American republic was not the power of Lenin or Robespierre. It was the power to regulate for "health, peace, morals, education, and good order of the people" in a way that benefited everyone, even if it burdened different people differently.[5] The aim was regulation to benefit everyone, if not directly then at least on balance.[6] Again, to use Cooley's words, "to insure to each the uninterrupted enjoyment of his own [rights] so far as is reasonably consistent with a like enjoyment of rights of others."[7]

The antithesis of regulation in the common good is a rule that takes from one person and gives to another.[8] The "powers of government" under this conception of the police power, as Michael Les Benedict summarizes the view, "could not be used for the benefit of one citizen at the expense of another, or one group of citizens at the expense of the rest."[9]

This is the idea of "neutrality," sometimes referred to as a rule against "class legislation." And it was a common idea at the Founding and throughout the early republic. The notion was expressly articulated in many state constitutions. In 1776, Virginia and North Carolina defined the very idea of a "commonwealth" in precisely these terms: "No men or set of men are entitled to exclusive or separate emoluments or privileges from the community, but in consideration of public service."[10] New Hampshire had a slightly different version: "Government [is] instituted for the common benefits, protection, and security of the whole community, and not for the private interest or emolument of any one man, family, or class of men."[11] And it was an ideal that continued throughout the nineteenth century. If anything was clear about the nature of a properly republican form of government, it was that such a government was to legislate for the common good.

The most obvious example of a law that would violate this principle of neutrality is legislation that changed the law applicable in a case currently being litigated, for the express purpose of changing the result of that litigation. Justice Samuel Chase expressly condemned such an act—a law that "takes *property* from A and gives it to B"—as a "*flagrant* abuse of *legislative* power."[12] More than thirty years later, Justice Story drew a similar judgment:

> We know of no case in which a legislative act to transfer the property of A to B without his consent has ever been held a constitutional exercise of legislative power in any state in the union.[13]

Just as strongly condemned was, as Andrew Jackson would put it, "any prostitution of our Government to the advancement of the few at the expense of the many."[14] Indeed, Jackson and his allies (including the future Supreme Court justice Stephen Johnson Field) "sought constitutional limitations to legislative power because they feared arbitrary and unequal legislation."[15] As described by Hannis Taylor a century ago:

> The primary purpose of the founders of American constitutional law was to wipe out the entire system of legislative despotism over life, liberty and property, based...not only upon a denial of the right to due process, but also upon the denial of the principles demanding generality and equality in the laws.[16]

Until the Civil War, these notions of neutrality as enforced through due process were enforced, if at all, in state courts only.[17] The federal Constitution had a due process clause in the Fifth Amendment ("No person shall be ... deprived of life, liberty, or property, without due process of law"), but that restriction applied to the federal government, not to the states. And except for one important blunder, *Dred Scott v. Sanford* (1857), and one effectively insignificant restriction, *Marbury v. Madison* (1803), there is no string of Supreme Court cases before the Civil War applying the Constitution to restrict the laws of Congress.

The Fourteenth Amendment, however, added a parallel due process clause to the Constitution, one now regulating the states ("nor shall any State deprive any person of life, liberty, or property, without due process of law"). And quite early in the history of the Supreme Court's interpretation of that clause, it signaled both the interpretive challenge of grafting onto the American Constitution this originally English ideal and a core meaning to the provision, at least as that judicial body understood it. Writing for the Court in 1877, Justice Samuel Freeman Miller commented:

> It is easy to see that when the great barons of England wrung from King John, at the point of the sword, the concession that neither their lives nor their property should be disposed of by the crown, except as provided by the law of the land, they meant by "law of the land" the ancient and customary laws of the English people, or laws enacted by the Parliament of which those barons were a controlling element. It was not in their minds, therefore, to protect themselves against the enactment of laws by the Parliament of England. But when, in the year of grace 1866 [*sic*], there is placed in the Constitution of the United States a declaration that "no State shall deprive any person of life, liberty, or property without due process of law," can a State make any thing due process of law which, by its own legislation, it chooses to declare such? *To affirm this is to hold that the prohibition to the States is of no avail, or has no application where the invasion of private rights is effected under the forms of State legislation.*[18]

Clearly, the amendment was meant to have an effect, Justice Miller believed—which is rather astonishing since, as we'll see, Miller effectively castrated the other important language of the Fourteenth Amendment, the privileges-or-immunities clause—and so he offered a simple example of what would plainly offend the terms of the amendment:

> It seems to us that a statute which declares in terms, and without more, that the full and exclusive title of a described piece of land, which is now in A., shall be and is hereby vested in B., would, if effectual, deprive A. of his property without due process of law, within the meaning of the constitutional provision.[19]

Again a transfer of property from A to B without due process: The aim of neutrality was to prevent this, and Miller believed the amended Constitution demanded it.

Miller also didn't object in *Barbier v. Connolly* (1885), when Justice Field added to his opinion that under the Fourteenth Amendment "class legislation, discriminating against some and favoring others, is prohibited."[20]

Whatever else was uncertain, due process was a command against class legislation. As one treatise summarized the view from the beginning of the last century:

> In those cases where the central problem is one of classification, it is evident that, unless the actual conditions surrounding the classification are such as to disclose a reasonable justification for the class distinction, the class distinction becomes an arbitrary discrimination. The determination, therefore of the constitutionality of the law depends upon the determination of the further question of whether there is a real distinction between the classes established, in view of the particular circumstances.[21]

"Arbitrary" in this context means without constitutional justification. Taking from A and giving to B is in this sense arbitrary, since, as defined, it is a transfer only.

Neutrality, then, is the first latent value in the concept of "due process," both at the Founding in the eighteenth century and at what is often referred to as the "Second Founding," the period after the Civil War in which the Thirteenth, Fourteenth, and Fifteenth Amendments were passed, along with a number of landmark statutes. To complain about neutrality is not to complain about process. It is to complain about the result. But the wrong result may well signal a mistake in process. It may demonstrate that something had to have gone wrong in the steps leading up to the legislation being enacted. The hard question, then, was whether that mistake would be corrected, and if so, by whom: courts or legislatures?

## Latent Values: Free Labor

Neutrality as a value is easy enough for us to understand. The second latent value from the Civil War period is more difficult. This value speaks to an ideal that is wholly foreign to us today. Or to the extent it isn't foreign, it is understood only as an exception to an otherwise dominant way of life. Yet this value wasn't born as an exception: as Jefferson and Lincoln understood it, it was the very model for America, an ideal to which everyone should aspire.

This value is captured in a certain picture about how Americans would work. It was a picture advanced not for efficiency's sake, though there was an inherent belief in its efficiency. It was advanced instead for the republic's sake. America would survive as a republic, these Founders believed, so long as it could preserve a certain ideal of work.

This ideal has many incarnations across our history. For our purposes, we can reprise just two: the first, Jefferson's, and the second, Lincoln's. Both of these incarnations are called "Republican," though Jefferson's Republican Party (in full, the Democratic-Republican Party) was not exactly Lincoln's Republican Party.

## JEFFERSONIAN REPUBLICANS

The Framers had a pretty dismal view about the progress of human society. Societies, they believed, like human beings, passed through a peak and then declined. As Gordon Wood quotes Samuel Stanhope Smith, "Human society can advance only to a certain point before it becomes corrupted, and begins to decline."[22] Indeed, it rises and falls in stages. In the first three, society advances: from hunting/gathering to pasturage and then to agriculture. In the final stage, commerce, it declines.[23] This fourth stage marks a society undone by corruption: a world of luxury and large factories, a nation of the very rich and the exceedingly poor. England, our founders believed, was in stage four, while America was somewhere between stage three and stage four.

From the Founding, those who would become what I'm calling Jeffersonian Republicans sought ways to cheat death by slowing this decline. Their correspondence is filled with rumination about whether such a slowing was even possible—is there a political fountain of youth?—and about the means for achieving it. Jefferson thought that America's endless frontier would be a perpetual supply of land for a growing population, thus slowing the growth of cities and all the corruption they inspired. And Madison and Jefferson both thought there were regulatory techniques that the new nation might deploy to delay decline—a kind of political Botox that through a mix of virtue and law would keep the young society young.

Many thought this idea foolish. As Thomas Malthus put it, anyone who expected the United States to remain a land with relatively little poverty and misery forever "might as reasonably expect to prevent a wife or mistress from growing old by never exposing her to the sun and air."[24] And indeed, even as many "were coming to suspect that the Revolutionary vision of a Republican society in which there would be no 'labouring poor'—where everyone would be independent and economically secure—was a chimera," many simply moved on to the question of how to make the final stages of society the most prosperous they could be.[25]

Yet many of the most important Founders did not accept this as America's fate. For these Founders, resisting this fate was the challenge of better governmental design. Like an architect discovering the flying buttress, or an engineer inventing the suspension bridge, these political architects sought a system that would secure the nation against this "race against time."[26]

The first years of the American republic convinced these Republicans that the Constitution alone was not that design. Mercantilists such as Hamilton embraced the idea of corruption as a means for building loyalty to the federal government. He wasn't scheming to slow our progress toward becoming England. To the contrary, he was eager to speed it up—as was a whole class of new merchants and traders who were more than happy to give up the relatively sparse life of the country for the aspiring wealth of a blooming aristocratic society. If people wanted to get rich, they would work harder. If other nations wanted to supply this new American greed, they'd be more likely to respect and support the United States.

This conflict—between the Republicans and their enemies—made it more and more doubtful, the Republicans feared, that we as a nation would achieve our true potential as a republic. As Drew McCoy puts it:

> As they endeavored to cope with the tensions and inconsistencies lurking in their vision, many Americans experienced an agonizing despair, prompting them to retreat toward traditional classical modes of expression that voiced serious doubts about the compatibility of commerce and republicanism.[27]

And as leaders such as Hamilton pushed the nation to encourage manufacturing, many wondered whether "under the pretext of nurturing manufacturers," as McCoy quotes one critic, "a new field may be opened for favouritism, influence, and monopolies."[28] "The new nation seemed to be afflicted by the very symptoms of the British political and moral economy," he continues, "that the Revolutionaries had risked their lives to escape."[29] The "disorder and unrest of the 1780s signified," Madison and others feared, "the decay of industry, diligence, frugality, and other republican character traits among the American people."[30]

This is why the Republicans looked to the election of 1800 as a kind of final chance to save the soul of the new nation. Based on the results, they believed they had their mandate. The "revolution of 1800," as McCoy describes Jefferson's view, was a "return to first principles, ... a restoration of original values and ideals that had been overturned or repudiated" during the first decade of the new republic.[31] Jefferson and his collaborators would use this mandate to squeeze the blooming America back into a properly Republican corset. Armed with the power of government, the Republicans would bind America to a path that would delay its own demise.

For Jefferson had a plan. As McCoy writes:

> Within the Jeffersonian framework of assumptions and beliefs, three essential conditions were necessary to create and sustain such a republican

political economy: a national government free from any taint of corruption, an unobstructed access to an ample supply of open land, and a relatively liberal international commercial order that would offer adequate foreign markets for America's flourishing agricultural surplus.[32]

Jefferson had a strategy to achieve this plan. That strategy had two parts, one that we remember and one that we conveniently forget.

The famous bit was the Louisiana Purchase, important to Jefferson because it bought his agricultural republic more time, as it enabled more and more of the growing population to acquire and cultivate land simply by moving west.

The less famous—let's call it infamous—part was America's first national industrial policy, with a very particular kind of industry in mind. The only manufacturing Jefferson supported was "domestic manufacturing," meaning manufacturing for domestic supply only. "Above all," McCoy summarizes, "the republic would not manufacture extensively for export, as England did, for then the whole decadent system of large urban manufactories and poverty-stricken landless laborers...might be transferred to the United States."[33]

To achieve this, Jefferson got Congress to impose a disastrous embargo on the United States for the express purpose of inducing household and domestic manufacturing, while stanching the drive to luxury.[34] As McCoy describes it, "The embargo...had finally forced Americans to realize their full potential in *household* manufacturing, a momentous achievement that had always been implicit in the Revolutionary impulse."[35]

Unsurprisingly, given the real constraints of actual economics, with this "momentous achievement" came a radical contraction in the growth of the U.S. economy. Writes McCoy: "Many Federalists insisted that Jefferson advocated a 'Chinese' approach to political economy and that his policies were therefore directed toward the creation of an isolated, barbarous, and crudely self-sufficient America."[36] Chairman Mao would have been proud; a hungry nation was not.

Jefferson's utopia had failed.[37] His party quickly gave up the social experiment at stopping economic and social progress. Wealth and luxury grew quickly. And in the early years of the nineteenth century, conditions made the ideal of a nation governed by the yeoman farmer unlikely. However essential such "independence" was to the idea of a republic, by the time Jefferson died, his republic had resolved to live without it.[38]


## LINCOLN REPUBLICANS

Throughout antebellum America, agriculture was the nation's business.[39] But the character of this agriculture was radically different depending upon the region in America. In the North, farms were small-scale family farms, and 80 percent of produce was consumed locally. In the South, while there were some family farms, the most important economic power was held by plantations. As historian Douglas Hurt describes, the plantation system "provided the basis for commercial agriculture in the antebellum South," even though "most farmers were not planters but small-scale operators without slaves."[40] The few, however, dominated. Notes Hurt:

> In the cotton South on the eve of the Civil War, 5 percent of the farmers and planters owned 36 percent of the agricultural wealth, while 50 percent owned about 6 percent and 40 percent of the population lived in slavery.[41]

And while one might say there were yeoman farmers everywhere if you excluded slaves from the story, the struggle over slavery made that understanding more and more contested.

Indeed, throughout the history of antebellum America, there was a constant battle to define how Americans should work. The traditional conception of work saw men as machines—tools to be owned and deployed as their masters choose. The enlightened conception of work saw men as humans—souls who could develop and grow as they came to learn and know more.

This enlightened conception inspired the free labor movement.[42] That movement was born against the background of a long tradition of oppressive regulation of labor. Throughout England and the United States, laws made it a crime to break a labor contract. This meant that individuals were bound to a particular craft or profession and were not free to move beyond it. If they left the job or profession to which they were committed—and were caught—they could well go to jail.[43]

This binding was inconsistent with a romantic, and increasingly compelling, ideal about the human condition. The Enlightenment dreamed of human progress; the ideal was an individual working his way through stages of development, from poverty to self-sufficiency. As he progressed, he would be free to move beyond his station to something more and better. Society's role was to provide the context for this progress. It was to secure the opportunity for an individual to become the best he could be.

To do this, however, progress needed a better reward than simply avoiding jail. The need for this better reward gave birth to the notion of "free labor."

Free labor in this sense obviously does not refer to laboring for free. It's not slavery, or volunteerism, or anything like that. Instead, free labor refers to the idea that individuals would be free to select their craft and, more importantly, free to move on. The free labor system, as perhaps the greatest historian of free labor (and much else), Willie Forbath, describes it, "was the phrase Antebellum Northerners, politicians, businessmen and labor leaders alike...used to describe their social and economic order....[Its] genius rested in the dignity and opportunities it afforded the laboring man."[44]

The "freedom" in free labor thus referred to economic independence. That independence required the ownership of productive property. In Abraham Lincoln's view, as Forbath describes, it "rested on the image of the 'working-man' as an artisan or petty entrepreneur[,] one who labored but also owned productive property."[45] It required that workers have the opportunity to move from one job to another. The right was, as Lincoln celebrated it, the "right to rise." And the commitment to a free labor system was a commitment to a system of laws that would secure the freedom of men to rise.

The "right to rise," however, did not mean a person was always, at every stage of his life, economically independent. It wasn't a government guarantee of the ownership of productive property—a kind of universal forty acres and a mule. It was rather the commitment to the possibility of moving up in the social or at least economic ranks. It was, in legal scholar Jedediah Purdy's words, a "narrative for a life."[46] As Lincoln described it, free labor was

> the just and generous and prosperous system [in which the] prudent, penniless, beginner in the world labors for wages for a while, saves a surplus with which to buy tools or land for himself; then labors on his own account for another while, and at length hires himself another new beginner to help him.[47]

As he promised, "The man who labored for another last year, this year labors for himself, and next year he will hire others to labor for him."[48] Lincoln, like Karl Marx, saw labor as the core engine of economic value. In his first message to Congress, Lincoln had criticized the "effort to place capital on an equal footing with, if not above, labor in the structure of government." Instead, Lincoln insisted, "labor is prior to and independent of capital. Capital is only the fruit of labor....Labor is the superior of capital and deserves much the higher consideration."[49] The difference between Marx and Lincoln was social mobility—Lincoln thought it central; Marx believed it a mirage.[50]

From a modern perspective, what's particularly interesting about this framing conception of free labor was that it was neither libertarian nor statist. Beyond slavery (which, again, the movement plainly condemned), the free laborer was to be protected from the consequences of his own agreements. The movement sought to limit the freedom of contract, so as to secure a more basic freedom for labor. Contract theorists, of course, have long noted that the practice of contract law is far more restrictive than the ideals of a pure contract theory. But here the contrast is particularly striking. The flaw in the traditional system of labor, free labor advocates believed, was that it gave too much freedom to the laborer. Despite his choice, a laborer should not be free to contract to certain restrictive conditions, and if he does, he should be relieved of that choice by a court's refusal to enforce that wrongful contract. The notion resonates with Cass Sunstein's conception of libertarian paternalism: the ideal is liberty, but certain paternal limits on that liberty are necessary to achieve the ideal.[51]

Like Jefferson, the motivation behind this movement was not purely economic. It was also and essentially political. The "ownership of productive property" was not "an end in itself," as Forbath describes; instead, "such independence was essential to participating freely in the public realm."

> The propertyless "servant" or "hireling" was an untrustworthy citizen. His poverty and "dependence" made him vulnerable to coercion, threatening the integrity of his opinions and his ballot. "Independence" in pursuing one's economic calling and "independence" as a citizen were entwined,...and a republic polity could not safely co-exist with a large permanent class of propertyless laborers.[52]

"Representative government," writes historian Eric Foner, "could only rest on a citizenry enjoying the personal autonomy that arose from ownership of productive property"—because only property-owning citizens could "subordinate self-interest to the public good."[53] Wage laborers didn't qualify for this sort of respect. For though only "free and self-owning persons could enter into wage contracts," still "to work for wages was to be dependent, to lose the autonomy requisite to citizenship."[54] Dependent individuals "lacked a will of their own, and thus did not deserve a role in public affairs."[55]

In this sense, then, there was a direct line back to Jefferson: the yeoman farmer was essential to democracy not because of his produce, but because of the independence of the character he would develop. Democracy depended, these Republicans believed, upon these independent souls. Dependent people, by contrast, could not support a republic. For dependence, as Jefferson wrote in his *Notes on the State of Virginia*, "begets subservience and venality, suffocates the germ of virtue, and prepares fit tools for the designs of ambition."[56] Thus, common between the two conceptions of the social order—Jeffersonian Republicanism and Lincoln Republicanism—was the view that the practices of economic life would help craft the virtues of a citizen.

In obvious ways, the free labor movement was consistent with the more famous movement for the abolition of slavery. But the free labor movement was not concerned primarily with the unfree labor of slaves—slavery was clearly not an appropriate model for labor. But it wanted much more than the end of slavery.[57] Indeed, some in the movement feared aligning the free labor movement with the abolitionist movement, precisely because they feared that their more general claims would be swallowed by the drama surrounding the fight against slavery. Those fears would prove correct: today everyone knows about abolitionism, few remember its more fundamental twin, free labor.

By the middle of the nineteenth century, the ideals behind the free labor movement began to attract political force. And the revived Republican Party was the most important subscriber to that movement. Its very first platform (1856) embraced free labor in its slogan: "Free Speech, Free Press, Free Men, Free Labor, Free Territory and Fremont."[58] (Fremont referred to General John C. Frémont, the first Republican candidate for president.) Each of these freedoms (save, of course, Frémont) was a required condition, the Republicans thought, for enlightened human development. "Free soil" would provide a continued opportunity for republican self-sufficiency, as the Jeffersonian ideals of the yeoman farmer would be secured with land. "Free labor" guaranteed the opportunity for progress for those who moved beyond the farm. And "free speech" would guarantee the continued political opportunity to challenge the forces of unfreedom wherever they might flourish. The specific motivation for this part of the slogan was Congress's practice of forbidding the reading in its chambers of petitions relating to slavery.[59] The challenge to that practice was the first successful free speech movement in the history of America. Yet it was just part of a more general fight for human freedom.

It is important to note that this was not a pro–African American party. Racism in the North as well as the South was as common as dirt. And there were plenty of openly racist members of the new Republican Party. Indeed, there were many who pushed for abolition not because it benefited blacks, but because they believed it would benefit whites. As one new Republican put it, "The question is not, whether black men are to be made free...but whether we white men are to remain free."[60]

These ambiguities notwithstanding, as the nation prepared for war many saw the impending struggle through the lens of the free labor movement, Lincoln in particular. As Foner describes:

> Slavery, [Lincoln] insisted, embodied the idea that the condition of the
> worker should remain forever the same; in the North, by contrast,
> there was "no such...thing as a free man being fixed for life in the
> condition of a hired laborer....Men, with their families...work for
> themselves on their farms, in their houses, and in their shops, taking

the whole product to themselves, and asking no favors of capital on the one hand nor of hired laborers or slaves on the other."[61]

And while most of us today are likely to believe the Civil War was fought to preserve the Union, fundamental to that conflict was the battle to end slavery and secure the ideal of free labor. One of these principles was backward-looking, while the other looked forward. The men who joined the Union Army wanted to preserve the Union—though most saw their fight as a fight to end slavery.[62] That was the look back. But they also wanted to establish for their children a nation of free laborers. That was the dream looking ahead.

This is the conception of the social order that I said framed this constitutional moment. And after the end of the war, practically every significant legislative act of the Radical Republican Congress was understood as a means for achieving this utopia of free labor among equal citizens. The statutes seeking equal rights and the constitutional amendments forging equality into our framing document did so—in part at least—because they were seen by many as a means to a substantive social end: a world in which as many citizens as possible would labor freely and responsibly, not in large factories as wage laborers, nor on large plantations as slaves in all but name, but as owners of the means of production, which they deployed to produce a modest but healthy economy. The ideal was both economic and political. Free labor would produce free citizens as well as bountiful wealth.

Thus, when the Civil War came to an end, the first ideas for reconstruction were all about creating the conditions under which free labor could flourish. As Foner describes:

> In a speech to Pennsylvania's Republican convention in September 1865, [Thaddeus] Stevens called for the seizure of the 400 million acres belonging to the wealthiest 10 percent of Southerners. Forty acres would be granted to each adult freedman and the remainder— some 90 percent of the total—sold "to the highest bidder" in plots, he later added, no larger than 500 acres. The proceeds would enable the federal government to finance pensions for Civil War veterans, compensate loyal men who had suffered losses during the war (not a few of whom lived in Stevens' southern Pennsylvania district), and retire the bulk of the national debt.[63]

Reconstruction would require something more than rebuilding destroyed facilities. It would require changing, as Stevens argued, "the whole fabric of southern society." Without such change, "this Government can never be . . . a true republic."

How can republican institutions, free schools, free churches, free social intercourse exist in a mingled community of nabobs and serfs? If the South is ever to be made a safe republic let her lands be cultivated by the toil of the owners or the free labor of intelligent citizens.[64]

Of course, such massive land redistribution never happened in the South—tragically. "Forty acres and a mule" was just one more broken promise, not the path to economic independence. The only slaveholders ultimately forced to provide their former slaves with land were slaveholding Native Americans, and of that group, only those who had sided with the Confederacy.[65]

Some held the view that "free labor assumptions—economic rationality, internal self-discipline, responsiveness to the incentives of the market—could never . . . be applied to blacks."[66] Despite this, the "unifying" purpose of the first administrative agency devoted to securing equality, the Freedmen's Bureau, "was the endeavor to lay the foundation for free labor society—one in which blacks labored voluntarily, having internalized the values of the marketplace, while planters and civil authorities accorded them the rights and treatment enjoyed by Northern workers."[67]

That was also a unifying purpose of the Civil War Amendments. Though the means deployed in each amendment are different, the end sought was the same: a society of free laborers. The Thirteenth Amendment (ending slavery) and the Fifteenth Amendment (removing race as grounds for restricting the right to vote) pursued those ends by helping blacks in particular. But the Fourteenth Amendment sought that end more neutrally. The first sentence of Section 1 of that amendment constitutionalized the right of citizenship. The balance of that section constitutionalized a system of privileges or immunities, due process, and equal protection that would help secure a world of free labor. The Fourteenth Amendment was not just about free labor, but we need to see free labor as an organizing ideal in the background of that amendment if we are to understand its meaning at the time.

The fight for free labor, however, was complicated by the fight for racial equality. Both ideals were embedded in the legal and constitutional changes of this second constitutional moment.[68] Yet each is distinct. The ability to pursue the conditions that supported free labor for blacks is distinct from the ability to pursue the conditions that support free labor generally, not to mention the political feasibility of doing so. And it is within that distinction, I suggest, that we can understand the story of substantive due process that I will tell in the balance of this chapter.

That story blooms with the Civil War Amendments themselves. In 1873, the Supreme Court declared that those amendments were about blacks and meant to protect blacks.[69] But then America turned its back on America's blacks. In the most shameful chapters of our history, Americans everywhere permitted white Americans to effectively reenslave African Americans throughout the South, and then more slowly in the North as well. Rights granted on paper in the Civil War Amendments were denied in practice. A society that declared it had no castes produced a racial caste throughout the nation, through a level of violence and corruption unmatched at any point in our history (save perhaps the "war on drugs" that is now waged in America's ghettoes).

But though the Civil War Amendments were rendered useless for their primary purpose of protecting African Americans, they were not useless for all purposes. If the amendments were meant to resonate on two channels— one achieving equality for blacks, the other securing the ideals of free labor— the faults of the first channel did not automatically silence the second. The defense of African Americans was dead for a century at least. But the struggle to protect the ideals of free labor continued through the judicial interpretation of these amendments.

So that we can see how this happened, I want you to make an extraordinary assumption about these Civil War Amendments. Assume with me for a moment that they had nothing to do with blacks in particular, but everything to do with creating the conditions for a free labor society in general. That like the Jeffersonian Republicans before them, the free labor Republicans had an ideal society in mind as they crafted their new constitution. But also like the Jeffersonian Republicans after the catastrophic embargo of 1807–1808, these free labor Republicans quickly came to see that after the Civil War, the preconditions for a free labor society were quickly disappearing. Rather than a world of small proprietors and small farmers, America was quickly becoming a world of wage laborers and workers in large factories. And that economic change threatened the Republicans' free labor ideals.

For the economic facts here could not be more stark. By 1860, more than 60 percent of Americans were employees.[70] A decade later, the census calculated that 67 percent of "productively engaged Americans were dependent for a livelihood upon employment by others."[71] For the first time in its history, postbellum America was a nation of wage earners. As a Massachusetts Bureau of Statistics of Labor report declared in 1873, wage labor was universal, "a system more widely diffused than any form of religion, or of government, or indeed, of any language."[72]

Of course, wage labor wasn't slavery. But most from the free labor movement believed that it also wasn't free labor. As Forbath puts it, "For a Lincoln or a Horace Greeley, the man who worked for wages all his life was almost as unfree as the slave in the South."[73] He was unfree not because he was chained to a job, but because he had none of the independence that was so central to the ideal of free labor. "When a man agrees to sell his labor," E. L. Godkin, editor of *The Nation* put it, "he agrees by implication to surrender his political and social independence."[74] "The rise of wage labor," writes Foner, "posed a profound challenge for the ethos that defined economic dependence as incompatible with freedom."[75] "Larger and larger masses of the population," Godkin wrote in 1867, were each year being "reduced to the conditions of hired laborers," "subjected to factory discipline," and "learning to consider themselves a class apart, with rights and interests different from those of the rest of the community."[76] Wrote one labor leader, "[Workers] do not complain of wage slavery *solely* on account of the poverty it occasions.... They oppose it because it holds the laboring classes in a state of abject dependence upon capitalists."[77]

The factory and wage labor system could not deliver a "right to rise." As Jack Beatty reports, one study of three hundred unskilled laborers in Newburyport, Massachusetts, between 1850 and 1880 found "not a single instance of mobility into the ranks of management or even into a foremanship."[78] "Fifty years ago we had millions of artisans working at their own homes, on their own account," one labor spokesman claimed in 1886. But now "the majority are in factories of the capitalists working as their wage-slaves. From being their own masters...they work for other masters."[79]

Again, Eric Foner:

> Throughout the nineteenth century, the "small producer ideology," resting on such tenets as equal citizenship, pride in craft, and the benefits of economic autonomy, underpinned a widespread hostility to wage labor, as well as to "non-producers" who prospered from the labor of others. The ideology of free labor would emerge, in part, from this vision of America as a producer's republic.[80]

These changes produced sustained conflict throughout the balance of the nineteenth century. As historian Amy Dru Stanley notes, "Wage labor had become a problem as serious as economic crisis or the relations between former slaves and former masters.... [R]elations of free contract were producing conflict in the North to an extent unforeseen when slavery was destroyed."[81] That conflict only grew, as policymakers recognized that not only was the wage labor system not delivering the promise of civic independence, it was not even delivering economic sustenance. "The jarring postwar changes in American life," Michael Ross reports Justice Miller as arguing, "had destroyed the free-labor society envisioned by antebellum Republicans and replaced it . . . with a dangerous landscape filled with the mansions of the rich and the tenements of the 'discontented, the unfortunate, and the poor.'"[82] And in this state of poverty, the family, as labor leader Samuel Gompers put it, "was not sacrificed on the altar of chattel slavery, but 'to the Moloch of wage slavery.'"[83] Study after study demonstrated that wage labor had "'unsexed men and women' and threatened 'coming generations' by drawing whole families into the labor market."[84] "The market in free labor" was "changing 'homes into houses.'"[85]

I report all this not to motivate a return to a free labor society. I am not Mao. I don't believe in steel mills in the backyard. We're far from a world in which each citizen is a small proprietor. (But maybe not so far, if we look forward—for isn't this the best picture of what robots and artificial intelligence could give us?) And the fact that the framers of the Civil War Amendments envisioned that world is not a command that we work to rebuild it. They assumed the conditions that would produce that world would survive. They were wrong. And the fundamental question their error creates is this: How do their amendments to the Constitution get read now? How do we interpret constitutional commands written for a world that has plainly and obviously disappeared?

This is an issue that reaches far beyond free labor. But it is a core issue that any practice of fidelity must struggle to understand, because constitutional texts are not simply erased when reality comes to contradict them. Instead, they morph. They become different, or adapted, to the newly discovered contexts.

This was the fate of the free labor movement. Changed circumstances rendered its original ideal impossible. Those same changed circumstances then threw into relief an essential ambiguity at the core of the concept of free labor. That ambiguity in turn divided the free labor movement. One side emphasized the "free" in "free labor" and focused its normative attention on securing the conditions within which labor contracting could happen freely. For this part of the divided movement, wage labor was as much a free choice for free individuals as becoming a blacksmith was. It didn't, inherently at least, make anyone any worse or better than the choice to become a butcher or a farmer or a factory worker. It was an individual exercising his autonomy to deploy his labor as he saw fit. And if the choice left the worker "dependent," at least, as Eric Foner writes that Adam Smith had argued, it was a dependency upon "the impersonal law of supply and demand rather than the decision of a paternalistic master."[86] It was an instance of free labor, however imperfect, those on this side of the ambiguity believed, and one that the law should protect.

To protect this kind of free labor, the law need only protect the freedom to contract. The latter, insisted the inheritors of the free labor movement, was entailed by the former.

But for those who focused on the "labor" part in "free labor," and who understood that movement as part of an aspiration to better humans and, more important, to secure their independence, the wage labor system was a step backward. The problem wasn't the idea of freedom of contract. The problem was that in a world of "scale and scope," "no actual 'freedom of contract' could exist between labor and capital."[87] If the anti-slavery ideal was, as labor leader Ira Steward wrote in 1873, "that every man has the right to come and go at will," the labor movement asked, "How much [is] this abstract right...worth without the power to exercise it?"[88]

As evidence mounted of the failure of the wage labor system to provide for even the basic necessities of workers and their families, wage labor was attacked.[89] And as the wage labor system grew, formerly independent artisans "found themselves reduced to the position of wage earners," and they "no longer moved in a 'sphere of equality.'"[90] The free market thus became an enemy of this branch of the free labor movement, while for the other branch, the free market was gold.

These two very different responses to the failure of the initial free labor ideals to materialize thus produced two very different political movements within America. One was what we now refer to as the libertarian or laissez-faire movement in American politics—a movement that emphasized the freedom to contract and sought ever stronger constitutional limitations on the ability to use government to muck about with that liberty. The other was the labor movement—a movement that sought ever stronger governmental support for the opportunity of labor to use its power, political and otherwise, to secure its own independence.

These two movements could not be more different, at least as they matured through the end of the nineteenth century. But the key is to recognize their common origin. They were born as siblings. Their mother was the idealism that in part gave us the Civil War Amendments. Their father was the war that turned that idealism into law. "Both outlooks," Forbath wrote,

> the courts' liberal orthodoxy and the labor movement's anticapitalist republicanism, had a common origin. They represented the increasingly divergent strands of the republican discourse that had dominated American political thought since the Revolution....[B]oth judges and labor leaders claimed to be speaking [for] the "Free Labor" and

"Antislavery" republicanism that knitted together the Northern working and middle classes during the Civil War.[91]

The labor movement saw in the ideals of free labor a world in which laborers enjoyed independence and integrity. It saw a constant struggle in American history against the lobotomized laborer Adam Smith had described in *The Wealth of Nations*, and over which the bloodiest war in American history had been fought. This movement was not embarrassed to rely upon government power to secure this independence and integrity. The "wage system," held Uriah Stephens, a founder of the Knights of Labor, was "an artificial and man-created condition, not God's arrangement."[92] Why, then shouldn't Americans push for different man-made constructs that would better achieve these republican ideals of independence? Whatever the means, this branch of the free labor movement sought to make good upon free labor ideals by further constitutionalizing the value of this sort of independence. When the economic conditions of the industrial revolution made it impossible to achieve that independence by relying upon an unregulated market alone, the labor movement inherited the objectives but sought to achieve them through very different means. Government would become a tool to secure the independence free labor required. Its activism would be an essential weapon, allowing workers to secure what the market alone did not.

The libertarian wing of the free labor movement, by contrast, was less concerned with results, more concerned with process. Opportunity, on this view, was the keystone to free labor. Choice unconstrained by government was its cardinal objective. Freedom didn't mean a guarantee of riches. It meant simply that whatever lot one had in life was mostly the consequence of one's individual choice. Or better, that the relevant independence was not independence from fate but independence from the will of another human being. History had shown that whenever the government was brought into that mix for the purpose of helping one side or another, it was not idealism but corruption that ultimately guided the government's hand. As Charles Francis Adams Jr. (grandson of President John Quincy Adams and no apologist for capitalism) wrote, "He who owns the thing knows that he must also own the legislature which regulates the thing."[93] This was an argument for limiting the power of the government to interfere. Wrote the social scientist William Graham Sumner: "The advocate of interference takes it for granted that he and his associates will have the administration of their legislative device in their own hands. . . . They never appear to remember that the device, when once set up, will itself be the prize of a struggle. . . . Who will get it?"[94]

The signal objective of these free labor idealists was thus to ensure that the corruption of government didn't limit the freedom of laborers. Preserve individual liberty, and you will achieve as much free labor as the world can support. Give up that liberty so as to secure the protection of labor, and you will enter a game that laborers can never win. For once the government was allowed to pick sides, labor was certain to lose in that battle eventually. Neutrality was thus the ruling norm for these libertarians. Keeping the government out was its means.

I don't mean to engage the obvious and familiar debates for and against each of these stylized positions. My aim instead is simply to demonstrate that their common origin complicated the relationship between the two. As Forbath puts it, "The judges who struck down the labor laws and the labor reformers who promoted them claimed to act on behalf of many of the same ideals: the workingman's 'independence,' the 'dignity of free labor,' its deliverance from 'coercion' and 'paternalism.'"[95] My claim is not that the libertarian view was true, nor that libertarianism was an obvious descendant of the free labor movement. Nor is it my view that the libertarian view was adopted by the Supreme Court justices who made it famous simply because it could claim the free labor movement as an ancestor. Rather, my only objective here is to show how one set of constitutionalized ideals could become a very different set of constitutional practices when carried into the midst of an industrial revolution, and that justices could in good faith claim the authority of a constitutional moment when striking down inconsistent legislative acts.[96]

Again, this may feel like praising the good manners of John Wilkes Booth as he entered Ford's Theatre to assassinate Abraham Lincoln. For it may seem that in looking for the fidelity in the substantive due process revolution, I am ignoring the gross infidelity of the Court when addressing race. For now, all I can do is acknowledge that weirdness. In Chapter 16, we will address it, understand it, and possibly defuse it.

Finally, we need to bracket an inconvenient bit of this history—the actual text under which the value of free labor lives. To the most ardent defenders of free labor, that text was the privileges-or-immunities clause of the Fourteenth Amendment. As we'll consider later in this chapter, that clause was quickly rendered useless. So the value that I'm describing gets relocated to the due process clause—not so much because anyone believes that's what the framers of these amendments meant, but because the justices believed that despite the complication with the privileges-or-immunities clause, this value was central to the framing of this part of the Constitution during the Civil War.

# Limits Realized

This (insanely) long preamble has tried to place in context the series of increasingly dramatic steps taken by the Court's conservatives to constrain the power of government. The pattern of this constraint parallels the story of the commerce power, though here there are more moving parts and more values that get voiced. As with the constraints on commerce, the limits here come slowly at first. But the dynamic with each is similar, and the parallels are instructive.

Put most simply, if crudely, at first the Court stands oblivious to the growing reach and significance of regulatory activity (as happened with commerce) and its conflict with the framing value of free labor. As with *Gibbons* and *McCulloch*, at first the Court ratifies formulae that rationalize an ever-expanding scope for regulation. But then, as with the commerce power, at a certain point conservatives become troubled by an obvious gap between what they think was the Framers' conception of the scope of government power and the actual scope of government power now openly and regularly practiced. That gap becomes an embarrassment. In response, the conservatives make up constraints on the scope of the government's power in order to restore their conception of a framing balance.

## THE INFIDELITY FROM FOLLOWING THE TEXT

Our parallel begins with two cases that reject any idea of a constitutional limit on the state's power to regulate. As with *Gibbons* and *McCulloch*, these cases see nothing in the text of the Constitution to restrict the scope of state power. They therefore reject any idea that the Court should impose the restriction itself.

### Slaughterhouse

In May 1862, Union general Benjamin Franklin Butler sailed into the harbor at New Orleans to take command of the city. Union forces had overrun Confederate troops, and this bastion of the South would be firmly controlled by the North for the balance of the war.

Butler had been commissioned a major general for political reasons. Appointed in the spring of 1861, he served until dismissed after a disastrous command of his troops in the First Battle of Fort Fisher. And while he had no feel for commanding men in battle, his true talents lay in his capacity to administer government. That talent showed itself in New Orleans. Upon taking command, he immediately implemented a wide range of reforms to improve the city. Central among these reforms was a regulation of butchery. From 1863 on, no longer were butchers free to slaughter animals wherever and however they wished. Instead, Butler's regulations closed all slaughterhouses north of the city, to avoid the waste from slaughtered carcasses traveling down the Mississippi into New Orleans.

The most dramatic effect of this regulation was not on butchery, however, but on disease. Before General Butler's regulation, New Orleans would regularly fall prey to a range of tropical diseases. After Butler cleaned up the city's water, the incidence of those diseases fell from thousands each summer to just a few. Regulations of butchery thus had an extraordinary police power effect, significantly improving the health of the community.

After the war, some of General Butler's ideas eventually became the policy of the state of Louisiana as well. In 1869, for example, the state passed an act "to Protect the Health of the City of New Orleans, to Locate the Stock Landings and Slaughter Houses, and to Incorporate 'The Crescent City Live Stock Landing and Slaughter House Company.'" Rather than allow unregulated competition among hundreds of butchers across the city, the act mandated that all butchery was to be done at a newly established "Grand Slaughterhouse," located south of the city.[97] That regulation had the obvious effect of displacing many butchers and forcing them to apply for the right to practice the trade of butchering.[98]

Butchers challenged the regulation as violating the Thirteenth and Fourteenth Amendments. In an opinion written by Justice Miller, the Court rejected their argument. We'll focus on the logic behind that rejection in Chapter 16. But as we're tracking a pattern of translation—a pattern that begins with failure, is marked in dissent, and eventually rises to success—let us focus on the dissents for now.

In an opinion that Roscoe Pound would later call "the fountain head" of a "reactionary line of decisions," Justice Field dissented from the decision upholding the regulation.[99] Butchery, Field insisted, was a "lawful calling," and every man had a now constitutionally protected "right to pursue lawful callings."[100] "Lawful calling" was code for a profession protected by the ideals of free labor. The Thirteenth Amendment had created this new right, or at least Field believed.[101] The Constitution, Field wrote, should now be read to protect that liberty against state regulations that aimed to restrict it.

Justice Joseph P. Bradley dissented as well, and echoed Field's view. He too read in these texts of the Second Founding a constitutional commitment to free labor ideals. As he wrote, the "rights to life, liberty and the pursuit of happiness . . . belong to the citizens of every free government."

For the preservation, exercise, and enjoyment of these rights the individual citizen, as a necessity, must be left free to adopt such calling, profession, or trade as may seem to him most conducive to that end. Without this right he cannot be a freeman. This right to choose one's calling is an essential part of that liberty which it is the object of government to protect; and a calling, when chosen, is a man's property and right. Liberty and property are not protected where these rights are arbitrarily assailed.[102]

What Louisiana had done by "granting [a] monopol[y] or exclusive privilege" to the Crescent City Live-Stock Landing and Slaughter-House Company, Field and Bradley held, was "an invasion of the right of others to choose a lawful calling, and an infringement of personal liberty."[103] Justice Noah Haynes Swayne dissented with a similar view: "A more flagrant and indefensible invasion of the rights of many for the benefit of a few has not occurred in the legislative history of the country."[104]

This was stirring rhetoric, but free labor had lost. And not surprisingly, as the state's argument for regulation here was indeed quite strong. Everyone conceded there was a public purpose to the regulation in eliminating the harmful health effects from unregulated slaughtering. The only dispute was whether there was another way, more respectful of free labor rights, to achieve that legitimate end. At this stage in the Court's constitutional jurisprudence, the Court hadn't developed an effective doctrine for weighing or narrowing the reach of governmental power. In modern terms, we could ask whether there was a less restrictive means to achieving the government's ends, where "less restrictive" means with less burden on the free labor right. That doctrinal tool did not exist in 1873. So all the Court could do was acknowledge the public purpose and leave to the legislature the issue of legitimate means. Free labor had made its claim and lost.

A much clearer articulation of the principles of free labor that underlay the Civil War Amendments comes in the later slaughterhouse monopoly case, *Butchers' Union Slaughterhouse v. Crescent City Slaughterhouse* (1884). Crescent City held the monopoly that had been upheld in the *Slaughterhouse Cases*. But in 1879, a decade after Louisiana had granted that monopoly to Crescent City, Louisiana's constitution was amended to abolish the power of a city to grant such a monopoly. On the basis of that abolition, Butchers' Union Slaughterhouse started slaughtering without Crescent City's approval. Crescent City filed a lawsuit to defend its original monopoly.

That monopoly, Crescent City argued, was a contract. The state had no power to breach that contract. Thus the 1879 state constitution could not abolish the rights that Crescent City had been granted. Whether granting that monopoly originally had been advisable or not, Crescent City argued, the constitution forbade a do-over.

The lower courts agreed with the monopolist. But the Supreme Court reversed. In an opinion again by Justice Miller, the Court held that the state had no power to contract away such a core part of its police power. While it was free to establish a monopoly, any law that did so had to be understood as contingent upon the continued desire of the state to secure such a monopoly. Miller did not hold that every contract that touched the police power was subject to this contingency. But any contract touching such a core part of the police power could not be understood to bind the state.[105]

Justices Field and Bradley concurred, but for reasons that were very different. They believed Louisiana was free to abolish the Crescent City slaughterhouse monopoly because they believed that monopoly had been invalid from the start. Neither justice was willing to concur, even eleven years later, with the position of Justice Miller in the *Slaughterhouse Cases* (1873) that the only privileges or immunities protected by the Fourteenth Amendment were federal. In their view, that amendment also protected the privilege of free labor. As Bradley wrote:

> The right to follow any of the common occupations of life is an inalienable right; it was formulated as such under the phrase "pursuit of happiness" in the Declaration of Independence, which commenced with the fundamental proposition that "all men are created equal; that they are endowed by their Creator with certain inalienable rights; that among these are life, liberty, and *the pursuit of happiness*."[106]

The right to pursue a common calling was "a large ingredient in the civil liberty of the citizen." And while such professions can be regulated under the police power, such regulation cannot defeat the core right. "This concession" that common callings can be regulated, Bradley wrote,

> does not in the slightest degree affect the proposition (which I deem a fundamental one), that the ordinary pursuits of life, forming the large mass of industrial avocations, are and ought to be free and open to all, subject only to such general regulations, applying equally to all, as the general good may demand.[107]

Justice Field was even more emphatic: "It cannot be admitted that, under the pretense of providing for the public health or public morals, [states] can encroach upon rights which those amendments declare shall not be impaired"— rights that included, for Field, the right of free labor.[108] Field too tied this right to the Declaration of Independence:

These inherent rights have never been more happily expressed than in the Declaration of Independence, that new evangel of liberty to the people: "We hold these truths to be self-evident"—that is, so plain that their truth is recognized upon their mere statement—"that all men are endowed"—not by edicts of Emperors, or decrees of Parliament, or acts of Congress, but "by their Creator with certain inalienable rights"—that is, rights which cannot be bartered away, or given away, or taken away, except in punishment of crime—"and that among these are life, liberty, and the pursuit of happiness, and to secure these"— not grant them, but secure them—"governments are instituted among men, deriving their just powers from the consent of the governed."

That declared the nature of the right. Field then immediately declared the free labor right as within the scope of the Declaration:

Among these inalienable rights, as proclaimed in that great document, is the right of men to pursue their happiness, by which is meant the right to pursue any lawful business or vocation, in any manner not inconsistent with the equal rights of others, which may increase their prosperity or develop their faculties, so as to give to them their highest enjoyment. The common business and callings of life, the ordinary trades and pursuits, which are innocuous in themselves, and have been followed in all communities from time immemorial, must therefore be free in this country to all alike upon the same conditions.[109]

It was Justice Bradley's opinion, however, that would presage the arc of the litigation strategy to defend this free labor right. Bradley believed a monopoly interfering with the right to pursue a common calling "abridges the privileges of citizens of the United States; it deprives them of a portion of their liberty and property without due process of law; and it denies to them the equal protection of the laws," for the reasons I've just rehearsed. At the core of those privileges was the right to pursue a common calling. Bradley (and three other justices) believed that right was protected by the privileges-or-immunities clause of the Fourteenth Amendment.

But it also, as Bradley argues, "deprives them of a portion of their liberty and property without due process of law, for it takes from him the freedom of adopting and following the pursuit which he prefers; which, as already intimated, is a material part of the liberty of the citizen." Bradley doesn't explain how this deprivation was accomplished without due process; his argument hangs on the idea that any process depriving citizens of such a fundamental privilege could not be proper.

And finally, Bradley insists the deprivation violates the equal protection clause:

> If it is not a denial of the equal protection of the laws to grant to one man or set of men the privilege of following an ordinary calling in a large community and to deny it to all others, it is difficult to understand what would come within the constitutional prohibition.[110]

Though these arguments are strongly made, they still leave plenty of room for regulation. The essence of the complaint Bradley, Field, and Swayne had made against the Crescent City monopoly was not that butchers were regulated, but rather that the regulation involved a monopoly. The city was free to banish butchers from the city; it would have been free to regulate the manner by which they did their work. What it couldn't do was to condition the right to work on the consent of a monopoly. The attack was on monopolies—"the bane," said Bradley, "of our body politic."[111] It was not an attack on the police power, which both Bradley and Field insisted survived the Civil War Amendments unmolested.

These ideals would echo in later opinions, striking the regulation of labor under the ideals of free labor. But here, they were rejected by the Supreme Court—again.

### Munn

The biggest change in the infrastructure of commerce after the Civil War was the explosion of railroads. While railroad infrastructure had grown quickly before the war—in 1830, there was thirty miles of railroad track; by 1840, there was three thousand miles; a decade later, that had tripled to nine thousand miles; a decade after that, it had tripled again—its real rise happens after the war. Between 1871 and 1900, the nation laid 170,000 miles of railway. In the South, the network of railways expanded from 11,000 miles in 1870 to 29,000 in 1890. Congress, as eager as any to ride this wave, authorized the first transcontinental railway in 1862, which was completed in 1869. By 1900, four more transcontinental railways existed.[112]

These changes made more of America dependent upon railroads. And as railroad companies became more concentrated, that dependency would produce a very predictable conflict: when owners of railroads increased rates, those dependent upon railroads petitioned their legislatures to check such increases in order to ensure that local production would not be held hostage to national infrastructure.

Those petitions produced a series of restrictive limitations on railroad charges in southern and midwestern states. The railroads challenged those restrictions. In 1877, in *Munn v. Illinois,* the Supreme Court reviewed the constitutionality of those challenges and upheld the power of the state to regulate rates.

*Munn* didn't involve railroads, at least not directly. *Munn* concerned grain elevators. Like railroads, grain elevators had become an essential facility in the economy of grain production. Located at critical railroad junctions, the elevators stored grain until shipment, and ownership of those elevators was concentrated. The thirty-one people who owned the nine firms that owned the fourteen grain elevators in the Chicago area had a "virtual monopoly" over grain trade between midwestern states and the eastern seaboard.[113] Those facts were sufficient, Chief Justice Morrison Waite believed, to justify the state's power to regulate them: "If any business can be clothed 'with a public interest, and cease to be *juris privati* only,' this has been. It may not be made so by the operation of the Constitution of Illinois or this statute *but it is by the facts.*"[114] That last line was crucial. Theorists of government power had long conceded that a monopoly could be regulated by the state. But most of these theorists were speaking of government-granted monopolies (for example, the slaughterhouses in the *Slaughterhouse Cases*). Where the state granted an exclusive charter, for example, to a bridge or ferry company, that charter was a monopoly; no one doubted the state could then regulate the monopoly that it had created, at least in the terms of its creation, even if the power of the state was limited by contract after the monopoly was created.

But in *Munn,* the state hadn't created the monopoly, or given the "virtual monopoly" its monopoly power. Instead, that power had been created "by the facts." Thus, as with *Gibbons,* the jurisdictional trigger was not law or logic, but facts in the world. And as with *Gibbons,* this meant that as the facts of connectedness changed, so too would regulatory authority change. Though the business here was new, the case, Waite held, simply "presents . . . a case for the application of a long-known and well-established principle in social science, and this statute simply extends the law so as to meet this new development of commercial progress."[115]

*Munn* thus rejected the argument for a constitutional limit on the state's regulatory power. Yet as with *Gibbons* and *McCulloch,* seeded within the opinion was at least an invitation for limits later on. As Waite wrote in response to Justice Field's dissent,

> From what has been said, it is not to be inferred that this power of limitation or regulation is itself without limit. This power to regulate is not a power to destroy, and limitation is not the equivalent of confiscation. Under pretense of regulating fares and freights, the State

cannot require a railroad corporation to carry persons or property without reward; neither can it do that which in law amounts to a taking of property for public use without just compensation.[116]

This was just the second case in the history of the federal courts which indicated that due process could limit the economic effects of state legislation.[117] It was a message that became a slogan to a generation of constitutional lawyers: Chief Justice Waite, and hence the Court, recognized that a line would have to be drawn. As he confessed in a letter after the decision, "The great difficulty in the future will be to establish the boundary between that which is private, and that in which the public has an interest."[118] It was a prescient insight from a chief justice that most considered mediocre at best.[119]

Justice Field's dissent did not invoke the latent value of free labor. It instead invoked the latent value of neutrality. Regardless of the importance of grain elevators, a regulation of their rates, Field argued, effected a transfer from one class (the owners) to another (the farmers). It was a transfer from A to B, and thus violated the principle of neutrality. Even if the business regulated was "affected with a public interest," Field believed, the Fourteenth Amendment now limited the legislature in the means it could adopt to achieve its ends. Even if the power of police (compare: commerce) reached this economic behavior, a latent value of neutrality (compare: federalism) restricted that police power.

Field lost, and the regulators won. This time, however, Field didn't have the support of Bradley. Indeed, Waite's opinion had been ghostwritten by Bradley.[120] He was not as committed to judicially enforced neutrality as he was to a judicial defense of free labor.

Yet as the scope of the *Munn* principle increased, the concern voiced by Field and his followers became more and more salient. And in a series of cases, courts began to explore the limit to the *Munn* principle. At first, the dispute was about whether the monopoly had to be de jure (as the grain elevators were not) or whether a de facto monopoly (as the grain elevators were) was enough. But a series of cases made clear that even a de facto monopoly was not necessary for the state to have the power to regulate.[121] Merely being significant or powerful within an economy was enough to render an activity regulable. Thus again, as with the commerce authority, less and less was immune from regulation. More and more became within the reach of government.

Practically, however, and for the fifty years after *Munn,* the scope of activities said to be "affected with a public interest" did not dramatically change. As Barry Cushman describes the list identified by Chief Justice William Howard Taft in 1923, there were three general classes:

1) Those which are carried on under the authority of a public grant of privileges which either expressly or impliedly imposes the affirmative duty of rendering a public service demanded by any member of the public. Such are the railroads, other common carriers and public utilities. 2) Certain occupations, regarded as exceptional...Such are those of the keepers of inns, cabs and grist mills....3) Businesses which though not public at their inception may be fairly said to have risen to be such and have become subject in consequence to some government regulation. They have come to hold such a peculiar relation to the public that this is superimposed upon them. In the language of the cases, the owner by devoting his business to the public use, in effect grants the public an interest in that use and subjects himself to public regulation to the extent of that interest although the property continues to belong to its private owner and to be entitled to protection accordingly.[122]

This list set the scope of activity that was regulable by the state. That scope was increasingly vast. *Munn* thus stood for the idea that the state's power would be equally vast—at least until the arguments from the dissent began to inspire more than a minority of justices.

Thus, these two cases—*Slaughterhouse* and *Munn*—set the framework for the period of the Court's acquiescence. The power of government—the values of neutrality and free labor notwithstanding—went unchecked. The dissenters registered their dissent. That objection was ignored.


## *Translating Limits*

Then, as with the commerce power, the justices woke up. In a string of cases ranging from labor regulation to the right of parents to teach their children German, the Court began to invalidate both state and federal laws in the name of due process.[123] One-step originalists—finding no real limit in the scope of police power regulation—began to see that they needed to take a second step.

The predicate for these cases was a decision in 1897 about a technical issue of contract law. In *Allgeyer v. Louisiana* (1897), a citizen of Louisiana had entered into a contract with a New York insurance company in New York to insure property held in Louisiana. The location where the contract was made was important (and conceded by the state of Louisiana). If the contract had been made in Louisiana, the Court held, then it would have violated Louisiana law. But because the contract was made in New York—even though made by correspondence between a resident of Louisiana and a corporation in New York—the question for the Court was whether Louisiana could punish defendants for a legal contract made in another state, just because it involved property in Louisiana.

In a stunning reversal of decisions made in the twenty-four years since the *Slaughterhouse Cases,* the Court relied on the free labor ideal to strike down Louisiana's law. Quoting Bradley from his *Crescent City* concurrence, Justice Peckham wrote, "The right to follow any of the common occupations of life is an inalienable right.... [T]o prohibit [anyone] from pursuing his chosen calling ... deprive[s] him (to a certain extent) of his liberty."[124] Likewise, the Court quoted Justice Harlan in *Powell v. Pennsylvania* (1888): the "enjoyment upon terms of equality with all others in similar circumstances of the privilege of pursuing an ordinary calling or trade ... is an essential part of [a person's] rights of liberty."[125] Of course, just because the right to "pursu[e] an ordinary calling" was a protected liberty did not necessarily mean "that in no such case can the state exercise its police power."[126] The issue had to be decided case by case. But it was clear nonetheless, *Allgeyer* held, that the liberty protected by the Fourteenth Amendment included the free labor right.

> The "liberty" mentioned in that amendment means, not only the right of the citizen to be free from the mere physical restraint of his person, as by incarceration, but the term is deemed to embrace the right of the citizen to be free in the enjoyment of all his faculties; to be free to use them in all lawful ways; to live and work where he will; to earn his livelihood by any lawful calling; to pursue any livelihood or avocation; and for that purpose to enter into all contracts which may be proper, necessary, and essential to his carrying out to a successful conclusion the purposes above mentioned.[127]

It is important, if confusing, that the Court did not go back on the holding that Miller had articulated in *Slaughterhouse.* Justice Peckham did not revive the privileges-or-immunities clause. Instead, the Court followed Bradley's suggestion in *Crescent City* that even if the right could not be grounded in the privileges-or-immunities clause, it could still be grounded in due process.

Seven years later, *Lochner v. New York* (1905) launched this idea into constitutional orbit. New York had passed a law to regulate bakers. In the view of its legislature, at least as it was defended, the law was meant to protect both bakers and the public. By limiting the number of hours a baker could work, the law would protect the health of bakers. Healthy bakers bake healthful bread. New York thus justified its regulation as a simple application of its police power. This was, as New York attorney general Julius Meyer wrote in his brief, almost too obvious for comment:

> The main purpose of the…law under discussion was to safeguard the public health; but another purpose…was to safeguard the health of those engaged in…making biscuit, bread, cake, and confectionery.[128]
>
> …
>
> Is it not true that the man who suffers with skin diseases, with tuberculosis and other affections [*sic*], may communicate some of the germs of his disorder to this product which is to be eaten by the mass of our people? Is it not equally true that, working as the baker does, at night, he is more likely to contract disease by reason of the impoverishment and deterioration of his physical system and his exclusion from the sunlight in which it is the privilege of most of us to do our daily work?[129]

In the lower court, Chief Justice Alton B. Parker (who would resign the same year to challenge Teddy Roosevelt as the Democratic nominee for president) cited page after page of Supreme Court authority upholding the power of the states to interfere with labor contracts for the purpose of protecting the public health or the health of the worker.

Most powerful in this long line of authority was *Holden v. Hardy* (1898), which upheld a maximum-hours regulation for miners. But in addition to *Holden*, Parker cited others:

> Statutes declaring a railroad company liable for damages to an employé although caused by another employé (127 U.S. 205); fixing the damages at double the value of stock killed when due to the neglect of a railroad company to maintain fences (129 U.S. 26); requiring locomotive engineers to be licensed, and providing that the railroad company employing them pay the fees of examination (128 U.S. 96); requiring cars to be heated otherwise than by stoves on railroads over 50 miles in length (165 U.S. 628); providing for immediate payment of wages by railroad companies to discharged employees (173 U.S. 404); prohibiting options to sell grain (184 U.S. 425); providing for inspection of mines at expense of owners (185 U.S. 203), and one declaring void all contracts for sales of stocks on margins (187 U.S. 606).[130]

Thus did the law seem absolutely settled in Parker's view. And while three of the judges on the New York Court of Appeals dissented from his opinion, their dissents were motivated more by the fact that the legislature had located the ordinance within its labor regulations rather than its health regulations—thus revealing, the dissenters believed, that the true intent was not health.

But the U.S. Supreme Court surprised Parker—and the world. By telling an employee how many hours he could work, New York was interfering with these bakers' free labor right: "The right to purchase or to sell labor is part of the liberty protected by this amendment, unless there are circumstances which exclude the right."[131] Nothing New York said, Justice Peckham found for the United States Supreme Court, was sufficient to justify this invasion of liberty. Indeed, New York had convinced Peckham that the law also violated the second latent value described above, that of neutrality. New York's law, Peckham held, was simple class warfare. This was, as Justice Chase had put it more than a hundred years before, taking from A (capital) and giving to B (some laborers). As Justice Peckham wrote:

> Many of the laws of this character, while passed under what is claimed to be the police power for the purpose of protecting the public health or welfare, are, in reality, passed from other motives. . . . It is manifest to us that the limitation of the hours of labor as provided for in this section of the statute . . . has no such direct relation to . . . the health of the employee, as to justify us in regarding the section as really a health law. It seems to us that the real object and purpose were simply to regulate the hours of labor between the master and his employees (all being men *sui juris*), in a private business, not dangerous in any degree to morals, or in any real and substantial degree to the health of the employees. Under such circumstances the freedom of master and employee to contract with each other in relation to their employment . . . cannot be prohibited or interfered with, without violating the Federal Constitution.[132]

Justice Peckham was dancing the two-step.

The dissents to this holding are justly famous. Justice Harlan spent many pages trying to establish that the justifications offered by the state were just fine. Justice Holmes had much less patience. As he wrote:

> This case is decided upon an economic theory which a large part of the country does not entertain. If it were a question whether I agreed with that theory I should desire to study it further and long before making up my mind. But I do not conceive that to be my duty, because I strongly believe that my agreement or disagreement has nothing to do with the right of a majority to embody their opinions in law. It is settled by various decisions of this court that state constitutions and state laws may regulate life in many ways which we as legislators

might think as injudicious or if you like as tyrannical as this, and which equally with this interfere with the liberty to contract.... The liberty of the citizen to do as he likes so long as he does not interfere with the liberty of others to do the same, which has been a shibboleth for some well-known writers, is interfered with by school laws, by the Post office, by every state or municipal institution which takes his money for purposes thought desirable, whether he likes it or not. The 14th Amendment does not enact Mr. Herbert Spencer's Social Statics.[133]

Yet from the perspective of translation, both dissents miss a central point.

The values Peckham tried to enforce were at least latent in the Civil War Amendments. It was certainly a fair reading of those values to understand them as blocking the state from interfering with an employee's choice to work however he wants. Holmes didn't see such a value in the Constitution, but for Holmes, at this point in his career at least, the Constitution was largely invisible. As we will see in Chapter 17, even when the Constitution stated expressly that the right to vote could not be denied on the basis of race, Holmes refused to enforce that right against a state plainly denying it on the basis of race.[134]

Likewise, Harlan was no doubt correct that the statute was consistent with a public concern for health. But he refused to even consider whether the state's concern for health was merely pretextual. That was beyond the Court's authority, Harlan believed:

> We are not to presume that the State of New York has acted in bad faith.... We cannot say that the state has acted without reason, nor ought we to proceed upon the theory that its action is a mere sham. Our duty, I submit, is to sustain the statute as not being in conflict with the Federal Constitution for the reason—and such is an all-sufficient reason—it is not shown to be plainly and palpably inconsistent with that instrument.[135]

Yet for the conservatives, the consequence of this presumption was the end to the limits of government. They therefore came to see their duty differently. The statute, as the Court read it, "took from A and gave to B."[136] Worse, it did so in the context of the free labor rights. It thus mixed the two latent values standing behind the due process limitation, and it challenged the Court to protect those values in the face of a growing practice by progressive legislators to simply ignore them.

Or at least, with respect to the free labor interest, the growing practice of ignoring one branch of the free labor movement. Recall that I suggested, following Forbath, that the free labor movement had divided soon after the Civil War Amendments were adopted. One part became libertarian; the other part became the union movement. The regulation at issue in *Lochner* was plainly consistent with the values of the labor movement faction, but it was inconsistent with the libertarian faction. The progressives were generally not libertarians. They were happy to defend the interests of labor, especially as capital seemed to them to deny laborers the independence the free labor movement was to be fighting for.

The Court thus did precisely what it would do thirty years later with the commerce power. As with the commerce power, there was nothing in the text of the Fourteenth Amendment that expressly enumerated the free labor limitations that Peckham imposed. There was instead a recognition that things had gotten out of control. The scope of regulation engaged by the state was far beyond the scope of regulation imagined at the Second Founding. And thus, in reliance upon this recognition, the Court crafted affirmative limitations on the scope of state power. Again, nothing in the text compelled it. These were, to put the matter pejoratively, made-up limitations on the government's power, but pursued to the end of preserving fidelity to at least one conception of what the framers at the Second Founding had established.

The pattern is thus a formula: there is a power of government; economic or factual integration removes any effective limit to that power; the government then legislates beyond traditional limits; the Court, in an act of translation, creates affirmative limits on the government's power, in order to restore the original value. Here that value was "the inherent and natural right of every man to freely labor with his head and his hands" as well as the protection against "class legislation, the most pernicious and most dangerous of all legislation."[137]

Like *Hammer* with the commerce power debate, however, *Allgeyer* and *Lochner* at first were just warning shots. Once again, the revolution took off slowly. Constitutional lawyers were uncertain, and the principle would not come into full bloom for a decade.[138] Three years after *Lochner*, in *Adair v. United States* (1908), the Court invalidated a federal statute that made it a crime to fire a railroad employee because he was a member of a union.[139] The right of liberty, Justice Harlan asserted, was a "personal right."

> It is not within the functions of government . . . to compel any person in the course of his business and against his will to accept or retain the personal services of another, or to compel any person, against his will, to perform personal services for another. The right of a person to sell his labor upon such terms as he deems proper is, in its essence, the

same as the right of the purchaser of labor to prescribe the conditions upon which he will accept such labor from the person offering to sell it. So the right of the *employé* to quit the service of the employer, for whatever reason, is the same as the right of the employer, for whatever reason, to dispense with the services of such *employé*.[140]

This was the right of free labor, made equal between the employer and employee. Seven years later, the Court affirmed that the same principle restrained the states. In *Coppage v. Kansas* (1915), the Court affirmed the constitutional status of the free labor right. And while it affirmed as well the power of the state to regulate, that power did not include the power to interfere merely to remedy inequality. It was in "the nature of things," the Court said, that there would be "legitimate . . . inequalities of fortune," but such inequality was not enough to justify a restriction on liberty.[141]

But history rarely follows a straight line. As the Court sought to uphold the liberty of the worker against the regulations of the state, its opinions were not always, or at least not obviously, consistent. In the same year as *Adair*, the Court upheld a limitation on the number of hours an employee could work—precisely the regulation it had struck down in *Lochner*. But these employees were women, not men, and Louis Brandeis had wowed the Court with the first "Brandeis brief," demonstrating, or so the justices thought, the public purpose (and sexism) implicit in this woman-protective legislation. As Barry Cushman has noted, when the Court "did not view a regulation of contractual prerogatives as also resulting in an improper legislative discrimination or redistribution of property," the free labor justices failed to secure a majority.[142] But when the two ran together during this period, the combination was viewed as a plain violation of due process.

World War I then put a complete stop on this revolution through translation. The war led the Court to relax constitutional constraints on the government. Industries were nationalized; competition was eliminated. As Robert Post has described:

> War mobilization entailed "the most sweeping extension of national power experienced by the country up to that time." The federal government took control of the operations of the nation's railroads, its telegraphs and telephones, and its shipping industries. It assumed authority to regulate the production and prices of food and fuel. It actively intervened to shape the priorities of the wartime economy. It instituted sharply progressive income taxes. It established national labor policies and agencies. It imposed national prohibition. Nothing like this explosion of federal regulatory power had ever happened before.[143]

We were a nation at war. And whether consistent with our Constitution or not, the Court did almost nothing to constrain Congress and the president while hostilities were alive. As the *New Republic* described it, the war had "forever exploded the myth that all we have to do is to leave things alone. . . . [T]he war has forced men to turn over to the state the chief means of production and to regulate monopolies, prices, wages and labor conditions. *Laissez-faire* has been adjourned. . . . We have entered upon the stage of state-capitalism in which all our main economic activities are subordinated to the public interest."[144]

Or maybe not forever. After the war, three new justices came to the bench in the 1922 term, and "almost immediately," as Post describes it, the Court executed "a flat reversal of direction."[145] Peace brought a feeling of general restoration. The emergency was over. The predicate justifying unprecedented national control had been removed. And under Chief Justice Taft, the Supreme Court vigorously used the due process clause to return government to simpler, more federalist and libertarian ways. As Post puts it, the "Court throughout the 1920s would aspire to re-establish the domain of the normal," but to its surprise, it would "find its vision and authority subject to increasingly sharp contestation."[146]

The resistance came on two fronts. First was a revived effort to cabin the scope of businesses "affected with a public interest." Thus, in a case regulating rates for meatpacking, Chief Justice Taft conceded that "the regulation of rates to avoid monopoly" was permissible.[147] But, as Cushman describes it, "the business of food preparation was unlike those . . . with respect to which 'fear of monopoly prompted, and was held to justify, regulation of rates.'"[148] The regulation was thus unconstitutional. Likewise, the Court invalidated statutes regulating the prices charged by ticket brokers, employment agencies, and gasoline retailers, each on the ground "that the business in question was not affected with a public interest."[149]

Second, the Taft Court revived the notion of free labor. The "common callings," as Taft referred to "the ordinary producer, manufacturer or shopkeeper," "must be free from 'minutely detailed government supervision.'"[150] This notion didn't stand alone. Instead, it buttressed the more restrictive sense of businesses "affected with a public interest" that the Court was developing. As Taft wrote, tying the two together:

> It has never been supposed, since the adoption of the Constitution, that the business of the butcher, or the baker, the tailor, the wood chopper, the mining operator or the miner was clothed with such a public interest that the price of his product or his wages could be fixed by State regulation.[151]

"To deny a person the 'property which is the fruit and badge of his liberty,'" Post quotes Justice George Sutherland as arguing, "is to . . . leave him a slave."[152] Similarly with Justice James Clark McReynolds:

> Take from the citizen the right to freely contract and sell his labor for the highest wage which his individual skill and efficiency will command, and the laborer would be reduced to an automaton—*a mere creature of the state.*[153]

But certainly the most dramatic and restorative of these free labor cases was *Bailey v. Alabama* (1911), plus the anti-peonage cases it would support.[154]

*Bailey* was all about free labor. It flowed from the view that "freedom in the making of contracts" was "an elementary part of the rights of personal liberty and private property."[155] Alabama had made it a crime to defraud a labor contractor by taking money for labor and not performing the contract or returning the money. But that law violated the core aim of the Thirteenth Amendment, as expressed in the anti-peonage statute, "by prohibiting that control [criminal law] by which the personal service of one man is disposed of or coerced for another's benefit." The Thirteenth Amendment hadn't prohibited labor contracts. It had prohibited criminal coercion as the means by which such contracts could be enforced.

This is the expression of the free labor ideal. The question is not whether the choice is voluntary but whether the contract involves state coercion. What was prohibited was a certain kind of deal, because that deal was inconsistent with the ideal of free labor. And that deal was prohibited regardless of whether the laborer had agreed to it or not. The question was not freedom; the question was free labor.

That was the issue in *Adkins v. Children's Hospital* (1923) as well.[156] The District of Columbia purported to have established a minimum wage for women working within the district's limits. Recall that in *Muller* (1908) the Court had upheld a maximum-hours regulation for women. The District of Columbia saw no difference between one regulation and the other. (Neither did Justice Holmes in dissent.) Thus, the District of Columbia believed it was free to protect women through minimum-wage regulation, just as it was free, under *Muller*, to limit the number of hours that women could work.

But the Court balked. Price was the essence of the liberty of contract. And as it was "no longer open to question" that the "right to contract about one's affairs is a part of the liberty of the individual protected by" the Constitution, the only question was how broadly that right would reach.[157] As in *Coppage* and *Adair*, what animated the Court's reasoning was the inequality in the application of the rule—the law accounted for the interests of women but did not account for the interests of employers. The law was thus not neutral, and because it imposed upon a protected liberty, that bias killed the law.

*Adkins* would be the final flourish in the line of judicial interventions to protect the free labor right. Though that right was no doubt important, as Barry Cushman has noted, it was not vigorously enforced.[158] As we will consider in Chapter 6, a decade later the seeds of its demise were planted in *Nebbia v. New York* (1934). Those seeds would blossom three years after that and reverse *Adkins* expressly. As I've argued, the Court was faced with two very different ways of making free labor real, given the changed circumstances of wage labor. Given that choice, the Court embraced what was called "liberalism" at the time (what we would call libertarianism), "discarding many of its democratic strands and fortifying its liberal ones."[159]

The alternative would have embraced the labor movement and would have strengthened labor's independence vis-à-vis capital. Both reactions were plausible. Both come from a common source. And more directly for purposes of this chapter, the judges following the liberal tradition, Forbath says,

> were not engaged in willful perversion of republican principles. Protecting workers' liberty of contract was not, to them, mere window dressing...To them, the two strands of substantive due process [one, coming from the republican tradition, holding a laborer is free if he is independent, owns productive property, and has positive rights to the fruits of his labor, the other, coming from classical liberal political economy, holding a laborer is free if he isn't legally tied to his job] expressed a single, central tenet...: the notion that individual ownership...was the essence of personal right and freedom.[160]

That central tenet had a corollary: if free labor meant the right to work free of regulations controlling how one worked, it also meant a right to manage. As Daniel Ernst describes the Vermont Supreme Court in 1887:

> "Every man has the right to employ his talents, industry and capital as he pleases, free from the dictation of others," it declared. The "labor and skill of the workman, be it of high or low degree, the plant of the manufacturer, the equipment of the farmer, the investments of commerce" were all comparable forms of legally protected property.[161]

"Wherever a piece of labor legislation was found to interfere with the capitalist's property rights," Forbath notes, "it was found also to infringe on the worker's right to 'dispose of' his 'property'...as he saw fit."[162]

This conception was increasingly contested during the very period in which it was being developed. In the face of rising and powerful economic forces that effectively constrained the power of individual workers to control their destiny, the labor movement "proclaimed the demise of the 'free labor system,' and its promise of freedom and independence through individual effort and upward mobility."[163] In its place, the labor movement demanded collective action and democratic support. Progressives responded warmly to this demand. Both Teddy Roosevelt and Woodrow Wilson "portrayed Americans as vulnerable to vast economic and social forces that only government could discipline."[164] Individuals, Wilson believed, were "limited in their powers of self-mastery and small before vast 'industrial and social processes' which could overpower them without the state's protection."[165] Roosevelt extended the idea in 1937, when he spoke, as Purdy describes quoting FDR, of "problems that 'without the aid of government had left us baffled and bewildered,' the victims of 'blind economic forces and blindly selfish men.'"[166] The values, Franklin Roosevelt asserted in 1932, were the same as the values of the "old free-labor idea." But the aim now was to "secure those old values in new times."[167]

In the end, these due process cases and the federalism cases before them "were both sentinels standing guard over a vision of liberty."[168] Very soon the Court would recognize that it couldn't support those sentinels anymore.

| Retreat

I'VE TOLD A STORY about the evolution of two doctrines of constitutional law, an evolution that follows a similar two-step pattern in both cases. With both the commerce clause and economic due process, the Court at first ignores a widening gap between a conception of the framing design and the emerging reality of government power. With both, at some point, conservatives react by deploying doctrine intended to close that gap. This is two-step originalism. It is, I have argued, a kind of translation. Those translations imposed limits on government power that weren't otherwise there.

And then, as I describe in this chapter and Chapter 7, the Court gave up. In a dramatic reversal (whether in a single term or over a couple of years is still debated), the Court resigned in its fight to impose limits on government power. It retreated. And for generations since, critics and apologists have tried to explain this dramatic about-face.

My aim in this chapter is to describe the retreat. In Chapter 7, I introduce two ideas that help us see this retreat as fidelity—not fidelity to meaning, but fidelity to role. As Marshall did at the beginning of the republic, the New Deal Court did in its middle: it bent its understanding of the law to reflect an understanding of its own institutional role.

## Retreat: Commerce

We left the story of the commerce clause just as the Supreme Court had invalidated yet another critical New Deal statute, this time regulating the production of coal. Coal production was local, the Court held in *Carter v. Carter Coal* (1936). Congress therefore had no power to regulate labor relations in coal production. And while Congress might have the power to regulate interstate prices of coal, the Court held that price regulation could not survive once the labor relations section was struck down—a clear and final blow to the idea that Congress might address a Depression directly.

*Carter Coal* was decided on May 18, 1936, and it fueled FDR's growing "rage" with the Court.[1] More important, it helped set a debate that would frame the 1936 elections—never directly, but always in the background. The Supreme Court had rejected FDR and his New Deal. What would the people do in response?

Six months later, the answer was unequivocal. FDR had won by a landslide, carrying every state except Maine and Vermont, defeating Alf Landon 523–8 in the electoral college, and with 60.8 percent of the popular vote.[2] His party had trounced the Republicans in Congress as well, ending up with a 333–102 majority in the House and a 75–21 majority in the Senate. And as he prepared for his second term, Roosevelt was confident that he had the upper hand—with Congress and the people for sure, and, he believed, also with the Court. The Court had tried to stop him. The American people had signaled in response that they were on his side. The battle with the Court was teed up. The only question for FDR was what the next step should be.

And then the Court blinked. In a series of decisions beginning in April 1937, the Supreme Court retreated from the line it had drawn just a year before in *Carter Coal.* Its retreat couldn't have been more dramatic: black was now white, and at least initially, the Court wrote as if black had always been white.

The break happened in a commerce clause case—*National Labor Relations Board v. Jones & Laughlin Steel Co.* (1937). The issue presented was precisely parallel to the issue decided in *Carter Coal*: did Congress have the power to regulate labor relations in manufacturing?

Under the rule of *Carter Coal*, the answer was pretty simple: manufacturing was local, and local activities did not directly affect interstate commerce. Despite the importance of the steel industry to the national economy, the steel industry was not within the jurisdiction of the national government— at least according to the jurisprudence of *Carter Coal*.

*Jones* reversed this reasoning: "Although activities may be intrastate in character when separately considered, if they have such a close and substantial relation to interstate commerce that their control is essential or appropriate to protect that commerce from burdens and obstructions, Congress cannot be denied the power to exercise that control."[3]

"Cannot be denied"? This from the very Court that thirteen months before had denied it explicitly!

Yet no longer. The careful formalistic parsing of "direct" from "indirect," "manufacturing" from "commerce," and "flows" from "termination" was gone: steel was a national industry, and Congress was free to regulate it.[4]

The second major commerce clause reversal came four years later, as yet another post-inauguration gift to FDR. (There had been other significant reversals immediately after *Jones*, and I will discuss them later in this chapter. They were not directly tied to the commerce power.) In *United States v. Darby* (1941), the Court expressly reversed *Hammer v. Dagenhart* (1918) on its way to upholding the Fair Labor Standards Act (FLSA).[5] The act banned interstate transport of goods made by workers not given the benefits of the FLSA. *Hammer* had rejected a law that banned the transportation in interstate commerce of goods produced by child labor. The FLSA also mandated standards for workers producing goods for interstate commerce.

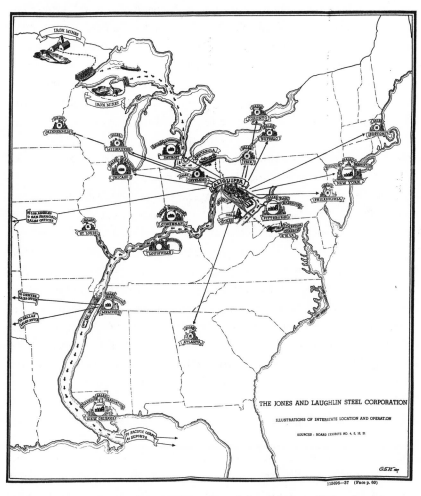

**FIGURE 2** Map: Graphic from *NLRB v. Jones & Laughlin,* 301 U.S. 1 (1937).

Once again, arguments made forcefully in the dissents before were now unapologetic holdings of majority opinions. Sure, manufacturing wasn't commerce. But shipping goods across state lines was interstate commerce, and subject to federal regulation. Even if the motive of that regulation was to affect what otherwise would be within the jurisdiction of the states, the federal regulation was proper. *Hammer* was to the contrary, but *Hammer* was now bad law.

Likewise with the limits created by *Carter Coal* on the ability of Congress to regulate the wages of employees producing goods to be sold in interstate commerce. Whether or not that production is interstate commerce, it certainly affects interstate commerce. The commerce power, the Court affirmed, includes the authority lent by the (now rediscovered) necessary-and-proper clause. The sum of that authority plainly authorized this regulation.

Finally, and in perhaps the most extreme case for two generations, in *Wickard v. Filburn* (1942) the Court upheld the Agricultural Adjustment Act of 1938.[6] That act aimed to regulate the market for certain agricultural products, including wheat, tobacco, corn, cotton, and rice, by regulating both the commercial sale of the products as well as home production of those products. Roscoe C. Filburn, a farmer, had complained that the statute regulated his "homegrown wheat"—wheat he grew on his land and which he intended to, and did, consume on his land. Nothing could be more intrastate than this, Filburn argued. Nonetheless, embracing a rationale that would have embarrassed even the government five years before, the Court held that this home consumption depressed market consumption, which in turn affected interstate commerce. Congress therefore had the power to control even the most local activity if, in the aggregate, it could argue that this local activity affected interstate commerce. Here, the Court held, it did.

Through this trilogy, the limits on Congress's commerce authority had been erased. Any attempt at translating the clause to preserve an alleged original meaning—by crafting limits on the otherwise expansive federal authority—had been forfeited. The Court returned to one-step originalism. It gave to Congress a breadth of power that would authorize it to regulate far beyond the limits that (at least the conservatives believed) the Framers had intended. Fidelity to the meaning of this original constitutional commitment had been surrendered.

## Retreat: Due Process

The retreat in the economic due process cases was slower than with commerce. To anyone reading carefully, the jig was up in 1934, when the Court held that milk production was "affected with a public interest," and therefore milk prices could be regulated by the state of New York. In *Nebbia v. New York* (1934), the Court held that even though milk production was not monopolistic and those engaging in milk production did not depend upon a public franchise, still the state was empowered to regulate the price of milk.

The authority the Court invoked for this effectively unlimited regulatory power (at least over goods within an economy) was *Munn v. Illinois* (1876)— as if nothing had happened in the almost sixty years since.

> It is clear that there is no closed class or category of businesses affected with a public interest, and the function of courts . . . is to determine in each case whether circumstances vindicate the challenged regulation as a reasonable exertion of governmental authority or condemn it as arbitrary or discriminatory. . . . The phrase "affected with a public interest" can, in the nature of things, mean no more than that an industry, for adequate reason, is subject to control for the public good.[7]

Any doubt about whether this was actually a retreat was finally resolved a month before the big break in the commerce clause cases. In *West Coast Hotel v. Parrish* (1937), the Court reversed its decision in *Adkins v. Children's Hospital* (1923) and upheld a statute that regulated the minimum wage of women. Arguments grounded in free labor and neutrality notwithstanding, the Court rejected the notion that due process could be used to invalidate a minimum wage law. The "liberty" in the due process clause might well have its "history and connotation."[8] But it was "liberty in a social organization which requires the protection of law against the evils which menace the health, safety, morals, and welfare of the people."[9] That means the interests that the state might protect may change as the "social organization" changes. The effort to hold fast to a framing conception of legitimate interests was rejected. *Adkins* and its ilk were overruled.

Then, as if to signal just how clearly his Court had understood the 1936 elections, Chief Justice Charles Evans Hughes added this final paragraph to the opinion:

> There is an additional and compelling consideration which recent economic experience has brought into a strong light. The exploitation of a class of workers who are in an unequal position with respect to bargaining power, and are thus relatively defenseless against the denial of a living wage, is not only detrimental to their health and well-being, but casts a direct burden for their support upon the community. What these workers lose in wages the taxpayers are called upon to pay. The bare cost of living must be met. We may take judicial notice of

the unparalleled demands for relief which arose during the recent period of depression and still continue to an alarming extent despite the degree of economic recovery which has been achieved. It is unnecessary to cite official statistics to establish what is of common knowledge through the length and breadth of the land. While in the instant case no factual brief has been presented, there is no reason to doubt that the state of Washington has encountered the same social problem that is present elsewhere. The community is not bound to provide what is in effect a subsidy for unconscionable employers. The community may direct its law-making power to correct the abuse which springs from their selfish disregard of the public interest.[10]

What the dissenters had been saying for almost fifteen years was now the law: governments were free to regulate as they wish, at least touching matters of economics. Any liberty interlude, during which Founding ideals had cabined burgeoning regulatory authority, was over.

Together, these reversals present the most difficult challenge for constitutionalists trying to justify the practice of American constitutional law across its history. If the Court was acting with fidelity, how were these reversals fidelity? And to the extent the reversals flowed from the decision of a single justice, what did that say about the function of the Court? As Indiana senator (and future Supreme Court justice) Sherman Minton put it just after *West Coast Hotel*:

> There will be four who favor interpretation in light of the times.... [T] here will be one justice who vacillates from one side to another. Thus the future interpretation would depend upon the frailty of one man.... [I am] unwilling that the future of the country be committed to the uncertainty of Mr. Justice Roberts's mind.[11]

There was no explicit amendment to the Constitution to justify the change (though FDR had been pressed to push for one).

There is no move of translation possible here—whatever the difference between 1937 and 1837, there was no real economic difference between 1937 and 1936. It may well be, as the *Wall Street Journal* opined just after the opinion, that "it can no longer be asserted with even a color of plausibility that the high bench interprets the basic law without reference to changing economic or social conditions."[12] But that reference in this case can't use those changes in facts to justify the changes in law. So what does justify it?

Bruce Ackerman has offered a brilliant and elaborate—and to many, quite convincing—theory of amendment to justify this "illegal" change, as well as the illegal changes of the Founding and Second Founding. I describe his theory more extensively in Chapter 21. If his were the only option for an account of fidelity, it would be an attractive and indeed edifying theory to embrace.

Yet I suggest that we can understand the New Deal reversals without the need to credit implied amendments to our Constitution. What's needed is a broader conception of fidelity, not a different understanding of amendment.

| Interlude

L ET'S PAUSE FOR a moment to introduce two ideas that will be central to the argument of the balance of the book, and essential to explaining this first retreat: *contestability* and the importance of *what seems to be so.*

## Contestability

Imagine the following examples of claims for justice made on behalf of different groups of people. You're going to find each of these claims to be ridiculous. I want you to think carefully about just why you think they're ridiculous:

- I speak to you on behalf of the dolphins of the world. These creatures implore you to stop your inhumane treatment of their species. Dolphins have a mental capacity comparable to humans; they are self-aware in just the way that humans are. Yet humans capture these creatures, murder them in tuna nets, and keep them like slaves in their zoos. No moral being could be so indifferent.
- I speak to you on behalf of teenagers, who while being tried as adults by a jury for crimes they are alleged to have committed are denied a jury of their peers, since children of their own age are excluded from juries. Children are citizens. There is no justification for excluding these citizens from juries.
- I speak to you on behalf of women who are insulted by being forced to use bathrooms separate from men. Women are no less human than men. They deserve no less dignity. Yet to be told that—merely

because they are women—they must use a separate public facility is a deep insult to their status and being. Government should ban this form of discrimination, or at least not participate in it, by segregating on the basis of sex bathrooms in public places.

It doesn't take much sleuthing to see the original claims these examples are meant to suggest. The first parallels a claim by African Americans against slavery, the second a claim by African Americans and women against exclusion from juries, and the third a claim by African Americans against segregation. Yet while each of the original claims that my examples parallel seems obvious and obviously correct to us, each of the parallels seems—and is—absurd, at least to us now. Why?

Think about two distinctions, and about how they together map a conceptual space.

First, a distinction between "contested" and "uncontested" issues: By "contested" I mean issues that normal people think normal people can disagree about. Not issues that people themselves are themselves necessarily uncertain about, but issues that everyone understands that normal people are allowed to have different views about.[1]

For example, you might be a Democrat. Your cousin might be a Republican. You might have strong views about your cousin's political allegiance. Indeed, it might make you quite angry. But you wouldn't say that his being a Republican makes him crazy or a nut. Normal people within this political society can be either Republican or Democratic. Party status (at least within this range) is contested.

An "uncontested" issue is, by contrast, one that normal people think normal people don't disagree about. For these issues, identifying yourself as someone who disagrees with the accepted view is enough to disqualify you as a normal person—or at least enough to make people wonder.

Think about views about pedophilia. Pedophilia lies within an uncontested discourse. Not because it has always been condemned (it hasn't), and not because every single person in America condemns it (they don't). Instead, pedophilia is an uncontested discourse because if you identify yourself as someone who believes in the "right" of an adult to have sex with a child, you have identified yourself as someone who, for us, is not normal. It would be a joke to say, "We can't leave our child with her. She's a Democrat." It would not be a joke to say, "We can't leave our child with him. He believes in child sex."

In both cases, the description is normative, not empirical. I'm not saying that something is contested merely because people, on average or even frequently, contest it. I'm saying it's contested because within a particular social context, people understand that normal people can disagree about it. The statement isn't a prediction of how people would vote; it is instead a prediction about how deviation would be understood.

Don't get caught up in the qualifications just yet. Of course, there are some who would die before hanging with a Republican. And of course there may be bright and otherwise "normal" people who believe in child sex. I'm not trying to describe a rule that describes individuals reliably; I'm instead describing a rule about *social meaning*.[2] Contested versus uncontested will be one distinction central to that rule.

The second distinction is between *foregrounded* and *backgrounded* discourses.

By foregrounded, I mean a discourse that is currently the topic of substantial discussion. If you scanned the newspapers or what's hot among the chattering class, you'd see lots of conversations around these issues. They describe what's on the table; what stuff we talk about; what kind of issues we know others are likely to want to know about. Whether we should have invaded Iraq was a foregrounded discourse a decade ago, but not so much today. So too is whether global warming is real, or whether evolution is true, foregrounded today. These are all matters about which people actually engage. They describe the activity of current social discourse.

"Backgrounded" discourses, by contrast, are the things we don't talk about. Whether Lincoln loved his wife. Whether Garfield's assassin was insane. Whether the Russian Revolution could have gone differently. We might imagine constructing a context within which such things could be discussed. (The hundredth anniversary of Alexander Kerensky's provisional government in Russia, for example.) But they are not the sort of things that people are talking about now. You could go for months not hearing about these sorts of things. If you heard about them three days in a row, you'd be spooked.

The distinction between foregrounded and backgrounded is a bit easier than contested versus uncontested: it is empirical. Big data could more easily describe that distinction than it could the one between contested and uncontested. But whether machines can understand it or not, the distinction between contested and uncontested is the stuff history is made of. It is the work of historians to reckon what was obvious in a context and what was perverse. And in the analysis that follows, though I don't pretend to be a historian, I offer an approach that assumes the substance of these distinctions and offers a reading on the basis of the assumption I make.

Throughout this discussion, "for whom" will be the central idea. For of course, the contestability of a discourse depends upon who we are considering. Whether or not you think evolution is a contested discourse, it is certainly not contested among scientists. No doubt there are a few who dissent.

FIGURE 3 Matrix: Original

|  | CONTESTED | UNCONTESTED |
|---|---|---|
| FOREGROUND | (1) | (2) |
| BACKGROUND | (4) | (3) |

But no doubt those dissenters are treated as the scheme I've described would predict. The same holds for global warming. Whatever the public's view, the view among scientists is very different. So to speak of contested or uncontested without specifying the relevant public is always incomplete.

Yet before we complete that sketch, it is critical to see the dynamic that I believe these two dimensions together could map. Let's put these two distinctions together in a four-box matrix (Figure 3).

As the matrix suggests, we can have contested issues that are foregrounded, and uncontested issues that are foregrounded. Likewise, background issues can be both contested and uncontested. Let's consider one of each:

1. Abortion is a foregrounded, contested issue. We as a nation continue to debate it. It is the center of political campaigns and political action. And while each of us might have a firm view of the issue—supporting a woman's right to choose or supporting the right to life—we recognize that a different view is "normal." We may choose not to associate with people who have that different view, but difference here is within the range of reasonable.

2. Quid pro quo sexual harassment is a foregrounded, uncontested issue. Movements to establish sexual equality continue to make this a salient social issue. Whenever instances of such abuse become known, they are spoken of. (Think of the #MeToo movement.) Yet the valence of these conversations is quite certain: if someone you knew started arguing in favor of quid pro quo sex in the workplace, that would mark that person not just as different, but as an outsider. And if he or she seemed genuinely puzzled about why the law bans conditioning opportunity at the workplace upon sexual relations, then we'd wonder about much more than just her read of current mores.

3. Infanticide is a background, uncontested issue. We don't talk about it much. Random instances may make the paper, but not because they're seen to question the basic moral judgment against it. Yet as with quid pro quo sexual harassment, if someone genuinely started questioning our resolve against killing infants after birth, that question would be a form of rhetorical self-immolation. Its effect would be to disqualify the speaker, not to advance the speaker's position.[3]

4. The fourth category—backgrounded, contested issues—may seem oxymoronic. If an issue is contested, why isn't it being discussed? But a simple test will suggest the idea. And the idea will suggest many cases historically of this critical category. The example I use here is "What is a button-down shirt?" Each year when I explain this category of social discourse to students, I ask them this question. I usually ask it through demonstration: I wear a shirt that has buttons down the front, but no buttons attaching the collar to the shirt. As some of you know, such a shirt is not a button-down shirt. Yet you who recognize this—if my twenty years' worth of samples is a measure of anything real—are a minority. The vast majority of my students (over 70 percent) believe a button-down shirt is any shirt with "buttons down" the front—whether or not it also has buttons on the collar.

This is a great, if trivial, example of a backgrounded contested issue. If we can foreground the issue, then we can get people to recognize the contest. But for different reasons for different issues, the question doesn't get placed on the table. In the context of a shirt, the issue never gets attention because in most cases a distinction is not needed. People thus don't notice their error (and trust me, it is an error).

But in other contexts and with other issues, the dynamic is different. Sometimes an issue doesn't get discussed because people don't think it is important (think about cruelty to dolphins). Sometimes it doesn't get discussed because people are reluctant to discuss it (think about issues surrounding gay rights in the 1970s). Whatever the reason, these issues remain buried: potential sources of argument or progress, but not until people are motivated to consider them. Box 4 is thus a set of resources for social entrepreneurs. These are the issues that we might get people to see differently. They are the source for new social movements.

This matrix gives us a way to understand how issues might evolve. Think about the history of quid pro quo sexual harassment. For most of the twentieth century, at least among legal sorts, quid pro quo sexual harassment was a backgrounded, contested issue (box 4). In the early 1970s, legal activists and scholars such as Catharine MacKinnon began to draw attention to the issue by arguing that practices of quid pro quo sexual harassment were instances of inequality.[4] Lawsuits quickly pushed the issue into the foreground. And amazingly quickly, a conservative Supreme Court ratified the view that quid pro quo sexual harassment violated Title VII (the federal employment equality law), even though it is absolutely certain that no one in 1964 was thinking about sexual harassment when they enacted Title VII. That resolution quickly moved the issue from box 1 to box 2, where I suggest it remains just now. We can hope (indeed, maybe just glimpse) that the issue will move from box 2 to box 3—resolved, but not a point of discourse because instances are either rare or unremarkable. But the recent revival through the #MeToo movement shows the issue is not going away anytime soon.

Movement from one box to another does not necessarily occur in any particular order or direction. I'm not arguing that progress is inevitable or regular. But for our purposes, the important point is this: the character of the discourse about an issue changes as it moves among these categories. It becomes easier—for a court at least—to take a position on a moral question if that issue stands within the uncontested space. It becomes more difficult if the issue is plainly seen as contested.

This matrix is thus a map of the character of social understanding. This map will be central to the argument in the balance of this book. It will be directly applicable when we get to the equal protection clause. But it is also critically relevant to the account I've offered of the evolution of the commerce power and economic due process.

For just as we can identify the way ordinary discourses can evolve or change, so too can we identify the way more professional or even academic discourses evolve or change. The history of science tells a rich story of disciplines with an approach that is at one time taken for granted and then is upended. Thomas Kuhn called these scientific revolutions.[5]

And even outside a particular discipline, we can recognize the way in which the truths from that discipline seem certain and accepted at one time, and then uncertain and contested in another. The mechanism of that change is hard to track or predict. I don't offer any machine in the pages that follow. But whatever the particular cause, we can map the movement of the social understanding of that discourse and see its effect, at least within certain professions.

By way of example, consider the field of economics and its relationship to constitutional law. As Herbert Hovenkamp has observed in his extraordinary book *Enterprise and American Law*:[6]

> The courts of the substantive due process era were guided by prevailing scientific doctrines much as courts are today. They took the law for what it was, a human creation and an intellectual activity, never able to transcend the world view in which it was formed. Judges trained in the classical tradition of political economy carried that intellectual baggage into their chambers. In the case of substantive due process, they carried American writers' unique perspective on political economy, which for them defined both the content of the property rights protected by the Constitution and the limits of the state's power to interfere.[7]

Judges "drew their wisdom," Hovenkamp suggests, "from outside...They simply accepted, and asserted as obvious, doctrine that had become part of the well-established consensus models of other disciplines."[8]

At the birth of the substantive due process era, the "prevailing well-established consensus models of other disciplines" came from classical economics. And classical economics, also called the classical model, had certain clear implications for social policy. Among these implications were (1) the importance of competition, (2) suspicion of government privilege or monopoly, and (3) a relatively narrow conception of market failure. That conception of market failure helped guide the courts in deciding whether to uphold a regulation or not. As Justice Harlan F. Stone described it late in the movement:

> The constitutional theory that prices normally may not be regulated rests upon the assumption that the public interest and private right are both adequately protected when there is "free" competition among buyers and sellers, and that, in such a state of economic society, the interference with so important an incident of the ownership of private property as price-fixing is not justified and hence a taking of property without due process of law.[9]

In the face of this assumption, regulators had to show a "substantial divergence between the 'public interest and private right.'" Who had established or proved the assumption was nowhere part of this argument. It was, instead, just part of the furniture of that judicial context—something that was just there, and nothing anyone had to argue about.

Of course, this wasn't the first time courts were so influenced. Nor would it be the last. Hovenkamp points to the beautiful example of the contrast between economic theory at the Founding—which was mercantilist—and the theory of classical political economy dominating at the time of the Civil War. According to mercantilism, monopoly privileges are essential tools of government policy. According to classical economics, monopoly privileges are an abomination, to be avoided at whatever cost. So as Hovenkamp describes:

> Under the strong view of the contract clause developed during the Marshall era, monopoly rights were considered essential to economic development and many prominent lawyers, including Joseph Story and Alexander Hamilton, believed they should be implied in charters for works of public improvements such as bridges. But under the strong view of substantive due process emerging in the 1870s, monopoly was an abomination and was not justified merely because it was expressly authorized in a state charter.[10]

Thus, in *Charles River Bridge* (1837), the Court made a "constitutional issue of whether a monopoly provision should be implied in a charter that did not explicitly contain one." Forty years later, *Slaughterhouse* "made a constitutional issue of whether a monopoly provision explicitly contained in a charter was invalid." As Hovenkamp concludes, "In less than four decades, a mere economic revolution had stood the Constitution on its head."[11]

Or consider the constitutional role of the "wage fund doctrine." As Hovenkamp describes, for almost all of the nineteenth century, liberals and conservatives alike opposed wage and hours legislation.[12] They did this because for almost all of that century not only did economic theory seem conclusive that such transfers would do no good, but also, and more important, the wage fund doctrine held that such transfers would ultimately harm the very workers they were intended to benefit. As described by a political economy textbook of the time:

> That which pays for labor in every country, is a certain portion of actually accumulated capital, which cannot be increased by the proposed actions of government, nor by the influence of public opinion, nor by combinations among the workmen themselves. There is also in every country a certain number of laborers, and this number cannot be diminished by the proposed action of government, nor by public opinion, nor by combinations among themselves. There is to be a division now among all these laborers of the portion of capital actually there present.[13]

The implications of this theory, as Hovenkamp has put it, "cannot be overstated. Any forced wealth transfer from capitalists to laborers would upset the equilibrium and spell disaster for the laborer."[14] Neutrality, from this perspective, wasn't just about fairness. It was about rationality. Class legislation over wages was simply self-defeating.

The wage fund doctrine grew out of classical economics. But as classical economics gave way to marginalism, marginalists discovered a deep flaw in the wage fund doctrine. According to marginalism, wages are not a function of previously invested capital. They depend instead upon the marginal contribution that a laborer makes to the value of a product. Among other things, this meant that minimum-wage legislation was no longer *necessarily* irrational or self-defeating. It could well be a bad idea, depending upon the facts at the time. But it wasn't an insane idea, which would have rendered it the sort of legislation that constitutional lawyers could simply rule off the policy table.[15]

So conceptually the point is this: as the background theory of economics changes, the sensibility of a constitutional doctrine can change as well.

Minimum-wage laws are simply crazy—self-defeating or worse—against the background of classical economics. They're not crazy against the background of marginalism. As economics evolves, the boundaries of constitutional sanity evolve as well.

It is here that the map of contestability becomes relevant to the history of this book, because concepts don't determine constitutional law—or at least they don't do so alone. Much more salient to the account I am offering here is the sociology of these background concepts. (Oliver Wendell Holmes Jr.: "The felt necessities of the time, the prevalent moral and political theories, intuitions of public policy, avowed or unconscious, even the prejudices which judges share with their fellow-men have had a good deal more to do than the syllogism in determining the rules by which men should be governed.")[16] Dominant theories create a kind of conventional wisdom. Over time they become taken for granted. They become the sort of thing "everyone knows." Even while they may be contested or challenged within a discipline, they can be taken for granted outside that discipline. And it is this taken-for-grantedness— this relative uncontestedness *for judges*—that will be most relevant to the constitutional debate that follows.

Because when an idea gets taken for granted—when it is the sort of thing that every sane soul "just knows"—then the important consequence for the law is that it is no longer necessary to justify that idea. At least among those who take it for granted, which for some ideas is practically every member of a political or legal elite, the idea becomes self-validating. One can simply assert it as truth, and one is not then responsible for the costs of that truth.

By contrast, when an idea is no longer taken for granted—when it is the sort of thing that every sane soul knows might be contested, or (at least for the relevant community) is contested—then to embrace that idea requires an argument. You say something about yourself if you agree, or disagree, with a contested idea. You mark yourself, and bear responsibility. To meet that responsibility, you must come forward with reasons.

This is precisely what happened to the ideas of classical economics, Hovenkamp argues. Among economists, the marginalist revolution began in the latter part of the nineteenth century. But for a generation schooled in classical economics, that birth meant very little. For them, accepted wisdom was what they had learned when they were still in the wisdom-learning mode—when, that is, they were still young. No matter what they were currently teaching young people at university, for that generation classical economics was still the accepted wisdom.

But as circumstances, such as the Great Depression, threw classical economics into doubt, judges couldn't rely upon its implicit policy conclusions anymore. They could still believe them, but they couldn't rely upon them in an opinion without advancing an argument. Thus, rendering classical economics contested had the effect of rendering certain legal moves unavailable—or at least unavailable without the judge or the court that was making these arguments *seeming* political by making them. Once the views are contested, to embrace them implicates the person embracing them, in a way that the person is not implicated when the views are simply taken for granted.

There are obviously a million qualifications necessary to make this notion usable in the context of actual cases or the actual evolution of constitutional doctrine. While the dynamic I am describing could occur in any field, the focus of this book is contestability among judges. And that contestability itself is highly contingent, both as to the field of knowledge that might become contested and as to the significance of that contest.

Take again the field of economics. As Hovenkamp argues, and as I will describe in greater detail in Chapter 8, economics was highly relevant to the constitutional jurisprudence of the period leading up to the New Deal. A certain theory of economics resulted in judicial activism—in the sense of judges invalidating legislative action—making sense. When that theory became contestable, the activism was harder to sustain. As I will describe, that difficulty induced a retreat from the practice of activism that marked the period before 1937.

But once the Court had retreated from activism within the economic domain, it was immune from any further evolution in the theories of economics—at least as they affect constitutional law. Thus while the Depression may have destabilized the old Court's activism, once economic legislation was reviewed deferentially, subsequent recessions, even the Great Recession of 2008, had no effect on constitutional jurisprudence. The embrace within economics of monetarism, or the rejection of Keynes, or the readoption of Keynes—all of these were significant in the history of economics and economic policy. But after the retreat by the Court, they were no longer significant to constitutional law.

This means that any account of the salience of contestability within a domain of knowledge is local and contingent upon the contours of the Court's jurisprudence. What matters in one period need not necessarily matter in a second period. Whether a domain of knowledge matters will depend upon the jurisprudential framework.

A second consideration is also important. In the story I tell here, I am constructing a modal judge. My focus is upon the kind of sensibility a modal judge would experience, given a certain contest or question.

This modal judge is a construct. The law uses the idea of the "reasonable person." I will use the idea of the "normal judge." We might speculate about particular judges and how close or far from the modal judge any particular judge is. But I am not aiming in this account to describe a theory of constitutional law as, say, Justice Anthony Kennedy would decide it. Some judges are immune to the considerations I will be presenting here. Some judges are overwhelmed by the considerations I present here. And in neither case is there any need, on the account I am offering here, for self-awareness. My theory is not that there is a hidden rule book that steers judges one way or the other. Instead, my account rests upon the recognition of what would seem appropriate to the well-socialized judge.

Thus, the better analogy is not a secret map, but politeness. Well-socialized sorts come to understand how to behave politely. Regardless of one's politics, one learns to adapt to the evolving understandings of the time. That understanding is not taught, in the sense of transmitted via lectures or continuing education seminars. It's what every decent person comes to know as he or she lives within the contours of contemporary society.

Maybe so-called political correctness is an even more compelling analogy. Whether one agrees with the substance or not, everyone in modern elite American culture recognizes the contours of political correctness. For most it is a constraint. For some (e.g., Donald Trump) it is an opportunity. Yet whether disabling or enabling, it is a reality we all come to understand, as normal, normative beings. If someone was clueless about the lines of political correctness, we'd wonder not just about their education (as if they had confessed they didn't know what the Thirteenth Amendment was) but whether they were in fact a native of modern America. And if they were, then we'd wonder whether they were in fact normal.

Judges, I submit, are particularly sensitive to these understandings. For in the main, judges are quintessentially well-adapted sorts within the legal community. We're not likely to recognize this, given the recent prominence of clear exceptions to this normalizing rule. Justice Scalia, for example, was not a potted plant. Resisting or rejecting what was taken for granted by others was at the core of his nature.

But the Supreme Court is not filled with justices like Scalia. Even more so for the judiciary generally. Judges are meant to be boring—in the best possible sense of that term. They are intended to fit in, at least within the field of their tribe. And while they all have individual characters and quirks, they are not, as a class, devoted to changing the world. They understand the world, or so they believe, and they intend to make their understanding part of the law.

That process of understanding, however, cannot escape the social reality of the time. And the dynamic we will see in detail as we work through the cases that follow reveals that time drives that dynamic.

No justice escapes this effect—not even Justice Scalia did. The only difference among justices is how broadly they are affected by it and how self-aware they are about how it plays out.

The sensitivity that we will track finds its easiest expression in the notion of "seeming." As I will argue throughout the balance of this book, courts will steer themselves depending upon how things "seem."

This raises an obvious question that we cannot avoid: Why should it matter what something "seems to be"? Why shouldn't we be asking what something *is*, instead of what it seems to be?

## Seeming

Imagine you're the boss of a big firm that's selecting a new advertising agency. Your lead analyst has been working on the problem for months. She finally completes her work, and in a presentation to you, she tells you that on the basis of her extensive analysis, Madison, Inc., is the best agency for your firm. The next day you discover Madison, Inc., has paid your analyst $10,000.

Or imagine you've been diagnosed with a rare disease. Your doctor recommends a risky, experimental drug to cure the disease. The next day a friend tells you that the doctor is a founder of the company producing the experimental drug.

Or imagine you're a lawyer litigating a major contract dispute between two large firms. The judge has spent weeks studying the evidence necessary to interpret the contract. He then releases a hundred-page opinion explaining his decision to find in favor of the plaintiff. A week later, you discover that the judge's wife has a modest number of shares of the plaintiff's stock.

Here's what I want you to think about in each of these three examples. In each, there is a judgment of some kind by some sort of expert or authority. In each, that judgment may well be true or correct. But in each, the final fact revealed renders that judgment suspect. It may well be that the judgment was reached independently. It may well be that the judgment was not affected at all by the suspect fact. Still, in each case, the central actor has an issue. No matter what this actor says, his or her judgment will be questioned. Epistemology (what we can reasonably believe is true) has overwhelmed ontology (what is in fact true).

If you look, you will begin to see these sorts of examples everywhere. Life is full of instances in which what one can credibly say is constrained not only by what's true, but also by the context in which one tries to say it. That context can render certain statements rhetorically impossible, meaning simply that uttering them there and then is certain to defeat the objective of convincing anyone of their truth. The context can also destroy the credibility of certain statements, making believing them difficult, and making it especially difficult to trust the utterer.

The reason that belief is difficult in each of these cases is that the judgment that needs to be made requires some form of expertise. Without the need for expertise, the conflict does not create trouble. If an auto mechanic says my tire is flat, even though I know he may have a financial reason for saying that, I can easily get out of the car and check. But I can't verify whether an experimental drug is really what I should take (at least not without consulting another doctor). And most people don't have the knowledge to verify whether the judge has made the right judgment about the contract dispute.

Each of these cases shows why appearance matters. Whatever the truth of the underlying judgment, it is important that the context of that judgment not give the appearance of impropriety—important, that is, for the institution that serves in that context. And because of this importance to the institution, appearance in these cases will often trump substance. A court reviewing the judge revealed to have a bias does not ask whether the judgment was correct; the court asks whether there was an apparent conflict, and if there was, it returns the decision to someone else. Confidence in the system depends upon being able to convince people that improper motives have not tainted the process. As ordinary people are not experts, the only way to so convince them is to return the judgment to someone not tainted.

For judges, at least within the American tradition, the objective no doubt is to decide cases correctly. But the burden of the argument in this book is that correctness alone is not enough. Sometimes a court must also ensure that it is behaving "judicially." Its decision, that is, should at least "seem judicial" to the audience relevant to the judge.

How that is done depends upon the rules. Sometimes the rules are, in context, clear. A court behaves judicially—and thus does not "seem political"— when it follows those clear rules, even when the consequence is political. If a Democratic candidate for president acknowledged that she was actually thirty years old (not the thirty-five required by the Constitution) and a Republican-dominated Supreme Court ruled her ineligible (bracketing a host of questions about whether the Court could or would ever review such a question), few would charge the Court with behaving politically. The political consequence is insulated by the clarity of the rule.

Sometimes, however, the rules are not clear—either because the subject is complex, or because the rules are simply indeterminate. When the subject is complex, a court behaves judicially when its decisions at least seem consistent.

Or, more weakly, when they don't seem inconsistent. When the subject is indeterminate, the Court behaves judicially when its actions don't seem to be guided by illicit motives—where "illicit" is institutionally determined.

In each case, the operative verb is "seem."[17] The motivating analysis is how things look. And that might lead you to think that I'm ignoring what's true, or what the right answer is. But again, the point is not to ignore what's true. The point is to emphasize that especially for institutions that depend upon public trust, what's true is not the only relevant consideration.

Think again about the cases at the start of this section. The analyst, the doctor, and the judge may all have been right in the conclusions they reached. The agency, the drug, and the plaintiff may well have been the correct choice in each circumstance. But that isn't enough to know what answer should be recognized. And as I'll argue as we work through the cases that follow, for purposes of fidelity to role, that answer is also not enough in reckoning how a court following fidelity will, or should, decide its cases.

Drawing these points together, we can summarize the "seeming" like this: Institutions must worry not only about what is, but also about what seems to be. And courts in particular must worry not only about what is, but also about what seems to be for them.[18]

Among the "seems" that will be most important to courts is "seeming political." All things considered, courts suffer an institutional cost if their judges behave in a way that seems political. Thus, a judge, especially a chief judge, keen to preserve the institutional stature of a court must reckon this institutional cost. And in reckoning that cost, she may be guided to decide cases differently.

More specifically, there may be cases in which the court decides in one way, even though the judges believe they would decide it differently if they didn't need to worry about the institutional costs to the court.

Of all the lines in this chapter, that line is the one you're most likely to resist. I don't mean to prove it now. Over the balance of this book, though, I mean to demonstrate that in fact this is what the Supreme Court has done, and that just such a recognition explains critical cases within our tradition. At the end of this book, I will suggest why such a conception also justifies these cases.

For now, my only objective is to map out the conceptual space that the cases will occupy. At the center of that conceptual understanding is this sensitivity to "seeming political."

---

If we put these two ideas together, "contestability" and "seeming," we have a glimpse of the dynamic in the balance of this book. Discourses or disciplines in the background of many areas of constitutional law evolve. As they do, what was contested becomes uncontested, and the other way around as well. When that status shifts, it will sometimes affect the freedom of an institution that depends upon that discipline. Sometimes, in other words, the institution, especially courts, must take this change into account. One consequence of that reckoning will be to change the way these institutions behave.

These changes are not all in one direction. There's no simple model to describe them. But as I will argue throughout the balance of this book, there is no way to understand, and hence justify, the work of our Supreme Court without also accounting for these changes. Like the foundation of an old house, as it shifts, cracks will open and floors will tilt. We must live with these changes, and first we must understand their source.

CHAPTER EIGHT | Accounting for Retreat

IN THE STORY SO FAR, I have described how the conservatives made up limits on the Constitution's power in the name, or so I have argued, of fidelity to original meaning. They then abruptly gave up. Whether it happened as a blowout or as a slow leak, the jurisprudence of the Supreme Court shifted dramatically in the period 1934–1941. Until that point, if only for a brief while, the Court acted vigorously to limit the scope of federal and state power. After that point, the Court no longer sought to limit the scope of federal and state power at all, at least not in the same manner. There was a fundamental change here for which fidelity must account—if, that is, fidelity can describe the Court's past.

The doctrine that was rejected in the 1934–1941 period, of course, was itself a change from an earlier past. As I described in Chapter 4, for much of the nineteenth century the Court allowed the effective commerce authority to grow essentially unchecked. As I described in Chapter 5, for much of the nineteenth century, the Court allowed states to regulate more and more, claims of free labor and neutrality notwithstanding.

But the changes that produced those shifts in the limits on federal and state power were themselves justified, the conservatives say, by fidelity to meaning. Perhaps it was done slowly, but on the account of translation that I have offered here, in those cases the Court was crafting limits on the government's power in the name of founding commitments expressed by the Constitution's original meaning (or meanings, as there are two constitutional moments, the framing and the Civil War, that account for the full range of values that guided the translation during this period).

The retreat of 1937 (the shorthand I will use to refer to the full range of changes between 1934 and 1941) has no such handy fidelity-to-meaning-based excuse. If there is a justification, it is found within the fidelity to role. On the account I offer here, the retreat of 1937 manifests a fidelity to role, for it reflects constraints on the institution of the Court that are independent of the constraints of meaning.

As I outlined in Chapter 2, such constraints can be either internal or external—or both. *Marbury* responded to an external constraint: Marshall's motivation was the fear that the very status of the Court as a constitutional adjudicator would be challenged by both Congress and Jefferson. That challenge was imposed on the Court from without. *Marbury* responded to that challenge by bending its reading of the statutory text to preserve (and establish) the institutional and constitutional role of the Court.

*McCulloch*, by contrast, responded to an internal role constraint: a very broad reading of what was "necessary and proper" was in a (different) sense necessary because anything more restrictive or substantive would have involved the courts in judgments that they couldn't sustain consistently over time. Discerning whether legislative action was really necessary, in light of an array of factual judgments, is not the sort of judgment within the ordinary ken of courts. Marshall thus avoided that morass by bending the plain meaning of "necessary"—at least a bit. His opinion thus steers the courts away from a plainly self-destructive jurisdiction.

The retreat of 1937 reveals strains of both internal and external constraints. Neither of the external constraints I focus on here, however, is the one that is ordinarily invoked in discussions of this retreat. And the internal constraint that I outline is more interesting and less discussed than the external constraints.

## An External Constraint Rejected

On February 5, 1937, ninety-four days after securing the most significant political mandate since the "Revolution of 1800," Roosevelt committed the most extraordinary political blunder of his career.[1] Frustrated by the Supreme Court's repeated rebukes, Roosevelt announced a proposal that would effectively enable him to pack the Supreme Court with justices who held a different view of the Constitution, one more favorable to the plans he wished to carry out. Under the scheme, for every judge who had more than ten years of tenure, was over the age of 70 ½, and refused to retire, Roosevelt would be entitled to appoint someone new. The President could appoint no more than six to the Supreme Court, and up to fifty judges (including Supreme Court justices) to all the courts. Very quickly, under this proposal, the nation would have a New Deal Supreme Court that would join its New Deal president and New Deal Congress.

It's not exactly clear how FDR expected that his scheme would be greeted.[2] The administration had rejected the idea of proposing a constitutional amendment. But the alternatives to amendment were not pretty. Keynesian economics had not yet fully penetrated FDR's understanding or the administration's, and so they believed (wrongly, of course) that the only way they could revive the economy was through the means the Court had already ruled unconstitutional. And as advisors looked back at the long precedent of mucking about with the number of Supreme Court justices, especially by Lincoln during the Civil War and by Grant after the war, they felt entitled to their "adjustments," or "court-packing." In their view, the economic war they were in the middle of may have been less bloody than a real war, but it was no less significant.

In that context of self-righteousness, it is easy to see why the particular strategy they embraced seemed so attractive. For it turned out that one of the leaders of the anti–New Deal forces, Justice James Clark McReynolds, had, when he was attorney general under President Wilson, crafted a similar court-packing proposal (as applied to lower court judges) that FDR would now copy for the Supreme Court.[3] To insiders, this looked like political karma, an institutional tit-for-tat. Justice for the anti-New Deal justice was too perfect to resist.

America, however, didn't get the joke. It certainly didn't remember the parallels with Grant. Instead, what many saw was a scary echo of the totalitarian leadership that was breaking out across Europe. Elected to power with an overwhelming mandate, an American president was declaring essentially that he could rise above constitutional constraints. Even Roosevelt supporters were anxious. And rather than rally around the president, the nation launched into a long and furious debate about the meaning of this extraordinary constitutional power grab.

Whether or not Roosevelt would have won the vote in Congress for his court-packing scheme, it's clear that as time went on he was losing the support of the public.[4] The administration had tried selling the proposal on the theory that it would improve judicial efficiency. No one took that argument seriously. When Chief Justice Hughes was finally asked to address the matter, he was able to demonstrate with numbers that, in fact, efficiency had increased during the period FDR had complained about.[5] More important— and quite obvious, as anyone who has run a meeting knows—was that adding more justices to the Court would not improve its efficiency. If anything, it would only slow down the judicial process. Hughes's testimony tore away the only shred of principled and neutral justification for court-packing. FDR's power grab was now plainly seen for what it was.

In the middle of this struggle, however, at least according to the conventional account, Justice Roberts switched sides. Though Roberts had written the opinion in *Nebbia* (1934) that had effectively ended the reign of substantive economic due process, he had been the critical fifth vote in *Morehead v. New York ex rel. Tipaldo* (1936).[6] That case held that a minimum-wage law was unconstitutional. Less than a year later, and after FDR announced his court-packing proposal, Roberts provided the crucial fifth vote in *West Coast Hotel* (1937), upholding a minimum-wage law. His vote to reverse in this case—and, much more important, in the *Jones & Laughlin* case—destroyed the chances that the court-packing proposal would be adopted, for now that FDR had his majority, what need was there for the scheme? His switch has since become known as "the switch in time that saved nine."[7] The burden then fell on Roberts, and the rest of the Court, to justify the switch.

To students of the Court at the time, even those who supported FDR's substantive agenda, Roberts's apparent switch was an embarrassment. As historian Marian McKenna describes:

> The same day the Court decided *Parrish*, Justice Brandeis wrote Frankfurter: "Overruling *Adkins* must give you some satisfaction," to which Frankfurter responded: "It is characteristically kind of you to think of the aspects of the Washington minimum wage case that would give me some satisfaction, but, unhappily, it is one of life's bitter-sweets and the bitter far outweighs the sweet." Following the *Parrish* ruling, Frankfurter wrote FDR: "And now, with the shift by Roberts, even a blind man ought to see that the Court is in politics and understand how the Constitution is 'judicially construed.' It is a deep object lesson—a lurid demonstration of the relation of men to 'the meaning' of the Constitution."[8]

In Frankfurter's view, at least at that time (he would later express regret for his letter to FDR), this was pure politics.[9] To save the Court from FDR, Roberts had sacrificed himself. Newspapers at the time did not miss the connection or read the reversals as unrelated to the threat.[10] Nor were they slow to argue that given the reversal, there was little reason left for Congress to adopt FDR's proposal to pack the Court.[11]

It is likely historically unfair to claim that Roberts switched because of the court-packing scheme. The Court voted in the *West Coast Hotel* case in

December 1936, long before FDR's proposal was announced.[12] (By contrast, Roberts's vote in the *Jones & Laughlin* case came after the court-packing idea had been announced.) It may be that Roberts felt impending political pressure. He certainly acknowledged as much in an interview a decade and a half later.[13] And it is certainly possible that he was preparing himself for a political run by aligning his position with the then-current position of the GOP.[14] We just can't tell. In Frankfurter's (later-expressed) view, Roberts's switch was justified in law.[15]

Yet it is not necessary to understand the shift of the Court as tied to the views of any single justice. There was an external constraint that led the Court away from its efforts at translation. That constraint is more general and pervasive than the akrasia of a single justice.

## An External Constraint Affirmed

By an external constraint, I mean a change that is not within the control of a court but which changes how a court's practice is understood. The court doesn't bring it about. But once it has occurred, it radically alters the institutional costs of the court continuing its practice in the same way as before.

The retreat in 1937 evinces three kinds of external constraints: one tied to politics, one tied to ideas, and one tied to power. Neither constraint was created by the Court, but once manifested, neither constraint could be ignored.

### POLITICS

While the conservatives' objective in preserving the framing meaning of the Constitution was always, in some sense, political, in the decades of its most important prominence, it hadn't triggered a popular partisan understanding. The formal lines that the Taft Court reintroduced were aimed, as Robert Post has described, at establishing a new normalcy after a radical expansion of federal power in the midst of the First World War.[16] "Normalcy" had no obvious or salient political valence. The ideal was to restore a balance that had existed before the disruption of the war. The Progressives had certainly attacked the Court's activism. But to most Americans, this was inside baseball. The idea that there were limits to how much the states and the federal government could regulate was not obviously politically suspect.

The Depression changed that meaning. The formal lines that had kept federal power apart from state power, and that had restricted government power generally, became partisan lines. One side favored intervention; the other side did not. And though American political parties were not purely ideological at this time, their battle with FDR couldn't help but frame the debate as a struggle either with or against the Democratic Party.[17] As FDR remarked in 1932, the Republican Party was "in complete control" of the Supreme Court.[18] Resistance was now not principled; it had been rendered partisan.

Roosevelt continued his effort to render the Court political in a Democratic victory address in early March 1937. Though on the defensive because of negative reaction to his court-packing plan, FDR did not mince words in his characterization of the motivations of his judicial opponents. It was, Roosevelt asserted, the "'personal economic predilections' of a majority of the Court" that was deciding these cases.[19] Five days later, in a fireside chat, he attacked the justices who refused to "act as justices and not as legislators."[20] The president had rejected the translator's argument: "There is no basis," FDR insisted, "for the claim made by some members of the Court that something in the Constitution has compelled them regretfully to thwart the will of the people." Those justices, the president claimed, were instead "den[ying] the existence of facts universally recognized."[21] At a press conference after the *West Coast Hotel* decision, he continued the attack: "Courts should be judicial and not legislative."[22]

These comments had an effect on the social meaning of the Court's actions, rendering those actions, and hence the Court, political. It was not these comments alone that were responsible, of course; no one person, not even a president, can control the meaning of the behavior of an institution. But these comments were part of a campaign to raise significantly the institutional costs incurred by the conservatives as they sought to preserve original meaning (or at least their understanding of it).[23]

## IDEAS

The second external change ties less to charges of partisanship and more to the collapse of a certain set of ideas that explained how an economy would work.

As I sketched in Chapter 5, standing behind the conservative justices' economic due process cases was a particular understanding of economics—a pre-marginalist, classical understanding of economics. For example, in rejecting wage legislation in 1923, Justice Sutherland described "the inexorable law that no one can continue indefinitely to take out more than he puts in."[24] That was as "orthodox a statement of the wage-fund doctrine as could be found in any nineteenth century manual of political economy."[25]

When the economy was working well, these theories and the institutions they implied were not questioned. As Thurman Arnold wrote,

> When institutions function adequately, the theories which support them also appear to be adequate, because they are never called upon to solve practical problems. The very success of the institution prevents anyone questioning its underlying theory.[26]

The devastation of the Depression, however, raised profound questions about the economy and how it actually worked. Those questions in turn forced the conservative justices into an increasingly uncomfortable position. The economic collapse of the Depression was the biggest in American history: between 1929 and 1933, real GNP of the United States had fallen by more than 30 percent. Unemployment had gone from 3.2 percent to over 24 percent. Prices during the same period declined by over 22 percent, and such "deflation of incomes and prices...increased the burden of debt, brought widespread defaults, and accelerated bankruptcies."[27]

This collapse was not just an economic event. Yes, it manifested massive economic shifts. But it also induced profound changes in social and economic philosophies. The change was not from one certainty to another certainty, but from relative certainty to profound uncertainty. The confidence of the 1920s was shaken, and no new confidence took its place. As Arnold would write:

> The lack of faith in the future is not caused by specific legislation or the advocacy of specific objectives. It is the failure of practical institutions to function which has raised doubts in the hearts of conservatives. Twenty years ago, no one worried about socialism, because it was thought to be impossible; just as water running up hill is impossible. Automatic economic laws prevented it. Today we see before us both fascism and communism in actual operation, with their governments growing in power. Economic law no longer prevents such types of control. The only bulwark against change is the Constitution. But with the disappearance of the economic certainties, the actual words of the Constitution no longer appear like a bulwark.[28]

If the economic theory of the conservatives were correct, the collapse the nation had just suffered could not have happened. Yet it did. That it did didn't mean the conservatives would then become socialists. But they did have to wonder: what had their theory missed? Again, Thurman Arnold in 1935:

> In times like the present, when institutions fail to function adequately, we rush to theories and principles as guides. Questions as to the

soundness of the law or the prevailing economic doctrines rise to the level of popular debate. Everyone becomes a reformer; everyone becomes a social planner. Constitutional law and economics are dragged out of the technical publications, which no one reads, to appear every morning in the local newspaper and every evening over the radio.... Sound economic theory and fundamental law are explained by everyone to everyone else. The separation between politics and economics is broken down and issues such as budget-balancing, public works, inflation, foreign trade and indeed all the theories of current economics are submitted to the people by political conventions. Bitterness and intolerance increase because partisans are compelled to argue about matters which formerly were taken for granted.[29]

As I described in Chapter 7, this change—from "matters which formerly were taken for granted" to matters now contested—raised a cost for the Court. Doctrines that earlier had been able to rest undisturbed on these formerly taken-for-granted matters could not now do so easily. Contestation alone would be enough to raise the institutional costs to any court that continued to rely upon the policy that had become contested, for what earlier had not needed to be defended (because taken for granted) now had to be defended (because contested).

Yet who was the Court, who were these justices, to be picking among and defending economic theories? This is the point that Holmes had telegraphed in 1905 in his dissent in *Lochner*, saying that the case was "decided upon an economic theory which a large part of the country does not entertain." But when Holmes made that point, the theories were, in the legal domain at least, not yet contested. After the Depression, the contestation was unavoidable. That left the Court stripped naked: what was their justification now for constitutionalizing laissez-faire—beyond, as FDR put it, their own "personal economic predilections"?[30] The clean and simple truths of classical economics, and the laissez-faire politics they seemed to imply, were fine to presume in a world in which prosperity was everywhere. But as those positions became uncertain, they rendered judicial doctrine that rested upon them politically costly. For once the economics was unclear, the doctrines needed a new defense. What was there to defend the justices' resistance to the program advanced by FDR—beyond, of course, their own politics? The Depression was obviously not simply a function of lazy workers. Something was missing from a theory that suggested it was. Judges, in turn, could no longer rely upon a theory that was plainly missing something so fundamental. Recognizing that, they stepped back. And thus did the retreat begin.

To politics and ideas, we must add a third factor that may have been the most important at the time and yet may be the hardest for us to reckon: power. Not the power of the president, but the power of the Court. For in the decision whether to give up on their translation of the Framers' design, the justices must also have recognized that they risked giving up on a critical part of their own institution's design.

For the threat faced by the Court was not just from Roosevelt. It was also from Congress. FDR wanted a statute that would give him the opportunity to pack the courts. His strongest opponents in Congress—especially Democratic senator Burton Wheeler—wanted a constitutional amendment that would give Congress the power to overturn decisions by the Supreme Court. Building upon a progressive idea that had been bouncing around for more than a generation, Wheeler believed that the principled way to respond to the impasse with the Court was not to give the president alone more power, but to give the democratic branch the power to veto the Court.[31]

Between the two proposed reforms, Wheeler's was certainly the less likely but clearly the more dangerous—at least to the Court's own conception of its role. Thus, even if the Court believed it could escape the frying pan of FDR's court-packing, there was no guarantee it could avoid the fire of a congressional-veto amendment.

*Unless* the Court gave up on its effort at translation. If the Court retreated, then both the court-packing plan and the proposed amendment would go away. And the project of translating the Framers' values could wait for another day.

This is fidelity to role of the *Marbury* kind. That is, it is fidelity to role of the institutional self-preservation kind. Congress was not going to destroy the Court, and FDR's reforms would not have done so either. But the Court could well view the changes that each threatened, and which both together made likely, as fundamental. Or at least fundamental enough to justify backing away from its own conception of original meaning.

## ALL THREE TOGETHER

In all three ways, these external constraints raised the institutional costs the conservatives faced in continuing their translation. At a minimum, if they persevered in the face of this contestedness, both political and conceptual, their behavior would come to seem political. More fundamentally, to persevere in the face of the threatened political response was reckless. The judges didn't produce the changes in politics or ideas. Yet they were subject to them. And the question they had to address was whether they would ignore them or whether, to preserve an institution that appeared increasingly under threat, they would accommodate them by retreating from translations that now seemed political.

The reality of this external constraint is supported by Justice Roberts's own words many years later, reflecting on the Court's position in the late 1930s. John Chambers quotes Roberts after his retirement: "It is difficult to see how the Court could have resisted the popular urge for uniform standards throughout the country—for what in effect was a unified economy."[32] In the face of strong democratic will, the safer path institutionally—both for the Court and for the republic—was to back down. In another quote from 1951, Roberts says that resisting FDR in the name of the Framers "might have resulted in even more radical changes in our dual structure than those which have been gradually accomplished through the extension of the limited jurisdiction conferred on the federal government."[33] As Burt Solomon understands it, Roberts "had switched sides...to save the American system of federalism—to prevent the central government from assuming a dictatorial power, as it already had done so disastrously in Germany, Italy, and the Soviet Union."[34] Again, I don't mean to explain the shift by the motives of a single justice. Yet this single justice gives us a clue to an understanding that was, no doubt, quite general. The justices were responding to force, not reason, and legal arguments could have only muted that effect here. In executing their "jurisprudential retreat," they chose, as political scientist Gregory Caldeira puts it, "between substantive policy and structural integrity. The Court wisely chose to give up on the substantive issues and preserve its structural integrity."[35]

## Internal Constraints: Recognized

The constraints on a court are not just external, as I have said. They are internal as well. The judicial role demands that judges not track political whim. It also demands that a court not develop doctrines that, when applied over time, can't help but seem arbitrary or random (and therefore a cover for simple politics). This was the insight I suggested that explains *McCulloch*—even if the ordinary meaning of the word "necessary" is restrictive, it wasn't a restriction that was meet for a court.

We can glimpse precisely this sort of constraint in the context of the post-1937 Court, through the extraordinary work of Barry Cushman's explicating the history of *Wickard v. Filburn*.[36]

As I've already described, in *Wickard* the Court reviewed a statute that purported to regulate homegrown wheat. Roscoe Filburn had grown twice as many acres of wheat as the federal government allowed. The Department of Agriculture fined him for his overproduction, even though he only intended the wheat for his own consumption.

The government defended the statute by arguing that whether or not Filburn's own action affected interstate commerce, the actions of everyone like Filburn certainly affected interstate commerce. If farmers generally grew wheat for their own consumption, that would depress the market for wheat. The statute's (come on, admit it: idiotic) objective was to raise the price of wheat by limiting its production.

As many have noted, *Wickard* is arguably the most extreme position that the Court took on its path from policing Congress's power to no longer policing Congress's power.[37] For in upholding this aggregative principle, the Court opens the door to a practically unlimited federal jurisdiction. If the test is not whether a particular activity affects interstate commerce, but whether *all similar activities added together* affect interstate commerce, it is hard to see what activities would not be within the reach of Congress.

Yet what Cushman's research revealed was that, initially at least, the Court was unsure. At the first conference in the spring of 1942, every justice except Roberts was convinced the law was constitutional. Roberts was unsure. To Roberts, the law seemed to regulate beyond anything the Court had ever upheld.

Roberts's concerns then began to trouble the other justices as well. As Cushman reports, "Eventually a majority...came to share Robert's reservations."[38] The Court was therefore not yet prepared to uphold the law. Justice Robert H. Jackson prepared two draft opinions in response, each directing the lower court to make more factual findings. The first draft didn't advert directly to the constitutional concerns the Court was having. But the second was more explicit. As Jackson wrote:

> We cannot blink the fact that if this Act...is to be sustained it regulates intrastate, in fact intra-farm, activities beyond any statute sustained by any former decision of this Court....The regulation appears to extend to matters which would not be thought of as commerce at all, for the penalty appears to be applied although the wheat sought to be regulated never leaves the farm on which it was produced and is never the subject of a sale of any kind or in any form.[39]

Jackson's skepticism, as he wrote in a letter to Chief Justice Stone, grew from the fact that the "activities [to be regulated] are neither interstate nor commerce," yet are to be regulated "because of their *effect* on commerce."[40] In May 1942, Jackson still seemed to believe that jurisprudence required an assurance that there was a direct enough link between these indirect effects and commerce. The link regulated by this statute, Jackson was coming to believe, was too attenuated.

In the memoranda written to his law clerk, Jackson outlined three ways to resolve the question presented in *Wickard.*

First, following *Knight,* the Court could return to the idea that "production and consumption not for commerce is exclusively within the control of the states."[41] Second, following *Swift* and *Shreveport,* the Court could hold that such production "is normally within the control of the state but is transferred to federal control upon judicial findings that it is necessary to protect exercises of the commerce power."[42] Third—and this was the truly new idea—the Court could hold that while such production is "normally within the control of the state,...it is transferred to federal control upon a mere Congressional assumption of control."[43] With congressional *ipse dixit,* federal power would thus expand.

The problem with the second approach, Jackson noted, was the difficulty that judges would have processing the "economic data as a factor in determining the scope of the commerce power."[44] Such an approach presumed to draw boundaries. But "all boundaries based on economic facts," Jackson wrote, were "vague and blurred."[45] The standards used to draw those boundaries had been "neither consistent nor well defined."[46] They were "judicial shibboleths," having "almost no value in weighing economic effects."[47]

These insights, Cushman argues, led "Jackson to despair of the enterprise" of cabining congressional power. As he quotes Jackson: "In such a state of affairs, the determination of the limit is not a matter of legal principle, but of personal opinion; not one of constitutional law, but one of economic policy."[48]

This view led Jackson to a truly radical position: that the Court could have "no legal judgment upon economic effects which [it] can oppose to the policy judgment made by Congress."[49] The "pretense of review [was] a shadow without substance."[50] That in turn counseled a "frank holding that the interstate commerce power has no limits except those which Congress sees fit to observe."[51] Yet frankness has its own cost—an institutional cost. And rather than suffer that cost as well, the Court chose instead to simply dissemble. As the final opinion of the Court demonstrates, Congress in effect was determining its own power, even if that fact was not expressed that frankly.

Jackson's recognition is fidelity to role. As in *McCulloch,* it is the product of a court recognizing that a practice, or a kind of judgment, is simply beyond its institutional ability. Jackson sees, and then confesses to the Court, what the Court can and cannot do. Judges haven't the capacity or training to make calculations of economic effect. Even if they tried, the inconsistency of results would only result in embarrassment. Better to recognize these institutional limits and give up the constitutional pretense rather than ignore the limits and weaken the Court. Again, as with *McCulloch*, the claim is not that no one in our constitutional system should make a judgment about whether the commerce power really reaches as far as this statute says it reaches. It is instead that the Supreme Court is not the institution that should make that judgment. Fidelity to meaning (this act is unconstitutional) yields to fidelity to role (we are not capable of crafting a legal test to reach that conclusion).

In the name of fidelity to the Founders' values, the old Court had crafted tools to limit the scope of Congress's power. When those tools became unusable, the Court withdrew. Congress might well be legislating beyond the scope the Framers had intended. But there was nothing the Court would do to stop it—at least for now.

## Constraints Combined: Implications

I have described two kinds of constraints that define the contours of fidelity to role. One kind of constraint is external; the other is internal.

The external constraint recognizes a cost when the character of the institution, or the institution itself, is threatened. That threat in these cases emerged from the likelihood of the Court's behavior seeming political, and from the unmeasurable threat to the independence of the Court posed by the political branches. The Court's behavior would seem political because the garb that had shielded it before had been rendered contested. It wasn't law deciding these cases. It was, as FDR had effectively tagged the old Court, the "'personal economic predilections' of a majority of the Court."[52] The genealogy of this kind of constraint reaches back to *Marbury*.

The internal constraint tags *McCulloch* as its ancestor. Here the Court is reckoning not the cost in a particular case of a certain rule of decision, but the costs in a line of cases. Where a certain rule demands a judgment beyond the capacity of a court—as a rule that would cabin congressional jurisdiction by tracking economic effects would—the Court retreats from such a rule because over time that rule would yield inconsistency. Inconsistency is costly only to the extent it is noticed. But if it is noticed, it weakens the institutional stature of the court.

These two constraints, in mapping the contours of fidelity to role, sometimes work together. Sometimes, we will see, they work separately. The retreat from the New Deal is a paradigm in fidelity theory, as it is the clearest example of these two separate constraints operating together.

Both internal and external constraints together made it too costly, institutionally, for the Court to continue its project of translation—both in the context of economic due process as well as in the context of federalism. Yet at least with federalism, the resolution had an obvious implication. If Jackson's view was that the Court couldn't enforce the limits of the Constitution because he couldn't craft a judicially administrable rule, that left open the possibility that other, more creative, justices could do so later. Necessity had forced the Court to give up its pursuit of fidelity to meaning. That necessity, however, could pass. And if it did pass, then a justice convinced of her duty to fidelity to meaning could ask, "How might we do this better?"

| Federalism II

A S I'VE TOLD THE STORY SO FAR, beginning roughly at the beginning of the twentieth century, the Supreme Court embraced a practice of fidelity that I've called translation. In the name of federalism, and with a commitment of fidelity to (at least their understanding of) the meaning of federalism, the Court radically changed the reading of the federal commerce power, to cut back on the scope of Congress's state-crushing authority.

That effort failed. By the late 1930s, the institutional costs of that judicial war were too great. And in a series of decisions, the Court signaled a retreat. The Court would no longer be in the business of policing the borders between legitimate and illegitimate federal authority. The task of guarding the henhouse had been given back to the fox.

Yet as I said at the end of Chapter 8, one clear implication of this analysis is that there remains an argument from fidelity that would justify a renewed effort at restricting the scope of federal authority. Put differently, if it is possible to restrict that authority without violating fidelity to role, fidelity to meaning could require it.

And so the Court has tried—and tried, and tried again. This chapter maps that series of attempts and failures. In Chapter 10, I describe some examples that are more hopeful.

## Charge and Retreat I: Tax Immunity

The story I told about *McCulloch v. Maryland* (1803) in Chapter 2 had a pretty big hole in the middle of it. I focused on the question of Congress's power to charter a bank. But to contemporaries of the case, that's *Hamlet* without the prince. The more dramatic (and bloody—literally, at least in a related case, *Osborn v. Bank* (1824)) question was whether the states had the power to tax the bank at all.[1] No doubt Maryland had the power to tax a Maryland state bank. But did it have the same power to tax the Bank of the United States operating within Maryland?

In *McCulloch*, the Supreme Court said no. "The power to tax involves the power to destroy," Chief Justice Marshall wrote. And the purpose of Maryland's tax was certainly to destroy the Bank of the United States. Yet it is in the nature of a federal constitution that the states do not have the power to destroy a federal institution. To avoid that power, Marshall announced a principle of intergovernmental tax immunity: the federal government would be free from state taxes.[2]

How broadly that principle would extend would be the subject of years of litigation. Does a federal judge have to pay state income taxes? Does she have to pay a toll on a state highway? (The short answer today is that federal officers can be taxed, so long as the burdens are not discriminatory or Congress doesn't exempt them.) These were hard questions. Yet at its core, one idea was certain: the states could not use their taxing power to defeat an otherwise legitimate exercise of federal power.

Yet what about the other way around? If the states can't tax the federal government, can the federal government tax the states, or state institutions?

Soon after *McCulloch*, states started pressing hard upon this obvious corollary: that as "the power to tax involves the power to destroy," and as the Constitution certainly didn't envision giving the federal government the power to destroy the states, it follows, these jurists argued, that the federal government shouldn't be able to tax states either. If Maryland couldn't tax the Bank of the United States, the United States couldn't tax a Maryland bank, or anything else tied to Maryland.

The argument has a nice symmetry, if not as much logic. After all, states participated in any decision to impose a federal tax on the states (originally quite directly, through the Senate, as state legislatures appointed senators), while the federal government didn't participate in the decision to tax the Bank of the United States.

But the pull of symmetry overwhelmed the demands of logic, and in 1870, the Supreme Court recognized a reciprocal immunity of states' "instrumentalities" from federal taxation.[3] A core principle of our federalist design, the Court held, was that neither government could tax the other.

One could well quibble with that principle, or deny it was really part of the original design. But for those who believed that it was, the challenge over time was how best to respect it. As the states became involved in more and more activities, they pressed the demand for immunity from federal taxation for those activities. Even when a state engaged in typically private activities—running a cement factory, for example, as the state of South Dakota did for more than eighty years—lawyers for the states argued that those activities too had to be immune from federal taxation. Intergovernmental tax immunity was thus creating a subsidy for socialism: an activity done by the state faced lower taxes than the same activity performed by private actors.

The simplest response to this growing demand for immunity was to grant it—always.[4] But the Court resisted that simple option. Instead, the Court tried to draw a more balanced line between activities that would be accorded immunity and those that would not. At first, it limited immunity to "historically recognized governmental functions," as distinct from "business engaged in by a State of a kind which theretofore had been pursued by private enterprise."[5] As the Court wrote in 1934,

> If a state chooses to go into the business of buying and selling commodities, its right to do so may be conceded so far as the Federal Constitution is concerned; but the exercise of the right is not the performance of a governmental function.... When a state enters the marketplace seeking customers it divests itself of its quasi sovereignty pro tanto, and takes on the character of a trader, so far, at least, as the taxing power of the federal government is concerned.[6]

Yet soon this historical conception was thought to be too rigid. The test thus shifted to the sort of activities a state "normally" engaged in. But then, as Justice Frankfurter describes, the idea of resting "federal taxing power on what is 'normally' conducted by private enterprise in contradiction to the 'usual' governmental functions [was] too shifting a basis for determining constitutional power and too entangled in expediency to serve as a dependable legal criterion."[7]

The Court had gotten itself into a jurisprudential mess, but again, for the best possible reasons (or at least the best possible if you believe intergovernmental immunity was indeed part of the framing design). The task of translating the immunity principle over time was not simple. The challenge of fitting it to radically different conceptions of what a government should do was not easy. As with the other translations we have seen so far—commerce and economic due process—at a certain point the will to continue began to wane.

And then in *New York v. United States* (1946), the Court, via Justice Frankfurter, signaled a very determined retreat. From that point on, the Court announced, it was no longer the job of the Court to craft the implied respect between federal and state governments by limiting federal taxing power in cases where such respect demanded it. Instead, the Court would insist only that taxes not be discriminatory—targeted only against state entities—and leave the rest of the question to Congress.

What justified this retreat was a plain statement of fidelity to role. As Frankfurter put it:

> Any implied limitation upon the supremacy of the federal power to levy a tax like that now before us, in the absence of discrimination against State activities, brings fiscal and political factors into play. The problem cannot escape issues that do not lend themselves to judgment by criteria and methods of reasoning that are within the professional training and special competence of judges.[8]

Frankfurter was not denying that there were issues of federalism to reckon. He wasn't asserting that the federal government had an obvious and unlimited power to tax, at least "in the absence of discrimination." He acknowledged that there were issues to resolve, but he believed them beyond the ken of a court. To resolve the issues properly would bring "fiscal and political factors into play," factors that were beyond the "methods of reasoning that are within the professional training" of judges. It was by recognizing the inherent limits on judges that the Court would express a fidelity to its own role, even if the consequence was that a value embedded in the original design would be lost. Fidelity to role would trump fidelity to meaning.

This doctrine too, like the retreat described in Chapter 8, yields to both internal and external constraints. Indeed, the fidelity to role analysis here is as crisp as any so far. Surveying the history and imagining the future, Frankfurter fears the ongoing uncertainty of a doctrine that cannot yield clear results. That internal inconsistency would then yield external costs: any line drawn will be seen by someone to have been drawn for political reasons, not judicial ones. The internal constraint may have been strong enough; but the external constant is certainly icing on the cake.

## Charge and Retreat II: Regulatory Immunity

The fight over the commerce power that ended in 1937 was a battle about the limits on the federal government's power to regulate individuals or businesses.

The claim of those modern federalists was that the jurisdiction of much of that regulation rested in the states. After the retreat, the best reading of the Court's position was also jurisdictional—that whatever the proper reach of federal power was, it was for Congress to adjudicate that question, not the Court. Fidelity to role, in other words, meant that the Court could not ensure fidelity to meaning—at least given the tools the Court had thus far used.

But as a parallel to the claim of intergovernmental tax immunity, federalists developed a distinct argument for intergovernmental regulatory immunity. Again, just as the states' power to regulate the federal government is limited, the claim of these federalists was that the federal government's power to regulate the states should also be limited. Here the beneficiary of this immunity would not be any citizen; it would be the state. But the state would enjoy this immunity, this argument went, as a consequence of the Constitution's federalism protections.

The first effective champion of this constructed doctrine of immunity was William Rehnquist, then an associate justice. In a series of dissents, Rehnquist pushed an argument of fidelity to the meaning of the original Constitution. He insisted that the Framers' Constitution had been badly mangled by post– New Deal Congresses. Again and again, he called upon the Court to return to the front of the federalism wars and to give judicial sanction to those who would restrict Congress's extra-constitutional behavior. At least when it came to the question of Congress's regulation of the states, Rehnquist believed, principles of federalism ought to limit federal authority.

Finally, in 1976, his dissent matured into a majority. In *National League of Cities v. Usery*,[9] the Court struck down the part of the Fair Labor and Standards Act that applied to state employees. Though the Court did not question Congress's power to regulate the wages and hours of employees generally (the battle that had ended with *Darby* in 1941), the question here was whether the fact that the employee worked for a state government made any constitutional difference. Was Congress's power vis-à-vis employees of U.S. Steel any different from Congress's power vis-à-vis employees of Pennsylvania?

If you look at the text of the Constitution, there's not much there to suggest that Congress's power would be any different. Article I, Section 8, which defines the core of Congress's regulatory authority, does not distinguish between that authority as applied generally and that authority as applied to state officials. One-step originalism would not give the future chief justice the constraint he needed.

Defenders of federalism, however, point to the Tenth Amendment. As it states, "The powers not delegated to the United States by the Constitution, nor prohibited by it to the States, are reserved to the States respectively, or to the people." On its face, this text too seems to do little to advance the federalist's argument. Certainly it establishes that the United States cannot exercise any power "not delegated to the United States." But the issue in *National League of Cities* was a delegated power—Congress's commerce power. And the Court did not question whether Congress's commerce power would reach this sort of economic activity. So how could a limitation on powers not delegated limit a power the Court believed was, in fact, delegated?

The answer is that Rehnquist was engaged not in reading a text, nor in writing an original text of his own, but in translating the text the Framers gave us. He was not applying a text as it would have been understood either in 1976 or in 1791. He was crafting a reading of the text that restored (at least part of) an original balance. He was making up affirmative limits on Congress's power—as Justice Brennan put it in dissent, he had "manufactured an abstraction without substance, founded neither in the words of the constitution nor on precedent"—as a way to preserve his understanding of the Framers' intended balance between federal and state authority.[10] This is two-step originalism, a translation of limits to restore a framing balance.

But the limits the Court imposed in *National League of Cities* were not the limits imposed by the old Court before the New Deal. They were instead different in both scope and style.

*Scope*: The old Court wanted to constrain Congress's power generally. The beneficiaries (if you assume limiting federal regulatory power is a benefit) would have been ordinary people (directly) and states (indirectly). The *National League of Cities* Court wanted to constrain Congress's power specifically. The only beneficiaries would be the states. The aim was therefore much more directly targeted to the federalist end—to preserve a domain of state autonomy within a federal system.

*Style*: The old Court tried to constrain Congress's power through formal categories. Congress could regulate commerce but not manufacturing; it could regulate directly but not indirectly. No doubt those lines were clear at some point, but over time, and in different contexts, they became inherently ambiguous.

In *National League of Cities*, the Court tried to constrain Congress's power through a substantive historical conception of the appropriate role for state autonomy. Congress was banned, the Court held, from regulating states "in areas of traditional governmental functions." Setting the wages of its employees was a "traditional governmental function." Congress could thus not invade that domain. But outside of this domain of tradition, Congress's power was not constrained. "Tradition" was thus the arbiter of Congress's power over states.

We can think of this "traditional governmental functions" limitation as another tool of translation. It aims at a line that might protect state sovereignty, even while echoing the test that Frankfurter criticized in *New York v. United States*. As with every tool, the question fidelity asks is whether that tool is usable. Does it push in a direction that fidelity to meaning supports? Does it do so in a way that does not threaten fidelity to role?

Let's stipulate for a moment that this rule did push in a direction that fidelity to meaning supports, for it is clear that the rule Rehnquist imagined would at least restore a freedom states would originally have had, even if the freedom is purchased rather than given. But does this tool advance fidelity to meaning in a way that doesn't threaten fidelity to role?

Certainly, the tool wasn't vulnerable to the formalism charge. (Don't think that I believe all formal rules are futile; my view is that the futility of a formal tool depends upon the context of its application, and we'll see lots of usable formal tools later on.) A tool triggered by "traditional governmental functions" looks to particular content, or a particular history. And so the question is whether this alternative was more stable and predictable than the one grounded in the formalisms embraced by the old Court.

It wasn't long before the answer to this question was clear. Not surprisingly, Rehnquist's test launched a new industry of litigation. Within five years of the test, there were almost twenty cases filed across the nation challenging some aspect of federal regulation as it applied to the states.[11] And very quickly, lower courts undertook faithfully to apply Rehnquist's new rule. These applications produced a list of laws that the lower courts thought violated the *National League of Cities* rule. And each time a violation was found, it was the Court's job to decide whether, in fact, the rule of *National League of Cities* invalidated a federal law.

These results should be kept in perspective. Despite the attention paid to the power of courts to invalidate laws of Congress, courts actually rarely do so. And whenever they do, it becomes incumbent upon the Supreme Court to review the decision of the lower court, since otherwise a federal law would not apply equally across the Union.

Against that background, the results produced by *National League of Cities* were quite dramatic. Compared to the norm, this case produced an extraordinary number of invalidated laws. It was not a pinprick. It was the beginning of a revolution.

Yet unlike some similarly revolutionary invalidations (for example, *I.N.S. v. Chadha* (1983), which, according to Justice Byron White, invalidated the one-house legislative veto, and hence invalidated more than two hundred other statutes), lower courts were not simply applying the same understanding to these different laws.[12] In each case, the lower court had to decide whether the law at issue invaded a "traditional governmental function." Very quickly, even the conservatives on the Court began to see that that test would never provide the certainty and consistency that would be required if it was to survive.

Less than a decade later, the Court confronted this problem directly. The case, *Garcia v. San Antonio Metropolitan Transit* (1985), raised the question whether municipal ownership of a mass transit system was a "traditional governmental function." The lower court held that it was, and invalidated Fair Labor and Standards Act regulations that applied to a state-run mass transit system.

But by now a majority of the Supreme Court had had enough. Justice Harry A. Blackmun, who had originally voted with Justice Rehnquist in *National League of Cities*, wrote the opinion for a majority of the Court, overruling *National League of Cities*. Blackmun's reasoning will be quite familiar.

Blackmun first reviewed the efforts of lower courts and the Supreme Court to layer precision on the rule that *National League of Cities* had established. The review was not hopeful:

> The controversy in the present cases has focused on the third *Hodel* requirement—that the challenged federal statute trench on "traditional governmental functions." The District Court voiced a common concern: "Despite the abundance of adjectives, identifying which particular state functions are immune remains difficult." Just how troublesome the task has been is revealed by the results reached in other federal cases. Thus, courts have held that regulating ambulance services, licensing automobile drivers, operating a municipal airport, performing solid waste disposal, and operating a highway authority, are functions protected under *National League of Cities*. At the same time, courts have held that issuance of industrial development bonds, regulation of intrastate natural gas sales, regulation of traffic on public roads, regulation of air transportation, operation of a telephone system, leasing and sale of natural gas, operation of a mental health facility, and provision of in-house domestic services for the aged and handicapped are not entitled to immunity.[13]

The Court had "made little headway in defining the scope of the governmental functions deemed protected under *National League of Cities*."[14] As with intergovernmental tax immunity, the first efforts had tried to peg power on a reading of history. But as in *New York v. United States*, crafting a historical test was impossible. "Reliance on history," Blackmun wrote, results in line-drawing of the most arbitrary sort; the genesis of state governmental functions stretches over a historical continuum from before the Revolution to the present, and courts would have to decide by fiat precisely how longstanding a pattern of state involvement had to be for federal regulatory authority to be defeated.[15]

But a non-historical standard was also doomed to fail. "Uniquely governmental functions" and "necessary government functions" both were lines that could not consistently be applied. Again, as the Court had learned in *New York v. United States* (though apparently forgotten), there were too many differences in the range of state activities to make these conceptual maps fit.

These failures transformed Blackmun into Frankfurter. Invoking the struggle over intergovernmental tax immunity, Blackmun wrote: "Any rule of state immunity that looks to the 'traditional,' 'integral,' or 'necessary' nature of governmental functions inevitably invites an unelected federal judiciary to make decisions about which state policies it favors and which ones it dislikes."[16] And that recognition led the Court to an obvious retreat:

> We therefore now reject, as unsound in principle and unworkable in practice, a rule of state immunity from federal regulation that turns on a judicial appraisal of whether a particular governmental function is "integral" or "traditional." Any such rule leads to inconsistent results at the same time that it disserves principles of democratic self-governance, and it breeds inconsistency precisely because it is divorced from those principles. If there are to be limits on the Federal Government's power to interfere with state functions—as undoubtedly there are—we must look elsewhere to find them.

There are limits, the Court had affirmed, "on the Federal Government's power to interfere with state functions"—"undoubtedly there are." These are just limits that a Court is incapable of enforcing without betraying a fidelity to role. The two-step again was thus over.

So once again, in the name of fidelity to meaning, justices had crafted made-up limits on the government's power. Those limits proved unworkable. In the name of fidelity to role, then, the Court "surveys the battle scene of federalism and sounds a retreat," as Justice O'Connor put it.[17] Role dominates meaning.

Here again, there is an interaction between the external and internal constraints on fidelity to role. The inconsistency inevitably produced by the underdetermined character of "tradition" stripped the enterprise of its non-political, or not necessarily political, character. Once it was clear that tradition couldn't even be said to be driving the result, all that was left was a bunch of Republican-appointed justices doing the work of a right-wing anti-government movement.

Rehnquist promised that the battle was not over. The "principle," he wrote, "will...in time again command the support of a majority of this Court." Justices Sandra Day O'Connor and Lewis Powell joined that view. After a lengthy dissent mapping the Court's struggle to preserve the principles of federalism in light of "the emergence of an integrated and industrialized national economy," Justice O'Connor affirmed fidelity's obligation: that the principle of federalism "requires the Court to enforce affirmative limits on federal regulation of the States to complement the judicially crafted expansion of the interstate commerce power."[18]

But *how* was still not clear. O'Connor suggested "weighing state autonomy as a factor in the balance when interpreting the means by which Congress can exercise its authority on the States as States."[19] But she acknowledged that such a method would produce no bright lines. Still, despite the repeated failure of non-bright-line tests in the past, she remained undeterred:

> Such difficulty is to be expected whenever constitutional concerns as important as federalism and the effectiveness of the commerce power come into conflict. Regardless of the difficulty, it is and will remain the duty of this Court to reconcile these concerns in the final instance.[20]

Echoing Rehnquist, O'Connor too believed that "this Court will in time again assume its constitutional responsibility."[21]

## Charge and Retreat III: "Economic" as a Line

On March 10, 1992, Alfonso Lopez, a senior at Edison High School in San Antonio, Texas, showed up at school with a .38-caliber handgun. He was arrested and charged under Texas law. The next day he was indicted by federal authorities under a law that made it a crime to possess a gun within a thousand feet of a school.

Lopez had no money for a lawyer, so the local court appointed a public defender. That lawyer, Jack Carter, as *Time* magazine described it,

> decided that his client's case was hopeless enough to warrant a bold gamble. In a move that is about the closest an attorney ever gets to throwing a Hail Mary pass in the final two seconds of the Super Bowl, Jack Carter conceded that Lopez had indeed broken the law—and then went on to argue that the law itself was [unconstitutional].[22]

The essence of Carter's argument was that Congress had gone too far. There was a limit, Carter argued, to the commerce power—there had to be a limit to the commerce power if the Framers' design made sense—and that in this statute, by trying to regulate the mere possession of guns near schools, that limit had been surpassed.

To the surprise of most constitutional scholars at the time, the Fifth Circuit Court of Appeals agreed with Carter. And to the shock of almost all constitutional scholars at the time, the Supreme Court agreed with the Fifth Circuit. For the first time in almost sixty years, the Court had invalidated a law that regulated ordinary citizens on the grounds that the law exceeded Congress's commerce power.

The opinion was written—here at least there was no surprise—by Chief Justice Rehnquist. Rehnquist surveyed the history of commerce clause cases and offered a framework with which to understand them. As he wrote:

> First, Congress may regulate the use of the channels of interstate commerce.... Second, Congress is empowered to regulate and protect the instrumentalities of interstate commerce, or persons or things in interstate commerce, even though the threat may come only from intrastate activities.... Finally, Congress' commerce authority includes the power to regulate those activities having a substantial relation to interstate commerce,..., i.e., those activities that substantially affect interstate commerce.[23]

There had been no showing that Lopez's gun had traveled in interstate commerce. That meant, according to Rehnquist, that Congress could reach it only if it could be shown that the activity regulated had a substantial relation to interstate commerce or substantially affected interstate commerce. As the Court wrote:

> Section 922(q) is a criminal statute that by its terms has nothing to do with "commerce" or any sort of economic enterprise, however broadly one might define those terms. Section 922(q) is not an essential part of a larger regulation of economic activity, in which the regulatory scheme could be undercut unless the intrastate activity were regulated. It cannot, therefore, be sustained under our cases upholding regulations of activities that arise out of or are connected with a commercial transaction, which viewed in the aggregate, substantially affects interstate commerce.[24]

Lopez's behavior fell outside of that catalog. Possessing a gun was not economic activity; as non-economic activity, it plainly did not substantially affect interstate commerce. Congress had crossed a line. More important, a line between proper and improper federal power had been found once again.

Just as important as the commerce power line, however, was the method of interpretation that the chief justice seemed to be announcing. We could call this method the "enumeration principle." The enumeration principle asks whether the theory the government has offered for interpreting the federal power at hand has any limit. If it doesn't, that creates a problem. Within a constitutional regime intended to limit power, an interpretation of a constitutional power that had no limit would conflict with the objective of the regime. If Congress, for example, could regulate any activity under the commerce power, then the whole purpose of a constitution that enumerated federal power would be defeated. Why enumerate if one power (commerce) gave you the authority to regulate everything?

That question proved difficult for the government. Asked by the chief justice to articulate a limit to the principle he was advancing, Solicitor General Drew Days could not. This led the Supreme Court to frame the motivation for its response: "We pause to consider the implications of the Government's arguments."[25] Days had walked into the enumeration principle buzz saw. If he couldn't articulate a limit, then his reading of the commerce clause was wrong. Another reading—one that entailed a limit—was necessary. A "stopping point" had to be found, for otherwise "we are hard pressed to posit any activity by an individual that Congress is without power to regulate."[26] The *reductio* (and two-step) returns!

*Lopez* thus stands within the line of cases stretching back to *Hammer* crafting affirmative limits on federal power, in the name of fidelity to the Framers' balance. To that end, it deployed a simple tool to restrict the scope of intrastate activities that might be reached by the commerce authority: as the Court had held before, Congress could regulate intrastate activities to "protect the instrumentalities of interstate commerce." That much wasn't new. The new bit was a limit on the scope of other intrastate activities that might be regulated under the commerce authority. On this test, only "activity [that] 'substantially affects' interstate commerce," not activity that merely affects interstate commerce, can be regulated pursuant to the commerce authority.

Many expected the *Lopez* limits would never again appear. Law professor David Currie thought *Lopez* was a "bolt out of the blue" intended to scare rather than direct.[27] Congress would be more careful in the future and the Court would not need to engage in any further intervention. The case would be remembered as a sport, but still a firm (if not clear) statement that there were limits beyond which the Court would not allow Congress to go.

Yet very soon after *Lopez*, the Court applied the same principle again—and this time not to a minor regulation carelessly framed in a time before the Court decided *Lopez*. Instead, this time the Court relied upon the *Lopez* tool to strike down a statute that was expressly crafted in light of the restrictions that *Lopez* had articulated.

The case was *United States v. Morrison* (2000).[28] In 1994, Christy Brzonkala alleged she was assaulted and raped by two Virginia Tech football players, Antonio Morrison and James Crawford. When the university failed to punish one of the students, she filed a lawsuit under the then recently enacted Violence Against Women Act (VAWA). That statute created a federal cause of action for victims of gender-motivated violence. The federal authority for this regulation was said to come both from the Fourteenth Amendment's equal protection clause and from the commerce power.

It is the second ground that concerns us here. Modeling itself on the Civil Rights Act of 1964, the VAWA was premised upon the claim—supported by extensive findings—that pervasive sex-based violence dampened the willingness of women to engage in economic activity.[29] That dampened demand affected interstate commerce. Indeed, as Congress found, it had a substantial effect on interstate commerce. As the bill's report from the Senate detailed:

> Gender-based crimes and the fear of gender-based crimes restricts movement, reduces employment opportunities, increases health expenditures, and reduces consumer spending, all of which affect interstate commerce and the national economy. Gender-based violence bars its most likely targets—women—from full participation in the national economy. For example, studies report that almost 50 percent of rape victims lose their jobs or are forced to quit in the aftermath of the crime. Even the fear of gender-based violence affects the economy because it deters women from taking jobs in certain areas or at certain hours that pose a significant risk of such violence.[30]

That argument might sound a bit strange: why premise a law against gender-based violence on the theory that it will chill the desire to shop? But in fact, it was an argument very close to this that was the keystone to the Court's decision upholding the 1964 Civil Rights Act. For obscure reasons living in the notes, lawyers from the Johnson administration defended that statute on the ground that discrimination against African Americans dampened their economic activity.[31] There was extensive evidence about the inability, for example, of blacks in the South to drive long distances because of unreliable access to hotels and restaurants. These were facts the Court expressly relied upon in *Heart of Atlanta Motel v. United States* (1964) when it upheld the Civil Rights Act as a regulation of an activity that affected commerce.[32] As the Court noted in that case:

> [The *Congressional Record*] is replete with evidence of the burdens that discrimination by race or color places upon interstate commerce. This testimony included the fact that our people have become increasingly mobile, with millions of people of all races traveling from State to State; that Negroes in particular have been the subject of discrimination in transient accommodations, having to travel great distances to secure the same; that often they have been unable to obtain accommodations, and have had to call upon friends to put them up overnight, and that these conditions had become so acute as to require the listing of available lodging for Negroes in a special guidebook which was itself "dramatic testimony to the difficulties" Negroes encounter in travel... [T]here was evidence that... racial discrimination had the effect of discouraging travel on the part of a substantial portion of the Negro community. This was the conclusion not only of the Under Secretary of Commerce, but also of the Administrator of the Federal Aviation Agency, who wrote... that it was his "belief that air commerce is adversely affected by the denial to a substantial segment of the traveling public of adequate and desegregated public accommodations."... [T]he voluminous testimony presents overwhelming evidence that discrimination by hotels and motels impedes interstate travel.[33]

Yet in *Morrison*, the Court rejected the very same dampening argument as it applied to gender-motivated violence. "Gender-motivated violence," the Court held, was not "economic activity." That distinguished the VAWA, since the Civil Right Act focused on discrimination in the "activity" of providing economic facilities—hotels, restaurants, and other public accommodations. Here, the "activity" (rape) was not economic. The Court thus used that distinction to further narrow the presumptive reach of the commerce authority: *Lopez* had required that activities substantially affect interstate commerce. *Morrison* added the requirement that it be *economic* activities that substantially affect interstate commerce.

The line was not perfectly bright. The Court didn't conclusively exclude non-economic activity from the reach of the commerce authority. But it did reject Congress's effort in VAWA to link the noneconomic activity of gender-based violence to the commerce power. And it did so with a mode of reasoning that is quite familiar. Congress had claimed that gender-motivated violence affected interstate commerce by deterring potential victims from traveling interstate, from engaging in employment in interstate business, and from transacting with business, and in places involved in interstate commerce;...by diminishing national productivity, increasing medical and other costs, and decreasing the supply of and the demand for interstate products.[34]

But if the Court accept this mode of reasoning, it would, as Chief Justice Rehnquist wrote,

allow Congress to regulate any crime as long as the nationwide, aggregated impact of that crime has substantial effects on employment, production, transit, or consumption. Indeed, if Congress may regulate gender-motivated violence, it would be able to regulate murder or any other type of violence since gender-motivated violence, as a subset of all violent crime, is certain to have lesser economic impacts than the larger class of which it is a part. Petitioners' reasoning, moreover,...may...be applied equally as well to family law and other areas of traditional state regulation since the aggregate effect of marriage, divorce, and childrearing on the national economy is undoubtedly significant.[35]

*Reductio ad absurdum:* Congress can't regulate this far because if it could, it could regulate everywhere. The principle of enumeration—if you enumerate powers, you must have a principle to interpret the powers that entails they are limited—entailed that this method of reasoning was flawed. For "under our written Constitution...the limitation of congressional authority is not solely a matter of legislative grace."[36]

The *Lopez* and *Morrison* line of authority was quickly understood to be something more than an aberration. Lower courts were thus encouraged to apply the tools the Supreme Court gave them to once again test the boundaries of federal authority. And there was no limit to the number of cases the lower courts got to review. Just as *National League of Cities* had, *Lopez* and *Morrison* launched an industry of litigation challenging the scope of federal authority—by one estimate, hundreds of cases had considered *Lopez* challenges by 2003.[37]

Yet the danger that this doctrine faced was in how it would be perceived in practice. Was this a principle of constitutional law, or was it a tool to strike down statutes unpopular with conservatives?

That question could only be answered over time by evaluating how the courts drew the line in other cases applying the test. And given the origin of the test—striking down a gun regulation and striking down a regulation designed to protect women, both laws opposed by conservatives but supported by liberals—there were many who were skeptical about the "principle" in this practice. Yet the most interesting outcome involved conservatives who pushed the principle of *Lopez* and *Morrison* in contexts in which the result would not appear conservative.

I was intimately involved in one such case, *Eldred v. Ashcroft* (2003), though I wouldn't count myself as a conservative wanting to prove the fidelity in *Lopez*. Nonetheless, in a case challenging Congress's extension of existing copyrights, the core argument followed an opinion of perhaps the most conservative member of the D.C. Circuit Court of Appeals, Judge David Sentelle. Congress, we argued, following Sentelle, said it had the power to extend existing copyrights. The Constitution said that copyrights could be secured for a "limited time." As Judge Sentelle argued, if Congress could extend any copyright so long as the extension was itself limited, what was the stopping point? The government's reasoning meant the clause had no limit—flatly contrary to the enumeration principle identified in *Lopez* and *Morrison*.

I pressed this argument directly in the Supreme Court:

> The opinion of the Court of Appeals suggests that alone among the enumerated powers, the Copyright Clause grants Congress effectively unbounded authority. Despite this Court's instruction in *United States v. Lopez*, 514 U.S. 549 (1995), *City of Boerne v. Flores*, 521 U.S. 507 (1997), *Kimel v. Florida Board of Regents*, 528 U.S. 62 (2000), and *United States v. Morrison*, 529 U.S. 598 (2000), that "the powers of the legislature are defined and limited," and that these limits are "not solely a matter of legislative grace," *Morrison*, 529 U.S. at 616, the Court of Appeals ruled that the most distinctive feature of the Copyright Clause—its grant of power "to promote the Progress of Science"—"constitutes [no] limit on congressional power."[38]

Yet the conservatives didn't bite. In an opinion written for seven justices by Justice Ruth Bader Ginsburg—an opponent of the *Lopez* and *Morrison* principle—the Court upheld the practice of extending existing terms largely on historical grounds. But what was significant from the perspective of perception was that the Court didn't even mention the core argument raised before it—*Lopez*. And while it might have been unsurprising that Ginsburg didn't mention the argument (as she didn't support the position), it was revealing that none of the five conservative justices who had recently invalidated a law protecting women even offered an opinion about why Judge Sentelle was wrong to say that this was precisely the same case. The result seemed selective: invoke *Lopez* where you don't like the regulation, ignore it where you do.

*Eldred* was but a blip in this struggle. The bomb was dropped by *Gonzales v. Raich* (2005).[39] Argued by one of the most brilliant libertarian law professors of our time, Randy Barnett, *Raich* attacked Congress's regulation of the possession of marijuana intended for personal medical use. Possession was not an economic activity, Barnett argued. On the principle of *Morrison*, Congress should therefore have no power to ban the mere possession of marijuana. No doubt, drug regulation is a popular conservative principle. But if the principle of *Lopez* was indeed a principle, then it should invalidate overreaching by Congress whether the law is one conservatives like or not. As a brief filed by a group of constitutional law scholars in support of invalidating the statute put it:

> Judges are not free to pick and choose which portions of the Constitution they will enforce, and...a decision to yield to the political process must be reconciled, in a principled way, with decisions to engage in more searching judicial review in other areas. The courts have enforced separation of powers principles, as well as "dormant" commerce limits on state regulation, notwithstanding the operation of strong "political safeguards" in those areas. Objections to judicial enforcement of federalism have often sounded in judicial competence and the difficulty of formulating manageable judicial standards for limiting Congress's power. But similar competence objections have been rejected in areas posing comparable or even greater difficulties.[40]

Yet by a vote of 6 to 3, the Supreme Court upheld the law. While *Lopez* had narrowed the scope of Congress's commerce power to activities that have a substantial effect on interstate commerce, and *Morrison* had narrowed it even more to *economic* activities that have a substantial effect on interstate commerce, *Raich* expanded the power to reach "an *economic 'class of activities'* that have a *substantial effect* on interstate commerce."[41]

Most revealing was the opinion of Justice Scalia. Scalia rightly and carefully dissected the scope and reach of commerce authority. And much more carefully than the Court had been doing, he traced the ultimate source of each bit in the *Lopez/Morrison* three-part catalog. While the first two parts, Scalia wrote, were plainly within the scope of the commerce clause (regulating the channels and protecting the instrumentalities of interstate commerce), the third part (economic activities that substantially affect interstate commerce) came from the necessary-and-proper clause. If Congress had the power to regulate economic activities that substantially affect interstate commerce, then that's just because Congress had the power to regulate activities not directly within the scope of the commerce power so long as regulating them is necessary and proper to regulating interstate commerce.

But here Scalia makes the absolutely correct *textualist* step: if the third part arises from the necessary-and-proper clause, then it can't be that the only activities that Congress can regulate are economic activities that substantially affect interstate commerce. As Scalia puts it, "Where necessary to make a regulation of interstate commerce effective, Congress may regulate even those intrastate activities that do not themselves substantially affect interstate commerce."[42]

The most common case in which this might be true, Scalia believes, is in the context of a "comprehensive regulation of interstate commerce." "The regulation of an intrastate activity may be essential to a comprehensive regulation of interstate commerce even though the intrastate activity does not itself 'substantially affect' interstate commerce."[43]

*Wickard* was thus Scalia's paradigm case. The activity in *Wickard* was local. It was also not commerce. But it could be regulated, Scalia wrote, not because in the aggregate the activity affects interstate commerce but rather because homegrown wheat could potentially disrupt federal regulation of the wheat market. It was thus "this potential disruption of Congress's interstate regulation . . . [that] justified Congress's regulation of that conduct."[44]

Justice O'Connor, in dissent, strongly criticized Justice Scalia's explication of the necessary-and-proper clause, labeling it "superficial and formalistic."[45] In response, Scalia wrote that O'Connor's criticism "misunderstand[s] the nature of the Necessary and Proper Clause, which empowers Congress to enact laws in effectuation of its enumerated powers that are not within its authority to enact in isolation."[46]

Yet one might well reply that Justice Scalia was missing the fidelity point: ignoring the necessary-and-proper clause had become a common and necessary technique for cabining the expanded scope of Congress's regulatory authority. Reading the clause the way Marshall did no doubt has a nice pedigree. But Marshall was not reading the clause in the context of a fully integrated national economy.

It is of course Scalia's prerogative to insist that the better way to restore original meaning is to read more carefully the "proper" in "necessary and proper." That was his technique in *Printz v. United States* (1997).[47] It was Justice Thomas's technique in his dissent in *Raich*. But that technique too risks the stain of selectivity. If it succeeded, the Court would have to be very careful about the character of the line it draws. More explicitly, it would need to make sure that it didn't simply strike down liberal laws while allowing the conservative laws to stand.

Only Justice O'Connor was clear about what the *Lopez* and *Morrison* line of cases had been about. As she wrote:

We enforce the "outer limits" of Congress' Commerce Clause authority not for their own sake, but to protect historic spheres of state sovereignty from excessive federal encroachment and thereby to maintain the distribution of power fundamental to our federalist system of government.[48]

That objective was just ignored in this case, O'Connor believed.

The Court's definition of economic activity is breathtaking. It defines as economic any activity involving the production, distribution, and consumption of commodities.

Most commercial goods or services have some sort of privately producible analogue. Home care substitutes for daycare. Charades games substitute for movie tickets. Backyard or windowsill gardening substitutes for going to the supermarket. To draw the line wherever private activity affects the demand for market goods is to draw no line at all, and to declare everything economic. We have already rejected the result that would follow—a federal police power.[49]

As Justice O'Connor acknowledged, *Raich* was the end of the *Lopez/Morrison* line.[50] As many commentators have argued, it seemed to signal a retreat from the technique of this latest effort to craft limits to the scope of federal commerce authority.[51] Though the line between commercial and non-commercial activity may be more tractable than the line between direct and indirect activity, if the Court applies the line in a way that finds Congress can regulate where the law supports conservative values but can't regulate where the law doesn't, then applying this line raises the concerns that fidelity to role focuses on. *Lopez* was a doctrine either badly conceived or badly marketed. If indeed the Court wanted it to survive as a core principle limiting Congress's power, it should have thought more about where and how it would be deployed, consistent with fidelity to role.

## Charge IV: "Activity" as a Line

The last example in this cycle so far has no clear retreat—yet. It doesn't even have a clear advance—at least as a constitutional holding in a Supreme Court case. But it is the most elegant and intelligent of the translation-based limits on Congress's commerce authority, and it was deployed with a fidelity to role brilliance that would have impressed even Chief Justice Marshall.

The translation arose in the context of the Patient Protection and Affordable Care Act (often known as just the Affordable Care Act (ACA) or

"Obamacare"). The law was President Barack Obama's signature legislation, extending health care to millions while simultaneously penalizing those who refused to purchase insurance. (The case also involved a question about Congress's power to condition spending, which I don't consider here but will consider more in Chapter 11.) The nub of Congress's justification for the mandate made perfect economic sense: people who fail to purchase insurance raise the cost of insurance for everyone else—not indirectly (the way failing to join a Sam's Club foregoes the benefits of bulk purchases enjoyed by others) but quite directly, since the uninsured will need health care, and when they can't pay for it, those who buy insurance will. As Congress estimated, the average family in America pays $1,000 more per year in higher premiums because other Americans fail to purchase insurance.[52]

The solution was to mandate that (practically) everyone purchase insurance. That mandate was enforced through a penalty that would be imposed by the federal tax system. If an individual failed to purchase qualifying insurance, the law would make that decision costly. If the penalty was more expensive than the insurance, then the hope was that people would buy the insurance rather than pay the penalty.

When Congress passed the ACA, there was an immediate debate among constitutional law professors about whether the act was constitutional. Could you force someone to enter an economic market, as a means to making that market operate more efficiently? Most law professors—on both the Left and the Right—thought the question was absurdly simple. Congress has the power to regulate activities that are in or affect interstate commerce. Health insurance is one of the biggest markets in our economy. If anything is interstate, health insurance is. And it followed that regulations to require individuals to participate in the health insurance market were plainly within the scope of Congress's commerce authority. Indeed, so certain was my colleague Charles Fried—a distinguished and prolific scholar who had served as a justice on Massachusetts's highest court and as Ronald Reagan's solicitor general to the Supreme Court—that he promised to eat his hat (made of kangaroo skin, no less) if the Supreme Court struck down the mandate.[53]

Yet Chief Justice John G. Roberts Jr. had a surprise for the law professors. Yes, health care is commerce. And yes, the activity of buying health insurance—or not—affects commerce. But what was regulated here was the act of *not* buying health insurance. And never before, Roberts insisted, had Congress required *under the commerce power* someone to enter a market and participate in it. As Roberts wrote: "As expansive as our cases construing the scope of the commerce power have been, they all have one thing in common: They uniformly describe the power as reaching 'activity.'"[54] The individual mandate in Obamacare, however, did not regulate an "existing commercial activity," said Roberts. It "instead compels individuals to *become* active in commerce by purchasing a product, on the ground that their failure to do so affects interstate commerce."[55] This, for the chief justice, was a bridge too far.

Roberts's argument is not historically persuasive. Justice Ginsburg had referred in her dissent to other examples of Congress requiring people to enter a market—for example, to purchase firearms to support a militia. Chief Justice Roberts distinguished those cases by insisting that they were grounded in powers other than the commerce power and therefore did not implicate the argument he was making. But my colleague Einer Elhauge had collected many other instances of Congress mandating that individuals enter into a market, some justifiable only on the basis of the commerce power.[56] These were not presented to the Court, but had they been, Roberts would not have had an easy reply.

Yet again, that's because Roberts was not reading but translating. His aim was not to understand how the commerce power could logically expand. It was to craft a limit on that expanse, in the name of fidelity to meaning. Elhauge charged that those challenging the law "want the justices to read into the Commerce Clause a *new* limiting principle, one that bars laws mandating the purchase of any product."[57] That's exactly right—they wanted a new limit. But the limit they sought aimed at an old value, federalism. Roberts was crafting the latest tool to cabin federal power in a context in which the Framers' original device—interstate versus intrastate commerce—no longer worked.

The real genius in Roberts's opinion, however, was not the crafting of this tool but the way he protected the tool in its crib. Roberts was not displaying the lack of "courage of his convictions," as Bruce Ackerman has charged.[58] He was revealing a deep and intuitive sense of fidelity to role. The fight against Obamacare had become deeply political. The identity of the Republican Party seemed fixed on abolishing the program; the identity of the Democrats was fixed on defending it. Certainly, had Chief Justice Roberts crafted an opinion striking down the law with this newly minted tool, the tool would have been tarnished with the presumptively partisan motivation that almost all would have attributed to Roberts and his Court.

So rather than invalidating the law, Roberts upheld it. Not under the commerce authority, but under the taxing power. After concluding that Congress had no authority under the commerce clause to mandate an entry into the insurance market, the Court concluded nonetheless that Congress had the power to tax those who refused to purchase insurance more heavily than those who complied. Congress had not called the financial burden a "tax." It had called it a "penalty." But that was marketing not law, and not a measure of the substance of the intervention. The essence of the statute was to increase the taxes paid by those who refused to purchase insurance. That regulation, even if beyond Congress's commerce authority, was perfectly constitutional under the taxing power, according to Roberts.

Yet the order of decision here raised an obvious question—and one that harkens back to a similar question that was raised before Chief Justice Marshall. If the statute was constitutional under the taxing power, why did the Court first determine that it was unconstitutional under the commerce authority?

The answer is familiar to anyone this deep into this book: Roberts was securing the latest translation by protecting it from a partisan framing. As it was, the decision was hailed as a masterstroke of judicial statesmanship—which it plainly was.

Of course, the bending here to secure the fidelity to meaning was not as significant as in earlier cases. The conclusion that Congress's taxing power enabled the mandate was wildly more secure than the conclusion about the commerce authority. Instead, the relevant bending here was against the ordinary norms of judicial restraint. There was no reason to reach the commerce power, given that the law was constitutional under the taxing authority.

No reason, except fidelity. Given the Court's views about the ongoing salience of limiting federal power, the crafting of a new tool was an expression of fidelity through translation. The Court had made up limits on federal power, in the name of restoring something of an original balance.

———

The history of judicially enforced limits on Congress's power in the name of federalism is the story of translations attempted, and then constraints of role realized. From the aborted efforts of intergovernmental tax immunity to the aborted efforts at intergovernmental regulatory immunity (*National League of Cities*) and to the now openly questioned (by its supporters) doctrine of substantive limits at the edge of commerce authority, the Court has enacted a constitutional thrust and parry. The Court plainly recognizes a continued obligation to find faith with the Framers' commitment to federalism. But except for its latest effort regarding the ACA, the Court has not yet identified the right tools to enforce that federalism limit, or at least tools that could survive the wide range of cases such tools must adjudicate.

Could it? Are there tools the Court could use that would better effect the federalist aims without suffering fidelity to role troubles?

In my view, there are. After one more example of translation on the Right, I catalog a range of more reliable federalist tools that might better effect this translation.

CHAPTER TEN | Immunity

A FINAL EXAMPLE OF TRANSLATION on the Right may be at once the least convincing yet most illustrative. It is the least convincing because no argument in this domain seems to move anyone, which is perhaps because the political stakes are so high. Nonetheless, it may be the most illustrative because there is a lesson to be drawn from this rewriting—if not for a theory of immunity, then at least for a theory of interpretive fidelity.[1]

As we've seen in the federalism cases that promoted tax immunity and regulatory immunity, "immunity" means a protection from some form of legal liability. It may mean complete protection from prosecution. It may mean partial protection from at least some forms of liability (e.g., damages).

Such immunity is not necessarily the right to get away with murder. It is instead the right to choose whether or not to subject oneself to the judicial process of another. That "right to choose" does not mean that there are no consequences from that choice. The right of free speech does not mean the right to be liked for what you say. Instead, the right to choose simply means that judicial process cannot be forced upon the individual or entity. Put differently, the individual or entity gets to decide whether the process will apply.[2]

"Sovereign immunity" is one such immunity. It refers to the right of the sovereign to choose whether it will be subject to legal process or not. In America, there are three types of "sovereigns" that might claim this kind of immunity—"we the people" (the ultimate sovereign in any regime of popular sovereignty), the states, and the federal government (the last two having sovereign authority delegated to them from the primary sovereign, the people).

The text of the original Constitution was explicit about one immunity only: the immunity of the people from process by the government, at least until representatives of the people (acting through grand or petit juries) yield. As our Constitution was originally understood, the federal government did not have the power to try or convict an individual unless a representative of "we the people" gave that person up. The grand jury was that representative, and it constituted the process by which we gave a person up to be prosecuted. The petit jury (the jury that ultimate decides the case) was the process by which we gave a person up to be convicted. Without convincing both juries to do what the government wanted, the government had no power to criminally punish one of our peers. So, without the assent of the grand and petit juries, an individual was, in this sense, immune. That doesn't mean that no one will be tried for criminal offenses. It means instead that the decision to convict one of us will happen only if we the people, so represented, agree.[3]

This same sense of immunity attaches to both the federal and state governments. The federal government, all concede, is immune from suit—unless it consents. It is a measure of its responsibility that it has through statute essentially consented in a host of important contexts.[4] And so too are states immune from suit—unless they consent. It is a source of frustration among many that states have not through statute consented to suit in a host of important contexts.

But the fact that there is a choice that both the federal and state governments must make gives both the opportunity to do right. It gives both the opportunity to demonstrate the kind of government that each is. And it gives the rest of us a way to understand and respond to the government that each demonstrates itself to be. We should have less respect for—and should democratically punish—governments that fail to live up to their responsibilities, especially when those responsibilities can't be enforced upon them.

The history of the judicial doctrine of immunity in America is a story of both rise and decline. In the sense I've described, the immunity of the people has radically declined.[5] The grand jury right is effectively meaningless today. Because of the plea bargain—97 percent of federal indictments now result in pleas—the check of the petit jury is increasingly the exception to incarceration, not the rule.[6] *Why* people committed to fidelity should have permitted this to happen is hard to understand. That a defendant would plead is understandable; the only way to check the abuse that might lead to improper pleading is a vigorous defense by "we the people," as represented in the grand and petit juries.

But the story of state immunity is different. In a series of decisions climaxing over the last few decades, the Court has articulated an ever-expanding scope for state immunity, against the contrary wish of Congress—all in the name of constitutional fidelity.

The problem with that moniker, however, is that there's no clear constitutional text upon which to hang this sovereign immunity campaign. Early in the struggle there was. The Eleventh Amendment explicitly secured at least some kind of immunity, as will be discussed shortly. But the campaign to constitutionalize immunity has long liberated itself from the confines of the text of the Eleventh Amendment. Today, the cause pursues a free-floating ideal of sovereign immunity, unmoored to any constitutional text.

And yet the conservatives battle on to defend it.

## Immunity Recognized

In 1777, a South Carolina merchant, Robert Farquhar, signed a contract with two agents of the state of Georgia. Farquhar was to give them a wide range of goods, including cloth, thread, silk, handkerchiefs, blankets, coats, and jackets; they were to pay him money. Farquhar performed; the agents did not. For seven years, Farquhar tried to get Georgia to pay. When he died, Alexander Chisolm, the executor of his estate, continued to prosecute the claim.

Chisolm petitioned Georgia directly. The legislature said the problem wasn't its. It had paid the agents Farquhar had contracted with. Chisolm, the legislature said, should sue them.

Those agents, it turned out—surprise, surprise—were not a fount of wealth.

So in 1791, Chisolm filed suit in federal court against the state of Georgia. Georgia was insulted, insisting that it could not be sued in federal court without its consent. The trial court agreed and dismissed the suit.

In the following year, Chisolm refiled his suit in the Supreme Court. Unlike *Marbury*, there was a plain hook in the Constitution's text for Chisolm's suit: this was a suit "between a State and Citizens of another State"—one of the explicit heads of federal jurisdiction enumerated in the original Constitution.

This time, however, Georgia did not even appear. The United States attorney general, Edmond Randolph, acting as private counsel to Chisolm, asked the Court to order Georgia to appear. The Court did so, and then postponed the case till the next term. In 1793, Georgia again did not appear. Perhaps in part miffed by this slight, two weeks later the Court decided in Chisolm's favor, holding that Georgia was responsible for the debt, and, implicitly, that the debt could be recovered in federal court against a nonconsenting state.

It's hard today for us to recognize just how astonishing this decision was at the time it was rendered. One part of that astonishment was simple, and pedantically legal: as Justice James Iredell argued in dissent, Chisolm had no legal (as opposed to moral) claim against Georgia, because everyone understood that a debt with a state was not enforceable in a court of law. Indeed, this is precisely how Hamilton had described the question in *Federalist* No. 81: the obligation of the state to pay its debts "flows from the obligations of good faith." It was as if the contract said, "The parties agree this document creates no enforceable legal obligation." Yet in *Chisolm v. Georgia* (1793), the Supreme Court ignored that implicit clause and enforced the agreement anyway.[7]

The other part of the astonishment was much more practical. After the Revolution, the states owed an enormous amount of debt to everyone. If any debtor, American or foreign, had the power to race to a federal court to enforce the promise of the state, many states would be driven into bankruptcy. Whether or not the Constitution contemplated this power in federal courts, many felt the Union could not survive it.

And so, in a very brief time, an amendment to the Constitution was proposed and ratified. This amendment does not use the word "immunity." Instead, the text limited the "extent" of the "judicial power":

> The Judicial power of the United States shall not be construed to extend to any suit in law or equity, commenced or prosecuted against one of the United States by Citizens of another State, or by Citizens or Subjects of any Foreign State.

The amendment was targeted against a judicial construction: the problem, according to the text of the amendment, is judicial power improperly construed. The amendment aims to correct that impropriety. As it specifies, judicial power will not extend:

1. "to any suit"
2. "in law or equity"
3. "commenced or prosecuted against one of the United States"
4. "by Citizens of another State"
5. "or by Citizens or Subjects of any Foreign State"

For modern readers, the precision of this text raises a number of obvious puzzles. First, why doesn't the amendment speak about a state's own citizens? Can a citizen of New York sue New York but not Pennsylvania? Second, the amendment speaks of "citizens or subjects of foreign states." Can France sue New York, even if a French citizen can't? Third, it speaks of "law or equity." But what about admiralty, another domain of federal jurisdiction?

These puzzles, in turn, led many to argue that where the Eleventh Amendment's text left gaps, the states have no immunity. "The Courts can't ignore claims of immunity in cases of types A, B, and C" gets read to mean that the Eleventh Amendment has acknowledged that there is no immunity in cases of types D, E, and F.

This inference is odd. If we presume that governments are born with their immunity intact, then on its own, an amendment designed to secure express constitutional protection for at least some of that immunity can't be read to remove immunity in all other cases. Whether that other immunity has been removed is a separate question. Once again, the question is what truth stands in the background, and we cannot glimpse that truth by looking at that text alone.

The justices (save Iredell) presumed that the Constitution had eliminated state sovereign immunity. The swift passage of the Eleventh Amendment suggests that those justices were wrong. If they were wrong, then there remained after the Eleventh Amendment an open and important question: Granted the Eleventh Amendment doesn't by its terms block certain kinds of lawsuits (e.g., a New Yorker suing New York), yet does state sovereign immunity in those cases survive nonetheless? Or more precisely, if we assume that by default immunity does survive, does Congress have the power to preempt it?

This language is important, because it suggests the framework within which the issue should be resolved: preemption. Courts sometimes speak of "abrogation," which invites a range of unnecessary connotations. Instead, here, as with every other question of whether federal policy can displace contrary state policy, the only relevant questions are, first, whether the federal policy maker intends it to displace contrary state policy, and second, whether something in the Constitution would block that displacement.

The answer to those questions is simple in some cases, not so simple in others. If Congress said, "Citizens of Pennsylvania are free to sue the state of New York," the answer is simple. Even though the intent to displace New York's immunity is clear, the Eleventh Amendment plainly bars it. But if Congress said, "Citizens of Pennsylvania are free to sue Pennsylvania," the intent to displace state sovereign immunity would be clear, but whether there is anything else in the Constitution to block that intent turns out to be a harder question.

We could get a start on answering that harder question by trying to understand why the gaps might have been left. Was there a reason to leave unresolved, at least on its face, the issue of whether a citizen could sue his own state? More precisely, could there be legitimate federal interest in giving citizens the right to sue their own state?

Law professor Bradford Clark says there couldn't have been, at least if one understands the original Constitution as the Framers did. According to Clark, the Framers didn't believe that Congress had the power to coerce the states to do anything. If that is true, then they didn't believe that Congress had the power to empower citizens to sue to coerce the states to do anything. If the suit was impossible, this account says, there was no reason for the Eleventh Amendment to forbid it.

But what about the express limitations placed on the states in Article I, Section 10? For example, states may not "pass any Bill of Attainder, ex post facto Law, or Law impairing the Obligation of Contracts." Wouldn't a citizen have the power to sue to enforce those? Not necessarily, Clark argues. All of these obligations, he insists, could be enforced without ever suing the state directly. As Clark puts it:

> [Regarding] prohibitions against coining money, emitting bills of credit, and making anything but gold and silver a legal tender in payment of debts[:] If a state violated any of these prohibitions, a creditor could simply refuse to accept improper payment and sue his debtor. If the debtor raised state law as a defense, the creditor could then assert its invalidity under the Constitution. A similar analysis applies to the prohibitions against bills of attainder and ex post facto laws (and, for that matter, to the comparable prohibitions on the United States). If a state initiated an action to enforce such a law against an individual, the Constitution provides a complete defense. A suit against the state would have been unnecessary to enforce these prohibitions.[8]

The one obvious exception to this happy coincidence of unnecessary suits and the text of the Eleventh Amendment might be the contracts clause. That clause forbids state laws "impairing the Obligation of Contracts." What if the state issues a bond, and then passes a law revoking that bond? Wouldn't a citizen have a claim he could raise directly against the state?

Clark again says no, because the contracts clause as originally interpreted applied to private contracts only. So if Pennsylvania passed a law canceling a contract, the aggrieved party in that case can still bring a suit against the promisor in the contract. The promisor will invoke the state law as a defense. But the promisee will invoke the Constitution to demonstrate the state law is invalid. No direct action against the state is necessary.[9]

By 1810, however, this happy coincidence had disappeared. In *Fletcher v. Peck* (1810), the Court interpreted the reach of the contracts clause to include state as well as private contracts. That clarification didn't initially raise any trouble, however, since Congress had not expressly secured, in the Judiciary

Act, a jurisdiction in federal trial courts to hear causes arising under the Constitution or laws of the United States. That happened much later, in 1875—and left such issues to be resolved in the first instance by state tribunals.

Clark's account is compelling, but a much simpler explanation might conclude that the framing of the Eleventh Amendment simply left the question open. Congress was not forbidden from empowering citizens to sue states, at least when such suits would implicate a federal interest. But likewise, by merely permitting Congress the option, those who framed the amendment didn't intend to automatically preempt that sovereign immunity. Congress had the option of empowering some citizens' suits. But that option didn't—on its own, or automatically—negate any residual state sovereign immunity. Whether it did depended upon the scope of federal power.

This reading is consistent with the Supreme Court's first case addressing the question whether a citizen could sue his own state. In 1874, Louisiana issued bonds. Five years later, Louisiana adopted a constitution purporting to repudiate the obligations of those bonds. Hans, a citizen of Louisiana, sued to enforce the bonds, the state constitution notwithstanding. The question the Court had to answer was whether the apparent hole in the Eleventh Amendment (since, again, it didn't bar suits by citizens against their own state) meant that, as in *Chisolm*, federal courts could be used to force the states to live up to their debts.

Speaking for a unanimous court, Justice Bradley rejected Hans's claim. It would be a "startling and unexpected" consequence of the "Constitution and the law" if out-of-state citizens were barred from suing a state while in-state citizens were not.[10] But that "anomalous" result was avoided in *Hans* because of a background understanding, taken for granted by those who framed the Eleventh Amendment, that fundamentally constrained the scope of government (judicial) power: "The suability of a state, without its consent, was a thing unknown to the law."[11] Sovereign immunity was thus presumed and would now be applied to constrain the judicial power even in contexts in which the Eleventh Amendment would not.

Even here, however, there is an important ambiguity that too few notice. In *Hans*, the Court holds that the state's presumptive sovereign immunity is enough to defeat the ability of a citizen to bring suit in federal court to enforce a contracts clause claim. The Court does not hold that Congress lacks the power, pursuant to the necessary-and-proper clause, to override that state immunity if it so desires. By default, the immunity is not overridden, but there's nothing in Bradley's opinion that would question Congress's power to override the default. And indeed, depending upon the claim at issue, it may well make sense to permit citizens to sue their own state to enforce a federal interest. The Eleventh Amendment would thus block Congress from giving that power to out-of-state citizens. But nothing in the Eleventh Amendment or in Bradley's opinion would block a statute that preempted state sovereign immunity for claimants not within the terms of the Eleventh Amendment.[12]

As federal power grew after the Civil War—both because of the particular rights protected by the Civil War Amendments and because of the growth of federal commerce clause authority—Congress began to act on this understanding of the limits to state sovereign immunity. As Clark describes, Congress began the "practice of regulating states as part of its broader legislative agenda, and eventually authorized suits by individuals against states to enforce congressional commands."[13] This new practice was challenged by the states, forcing the Court to revisit the question not yet answered in *Hans*: does state sovereign immunity have some special constitutional sanction, or put differently, is there a reason that Congress would be blocked from preempting it?

At first the Court didn't see much of a problem (originalism, step one). In *Parden v. Terminal Railway* (1964), the Court resolved the question against immunity.[14] State law had a presumed immunity. But that state interest, like any state interest, could be overcome by a competing federal interest, at least if the federal interest was expressed in a law itself constitutional. If Congress acts pursuant to an enumerated power and passes a law that could benefit from the ability to sue states in federal court, then the necessary-and-proper clause would authorize the federal government to preempt that state immunity.

But then the Court balked (translation, step two). Just at the moment that the federalism translations described in Chapter 4 were beginning to take off, the Court evinced a similar translation with respect to immunity. In the face of a massively expanded federal jurisdiction, exercised now in a wide range of regulatory contexts, the Court began to deploy immunity to carve back federal intrusion on the judgment of the states, in order to more effectively preserve state autonomy.

At first, the limits were tame. In 1985, the Court erected a "clear statement rule," to require that Congress clearly express its desire to preempt state sovereign immunity.[15] But clear statement rules are not much of a burden, once Congress learns how to speak clearly. So, a decade later, the Court crossed the constitutional Rubicon: in *Seminole Tribe of Florida v. Florida* the Court expressly prohibited Congress from using its affirmative power to preempt state immunity in federal courts.[16]

And then, three years later, in *Alden v. Maine* (1999), the Court took what seemed to some to be the most extreme step possible—at least from the perspective of the Constitution's text, and at least if one believed that the sovereign immunity doctrine was an outgrowth of the Eleventh Amendment. In *Alden,* the Court held that Congress couldn't even impose liability on the states in *state* courts.[17]

Let's be clear about the meaning of this holding. The Eleventh Amendment speaks only of the judicial power of the United States. It says nothing about the judicial power of the states. Yet *Alden* held that Congress had no authority to empower citizens to sue states in state courts. The source of that restriction on Congress's power could not be the Eleventh Amendment. Instead, as Justice Anthony M. Kennedy wrote, quoting Justice Scalia:

> Although the text of the Amendment would appear to restrict only the Article III diversity jurisdiction of the federal courts, "we have understood the Eleventh Amendment to stand not so much for what it says, but for the presupposition [...] which it confirms."[18]

That "presupposition" was, as in *Hans*, the existence of state sovereign immunity. But unlike in *Hans*, the presupposition here includes the extra argument that Congress can't preempt that state policy. Whereas in *Hans*, Congress may well have had the authority to preempt state sovereign immunity, after *Alden*, it plainly does not—except with respect to the federal authority embodied in the Civil War Amendments, which, as the Court wrote in *Alden*,

> fundamentally altered the balance of state and federal power struck by the Constitution. When Congress enacts appropriate legislation to enforce this Amendment, federal interests are paramount, and Congress may assert an authority over the States which would be otherwise unauthorized by the Constitution.[19]

How could this possibly make any sense, at least as a matter of fidelity? Whether or not sovereign immunity was presupposed by the Framers, how did it now get converted into a constitutional bar?

The answer is—surprise, surprise!—translation.

The scope and reach of federal regulation has grown dramatically. As in the other federalism cases, that growth is seen by conservatives to skew an original and intended constitutional balance. And so, to restore that balance, the Court crafts a constitutional limitation on Congress's authority where before there had been none. Congress may have the authority to preempt state regulation (pursuant to the commerce clause) in every traditional sphere of state life. But it would not have the power to preempt the right of the state to control whether and when to waive its own immunity.

This rule is thus quite important, and it has a feature that we should not overlook. Unlike the limits discussed in Chapters 4 and 9, the limits discussed here do not leave to the states an exclusive jurisdiction the federal government may not touch. They instead give the states an unfettered right to choose whether to be subject to federal judicial control, at least through money damages. This does not exempt states from the responsibility to obey federal law. It simply exempts them from being compelled *through money* to obey federal law. As with all immunity, state sovereign immunity leaves the state with the choice about whether to do the right thing or not. By giving the state the choice, the doctrine expresses a respect for the integrity and autonomy of the state. That respect is the core of any sovereignty doctrine, which federalism plainly is. And its effect is to better carry into effect framing ideals about the proper place of states in the Constitution's design.

Seen in this way, the doctrine is an obvious translation. And like many translations, its current expression has little connection to the actual text of the constitution. Yet it has a strong connection to the original meaning, at least as the conservatives understand that meaning. The doctrine does not secure to states the full freedom that the original balance did. But it gives them an important part of that freedom, and perhaps more important, it does so in a manner that expresses respect for them as sovereigns. It restores something of the original design, through made-up limitations on the scope of federal power. That restoration is justified only if the claim to fidelity is real.

Unlike the other examples of translation described in Chapters 4 and 9, in this case there is no retreat. Or at least none so far. The translation that is the state sovereign immunity doctrine is growing. It has yet to encounter a resistance that triggers concerns about role. That's not to say it won't, someday, in some context. But as we'll consider further in Chapter 11, the striking feature of this immunity doctrine is the simplicity with which it can be enforced. There are no hard lines to draw. Unlike "manufacturing" versus "commerce" or "direct" versus "indirect," there are no distinctions here that are likely to be rendered false or unstable. As we'll consider in Chapter 11, immunity doctrine is a usable tool of translation, precisely because its deployment does not trigger fidelity to role.

CHAPTER ELEVEN | Usable Tools

W E'VE SURVEYED A RANGE of examples of two-step originalism—translation—on the Right. Before we turn to the same on the Left, it will be useful to draw together some lessons about what makes these translations succeed or fail. Is there a technique that helps? Is there an approach doomed to fail?

As the examples evince, sometimes context is a hurricane, and no matter what the Court does, it won't be able to hold on to its particular translated view. But sometimes the wounds are self-inflicted, and a fidelitist keen to avoid such wounds would be wise to keep in view what works and what does not.

In this chapter, I sketch five successful tools of translation. These devices achieve the translator's objective without triggering a retreat because of fidelity to role. My claim is not that they must, or will always, work in this way. Tools, like readings, are contingent upon context. My claim is only that they have worked so far, and that they contain properties that suggest why they will work in the future.

I call these devices "usable tools." The tool metaphor is important. We should see these techniques as the means to an end of two-step originalism. They are independent of that end, but they enable it, by achieving, in a stable and predictable manner, the limiting objective sought by the Court. Not perfectly, and sometimes not even close to the dimension of substance. But these are the limits that stick, and we should learn something about why they stick.

# Immunity

After Chapter 10, the easiest and most obvious example of a usable tool is immunity. The doctrine supports the value of federalism.[1] It leaves to the judgment of the state whether and how to obey the regulatory demands of the federal government, at least vis-à-vis the remedy of damages. In the ordinary case, the federal government cannot order, it can only ask. Within the limits of an injunctive jurisdiction, the states can choose whether and how to comply with the federal command.

As it has been crafted so far, the standard is clear and administrable. The doctrine won't produce inconsistencies in administration that would render the actions of the Court suspect. Congress, moreover, has plenty of cheap ways to achieve much of its regulatory objectives despite the constitutional rule. Courts remain open, for example, to enjoin compliance in appropriate cases. That injunction, especially today, has real costs. The only limitation on Congress's power is the use of money damages to manage state incentives. No doubt, that's a constraint. But it is a stable constraint, not one likely to veer out of control.

At least, that is, so long as the line between Congress's Article I authority and the Civil War Amendments authority remains clear. State immunity does not extend to block efforts by Congress to make states amenable to suit to protect the rights enumerated in the Civil War Amendments. There's a good originalist reason why that line should not be as stable or clear as it now is, and we'll consider that argument in Chapter 16. But for now, the reach of the Civil War Amendments is known. Within that scope, Congress can regulate states more broadly pursuant to those amendments than they can pursuant to Article I.

# Clear Statement

A second stable and effective technique to achieve the values of federalism has been the clear-statement rule. This rule simply requires that Congress use certain magic words when trying to regulate in a particular domain. That requirement is easily met. The standard is easily enforced. The result is thus unlikely to get out of control.

Consider, for example, *Gregory v. Ashcroft* (1991).[2] At issue was whether the Age Discrimination Act applied to state judges who, under the state constitution, were required to retire at age seventy. Under *National League of*

*Cities*, the Court might have had to determine whether regulating the age at which states may force their judges to retire was a regulation of "states as states." *Garcia* disposed of that rule, and replaced it with a rule that relied upon the political process.[3]

*Gregory* sought to improve this political process through the use of a clear-statement rule. Said the Court, affirming the rule of *Garcia*, "Congress may legislate in areas traditionally regulated by the States," but the Court will not assume that Congress exercises this power "lightly."[4] Therefore, before assuming that Congress has exercised this power, "it is incumbent upon the federal courts to be certain of Congress's intent."[5] To be certain, the Court requires that Congress speak with particular clarity when it attempts to so regulate. Citing a clear-statement case from the Eleventh Amendment context, the Court said, "If Congress intends to alter the "usual constitutional balance between the States and the Federal Government," it must make its intention to do so "unmistakably clear in the language of the statute."[6]

With this device, the Court measures Congress's statute against an implied standard of certainty, to measure whether the Court believes that Congress really intended to reach as far as it apparently did. Where a statute is ambiguous, or where a particularly strong state interest or individual right is being overridden by governmental action, then the Court will require of Congress that it make its intent clearer. The Court will not presume, from simple ambiguity, that Congress intended to invade a domain of state regulatory interest.

The contexts within which the Court has applied the clear-statement rule are many. They range from individual rights cases to Eleventh Amendment cases and to cases where the fear is Congress's invasion of a traditional state function.[7] In each case, the notion is simply that any intent to change the constitutionally preferred status quo must be demonstrated by clear language in the statute.[8] But it should be plain that in setting out such a rule, the Court is setting out a constitutionally preferred status quo. And by increasing the costs of deviating, it is reducing the number of deviations.

The advantage of the clear-statement rule is twofold. First, it functions primarily as a channeling device. It requires simply that Congress be certain of an intent to alter a presumed constitutional balance. Second, it can achieve this function without requiring of the Court some impossible interpretive task. Determining whether a statute is sufficiently clear is an activity within the ordinary ken of the Court. We can expect, then, that the Court's adjudication of these cases will yield a fairly consistent line of authority.

# Spending

The third example of a usable tool isn't actually a tool of the Supreme Court, or at least not yet. It was instead proposed by Justice O'Connor in dissent, and if it is adopted, it would, in my view, advance a significant federalism interest in a manner that would be reliably administered.

The tool would regulate Congress's spending power to ensure that power doesn't swamp any competing federalism interests. The concern motivating this tool is that Congress's purse is so full that, in practice, it can buy any behavior by the states that it wants. And while from some perspective, being bought isn't inconsistent with autonomy, there are plenty of important federalist systems that try hard to avoid excessive control exercised through the purse.

The Supreme Court, so far at least, has not tried to restrain federal spending power in any meaningful sense. In *South Dakota v. Dole*, the Court articulated a test purporting to regulate the spending power. In reality, the test does little to restrain Congress's policymaking through spending power.

But in her dissent in that case, Justice O'Connor did sketch a test that would restrain the scope of Congress's spending power in a manner that would be perfectly administrable. As she stated the rule, Congress would be free to condition grants to the states so long as the conditions related directly to how the money granted would be spent. Conditions unrelated to how the money was to be spent were forbidden. So, for example, Congress would be free to condition a grant to support the building of highways upon 10 percent of that money being spent to fund equipment that could detect when drivers were under the influence. It would not be free to condition a federal grant on the state's lowering the speed limit to 55 mph.

O'Connor's distinction might well be criticized as more formal than real. And one might well question whether it actually does much to limit federal policymaking through spending. No doubt, it echoes with the efforts of the pre–New Deal Court to restrict the scope of Congress's power to regulations that "directly" regulate commerce.

But from the perspective of fidelity to role, her rule has obvious appeal. It achieves something in its objective of protecting the autonomy of states. But it does so in a manner that also protects the institution of the Court. The rule has a clear federalism-related purpose. It wouldn't be administered in a way that created problems for the Court. It thus is a model of a usable tool deployed to advance federalist ends.

The Supreme Court has not embraced O'Connor's tool. Indeed, in its latest and most dramatic spending clause case, the Court struck down a condition in the Affordable Care Act that would require the states to meet certain minimal obligations in order to continue to receive Medicare funding.[9] The Court, through Chief Justice Roberts, invalidated that spending clause condition, not because it was unrelated to health care but because it was a surprising shift in the focus of Medicare—away from its traditional domains and toward a program of national health insurance—and because the economic consequence for states of choosing not to follow the mandate was so great as to remove any meaningful choice.

This approach to the spending power is closer to the approach seen in other federal systems, such as Germany. And it certainly advances fidelity to meaning objectives, at least for those who believe fidelity requires better protection of state autonomy. But the line drawn by the Court is a fuzzy one. And while the political process may dampen the frequency of such regulation, it's not clear that over time the line will remain, or be perceived to be, stable. We'll see.

## Commandeering

The fourth example is as specific a rule as the spending rule, but perhaps less significant, if only because the "invasion" is less common. This is the rule against "commandeering" announced by the Court in *New York v. United States* (1992) and *Printz v. United States* (1997).[10]

*New York v. United States* involved a federal program designed to deal with the problem of nuclear waste. Among its many provisions was one set of requirements that constituted the "commandeering" that the Court held unconstitutional. In these regulations, Congress gave the states a choice: either enact certain regulations specified by the federal government, or take title to that state's nuclear waste.

The problem with this your-money-or-your-life "choice" was that the federal government had no power to mandate either alternative. The government couldn't force the states alone to take title to spent nuclear waste. That rule would conflict with the principles of an earlier case in which the Court held that to force states to take title to property of negative value would be in essence to tax the states. This earlier case clearly indicated that a discriminatory tax against the states would be unconstitutional.[11]

Neither could the federal government force the states to enact certain regulations. Even though these regulations were otherwise within the scope of the federal government's power (meaning that the federal government could have enacted them itself), the federal government couldn't direct the states to enact them for it. "By directly compelling [states] to enact and enforce a federal regulatory program," the federal government was "commandeering" the states in the exercise of their sovereign power.[12] This, the Court held, was unconstitutional.

This rule serves obvious federalism interests. If a state is being forced to pass an unpopular law, the state will be bearing the political costs even though it was Congress that was making the political choice. The rule protects the state against this unfair attribution, preserving responsibility when the state is in fact responsible.

But the rule advances federalism interests in a manageable and stable way. "Commandeering" has a logical form. It can be identified from the structure or language of a statutory rule. It is not vulnerable to uncertain history (as "traditional state functions" was). Nor is it vulnerable to arbitrary formal limits ("direct" versus "indirect"). A court applying the doctrine can easily determine whether the condition has been violated. If it is, the court can easily remove the offending rule. The rule is meaningful and administrable— necessary and sufficient conditions for a usable tool.

## Simple Formalism: Non-Activity

The final example is also the most recent—the formal line between activity and non-activity drawn in *Sebelius* (2002). Like every other formal distinction in the history of the commerce authority—direct versus indirect, commerce versus manufacturing, and so on—this line is crafted. It tracks a category that is imposed based on economic facts. But as we saw with commandeering, a tool is not unusable because it is formal. A tool becomes unusable when it is unreliable, unpredictable, or too easily tracked to political motivations.

This line between activity and non-activity has not had the chance yet to be vulnerable to that attack, though time will tell. Rarely does a Court launch a new tool of translation expecting it will fail. But like commandeering, this new formalism is less vulnerable than the old. The tool it crafts may not have frequent or general application. But where it applies, it applies reliably, and to the end of protecting federalism interests, in the name of framing federalism values.

———

Each of these tools has a common form. As applied in the context of federalism cases, they advance federalism interests in a manner that the Court could administer easily. They give the Court, in other words, a way to advance a particular conception of fidelity to meaning, consistent with fidelity to role. They effect the second step in a practice of fidelity.

No doubt, the conservatives' view about the limited reach of federal authority can be questioned. Were the Court to come to the view that fidelity to framing values does not require ongoing policing of the reach of federal power, then it could be relaxed. But to the extent we see a continued effort by the Court to carve back the scope of federal authority—in the name of fidelity to framing values—we can expect the Court to evolve tools that are similar to these.

The only question is whether the Court will acknowledge just how "made up" these doctrinal limits will always be. As law professor Richard Fallon has demonstrated powerfully in his writing, the work of doctrine is always constructive and creative, and the test of that work is efficiency and fidelity: Does it respect values properly deemed constitutional? And does it give courts a way to enforce those values efficiently and without inducing unnecessary regulatory uncertainty?[13]

The early efforts by the conservatives failed this efficiency test, even if they advanced values properly deemed constitutional. The later efforts suggest that even courts can learn.

| Elements of Translation

L ET'S RECAP THE ARGUMENT so far.
I've described a pattern of constitutional interpretation that is grounded ultimately in two conceptions of fidelity. One is fidelity to meaning; the other is fidelity to role.

Fidelity to meaning asks the Court to read the Constitution in light of the current interpretive context so as to preserve its original meaning. That is different from saying the Court should read the Constitution as the Framers would have. That's the question of the one-step originalist. The aim of the two-step originalist is to take what the Framers would have done in their context and to find an equivalent in this context, so as to preserve meaning across contexts. To use the central animating metaphor, the goal is to translate the original text in the original context to a new context. Like the translator making sense of *Hamlet* in twenty-first-century Harrisburg, the aim is to preserve meaning across very different contexts.

Such preservation may not always be possible. Contexts may change too dramatically to make it meaningful to speak of preserving meaning across contexts. The Second Amendment may be a perfect example of such a failure: so radically has the original context been changed that any effort at preserving original meaning could make no sense.[1]

But where a meaningful equivalent is possible, the cases presented so far demonstrate at least the will of the Court to take extraordinary steps to realize as much of that equivalence as possible.

These steps are extraordinary in the literal sense that they go beyond ordinary interpretation. What guides the reading of a particular clause is not simply a text accompanied by ordinary assumptions about the meaning of the words in that text. It is instead an understanding of how that clause would have functioned originally that guides how the clause is read today.

The product of that extraordinary practice, at least in the cases we've seen so far, is a set of artificial or constructed limits on the scope of the government's power and Congress's power. Whether limiting federal power to protect the states or limiting state power to protect private economic activity, these translations look to Founding ideals to justify their counter-majoritarian results. It is not the will of the Court that limits the democratic branch, or so goes the assertion. It is the will of the people, properly adjusted to the circumstances of the time.

This practice, however, is not costless. The act of translation, like any judicial act, reflects back on the institution doing the translating. And this reflection gets reckoned. Courts take account, I submit, not just of whether their decision is right, but also of how their decision will be understood. How courts perform this reckoning is something I've not described. While I've pointed to at least one self-conscious reckoning, the best judges, I suggest, have an intuitive sense of what seems appropriate. That sense constrains the range of possible interpretations. That constraint can even block the "correct" interpretation of a particular text, at least if that interpretation is too costly for the judicial institution.

I've named this constraint "fidelity to role." And my argument is that this constraint on interpretive fidelity is itself justified—not on interpretive grounds, obviously, but on institutional grounds. Where the interpretive context makes it no longer possible for the Court to sustain a particular interpretation, the Court retreats. Getting it right is important, but appearing non-political can be much more important.

This pattern of advance and retreat, I have argued, explains much of the history of conservative translation. It also suggests a continued practice of conservative translation in the future. Put differently: The current balance of federal and state authority is no doubt wildly different from what the Framers imagined. That means there remains plenty of work that the Supreme Court might do to restore that balance, subject to fidelity to role, and if only it can be done in a way that makes the argument for fidelity its most salient feature.

But conservatives are not the only translators. In the next section, we consider translations that have no obvious political valence. These build on the dynamic of contestability at the core of the conservative retreat and illustrate more fundamentally how the balance of power within a constitution remains contingent upon the balance of public understanding.

SECTION TWO | Fidelity in the Middle

| Brooding Omnipresences

H ARRY TOMPKINS HAD A BAD NIGHT on July 27, 1934. On his way home after hanging out with a friend, he was dropped off a few blocks from his house. That was at about 2:30 a.m. His home was located on a dead-end street, near the tracks of the Erie Railroad, in Hughestown, Pennsylvania. Harry decided to walk the last couple of blocks on a "well-worn footpath adjacent to the tracks."[1] A train approached, but as it was dark, Harry could not see that there was an object protruding from the train. The object struck Harry, throwing him onto the tracks. The train then crushed his right arm. Harry lost his arm the next day.[2]

Tompkins's accident gave rise to one of the most important lawsuits in the history of American jurisprudence. In August 1934, Harry's lawyers filed suit against the Erie Railroad in New York City. That court had to decide what law it would apply. The accident had happened in Pennsylvania. The lawsuit was brought in New York. But Harry's lawyers asked the court to apply neither the law of New York nor the law of Pennsylvania, but instead "federal general common law"—a law that stood somewhere between, or above, or below, though no one quite knew how to think about precisely where that law was.

You've probably heard of common law. This is the law articulated by courts within the Anglo-American legal tradition. Such law may begin with a statute—like the Sherman Act—but then grow or evolve as courts apply the statute over time. Or it might begin with tradition and then get codified into a statute. That was the history of contract law, and of much of property law. And it was also the history of the law that Harry Tompkins needed to rely upon—the law of negligence, or tort.

Tort law regulates whether the victim of an accident will or will not get compensated by the person or corporation that caused, or is held responsible for, the accident. As it has evolved, the typical tort claim is that someone was harmed because someone else was negligent. "Negligence" is a judgment about how someone should have behaved. That standard is set, ordinarily, based on how a "reasonable person" would have behaved.

In some jurisdictions, at least at the time of Harry's accident, the victim was not allowed to recover for negligence if the victim was also a trespasser at the time of the injury. Such was the law in Pennsylvania. So Harry's lawyers needed to find a way to get a court to apply a different law. That's why they filed their lawsuit in New York. And that's why they asked the judge to ignore Pennsylvania law and apply its own version of tort law, expressed as federal general common law.[3]

The general common law is said to have been born in the federal legal system in 1824. One of America's greatest judges, Joseph Story, was called upon to decide another case involving New York law. That case involved a debt, and the debt involved parties located in Maine and New York. In the language of contract law, the question was whether there was "consideration" for the promise to pay that debt. If there was, the court could enforce it. But to answer that question, Story had to decide which law he was going to apply. And in an opinion that has been misunderstood for generations, Story decided that he would apply neither the law of Maine nor the law of New York. Instead he would apply "the general common law" to resolve the question of whether there had been consideration.

To the modern lawyer, Story's decision to ignore the law of New York seems odd. The federal statute that regulated the courts in their choice of law at the time read:

> The laws of the several states, except where the constitution, treaties or statutes of the United States shall otherwise require or provide, shall be regarded as rules of decision in trials at common law in the courts of the United States in cases where they apply.[4]

That seemed to suggest that Story should apply New York law to decide the case.

But Story didn't believe that New York law applied to the case. That language from the law, Story reported, had been interpreted by the Supreme Court "to be limited in its application to state laws strictly local" (meaning statutes) as well as "rights and titles to ... real estate, and other matters immovable ... in their nature."[5] "It never has been supposed by us," Story explained, that the section did apply, or was designed to apply, to questions of a more general nature ... as, for example, to the construction of ordinary contracts or other written instruments, and especially to questions of general commercial law, where the state tribunals are called upon to perform the like functions as ourselves, that is, to ascertain, upon general reasoning and legal analogies, what is the true exposition of the contract or instrument, or what is the just rule furnished by the principles of commercial law to govern the case.[6]

This has been called the "brooding omnipresence theory of law."[7] But it's not quite fair to call it that—yet. Because in this limited form, what Justice Story is describing is not so peculiar. And the key to seeing why is to focus on the phrase "contract or instrument."

The questions at issue in *Swift* involved a commercial transaction. Swift was, in the technical terms of commercial law, a "holder in due course" of a "bill of exchange." A bill of exchange—basically a check—is a written order by one person (the drawer) telling another person (the drawee) to pay a third person (the payee) an amount of money. The trick—and a really valuable trick it is—with such instruments is that they can be "negotiated." If I have a bill of exchange that orders Marshall to pay me $100, I can sell it to you, and then Marshall will pay you. You might give me $100 for that bill if you really trust Marshall and me. Or you might give me less, reflecting the chance that Marshall may not pay, or I might be a fraud.

These instruments operate within a market—or better, many markets. The state is meant to police those markets to avoid force or fraud. But beyond that policing, the role of the state is to let the parties transact as they wish. Think of a court interpreting a contract, working as hard as it (or its law clerks) can to figure out what the parties to that contract actually wanted to do. The aim is to facilitate a transaction while remaining neutral between the parties in that facilitation.

That's the type of activity that the Supreme Court was engaging in when it decided the precise question that *Swift v. Tyson* presented: deciding what rule best facilitated the intent of the parties to a "bill of exchange." But that decision is not easy. The whole purpose of a bill of exchange is to enable people who never actually meet to engage in commerce. I buy a computer from you in Chicago. I give you a check. You then travel to California with that check and endorse it over to Sam. Sam takes it to the bank to cash it. The bank is supposed to give Sam the money, even though Sam doesn't know me, and even though he has no clue why you had a check from me. In a world without the Internet, commerce depends upon an efficient system of exchange that doesn't itself depend upon everyone knowing everything there is to know about everyone else's business. So "the intent of the parties" is not actually a real intent; it is instead the intent we presume everyone has when they engage in this form of commerce.

It was Justice Story's whole purpose in life to craft a body of law that would support an efficient system of commerce—"law merchant," as that body of rules and principles is traditionally called. As a jurisprudential founder of American law, Story's "life's work," as Herbert Hovenkamp has put it,

> was devoted to developing a uniform body of commercial legal rules that would do two things at the same time. First, they would bind the states of the United States into a unified nation; second, they would encourage America's participation in world markets. Justice Story used every scholarly vehicle to support this idea, including his commercial treatises on bills of exchange and promissory notes, his pathbreaking treatise on conflict of laws, and his judicial opinions in cases such as *Swift v. Tyson*.[8]

Think of it as the rules of the game: Story, and every other common-law judge across the common law world, was working to devise rules that would best enable commerce to happen. Yet those rules were ultimately grounded in the expectations and desires of the parties to these instruments. There is a law here, in these rules of the game, but this law is essentially bottom-up. It expresses what we all in some sense agree to when we participate in the bill-of-exchange game.

Now compare those rules of law to a very different kind of rule of law—say, for example, criminal law. Criminal law says I can't just steal your computer. I may want to—it may be a nice computer, and it would be even nicer if I could get it for nothing. But you obviously don't agree with that, and criminal law is obviously on your side. If I take your machine, the law makes me liable, both to you (to return the machine) and to the state (to be punished for my crime). And the job of a judge enforcing that law is not to suss out what my intention may have been. Her job is to suss out what the law is, and whether I have violated it. That law is top-down, imposed by the state. My agreement or consent to that law is fundamentally irrelevant.[9]

This is the distinction between "top-down" law, or law as the "normative command of the sovereign," to use law professor Ernest Young's phrasing, and "bottom-up" law, or customary law (such as the law merchant), that "arises out of the practices of predominantly private actors."[10] Courts to this day continue to apply both, and it is not particularly troubling that they do, so long as the law at issue is genuinely customary. So long as those subject to the reach of customary law are free to change the law by saying something different, that law is not normative or regulatory in any obvious way. I'm not troubled if the default term in a contract says I have to accept by email, so long as I'm free to change that to certified mail. The custom just specifies what the rule is if we don't say something different. That's not a rule, that's a convenience.[11]

Just as important, too, is the source of the authority that the court is seeking. If the common law is custom, then the court is seeking the law in the custom of others. It might be confused about how well or completely it is deferring to the judgment of others. We are all blind to the effect of our own bias, and have always been. But the structure taught that the authority was outside of the judge. It was the judge "trying to follow the practices of others," as Young puts it, rather than "choosing the best practice by [the judge's] own lights."[12]

This distinction between top-down and bottom-up law is critical if we're to understand the relatively harmless activity that Story was actually engaged in when deciding *Swift v. Tyson*. Story and the Supreme Court were not imposing top-down rules to govern bills of exchange everywhere. They were articulating what they understood to be the best exposition of the understandings or custom of those engaged in this kind of commerce everywhere. And as that articulation applied to the facts in *Swift*, the result was not terribly surprising. A bill of exchange was an international instrument. While New York was perfectly free to change the rules governing bills of exchange *for New Yorkers engaged with other New Yorkers*, it was not free to change the rules for others. So when deciding whether to allow Swift to collect, the rule that the Supreme Court would apply was the general rule that governed bills of exchange generally. Story was something of an expert in that subject. He had literally written the book(s) about bills of exchange. So he was perhaps the best judge in America to describe the customary rules that would govern bills of exchange, except where local law had effectively changed them.

I rehearse the facts because they are so completely misunderstood by lawyers and judges today. The account of who Story was and what he was doing has been completely rewritten. And, in fact, it is the rewriting, not the original truth, that will be important to the story I tell in the balance of this chapter. But before we so willfully slander the brilliance of this extraordinary justice, we should remark certain facts. First, Justice Story was not divining the law of commerce from the will of God, or any other "brooding omnipresence." Yes, he was placing the power of his Court behind the rule he described, but he was doing so in the same way any judge puts the power of her court behind her interpretation of a contract. Story was interpreting a commercial instrument—a kind of contract—against the background of a certain custom within commerce, that of New York.

There is a second point that is systematically ignored when considering Justice Story and *Swift*. Much is made of part of the passage that I quoted above—"to be limited in its application to state laws strictly local"—suggesting (at least if "laws" means statutes) that the rule of *Swift* was limited to the common law. In this view, if New York had enacted the rule that Tyson was trying to rely upon to escape his debt, Story would have followed that statute, despite its conflict with the general law.

Yet that was just not true. As Herbert Hovenkamp has brilliantly shown, the rule of *Swift* reached beyond the common law. Indeed, a unanimous Supreme Court applied it to a statute directly just thirteen years after *Swift*.[13] In *Watson v. Tarpley* (1855), the Supreme Court reviewed an application of a state statute to defeat the operation of the general law governing bills of exchange.[14] The Supreme Court reversed the decision and held that the statute could not be applied. The reason followed directly from *Swift*: Mississippi was free to change the rules for bills of exchange *within Mississippi*. It was not free to change the rules—whether through the common law or through statutes—for people who were not within the jurisdiction of Mississippi.

Thus, *Swift* was not about the common law versus a statute; it was about improperly applied local law versus the custom of a commercial practice. And that custom was not some "brooding omnipresence." The understanding of that custom came from careful study of the actual practices and transactions that occurred within this commercial field. Properly understood, nothing Justice Story was doing was either surprising or weird—even for us today. Indeed, properly understood, what he did then is what any judge today should do again (bracketing the certainly wildly complex evolution of conflicts of laws).

Again, though, that is not how Justice Story's story is told. Instead, in the modern understanding, Justice Story is charged with launching a practice that over time morphed into an incredible monster. As the practice of federal general common law grew, it took on a wholly different character. The doctrine evolved to include much more than custom. The common law that it presumed to articulate was not just the implied terms of a commercial contract. Instead, federal general common law began to reach far beyond the law of implied terms, to include law in a more normative sense—including, eventually, torts. As Tony Freyer describes, "Between 1842 and the end of the nineteenth century the *Swift* doctrine underwent a gradual but fundamental transformation."[15] By the 1880s, "the general law included 26 distinct doctrines."[16]

This was mission creep.[17] And as time passed, it raised significant concerns. For as the one-step originalist allowed the law moved from supplying implied terms to regulating rules of conduct, the law moved from descriptive to prescriptive—from bottom-up to top-down. It moved, that is, from the position of simply ratifying the choices made by others in a contract to the position of choosing the rules that should be imposed upon others in contexts far beyond a contract. "A court enforcing a customary rule of commercial law is engaged in a quite different enterprise than, say, a court formulating a common law doctrine of products liability," writes Young.[18] He goes on: "The shift away from customary law to normative lawmaking put the question of legislative authority front and center."[19]

This change raised two questions. First, a federalism question: The domain of these issues was any matter presumptively within the domain of state law. So why were *federal* courts deciding what were essentially state law questions? Second, a separation-of-powers question: The domain of these issues was any matter that was presumptively a matter of policy. So why were federal *courts* deciding these policy questions rather than a state *legislature*?

We will return to these questions later. But I raise them now to introduce an idea that will be central to the argument of the balance of this book. To understand how federal general common law evolved from a gap-filling technique to a "brooding omnipresence," we need to understand a bit more about the nature of law as it came to be understood at the time.

This will be the hardest bit for us moderns to get, because it is hard to see what one takes for granted. But as Hovenkamp has described, the nature of law, or of how law was understood, has changed dramatically over the past two centuries—though as we look back, we're likely to miss just how advanced Justice Story was. As Hovenkamp writes, Story's jurisprudence

> reflects the legal world going through a painful transition from universalism to nominalism. At one extreme is the view that there is one universal set of moral and legal rules and the State's job is merely to identify the correct rule. At the other extreme is the view of the legal realists that a rule is whatever the state declares it to be. Story stands halfway between: too much a realist to believe that rules transcend sovereigns, yet too faithful to doubt that in fact some principles are better than others.[20]

Yet whether that earlier jurisprudence is fairly ascribed to Story or not (and I agree with Hovenkamp it is not), the world of legal thought came to see Story as part of that earlier view. For those holding that view, the law was perceived as more natural than it is for us today—natural in the sense of being derived from nature and thus being something all people could reason about and, if they reasoned carefully enough, come to view in the same way.

Think about math, or about how most philosophy is done today. Philosophers (in the Anglo-American tradition at least) believe they are seeking the truth. Many philosophers, from many different perspectives and traditions, all work hard to describe the nature of this truth, as it applies, for example, to free will, or knowledge or beauty. Within a certain tradition at least, they don't believe that they are trying to discover the truth as certain important philosophers have *made* it. They believe that they are trying to discover the truth as every philosopher from the beginning of time has tried to *find* it. There is a truth about truth—or about meaning, or consciousness, or beauty—out there. Philosophers are engaged in the enterprise of discovering that truth and revealing it to the world.

So too were nineteenth-century lawyers, at least with respect to law, at least as they were described to the world by legal theorists at the end of the nineteenth century. Law was thought to be a certain kind of science—at least within the tradition of American and English law, at least in the first three-quarters of the century. In this tradition, judges and lawyers were trained in that science, just as philosophers today are trained in philosophy. They practiced that science by working out the truth about certain principles of law. And for many years, they were considered—by the public at least—to actually be finding those truths through the practice of law. As American lawyer Justin Zaremby puts it:

> Careful analysis of judicial precedent would yield firm principles that judges could then apply in individual cases. This discoverable law was accessible at all times through the use of a unique form of reasoning— legal reasoning—and stood above the politics of the time.[21]

Jurists sustained that view by deriving what seemed to be consistent and sensible "principles" of law. So long as the results were in fact consistent and sensible, it was at least plausible that those principles were as jurists found them because they were in fact true. Such a view emboldened federal courts, none more so than the Supreme Court in *Gelpcke v. City of Dubuque* (1863) when it rejected a state court construction of a state constitution that would have invalidated a state bond by remarking, "We shall never immolate truth, justice, and the law, because a State tribunal has erected the altar and decreed the sacrifice."[22]

But the conditions that made it possible for these decisions to be seen as consistent and sensible were very particular. In England, the conditions were sustained by a highly concentrated judiciary. There were never more than half a dozen judges on England's high court.[23] Those judges could maintain the appearance of consistency because they could easily conspire to keep the results consistent.

In America, the conditions were more difficult to sustain. The country had hundreds of judges, working thousands of miles apart from each other. And while that multitude made it difficult to demonstrate consistency, at least for a while it also made it difficult to demonstrate inconsistency. The law was as you wanted to believe it was—and for judges, that meant it was consistent.

Until the rise of a company called West Publishing. Beginning in 1872, and then moving ahead in earnest in 1879, West started organizing the decisions of America's common-law courts. The company published the decisions, but also wrote summaries of the holdings and built a scheme to organize the reasoning of the judges writing the opinions behind those holdings. West's Key Number System made it easy to see how different courts were deciding the same questions. And that made it easy for jurists to see an inconvenient truth: the emperor was wearing no clothes. Rather than an archive of consistency, the West system reported incredible variation. The idea that judges were discovering the true principles of the law became harder and harder to sustain. Either a whole bunch of judges were pretty bad discoverers, or there was no truth here to be discovered.[24] Writes legal academic Robert Stevens:

> The extraordinary number of jurisdictions and judges in the United States made highly unlikely the same kind of manageable case law as in England; the establishment of the National Reporter System by the West Publishing Company in 1879, designed to produce exhaustive rather than selective reporting, assured that anything like the English approach was bound to perish. English judges found it relatively easy to appear to select precedents only from a clear-cut stream of cases, whereas American judges had a wide area of selection, which emphasized their creative discretionary role.[25]

These material conditions of inconsistency created a clear motive for the law to reconceptualize itself. If judges were discovering truth, why were there so many errors (as evinced by the inconsistencies)? And if they were not actually discovering a truth, then why should the public obey them? What was their authority? What made it appropriate for the public to listen to these men in black robes?

The anxiety that this question created drove the development of a school of jurisprudence—what today we call "positivism." The law, the positivists believed, was the law not because it was the truth. The law was the law because the sovereign—who might or might not be democratically accountable—said it was so. And when the judges spoke, the only question the public need worry itself about was whether the judges spoke for the sovereign. Positivism was perfectly compatible with judge-made law. The sovereign could easily say, "I delegate to the judges the task of crafting the law of tort." But at each moment, the relevant question was whether the sovereign had authorized the judges, not whether the rules of the judges were "true."[26]

Positivism was not new in the late nineteenth century. John Austin, its most famous father, laid the foundations of the school in the middle of the nineteenth century. His work had strong adherents across the world from early on.

But my point is less about the philosophical possibility than about the practical necessities. And as the practical reality of the common law's diversity became clearer, the conceptual possibility of federal general common law became more complex. The conflict forced a critical question: Who was responsible for a given bit of law?

In America, it turns out, that is a complicated question. Because in the theory of American government, there are at least three entities that call themselves "sovereign." As I described in Chapter 10, there is us, the people. We are the ultimate sovereigns in a republic of popular sovereignty. But we, the sovereigns, have also delegated our sovereignty—twice. Some of our power we have delegated to the federal government. Some we have delegated to the state governments. So when a judge says he or she speaks for the sovereign, we have to ask, which sovereign, and how?

And this is why the question became so troubled for the Supreme Court in *Erie Railroad Co. v. Tompkins*. Recall when *Erie* was decided—1938. And remember what was happening in the federal judiciary in 1938: as I described in Chapter 6, the Supreme Court had just given up on the enterprise of limiting federal power in the name of protecting federalism. The Court had just signaled it would no longer restrain Congress in its efforts to regulate what Congress viewed as national issues. It had just signaled it would not limit the power of the states to regulate economic and social issues.

But what about the power of the federal courts? Because as Justice Brandeis surveyed the question of "federal general common law," it raised two very different kinds of questions. The substantive law at issue in Harry Tompkins's case was tort law. Whether or not it could, Congress had not tried to set national standards to govern the law of negligence. This was, as it was, quintessentially, a state law question.

Yet if courts weren't "finding law" but were instead making it, why were *federal* judges making *state* law? That question in turn raised a second: if this was lawmaking and not law-finding, why were federal *judges* engaged in lawmaking rather than Congress or, better, state legislatures?

These two questions resolved themselves into one of the most important opinions in the history of American federalism in the last century.[27] "There is no federal general common law," Brandeis declared in *Erie*—ninety years of case law notwithstanding. That was because, first, "Congress has no power to declare substantive rules of common law applicable in a state whether they be local in their nature or 'general,' be they commercial law or a part of the law of torts," and second, "No clause in the Constitution purports to confer such a power upon the federal courts."[28] This was not the job, Brandeis was saying, of either *federal* courts or federal *courts*. The one-step would become the two-step, so that the scope of judicially crafted state law would be shrunk.

The contrary doctrine, said Brandeis, was the product of a "fallacy." Quoting Holmes, Brandeis wrote:

> The doctrine rests upon the assumption that there is "a transcendental body of law outside of any particular State but obligatory within it unless and until changed by statute," that federal courts have the power to use their judgment as to what the rules of common law are; and that in the federal courts "the parties are entitled to an independent judgment on matters of general law":
>
> But law in the sense in which courts speak of it today does not exist without some definite authority behind it. The common law so far as it is enforced in a State, whether called common law or not, is not the common law generally but the law of that State existing by the authority of that State without regard to what it may have been in England or anywhere else.
>
> . . .
>
> The authority and only authority is the State, and if that be so, the voice adopted by the State as its own (whether it be of its Legislature or of its Supreme Court) should utter the last word.

*Swift,* Brandeis concluded, again quoting Holmes, was "an unconstitutional assumption of powers by the courts of the United States which no lapse of time or respectable array of opinion should make us hesitate to correct."[29]

Yet Brandeis was saying both too little and too much. If the doctrine of *Swift* had been limited to the articulation of the default terms in commercial contracts, it's hard to see how or why that would have raised any constitutional question. So limited, *Swift* was a rule for reading contracts. Federal courts interpret contracts all the time. No one believes that there is any constitutional issue presented if a federal court interprets that contract on its own. Charging Story with a constitutional violation was going too far.

But Brandeis's opinion didn't go far enough in explaining just how or why the doctrine of *Swift* had morphed into the monster that he felt he must slay. Missing was any account of why or even how the law had evolved from the naturalist view of Justice Bradley to the positivist view of Justice Holmes. As federal general common law moved beyond custom to control, what made that transformation make sense? What made it happen? Was it because the natural-law philosophers took over? Was it because the formalism their philosophy taught paid off? Or was it because the nationalizing uniformity that *Swift* evinced actually expanded beyond the scope of commercial law?

Maybe that's an unfair question. It wasn't Brandeis's job to write a dissertation on American jurisprudence. Neither is it true or fair to see this change as driven by a change in philosophy alone. As many have demonstrated, there is no logical connection between the result in *Erie* and positivism, nor any logical inconsistency between positivism and *Swift*.[30] And in any case, Brandeis had no special affinity for or connection to the Framers' views about anything. Tracking change from a framing view was not a Brandeisean mission.

Yet law is a culture, not a logic board. And even if there is no logical necessity between the result in *Erie* and a by-then-dominant legal philosophy of the time, there is certainly a cultural connection. Certain cultures make certain moves easier and other moves harder. And while I would agree with Hovenkamp and with Jack Goldsmith and Steven Walt that the increasingly obvious conflicts between federal general common law and state common law created a strong motive for reform, the way they understood the nature of law at the time—especially given the extraordinary political struggle that had just been resolved—made acting on that motive easier. The legal culture gave jurists like Brandeis the tools they needed to do what they did. That's not to highlight the "irrelevance" of culture. It's to emphasize the incompleteness of an approach that exhausts inquiry at the "conceptual[] or normative[]" level.[31]

Thus, it's no surprise that Brandeis is not wholly reflective about why he thinks as he does. It's no surprise that he is untroubled that the way "law in the sense in which courts speak of it today" may be different from how the law was spoken of before (or at least how he thought it had been spoken of).[32]

But it should be a surprise that another equally famous Supreme Court justice, Antonin Scalia, did the same thing. Scalia was an icon of originalism, committed throughout his career to finding and applying the original meaning of a constitutional text. So to be consistent, he would have a clear obligation to explain how the understanding of the law had changed. Or more directly, he would have an obligation to explain which view—the Framers' view or the modern view—a judge should follow. And at a minimum, if he was to follow what he thought was a modern view of the law and reject what he thought was an original view, he should account for that change.

Remember the puzzle of Chapter 1. As I argued there, the Framers had a view about the nature of constitutions. That view, roughly put, is that no constitution could constrain the constituent power of the people. The people had an "unalienable right," as Jefferson put it, to "alter or abolish" their constitution. *How* they could do that is a hard question. That they *could* do that was not, at least for the Framers.

But how, I asked in Chapter 1, should an originalist answer the same question today? Because I take it (though I hope I'm wrong) that, the Yale lawyers notwithstanding, most practicing lawyers today would deny the perpetual right of revolution. Most today would read Article V of the Constitution (remember, the article that governs amendments) as the *exclusive* mode by which the Constitution can be changed. So, between the Framers' view and our view today, which backgrounded, taken-for-granted views should an originalist follow? Who, in other words, should *govern*—them or us?

That same puzzle exists with the question raised by *Erie.* If we assume, as Scalia does, that the Framers had a different view of the nature of law (bracketing the question of whether this assumption is correct), whose view should an originalist follow? Theirs or ours?

There are times when Scalia struggles with this question openly and honestly. There are also times when he treats the answer as obvious. *Erie* is an obvious case for him. Scalia feels himself bound to follow the modern view and ignore what he takes to be the original view—and he doesn't in any way object to this binding. Though an originalist, he doesn't even pause to consider whose view should control, theirs or ours. Instead, he takes it as undebatable that our modern view should control our approach to federal general common law.

Or at least this was the Scalia on display in an extraordinary case decided in 2004. The issue in that case, in part, was the scope of customary international law. Remember, the law merchant was part of customary international law as well. That was the law that Story appealed to in *Swift.* As I've described, customary international law was very much a part of the legal universe at the framing—so much so that the first Congress enacted a statute that explicitly gave to federal courts jurisdiction over "all causes where an alien sues for a tort only in violation of the law of nations or a treaty of the United States."

This law was the Alien Tort Statute. And in *Sosa v. Alvarez-Machain* (2004), the Court had to determine the scope of that statute today. Given that the substance of customary international law had changed dramatically in the 213 years since the Founding, did the federal courts have an ever-growing list of wrongs that the Alien Tort Statute was meant to right? Was the job of the courts to follow the understanding of the Framers and permit customary international law to control the scope of a federally enforced right?[33]

These issues raised the anxiety Brandeis had felt in *Erie* to a whole new level, because now the substance of the law was not evolving in federal courts within a federal system. Customary international law—or more specifically, as it was implicated in *Sosa*, the customary law of human rights—now evolves mainly as law professors write ever more compelling law review articles arguing for its never-ending expansion. It may well be that the community of human rights lawyers comes to view some wrong as a violation of a human right. But can it really be that such a judgment by law professors translates into a federal cause of action?

The very thought was inconceivable to Justice Scalia (and the other conservatives). And thus the only conceivable result was one that rejected the law as (Scalia thought) Story saw it and embraced the law as Brandeis described it. The Court, in an opinion by Justice Souter, had rejected the idea that the law would evolve automatically. But Souter had left open the possibility that some new wrong would be recognized as within the scope of that federal right.

For Scalia, that was a loophole too far. As he wrote in *Sosa*:

> Because today's federal common law is not our Framers' general common law, the question presented by the suggestion of discretionary authority to enforce the law of nations is not whether to extend old-school general-common-law adjudication. Rather, it is whether to create new federal common law. The Court masks the novelty of its approach when it suggests that the difference between us [members of the Court] is that we would "close the door to further independent judicial recognition of actionable international norms," whereas the Court would permit the exercise of judicial power "on the understanding that the door is still ajar subject to vigilant door keeping." The general common law was the old door. We do not close that door today, for the deed was done in *Erie*. Federal common law is a new door. The question is not whether that door will be left ajar, but whether this Court will open it.[34]

Yet one might well have wondered why, for an originalist at least, "today's federal common law is not our Framers' general common law." Did an amendment to the Constitution change it? Or is it just the "evolving standards of [jurisprudence]," to remix *Trope v. Dulles* (1958), that justify reading the Constitution differently today from how the Framers would have? And if we can read the Constitution differently because our view of "what the law is" evolves, what other evolution counts? What else can we read differently? For an originalist, which domains of truth or knowledge or value are permitted to evolve? Which ones must stay static?

We will return to the puzzle of how Scalia should have seen it below. For now, recognize the pattern in these cases that we will see repeated elsewhere: a doctrine of law rests upon a conceptual foundation; that foundation crumbles; the doctrine must shift.

*Erie* is the paradigm case. Call the pattern the *Erie* effect.

In *Erie*, the doctrine was the practice of federal general common law. That practice rested on a foundation. That foundation was (in part, not completely) a way to view the activity of common-law lawmaking. Against the background of naturalism—or better, within a culture that practiced naturalism or its cousin, formalism—that view minimized the constructive aspect of common-law lawmaking. Scalia suggested that the judges understood this constructive aspect but put it to one side:

> I am not so naive (nor do I think our forebears were) as to be unaware that judges in a real sense "make" law. But they make it *as judges make it*, which is to say *as though* they were "finding" it—discerning what the law *is*, rather than decreeing what it is today *changed to*, or what it will *tomorrow be*.[35]

But this is to read a great deal into their actions. What jurists did, at least originally, was to engage in a practice that they believed gave them answers—indeed, truths. Like philosophers in a philosophy workshop, they worked the problems out, and when they were finished, they believed they had a truth. That belief grounded the practice of federal general common law.

Yet over time, many factors cracked this foundation. At a certain point, it could stand no longer. When it collapsed, the practice it had supported had to shift. Federal general common law was dead. From *Erie* forward, federal courts would have to follow state courts on state law. Or more precisely, to the extent state law would be displaced, federal courts would not be in the business of displacing it. As Bradford Clark has explained,

> *Erie*'s constitutional holding is best understood as an attempt to enforce federal lawmaking procedures and the political safeguards of federalism they incorporate. In other words, *Erie* reflects the idea that the Constitution not only limits the *powers* granted to the federal government, but also constrains the *manner* in which the federal government may exercise those powers to displace state law.[36]

As with the retreat of the old Court in the commerce and due process cases, the trigger was a kind of contestability. The world didn't necessarily move from naturalist to positivist. It is more accurate to say the world moved from a place where naturalism was relatively uncontested to a place where naturalism was increasingly contested. That contestation then forced a retreat. Because to hold steady when the surrounding world is in doubt is to take sides in a contest that the Court itself had no jurisdiction to resolve. Given how the old practice was viewed, it was inappropriate for the Court to continue it. The retreat—as with the retreat on substantive due process and the commerce clause—was thus motivated by a conception of the judicial role, given a culture of law. Conservative and limited, that role demanded that in the face of the emerging understanding of "law in the sense in which courts speak of it today," the judicial practice of federal general common law must go.[37]

When Scalia wrote about *Erie* in *Sosa*, that contest was long resolved. If the view of naturalism had been relatively uncontested in the time before Harvard Law School dean Christopher Columbus Langdell, and then became increasingly contested in the period leading up to *Erie*, our view about naturalism today is again relatively uncontested.

But our view now is uncontested in precisely the opposite way. We now reject it, and unambiguously so. And if a judge today spoke today as a naturalist did in 1860, her words would be striking and weird.[38] To us, they would be a pretense, even if 175 years ago they would have been ordinary.

Yet Scalia embraced the modern way of speaking. He yielded to the modern uncontested view, even though the uncontested view he yielded to is the exact opposite of the view most likely adopted by the Framers.

This is the right response. Fidelity to role should teach at least this much: that we cannot spit into the wind of what everyone knows is true, whether or not that "truth" conforms to what the Framers may have thought.

Yet to anticipate just a bit, it is not Scalia's consistent response. Over the next few chapters, we will track this inconsistency in Scalia. And in the end, I will argue that we can draw from the inconsistency an important lesson about fidelity. To telegraph the answer just a bit: Scalia is certainly right about *Erie* and (as we'll see in Chapter 14) executive power. Which is why Scalia is certainly wrong (as we'll see in Chapter 22) about equality.

———

There was an understanding about the nature of law that was taken for granted by those charged with its enforcement. That nature made certain practices easier. That understanding was then rendered contestable, as technology revealed its pretense was just false. Contestability in the understanding rendered the practices that depended upon that understanding vulnerable. Courts thus shifted the practice, in light of that vulnerability. This is the *Erie* effect. We will see it again.

CHAPTER FOURTEEN | The Executive

THERE ARE SEVEN GOVERNORS on the Federal Reserve Board. They exercise an incredibly important policymaking power. They meet regularly throughout the year and decide whether to change the monetary policy of the United States. They might decide inflation is too high, and cut the money supply. They might decide the economy is growing too slowly, and lower interest rates to spur investment. Within an incredibly broad statutory framework—to "maintain long run growth of the monetary and credit aggregates commensurate with the economy's long run potential to increase production, so as to promote effectively the goals of maximum employment, stable prices, and moderate long-term interest rates"[1]—the governors are meant to tune monetary policy for the good of the nation.

What's striking about these (monetary) policymakers is how far removed they are from the democratic process. They are not elected by the people. They are appointed by the president. Yet even that appointment is restricted: the president nominates the governors, and they are confirmed by the Senate. Once appointed, a board member can only be removed by the president "for cause," at least according to the statute. Thus, the Federal Reserve Act creates within the core of our government a policymaking body that affects some of the most important national economic issues that our government addresses, but which none of the democratically elected representatives of our government actually controls.

Is that really legal, under our Constitution?

———

From the very beginning of our republic, there has been a fight about the nature of presidential power. That fight occurred because no one knew precisely who that president would be.

The Framers were pretty clear about who they *didn't* want the president to be. They wanted, in their Constitution, to guarantee that the president wouldn't be a king. King George III was precisely the executive the Framers rejected. Willful, entitled, and empowered, George III had destroyed the greatness of Britain, or so the Framers believed. He was who our president would not be.

But neither did the Framers want the executive they already had under the Articles of Confederation—effectively no executive at all. The Articles had created a Congress, and Congress was in charge of everything. The executive power in Congress was not independent of Congress. It was as Congress decided.

Thus, the Framers created a president who was to stand between these two extremes. That president was given certain enumerated powers. But unlike the enumerated powers of Congress, the Constitution does not say that the enumerated powers given to the president are all the powers the president has. Instead, Article II, Section 1 states, "The executive Power shall be vested in a President of the United States of America." And then in Sections 2 and 3, the Framers proceeded to enumerate at least some of that executive power:

> Section 2. The President shall be Commander in Chief of the Army and Navy of the United States, and of the Militia of the several States, when called into the actual Service of the United States; he may require the Opinion, in writing, of the principal Officer in each of the executive Departments, upon any Subject relating to the Duties of their respective Offices, and he shall have Power to grant Reprieves and Pardons for Offenses against the United States, except in Cases of Impeachment.
>
> He shall have Power, by and with the Advice and Consent of the Senate, to make Treaties, provided two thirds of the Senators present concur; and he shall nominate, and by and with the Advice and Consent of the Senate, shall appoint Ambassadors, other public Ministers and Consuls, Judges of the supreme Court, and all other Officers of the United States, whose Appointments are not herein otherwise provided for, and which shall be established by Law: but the Congress may by Law vest the Appointment of such inferior Officers, as they think proper, in the President alone, in the Courts of Law, or in the Heads of Departments.
>
> The President shall have Power to fill up all Vacancies that may happen during the Recess of the Senate, by granting Commissions which shall expire at the End of their next Session.

Section 3. He shall from time to time give to the Congress Information of the State of the Union, and recommend to their Consideration such Measures as he shall judge necessary and expedient; he may, on extraordinary Occasions, convene both Houses, or either of them, and in Case of Disagreement between them, with Respect to the Time of Adjournment, he may adjourn them to such Time as he shall think proper; he shall receive Ambassadors and other public Ministers; he shall take Care that the Laws be faithfully executed, and shall Commission all the Officers of the United States.

What a mess! This list of powers and duties seems to have no rhyme or reason behind it. Some of the powers are great, such as the power of commander in chief; some of the powers are tiny, such as the power to require written opinions from the heads of the departments. And some of the powers are written in a way that seems intended to be hopelessly obscure: he "shall take care that the Laws be faithfully executed"—by whom, and how?

Law professor (and former judge) Michael McConnell has given us perhaps the best account of this hodgepodge.[2] The Framers essentially began with a list of the royal prerogative powers. They then assigned each of those powers to either Congress, the president, or the president with qualifications. The scope of some of these powers was altered, as McConnell explains, "in light of their intention to create a republic and not an elective monarchy."[3] And then to top it all off, the Framers made clear in Article I that Congress was to fill in the details. As the necessary-and-proper clause makes clear—remember, from *McCulloch v. Maryland* in Chapter 2—it is Congress that has the power to

make all Laws which shall be necessary and proper for carrying into Execution the foregoing Powers, and all other Powers vested by this Constitution in the Government of the United States *or in any Department or Officer thereof.*[4]

Congress was thus the policymaker. The president was to be Congress's policy executor.

As we saw in Chapter 2, from the very beginning it was clear that Congress had the power to draft at least some of the executive departments to the task of executing Congress's policy. This was Chief Justice Marshall's point in *Marbury v. Madison* (1803): Sometimes when an executive officer acts, he is carrying out the policy of the president. Sometimes he is carrying out the policy of the law. When he is carrying out the policy of the law, then at least in principle, assuming a court with the proper jurisdiction, a court could order the executive officer to obey the law.

When the early Supreme Court considered this power, it referred to such duties as "ministerial." The clear sense of that description was that the officer has no discretion under the law. In *Marbury*, the Court gave the example of a statute that required the secretary of state to provide a copy of a patent upon the payment of a dime. That rule was clear. No one need interpret anything. If a person tendered the ten cents and the secretary of state refused, then a court would have a clear basis upon which to order the officer to obey the law.

Or likewise, when Congress ordered the postmaster to pay certain agents who had carried the mail, the Court did not hesitate to order the postmaster to obey the law.[5] As the Court explained:

> The theory of the constitution undoubtedly is, that the great powers of the government are divided into separate departments; and so far as these powers are derived from the constitution, the departments may be regarded as independent of each other. But beyond that, all are subject to regulations by law, touching the discharge of the duties required to be performed.[6]

It follows from this explanation, however, that not "every officer in every branch of that department is under the exclusive direction of the President."[7] Whether an officer is or not depends upon the nature of the duty.

> There are certain political duties imposed upon many officers in the executive department, the discharge of which is under the direction of the President. But it would be an alarming doctrine, that congress cannot impose upon any executive officer any duty they may think proper, which is not repugnant to any rights secured and protected by the constitution; and in such cases, the duty and responsibility grow out of and are subject to the control of the law, and not to the direction of the President.[8]

If you're this far into this book, you'll already recognize that clarity is a function not of (legal) nature but of (legal) culture. What might be clear to one culture is not necessarily clear to another. Or put differently, what might seem void of any discretion in one culture might seem dripping with discretion in another. And if that is true, then an assignment that could be perfectly appropriate in one culture (because appearing perfectly ministerial in that culture) might seem wholly inappropriate in another culture (because appearing inherently discretionary in that culture).

Consider an example by analogy that will illustrate the point I'm suggesting here. Imagine there's a disease that traditionally has been treated by a doctor. It's a serious disease. The doctor needs to monitor its progress constantly.

As she watches its progression, she adjusts the treatment. Because the disease affects every part of the body, her knowledge must be broad to be able to understand its progression and treat it.

Then imagine that a cure is discovered, and it requires just a few injections. The injections are to be given every twelve hours for three days. After the third day, in 99 percent of the cases, the patient will be restored to health.

Before this cure is discovered, it's obvious why the patient must be monitored by a doctor. In that context, discretion and judgment are clearly required. We require such judgment to be exercised by someone with extensive experience.

But after the cure is discovered, it's equally obvious that there's no reason to insist that the patient be treated by a doctor. A nurse could administer the injections. A nurse could easily monitor whether anything unexpected has happened. The nurse might have to exercise discretion when administering the treatment—for example, should the injections be given on an empty stomach? But that discretion is cabined within a clear set of objectives. The treatment is now simply "ministerial."

This progression could happen the other way around, of course. It could be that medicine believed it had a simple cure, but then discovers the cure does not work for a significant class of patients. Assigning the treatment to someone not fully trained in the profession would then no longer make sense. Instead, that treatment should be done by someone with real institutional experience.

I am emphasizing the contingency behind the idea of "ministerial" because, as we will see, it reveals an important and potential gap in the democratic accountability of the executive. And as I'll argue below, the doctrine that I'm tracking in this chapter on the executive can best be understood as a response to that gap in accountability. In a single line: the history of the Court's evolving jurisprudence regarding executive power can be understood as the product of an evolving understanding of this gap. That dynamic will parallel *Erie*, because the story is yet another example of an *Erie* effect.

## Removal as Democratic Accountability

In the 1980s, fiscal conservatives in America were obsessed with budget deficits. Ronald Reagan had campaigned on the importance of fiscal responsibility. Once president, however, he became less concerned about a ballooning federal deficit and more enamored of supply-side tax cuts. Reagan cut taxes dramatically, believing, or so it is said, that by cutting the marginal tax rate, he could actually increase total tax revenues. Most economists said that wasn't possible. It turned out that most economists were right. Rather than increasing federal revenue, Reagan dramatically decreased federal revenue—while radically increasing the amount that America was spending on defense. The result was the biggest budget deficit since Franklin Delano Roosevelt.[9]

Many believed this deficit was "structural," meaning that without significant changes in the structure of spending—or the structure of the institution authorizing spending—the deficit would not disappear. Some, following this insight, pushed for a constitutional amendment to force Congress to balance the budget. Others, following this insight, pushed for a change in the process by which Congress spent its money.

The constitutional amendment came to nothing. But in 1985, Congress did change the budgeting process in a pretty substantial way. Under the terms of the Gramm-Rudman-Hollings Act, Congress was given a target budget deficit in each of the following five years. If it met that target, then all was fine. If it missed it, then the statute made the comptroller of the Treasury the budget master in chief. Based upon estimates from the Congressional Budget Office and the Office of Management and Budget, the comptroller was to report to the president an amount the president must sequester. That amounts determined how much the budget would, effectively, be cut.

In the history of executive officers, the comptroller has always held a special place. When the Framers set up the first departments of the new federal government, they differentiated strongly between the executive departments that were meant to help the president carry out the president's constitutional powers, and departments that were meant to help Congress carry out Congress's constitutional duties. The statute establishing executive departments provided for a relatively simple structure: there is a head of the department, who does what the president says, while the people working for this department head do what the head says. On the other hand, the statute establishing the departments serving Congress created a structure that was wildly more articulated than anything specified for executive departments.

The Treasury was conceived of as a department serving Congress. Congress had the power to tax and appropriate. No spending could occur except through its action. And Congress had the responsibility to ensure that the nation's money was spent as they had directed. That was the comptroller's job. In the early republic, it was a crucial job, both to ensure efficiency and to give the states confidence that the people's money was being spent properly. Alone among the executive officers given the power to prosecute (that is, to bring criminal actions against individuals), the comptroller was believed, at least by some, to be free of the president's control. Someone needed to make

FIGURE 4 Great Departments Chart: Original.

|  | FOREIGN AFFAIRS | WAR | TREASURY |
|---|---|---|---|
| DENOMINATION | An act for establishing an **Executive Department**, to be denominated the Department of Foreign Affairs. | An act for establishing an **Executive Department**, to be denominated the Department of War. | An ACT to establish the Treasury **Department** |
| ESTABLISHING | Be it enacted, &c., That there shall be an **Executive Department**, to be denominated the Department of Foreign Affairs; | Be it enacted, &c., That there shall be an **Executive Department**, to be denominated the Department of War; | Be it enacted, &c., That there shall be a **Department** of Treasury, |
| HEAD OFFICER | and that there shall be a principal officer therein, to be called the Secretary for the Department of Foreign Affairs, | and that there shall be a principal officer therein, to be called the Secretary for the Department of War, | in which shall be the following officers, namely: A Secretary of the Treasury, to be deemed head of the Department, a Comptroller, an Auditor, a Treasurer, a Register, and an assistant to the Secretary of the Treasury, which assistant shall be appointed by the said Secretary. |
| HEAD OFFICER'S DUTIES | who shall perform and execute such duties as shall, from | who shall perform and execute such duties as shall, from | §2. And be it further enacted. That it shall be the duty of |

(continued)

FIGURE 4 Continued

| | FOREIGN AFFAIRS | WAR | TREASURY |
|---|---|---|---|
| | time to time, be enjoined on or entrusted to him by the President of the United States, agreeable to the Constitution, relative to correspondences, commissions, or instructions, to or with public ministers from foreign States or princes, or to memorials or other applications from foreign public Ministers, or other foreigners, or to such other matters respecting foreign affairs as the President of the United States shall assign to the said department. And furthermore, that the said principal officer shall conduct the business of the said department in such manner as the President of the United States shall, from time to time, order or instruct. | time to time, be enjoined on or entrusted to him by the President of the United States, agreeably to the Constitution, relative to military commissions, or to the land or naval forces, ships, or warlike stores of the United States, or to such other matters respecting military or naval affairs, as the President of the United States shall assign to the said department, or relative to the granting of lands to persons entitled thereto, for military services rendered to the United States, or relative to Indian affairs. And furthermore, that the said principal officer shall conduct the business of the said department in such manner as the President of the United States shall, | the Secretary of the Treasury to digestand prepare plans for the improvement and management of the revenue, and for the support of public credit; to prepare and report estimates of the public revenue and the public expenditures; to superintend to collection of the revenue; to decide on the forms of keeping and stating accounts and making returns, and to grant, under the limitations herein established, or to be hereafter provided, all warrants for moneys to be issued from the Treasury, in pursuance of appropriations by law; to execute such services relative to the sale of the lands belonging to the United States as may be by law required of him; to |

|  | FOREIGN AFFAIRS | WAR | TREASURY |
|---|---|---|---|
|  |  | from time to time, order or instruct. | make report and give information to either branch of the Legislature, in person or in writing(as he may be required) respecting all matters referred to him by the Senate or House of Representatives, or which shall appertain to his officer; and generally to perform all such services relative to the finances as he shall be directed to perform. |
| INFERIOR OFFICERS | §2. And be it further enacted, That there shall be in the said Department an inferior officer, to be appointed by the said principal officer, and to be employed therein as he shall deem proper, and to be called the chief clerk in the Department of Foreign Affairs; | §2. And be it further enacted, That there shall be in the said Department an inferior officer, to be appointed by the said principal officer, and to be employed therein as he shall deem proper, and to be called the chief clerk in the Department of War; | §3. And be it further enacted. That it shall be the duty of the Comptroller to superintend the adjustment and preservation of the public accounts; to examine all accounts .... §4. And be it further enacted. That it shall be the duty of the Treasurer to receive and keep the |

(*continued*)

FIGURE 4 Continued

| | FOREIGN AFFAIRS | WAR | TREASURY |
|---|---|---|---|
| | | | moneys of the United States, and to disperse the same upon warrants drawn by the Secretary of the Treasury.... §5. And be it further enacted. That it shall be the duty of the Auditor to receive all public accounts, .... §6. And be it further enacted. That it shall be the duty of the Register to keep all accounts of the receipts and expenditures of the public money,.... |
| REMOVAL POWER | and who, whenever the said principal officer shall be removed from office by the President of the United States, or in any other case of vacancy, shall during such vacancy, have the charge and custody of all records, books and papers appertaining to the said department. | and who, whenever the said principal officer shall be removed from office by the President of the United States, or in any other case of vacancy, shall during such vacancy, have the charge and custody of all records, books and papers appertaining to the said department. | §7. And be it further enacted. That whenever the Secretary shall be removed from office by the President of the United States, or in any other case of vacancy in the officer of Secretary, the assistant shall, during the vacancy, have the charge and custody of the records, books, and papers appertaining to the said officer. |

|  | FOREIGN AFFAIRS | WAR | TREASURY |
|---|---|---|---|
| INDEPENDENCE | §3. And be it further enacted, That the said principal officer, and every other person to be appointed or employed in the said department shall, before he enters the execution of his officer or employment, take an oath or affirmation, well and faithfully, to execute the trust committed to him. | §3. And be it further enacted, That the said principal officer, and every other person to be appointed or employed in the said department shall, before he enters the execution of his officer or employment, take an oath or affirmation, well and faithfully, to execute the trust committed to him. | §8. And be it further enacted. That no person be appointed to any officer instituted by this act, shall directly or indirectly be concerned or interested in carrying on the business of trade or commerce, .... |
| TRANSITION | §4. And be it further enacted, That the Secretary for the Department of Foreign Affairs, to be appointed in consequence of this act, shall, forthwith after his appointment, be entitled to have the custody and charge of all records, books, and papers in the officer of Secretary for the Department of Foreign Affairs, heretofore established by the United States in Congress assembled. | §4. And be it further enacted, That the Secretary for the Department of War, to be appointed in consequence of this act, shall, forthwith after his appointment, be entitled to have the custody and charge of all records, books, and papers in the officer of Secretary for the Department of War, heretofore established by the United States in Congress assembled. | |

sure no one's hand was in the till. And the only way to ensure that was to ensure that the office of the comptroller was not dependent on the people he was meant to be checking. He would be "independent"—meaning he could not be removed by the president—but the job he was meant to do independently was fairly clear and precise.[10]

Over the history of the federal executive, there have been others charged with administering federal statutes that Congress has also tried to make independent. But perhaps none of these efforts is more famous (or more pathetic) than the effort to protect the commissioners of the Federal Trade Commission (FTC).

The FTC had been established to be a kind of referee over interstate commerce. It was empowered to:

1. Prevent unfair methods of competition, and unfair or deceptive acts or practices in or affecting commerce
2. Seek monetary redress and other relief for conduct injurious to consumers
3. Prescribe trade regulation rules defining with specificity acts or practices that are unfair or deceptive, and establishing requirements designed to prevent such acts or practices
4. Conduct investigations relating to the organization, business, practices, and management of entities engaged in commerce
5. Make reports and legislative recommendations to Congress[11]

Through its commissioners, the FTC exercised an extraordinary (for its time) control over interstate trade. And to ensure the independence of the commissioners from political influence, they were appointed to fixed terms, and could not be removed except for cause.

When President Franklin Roosevelt took office, he wanted to make sure that the whole of the federal executive was answerable (or at least sympathetic) to him. So he wrote one of the existing commissioners, William E. Humphrey, and asked for his resignation. Humphrey did not want to resign. The president wrote him again. Humphrey refused again. FDR then wrote him a third time, informing him that he was "hereby removed" as a commissioner. Humphrey did not believe the president had the power to remove him. So for the last four months of his life, Humphrey showed up at the FTC building each day and sat pathetically in its front hall, insisting that he was still a commissioner and that the government still owed him his salary.

It was, apparently, a very depressing occupation. On Valentine's Day, 1934, Humphrey died, and his estate began a lawsuit to recover his lost wages.

The estate's argument in *Humphrey's Executor v. United States* was straight-forward. Humphrey had been appointed a commissioner. The president could fire him only for cause. The president had no cause to fire him. So his removal was illegal, and his estate was entitled to his wages through his death.

The president's argument was straightforward as well. The power to remove was inherent in the power to appoint. Because the president had ap-pointed Humphrey, the president had a constitutional power to remove him.

In the Supreme Court, the president lost. Humphrey, the Court observed, had been charged with a certain duty. That duty depended upon him being free of political control. According to that duty, he was to determine "unfair methods of competition in commerce." That required judgment, the Court believed, a judgment that Humphrey could make fairly and truly. There was nothing problematic in Congress giving an officer the duty to make such a judgment. To the contrary, it was an effective way to carry out Congress's own policy.

Now step back for a minute. The Court suggests that the statute required commissioners to make a judgment that a certain practice was unfair. Not unfair in a loosey-goosey sense, but unfair objectively.

What must you believe in order to believe that this claim—that some method is an "unfair method of competition in commerce"—is true? What is the view of the world—or at least legal science—that you would have to have for that claim to make sense? To believe, that is, that it makes sense to charge an officer with the duty to make such a judgment?

The answer is that you must believe that there is such a thing as an unfair method of competition, and that an agent could discover it. And if you began to doubt that such a thing was discoverable, you would in turn begin to doubt whether an agent could actually be charged with finding it. The plau-sibility of the claim that Humphrey was carrying out a ministerial duty im-posed upon him by Congress thus turned upon the plausibility of the claim that there is a thing for him to find.

So spin ahead to the Gramm-Rudman-Hollings Act, and consider again the judgment that act imposed upon the comptroller if Congress couldn't come up with a way to hit the deficit targets. The comptroller was supposed to "exercise his independent judgment and evaluation with respect to" the estimates of the amounts to be sequestered. Could he do that fairly? Or, in the terms of *Humphrey's Executor*, could he do it truthfully?

This was the question that the D.C. Circuit Court of Appeals struggled with when the act was challenged. Was it consistent with our system of gov-ernment for an officer such as the comptroller to be given this sort of power? To whom was he answerable? How was he accountable?

In its opinion (said to be written by Antonin Scalia, who was then sitting on the appeals court), the court struck down the Gramm-Rudman-Hollings Act. And it did so in part based on exactly this question. As the appeals court wrote, describing the evolution of cases examining the president's removal power:

> These cases reflect considerable shifts over the course of time, not only in the Supreme Court's resolutions of particular issues relating to the removal power, but more importantly in the constitutional premises underlying those resolutions. It is not clear, moreover, that these shifts are at an end. Justice Sutherland's decision in *Humphrey's Executor*, handed down the same day as *A. L. A. Schechter Poultry Corp. v. United States* (1935), is stamped with some of the political science preconceptions characteristic of its era and not of the present day.... It is not as obvious today as it seemed in the 1930s that there can be such things as genuinely "independent" regulatory agencies, bodies of impartial experts whose independence from the President does not entail correspondingly greater dependence upon the committees of Congress to which they are then immediately accountable; or, indeed, that the decisions of such agencies so clearly involve scientific judgment rather than political choice that it is even theoretically desirable to insulate them from the democratic process.[12]

What Scalia is remarking upon is something that should be very familiar to the readers of this book. Like the realist criticizing the "brooding omnipresence" inspired by *Swift,* here Scalia, ever the realist, is expressing skepticism about the "scientific judgments" presumed to stand behind the judgments of independent regulators. As a legal realist in the context of *Erie*, Scalia insists that the choice about the common law is always a choice about politics. As a scientific realist in the context of delegations of executive power, Scalia insists that scientific judgment is also only politics. And if it is always and only politics, then, Scalia insists, it must be a judgment that the president is responsible for. For without that ultimate presidential check, governmental power is being exercised without anyone being held democratically responsible.

Notice the pattern, because we've seen it before. It is the *Erie* effect. There is a legal practice that rests upon a conceptual foundation. Here the practice is scientific policymaking. The foundation is the belief that such policymaking is something more than simply political choice.

That foundation is then shaken. Confidence in the (political) independence of so-called scientific policymaking is shaken. And once that skepticism is recognized, then the delegation of judgment to these "independent policymakers" becomes democratically problematic. For who is this administrator to be making fundamental policy judgments for the nation? (Recall: "Who are federal judges to be deciding matters of state-law policy?")

Once that framing sticks, the Court must adjust to restore an appropriately democratically accountable structure. And it does so by striking down any statute that does not reserve to a democratically elected executive ultimate responsibility for these fundamentally political policy decisions. Or at least, on this view, it should strike down the provision that removes the ability of a democratically responsible agent to control this "independent" agent who is now no longer viewable as independent. Put differently, the Court should translate the existing regime into the new conceptual space, preserving the value of democratic accountability along the way.

The Supreme Court eventually struck down the statute that Scalia was reviewing on the Court of Appeals, though not for the reasons that Scalia offered. Yet soon after his promotion to the Supreme Court, Scalia continued to develop his translation of the executive power.

Everyone recalls the scandal of Richard Nixon. When it became clear that there was likely criminal behavior at the highest level of the administration, Nixon's attorney general, Elliot Richardson, appointed a special prosecutor, Harvard law professor Archibald Cox. Cox was charged with ferreting out evidence of criminal behavior. When he got too close, Nixon ordered his attorney general to fire the special prosecutor. Richardson refused, and Nixon fired Richardson. Richardson's deputy, William Ruckelshaus, also refused. So Nixon fired Ruckelshaus as well. Nixon then directed the acting head of the Justice Department, Solicitor General Robert Bork, to fire the special prosecutor. Bork complied, and America stood stunned at the idea that the president would have the power to fire the person trying to determine whether the president had violated the law. (No doubt, this was not the last time America would be stunned by this.)

The attorney general hired a new special prosecutor, Leon Jaworski. That prosecutor succeeded in uncovering the evidence that would eventually force Nixon to resign. America looked at the whole saga and saw one clear hero—the special prosecutor. A man (and at the time it was only ever a man) above politics, simply enforcing the rule of law.

In 1978, Congress decided to make this good idea permanent. In the Ethics in Government Act of 1978, Congress established a process whereby anytime there was "receipt of information that [the attorney general] determines is 'sufficient to constitute grounds to investigate whether any person [covered by the act] may have violated any Federal criminal law,'" a special prosecutor must be appointed.[13] The obligation to appoint the special prosecutor was first with the attorney general. If the attorney general refused, then an application could be made to a special court of judges. And once a special prosecutor was installed, he or she could not be removed except "by the personal action of the Attorney General" and then "only for good cause, physical disability, mental incapacity, or any other condition that substantially impairs the performance of such independent counsel's duties."[14]

In the early 1980s, a pretty important squabble developed between President Reagan and Congress about the enforcement of environmental policy. Congress was convinced that the president was not properly enforcing the law. The president was anxious that Congress not intrude into his domain of executive discretion. When one of his lawyers, Ted Olson, was called to testify about the administration's policy, it became clear that there was more to the story than Olson was revealing. Olson amended his testimony; Congress alleged he had lied. And a process was begun to get a special prosecutor appointed to investigate whether Olson had in fact lied, and whether he had conspired to violate federal law. Alexia Morrison (a woman, finally!) was appointed to pursue the charges.

Olson (and his co-accused) cried foul. This law, they challenged, violated the Constitution, because the decision whether or not to prosecute an individual was a highly political one, and if it was a political decision, then it had to be, ultimately, the president's decision. Congress can't shift such a critical aspect of the executive power to someone the executive did not control. The law under which Morrison was operating as special prosecutor was therefore unconstitutional, they claimed. The Court of Appeals for the D.C. Circuit agreed, and very quickly, the question of the scope of executive power under the Constitution was again before the Supreme Court, as *Morrison v. Olson* (1988).

In an opinion by Chief Justice William Rehnquist, the Supreme Court disagreed with Olson. There was no reason Congress couldn't vest the judgment about whether to prosecute in someone other than the president. This prosecutor, the Court concluded, was an "inferior officer." (That's a category in the Constitution, not a professional slight.) The Constitution permitted Congress to vest the appointment of inferior officers in people or entities other than the president. And while the appointment in this case placed this executive power outside the executive branch (since it was vested in the courts), that did not sufficiently infringe on the domain of executive power. It did a bit, Rehnquist acknowledged, but not too much. Six justices joined · the chief (Justice Kennedy did not participate in the case). That left just one in dissent—Scalia.

In what is perhaps his most famous dissent, Scalia attacked the Court's reasoning aggressively. As he wrote:

That is what this suit is about. Power. The allocation of power among Congress, the President, and the courts in such fashion as to preserve the equilibrium the Constitution sought to establish—so that "a gradual concentration of the several powers in the same department," . . . can effectively be resisted. Frequently an issue of this sort will come before the Court clad, so to speak, in sheep's clothing: the potential of the asserted principle to effect important change in the equilibrium of power is not immediately evident, and must be discerned by a careful and perceptive analysis. But this wolf comes as a wolf.[15]

Scalia's opinions were often a powerful mix of theory and practicality. The theory here was his conception of executive power—and the idea that Congress had no power to restrict the scope of the president's core executive power at all. He buttressed his theory with ample citation of history. That history, it turns out, was flawed.[16]

But it was the argument from practicality—or as he put it, the "fairness"—that was most prescient. "Only someone who has worked in the field of law enforcement," Scalia observed, "can fully appreciate the vast power and the immense discretion that are placed in the hands of a prosecutor with respect to the objects of his investigation."[17] The only check on this "immense discretion," Scalia wrote, was political. It is the "President [who] pays the cost in political damage to his administration"—either by prosecuting too aggressively or by not prosecuting enough.[18]

Yet under the Ethics in Government Act, high-ranking officials lived under a different system. The choice to prosecute or not was not exercised by the president (or his designates). It was instead exercised, in effect, by a statute. And that meant that the actual prosecution need not be constrained by political judgment. Judges decided whether to prosecute or not. And the prosecutor decided how broadly or aggressively to prosecute. As Scalia wrote (almost conjuring in his vividness the next famous special prosecutor, Ken Starr, with his words):

An independent counsel is selected, and the scope of his or her authority prescribed, by a panel of judges. What if they are politically partisan, as judges have been known to be, and select a prosecutor antagonistic to the administration, or even to the particular individual who has been selected for this special treatment? There is no remedy for that, not even a political one. . . . So, if there is anything wrong with the selection, there is effectively no one to blame.

The independent counsel thus selected proceeds to assemble a staff. As I observed earlier, in the nature of things this has to be done by finding lawyers who are willing to lay aside their current careers for an indeterminate amount of time, to take on a job that has no prospect of permanence and little prospect for promotion. One thing is certain, however: it involves investigating and perhaps prosecuting a particular individual. Can one imagine a less equitable manner of fulfilling the executive responsibility to investigate and prosecute? What would be the reaction if, in an area not covered by this statute, the Justice Department posted a public notice inviting applicants to assist in an investigation and possible prosecution of a certain prominent person? Does this not invite what Justice Jackson described as "picking the man and then searching the law books, or putting investigators to work, to pin some offense on him"? To be sure, the investigation must relate to the area of criminal offense specified by the life-tenured judges. But that has often been (and nothing prevents it from being) very broad—and should the independent counsel or his or her staff come up with something beyond that scope, nothing prevents him or her from asking the judges to expand his or her authority or, if that does not work, referring it to the Attorney General, whereupon the whole process would recommence and, if there was "reasonable basis to believe" that further investigation was warranted, that new offense would be referred to the Special Division, which would in all likelihood assign it to the same independent counsel. It seems to me not conducive to fairness. But even if it were entirely evident that unfairness was in fact the result—the judges hostile to the administration, the independent counsel an old foe of the President, the staff refugees from the recently defeated administration—*there would be no one accountable to the public to whom the blame could be assigned.*[19]

Voilà! Proof that Scalia could see the future. For it was only six years later that Ken Starr (a Republican) was appointed by three federal judges (all Republicans) to investigate Bill Clinton (a Democrat). Starr's charge was originally to investigate possible crimes related to the Whitewater Development Corporation. When he concluded that there was not sufficient evidence of a crime, he expanded his investigation to include other alleged scandals, including allegations regarding the White House Travel Office, allegations about political involvement in the FBI, and, finally and most important, allegations of perjury regarding the president's relationship with White House intern Monica Lewinsky. No one who lived through this incredible spectacle could miss the insight behind Scalia's opinion or the point he was making. Ken Starr was the nightmare that Scalia had predicted. Even Chief Justice

Rehnquist must then have recognized the monster he had unleashed—and if not at that moment, then certainly as he presided over the trial after the impeachment of President Clinton.

No one can say for sure how the Court would rule if asked to decide the issue in *Morrison* again.[20] But it is clear that the innovation would now be infinitely more difficult to defend. The Ken Starr debacle has made it impossible for anyone to miss the politics built into the appointment of a special prosecutor. Those politics have rendered the idea of delegating such authority outside of political responsibility difficult, at a minimum. Not because Scalia argued it was so, but because an event in the real world suddenly made it impossible for anyone to see it any differently.

This again is an *Erie*-effect problem. There is a practice (the practice of appointing a special prosecutor) that rests upon a conceptual foundation (the belief that the prosecutor exercises power apolitically). That foundation is shaken (here, by the earthquake called Ken Starr). And once the foundation has been shaken, the practice must shift. The change makes the Court more sensitive to the political discretion that has been vested outside of the democratic order. Just as *Erie* relocated the power to make state law by removing it from federal judges, in the post–Ken Starr era the Court might well be justified in relocating the discretion to engage prosecution more directly to be within the control of the president.

Certainly that would have been Scalia's translation. Any statute that purported to restrict the scope of control of this inherently political activity by the only democratically responsible agent—the president—must either be struck down or "interpreted" to permit that control. Seeing the gap in democratic accountability, the Scalia translation would act to restore democratic accountability.

———

So now return to the example that began this chapter, the Federal Reserve, and let's ask what Scalia should have said about the discretion that has been vested in officers of the government who themselves have been rendered independent of the president.

Notice that the answer is highly contingent upon the state of economics. If there's a clear and uncontested view about how monetary policy should work, the problem of the Fed is less pronounced. If it is relatively uncontested that policy X advances the economic interests of Americans generally, then there's not much problem in Congress delegating to the Fed the task of advancing that policy. No doubt, that task will involve steps of judgment. Any monetary policy is complicated. But those elements of discretion would be within the bounds of clear policy. That clarity, if it is uncontested, should suffice to satisfy the Court that the Fed is exercising its duty under the law.

But if policy X is not uncontested—if the claim that it advances the economic interests of Americans generally is not accepted generally, or if the policy is seen to advance the interests of some (Wall Street) while retarding the interests of others (Main Street)—then from Scalia's perspective at least, tasking the Fed with the job of implementing that policy should raise serious constitutional questions. If the comptroller can't be charged with choosing between Wall Street and Main Street, why can the governors of the Federal Reserve? Where in the Constitution does it validate a gap in democratic accountability when it is monetary policy at stake but not fiscal policy?

These considerations point in the direction of a prediction. No doubt the Court has a million ways to avoid deciding a case. And it is certainly possible that it could avoid ever deciding a case that challenged the Fed. But if it did face that challenge—in a context in which economic theory was in turmoil—then the *Erie* effect would predict that the Court would find a way to pull the governors back into the political realm. Whether that means striking down the removal rules for the Fed or reading an implied ability of the president to remove Fed governors regardless of cause is a detail. The principle is the argument: the changing understanding of the practice of government actors forces the Court to reconsider the practice.

There are two points to keep clear. First, the act of adjusting to an *Erie* effect is an act of both fidelity to meaning *and* fidelity to role. The premise of the argument is that a practice can no longer be seen as respecting a core principle of democratic accountability. That core principle is a principle of meaning. And when, in response, the Court takes action to respect that core principle, that is fidelity to meaning.

But how the Court responds must account for its role. *Erie's* response was the easiest—the Court required the judiciary to give up part of its own power. Like Marshall in *Marbury*, humility helps hide the act of construction.

If that response is not available, then the Court may have to become more activist. The simplest active response is to strike down any statute that purports to limit the removal power of the president. That would secure democratic accountability by tying the decision-maker to the president. And indeed, this is precisely what I would predict the Supreme Court would do if it took seriously charges made against the Fed.[21]

Second, these accommodations reveal something important about the importance of the present context—or more precisely, about the understandings embraced by the present context. And to make the point most sharply, let's make the point against Scalia directly.

In both *Erie* and the executive power cases, Scalia pushed a judicial response that took for granted a modern understanding of the nature of the legal foundations at issue. He relies upon the view "that we all have" in the current context. We all understand that common-law lawmaking is *lawmaking*. We are all therefore troubled when that lawmaking is vested in an actor with inferior democratic accountability.

In *Sosa*, that meant there should be no expansion of the scope of the customary international law that might be remedied under the Alien Tort Act. If there are more wrongs to be righted by that statute, that is for Congress to decide, not the Courts.

And in the case of the independent agencies and special prosecutor, that meant that the president must have removal power, regardless of what the statute now says. We can't help but see the actions of these officers as political, Scalia says, and hence we need to read the Constitution in a way that respects what we now know is true.

But is this the only context where "what we now know is true" should matter? Or matter to the originalist? More sharply, why is it that in these contexts, the originalist can ignore what the Framers believed, merely because we believe we know better, but in other contexts, we are constrained by their beliefs? What makes the nature of law meet for evolving standards, but the nature of justice not?

This is the core question that I will press in the next section. But it is important to say precisely why it is an invisible question in the context of the executive. For though I've called these "translations in the middle," "middle" isn't quite the right word. These are not translations that advance the views of those who stand between people on the Right and people on the Left. These are translations of both people on the Right and people on the Left. There is no party in America that makes cabining executive power a principle of that party. Or more precisely, the only time a party advances that idea is when the other party is in power.

So that means that the politics, or values, embedded within these cases are in the background. There's no problem embracing the conception of law grounding *Erie* because there is no perceived political choice in embracing the conception of the law grounding *Erie*. It is the nature of the world, not the political views of the judge, that seems to guide these conclusions.

The puzzle for the originalist is why that should matter.

SECTION THREE | Fidelity on the Left

A T THE START OF THIS BOOK, I described a series of translations pushed by justices we typically think of as on the Right. These translations aimed at limiting governmental power, whether federal power or state power. The beneficiaries of those limitations were states (in the sense that the limits promoted state autonomy) and businesses (in the sense that the limits disabled at least some commercial regulation). They weren't the only beneficiaries. But the thrust and character of these translations had this feature. And thus, the politics they were generally understood to embrace was the politics of the Right.

In this process, we observed a pattern. Over time, a core provision of the Constitution falls out of tune. At first, the Court accepts the dissonance, despite the dissents of some. Eventually, the dissonance grows to be too much. Eventually the dissenters capture a Court, and craft new limits on the government's power. Those new limits are said to restore a balance said to have been entrenched by the Framers.

That was translation, and often translation of a fairly aggressive sort. To preserve the meaning of an original text, the Court grafts limits on the scope of government power.

Yet over time, in each of these cases save the last, the act of translation itself eventually causes dissonance. Sometimes that dissonance was external—as with FDR's efforts to respond to the Depression resisted by the old Court. Sometimes that dissonance was internal—as the Court, after *National League of Cities*, found itself being forced to resolve scads of cases striking down federal law. Either way, the translation put pressure on the institution of the Court. Eventually the Court yielded to that pressure. That yielding, I argued, was the product of a fidelity to role.

Thus, the interaction between the fidelity to meaning and fidelity to role in Section 1 produces a conflict. Fidelity to role is a retreat on fidelity to meaning. Or put differently, fidelity to role forces the court to compromise on fidelity to meaning.

In Section 2, we considered translations with an ambiguous political valence and with a particular application of the dynamic from Section 1. This dynamic I called the *Erie* effect. There is a way of viewing the world that is the product of our understanding of science or law. That way of viewing the world is, for us at any particular time, experienced as truth. That truth is in turn a conceptual foundation for a certain practice of law.

That truth can change. And when it does, legal doctrine that rests upon the foundation it built gets rendered vulnerable. In response to that vulnerability, the Court must redraw boundaries, to preserve as much as it can, given the parts that have been rendered contested—or worse.

Here again, as in Section 1, there is a relationship between fidelity to role and fidelity to meaning. Yet this time, the relationship is complementary. The two-step harmonizes with democratic theory; it doesn't challenge it. Translation is always about carrying meaning into a different world. In these cases, those changes create a democratic accountability gap. The translations help close that accountability gap by making the institutions more responsible democratically.

Two points are important to flag before we continue.

First, translations on the Right are all examples of the Court making up limits on governmental power, in the name of fidelity to an original meaning. Them's fighting words, I understand, but we should underline them before we turn to the examples where those fighting words are actually deployed.

Second, translations in the middle show us that when the foundations crack, even the originalist does not fight emerging truth. Scalia didn't commit himself to returning to the world of *Swift*, or to the confidence of scientific policymaking. Instead, he took the world as he found it—including the truths he couldn't help but believe—and then, subject to them, he practiced his originalism.

These two considerations enable us to see differently what I'm calling the translations on the Left. They will have the same form. With each, there is a vulnerability to how the world came to be seen. With each, there is an effort to preserve an original ideal against changes that defeat that original value. As with translation on the Right, the translator comes to see that one-step originalism creates a dissonance with framing values. She thus takes a second step, crafting affirmative limits on this expanded governmental power for the purpose of restoring a framing balance. Those affirmative limits get enforced though made-up or constructed tools—elements of legal doctrine designed to effect the limit on power identified.

Yet the beneficiaries of these limits on both federal and state power are typically (there is one exception) individuals, not states or corporations. The aim with this translation is to secure individual liberty—to limit invasions of individual liberty occasioned by power that reaches beyond what was originally intended.

Again, this line between Right and Left is not perfect. Translations animated by free labor ideals, for example, protected individual rights. And translations protecting First Amendment values, originally motivated by a desire to protect individuals from speech regulations, have now become important tools limiting the power of the state to regulate corporations. The political valence I describe is simply consistent with how most describe these interpretations. My aim in this book generally is to remove the sense that translation is ideological, by showing how common it is on both sides.

| Privacy I

I N THE MOST NATURAL SENSE of the term, there is no "right to privacy" expressed in the Constitution. That is, there is no right to be free of government surveillance, or free of any government search. What rights there are are the result of an affirmative limit on the power of government—at first just the power of the federal government, but later the power of the states as well. These public actors are forbidden, the Constitution directs, to carry out "searches and seizures" that are not themselves "reasonable."

That limit comes from the Fourth Amendment. As the amendment states:

> The right of the people to be secure in their persons, houses, papers, and effects, against unreasonable searches and seizures, shall not be violated, and no Warrants shall issue, but upon probable cause, supported by Oath or affirmation, and particularly describing the place to be searched, and the persons or things to be seized.

This text bundles together two very different requirements: people's security against unreasonable searches and seizures, and a rule about warrants. To understand what these two parts were intended to do, we need to understand a bit more about the context within which they were crafted. In particular, we need to understand more about the legal context within which both parts were intended to function. Consider each in turn.

Imagine you're an officer at the time of our Founding, trying to investigate a crime. Already it's likely that there are many bits of your imagination inconsistent with the reality at the Founding—for example, the idea of a police department was alien in America till late in the nineteenth century. Nor were there "police officers" in our modern sense of the term. But for our purposes, these anachronisms are not relevant. Whoever the police were, whatever the officers were, what constrained them in the work they were to do?

Some of the constraints were legal. The most important of these was the law of trespass. If an officer entered your land without your permission, he was a trespasser. That meant he was liable for damages for the unauthorized entry upon your land—unless either (1) his search was "reasonable," (2) he found contraband on your land, or (3) he had a warrant. Whether or not the search in this context was reasonable depended upon the judgment of a jury; whether or not he found contraband depended upon whether you had contraband and whether he was good at finding it; whether or not he had a warrant depended upon whether he could convince a judge that there was "probable cause" that a crime had been committed.[1]

Searching without a warrant was thus a gamble—if the search was found to be "unreasonable" and no contraband was found, the officer conducting the search could be personally liable for damages. To avoid that potential, the officer could secure a warrant. The private incentives of the officer were thus used to increase the protections for privacy of the public.[2]

The Framers apparently liked this sensible system, because their Fourth Amendment constitutionalized it. After the Fourth Amendment was ratified, certain features of this design could not change without also changing the Constitution.

So, what was the danger the Framers were avoiding? King George III, version 2.0: a federal government that, against the background of state trespass law, passed a law that directed federal courts to issue warrants without any showing of probable cause, or without specifying precisely what was to be searched. Such a law would be inconsistent with the Fourth Amendment (since inconsistent with the rules about issuing a warrant) and thus unconstitutional. And because unconstitutional, it would not supersede state trespass law. Federal agents acting under such a law would thus face the same risks that they would face without any warrant at all—namely, they had better hope they got it right!

This law of trespass thus sat in the background of the Fourth Amendment. And standing behind it was one more assumption that the history of technology has thrown into relief: that the only effective way to search was to physically enter someone else's property. Because of that (physical) nature, and given the technology of 1790, trespass law was a meaningful legal protection for privacy. So long as entering was a necessary step to effective spying, laws against entering without permission were effective protections of privacy.

Early in the twentieth century this technical assumption changed— dramatically. As telephones moved from businesses into the home, any private activity that would have been protected by a rule against physical invasions was increasingly no longer protected, at least technically. If the government could tap a telephone wire once it left your property, the government could listen to your intimate secrets as you discussed them on your telephone. And thus, very early in the twentieth century, the question was raised whether such a trespassless invasion of privacy would violate the Fourth Amendment.

In *Olmstead v. United States* (1928), the Supreme Court held that it did not.[3] Roy Olmstead and twenty of his associates had organized one of the largest criminal syndication rings in the nation. Based in Seattle, the ring reached far beyond the Northwest. It drew into its orbit contraband produced across the West Coast and far into the heartland of the nation.

And it used the telephone to do so. Like much of commerce and social life, by the 1920s crime had moved to the wires as well. The telephone had become something unimagined by its inventor, Alexander Graham Bell. (Bell thought the idea of a machine that would ring in one's home without announcement too extreme to be accepted; he thought his invention would be used to deliver music, not telephone calls. Apple's iPhone was more the world that Bell imagined.) It had become a place where citizens lived a good part of their life. Intimate conversations, political debate, commercial transactions, and, of course, crime all happened on the phone. And telephone companies profited greatly from general and undifferentiated use.

That life depended, however, upon the users believing that their conversations were private. The telephone companies knew that. If people thought their every conversation was being listened to, they would speak less. So contracts with telephone companies explicitly promised privacy on the line. When it became known that the government was breaching this bond, the telephone companies objected vigorously to the government's use of its property to investigate crime without judicial authorization. As one phone company brief observed, "It is of the very nature of the telephone service that it shall be private. . . . The wire tapper destroys this privacy."[4]

But as crime moved to the wires, federal agents believed they needed to move to the wires as well. Investigating crime on the wires was difficult using ordinary means of police surveillance. So the agents followed the criminals and shifted their investigations to telephones. As a telephone line left the home of a suspect, an agent attached a tap to the line to enable the investigators to listen in.

This progression raised an important question: did they need a court's permission to do so? No doubt, they hadn't trespassed, at least on the property of Olmstead or his associates. But did they need a warrant nonetheless? Had they broken into the headquarters of the ring to search the files, they would have required a warrant. Had they opened up the mail traveling to and from the headquarters, they would have required a warrant. Did they need a court's permission to listen without trespassing?

In an opinion authored by Chief Justice (and former president) William Howard Taft, the Supreme Court held they did not. The Fourth Amendment was intended to limit any immunity for trespass that the government might create. But in this case, the government had not trespassed. The government had instead simply listened to conversations without the participant's knowledge or consent. Historically, the government had, at least technically, always been allowed to listen to conversations without the participant's knowledge or consent—so long as there was no trespass. There was no legal problem, for example, with an officer standing outside someone's window (on a public sidewalk, at least), and listening in. That was all, the Court held, that had happened here, even if the technology for this eavesdropping had changed. As Taft wrote for the Court:

> The amendment does not forbid what was done here. There was no searching. There was no seizure. The evidence was secured by the use of the sense of hearing and that only.... The language of the amendment cannot be extended and expanded to include telephone wires, reaching to the whole world from the defendant's house or office.[5]

One-step originalism had rendered life on the phone not private.

Taft's opinion would be the law for forty years. Yet it inspired a dissent by Justice Brandeis that will guide constitutional interpretation for many generations more. For at the core of Brandeis's dissent is an understanding of the problem at the core of this book: change. Yes, when the Fourth Amendment was written, it was written to reinforce the law of trespass. That's because trespass was the most significant way in which the privacy of individuals could be invaded. But by 1928, that technical fact had changed. And the job of the Court, as Brandeis wrote in dissent, was to interpret the Constitution in light of that change. The Court must not "place an unduly literal construction upon it."[6] Instead, just as it had "sustained the exercise of power by Congress, under various clauses of that instrument, over objects of which the fathers could not have dreamed," so too must its clauses guaranteeing liberty have a similar "capacity of adaptation to a changing world."[7] Citing the Court's earlier decision in *Weems v. United States* (1910), Brandeis wrote: "Time works changes, brings into existence new conditions and purposes. Therefore a principle, to be vital, must be capable of wider application than the mischief which gave it birth."[8]

This way of reading begins with the "mischief which gave" the right its "birth." When the Fourth Amendment was crafted, Brandeis observed, "'the form that evil had theretofore taken' had been necessarily simple." But changes in technology meant that "subtler and more far-reaching means of invading privacy have become available to the government. Discovery and invention have made it possible for the government, by means far more effective than stretching upon the rack, to obtain disclosure in court of what is whispered in the closet." Those technologies made it possible for the government to invade "the right to be left alone—the most comprehensive of rights and the right most valued by civilized men."[9] To protect that right, Brandeis argued, the amendment must be read to reach invasions even absent trespass. This was the two-step, which, had it prevailed, would have rendered the wires private.

Taft's opinion, by contrast, doesn't translate. It is instead simple one-step originalism. As with the due process clause discussed in Chapter 5 and the power of Congress described in Chapter 6, in this first stage of the life of privacy, the Court permits the effective scope of privacy to shrink. Or put differently, the Court does not initially register how changing contexts could render the original meaning of the Fourth Amendment's protection different. Justice Brandeis had argued powerfully for a different result. He had even offered translation as the guide to achieve that different result. But at the height of the war over prohibition, the Court was not about to disarm the army.

This is the first step in a pattern we've seen before: A dissenter registers a gap between the Constitution as read and the Constitution as originally meant. The Court ignores that gap. Instead, it applies a simple textualism to permit the government to go where the dissenter claims the Framers never would have permitted the government to go. The dissenter loses in the first step, though his argument, if effective, festers.

In this case, as before, the dissent does fester. Brandeis's words get repeated again and again. A generation of lawyers gets raised asking the dissenter's question. And eventually that question wins over a later Court. In *Katz v. United States* (1968), the Court again considered whether the Fourth Amendment offered any protection when the search occurred without a trespass.[10] This time, its answer was radically different.

Charles Katz had found himself on the wrong side of another war of prohibition—not against alcohol, but against gambling. Katz had used the phones to transmit gambling information to clients in many states. Federal agents bugged the payphone that he used. Katz was convicted on the basis of that evidence, and like Olmstead before, his lawyers argued that such evidence should not be permitted.

This time, the Court agreed. By a 7–2 vote, the Court rejected trespass as the only basis upon which privacy could be protected: "The reach of that

Amendment cannot turn upon the presence or absence of a physical intrusion into any given enclosure." Instead, *Katz* held that the trigger to the Fourth Amendment's protections would be whether there was an invasion of one's "reasonable expectation of privacy."

Courts would eventually define the space within which one could reasonably expect privacy. But at a minimum, *Katz* meant that space was not limited physically. It could extend to a telephone conversation—even a conversation on a payphone. And thus, if the government wanted to invade a space that possessed a "reasonable expectation of privacy," it would need a judge (with a warrant) to make it legal. "The mandate of the [Fourth] Amendment," the Court held, "requires adherence to judicial processes."

This is fidelity to meaning, effected through translation. The aim is to preserve an original meaning. It achieves that result in light of a changed factual reality. The technique is precisely the technique of the conservatives: in the name of a Founding value, the Court makes up a limit on the government's power. That limit, if properly executed, compensates for a change brought about by technology. At the Founding, the imperfections of technology had secured a certain freedom; improvements in technology were removing the freedom it once secured. By translating the original protection, the Court was using law to preserve something that technology had erased. The aspiration was to draw a line around private spaces that reflected our current understanding of privacy, in light of the current potential of technology and ownership.

Whether the law successfully protected privacy or not is a question to which we will return. But to answer it fully, we need to introduce a second line of privacy translation. This translation also affected the scope of what people call "criminal rights." Because of that, as I will argue in the next section of this chapter, this translation had the unintended effect of weakening the effective protection of *Katz*.

## Translation II: Exclusion

As anyone who has ever watched a crime show knows, the Constitution has been read to give criminal defendants a "get out of jail free" card—if, among other circumstances, the police violate the defendant's rights when gathering evidence for his trial. If the police search a criminal's home without a warrant (and without one of the million currently recognized exceptions to the warrant requirement), then the fruits of that search can be excluded from the trial, with the result that sometimes the criminal goes free.

But as every first-year law student learns, in fact there's nothing in the text of the Constitution that actually requires the exclusion of evidence obtained contrary to the Constitution. Instead, the exclusionary rule is a judge-made remedy for the violation of a judicially recognized constitutional right.

Why? Or how?

As I described earlier in this chapter, in the world the Framers occupied, there was an important technical reality: searches, ordinarily at least, required a trespass, which exposed the trespasser to legal liability. Yet that world also contained a pragmatic presupposition: specifically, that the potential of a trespass action worked. That because of the nature of courts and the availability of legal remedy, the threat of a lawsuit against agents of the government was sufficient or at least effective to protect citizens against overly invasive government officers. (Remember, of course, that those officers were few—organized police only emerge in the late nineteenth century. But even if the officers were not police, the point is the same: trespass law was a constraint.)[11]

The nineteenth century changed this presupposition too. Whether intentionally, or not, the effectiveness of the trespass remedy as a limit on police authority faded.[12] As police became more professional, the number of regulated officers increased; as the court systems became costly and congested, the ability of individuals to defend their privacy through trespass actions evaporated. Over time, the effectiveness of private trespass actions as a way to control government misconduct decreased.[13] That loss of an effective remedy to regulate public officials pushed the Court to consider alternatives.

The exclusionary rule became that alternative. First applied within federal courts only, and then in 1961 to states as well, the exclusionary rule forbids convictions on the basis of unconstitutionally acquired evidence. Though not expressed in the Constitution, the Court described the rule as implied by personal privacy. If you had one, the Court maintained, you had to have the other.

At first the Court spoke as if that implication was obvious and inevitable. The real harm, Justice Bradley for the Court observed in *Boyd v. United States* (1886), was not the physical invasion. The harm was the use in a court of what was wrongfully seized. It was the use, then, that was unconstitutional. Likewise in *Weeks v. United States* (1914): since the purpose of the Fourth Amendment was to provide security, "the duty of giving to it force and effect is obligatory upon all entrusted under our Federal system with the enforcement of the laws."[14]

But in the struggle to resolve whether the same rule applied to the states, courts began to acknowledge that any justification for an equivalent exclusionary rule applied against the state was more contingent than compelled.

The twentieth century revealed that there was no effective control of unconstitutionally behaving officers. Before the exclusionary rule was applied, prosecutors were willing to confess the violations, but they still felt entitled to introduce the unconstitutionally acquired evidence. Over time, courts became increasingly willing to acknowledge that their remedy—exclusion—was a necessary accommodation to the otherwise absent protection for the values articulated by the Constitution.

An opinion by California Supreme Court Chief Justice Roger J. Traynor's opinion in 1955 is indicative. Police had broken into the homes of the defendants and placed microphones on the property. That breach was not immunized by a warrant. Nonetheless, the prosecutor offered the evidence from that violation in the trial to convict the defendants. As Traynor remarked, without any effort to hide his frustration:

> Without fear of criminal punishment or other discipline, law enforcement officers, sworn to support the Constitution of the United States and the Constitution of California, frankly admit their deliberate, flagrant acts in violation of both Constitutions and the laws enacted thereunder. It is clearly apparent from their testimony that they casually regard such acts as nothing more than the performance of their ordinary duties for which the City employs and pays them.[15]

Then, after reviewing the common-law system, the Court concluded:

> Experience has demonstrated, however, that neither administrative, criminal nor civil remedies are effective in suppressing lawless searches and seizures. The innocent suffer with the guilty, and we cannot close our eyes to the effect the rule we adopt will have on the rights of those not before the court.[16]

These facts led the court to adopt the exclusionary rule in California, a decision later affirmed by the California legislature by statute.[17]

Once again, this was translation. There was nothing in the text of the Constitution that compelled this result. But courts crafted affirmative limits on the government's power in order to secure a certain protection against unconstitutional action. Though it is impossible to calibrate accurately or to compare, by the twentieth century courts increasingly recognized that the Constitution, in the context of institutionalized policing, was providing much less protection than intended. The judicial response was to craft a tool to restore an original balance. The exclusionary rule was that tool.

Of course, an exclusionary rule is not the only possible response to the failure of trespass or tort law to protect privacy. Conceptually at least, the

Court had two clear alternatives. It could have tried to redefine the law of trespass, so as to ensure that it gave the citizens the protection that was required. Or the Court could have simply excluded the fruit of an illegal search from any criminal prosecution.

The first remedy may have been more faithful to the Framers' substantive scheme. They wanted to protect the guilty, or the likely-enough-to-be-guilty-to-be-prosecuted, but they were perhaps even keener to protect the innocent, who would be harassed by government officials even if the government officials didn't subsequently prosecute them. So, finding a way to revive trespass law so as to protect the underlying interest in privacy more efficiently could have more directly translated the framing ideals into the modern context.

Yet that level of judicial activism—effectively crafting a uniform state law of trespass—obviously conflicted with a narrower conception of fidelity to role. The Supreme Court was not about to get into the business of legislating trespass rules, or overlaying trespass rules with a set of Fourth Amendment requirements (as it did, for example, with defamation actions against state officials).[18] Given the diversity of laws in a wide range of jurisdictions, that was the work of a law reform committee, not of the Supreme Court.

So instead, the Court opted for a remedy that could be more easily implemented: exclusion. The states could protect trespass however they wanted, but the Court would not entertain any evidence that was obtained in violation of the Constitution. Even if a murder was involved, the Court argued, it was better that the criminal go free—though it would be the law that set him free:

> Nothing can destroy a government more quickly than its failure to observe its own laws, or worse, its disregard of the charter of its own existence. As Mr. Justice Brandeis, dissenting, said in *Olmstead v. United States*, "Our Government is the potent, the omnipresent teacher. For good or for ill, it teaches the whole people by its example.... If the Government becomes a lawbreaker, it breeds contempt for law; it invites every man to become a law unto himself; it invites anarchy."[19]

## Privacy Plus Exclusion

Both of these innovations—liberating the scope of privacy protections from trespass law and complementing the remedy for privacy violations with an exclusionary rule—can be understood as acts of translation. Both preserve a framing value, by crafting limits on the scope of the government's power. Neither limit is expressed in the text of the Constitution itself. But both aim at preserving an original meaning of the Constitution within a radically different context.

Yet in the interaction between these two innovations, we can see a critical, if unintended, effect: even if the indirect beneficiary of this system was to be all of us, the direct beneficiary is the (presumptive) criminal. Every time the Court announces that a new space falls within the "reasonable expectation of privacy," it delivers to the criminal defense bar a new tool to secure a client's freedom. The static effect, at least, is to increase the cost of criminal law enforcement. And the dynamic effect of that, as Judge Richard A. Posner and others have argued, may well be to radically increase the penalty for those actually convicted.[20]

Yet regardless of its effect on the criminal, this dynamic can be costly for the protection of privacy for all of us. Because as the effect of the exclusionary rule becomes contested—as the commitment of Holmes that it is "less evil that some criminals should escape than that the government should play an ignoble part" weakens—the judicial cost of recognizing these domains of privacy goes up.[21] The system tethers *our* privacy to the willingness of judges to let *them*— the guilty—go free. No doubt, if every judge were a former staff attorney at the ACLU, that might not be a terrible thing. But obviously that is not the case. The architecture of the system thus sabotages a system of privacy protection. For systematically, over time, most ordinary judges would stretch to ensure that the guilty go to jail, the Fourth Amendment notwithstanding.

The history of the Supreme Court's Fourth Amendment jurisprudence is consistent with this prediction. In *Katz*, the Supreme Court could brag "that searches conducted outside the judicial process, without prior approval by judge or magistrate, are *per se* unreasonable under the Fourth Amendment— subject only to a few specifically established and well-delineated exceptions."[22] Yet since that time, the few have become the many. As legal scholar Yale Kamisar has written, "*Mapp* and its progeny have brought about a great clarification and simplification of the law of search and seizure—almost always *in favor* of the police."[23] The "tendency," as Thomas McInnis writes, summarizing the work of others, has been "for the Court to rewrite the Bill of Rights and lessen its protections for criminal defendants."[24]

This forever shrinking scope for privacy's protection is the natural consequence of asking government officials to define the scope of privacy: over time, privacy shrinks. And this dynamic highlights the one clear mistranslation of the Framers' design built into the *Katz/Mapp* system for protecting privacy: the erasure of the jury. The original privacy right, protected through trespass actions, was enforced by a jury. The jury, in turn, was meant to reflect attitudes of the people. Those attitudes might become more or less sensitive to the importance of privacy. But they are not systematically biased.

Government officials, by contrast, are. And by constitutionalizing the protection of privacy—by removing its scope from the jurisdiction of juries, deciding on the basis of what's "reasonable," and vesting its scope in the judgment of courts—this particular translation of the Fourth Amendment was destined to shrink the scope of the amendment's protection. When the only context in which the scope of privacy gets raised is the trial of a drug dealer, a murderer, or a rapist, it should be no surprise that the scope would shrink.

This failure parallels the failure I identified with translation and federalism. In that context, the source of failure was the institutional capacity of the courts to craft lines that could cabin federal authority without seeming arbitrary or political. In this context, the source of the failure is the institutional capacity of the courts to systematically "do the right thing" (protect civil rights) when the consequence of not is that vicious criminals go free. I admire, but in some way can't begin to understand, a judge who upholds the Fourth Amendment but lets a known child rapist go free. I would be surprised to discover that most judges would do the same thing—at least if the question was close.

This parallel failure invites a parallel response: Are there better, more usable translations of privacy for the Court to use? Could we imagine a different system that didn't systematically bend the Constitution against privacy?

Here, I suggest, could be the most important consequence of recognizing our tradition as a tradition of translation: we might just relax a bit when we recognize these shifts in doctrine. Because by viewing these shifts—such as *Katz* reaching beyond trespass or *Mapp* extending the exclusionary rule to the states—as efforts at fidelity, we can acknowledge the inevitable limits that a court will face over time. What works at one moment won't work at another. (Steiner: "Each age translates anew.")[25] And what a court needs when it recognizes failure is the freedom to try again: "Our aim is to preserve X. We have tried techniques A and B; they've proven too costly. We'll now try C."

This kind of transparency is difficult for a court. At least in a context that is not open to the dynamic of translation, it is hard to explain change, and even harder to justify it.

That truth, however, should guide the Court as it contemplates strategies for effecting better translations. In particular, it should guide courts to consider empowering other, less constrained institutions to bring about the translation that might be too costly for a court.

This point is clearest in the context of privacy law. As I described, the exclusionary rule was a second-best solution to the problem of increasingly ineffective trespass law. It was a remedy the Court could apply, but it is imperfect.

Yet the Court could acknowledge its imperfection and invite states to offer something better. And if the states offered the Court something better than an exclusionary rule, then the Court could accept it as a way to protect the constitutional interest without tying that interest to the least desirable advocates.

Imagine, for example, a state created a procedure that considered the question of whether a search violated a right to privacy without revealing to the fact-finder whether contraband was found. Imagine this proceeding was cheap and quick, and attorney's fees were paid to victorious claimants. And imagine finally that the only remedy for a Fourth Amendment violation was this civil remedy. Innocent people could easily vindicate the violation of their rights, and guilty people could be compensated for the violation of their rights (even if they could only use that compensation to buy cigarettes in prison).

Others would certainly argue about whether such a remedy is adequately respectful of the importance of the Fourth Amendment protection. But that's not the question that I would focus upon. The question I would ask is whether this alternative is better able in the long term to avoid the fidelity to role costs that the current system suffers. Again, we could imagine judges as Hercules. Or we could imagine judges as ordinary sorts really keen to keep cop-killers off the streets. I wouldn't call the latter sort of judge a bad person. Let's call him or her an ordinary person. My point is that we should craft constitutional doctrine in light of the ordinary person and select tools that can be used by such a person.

Unfortunately, of course, states have not experimented in this way. But the reason, I suggest, is that the Court has discouraged such experiments. Because the Court has allowed itself to view its interpretations as expressions of what the Constitution requires—as opposed to accommodations to changing circumstances—it has closed off the opportunity for other, more capable institutions to craft better alternatives.

The clearest example of this refusal is in the context of the *Miranda* rule. Again, as everyone who has ever watched any police show knows, the Constitution has been interpreted to "require," it is said, a warning whenever the police arrest an individual. As Chief Justice Warren articulated that warning:

> If a person in custody is to be subjected to interrogation, he must first be informed in clear and unequivocal terms that he has the right to remain silent.... The warning of the right to remain silent must be accompanied by the explanation that anything said can and will be used against the individual in court.... Accordingly, we hold that an individual held for interrogation must be clearly informed that he has the right to consult with a lawyer and to have the lawyer with him during interrogation.... In order fully to apprise a person interrogated

of the extent of his rights under this system then, it is necessary to warn him not only that he has the right to consult with an attorney, but also that if he is indigent a lawyer will be appointed to represent him.[26]

But the Court in *Miranda* was as explicit about its method as the Court ever gets. This was a remedy intended to translate the protections of an older era. As the Court explained:

Our holding is not an innovation in our jurisprudence, but is an application of principles long recognized and applied in other settings.[27]

Then, quoting *Weems,* the Court continued:

Rights declared in words might be lost in reality. And this has been recognized. The meaning and vitality of the Constitution have developed against narrow and restrictive construction.[28]

The particular development that mattered here was the rise of the professional police force. Professional police advanced a practice of professional interrogation. But that interrogation happened far from the courts. Its essence was isolated and prolonged, with no neutral or adversarial component permitted at all. This created a radically different circumstance from the ordinary way in which criminal prosecution had happened initially and throughout much of American history. This difference in circumstance mandated a different scope for the protections against self-incrimination.

Almost immediately after specifying these warnings, however, the Court signaled they may be temporary. The Court wasn't saying that hidden in the Bill of Rights it had found this required warning. It was saying that in light of the changes in context, this warning would restore an essential framing protection. Yet there was no reason to believe that this was the only way to effect a restoration. There were a host of ways for the police to provide the kind of protection the *Miranda* warnings intended, without the warnings themselves. All the Court was saying was that it was crafting one and inviting legislatures to do better. As Chief Justice Warren wrote:

It is impossible for us to foresee the potential alternatives for protecting the privilege which might be devised by Congress or the States in the exercise of their creative rule-making capacities. Therefore we cannot say that the Constitution necessarily requires adherence to any particular solution for the inherent compulsions of the interrogation process as it is presently conducted. Our decision in no way creates a constitutional straitjacket which will handicap sound efforts at reform, nor is it intended to have this effect. We encourage Congress and the States to continue their laudable search for increasingly effective ways of protecting the rights of the individual while promoting efficient enforcement of our criminal laws. However, unless we are shown other procedures which are at least as effective in apprising accused persons of their right of silence and in assuring a continuous opportunity to exercise it, the following safeguards must be observed.[29]

This was a clear invitation to the states to innovate. So imagine, for example, that a state accepted this invitation and enacted a rule that forbade any confession that was not recorded on videotape and forbade any interrogation to continue beyond some maximum time (grounded in solid psychological research). That rule too would nicely restore an original protection of having a magistrate present during questioning. And it would seem—consistent both with the understanding that *Miranda* was a translation, and with the language of the Court in *Miranda*—that the Court should encourage just such a response by the states, and retreat from the constitutional rule where it judges that response in good faith.[30]

Yet the Court has refused this invitation so far, primarily because states have failed to accept. As criminal justice researcher Paul Cassel wrote:

> *Miranda* itself seemed to invite exploration of alternatives, explaining that "[o]ur decision in no way creates a constitutional straitjacket which will handicap sound efforts at reform." The Court's invitation, however, was in reality empty because it did not specify what alternatives would be deemed acceptable. In the quarter-century since *Miranda*, reform efforts have been virtually nonexistent.[31]

It may be that the refusal makes sense in a particular case. It may be that a particular alternative was not as protective of the original right. But it is a mistake, I believe, for the Court to so completely discourage the search for better translations of the Framers' values by institutions with more robust structural capacity. From the perspective of fidelity to meaning, it is difficult for the Court to craft new institutions or structural innovations not found within the Constitution. And from the perspective of fidelity to role, it would be far better for the Court to retreat from apparently arbitrary and made-up limits on government's power, at least where the legislature has done the important work of translation itself.

———

Thus, our first example of translation on the Left. To preserve an original value of privacy, the Court has crafted affirmative limits on the government's power. One set of limits extends the scope of privacy beyond physical space alone.

Another set of limits restricts the use of illegally obtained evidence within a criminal trial.

These are translations. Yet, as with translation on the Right, these translations on the Left get resisted, too, and this time through death by a thousand cuts. In case after case, the abstract value of privacy gets weighed against the real value of security. Not surprisingly, over time, privacy loses.

It need not. It would be perfectly possible for the Court to encourage legal innovation here. No doubt, the judgment of the Court in response to such innovation might seem arbitrary; and no doubt, to be effective, the Court should be strict in ensuring that the state-grounded alternative is better than the Court's. But once we have identified the value that we believe the Constitution must protect, we should be pragmatic about the institution best able to design that protection. In my view, that institution is not the Court. And if we don't free the Court from that obligation, then the scope of privacy protected by the Fourth Amendment will continue to shrink.

## CHAPTER SIXTEEN

Equality I

I T WAS MIDDAY ON EASTER SUNDAY, April 13, 1873, when the catastrophe became unstoppable. About 150 citizens, all but a few of them African American men, had been holed up inside the courthouse in Colfax, Louisiana. About an equal number of African American women and children were surrounding the courthouse, in what must have looked like a refugee camp. Marching toward them were a paramilitary force of at least 140 men who were committed to winning a fight for "white supremacy."[1] The African Americans were Republicans. They claimed the right, by virtue of a recent but contested election, to the government of Colfax. The whites soldiers—the terrorists—were Democrats, and they too claimed the right to the government of Colfax. Both sides were armed. The whites had more guns than the blacks.

The leader of the whites, Christopher Columbus Nash, ordered the blacks to leave the courthouse. When they refused, he gave the women and children around the building thirty minutes to evacuate. At noon, the white forces started firing. Though the courthouse was poorly defended, the battle remained at a standstill for at least two hours. Then the whites pulled a cannon to the side and behind the building, giving them a direct shot at blacks who had been firing from the trenches dug in front of the building. Some of the defenders panicked and fled. Nash ordered them pursued. And then, by threatening his life, Nash secured the aid of an African American, Pinckney Chambers. Handing Chambers a lit torch, he ordered the man to cross the 100 yards that separated the terrorists from the courthouse. Amazingly, Chambers succeeded unharmed, and then proceeded to ignite the cedar eaves of the courthouse. The fire spread quickly, and the souls inside realized they had to get out. The leaders jury-rigged a flag of truce, held it out the door, and asked permission to leave. They were promised safe passage if they left immediately. The blacks complied with their promise. The whites did not. As the defenders left the building, the terrorists shot them. Between those shot running away and those killed in the fire, some estimate that as many as 280 black Americans died that day in Colfax, Louisiana.[2] Charles Lane believes the best estimate is between 62 and 81.[3] Two whites were killed.

It was the largest massacre in the period of Reconstruction. It was not the only one, though. A line could be drawn from Colfax through much of the rebel South, connecting hundreds of acts of violence, killing thousands of black Americans, all with the purpose of reestablishing the hierarchy of power that had existed in the South before the Civil War. Eight years after the Thirteenth Amendment had been ratified, five years after the Fourteenth, and three years after the Fifteenth, thus was white dominance across the South expressed.

On the very next day after the Colfax massacre, April 14, 1873, the Supreme Court of the United States announced a decision in a case that modern readers believe marks the beginning of the end for the judicial defense of African American rights under the still newly enacted Fourteenth Amendment to the Constitution. As the story goes, while the *Slaughterhouse Cases* (1873) did not directly involve the rights of African Americans, the decision demonstrated that the Court was eager to narrow the reach of the newly enacted Civil War amendments. That eagerness continued through a series of cases, each more restrictive than the last. In the end, according to this view, despite a few exceptions, the history of the Court in the nineteenth century is the history of weakness and cowardice. It is a story not of fidelity but of infidelity, with the tragic consequence being the freedom of five generations of black Americans lost, and the lives of literally tens of thousands ended in violence or poverty.

The history of the Civil War Amendments (Thirteenth, Fourteenth, and Fifteenth) includes the hardest bits of the history of the Constitution for modern readers to understand. To us, the amendments scream with hopefulness. And yet little in the first ninety years of the life of those amendments was in any sense hopeful. Yes, slavery ended. But so much of the Thirteenth Amendment's potential for erasing the "badges and incidents of slavery" was never realized. The Fourteenth Amendment has become the central tool forcing equality within our legal and political society. But for generations, the amendment stood mute, like the pathetic Corporal Upham in *Saving Private Ryan*, doing nothing as murder surrounded him. And while the Fifteenth Amendment did formally end the exclusion of black men from the right to vote, so effectively did southern governments eventually bar blacks from

voting—through poll taxes, literacy tests, the white primary, and the like—
that when the Court was finally asked to enforce the amendment against the
state of Alabama, Justice Holmes practically laughed.[4] There was promise in
these constitutional texts. That promise was lost. And to most modern lawyers, it is the "cowards" or the "racists" on the Supreme Court who bear the
responsibility for that loss.[5]

The Civil War Amendments in general, and the Fourteenth Amendment
in particular, are the richest parts of our Constitution for illuminating the
contours of fidelity theory. Yet the pattern for these bits of constitutional text
is, in effect, the inverse of the pattern described in Section 1. Rather than
translation pushed back by the constraints of role, here the role constraints
came first, and translation happens later. The real story, in other words, of the
first years after these fundamental amendments to the Constitution of 1787
is of a court striving to synthesize two constitutional moments, while deeply
sensitive to its own tenuous ability to push a nation where it clearly and
plainly and obviously did not want to go.

That's not to say that the Court was filled with Radical Republicans (that
is, pro-egalitarians) in robes, forced to hold back despite their strong desire to
remake American culture, especially the culture of the South. The Radical
Republicans were in Congress. The judges were judges. They were not going
to push. But in our hasty condemnation of their actual work, we miss how
much they did to make equality possible—if, that is, the political branches had
only been willing to pull their own weight too. It was politics first that failed
African Americans in the post–Civil War period. And it is amazing to me that
anyone would imagine that in such a context, the judges could do any better.

Yet from our perspective, this political tenuousness is the part we're most
likely to miss, just as we miss the uncertainty that Marshall faced in *Marbury*.
The judges on the Supreme Court did not believe that they had the power to
remake society on their own but simply chose not to use it. Instead, the
judges were constantly sensitive to how much they could do. Indeed, the rich
history of this period reveals many points at which the judges bend to make
the future possible, even while allowing white terrorists to push that future
further and further back.

## Constitutional Texts

The bloodiest war in American history yielded three extraordinary amendments to the Constitution. (Not easily and not without significant question,
as Bruce Ackerman has reminded us. I will address that history in Chapter 21.)

The first resolved the issue the Civil War had come to stand for: slavery. The second has been the most generative text in the Constitution, securing for citizens "privileges or immunities" against state "abridgment," as well as "equal protection of the laws" and "due process." The third removed race as a reason to deny the vote to any male citizen. Few doubted the first of these three would be the consequence of the Civil War. It was enacted the same year the war ended. Few believed the third would ever be enacted. The commitment of President Grant made it happened five years later. And an emboldened and committed Congress essentially forced southern states to embrace the amendment between these two as a condition for readmittance to the Union.

These three amendments together did something that no earlier part of our Constitution had tried to do: they tried to change us. These were the first transformative amendments in our constitutional tradition. Every other part of our Constitution purported to constitutionalize existing practice or ideas. These amendments sought to change existing practice or ideas. Certainly, more than their framers ever understood, these amendments were meant to reach deep into American society and move it. Both in the South and the North, to give these amendments their full force would be to give America a new beginning.

Though the Fourteenth Amendment is chock-full of interesting post–Civil War cleanup, the overriding value at the core of each amendment was equality. The Thirteenth and Fifteenth Amendments expressly identify those who were to benefit from that new equality—black Americans (all slaves for the Thirteenth Amendment, black males for the Fifteenth). The first version of the Fourteenth Amendment also expressly limited its protection to blacks.[6] But after extensive debate among the Radical Republicans, the Fourteenth Amendment was extended beyond protection on the basis of "race, color, or previous condition of servitude." Instead, its target became class legislation generally, whether that legislation harmed blacks or any other group of Americans.

As we'll see, this expansion is critical in the history of the amendment. Yet equally critical is the way in which it was not, in principle, a change to American law. The principle of equality and due process had long been a part of the American tradition. But it was an equality principle that was not applied equally. The addition crafted by the Fourteenth Amendment was a guarantee against the failure of the state to live up to these principles. If the state failed to secure equality, the federal government could step in.

Yet in expanding the reach beyond a specific group, the amendment opened up a host of unresolved questions. The aim of the Fourteenth Amendment was clearly to target class legislation. But what would it take for legislation to be seen as affecting a class? Every law distinguishes among some relative to others. Yet certainly not every law is class legislation in the sense the framers of the Fourteenth Amendment meant it.

Working out how or how far that protection would reach is the core interpretive struggle of the Fourteenth Amendment. We will track that struggle in the balance of this section. But it is important to flag up-front what exactly we are tracking—or translating for—as the Court applies this equality principle across time.

In a sense that will become clearer over the course of this section, we should understand that at the core of this judgment about equality is a judgment about social meaning. Not every logically equivalent distinction will be seen to trigger an equivalent concern about equality. That's because equality claims are not the product of logic. They are the product of social understanding, or social meaning. Those understandings change. As we'll see, the Court translates the equality clause to track those changes. That translation applies the amendment differently across time. Those differences in context preserve meaning across time.

Yet the striking fact about the Civil War Amendments is that they are all but invisible (at least to African Americans) for almost the first century of their existence. How did the Court allow that to happen? This is the critical fact to explain. The dominant explanations rest upon infidelity; the explanation I mean to offer here is consistent with fidelity.

## The Conventional Account

On the conventional account of the Reconstruction Court, the justices worked hard to undo the revolutionary changes made by the post–Civil War Republican Congress. In the very first opportunity he was given, Justice Samuel Freeman Miller slaughtered the privileges-or-immunities clause of the Fourteenth Amendment, thereby radically restricting the rights anyone could claim federal protection for. On the view of many scholars, this was not just an accident. As Richard Aynes summarizes the view of many scholars, "Miller deliberately attempted to defeat the force of the amendment."[7] Then, in a demonstration of extraordinary activism, Justice Joseph Bradley inserted himself into the trial of the white terrorists of Colfax, and when he disagreed with an incredibly decent and committed district court judge, he wrote an opinion to stop the prosecution. The other members of the Supreme Court agreed with their brother, and with extraordinary obtuseness they invalidated the indictments against these terrorists, letting them go free. So for the worst massacre of the Reconstruction era, there were no successful criminal prosecutions. Bradley is then said to have participated in one of the most outrageous corruptions of American political history, when in exchange for the withdrawal of federal troops from the South, the Democrats permitted Rutherford Hayes, the Republican candidate, to become president, even though he had lost the popular vote to the Democratic candidate, Samuel Tilden. Seven years later, Bradley confirmed his sin in one of the Supreme Court's most obtusely written opinions about race, the *Civil Rights Cases* (1883). Striking down the last Civil Rights Act the United States Congress would pass until 1957, Bradley signaled that he—and the Court—had had enough.

> When a man has emerged from slavery, and by the aid of beneficent legislation has shaken off the inseparable concomitants of that state, there must be some stage in the progress of his elevation when he takes the rank of a mere citizen, and ceases to be the special favorite of the laws, and when his rights as a citizen, or a man, are to be protected in the ordinary modes by which other men's rights are protected.[8]

A dozen years later, the Supreme Court would affirmatively uphold racial segregation in public accommodations as mandated by law.[9]

This account is familiar. It is also just wrong. That's not to say that the opposite is true—the history of the Reconstruction Court is not the story of bold and brave justices sacrificing every ounce of judicial power to defend the former slaves. But the conventional account moves too quickly, crudely, and at places, stupidly. In these sins, it obscures a dynamic that will be familiar once we slow the story down. For we have seen this dynamic before.

To help with that recognition, let us recall the account I have offered of the New Deal Court. In that case, I argued, the conservatives had a conception of fidelity that eventually had to yield. Fidelity to meaning yielded to fidelity to role. The conservative's conception was that federal power must be limited to protect the regulatory jurisdiction of the state. That was the meaning to which the old Court was committed. At a critical point, I argued, fidelity to meaning had to surrender because of a fidelity to role. To continue to craft limits on the scope of the federal government's power would be seen as political—the act of conservative Republicans, not justices of the Supreme Court—and it could not continue to be seen as judicial since, as Justice Jackson argued, there was no line in law to be drawn. The Court did not face extinction—as other courts in other jurisdictions have when confronting a strong popular will (South Africa, when challenging the National Party in the 1950s; Russia's Constitutional Court in 1993, when challenging Yeltsin).

It is a measure of the strength of our traditions that FDR's court-packing plan was so effectively resisted, even at the zenith of his political power. Yet even though the justices did not fear for their Court, they did fear for the jurisprudence. The Court thus retreated from the defense of federalism, waiting to try again.

On this view, the Constitution was not amended in 1936—as, for example, Bruce Ackerman's account asserts—but instead the Framers' view was held hostage.[10] And while we could argue about whether and how much the Framers would have resisted the federal power that has emerged, my argument from fidelity insisted that the Court's acceptance of the relatively unlimited power of Congress expressed not a new reading of the Constitution but a fresh understanding of its own limited role. Even Justice Jackson saw that Congress had gone too far. But even Jackson saw there were limits to what the Court should do in response.

This story reversed is the interpretive story of the Civil War Amendments. Or at least, that is the burden of the argument in the balance of this chapter. My claim is that we should understand the post–Civil War Court as yielding to a political reality no doubt more extreme than the reality of post–New Deal America, but similar in character. Just as with the New Deal, the America that the post–Civil War judges confronted was not going to yield to strong holdings of interpretive fidelity. Just as with the New Deal, in the Reconstruction era an argument of fidelity would have to wait until it could again return. The incredible reversals from the mid-1870s on do not, as Michael McConnell suggests (applying Ackerman's theory of constitutional moments), effectively constitute an amendment to the Constitution that negated the Civil War Amendments. Rather, the reversals were a Court operating under *force majeure*, preserving the structure of a constitutional claim at least until the time when it could be effectively asserted again.

We miss this account today for both political and historical reasons. It is hard politically for students of the Constitution to see the post–New Deal Court as similar to the post–Civil War Court. That's because most of us agree with much of the post–New Deal Court and disagree with practically everything of the post–Civil War Court. And it is hard historically because we don't yet have a fair and complete account of the extraordinary story of the end of Reconstruction and the rise of the "redeemers," the white southerners who waged war against equality with violence. The pathetic weakness of federal law enforcement at the time is almost impossible for us even to conceive. Moreover, the effectiveness of the campaign to discredit the Reconstruction governments of the South was truly extraordinary. Somehow, a campaign of white terrorism in America got framed as the story of virtue overcoming corruption. How that happened is a story far beyond the reach of this book. My only aim here is to retell the history enough to see the parallel to the post–New Deal court.

I doubt that federalism as the conservatives push it will ever have its *Brown v. Board* moment. As a nationalist, I hope it doesn't. But that fact should not blind us to the parallels that exist between these two moments of extraordinary constitutional resistance. They are the same in kind, however difficult that is for us to accept.

# Background

One clue that the conventional account is incomplete is the biographies of the justices themselves. All but one within this period had been appointed by Lincoln, Grant, or Hayes. These were Republicans, with Grant committed to the cause of equality even more clearly than Lincoln. No doubt, these justices were Union men first. Yet every one of them was appointed with a clear understanding that their job was to deliver on a promise that the Union had made to the African Americans that the war had freed.

They launched on this project carrying assumptions that most serious people took for granted at the time. Some of these assumptions were jurisprudential—touching upon the nature of law. Some were constitutional—about the scope of the change in federalism that the Civil War Amendments were meant to effect. And some were political—about the consequences of active enforcement by the courts of judicially mandated equality. These assumptions constrained the Supreme Court. And if we're to understand that constraint, we need to understand these assumptions more fully.

## ASSUMPTION I: ON THE NATURE OF "RIGHTS"

The first assumption will be familiar after the discussion of *Erie v. Tompkins* (1938) and its protagonist, *Swift v. Tyson* (1842). This is an assumption about the nature of rights. For the justices of the Supreme Court, and especially the most intellectually prominent justices on the Court, most rights were natural. They existed before governments, and they existed whether or not a government recognized or protected them. That's not to say that a government couldn't create a new or different right. As the Court would hold, for example, the Fifteenth Amendment had created a new right—the right to vote without being discriminated against on the basis of race, a right never known to American society before. But all the rights that anyone cared about, at least before the Civil War, were the rights that God had given man. Governments could respect what nature had given us by protecting those rights through legal process. But regardless of whether governments protected them, none could deny that they existed.

The evidence for this truth has been powerfully and extensively reviewed by others.[11] We see an echo in the text of the Ninth Amendment to the Constitution: "The enumeration in the Constitution of certain rights shall not be construed to deny or disparage others retained by the people." My aim here is not to establish or to defend this naturalism. It is simply to introduce it, so that a big slice of what the Reconstruction Courts did will begin to make sense. On their view, rights were natural. On their view, the primary defender of these natural rights had to be the states. But on their view, if the Constitution itself created a right beyond those given by nature, Congress had extraordinarily broad power to protect and enforce such created rights.

One particularly important example of a right created by the (pre–Civil War) Constitution was the right of rendition. Article IV, Section 2 of the Constitution provides as follows:

> A Person charged in any State with Treason, Felony, or other Crime, who shall flee from Justice, and be found in another State, shall on Demand of the executive Authority of the State from which he fled, be delivered up, to be removed to the State having Jurisdiction of the Crime.

This clause, of course, is general. But it was an essential part of the Constitution's design because it enabled southerners to secure the return of fleeing slaves. Congress gave effect to this clause with the Fugitive Slave Act of 1850. That act—aggressively and with powerful effect—gave southerners the ability to recover runaway slaves.

Congress's power to enact the Fugitive Slave Law was challenged. But its validity followed directly from this naturalist division in the nature of rights. Before Article IV, Section 2, no slave owner would have had any right to recover a fleeing slave. Indeed, the law in most northern jurisdictions would have recognized a slave escaping to that jurisdiction as free. No one has a natural right to demand the recovery of someone who is free. So, before the Constitution, no such right to recover a freeing slave could have been asserted.

The Constitution thus created the right to recover people illegally escaping slave territory, even if state law recognized him as free. And therefore, exercising the power of the necessary-and-proper clause, Congress secured this newly created right through the Fugitive Slave Act. We recoil—and rightly so—at the injustice of that act, premised upon the still not fully recognized (and I mean not fully recognized by us) injustice of slavery. But whether just or not, what the Fugitive Slave Act did was demonstrate just how powerful the federal government's power to protect rights could be—at least if those rights were created by the federal Constitution.

This distinction was critical to the justices interpreting the Civil War Amendments. In their view, those amendments *both* created *and* recognized fundamental rights. Following this view, when the amendments created a right, Congress had enormous power. But when they simply recognized rights created elsewhere and forbade the states to abridge those rights, then Congress's power was derivative only. Congress could provide a remedy when the state violated the right. But unless the state violated the right (or, possibly, failed adequately to protect the right), the federal government had no power with respect to that right.

That is the first assumption we must keep clear to understand the post–Civil War justices. The second assumption is about the nature of the Civil War Amendments themselves.

## ASSUMPTION 2: ON THE NATURE OF THE AMENDMENTS

There are three ways to understand the Civil War Amendments, at least in principle. First, one could view them as repealing the federalism that preceded the Civil War. Second, one could see them as just modifying that federalism, in important but limited ways. Or third, one could view the amendments as aspirational only, changing nothing in the actual balance of power between the federal and state governments, but speaking nonetheless to the ideals the new republic was committed to. There were lawyers and politicians who subscribed to each of these readings. The third was the rarest, though certainly it was an argument made by lawyers resisting federal legislation affecting the South. The first was not uncommon, but again, it was a distinctly minority view.

By far the most common view among lawyers and politicians attentive to the law was that while the war had remade federalism, it had not abolished it. That meant the justices had to synthesize the federalism of the first republic, with the amendments brought about after its Civil War. They had, in other words, to find a way to give meaning to both bits of constitutional meaning, but without denying the truth of either.

This is thus an act of interpretive *synthesis*. Its aim is to read two sources together and fix upon a final reading that makes sense of both. Not every constitutional change requires an act of synthesis. For example, the Twenty-First Amendment simply repealed the Eighteenth Amendment. There is no continuing Eighteenth Amendment jurisprudence, and no need to conform the Constitution to the values inhering in that earlier amendment. But when an amendment, or a series of amendments, is understood as modifying rather than repealing what went before, the aim of the interpreter must be to have both parts make sense together. The result must synthesize the different traditions.

And that, in my view, is what the post–Civil War justices believed they were doing. It wasn't a revolution they were reading, it was a reform. Fundamental and critical, but continuous with what had happened before.

For how could it be any different? The North had waged war against an illegally seceding South. It was a war to preserve the Union. Once victory was secure, the North was not about to negate the Union it had just defended. The old Constitution would be changed, but the old Constitution would survive.

## ASSUMPTION 3: ON REMAKING SOCIETIES

Finally, the political assumptions: No one knew how a people defeated in a civil war would respond to that defeat. No doubt, everyone had a hope; they just had no clue. Would the South continue to resist, even after slavery had been abolished? Or would it yield and join in the cause of securing at least equal civil rights to the newly freed slave?

Even more uncertain was how best to encourage the South to yield. Was force going to be effective? Or would forgiveness be more effective? Would an aggressive judicial stance push southerners to give in? Or would a more accommodating approach that emphasized "with all due deliberate speed" be more effective?

No one knew the answers to these questions in 1865—and unsurprisingly so, because governments had so rarely confronted such a fight. (Even to this day, it has been rare.) And though in hindsight we can see the extraordinarily horrific consequences that flowed from the unwillingness of the North to continue to demonstrate force, that hindsight should not be confused with willfulness on the part of the post–Civil War agents of the Civil War Amendments. They were wrong about what their weak response to southern terrorism would produce. But evil is not inferred from error.

These are the assumptions—all too vague to mean much just now. But upon that outline I want to craft a story of the post–Civil War Court that at least saves it from the charge of racist evil.

Following the work of political scientist Pamela Brandwein, I will tell this story in periods.[12] She begins later than I do, so I will frame the earlier period as "period o." In that period, there is hope that courts will contribute to the construction of an equal society. And there is a clear indication in the words of the judges that the Constitution as amended would ensure that equality.

Except for the last period we will explore, not all the opinions that we will discuss are from the Supreme Court. However, except for one, they are opinions written by Supreme Court justices. (The exception is written by a judge who would become a Supreme Court justice.) Yet despite arising in the main from circuit courts, these opinions speak volumes about the understanding of the law at the time. Jurists of the nineteenth century held circuit court opinions in high regard. We should as well.

## Period o: Hope

Early in the morning of May 1, 1866, three white men broke into the home of an African American woman living in Nelson County, Kentucky, Nancy Talbot. The three men were apprehended and were charged with the intent to burglarize her home, as well as commit other damage. (As one paper at the time reported, "a number of constitutional Democrats wishing to vindicate their claim to the title of the 'superior race' and resolving to show their abhorrence of 'nigger equality' broke into the house of Nancy Talbot, a colored woman in Nelson county, destroyed the furniture, and committed other acts of violence.")[13] A Kentucky statute forbade her from testifying against the white defendants. Without her testimony, the defendants would go free.

Three weeks before Talbot's home was invaded, Congress had passed the first Civil Rights Act, applying and extending the proscriptions of the Thirteenth Amendment. That law required that Talbot and every other African American "shall have the same right . . . to make and enforce contracts, to sue, be parties, and give evidence, to inherit, purchase, sell and convey real and personal property; and to full and equal benefit of all laws and proceedings for the security of person and property as is enjoyed by white citizens." White citizens, Talbot claimed, would have had the right to testify against people who had broken into their homes. Because of this law, she claimed, she should have that right to testify as well.

The Thirteenth Amendment had ended slavery. On first glance, one might wonder just why the right to testify in court has anything to do with slavery. But in an extraordinary opinion by Supreme Court Justice Noah Swayne, riding circuit, the court connected the aim of the Civil Rights Act of 1866 to the purpose of ending slavery. Slaves had not just been forced to work. They had also been denied every essential civil right. The aim of the amendment, Swayne determined, was not merely to end the practice of forced labor. It was also to enable Congress to "consecrate[] the entire territory of the republic to freedom, as well as to free institutions."[14]

To do that would require more than simply ending the practice of forced labor. It would also require enabling former slaves with the same civil rights that non-slaves had. Without that protection, abolition

> would have been a phantom of delusion. The hostility of the dominant class would have been animated with new ardor. Legislative oppression would have been increased in severity. Under the guise of police and other regulations slavery would have been in effect restored, perhaps in a worse form, and the gift of freedom would have been a curse instead of a blessing to those intended to be benefited. They would have had no longer the protection which the instinct of property leads its possessor to give in whatever form the property may exist.[15]

To empower Congress to secure these equal rights, the Thirteenth Amendment included an unprecedented clause. Section 2 expressly gave Congress the power "to enforce [the Thirteenth Amendment] by appropriate legislation." It was pursuant to that power that Congress, Swayne held, had properly passed the 1866 Civil Rights Act, which had firmly and clearly established the equality of civil rights within America.

What's striking about *United States v. Rhodes* (1866) is not the result. It is the clarity and simplicity of its opinion. Even without the Fourteenth Amendment, the court found ample power in Congress to remake the rights that had attached to the "servile race" within the states' jurisdictions. The amendment did not simply manumit African Americans. It empowered them as citizens. And while, as was understood at the time, that civil status didn't necessarily imply political rights, it was at the core of any understanding of republican government that being a citizen must mean possessing equal civil rights.

That clarity was echoed in a second extraordinary case, *United States v. Hall* (1871), decided five years later by a future justice of the Supreme Court, William Burnham Woods. Black Republicans had organized a meeting in Eutaw, Alabama, to determine and rally in favor of Republican candidates for elected office. White Democrats were not happy that the meeting was happening. The whites incited a riot, attacking the Republicans, whether white or black. Two were killed and more than fifty wounded. Two whites were indicted under the newly enacted Enforcement Act of 1870.

Section 6 of that act had made it a crime for "two or more" to "band or conspire together" with "intent to violate [the Enforcement Act] or to injure, oppress, threaten, or intimidate any citizen with intent to prevent or hinder his free exercise and enjoyment of any right or privilege granted" by the Constitution. John Hall and William Pettigrew had done precisely that, and the question that Woods had to answer was whether Congress could enact such a protection.

The rights at issue were the right to free speech and the right to peaceably assemble. These rights were expressed in the Bill of Rights. But no one at the time believed they were created by the Bill of Rights. Instead, as I described, these rights were considered as having been given to man from God. And the only question for man was how far or how effectively governments would go to protect them.

Woods began his opinion by rehearsing familiar constitutional law. Before the Civil War Amendments, the federal Constitution protected the Bill of Rights by constraining the federal government only. But in Woods's view, the Fourteenth Amendment had now added to their protection. Under the Fourteenth Amendment, the rights to speak freely and to peaceably assemble were among the "privileges or immunities" protected by the Fourteenth Amendment. After that amendment, "congress is forbidden to impair them by the first amendment, and the states are forbidden to impair them by the fourteenth amendment."[16] Congress had the power, Woods held, to secure both protections through legislation designed to remedy the failure of each to protect these rights. Such legislation could attack both "unfriendly or insufficient state legislation," because the Fourteenth Amendment not only protected certain rights, it also "prohibits the states from denying ... the equal protection of the laws." And "denying"—here Woods makes an incredibly important move—"includes inaction as well as action and denying the equal protection of the laws includes the omission to protect, as well as the omission to pass laws for protection."[17]

This insight was not Judge Woods's alone. Indeed, in one of the most important (and not sufficiently famous) letters of American constitutional history, he had asked his friend Justice Joseph P. Bradley about this question precisely. Could Congress legislate against state action as well as state inaction? Did the Constitution require that the state actually do something bad before Congress could use its power to coerce it to do something differently?

Bradley could not have been more clear:

Denying includes inaction as well as action. And denying the equal protection of the laws includes the omission to protect as well as the omission to pass laws for protection. [And as it would be] unseemly for Congress to interfere directly with state enactments and as it cannot compel the activity of state officials, the only appropriate legislation it can make is that which will operate directly on the offenders and offenses and protect the rights which the amendment secures.[18]

As Brandwein notes, Woods copied Bradley's language in his opinion almost verbatim, to find that the failure of Alabama to protect black Republicans was a violation of the Enforcement Act—at least with respect to these rights, "and the other rights enumerated in the first eight articles of amendment to the constitution of the United States." Those, Woods held, "are the privileges and immunities of citizens of the United States," and because they are "secured by the Constitution,... Congress has the power to protect them by appropriate legislation."[19]

As we'll see, Woods's reading of the meaning of the privileges-or-immunities clause would not survive in the Supreme Court. But with the support of Bradley, like Swayne in *Rhodes,* he offers a clear and powerful conception of an empowered Congress against a recalcitrant South. In their hands, the Fourteenth Amendment had at the very least extended the protections of the Bill of Rights against the states. And given the broad conception of "deny," it had made inaction as culpable as action.

This understanding of responsibility was confirmed in a third case from this first post–Civil War period. In *United States v. Given* (1873), Delaware officials had failed to enable blacks to vote by failing to qualify blacks as they would have qualified whites. As in *Hall,* Supreme Court Justice William Strong, riding circuit, affirmed that the failure of a state to act could trigger the remedial power of Congress under the Civil War Amendments. "It was not intended to leave the right without full and adequate protection," Strong wrote in his opinion. "Earlier prohibitions to the states were left without any express power of interference by congress; but these later, encountering as they did so much popular prejudice and working changes so radical, were fortified by grants to congress of power to carry them into full effect—that is, to enact any laws appropriate to give reality to the rights declared."[20] The rights at issue in *Given* were no doubt clearer than those at stake in *Hall.* As we'll see, the Court would view the Fifteenth Amendment right as a new right, created by the Constitution, and thus amenable to the full power of Congress. But that power policed both action and inaction, just as *Hall* had held.

The fourth and final case from this period is also the most familiar (though it arises temporally after the second period begins): *Strauder v. West Virginia* (1880). Taylor Strauder, an African American, had been indicted for murder. He wanted his guilt to be determined by a jury that included African Americans. West Virginia law forbade blacks from serving on a jury. Invoking rights under the Civil Rights Act, Strauder wanted his case removed to federal court.[21]

His right to removal depended upon the Supreme Court concluding that the exclusion of blacks from the jury was a violation of equal protection. In an opinion whose clarity continues to inspire to this day, the Court, through Justice Strong, declared that a law that excluded blacks from juries was a "discrimination" that "ought not to be doubted."[22] Such an exclusion was

> practically a brand upon them, affixed by the law, an assertion of their inferiority, and a stimulant to that race prejudice which is an impediment to securing to individuals of the race that equal justice which the law aims to secure to all others.[23]

The state was free, the Court held, to place that "brand...of...inferiority" on women, non-freeholders, non-citizens, or people who had not yet arrived at the age of majority. But if the Civil War Amendments meant anything, they meant that the state was not free to so stigmatize black men.

If these were the only cases we had from the post–Civil War period, it would be hard to read them as anything other than faithful to the plain meaning of those amendments. They evince the best of one-step originalism, crafting an empowering meaning from these dramatic constitutional texts, subject to the framing understandings of an original context. The cases affirm a strong role for the federal government in defending the rights of the freedmen. They make clear that Congress has ample authority to intervene to protect rights if necessary. That the Constitution was meant to ensure equal *civil* rights was not controversial. That the Fourteenth Amendment meant to incorporate the Bill of Rights would only later be rendered controversial.[24] And that an exclusion by law on the basis of race was an assertion of inferiority is a claim that no one from that time (or now; we will put aside the end of the nineteenth century) could reasonably deny. The courts in these cases interpret and apply the amendments as the framers would have intended. They evince a clear commitment by these jurists to fidelity to the framers' law.

## Period 1: Caution

Then the storm clouds began to gather, and this hopeful and empowered reading of the Civil War Amendments falls into the shadows. Much more prominent are cases that (properly interpreted) are much more ambiguous about just what the Civil War had wrought.

The first case is one we've seen before.[25] In Chapter 5, I described the aspiration of the libertarian justices to establish constitutional support for the ideals of free labor. Louisiana had established a monopoly to control butchers in the city of New Orleans. The libertarians believed that monopoly violated a fundamental right of all free men to labor freely. These justices didn't deny the power of Louisiana to regulate butchery. Rather, they denied that such a power included the power to establish a monopoly.

I've already noted, following Herbert Hovenkamp, how dramatically different this ideal was from the ideals of economics at the Founding. Monopoly was a tool of government for the Americans who crafted the Constitution. By the Civil War, that view had been inverted, at least for many. Now monopoly was the enemy, both because monopoly denied the laborer his free labor rights and because, as Andrew Jackson had so powerfully insisted, monopoly was a constant source of governmental corruption.

Yet the plaintiffs who challenged Louisiana's monopoly were not theorists. They were not motivated by a purity like Adam Smith's. They were driven instead by a strong desire to stop Louisiana's biracial legislature from achieving the equality that that extraordinary body had sought.

Louisiana was a mix of potential and disaster. Because it had been occupied by the Union Army during the last years of the war, it was among the first states to be "reconstructed." In 1868, a majority-black state constitutional convention crafted a remarkable constitution defending equality. The "black codes" were ended, and the right to vote was extended to all males, regardless of race. Schools would be public and integrated. The first election after that constitution produced the first biracial legislature in the state's history.[26]

Yet there was a dark side in Louisiana as well—a side committed to restoring white dominance within southern culture. That war would continue on many fronts. But the part I want to focus upon here is the legal front.

New Orleans was home to some of the greatest legal talent available to the white supremacist movement. That talent worked together to undo the revolution that the Civil War Amendments had intended. Leading that cabal was a former United States Supreme Court justice, John A. Campbell. A bitter man who had tried to negotiate a compromise before the war began, resigned to join the Confederates once that failed, and then failed again to negotiate peace at the war's end, Campbell had been jailed for six months after the war before being released to his home in New Orleans. That experience left this talented lawyer committed to continuing the war through his briefs and his arguments. *Slaughterhouse* was his first important battle.

From our perspective, it is hard to appreciate the real genius in Campbell's strategy. We today take an activist state—whether federal or state—for granted. We assume that the state has the power to intervene to remake society. We don't doubt that Congress could pass a tax to redistribute wealth from the richest to the poorest. We understand the role of the state to include ensuring everyone an equal opportunity, even if that includes taking from some and giving to others.

Campbell didn't believe the power of an activist state should be taken for granted. And his great brilliance was to recognize how the very amendments that egalitarians believed would secure equality to former slaves could be used to ensure the permanent inequality of those very same people.

At the very least, the amendments achieved a legal equality between blacks and whites. Anyone born in America was a citizen, color notwithstanding. Everyone was entitled to the same privileges or immunities. Everyone, regardless of race, was guaranteed due process of law. And everyone was promised the equal protection of the laws. If life was a contest, what these amendments meant at a minimum was that everyone would compete subject to the same rules. The field would no longer be tilted to benefit one side more than another.

Yet not everyone began this contest at the same starting line. After the war, blacks were formally free, but whites still had all the assets, both intellectual (education, training, experience) and physical (land, wealth, housing, and transportation). Blacks had skills, but they were the skills of the least-paid members of any developed economy. They didn't start this contest with any wealth or education. And except in a very few places, they certainly didn't begin it with any affection from those who had the assets.[27]

Campbell's insight was that this victory of equality would be tiny if government was not free to redistribute. If the only role of government was the minimal role of enforcing contracts and protecting property, then so long as whites had all the assets it didn't matter that blacks could engage in this civil economy freely. A culture of white supremacy could reestablish itself simply through the enormous economic power whites would have over blacks. The whites would start the contest far ahead of African Americans, and if the state had no power to redistribute, there was no way the whites would lose.

The *Slaughterhouse Cases* was this argument's critical chance. At its core, the regulation at issue in *Slaughterhouse* was importantly redistributive. While on its surface the law seemed focused on a very public benefit—the creation of safe and sanitary conditions for the slaughter of cattle—everyone recognized that its most important effect was to give African Americans an opportunity to enter the profession of butchery, an opportunity they otherwise would never have.

As I described in Chapter 5, New Orleans had seen the results of an important experiment in public health conducted during the war. Union General Benjamin Butler was disgusted by the practice of butchery in the city of New Orleans. Butchers slaughtered animals everywhere, and the detritus of their work poured into the city's water. Butler ordered the trade out of the city and required that no animal remains be dumped in any water flowing into the city. The residents bitched about the change, but everyone soon noticed that fewer people in New Orleans fell ill and died.

When the war ended, things went back to their old ways—both the practice of butchery and the incidence of disease. So in 1869 the legislature determined that it would restore the best of the Union occupation by restoring the regulation of butchery.

Yet rather than simply requiring butchers to move, or requiring them to adopt new and sanitary practices, the legislature created a monopoly over butchery within New Orleans. And here was the critical redistributive key within that regulation. The monopoly, the Crescent City Live-Stock Landing and Slaughterhouse Company, was required to permit anyone to be a butcher who satisfied certain minimal conditions. The profession had been an informal cabal before, but now it was, for the first time ever, open to anyone regardless of race. Had the legislature simply required all butchers to move downstream of the city, the sanitary objective of the law would have been secured. But by creating the monopoly and regulating access to the monopoly right, Louisiana sought another important objective as well—the securing to all—blacks especially—of access to this critical free labor resource.

It was this redistributive objective that Campbell's lawsuit would undo. Regulating butchers was one thing. But by formally barring anyone from being a butcher without permission from a monopolist, Campbell said, Louisiana was violating a fundamental right: the right of "free labor." Every freeman had a right to "the common callings," and butchery was the quintessential "common calling." Louisiana's effort to regulate this common calling was a violation of this fundamental right. And now, after the Civil War Amendments, Campbell argued, it was a violation that could be remedied using the tools of the Civil War Amendments.

In this fight, Campbell deployed both the Thirteenth and Fourteenth Amendments. Under the Thirteenth Amendment, Campbell linked the regulation to slavery. The Thirteenth Amendment declared:

> Neither slavery nor involuntary servitude, except as a punishment for crime whereof the party shall have been duly convicted, shall exist within the United States, or any place subject to their jurisdiction.

To ban slavery was to secure the right of free labor. A monopoly purporting to regular or control a common calling was a regulation that violated the right of free labor. It was, in essence, "slavery."

Under the Fourteenth Amendment, the argument was less obvious. The Fourteenth Amendment secured "privileges or immunities" to every United States citizen. The right of free labor was, Campbell argued, one of these privileges or immunities. Louisiana had denied the citizens of Louisiana the privilege of free labor by purporting to vest that privilege in the hands of a private monopoly. This was "class legislation"—targeting a (presumptively white) butchers' class. It was precisely this sort of law that explained why the framers of the Fourteenth Amendment went beyond protecting blacks only.

The Supreme Court, through Justice Miller—a physician and anti-slavery Unionist—rejected Campbell's arguments.

The Court was quick to reject the slavery argument. Not every regulation of labor—even a regulation of the "common callings"—would be deemed slavery. Louisiana hadn't banned butchery. It hadn't even denied anyone the right to be a butcher. To the contrary, anyone who wanted to could become a butcher. They simply needed to follow the regulations of the Crescent City monopoly.

History has accepted this part of the opinion as obvious and true. It is the second part that has been criticized so violently. For in rejecting Campbell's argument that the Crescent Street monopoly violated the privileges-or-immunities clause of the Fourteenth Amendment, the Court, history's verdict has it, erased that clause from the Constitution. Modern observers insist that the Court's reading of the clause rendered it otiose. There was no reason, these critics say, for the framers of the Fourteenth Amendment to include the privileges-or-immunities clause if its meaning was as Justice Miller rendered it.

There is little doubt that Justice Miller rendered the Fourteenth Amendment differently than how most in Congress believed it would be read.[28] And for the reasons offered by John Harrison in his masterful work *Reconstructing the Privileges or Immunities Clause* (1992), there's little doubt the clause would have been a better foundation for the Court's (eventual) equality jurisprudence.[29] But by reading the opinion in light of what happened later, lawyers and historians both misread what Miller actually said and therefore—and more importantly—what he left open.

The specific question that the Court had to address in *Slaughterhouse* was whether an *unenumerated* right—one that was, moreover, just recently recognized, if recognized at all—could be enforced against the states via the privileges-or-immunities clause of the Fourteenth Amendment. If there was a free labor right violated by the erection of a monopoly, then that right was written nowhere and had been recognized, if at all, only recently.

We should pause to recognize what must have been obvious to the Court as it considered this question. This was not the only privileges-or-immunities claim that was being pressed in the federal courts at the time. It was not the only law that distinguished one class from another. Campbell said there was a fundamental liberty to free labor that the privileges-or-immunities clause protected. As we'll see more completely in Chapter 17, Myra Bradwell said this same privilege entitled her to be a lawyer in Illinois.[30] And Mr. F. Bartemeyer said that same privilege entitled him to sell liquor, the temperance movement notwithstanding.[31] From the perspective of the Court, the Fourteenth Amendment had threatened to unleash an enormous amount of new litigation, most of which had absolutely nothing to do with the animating purpose of the Fourteenth Amendment. And none of the justices could have been oblivious to the institutional costs of this deluge.

This fact annoyed the justices—Justice Miller in particular. Miller hated Campbell as a "traitor." He saw Campbell's efforts as the continuation of the treason that he had committed when he resigned from the Court to give aid to the enemy. As he wrote:

> I have neither seen nor heard of any action of Judge Campbell's since the rebellion which was aimed at healing the breach he contributed so much to make. He has made himself an active leader of the worst branch of the New Orleans democracy. Writing their pronunciamentos, arguing their cases in our Court, and showing all the evidences of a disconcerted and bitter old man, I think no man that has survived the rebellion is more saturated today with its spirit....[H]e deserves all the punishment he...can receive, not so much for joining the rebellion as for the persistency with which he continues the fight.[32]

Miller had no patience with the clever efforts of white southerners to turn the amendment against equality.[33] And, more significant, Miller could not begin to understand how the Supreme Court in particular, or the federal judiciary in general, could ever police the exploding docket of claims grounded in the text of the Fourteenth Amendment.[34]

There was good reason for Miller to worry.[35] After the Civil War Amendments, the Supreme Court was flooded with appeals raising a wide range of questions. By the time of *Slaughterhouse*, the Supreme Court's docket had quadrupled from its 1860s level.[36]

So what Miller did was to offer a reading of the privileges-or-immunities clause that did two things, only one of which we even remember anymore. First, the opinion decapitated this new industry of litigation by narrowing the scope of judicially enforceable rights to those that were explicitly federal. The privileges or immunities spoken of in the Fourteenth Amendment belonged to citizens of the United States, not the citizens of the states. Section 1 of the amendment, Miller held, had created the distinction between federal and state citizenship, and the privileges-or-immunities clause was referring to the federal citizenship and not state citizenship.[37] Thus the only privileges or immunities about which anyone could complain in a federal court were those that were federal. And these, as Miller enumerated them, seemed quite thin. Miller points to

> the prohibition against ex post facto laws, bills of attainder, and laws impairing the obligation of contracts. But with the exception of these and a few other restrictions, the entire domain of the privileges and immunities of citizens of the States, as above defined, lay within the constitutional and legislative power of the States, and without that of the Federal government.[38]

Miller then proceeded to enumerate examples of these "few other restrictions":

> But lest it should be said that no such privileges and immunities are to be found if those we have been considering are excluded, we venture to suggest some which owe their existence to the Federal government, its National character, its Constitution, or its laws.
>
> One of these is...the right of the citizen..."to come to the seat of government to assert any claim he may have upon that government, to transact any business he may have with it, to seek its protection, to share its offices, to engage in administering its functions. He has the right of free access to its seaports, through which operations of foreign commerce are conducted, to the sub-treasuries, land offices, and courts of justice in the several States." Another...is to demand the care and protection of the Federal government over his life, liberty, and property when on the high seas or within the jurisdiction of a foreign government.... The right to peaceably assemble and petition for redress of grievances, the privilege of the writ of *habeas corpus*, are rights of the citizen guaranteed by the Federal Constitution. The right to use the navigable waters of the United States,...all rights secured to our citizens by treaties with foreign nations, are dependent upon citizenship of the United States and not citizenship of a State. One of these privileges is conferred by the very article under consideration. It is that a citizen of the United States can, of his own volition, become a citizen of any State of the Union by a *bona fide* residence therein, with the same rights as other citizens of that State. To these may be added the rights secured by the thirteenth and fifteenth articles of amendment, and by the other clause of the fourteenth, next to be considered.

But it is useless to pursue this branch of the inquiry, since we are of opinion that the rights claimed by these plaintiffs in error, if they have any existence, are not privileges and immunities of citizens of the United States within the meaning of the clause of the thirteenth amendment under consideration.[39]

To the modern reader, the list is a hodgepodge. And, most important, on a quick read it leaves open a critical question—do the federal privileges or immunities include, as Judge Woods had concluded in *United States v. Hall* (1871), the Bill of Rights? Because if they did, then the Fourteenth Amendment's privileges-or-immunities clause wouldn't be a "nothing." Indeed, to the contrary, it would have worked a radical change on the scope of federal authority, if not relative to the dreams of some who drafted the Fourteenth Amendment, then at least relative to the jurisdiction of the Court before the Civil War.

Finally and fundamentally, what is Congress's role in determining the privileges or immunities that a citizen might invoke in federal court? Is it nothing, as Miller had indicated, or if not, how far could Congress reach?

The question about whether the Bill of Rights would be enforced against the states has inspired the most controversy among scholars. It's clear that among the justices at least, before the Civil War, the Bill of Rights was enforceable only against the federal government.[40] That's not to say that those rights did not obtain against the state governments. Remember, fundamental rights were natural. They existed whether or not they were recognized by government. So just because the constitutional amendments gave anyone the ability to sue a state, that didn't mean a state was free to ignore the rights recognized in those constitutional amendments.

But the real question at the time of the Fourteenth Amendment was whether the privileges-or-immunities clause would operate to make the Bill of Rights applicable to the states too. If one of the privileges of United States citizens was the privilege of the Bill of Rights, did the Fourteenth Amendment now make that privilege enforceable against the state?

There is little doubt anymore that the leaders in Congress who had drafted and passed the Fourteenth Amendment believed that it would incorporate the Bill of Rights. As Richard Aynes writes, summarizing the history:

[Ohio representative John] Bingham indicated in at least three Fourteenth Amendment–related speeches that it was his intent that the Bill of Rights be enforced against the states. The spokesman for the Amendment in the Senate, Jacob Howard, indicated that among the privileges and immunities of citizens were the Bill of Rights, and he read most of Amendments I through VII on the Senate floor. Neither of these spokesmen was contradicted by any other Representative or Senator.

As far as it can be determined, there were only three constitutional law treatises published after the Fourteenth Amendment was proposed but before it was adopted, which also spoke to the question of the meaning of the Amendment. All three of these treatises indicated the Amendment would enforce the Bill of Rights against the states.[41]

On this account, the framers of the amendment at least meant it to incorporate the Bill of Rights against the states. And it is clear that the Supreme Court did not recognize this incorporation under the privileges-or-immunities clause—ever.

Yet strictly speaking, though the Court would eventually and expressly reject the argument that the privileges-or-immunities clause incorporated the Bill of Rights, Miller's opinion does not on its own resolve the question. He goes more slowly. Miller expressly identified among the list of potential federal rights that might find enforcement through the privileges-or-immunities clause "the right to peaceably assemble and petition for redress of grievances." This language echoes the First Amendment. In hinting that the First Amendment could now be enforced through the Fourteenth Amendment's privileges-or-immunities clause, Miller is, at a minimum, leaving the question of incorporation open. Certainly, he didn't need to resolve it in order to resolve the *Slaughterhouse Cases*. No one believed that the Bill of Rights banned monopolies. Thus, the proper thing for Miller to have done was to leave the question unresolved—as he expressly did later in the opinion with respect to the scope of the equal protection clause.

So the federal privileges or immunities may or may not include the Bill of Rights. But is that all it might include? Even if Miller left the door open to incorporation, did he close it for everything else?

Once again, speaking precisely, the answer is plainly no. As I quoted from Miller's opinion earlier, among the federal privileges or immunities that Miller said the courts might secure were those that "owe their existence to the Federal government, its National character, its Constitution, *or its laws.*" This language clearly indicates that a properly enacted law might provide the basis for a privileges-or-immunities claim in a federal court, and thereby displace any state immunity that might otherwise stand in its way. Whether such a law was constitutional, of course, is a separate question. That depends upon its nature or scope. But it was quite clear that Congress was understood to have enormous interpretive power by virtue of Section 5 of the Fourteenth

Amendment ("Congress shall have power to enforce, by appropriate legislation, the provisions of this article"), just as it had by virtue of Section 2 of the Thirteenth Amendment ("Congress shall have power to enforce this article by appropriate legislation").

This is the powerful point made by law professor James Fox in an extraordinary work published in 2002.[42] Most took for granted the constitutionality of the first great civil rights act passed by Congress, the Civil Rights Act of 1866. The core provision of that act provided that all citizens

> shall have the same right, in every State and Territory in the United States, to make their rights and enforce contracts, to sue, be parties, and give evidence, to inherit, and obligations purchase, lease, sell, hold, and convey real and personal property, and to full and equal benefit of all laws and proceedings for the security of person and property, as is enjoyed by white citizens, and shall be subject to like punishment, pains, and penalties, and to none other, any law, statute, ordinance, regulation, or custom, to the contrary notwithstanding.[43]

When Congress passed that act, it believed it was exercising its power under the just-ratified Thirteenth Amendment. But how could Congress regulate the making of contracts or the sale of land under a provision that banned slavery and involuntary servitude?

The answer, Fox argues persuasively, was that Congress believed itself entitled to interpret the meaning and scope of the Thirteenth Amendment. And under a broad reading of Section 2 (as informed by the Supreme Court's reading of the equivalent power within the original Constitution, the necessary-and-proper clause), Congress could enforce that amendment by ensuring that African Americans would no longer suffer any "badges or incidents" of slavery. By establishing a federal right to what everyone understood to be the civil rights of any free white man, Congress believed it was enforcing the equality ideal at the core of the Thirteenth Amendment.

Not everyone was convinced, of course. And the questions about the constitutional foundations for the Civil Rights Act of 1866 led some in Congress to push for an even stronger constitutional foundation. That would be the Fourteenth Amendment. Yet the important point is this: on this reading of Congress's interpretive power, Congress would clearly have the right to define a federal privilege related to the substantive scope of the Fourteenth Amendment— recognizing, of course, that the substantive scope was broad, given the *McCulloch*-like power secured by Section 5 of the Fourteenth Amendment.

On this understanding, then, Miller's opinion in *Slaughterhouse* left open the door to the recognition of more privileges or immunities—at least if

Congress secured them through its laws. The Court was not going to be in the business of recognizing unenumerated rights. It might eventually recognize the enumerated rights in the Bill of Rights; that question was unresolved. But by the language of his opinion, it seems plain that Miller would have recognized privileges expressed in federal law beyond those enumerated expressly in the opinion.

So, consider a hypothetical. Imagine there was a revival of the free labor movement in America. And imagine Congress passing a law to support it. Imagine that this law, under the power of the commerce clause, said, "It shall be the privilege of every citizen of the United States to labor in the common callings, any state-created monopoly notwithstanding."

Then imagine New Orleans creating a new slaughterhouse monopoly—this one without the guarantee that anyone could work for the monopoly if they lived up to the terms of the house. A butcher in New Orleans then brings a lawsuit claiming Louisiana has violated one of his privileges by creating this monopoly. There is nothing in the opinion of Justice Miller that would deny that butcher his claim. The claim would be grounded in a law; the law would be constitutional by virtue of the commerce power; by its express terms, it secured to U.S. citizens the privilege of a free labor right against state-created monopolies. Under the reasoning of the *Slaughterhouse Cases*, that butcher should win—even though the actual butchers in the *Slaughterhouse Cases* clearly did not win.

But if that's true, then why didn't Miller at least entertain the idea that there was a fundamental right to labor? Why force Congress to get in the mix?

The answer to that question has a strong echo with the fidelity to role considerations that we saw in Chapter 8. Miller's clear anxiety regarding the Civil War Amendments was not that they might help blacks. It was that they would open the floodgates of litigation in the Supreme Court. In *Davidson v. New Orleans* (1877), Miller complained that "the docket of this court is crowded" with cases asking the Court to strike offending state litigation.[44] Miller had made a similar point in the *Slaughterhouse Cases* four years before: if the Court entertained enforcement of this unenumerated right, then that would

> constitute this court a perpetual censor upon all legislation of the States, on the civil rights of their own citizens, with authority to nullify such as it did not approve as consistent with those rights, as they existed at the time of the adoption of this amendment.

The "as it did not approve as consistent with those rights" language is the tell. How was the Court ever to know? How could it enforce such a jurisdiction consistently? How would it avoid appearing political as it picked some rights it liked and some rights it didn't?

Miller's point is not that such a jurisdiction would have been inconceivable. It was instead that such a jurisdiction was just not conceived by the framers of the Fourteenth Amendment. There was nothing to suggest that the framers of that amendment meant "to transfer the security and protection of all the civil rights which we have mentioned, from the States to the Federal government."[45] And more directly:

> When, as in the case before us, these consequences are so serious, so far-reaching and pervading, so great a departure from the structure and spirit of our institutions; when the effect is to fetter and degrade the State governments by subjecting them to the control of Congress, in the exercise of powers heretofore universally conceded to them of the most ordinary and fundamental character; when in fact it radically changes the whole theory of the relations of the State and Federal governments to each other and of both these governments to the people; the argument has a force that is irresistible, in the absence of language which expresses such a purpose too clearly to admit of doubt.[46]

And when it was so hard to tell, the better strategy, as he would write in *Davidson* (1877), was to go slowly:

> There is wisdom, we think, in the ascertaining of the intent and application of such an important phrase in the Federal Constitution, by the gradual process of judicial inclusion and exclusion, as the cases presented for decision shall require, with the reasoning on which such decisions may be founded.[47]

Thus, on this reading of Justice Miller's opinion, *Slaughterhouse* did just one thing: it shut down an industry of litigation that was trying to transform unenumerated rights into weapons against state legislation—and in particular, legislation that might effect racial redistribution. The opinion did not resolve the question of whether the Bill of Rights would be incorporated. And it did not foreclose Congress from establishing new privileges that could then be enforced by virtue of the privileges-or-immunities clause. The opinion thus respected the assumption that federalism survived. And it respected the role of Congress in articulating the rights and privileges that citizens of the United States would possess. The only people disrespected by this opinion were the opportunistic and treasonous lawyers who were trying to leverage the words of the Civil War Amendments into a tool by which its objectives could easily have been defeated.[48]

My point so far is just this: On the day after "freedom died," to borrow the title from Charles Lane's extraordinary account of the Colfax Massacre, Justice Miller did not massacre the Fourteenth Amendment. He did cabin the power of the courts to "discover" fundamental rights, expressed as "privileges or immunities," that could be deployed in federal courts against the states. And no doubt, he and the Court felt themselves constrained to read the Fourteenth Amendment as an *amendment* and not as a *revolution*. But there was plenty of room to secure the rights of African Americans under the framework of his actual opinion. At the very least, it affirmed—now on two grounds, the Thirteenth and Fourteenth Amendments—the constitutionality of the Civil Rights Act of 1866. Beyond that minimum, it left open the possibility of other privileges or immunities being grounded in federal laws too. And it left unresolved the question whether by force of the amendment alone, the Bill of Rights was now incorporated against the states. There was no reason for civil rights activists to despair after the *Slaughterhouse Cases*. To the contrary, if the Civil War had now shifted from the battlefield to the courtroom, Miller had executed a brilliant defeat of the rebel forces.

## *CRUIKSHANK* REREAD

The second great moment of Supreme Court betrayal—at least on the conventional account that I recounted earlier in this chapter—is *United States v. Cruikshank* (1876). Growing out of the Colfax Massacre, the case involved the few leaders of that massacre that the U.S. attorney in New Orleans, James Beckwith, could prosecute. Beckwith had initially indicted ninety-eight people. Only nine could be located and moved to New Orleans for trial. After two trials over many months, in *Cruikshank* the Supreme Court dismissed the indictments against the three of those nine actually convicted. That decision, legal scholars tell us, "may well have been the single most important civil rights ruling ever issued by the United States Supreme Court." It "belongs at the center of our pedagogical canon" as "a dramatic demonstration of the judiciary's capacity to alter the course of political development," "almost strangling the Equal Protection Clause in its infancy."[49]

To evaluate these claims, it is important to place the case in its context, and its context begins with the dates.

As I've described, the Colfax Massacre happened on Easter Sunday, April 13, 1873. On February 24, 1874, the trial of nine defendants began. Less than a month later, the jury acquitted one defendant, and the judge declared a mistrial for the other eight. On May 18, 1874, the second trial began. Just over three weeks later, on June 10, 1874, the jury found three defendants guilty and acquitted five others. Two weeks after that, the verdict was thrown into doubt when Supreme Court Justice Joseph Bradley, riding circuit, declared a critical part of the Enforcement Act unconstitutional. His view was not shared by the other judge hearing the case, Judge William Burnham Woods. Their disagreement was then taken up to the Supreme Court. The Supreme Court heard argument on the case across three days, beginning on March 30, 1875. Just under a year later, and almost three years after the massacre had occurred, on March 27, 1876, the Supreme Court threw the convictions out.[50]

There is no doubt that this long delay between Bradley's circuit court opinion and the decision of the Supreme Court had profound consequences in Colfax and across the South. Bradley's decision was hailed in New Orleans by supporters of the white terrorists.[51] As James Pope recounts:

> Whites celebrated in Colfax by holding a mass meeting, riding out in the night, and slitting the throat of Frank Foster, a black man who happened to be walking along the road. Two days later, Christopher Columbus Nash, the first named defendant in the *Cruikshank* indictment, led an armed force to a nearby town and ejected five Republican officials from office. In August, a crowd of whites that reportedly included Nash marched to the Republican stronghold of Coushatta and murdered three leading African Americans, torturing one to death in front of a crowd. The next day, armed white supremacists executed six white Republican office holders, one of whom had warned that resistance would be futile "thanks to Justice Bradley." Coushatta marked the first time that white supremacists had staged a massacre of their own race. Within two months of Bradley's ruling, the incidence of terrorism had already risen so sharply "that contemporary observers described the mayhem as a new phase in the South's rebellion against national authority begun in 1861."[52]

Quickly—and no doubt relatedly—similar violence spread across the South. Again, Pope:

> During the three months following the ruling, White Leagues ousted Republican officials from twelve Louisiana parishes. Democratic Party leaders launched a campaign of terrorist assaults on Republican-controlled towns and cities across the South including, most spectacularly, New Orleans, Louisiana (September 14, 1874), Eufaula, Alabama (November 3, 1874), Vicksburg, Mississippi (December 7, 1874 and September 2, 1875), Yazoo City, Mississippi (September 1, 1875), Clinton, Mississippi (September 5, 1875), Friar's Point, Mississippi

(October 2, 1875), and Hamburg and Ellenton, South Carolina (July 4 and September 16, 1876). At the same time, the Democrats forthrightly called for a "white man's government," disapproved Klan-style violence, and characterized the paramilitary actions as self-defense. These tactics helped the Democratic Party to regain control of Alabama (47% black) in 1874 and Mississippi (more than 50% black) in 1875.[53]

Moreover, as a result of Bradley's opinion, the Justice Department determined to pause all Enforcement Act prosecutions until the Supreme Court could rule.[54] "Rates of conviction in southern civil rights prosecutions," Pope writes, "fell from 36–49% in 1871–1873 to less than 10% after 1874."[55] As Louisiana's governor, William Pitt Kellog, commented, the opinion "establish[ed] the principle that hereafter no white man could be punished for killing a negro."[56] As law professor Robert Kaczorowski notes, southern conservatives believed Bradley's view had been confirmed in advance by the Supreme Court, as he had returned to Washington before issuing his opinion.[57] And as LeeAnna Keith writes, the release of the

> remaining Colfax prisoners provided the occasion for strident boasts and gala celebrations. "All hail to the judge," wrote the Alexandria *Caucasian*, for when the prisoners emerged, "free and unfettered, we felt that their release was our release from a thralldom worse than death."[58]

Historian James Hogue documents the spread of "White Leagues" across the South tied directly to Bradley's opinion.[59]

A similar story can be told once the Supreme Court affirmed Bradley's opinion in March 1876. Beginning in July of that year, white terrorists spread across South Carolina to intimidate blacks and prevent them from voting. President Grant, in the last months of his second term, tried to stop the violence by ordering federal troops to restore order. He was too late. The effect of the violence would remain.

Pope and others link this result to Bradley's (and the Court's) purpose. In support of his claim, Pope points to Bradley's support for slavery before the war, support for an amendment to make slavery permanent (something, we shouldn't forget, that Lincoln had supported as well), and his very negative views about the laboring capacity of the recently freed blacks. These attitudes suggest to Pope that Bradley intended the violence that followed from his decision. That somehow, or for some reason, he actually wanted the incredible instability that the courts' decisions immediately unleashed.

This, if true, would have been extraordinarily bizarre. Whatever else Bradley (and the rest of the Court) was, he was committed to the Union and to ending the strife across the South. The election of 1872 had—foolishly—convinced northerners in general, and the Court in particular, that the problem of the Klan had been solved. That year, Frederick Douglass declared that the "scourging and slaughter of our people have so far ceased."[60] Rather than intending to undo the amazing peace the nation had seen during that election, it is much more likely that Bradley (and the Court) had no clue about what would follow from dismissing the *Cruikshank* indictments. No doubt, others closer to the battle had a clearer sense. The U.S. attorney who had issued the indictment that Bradley dismissed, James Beckwith, predicted violence from the moment he came to fear that Bradley would do what he did. His insight looks obvious to us today, but if it was so obvious then, why didn't the Justice Department jump full force into punishing violence under the narrower scope that Bradley had set?

The answer is the set of facts most relevant to the political actors at the time, yet completely forgotten by us today. Already in 1874, the North was growing weary with the continued costs of the Civil War. We should remember the time scale here: the war of peace had already been waged for twice as long as the war of aggression had. People everywhere, including the North, were keen to move on.

And then there was weariness with President Grant. Grant had been re-elected in 1872 in a landslide. But after the economy collapsed in 1873, a series of scandals marred the administration, and voters grew impatient. Corruption seemed to hover over the Executive Mansion (unfairly) Corrupt too was the way that most viewed (also unfairly) the Reconstruction governments in the South.

So in 1874, for the first time since the Civil War, the Democrats gained control of the House of Representatives. Republicans lost ninety-three seats—one of the largest swings ever in a single election. That shift in control meant that Democrats had direct control over the budgets of the various departments, which in turn meant that the newly established Justice Department would have a difficult time increasing support for southern prosecutions. The attorney general, George Williams, thus directed U.S. attorneys to cut back and take on only the clearest or most important cases.[61]

This is the most obvious reason the U.S. government didn't jump into the prosecution of the growing list of white terrorists: there was neither the political will (certainly not among Democrats and increasingly not among northern Republicans) nor the resources (in the Justice Department after the Democrats gained control of the House). That reality, in turn—and maybe conveniently—convinced many that patience was the best response to the revival of white violence in the South.

It is hard to overstate the tragedy in the accidents within this period of history. Prime among these was a financial crisis. The Panic of 1873 caused a depression in the United States and Europe that lasted until 1879. The causes of that collapse were partially local and partially global. The local flowed from post–Civil War inflation and then the monetary policy of strict compliance with a gold standard. It was this event that weighed more than anything else on the minds of voters in 1874. One extraordinary text we have from the period was written by one of the first black Republican leaders of Mississippi, John R. Lynch. Lynch sketches the period of Reconstruction through the election of 1874 in incredibly hopeful terms. He describes a Republican Party in the South that was increasingly mixed. Former white leaders in the South—the Bourbons—joined the party with a commitment to effecting civil and political equality (though certainly not social equality) across the South. After Grant's victory in 1872, the writing seemed to be on the wall: the North had won, which meant civil equality would be affirmed.

But the 1874 elections changed all that. And immediately after the Democrats' victory, a more populist force in the Democratic Party pushed white southerners to abandon the Republican Party. Before that election, Lynch wrote, "race proscription and social ostracism had been completely abandoned. A Southern white man could become a Republican without being socially ostracized."[62] But after 1874, "there was a complete change of front. The new order of things was then set aside, and the abandoned methods of a few years back were revived and readopted."[63]

The election was framed as a referendum on Reconstruction. Foolishly and wrongly, of course—but in politics, such adjectives don't much matter. The reality was that for whatever reason, power passed to the Democrats, and white Southerners were then taught (again) which party they had to support. This brief moment of hopefulness in America was over—ended in part by the greediness of some corrupt Republicans, but in the main because of an exogenous shock to the system caused by a depression.

Many have wondered what would have happened had Bradley and the Court gone the other way in *Cruikshank*. It is likely the mayhem that followed Bradley's circuit court opinion in 1874 would have been avoided. Had the 1873 depression never happened and had the Republicans retained control of Congress, there could have been a sustained and vigorous response to any revival by the Klan after 1872. Certainly Grant would have supported such a response; indeed, he repeatedly tried to intervene but was restricted by both Congress and his limited treasury.

Yet it is equally likely, as Pamela Brandwein and others have noted, that the renewal of vigorous enforcement could have backfired in the North.

Northern voters had been exhausted by the war; they were even more exhausted by the peace. A decade after the end of the war, the real fear among Republicans was not the loss of black Republican votes in the South but the loss of many more white Republican voters in the North.

Pushing against the conventional wisdom about this period in the Court's history, Brandwein argues that we should read these opinions more carefully by more conscientiously placing them in their historical and legal context. For what's striking about Bradley was just how proud he was of his *Cruikshank* circuit court opinion. In a move unusual for the justice, he had copies of the opinion made and circulated to fellow justices, to other judges across the South, and to his friends (and supporters of the Fourteenth Amendment) in Congress. He obviously didn't do this because he was proud that he had discovered a way to subvert the Fourteenth Amendment. He did it because he believed he had done something great.

Bradley's aim in crafting his circuit court opinion was to synthesize the Civil War Amendments with the dominant legal theory of the day, to the end of clarifying precisely how an Enforcement Act prosecution could proceed constitutionally. That synthesis built upon the distinction that I introduced in the beginning of this chapter—between the rights created by the Constitution and the rights recognized or secured by the Constitution. This distinction would imply that Congress had ample power under the Thirteenth and Fifteenth Amendments, since those were rights the Constitution created. It would frame quite precisely what the government would have to prove under the Fourteenth Amendment, if it was to protect rights that the Constitution had not created but only secured.

According to that distinction, rights created by the Constitution can be enforced by Congress directly. Bradley viewed the Thirteenth Amendment as creating just such a right. Because natural law was the law of liberty and there was no slavery in the state of nature, natural law therefore had no reason to articulate a right against slavery. So the Thirteenth Amendment had to add a right to the default rights given to us by God. As Bradley wrote,

> [The Thirteenth Amendment] is not merely a prohibition against the passage or enforcement of any law inflicting or establishing slavery or involuntary servitude, but it is a positive declaration that slavery shall not exist. It prohibits the thing.[64]

And Congress was not limited to "prohibiting the thing." To the contrary, Bradley held that Congress had the "power to legislate for the entire eradication of slavery" *and* "the power to give full effect to this bestowment of liberty on these millions of people." Liberty, in Bradley's view, was more than a prohibition against slavery; it operated to give Congress the power to make the former slave "a citizen and placed on an entire equality before the law with the white citizen." This power thus justified Congress's Civil Rights Act of 1866, for the plain purpose of that act was to ensure that in every civil right, ex-slaves would have the same privileges as white people.

This power was limited, however, by the nature of its source. It would certainly authorize Congress to punish people who interfered with laws attempting to secure liberty to ex-slaves. But it would not authorize Congress to punish crimes generally. The test was whether a law was protecting against violations that were targeting people on the basis of "race, color, or previous condition of servitude." If the law was, it was constitutional. If it was not, it was not. Or as Bradley summarized it, for a law or prosecution under the authority of the Thirteenth Amendment to be constitutional, it must target "a design to injure a person or deprive him of his equal right of enjoying the protection of the laws, by reason of his race, color, or previous condition of servitude."[65] Bradley gave an example to make this point clear:

> If in a community or neighborhood composed principally of whites, a citizen of African descent...should propose to lease and cultivate a farm, and a combination should be formed to expel him and prevent him from the accomplishment of his purpose on account of his race or color, it cannot be doubted that this would be a case within the power of congress to remedy and redress.[66]

By contrast, Bradley offered an example of a law that went too far under this reasoning:

> If that person should be injured in his person or property by any wrongdoer for the mere felonious or wrongful purpose of malice, revenge, hatred, or gain, without any design to interfere with his rights of citizenship or equality before the laws, as being a person of a different race and color from the white race, it would be an ordinary crime, punishable by the state laws only.[67]

One could well quibble with Bradley's precise framing. Recognizing that slavery need not be tied to race or color alone, Bradley could have framed the test on a more general basis: whether a given law purported to establish caste or enforce inequality on the basis of any "suspect class" (as the law would describe it seventy years later.)[68] As Stephen Calabresi and Julia Rickert make clear, certainly an animating purpose of the Fourteenth Amendment was to eliminate "caste."[69] But clearly, at least with respect to the amendment's paradigm case, Bradley's opinion gives Congress extraordinary latitude to act directly against people who, by their wrongs, attempt to reestablish the inequality of African slavery.

Bradley's view of the Fifteenth Amendment is even more empowering. The Fifteenth Amendment provides as follows:

> The right of citizens of the United States to vote shall not be denied or abridged by the United States or by any State on account of race, color, or previous condition of servitude.

Anyone seeking to interpret that amendment narrowly would focus on the "or by any State" language, to claim (as courts would later claim) that this amendment can be violated only by "state action." That conclusion would mean that Congress was empowered to enforce the amendment only against a state that acted to violate it. Individuals, on this reading, could not be prosecuted under the amendment.

Bradley rejected that narrow reading of Congress's power. In an extraordinary interpretive jujitsu, Bradley asserts that although the amendment is framed in the negative, "and therefore, at first view, apparently to be governed by the rule that congress has no duty to perform until the state has violated its provisions, nevertheless in substance, it confers a positive right which did not exist before." That previously nonexistent "positive right" is the right not to be discriminated against on the basis of race when it comes to the political right of voting. And because that positive right is not a natural right, the effect of the Fifteenth Amendment was to give Congress extraordinary power to enforce this new constitutional protection—the protection of "conferring upon them an equal right to vote with that enjoyed by white citizens."[70]

Yet as with the Thirteenth Amendment, this power too was confined in its scope. The right is not a right to vote. It is a right not to be discriminated against on the basis of race as regards the right to vote. The amendment "does not confer upon congress any power to regulate elections or the right of voting where it did not have that power before, except in the particular matter specified."[71] Instead, what it does is "confer upon congress the right of enforcing the prohibition imposed against excluding citizens of the United States on account of race, color, or previous condition of servitude."

Bradley does not stop there. Not only was this an affirmative right, but it was a right that could be enforced against individuals as well as the state. As Bradley reasoned, to limit the right to actions against the state would render it a nullity. If a state violates the amendment, the state is not about to give the victim a remedy against the state in state court. Therefore, the "only practical way in which congress can enforce the amendment is by itself giving a remedy and giving redress."

This is true, Bradley writes, even if state law already gives African Americans the right to vote equally. There is no problem with both state and federal laws protecting the rights of black voters concurrently—after all, state and federal laws do this in many different contexts. Thus, as Bradley summarizes his view about the Fifteenth Amendment:

> Congress has the power to secure that right not only as against the unfriendly operation of state laws, but against outrage, violence, and combinations on the part of individuals, irrespective of the state laws.

Other discriminations, however, are not regulated by this amendment. The state can deny the right to vote to women and to children. Neither would the amendment reach "outrage, violence, and combinations on the part of individuals" to deny Republicans the right to vote—since there were white Republicans (and a growing number until 1875 at least) in the South as well as blacks. The essential trigger to the proper enforcement of a Fifteenth Amendment claim is discrimination on the basis of "race, color, or previous condition of servitude." In Bradley's view, once that element is shown, the full power of Congress can be brought to remedy the infringement.

After defining the scope of Congress's power under the Thirteenth and Fifteenth Amendments, Bradley summarized his theory so far:

> The war of race, whether it assumes the dimensions of civil strife or domestic violence, whether carried on in a guerrilla or predatory form, or by private combinations, or even by private outrage or intimidation, is subject to the jurisdiction of the government of the United States; and when any atrocity is committed which may be assigned to this cause it may be punished by the laws and in the courts of the United States; but any outrages, atrocities, or conspiracies, whether against the colored race or the white race, which do not flow from this cause, but spring from the ordinary felonious or criminal intent which prompts to such unlawful acts, are not within the jurisdiction of the United States, but within the sole jurisdiction of the states, unless, indeed, the state, by its laws, denies to any particular race equality of rights, in which case the government of the United States may furnish remedy and redress to the fullest extent and in the most direct manner.[72]

*This* power of Congress is as broad here as it could be. Any limit is simply to affirm the second assumption that I outlined at the beginning of this chapter—namely, that the Civil War Amendments did not abolish the principle of federalism. As Bradley explains:

Unless this distinction be made we are driven to one of two extremes
—either that congress can never interfere where the state laws are unobjectionable, however remiss the state authorities may be in executing them, and however much a proscribed race may be oppressed; or that congress may pass an entire body of municipal law for the protection of person and property within the states, to operate concurrently with the state laws, for the protection and benefit of a particular class of the community.[73]

Bradley had thus articulated a powerful Goldilocks principle that swims between both constitutional extremes—Congress has all the power of municipal law, but *only if* the aim of its regulation is to remedy "the war of race."

We should pause to emphasize a point that should be obvious. If you accept that the Civil War Amendments were not meant to abolish federalism, Bradley's framework still gives Congress extraordinary power. In its simplest terms, Bradley says that if the cause of the wrong is "the war of race," Congress's power under the Thirteenth and Fifteenth Amendments is as broad as Congress's power could ever be. For a justice committed to restoring the power of the South, that is a very odd position to take—which makes it difficult to accept the claims of modern scholars that indeed that was Bradley's purpose.

Bradley then turned to the Fourteenth Amendment. The government had claimed, Bradley wrote, that the Fourteenth Amendment "empowered [Congress] to pass laws for directly enforcing all privileges and immunities of citizens of the United States by original proceedings in the courts of the United States."

But according to the distinction between created and recognized rights, this claim was obviously too broad. With respect to privileges or immunities created by the Constitution, the reasoning just given for the Thirteenth and Fifteenth Amendments would mean that Congress had the power "to pass laws for directly enforcing" such rights. But if the right was not one created by the Constitution—or presumably, following *Slaughterhouse*, by its laws—but instead was merely recognized or protected by the Constitution, then Congress's power would be less. As Bradley expressed this essential contingency:

[As] that subject matter may consist of rights and privileges not derived from the grants of the constitution, but from those inherited privileges which belong to every citizen, as his birthright, or from that body of natural rights which are recognized and regarded as sacred in all free governments; and the only manner in which the constitution recognizes them may be in a prohibition against the government of the United States, or the state governments, interfering with them.[74]

"It is obvious, therefore," Bradley concludes, "that the manner of enforcing" any alleged privilege or immunity "will depend upon the character of the privilege or immunity in question." If the privilege or immunity is protected by the Fourteenth Amendment against state governmental abridgment only, then "there will be nothing to enforce" until the state government abridges it. Congress can pass laws that will stand at the ready, but "they can have no application until it occurs." For these rights, a delict by the state must be alleged to have happened first.[75]

What would that wrong by the state be? We will consider this point more extensively in the section on the *Civil Rights Cases* (1883) later in this chapter, but it is important to note here that Bradley's consistent view since 1870 had been that a state could violate its obligations not to abridge certain rights through either action *or inaction.* If a state denies blacks the right to own property, that is a direct violation of the rights protected by the Fourteenth Amendment. But Bradley also believed that if a state refused to protect a right to property based on race that too would violate a right protected by the amendment. If, for example, a state enforced trespass laws to protect whites but refused to do so to protect blacks, that would violate the obligations of the amendment, in Bradley's view—even though the wrong was the state's refusal to act, not the state's action.

I've already alluded to the evidence for Bradley's early view: the correspondence with Judge William Woods in *United States v. Hall* (1871). In his letter to Woods, Bradley had offered a view of Congress's power that included the power to remedy inaction as well as action.[76] This conclusion too secures to Congress ample power—at least, against the background of the two assumptions that began this chapter. If you accept that rights can be of different types (some are created, while some are merely secured) and if you accept that the Civil War Amendments were not meant to abolish federalism, then Bradley's framework is perfectly unobjectionable. Indeed, it is more protective of Congress's power to secure equality than the rules recognized by the Supreme Court today. This is not the opinion of a justice trying to cut down the potential of the Civil War Amendments. It is the opinion of a justice making sense of those amendments against the background of the existing reality of midcentury American jurisprudence.

Yet as hopeful and impressive as this part of Bradley's opinion is, to the modern reader everything that follows from this point in his opinion is just bizarre. After marking out a powerful (and, in my view, quite adequate) constitutional foundation for enforcing the rights of African American citizens throughout the South, the opinion then strikes down each of the charges of the indictment for failing to live up to the test that Bradley had just sketched.

The first count alleged a conspiracy against the right "to peaceably assemble together with each other, and with other citizens, for a peaceable and lawful purpose." In a point ordinarily missed by commentators, Bradley concedes that this right, originally articulated in the Bill of Rights, is now incorporated against the states ("Grant that this prohibition now prevents the states from interfering with the right to assemble, as being one of such privileges and immunities").[77] But because this right was not created by the Constitution but instead is a natural right that preceded the Constitution, Congress may regulate it only if its enforcement is conditioned upon some failure by the state. Because count one did not allege any such failure, the count was therefore invalid.[78]

The second count alleged "a conspiracy to interfere with certain citizens in their right to bear arms." This count, Bradley believed, "is open to the same criticism as the first." Yet that assertion is fundamentally ambiguous. Is Bradley saying the Second Amendment is also incorporated against the states, but that Congress had not conditioned the statute's application on any state failure (the precise analog to its striking down of count one)? Or is he making a different criticism—that the Second Amendment is not incorporated against the states? Either way, once again the count was not sufficiently contingent upon state delict. It was therefore struck down.

The third count charged "a conspiracy to deprive certain citizens of African descent of their lives and liberties without due process of law." This count was properly focused on race. Yet once again, there was no allegation of state delict. Because the right of due process was secured, not created, by the Constitution, a failure by the state was essential. That failure was not alleged.

Bradley's rejection of the fourth count introduced a new principle to the story. That count had charged "a conspiracy to deprive certain colored citizens of African descent, of the free exercise and enjoyment of the right and privilege to the full and equal benefit of all laws and proceedings for the security of persons and property which is enjoyed by the white citizens." Bradley acknowledges that this language tracks the (perfectly constitutional) Civil Rights Act of 1866. But he insists that the indictment did not allege that the deprivation was "on account of their race, color or previous condition of servitude." "Perhaps such a design may be inferred," Bradley observes, "from the allegation that the persons injured were of the African race, and that the intent was to deprive them of the exercise and enjoyment of the rights enjoyed by white citizens." You think? To the modern reader, the point is as obvious as mud. But to Bradley, whether the point was obvious or not, this was a criminal prosecution, and according to the strict rules of pleading at the time, such an essential fact "ought not to have been left to inference; it should have been alleged." Moreover, the charge was too vague, Bradley said, because it didn't allege the specific acts that might constitute the conspiracy to deny "free exercise and enjoyment" of any rights. Those same defects sank the fifth and eighth charges.

That left counts six and seven. The sixth count seemed to get very close to the wrong Bradley had indicated that Congress could remedy. The government charged the defendants with interfering with "the exercise and enjoyment of [the victims'] right to vote at any election." Moreover, the indictment named the race of the people whose rights were so infringed. But here Bradley attacked the statute itself, which didn't limit its scope to interference based on race (the essential predicate for Fifteenth Amendment enforcement). Thus, Bradley held, because the statute was flawed, it could not support a charge based on race.[79] The same with count seven, which charged an intent to injure or oppress African Americans because they had exercised their right to vote. Once again, had the statute supporting the count been limited to offenses based on race, it would have sufficed. As it was, it reached too broadly.

The remaining eight counts simply repeated the first eight but added the charge of murder as part of the violations in each. Bradley dismissed them all for the same reason he had dismissed the original eight. Adding murder as an offense didn't change the original flaws. To put it differently, if the counts were flawed before, their flaws were not cured by adding the wrong of murder.[80]

Because Bradley's was a circuit court opinion, we are likely to miss its significance at the time. It was the practice of courts in the nineteenth century to pay more attention to circuit court opinions than we do today, especially when the opinions were written by Supreme Court justices and especially when the opinions are so carefully and precisely articulated. Bradley had carved in stone the law constraining how the federal government might prosecute white terrorism. His opinion, Brandwein reports, was cited more frequently as "the authoritative statement in *Cruikshank*" than the ultimate Supreme Court opinion would be.[81] All that remained was vindication by the Supreme Court—or an embarrassing reversal.

## *CRUIKSHANK* IN THE COURT: BRADLEY
## (ALMOST) CONFIRMED

The Supreme Court did not embarrass. Indeed, it adopted Bradley's reasoning almost completely—though, critically, it did not find that any part of the Enforcement Act was unconstitutional. The Court embraced Bradley's distinction between created and secured rights; it embraced Bradley's view that the Civil War Amendments did not intend to eliminate federalism; and it enforced Bradley's strict reading of the pleading requirements.

Thus, in examining the first count (and the ninth, where the charge of murder was added), the Court distinguished between two rights of assembly: one that preexisted the Constitution, and one the Constitution created. The former could only be enforced within the states; the latter (the right to petition Congress) had not been alleged to have been violated by the defendants.

It is important to note that Chief Justice Waite does not assert, as Bradley did, that this right was now incorporated against the states. This is a crucial restriction on Bradley's reasoning. And this restriction continues to the second (and tenth) counts as well, where the Court rejects the idea that a state could be charged with violating the Second Amendment, since that amendment "has no other effect than to restrict the powers of the national government." In his *Slaughterhouse* dissent, Bradley suggested more than this.[82]

Waite strikes down the third count (and the eleventh) for the same reason Bradley did: it did not allege any fault by the state, and it seemed to reach any deprivation, regardless of race. The failure to allege race was also fatal to the fourth, sixth, and seventh (and twelfth, fourteenth, and fifteenth) counts. Even if race could be inferred, it was "material" to the indictment and thus must have been alleged. Likewise with the fifth and eighth (and thus, thirteenth and eighteenth) counts, where the Court concluded, as Bradley had, that the counts did not state the material facts necessary to the indictment with adequate specificity.

In its essence, Waite's opinion is Bradley's. It differs in three important respects: first, it does not question the constitutionality of the Enforcement Act; second, it does not acknowledge that certain amendments in the Bill of Rights were incorporated against the states; and third, it is just much less clear or obvious what the precise reach of the opinion is. The opinion is a mess—which might explain why it is almost invisible in modern casebooks retelling this period of American history.[83]

So, what might explain the last point? By answering this, we may well see a way to understand just what was going on.

Chief Justice Waite was famously not a genius (*The Nation* said he was "at the front rank of second-rate lawyers")[84] He was Grant's fourth choice for chief justice, and before his elevation to the Court he had been a relatively obscure lawyer in Ohio. He had served as counsel before the *Alabama* tribunal in Switzerland, which established perhaps the first clear precedent for arbitration to resolve international law claims, and his success there earned him some notoriety. But he was not a leading light in the constellation of nineteenth-century American jurists.

Yet the confusion in this opinion is not likely due to a failure in judicial craft. According to Brandwein, the obscurity was likely intentional. While dismissing the indictments against the perpetrators of the Colfax Massacre, the Court was nonetheless crafting a set of rules that would enable future prosecutions to comply with the Enforcement Act. But it did so, as Brandwein puts it, in "coded language."[85] To anyone schooled in the law at the time and aware of Justice Bradley's opinion, the meaning would be clear—namely, that there was an obvious way to prosecute white terrorists under the Enforcement Act and the Civil War Amendments. To the general public, however, the meaning would be very different,[86] and much more as modern lawyers read it—that the laws of the United States would not sanction the continued efforts to prosecute in the (soon-to-be post-) Reconstruction South.

But why would the Court want to assert one meaning to the lawyers of the time and another meaning to the general public?

While Brandwein's extraordinary work doesn't frame it like this, this is a perfect example of Berkeley professor Meir Dan-Cohen's device of "acoustic separation."[87] As Dan-Cohen describes, sometimes decision-makers benefit from being able to utter one rule to one population and another rule to a different, "acoustically separated" population—meaning a second population that won't understand the first. The simplest example of this is the principle that "ignorance of the law is no excuse." We all know this principle, and we repeat it openly and strongly. But as Dan-Cohen demonstrates, the actual reality of the rule is that it forgives ignorance, at least in the sense that a defendant who demonstrates actual ignorance is accorded a lesser punishment (or no punishment at all).

Why would it make sense to have a rule that says one thing to the general public, but a different thing to actual defendants? Well, it's a good thing, for example, Dan-Cohen sensibly argues, that the public believe that ignorance is no excuse, because then the public works hard to learn the law. But once someone has actually been charged with an offense he did not recognize as an offense, there's no reason to treat him harshly. If the law can obscure the fact that he is forgiven, it gets the best of both worlds—ex ante, a strong incentive for people to know the law; ex post, forgiveness for those who innocently violate the law.

A similar dynamic was happening here, Brandwein suggests. The aim of the Court, she argues, was to enable future prosecutions. But not in a way that would excite anti-Republican votes in the still-simmering South. So the Court crafted an opinion that sets a clear path for continued prosecution but mutes the clarity of that message, so as not to feed the anti-Republican campaigns that were brewing across the South—especially as the South approached the critical centennial election of 1876. (Remember, *Cruikshank* was decided just months before.)

This is an important and sensible account, consistent with fidelity to role. The point isn't that the Court was hiding anything. Rather, the Court was avoiding its opinion being used in a political way to create an impression that wasn't, in fact, true. Southern enforcement continued to be possible; the only question was whether the political branches would continue to support that enforcement.

The great virtue of Brandwein's theory is that it is testable. The claim of conventional wisdom about this period is that after *Cruikshank,* prosecutions by the Justice Department end. *Cruikshank*, on this view, kills the Enforcement Act. And 1876 marks the moment when a "compromise" between Republicans and Democrats gives the Republicans the presidency, but with the promise that Reconstruction would end. But on Brandwein's view of the *Cruikshank* opinion, the ability to prosecute under the Enforcement Act continues, and, at least where there is political will, prosecutions would continue to occur.

The data support Brandwein's account.[88] As Department of Justice statistics confirm, at least after the initial two years of the Rutherford Hayes administration, prosecutions under the Enforcement Action return. They grow significantly under James Garfield and Chester Arthur's administrations. They disappear during the presidency of (Democrat) Grover Cleveland but return under (Republican) Benjamin Harrison. And they only finally end once the Democrats take control of Congress again and the presidency in 1893, and when they can finally repeal the Enforcement Acts in 1894 as they relate to voting rights.[89] *Cruikshank* left the Justice Department plenty of legal resources to enforce equality. Indeed, it left the U.S. attorney in New Orleans, James Beckwith, with plenty of ground for reindictment if he so chose. What the Court couldn't do was to create the political will to continue the defense of African Americans in the South, or to provide the material resources necessary to do so. That necessity was beyond their ken and institutional competence. They had no choice but to leave that bit to others.

What this shows is that the real history of this period is not the story of Congress and the executive doing everything they can to defend African Americans, and then the Court stepping in to thwart them. To the contrary, the story of this period is one of enormous political weakness, which sets the limits on the executive and then on the courts.

That story begins with the massacre at Colfax. The rich history of this terrorism—and here I draw again from Charles Lane's *The Day Freedom Died*—is the story of real political will, at least at first. At the center is the story of a committed prosecutor. James Beckwith worked tirelessly to bring the terrorists to justice. But his day-to-day fights were not primarily judicial. They were the practical fights with his own government for the resources necessary to bring terrorists to justice.

This is the part of the story that from the perspective of the modern American federal justice system will seem the most difficult to understand. Yet here's a single incident that might suggest the limits, and the story of this incident could be multiplied again and again.

In 1873, Beckwith needed to arrest the criminals he intended to prosecute. To do that, he would first have to move a contingent of U.S. marshals up the Mississippi, then find and arrest the defendants. After the arrests those marshals would move the defendants back down the Mississippi and hold them in prison.

To do all this, Beckwith needed a steamboat and some effective marshals. At first he turned to the U.S. Army. As he wrote to the attorney general, George Williams, there was no chance that the state's forces could successfully arrest the people Beckwith had indicted. "Cannot the War Department be induced to permit the mounting of some infantry to aid in the arrest?," Beckwith asked.[90]

Despite Williams's early promise of support, he declined Beckwith's request. Indeed, he questioned Beckwith's strategy. Rather than prosecuting the ninety-eight people Beckwith had proposed indicting, Williams recommended that Beckwith select six to twelve who were "ringleaders and most responsible," and prosecute them. That would be enough, Williams believed, to have "the desired effect to vindicate the law and induce the future observance of it by the people."[91] Beckwith was free to use infantry to arrest the select few Williams wanted him to prosecute. Yet Williams asked him to cut costs by using horses from the parish where the arrests would be made. Williams was clearly out of touch.

Beckwith responded that fall with a new plan. Working with a U.S. marshal, he pulled together a strategy for arresting the terrorists that would require no new infantry but would require the U.S. government to provide him with thirty days' worth of food (and fodder) on credit, as well as the cash necessary to cover the costs of a steamboat to travel up the Mississippi to Colfax. Yet the federal government declined to supply even this tiny bit of support.

Yet Beckwith persisted. He and the U.S. marshal came up with a revised plan, this time for ten days rather than thirty. Using a steamship Governor Kellog had purchased with his own money—a contribution, as Charles Lane describes, "that demonstrated the governor's strong personal stake in establishing respect for the law in the most violent rural parishes of Louisiana"—the expedition to Colfax began, six months after the massacre had occurred.[92] It would take two weeks for the ship, *Ozark*, to reach Colfax, and with support from the infantry at Pineville, they would fight for two more weeks to arrest just seven of the people Beckwith had indicted. (Two more defendants would be captured before the beginning of the first trial.)

But securing the presence of the defendants was just the first step in Beckwith's prosecution. He then had to consider how he would get the testimony of the witnesses to the crimes that had been committed.

The defense surely faced the same challenge. But almost immediately, 120 people volunteered to travel to New Orleans to testify on behalf of the accused. The defense team organized fundraisers to cover the costs of this army of defenders. Thanks to the donations to this fund, the prison in which the terrorists were held was quickly converted to provide "hotel-like accommodations."[93]

The prospects were not as promising for the prosecution. Beyond two Republican leaders, not a single white volunteered to testify for the government. Against long-standing tradition, the government would have to rely on the testimony of African Americans. All that Beckwith could offer them was a small per diem and the costs of transportation. He could not promise any real safety from the almost certain retaliation of the terrorists in Colfax. Nevertheless, in an extraordinary show of bravery, given the risks they faced, dozens of African Americans appeared in New Orleans to help Beckwith to try to convict the terrorists.

As I've noted, the first trial failed to do that. The second convicted just three—not of murder, but of conspiring to violate the victims' civil rights. New Orleans was astonished, and white New Orleans reacted, as Lane has described, "with fury."[94]

But then Justice Bradley appeared to save the day—from the perspective of the defendants and the raging white southerners. Notified by Judge Wood of the verdict, Bradley responded that he would send an opinion. Beckwith insisted he deliver the opinion in person, forcing Bradley to travel from the District of Columbia by train to deliver the opinion, and then an hour later board a train back to Washington. Bradley's opinion forced the prosecution to stop, as Bradley believed the indictments were flawed and that the Supreme Court would have to resolve the matter.

My point in telling this story here is to make obvious to us what was certainly obvious to everyone then: that the real constraints on prosecution in the 1870s in the South were practical and political, not legal. They were the constraints of building and prosecuting a case without the funds or force from the federal government necessary to make prosecution possible.

Had the Justice Department authorized the resources, and had the army provided the force, then any ultimate failure of prosecution would fairly be placed at the foot of the judiciary. But long before we get to any failures of the judges, we must confront the complete failure of the politicians in the federal government to support the enforcement of the law.

That failure should have been predictable. A nation exhausted by the Civil War was not likely to be willing to fund an endless continuation of that war almost a decade after the peace had been declared. There was enormous pressure even within Republican administrations to cut back on the force that supported Reconstruction. That pressure was amplified at every election, as Democrats used the continued engagement within the South as an argument for their own political victory. The election of 1874 finally gave white Democrats the ability to say, "The people are with us." The defeat of the Republicans in that election was read as a mandate against Reconstruction. It was certainly a cause for the Justice Department to tread carefully going forward.

More crucial still, the story that was being told about Reconstruction itself was not pretty. Leading journalists quickly turned against Reconstruction, convinced it was nothing more than carpetbaggers profiting from the enormous corruption enabled, they believed, by blacks too easily bent by the corrupters.[95] Story after story recounted corruption after corruption, without any careful coverage of the outrage being crafted against equal rights for blacks.[96]

This was an enormous political and moral failure. There is no excuse for the North's willingness to allow slavery 2.0 to prosper. My purpose is not for a moment to minimize the immorality or wrongness in this failure.

Yet we need to be clear about the source of the failure. The period 1865 through 1896 is not a time when the political branches were unified and committed to delivering on the promise of equality for blacks. To the contrary, there was at first a slowly brewing resistance, and then an overwhelming political capitulation to the forces of terrorism.

Throughout the period ending in the second Cleveland administration there was a continued effort by Republicans and (except for the first two years of the Hayes administration) by Republican administrations to do whatever they could. Prosecutions continued. But these prosecutions were tiny compared with the force that would have been necessary to make them ultimately effective. For this story to have turned out differently, the North would have to have sent large numbers of highly visible troops to the South for at least a decade more, to deliver a clear and unbending message to the South that terrorism would not be tolerated.

Maybe this would not have been necessary. Maybe the energy necessary to defend the peace that prevailed in the 1872 elections would have been small.

But once the depression unleashed its fury and the Democrats claimed victory, the cost of continuing the enforcement of Reconstruction was going to be extraordinary. Had Grant not become beleaguered by the criminals surrounding him, maybe he could have delivered on his forceful promise to enforce peace in the South. The political resolve needed to do that is certainly imaginable, even if events made it impossible.

And yet even this resolve may have created an enormous threat. For the final bit of history that modern readers are most likely to miss was the extraordinary uncertainty about the survival of the Fourteenth Amendment itself.

## THE TENUOUS AMENDMENT

The story of the passage of the Civil War Amendments is not uncomplicated. Unlike, say, the Twenty-Sixth Amendment, which lowered the age of voting to eighteen, there isn't a simple list of state ratifications, in which three-fourths of the states were in favor of each of the three amendments.

Instead, described most simply but fairly: the North forced the South to adopt these amendments. Literally, in some cases, with troops outside the legislative chambers, the message was direct and clear—pass them or else.[97]

Because of this, it is not surprising that there was a growing question about whether Congress actually had the power to force states to adopt an amendment. By what power could Congress coerce a state to ratify an amendment? And if it did not have such power, was an amendment so coerced actually constitutional?

The seeds to this question were planted in a case that modern readers consider a moment of great judicial resolve—*Ex parte Milligan* (1866).[98]

Lambdin P. Milligan had been a vocal opponent of the war, believing the South was entitled to secede (and hence that undertaking the war in order to preserve the Union was unconstitutional). In September 1864, he was arrested in Indiana and charged with treason and with plotting to aid the enemy. Milligan was tried by a military tribunal, convicted, and sentenced to death. When he appealed his conviction to the Supreme Court, his argument was simple and (from a civil rights perspective) quite powerful: there was no power within the United States military to try civilians, so long as there were civil courts that could have tried him instead.

The Supreme Court agreed. As the Court wrote, persons living in states "where the courts are open, if charged with crime, are guaranteed the inestimable privilege of trial by jury." Indiana had not rebelled against the Union. Its citizens therefore had to be tried in civil courts. Martial law and military courts were limited, the Court held, to "actual war." And whether there was an actual war was a question of fact that could be resolved by the courts, not a judgment simply relegated to the political branches.

But if this was true, how far would that principle extend? If the extraordinary powers of a military occupation were contingent upon active rebellion, then when the active rebellion ended, did the federal government have the power to tell the states to do anything? Even more important, after Andrew Johnson had declared in April 1866 that the rebellion was over, did Congress have any continuing extraordinary power?

Congress of course disagreed with Johnson's assessment. In 1867, it passed the first Military Reconstruction Act, which divided the South (Tennessee excepted) into five regions, each to be governed by a military commander. The law was passed just a month shy of two years after Grant had accepted Lee's surrender at Appomattox. Yet it imposed military rule and required the ten states so governed "to write new constitutions that provided the elective franchise to all male citizens, regardless of race, and to ratify the Fourteenth Amendment in order to qualify for representation in the U.S. Congress."[99]

But *Ex parte Milligan* had raised serious questions about this law. If Milligan couldn't be tried by a military tribunal because the civil courts survived, by what power did the federal government impose martial law on the South years after the Civil War was declared over?

Southern lawyers tried a number of strategies to get the Supreme Court to answer that question precisely. In *Mississippi v. Johnson* (1867), Mississippi asked the Court to enjoin President Johnson from enforcing the Military Reconstruction Act. The Court ducked the question by holding it had no power to tell a sitting president not to enforce a law.[100]

Georgia then asked the Court to enjoin not the president but an officer below the president. This time, in *Georgia v. Stanton* (1868), the Court ducked the question by invoking the "political question" doctrine:

> That these matters ... call for the judgment of the court upon political questions, and, upon rights, not of persons or property, but of a political character, will hardly be denied. For the rights for the protection of which our authority is invoked, are the rights of sovereignty, of political jurisdiction, of government, of corporate existence as a State, with all its constitutional powers and privileges.[101]

These two defeats finally taught the southern lawyers an important lesson about how the acts of Congress had to be challenged—not through broad declarations of political power but, as in *Ex parte Milligan*, through the determination of the individual rights of some wronged individual.

*Milligan* was set in Indiana. Yet its reasoning threw into doubt the military courts across the South—at least after the rebellion had ended. So, building on that opinion, southern lawyers brought a precisely parallel claim in Mississippi on behalf of William McCardle. McCardle had published a newspaper. His paper attacked military Reconstruction. In 1867, he was jailed for his "incendiary" articles. McCardle's lawyers appealed to the Supreme Court. A terrified Congress responded by removing the Supreme Court's jurisdiction to review cases like his—after his case had been argued. The basis for this power in Congress was express in the Constitution. The Supreme Court accepted that Congress had the power to shut it up. It refused to decide whether McCardle's imprisonment was legal.[102]

McCardle's case was argued under an 1867 statute granting the Court jurisdiction to hear cases of *habeas corpus*. But the southern lawyers soon recognized that was not the only statute that gave courts the power of *habeas corpus*. Immediately after the decision in *McCardle*, they raced to file a suit challenging the conviction of Edward Yerger by a military tribunal in Mississippi based on another *habeas* statute—this one from 1789. When a lower court held that the repeal of the 1867 statute also repealed the 1789 statute, Yerger's lawyers appealed to the Supreme Court. This time the Court found it had jurisdiction. The repeal of the 1867 *habeas* statute should be read narrowly, the Court held. That meant Yerger was now free to press his case in the lower court.

This was a time bomb—and it was ticking. And with this decision, terror broke out in (Republican) Washington. The politicians' fear was that when the Supreme Court got a chance to hear the merits of Yerger's case, it would finally decide that the same principles that applied in Indiana applied in Mississippi. And if that was true, then the Republicans feared, the Military Reconstruction Act would be declared unconstitutional as well.

That holding, in turn, would have threatened not just the convictions by military tribunals. Much more important, it would also have threatened the Fourteenth Amendment itself. Because if Congress had no power to try traitors in military courts—since the state was at peace—how could Congress force the state to adopt an amendment to the Constitution when the state was at peace?

The lawyers for the government wisely did not want to risk it. They quickly settled Yerger's case, thereby depriving the Court of its opportunity to declare the Reconstruction Acts unconstitutional—in Yerger's case, at least. But there were still other cases, and other opportunities to embarrass the legal status of military Reconstruction. The final clear test grew out of Texas.

In *Texas v. White* (1869), Texas tried to force the Court's hand with a very different strategy. The underlying case involved a bond. Filing its case in the Supreme Court, Texas sued bondholders that it claimed had never paid for the bonds. Texas could sue in the Supreme Court only if it was recognized as a state.

Texas believed that however that jurisdictional question was resolved, it would create real problems for Republican Reconstruction. If Texas was a state, then Congress had no power to regulate it as it was being regulated under the Reconstruction Act. And if Texas was not a state, then it had no power to ratify an amendment—such as the Fourteenth Amendment—as a condition to being readmitted to the union. The lawyers for the South thought they had finally cornered the lawyers for the North.

Yet again, the Supreme Court dodged the bullet. Yes, Texas was a state. But the Constitution required the federal government to guarantee that Texas would have a "republican form of government." Reconstruction was the means by which that guarantee was being effected. And the Court was not going to limit the extent of this fundamental guarantee by deciding whether the Reconstruction Act did more than the republican-guarantee clause required.

Still, the race in the courts continued. Congress was fearful that another military tribunal case would find its way to the Supreme Court. The longer Congress refused to readmit states, the longer the Military Reconstruction Act remained in effect, and thus the greater the chance the Court would declare it unconstitutional. The "prospect of more cases on the horizon" led Congress "to put an abrupt end to military Reconstruction and readmit the remaining ex-Confederate states as quickly as possible."[103] The North had to secure peace if the Fourteenth Amendment was to survive.

*This* was the central obsession in the North during this period. And the key strategic decisions were all designed to avoid a determination by the Supreme Court that the Military Reconstruction Act was unconstitutional and hence that the Fourteenth Amendment was not law. The Republicans' aim was therefore to move as quickly as they could into a period of relative quiescence, so as to avoid the press for judicial resolution.

Finally, the resolution of these cases gives the lie to the claim that the Reconstruction Court was simply aiming to undo what the Civil War had wrought. It would have been trivially easy—at least judicially—for the Court to have struck down the Military Reconstruction Act, had it been so motivated. *Ex parte Milligan* was the simple road map.

Yet the Court didn't. Instead, invoking a power practically never acknowledged by the Court—the republican-guarantee clause—the Court crafted a constitutional free pass for the Reconstruction Congress. This was where a willful and anti-Reconstruction Court would have acted willfully. That it didn't tells us something about this Court.

---

These stories together resonate along a single theme: that the peace, as much as the war, was precarious and uncertain. Grant had defeated Lee's army at Appomattox. That victory would come to be known as the end of the Civil War. (Some continued to fight, though, including those who conspired to decapitate the federal government by assassinating Lincoln, Grant, Secretary of State William H. Seward, and Vice President Johnson. Seward was seriously wounded; Johnson's attacker lost his nerve; Grant had left town.)

Yet military victory did not end the political conflict. For a generation at least, the struggle to reunify America dominated federal politics. As that struggle lengthened, the willingness of anyone in any position of power to continue the fight weakened. Congress gave up first, the president next. When Rutherford Hayes became president in 1877, he withdrew federal troops from the South. The Union had officially retreated. And so too would the Court.

In this post–Civil War period, then, the argument of fidelity goes like this: The Supreme Court, and lower courts, worked initially to synthesize the Civil War Amendments within the legal framework they inherited. That framework was changed in part by those amendments, but it was not obliterated. Instead, at least according to the Court, the amendments presupposed this original legal framework. The job of the judges then was to give sense to the amendments against the background of that framework.

Initially they did this successfully. *Slaughterhouse* did not massacre the privileges-or-immunities clause. It denied the clause's relevance in one extreme class of cases but left open the question of its application to many other core privileges of federal citizenship—namely, the Bill of Rights—and any federal law establishing a privilege that Congress could lawfully pass.

Likewise, *Cruickshank* didn't terminate the ability of the federal government to prosecute terrorism in the South. Indeed, the decision left the Enforcement Act untouched and did nothing more than channel the mode by which prosecutions had to proceed. And while some might worry that the elements of proof required by the Court—that the crime was racially motivated and that the state had failed to act—would make prosecutions practically impossible, the actual history suggests the contrary.[104] The bar of proving racial motivation was not high, and the ability to show the failure of the state to act was quite direct.

Thus, given the legal framework of natural rights, and assuming the amendments did not intend to abolish federalism, these decisions are fair, even quite good, with respect to fidelity to meaning. The one clear exception—Miller's narrowing of "privileges or immunities"—reflects a fidelity to role desire to avoid putting the Court in the middle of an endless task supervising state regulation. As Miller left it in *Slaughterhouse*, there was plenty of room to secure federal privileges. They were not secured—but that happened later, as the political and social context of America turned radically against protecting African Americans.

The story then, is of the law left open to being used by the political branches to defend equality—to the extent the political branches so desired.[105] It is also the story of the political branches resolving again and again to leave the former slaves to their own defense. Maybe the Court could have done more. But between the sins of the Court and the sins of the politicians, there is simply no moral equivalence.

## THE *CIVIL RIGHTS CASES* UNDERSTOOD

And then finally, there is the *Civil Rights Cases* (1883), certainly the hardest of these first-period cases for modern readers to accept, if only because of the caveman-like rhetoric shot through the opinion. Here is Justice Bradley, the modern view has it, finally revealing his true self—racist, and openly rejecting the commitments of the Fourteenth Amendment—just seven years after he had engineered the great compromise that made Rutherford Hayes president in exchange for ending Reconstruction in the South. (For the record, there is no good evidence for this latter, absurd claim.)

There is no doubt that the language in Bradley's opinion reflects an attitude of the time:

> When a man has emerged from slavery, and by the aid of beneficent legislation has shaken off the inseparable concomitants of that state, there must be some stage in the progress of his elevation when he takes the rank of a mere citizen and ceases to be the special favorite of the laws, and when his rights as a citizen, or a man, are to be protected in the ordinary modes by which other men's rights are protected.[106]

But the decision in the *Civil Rights Cases* is neither surprising nor, given the legal understanding of the time, even necessarily wrong. What *is* striking is not what the Court did but what Congress did, because there was a clear way to craft this statute, the last civil rights statute that would be passed by Congress for eighty-two years. Indeed, Justice Bradley had explained as much in his (to them very well known) *Cruikshank* circuit court opinion. The puzzle is the stubbornness of the act's principal author, Charles Sumner.

The Civil Rights Act of 1875 was born in 1870. The brainchild of one of America's greatest civil rights activists, Massachusetts senator Charles Sumner, the act aimed to secure to African Americans equal access to "public accommodations." Originally, the act reached much further than just that. In its original form, it would have banned discrimination in schools, cemeteries, churches, juries, transportation, and public accommodations. But in the long fight to secure its passage, the sponsors of the legislation stripped out its most controversial features. Even then, the law did not pass until Sumner had died and a lame-duck Republican Congress sought an appropriate way to honor his incredible work. The 1875 act was that way.

As interpreted by the Court (and by its lone dissenter, Justice John Marshall Harlan), the act purported to secure to African Americans the right not to be discriminated against on the basis of race in the enjoyment of, or access to, "inns, public conveyances on land or water, theaters, and other places of public amusement." Could the Constitution support the granting of such rights?

Justice Bradley, for the Court, concluded it could not. Rights, as we've seen Justice Bradley believed, are either created by the Constitution or merely secured by the Constitution. If there was such a right not to be discriminated against in public accommodations, Bradley maintained, the Constitution had not created it but only secured it. That meant, in Bradley's view, any power that Congress would have over such rights could only be indirect. If a state denied to its citizens the protection of such a right—or more precisely, if it denied protection to some and not to others—then Congress could remedy that denial. But critically (and incredibly stupidly, after Bradley's *Cruikshank* opinion), the Civil Rights Act did not condition its application upon any failure by the state, whether action or inaction. As Bradley wrote,

> It applies equally to cases arising in States which have the justest laws respecting the personal rights of citizens, and whose authorities are ever ready to enforce such laws, as to those which arise in States that may have violated the prohibition of the amendment.[107]

That meant, according to the framework Bradley has sketched, the law could not be sustained under the Fourteenth Amendment.

Neither could it be upheld under the provisions of the Civil War Amendments—specifically the Thirteenth Amendment—that gave Congress direct authority to regulate. Bradley acknowledged again the position he had first made clear in his *Cruikshank* opinion, which was that the Thirteenth Amendment gave Congress the power to legislate directly not just to end slavery but to secure the equal liberty of the just-freed slaves. As he wrote, beyond declaring slavery illegal, the amendment has a reflex character also, establishing and decreeing universal civil and political freedom throughout the United States; and it is assumed, that the power vested in Congress to enforce the article by appropriate legislation, clothes Congress with power to pass all laws necessary and proper for abolishing all badges and incidents of slavery in the United States:

So the question for the Court was whether a

denial to any person of admission to the accommodations and privileges of an inn, a public conveyance, or a theatre, does subject that person to any form of servitude, or tend to fasten upon him any badge of slavery?

Bradley concludes that it does not:

It would be running the slavery argument into the ground to make it apply to every act of discrimination which a person may see fit to make as to the guests he will entertain, or as to the people he will take into his coach or cab or car, or admit to his concert or theatre, or deal with in other matters of intercourse or business.[108]

If equal access to public accommodations had been a civil right, then the story would have been different. But because it was, in Bradley's view, just a "social right," Congress could not regulate it directly. Thus, under neither the Thirteenth nor Fourteenth Amendment could this law be sustained.

Justice Harlan dissented. Yet what's striking from our perspective is not the difference between Harlan and his brothers but the common ground. Like the Court, Harlan distinguishes between rights that can be protected directly and those that can be protected only indirectly. Harlan, like the Court, believes that the only rights that Congress can protect are civil rights, not social rights. As he comments:

I agree that government has nothing to do with social, as distinguished from technically legal, rights of individuals. No government ever has brought, or ever can bring, its people into social intercourse against their wishes. Whether one person will permit or maintain social relations with another is a matter with which government has no concern. I agree that if one citizen chooses not to hold social intercourse with another, he is not and cannot be made amenable to the law for his conduct in that regard; for ... no legal right of a citizen is violated by the refusal of others to maintain merely social relations with him.[109]

But the key difference between the Court and Harlan is that Harlan viewed the rights being protected by the Civil Rights Act of 1875 as *civil* rights, not *social* rights. And he believed as well that such civil rights could be protected by Congress directly, not just through the Thirteenth Amendment but also through the citizenship clause of the Fourteenth Amendment.

Let's consider these foundations in turn.

Harlan, following Sumner, maintained that the rights that the act protected were public, not private. The act secured equality in "public conveyances." These, Harlan insisted, were paid for—directly or indirectly—by the public. Surely that meant that the operators of those conveyances could be charged with an obligation not to discriminate against any member of the public.

The same with inns: the law had long recognized a special legal status with inns. As Harlan wrote:

> The word "inn" has a technical legal signification. It means, in the act of 1875, just what it meant at common law. A mere private boarding-house is not an inn, nor is its keeper subject to the responsibilities, or entitled to the privileges of a common innkeeper. "To constitute one an innkeeper, within the legal force of that term, he must keep a house of entertainment or lodging for all travelers or wayfarers who might choose to accept the same, being of good character or conduct."[110]

This special legal status, Harlan maintained, meant that access to an inn was not just a question of private choice. "The law gives [the innkeeper] special privileges, and he is charged with certain duties and responsibilities to the public." The Civil Rights Act of 1875 aimed simply to ensure equality in that public right.

And finally, with respect to amusements. Harlan read that language narrowly, suggesting it applied only to those amusements that required a license to operate. That license meant that the amusement was not purely private. As with inns, a license imbued those businessess with a public purpose, which the act of 1875 was simply ensuring would be extended equally.

In each case, Harlan insisted that the role of the state rendered public certain choices that otherwise might have been seen as private. That rendering meant that these rights were civil, not social. And that meant that Congress had the power under the Thirteenth and Fourteenth Amendments to ensure those civil rights were not denied on the basis of "race, color, or previous condition of servitude."

It's clear that if Bradley (and the Court) had seen these rights as civil rights, then Congress would have had the power to secure them. But as Brandwein powerfully demonstrates, this view was, at the time, highly contested.[111] Certainly, Radical Republicans viewed these rights as civil rights. But moderate Republicans (and all Democrats) viewed them as social. And however compelling Harlan (and Sumner's) legal reasoning might be, it ran headlong into a public attitude that refused to see these rights as anything other than social.

The best evidence for this reality comes, as Brandwein evinces, from the popular press. To a modern reader, it is striking just how sophisticated the popular press was at the time in its reporting and understanding of Supreme Court opinions. There are maybe one or two national newspapers today that could match the seriousness of their analysis. At that time, there were many.

As Brandwein reports, in response to the Court's decision in the *Civil Rights Cases*, every major newspaper, north and (obviously) south, endorsed the Court's conclusion. And they did so precisely because they viewed the domain being regulated by the law as essentially private. Harlan notwithstanding, they considered this case to be about the power of the government to regulate social rights; they did not see this case as questioning the power of the government to secure a civil right.

More important, to the extent the rights weren't private, these papers observed, state law already forbade discrimination. And to the extent such discrimination was permitted, state law notwithstanding, then, these papers argued, Congress would be perfectly entitled to hold the states responsible. Indeed, Bradley had made this point directly:

> Innkeepers and public carriers, by the laws of all the States, so far as we are aware, are bound, to the extent of their facilities, to furnish proper accommodation to all unobjectionable persons who in good faith apply for them. If the laws themselves make any unjust discrimination, amenable to the prohibitions of the Fourteenth Amendment, Congress has full power to afford a remedy under that amendment and in accordance with it.[112]

But to do this, Bradley and the commentators insisted, the federal law had to be conditioned upon some failure by the state. The Civil Rights Act of 1875 was not.

The triggering failure by the state could be either an act or an omission. The modern reader is likely to miss this point when reviewing Bradley's opinion. This fundamental idea, expressed by Bradley first in the letter to Judge Woods, is a central part of his (at this point, the Court's) understanding of "state action." On this view, a state denies a right when it acts affirmatively to take it away (for example, denying the right to contract to blacks). And a state denies a right when it refuses to enforce it. So a law may say nothing about blacks not being entitled to contract, but if the courts refuse to enforce contracts with blacks, that inaction is a deprivation as much as the action of passing a statute. Thus, if state law forbids discrimination in access to inns, yet the courts refused to enforce that rule when asserted by blacks, that would plainly, on Bradley's view of the law, be a denial of equal protection, and remediable by federal legislation.

Tragically, the Civil Rights Act of 1875 did not so condition its application. Charles Sumner was a brilliant activist. Yet he was also extraordinarily stubborn. He was convinced that the rights he wanted to protect could be protected directly. Yet he was long dead when that argument was considered once again by the Court—and rejected. And perhaps the greatest mistake of his career was in not compromising on this one belief and thereby crafting a statute that Bradley could endorse.

Harlan had one more argument, however, that Bradley's opinion just does not engage: that the citizenship clause of the Fourteenth Amendment should be understood as the creation of a new right—namely, the right to be free of racial discrimination in the provision of civil rights—and that, consequently, Congress should be able to enforce that right directly.

This was a great argument then. Law professor Jack Balkin has picked up the argument today.[113] But the Court did not engage it because it was not raised by the parties, and hence it was not before the Court when Bradley wrote his opinion. After Bradley had read his opinion at the announcement of the judgment, Harlan noted his dissent. But it would be months before he actually published his opinion. And while it was unlikely that the argument would have changed the result, it would have been useful and important for Bradley to have addressed it. Was there in fact another new right that Congress had the power to enforce directly? And if so, how far could it reach? Was this a right that Bradley in his *Cruikshank* opinion had missed? This mistake was not Sumner's. This was the lawyers' mistake.

There is finally one more reason that the Court was unlikely to reach as far as the Civil Rights Act reached. We're unlikely to see this point now, but it was central to the opposition raised against the law then.

As we look back on the inequality of the time, we're likely to think that the only target of unfavorable access was blacks. Yet of course, that was not America in the late nineteenth century. In addition to signs declaring "whites only," there were signs declaring "no Irish," "no Catholics," "no Jews," "no Yankees," "no Chinese," "no Indians"—whatever a people or a place thought wrong or distasteful or beneath them, it tried to bar. Against the background of these practices, the Civil Rights Act of 1875 had a very special meaning to nineteenth-century readers—not the meaning of equality for all, but the forbidding of one kind of discrimination among many, for one favored class.

This is why many would refer to the act as "special legislation." And in a sense, it was. It mandated equality on the basis of race but permitted inequality on the basis of many other critically identical aspects of identity, including ethnic origin and religion. Thus, even if Harlan was correct that in the Fourteenth Amendment there was a new right to equality that Congress had the power to enforce directly, selective protection of that right raised a red flag in the minds of the public and the judges. Had Congress forbidden discrimination on the basis of ethnic origin—as modern civil rights acts do— then the charge of "special legislation" may not have stuck. And maybe then, just possibly, the Court could have seen the right that Harlan raised only in a dissent published months after the opinion.

All this makes the Court's decision not good but understandable. Depending upon your view of the citizenship right, it might make the Court's decision defensible. (I think Harlan and Balkin have the better of the argument, though it would have helped had the argument been made to the Court before it decided the case.)

Yet as Brandwein emphasizes, we should recognize something critically important about how far this decision did not reach. Whether or not the law would allow those running "public accommodations" to accommodate the private wishes of their customers by providing separate cars or separate rooms at a restaurant, it was clear to even the defenders of the *Civil Rights Cases* that those private prejudices could *never* be embodied in or enabled by the law. As the *Chicago Tribune* wrote after the *Civil Rights Cases* were decided (and the *Tribune*, like every other major paper, strongly supported the result in those cases):

> If a negro be ejected from a hotel, a sleeping-car or a theatre, the courts are open to him to sue for damages just as they would be open to the white man under the same circumstances. The corporation or individual responsible for the ejection cannot set up the color or race of the negro in justification, for there is no local law authorizing such discrimination, and *if there were it would be under the decision held to be unconstitutional and void.*[114]

Yet of course, what would have been "unconstitutional and void" in 1883 became the law a baker's dozen years later. In 1896, the Supreme Court jumped the shark: in *Plessy v. Ferguson,* the Court upheld the power of the state not just to *permit* private discrimination in public accommodations but to *require* that discrimination as well. That holding was a huge leap, not just logically but factually, from the assumptions that reigned at the time the *Civil Rights Cases* were decided.

In the end, we, citizens of a republic that continues to feel the poison of racial inequality a century and a half after the end of the Civil War, cannot help but see Harlan's as the stronger argument. Given what happened in the balance of that century through the middle of the twentieth century, it is impossible to believe that it was time to assert about former slaves (as Bradley had in the *Civil Rights Cases*) that "there must be some stage in the progress of his elevation when he takes the rank of a mere citizen." Who knows whether enforcing a public accommodations act in 1883 would have made any difference. Maybe it would have triggered an even more forceful reaction by white supremacists. Yet from our perspective, it seems like just one more opportunity that the nation wasn't given a chance to try.

So, my purpose in this very extended analysis of what I've called (following Brandwein) the first period of Reconstruction is not so much to defend these decisions—though they are much stronger than most give them credit for. My aim instead has been to make them make sense in the context within which they were rendered. I've tried to do that by engaging in the practice of a careful translator. The first step of any translation is to make the text understandable in the context within which it was written, and specifically to bring to the foreground those aspects of the context that would otherwise be invisible to us today.

The Court in this first period didn't abandon the commitments of the Civil War Amendments. It integrated those commitments into a legal context that the judges took for granted. Given how they understood rights, the Thirteenth and Fifteenth Amendment rights would look very different from the rights protected in the Fourteenth Amendment (bracketing whether Harlan was correct about the citizenship right or not). Those differences would matter as the Court interpreted the reach of those amendments against the framework of federalism.

Likewise with the nature of the rights thought to be essential to citizenship. Everyone denominated those rights as civil, not social. And indeed, framed like this, that distinction survives to this day. I take it that even the most committed supporter of equal rights legislation would reject the idea that the government could regulate whom one was friends with. We, like they, believe there is some space the government cannot reach, even if it is reaching for the most important type of interest it could have—equality.

Instead, what we see in the *Civil Rights Cases* is an example of perpetual contestation. And while Harlan certainly had the stronger view—that it should be Congress that draws that line and not the Court—that there was a line to be drawn between civil and social rights was not a crazy thought, or a thought of extreme racists only.

So yes, had the citizenship right that Harlan identified been articulated in the briefs and engaged by Bradley, there is a chance the Court could have decided differently. And had Sumner not stubbornly refused to take a clear signal from the Court about how to protect rights deemed natural, then there's a chance the last civil rights act Congress would pass until the mid-twentieth century could have survived. And had it survived, then maybe it would have been more difficult for the Court to embrace legally enforced segregation.

Yet there was a growing political reality that would increasingly render anything more by the Court difficult at least, and maybe impossible. This is the analogy I meant to draw with the post–New Deal cases. A cultural or legal *force majeure* left the Court with little it could practically do. And it did little.

There are cases in this period that throw doubt on this more forgiving reading, and others that support it. In *United States v. Reese* (1876), a companion to *Cruikshank*, the Court threw out Sections 3 and 4 of the Enforcement Act of 1870.[115] Those sections were grounded in the new right created by the Fifteenth Amendment. But the provisions didn't limit themselves to refusals on account of race. Sections 1 and 2 did. But Sections 3 and 4 used the phrase "as aforesaid." The limit, Chief Justice Waite instructed, had to be express.

Modern readers see this as suspiciously too strict. "As aforesaid" actually *said* the sections were limited to race. Why was the Court dictating legislative draftsmanship? But as political scientist Leslie Goldstein has noted, though the original indictment was drawn under the 1870 statute, that statute had been recodified in 1874. Under the new codification, "as aforesaid" had been removed. *Reese* was then perfectly correct as to the statute then in effect—and it was open to Congress to fix the error in codification by amending the two sections to add back a limit to race.[116]

Four years before *Reese*, the Court had read the right of African Americans to testify in court extremely narrowly. Though the Court recognized the Civil Rights Act had established that right, in *Blyew v. United States* (1872), the Court held it could not be enforced except by parties directly affected by an action. Witnesses who were not parties were not directly affected.

This reading of the Civil Rights Act is hard to defend. Yet what's striking is that its author is the justice who wrote the most aggressively pro-equality opinions of the period, William Strong, and the dissent is by the justice who has been most strongly vilified in this period, Bradley. The narrowness in Strong's opinion is hard to understand; the breadth in Bradley's dissent is hard to associate with someone said to be committed to overturning the effects of the Civil War Amendments. Wrote Bradley:

> To deprive a whole class of the community of this right, to refuse their evidence and their sworn complaints, is to brand them with a badge of slavery; is to expose them to wanton insults and fiendish assaults; is to leave their lives, their families, and their property unprotected by law. It gives unrestricted license and impunity to vindictive outlaws and felons to rush upon these helpless people and kill and slay them at will, as was done in this case. To say that actions or prosecutions intended for the redress of such outrages are not "causes affecting the persons" who are the victims of them, is to take, it seems to me, a view of the law too narrow, too technical, and too forgetful of the liberal objects it had in view.[117]

On balance, then, this first period is not the embarrassment that modern scholars suggest. The embarrassment was the political class turning its back on a liberated people That embarrassment was not the Court's. The Court was strict in cases it could have been more forgiving in, and it was obtuse to the practical consequences of its hesitation. But this was not a Court committed to reversing the commitments of the Civil War Amendments. It was a Court, like any court, that had no ability to force the political branches to act against the increasingly solid view of an exhausted people.

| Equality II

I F THE FIRST AND SECOND PERIODS after the Civil War are not moments
for embarrassment, the third period plainly is. No doubt, in the period
from *Plessy* (1896) to *Brown v. Board of Education* (1954), the Court is no
worse than any other branch of our government. But the bending that the
Court permits likely encouraged these other branches to bend even more.
Indeed, the clearest sin of the Court during this period may well be the sin of
the collaborator. Maybe there was little it could have done to resist the growing racism of this period, but it didn't need to do so much to encourage it.
Instead, the Court was too slow to recognize the value of principled dissent,
and too cowardly to deploy it consistently in the context of the violence that
racism was producing.

## Period 2: 1896 Through 1954

The Court's cowardice, of course, was not limited to race. One of the most
dramatic stories of the law of civil rights is the story of the birth of an enforceable First Amendment. When dissenters challenged Woodrow Wilson
in his decision to take America to war, Wilson responded with incredible
brutality, invoking the newly enacted Sedition Act of 1918, which built
upon the Espionage Act of 1917, and prosecuting many, including Socialist
presidential candidate Eugene Debs. At first the Supreme Court gave this
outrage a pass—no doubt, in part, for fidelity to role reasons, realizing the
Court was not about to question a president in the middle of an ongoing
struggle to get Americans to support a war.

But eventually even the realists were shocked into speaking. Justice Holmes had famously written an opinion for the Court upholding convictions under the Espionage Act of 1917 of defendants accused of circulating pamphlets "alleged to be calculated" to obstruct recruitment to the military. The First Amendment, Holmes said, may well reach beyond prior restraints. But "the character of every act depends upon the circumstances.... The most stringent protection of free speech would not protect a man in falsely shouting fire in a theatre."[1] So Holmes concluded that resisting the draft when the nation was at war was similarly outside the scope of protection.

Likewise, in the same year, Holmes, writing for the Court, upheld the conviction of a publisher of a German publication opposing the war. On the record, Holmes wrote, the Court couldn't conclude that the writing might not "kindle a flame." That was enough to support this speech crime.[2]

And finally, it was Holmes who wrote the opinion that sent Debs to jail for a speech he had made in Canton, Ohio.[3]

Yet then Holmes reversed himself. In *Abrams v. United States* (1919), Holmes dissented from an opinion that sent socialists to prison for up to twenty years. He (joined by Justice Brandeis) dissented again six years later in a case that sent an anarchist to prison for publishing a manifesto.[4] And then two years after that, Brandeis (joined by Holmes) wrote the clearest and most powerful statement of the modern conception of the First Amendment—that the right to speak freely can be limited only "to protect the state from destruction or serious injury." That can't be shown unless the speech "is intended to produce[] a clear and imminent danger."[5]

This was an incredible flip. Remember, it was Holmes who chuckled in *Giles v. Harris* (1903) when blacks in Alabama asked the Court to use its power to end the systematic violation of the Fifteenth Amendment in that state.[6] That was Holmes the realist, motivated by a clear sense of the limits on what the Court could do. But by *Abrams*, Holmes had come to recognize that the question was not just the power of the Court to order specific results, but also the moral force the justices had to seed the political space with the ideals that were actually part of our constitutional tradition. *Giles v. Harris* (1903) would have been a very different case if for technical reasons the Court did nothing but, in dissent at least, flagged the outrageousness of the conditions across the South for blacks wanting to vote. That effect may not have been as clear to the justices before they saw the vitality of Justice Harlan's dissent in *Plessy,* the case we will turn to presently.

Yet beyond Harlan in *Plessy,* there was not much principled opposition in the Supreme Court to the racism that raged across this period. Instead, in this second period, America was dominated by racism at every level of government.

This wasn't Europe circa 2016, when racism was tied to class. The racism of America cut across class. Woodrow Wilson showed—and celebrated—*Birth of a Nation* in the White House. And Teddy Roosevelt was not much better. (In 1905, he declared that "race purity must be maintained.")[7] Indeed, it is hard to find any national leader of stature—save the leaders among African Americans—who, like Grant or Garfield or Sumner or Stevens, was an open advocate for racial equality. This was a dark period in American history. Almost no one with any power seemed even to care. C. Vann Woodward is certainly correct that where we were by the turn of the twentieth century had been in no sense preordained at the end of the Civil War.[8] Things could have gone very differently. But as things did go, by the birth of the third period of civil rights, America had turned its back fully on the commitments of the Civil War Amendments—except (adding insult to injury) as they might benefit corporations or the wealthy.

To understand how this extremism was possible, we must begin with this racist culture. To remix Shakespeare a bit, how was it bred? In the heart, or in the head? How begot? How nourished?

The psychology that created this racism is no doubt complex. Its mechanisms are many and overlapping. Yet from our perspective, the important thing to see in this period is the many different sources that whites would draw upon for the social conclusion that blacks "were" or "must be made to remain" unequal. For whites at this time, this was a "truth" that was supported on many fronts.

It was supported first by a kind of social cognitive dissonance. The enterprise launched by Lincoln and affirmed by Grant had obviously failed in the South. The Civil War, and the Civil War Amendments, had not produced a world in which African Americans were equal citizens in America. Of course, this was not unintended—at least by the white terrorists in the South who marched forward to "redeem" southern culture. Through force and intimidation, blacks were kept away from the polls. That absence meant there was no local political support for equality to replace the federal legal support that would be withdrawn. African Americans in the South then fell into an abyss of poverty and hopelessness. In 1870, "per capita black income, as a share of per capita white income..., was roughly 0.25."[9] That number would never cross 0.5 until the middle of the twentieth century.[10]

This reality needed explanation—at least for the Americans at the end of the nineteenth century. The weakness of northern whites was an inconvenient truth, better forgotten or excluded. Much more convincing to them would be an account that tied the failure to blacks themselves. Equality was not achieved, on this account, because blacks were, in their nature, not equal to whites. They were lesser, or inferior, and that fact about them—not the weakness of whites in living up to a constitutional commitment—explained the truth about southern society.

This view about black responsibility for black failure certainly had support in the law. Recall again Justice Bradley's truly ignorant statement in the *Civil Rights Cases*—"there must be some stage in the progress of his elevation when he takes the rank of a mere citizen."

But law alone does not account for or justify the reality of the American South. Instead, America needed something more solid to explain the embarrassment that was the South.

That something more would be science.

## THE VIOLENCE OF SCIENCE

*Slavery . . . was a matter of economics, a question of income and labor, rather than a problem of right and wrong, or of the physical differences in men. Once slavery began to be the source of vast income for men and nations, there followed a frantic search for moral and racial justifications.*

—W. E. B. Du Bois[11]

It is a truth of human psychology that when we do something bad, we enter a market for rationalization. We desperately want a reason why what we know we shouldn't have done was something that in fact we should have done. We want to believe we're good and right, even when we know that we've betrayed ideals that we inherited. Maybe our forebears were wrong. Maybe their ideals were false. Maybe we know more than they knew. Maybe if they knew "the truth" as we do, they too would see the error of their ways.

This was the dynamic of social psychology after Reconstruction. A brave and lonely president had led a nation to save itself. In the process, the institution of legalized slavery had been abolished. Those goods were sacrosanct, and none would question them now. But millions of other ideals of civil and political equality, and the more fundamental ideal of free labor, would be challenged, questioned, and eventually rejected—at least as they related to race.

By the end of the nineteenth century, "everyone knew" why racism was right. This came about because white America wanted to "know" this, and because science delivered what whites wanted. "As long as the traditional order . . . was not challenged," historian George Fredrickson writes, "by a radical ideology calling for revolutionary change, it was not necessary to bring ideo-logical consciousness to social assumptions."[12] But as the struggles for equal-ity continued to simmer, the resistance continued to seek scientific shelter.

This was the birth of "scientific racism"—the effort to render as fact the impossibility of equality. As Nancy Stepan describes:

> By the middle of the nineteenth century, a very complex edifice of thought about human races had been developed in science that was sometimes explicitly, but more often implicitly, racist. That is to say, the language, concepts, methods and authority of science were used to support the belief that certain human groups were intrinsically inferior to others, as measured by some socially defined criterion, such as intelligence or "civilised" behaviour. A "scientific racism" had come into existence that was to endure until well after the Second World War.[13]

This "complex edifice" became an organizing principle. "Increasingly, the moral claim," Stepan writes, "to equality of treatment was taken to be a matter not of ethical theory but of anatomy."

> If all races were found to be anatomically and physiologically alike, then the rights and privileges enjoyed by the European would be guaranteed for all peoples. The appeal to nature in deciding what was in reality a moral issue was fatal, but one made by the anti-abolitionists and eventually the abolitionists alike. Nature was now the arbiter of morality.[14]

This "racist thought," Fredrickson argues, "did not reach its crescendo until the end of the nineteenth century, when it latched on to Darwinism—a more convincing scientific support than the earlier theory that blacks had been cre-ated separately by God before Adam and Eve had begotten 'the superior white species.'"

> But pseudoscientific Darwinian racism did not differ from the pre–Civil War variety in its basic assumptions about the differences between blacks and whites. What gave the reformulated doctrine its new virulence was its association with an aggressive southern campaign for the legal segregation and disenfranchisement of the blacks who three decades earlier had been freed from slavery.[15]

"Scientists were entrusted," Elazar Barkan argues, "with the tasks of discrim-inating between fact and opinion and defining the social and political dis-courses of race."[16]

As advocates claimed to be relying upon the "truths" of science to defend separation and, eventually, legally enforced segregation, courts found themselves constrained. That's not to say that they resisted the constraint. It's simply to note that whether they wanted to or not, "truth" was a boundary. "For most of the period," Herbert Hovenkamp has written, "the Court closely tracked prevailing scientific opinion on race. No responsible judge would have believed that the fourteenth amendment required the state to do something manifestly unreasonable or grossly injurious to the public health or welfare."[17] Instead, where "genetic determinism" had "created a situation in which strict racial segregation appeared to be socially prudent," the Court was not about to spit into the wind of such prudence.[18]

These scientists were not necessarily evil. They were not even necessarily anti-egalitarian. Instead, as Stepan remarks, "the scientists who gave scientific racism its credibility and respectability were often first-rate scientists struggling to understand what appeared to them to be deeply puzzling problems of biology and human society."[19] Indeed, "most," Stepan argues, "were not consciously racist."

> Many were instead people of humane outlook, opponents of slavery, decent individuals who would have been shocked by any charge that they were racists. Their work is on the whole not filled with race hatred. In fact, what makes the history of race science so interesting is that so many of the outstanding scientists of the past believed that biological races were the key to the most pressing problems of the day—the future of the Americas, the fate of the European in the tropics, the extinction of peoples, the role of Britain in Europe.[20]

Yet as Einstein would learn when he saw his insights used to create atomic weapons, the enlightenment of the discoverer does not determine the use of the discovery. There were people who sought to secure inequality who would use these scientists' work to do so if it would help.

No doubt, there were dissenters among the scientists. In 1894, Franz Boas, newly elected head of the Anthropological Section of the American Association for the Advancement of Science, caused a stir when he signaled his "skepticism" about "prevailing attitudes toward the colored races."[21] And nothing in this history should suggest any kind of determinism. As Barkan puts it, this recognition "should not lead to a reductionist conclusion that science determined politics, nor the reverse, that politics determined science. Rather the two were strongly intertwined."[22] Yet, intertwined as they were, they created an important constraint for courts.

It is impossibly hard for us today to understand the power of the ideals of scientific racism. Our brains don't allow us to unlearn. And if we've learned anything, we've learned about the bullshit in these "scientific" claims.

So, to see the power of those ideals, we need to imagine ourselves in a place where we didn't know what we now know. When it wasn't simply scum or scoundrels who uttered such words, but the very best of society. In that world, it was the ideal of equality that was crazy. And to understand that world, we need to imagine a way to credit that normal, even if we now believe it is just nuts. Here's an exercise that might get us close.

There is a taken-for-granted (or, in the terms used in Chapter 7, uncontested) view within our society today about children. That view is not that we hate children (though some do). It is not that we consider children to be a different species (though, as any parent will attest, sometimes we wonder). It is instead that we believe children are different. They don't reason as completely. They haven't understood as much. They can't control their emotions as fully. They are, in a word, immature. For any particular child, that will change (or so we can hope). Their condition is temporary. But no one who has spent any time with children can doubt that there is something profound that separates them from us—even if there is something even more profound, love, that binds us to them.

Science confirms this difference.[23] Children are cognitively and psychosocially different.[24] They make choices differently.[25] Their potential for useful and effective rehabilitation is different.[26] These are differences grounded not in culture or stereotypes but in the best available science about brain and emotional development.

Of course, there are dissenters to these views. There are some who believe that while children are different, they are not so different as to justify the radical difference in rights they enjoy.[27] Yet we recognize these dissenters as different. Sometimes harmlessly different (there are people who want to impanel a shadow Congress of twelve-year-olds—I say go for it). Sometimes dangerously different (pedophiles). But whether harmless or not, such dissenters mark the boundary between what normal people think and what normal people don't think. Being on the right side of this boundary in many important contexts is a necessary condition to being accepted within our society today.

Consider, then, against this background of what we all know is true, a claim by a fourteen-year-old for "equal rights"—the right to vote, the right to sit on a jury, the right not to be segregated on the basis of age. "We are treated differently," the boy claims. "That difference violates the constitutional command of equality."

There's no doubt that this precocious kid is right about the difference. Kids are treated differently. They do get fewer privileges or rights (depending upon how you see them) than adults. But for the kid to prevail in his claim for equal rights, he must do more than simply identify a difference. For (1) from the fact that a law imposes burdens differently, it doesn't follow that the law is discriminatory. (Every law imposes burdens differently; not every law is discriminatory.) And (2) even if a law is discriminatory, it may well be that the discrimination is justified. These two claims will be helpful for understanding the argument that follows, so let's rehearse them a bit before moving on.

Regarding the first point, *different treatment does not mean "discrimination."* I've put the word "discrimination" in quotes here because I want to suggest a particular, if familiar, sense of the term. In this particular sense, discrimination is narrower than distinction. It is also richer. The *Oxford English Dictionary* defines it as "the making of distinctions prejudicial to people," where the word "prejudice" evokes a complex set of ideas that resonate with equality. That certain distinctions would be *seen as* prejudicial depends upon the *social meaning* of those distinctions.[28]

Put somewhat obscurely and circularly, we recognize the possibility of "the making of distinctions prejudicial to people" only when we recognize the particular people involved as having a valid claim to equality.

In the example I've used, we don't "discriminate" against children, even though we impose different burdens upon them and grant them different benefits.

Neither do we "discriminate" against dolphins, even though we grant them different privileges than humans.

But to deny the right to vote to African Americans—for us, today—is to "discriminate" against African Americans. The difference in these cases tells us not about the logic of "discrimination." It tells us instead something about us. We could imagine societies where the judgments would be different. But we occupy a society in which we would acknowledge our precocious fourteen-year-old's claim that he was being treated "differently" but reject his claim that he was being "discriminated" against.

Or even if we didn't reject that claim, we'd have an answer to it. That answer is the second point: *discrimination can sometimes be justified.* Even if one believes a law that draws a distinction is discriminatory, that discrimination can, in certain cases at least, be justified. Under current law, for example, if a prison segregates inmates on the basis of race, that act is plainly discriminatory. But if that act is done in the context of a riot, or a similar threat to safety, that discrimination is nonetheless justified. The Constitution places a significant burden on the government to establish that the discrimination is justified. But in this context, the government is likely to meet that burden.[29]

This is an obvious point, too often forgotten. As we evaluate judgments about whether certain practices are constitutional or not, we can properly evaluate those judgments only if we understand something about what those who made those judgments believed. Why they believed what they believed is not, for the moment, important. For now the point is this: if they believed it, what did it mean for claims about "equality"?

Let's return now to our hypothetical precocious fourteen-year-old. When we deny fourteen-year-olds the right to vote or the right to sit on a jury, or when we segregate them on the basis of age, is that "discrimination"?

The answer differs depending upon the example. I take it the first two are plainly discrimination—based upon a prejudgment about kids, we deny them a certain right. But I also take it that such discrimination is perfectly justified: it is limited (until they get older), and it turns upon a fair estimate of their capacity.

The segregation example, however, is different. In this case, I would argue the distinction doesn't even rise to the level of "discrimination." There's no stigma associated with such age discrimination because the social meaning of such distinctions has nothing to do with harming or demeaning anyone. Education is progressive. It is not harmful to recognize differences in progress. Of course, particular kids may feel differently. They may feel that being forced to associate only with people their own age does indeed stigmatize them significantly. But if they have that view, then "it is not by reason of anything found in the act, but solely because [they] choose[] to put that construction upon it."[30] (Yes, I recognize the parallel here. That's my whole point.)

You might well think I've made the story more complicated than it needs to be by distinguishing between distinctions that are discriminations and discriminations that are justified. Hold that skepticism till we're finished with the cases. My only point so far is to get you to recognize (1) a way of looking at a group of people, (2) that you certainly share that way of looking, at least when it comes to some groups of people, and (3) that this way of looking at others yields the conclusion that the distinctions the law draws today about children are fully justified.

Obviously, African Americans are not kids. Nor are women, aliens, the elderly, and so on. But if you believed African Americans burdened, relative to whites, in a related way—if you really believed it, with your beliefs backed up by the most (absurd but) mainstream science—how could that affect your judgments about whether certain Fourteenth Amendment distinctions were discrimination? And how would it affect whether any such discriminations were justified? Recall again the quote from Herbert Hovenkamp, writing of this time:

> For most of the period the Court closely tracked prevailing scientific opinion on race. No responsible judge would have believed that the

fourteenth amendment required the state to do something manifestly unreasonable or grossly injurious to the public health or welfare.[31]

It is against the background of this way of understanding discrimination, and the cultural background of late nineteenth-century America, that we should begin to consider the most infamous case from this era, *Plessy v. Ferguson* (1896). This is the first case in what I've called period 2. Following Brandwein, it is the first case to mark clearly just how far the Court had fallen from the ideals of equality.

*Plessy* began as a fight about which railroad car the plaintiff had the right to sit in. Homer Plessy had purchased a ticket on the East Louisiana Railroad. He had tried to sit in the whites-only car on that train. All trains in Louisiana were required by law to have seating sections, "separate but equal," for whites and non-whites. Plessy insisted he was entitled to a seat in the white section.

Plessy grounded his argument on the fact that, based on his ancestry, he was seven-eighths white. That should, he believed, entitle him to all the privileges of being white, one of which was the privilege of sitting with other whites. The railroad had denied him this privilege, and Plessy sued for damages—including the damage of taking his "property," namely, the property of being white.

As the case was decided by the Supreme Court, the sole question was whether the statute that required segregation based on race violated the Constitution. To answer that question, the Court embraced the distinction among rights that had guided it in the *Civil Rights Cases*—civil rights, political rights, and social rights. No doubt, the Court acknowledged, the state would have no power to legally burden the civil rights of blacks relative to whites. And no doubt, as the Court had recently held, it would have no power to legally burden the political rights of blacks relative to whites.[32]

But social rights, the Court suggested, were not within the scope of federal power. States were not obligated to regulate them to make sure they were "equal." And as everyone recognized, social rights were not in any sense equal in the United States—either then or now. Whites did not equally wish to associate with blacks. Blacks did not equally wish to associate with whites. Men did not equally wish to associate with women. The rich did not equally wish to associate with the poor. Non-Irish did not equally wish to associate with Irish. These truths were undeniable. Social reality was a radically unequal space. And the only question raised in the *Plessy* case, as the Court viewed it, was whether the law could recognize these inegalitarian preferences and support them through legislation. Put differently, could the state use law to give legal effect to social rights?

Think of it as a kind of zoning regulation, but social zoning rather than physical zoning. Can the law draw lines that reflect the social preferences of its citizens, and enforce those lines through civil or criminal penalties?

Because of course, the law does this today in all sorts of ways. There are bathrooms designated for men and bathrooms designated for women, reflecting the social preference of most that they be permitted to use a bathroom with only members of their own sex. (Bracket the fight about transgender individuals' use of a bathroom; that's a different battle.) Presumably a law today that required "separate but equal bathrooms" (segregating on the basis of sex, not race) would not violate the Constitution. So why would a law that segregated on the basis of race—whether bathrooms or railroad cars—be unconstitutional?

The Court in *Plessy* acknowledged the law was drawing a line. It was, as the Court wrote, "impl[ying] a legal distinction between the white and colored races." But the law draws many such distinctions. What would make this legal distinction problematic but other ones not?

In the Court's view, the answer was found in the nature of the intent necessarily implied by the legal distinction itself. The Court pointed to the extraordinary case of *Yick Wo v. Hopkins* (1886), in which the Supreme Court had held that an ordinance applied to ban Chinese nationals from operating laundries was a legal distinction that was also a discrimination, because it was applied "for the annoyance or oppression of a particular class."[33] As the Court wrote, if the ordinance had been

> applied and administered by public authority with an evil eye and an unequal hand, so as practically to make unjust and illegal discriminations between persons in similar circumstances, material to their rights, the denial of equal justice is still within the prohibition of the Constitution.[34]

But in *Plessy*, the Court believed the segregation of Louisiana was not enacted with "an evil eye and an unequal hand." Louisiana had not denied African Americans the right to ride on a railcar, in the same way that San Francisco was trying to deny Chinese the right to run laundries; rather, it was giving legal effect to an existing social prejudice. All legislation must be tested, the Court insisted, against the background of the "established usages, customs, and traditions of the people." And against those, and in particular against the background of this existing social prejudice, this law was "reasonable." As law professor Michael Klarman remarks, "Segregation seemed a reasonable response to escalating white-on-black violence and an overwhelming white consensus behind preserving 'racial purity.'"[35]

And of course, it was "reasonable"—in the context of the late nineteenth century, years after the birth of scientific racism, and long into the normalization of a political and economic culture that recognized two clear classes in America and supported the separation of each. Indeed, it was the very essence of the idea of "reasonable," as it was precisely what practically everyone within a dominating class believed. "Reasonable" is inherently relative, which means, obviously, that much that is "reasonable" across the history of humankind is just flat-out wrong.

In this sense, then, there was nothing bizarre in the Court's opinion itself, for the opinion reflected attitudes that the culture had come to take for granted. The inferiority of the African race was a truth for the elite of the time, not opinion. And against the background of that truth, it was Justice Harlan's view that would have struck most people as crazy. "There are no castes here," Harlan had declared in his dissent in *Plessy*. What could that possibly mean? In the United States children did not have the same rights as their parents. Were they a caste? In the United States women did not have the same rights as men. Were they a caste too?

What was operating in *Plessy* was the normal view of a racist society. Normal people saw the appropriateness of race-based segregation. It was as obvious to them as separate bathrooms for men and women are to many today.[36] Justice Henry Billings Brown affirmed that normal view not with argument but with a description of what was plainly considered reasonable at the time, which included race-based segregation. Justice Brown did not need to defend that claim. It was shared by everyone in 1896—including Homer Plessy! Or practically everyone, at least, and certainly almost everyone who mattered to the world of power.

Against the background of how the world was seen (at least by this unreconstructed elite), there was no harm in *Plessy*. In much the same way as we today would view segregating kids by age or public bathrooms by gender, the Court saw no harm flowing from a segregation on the basis of race. Of course, the Court saw no harm because it viewed African Americans as different. From our perspective, it was that move that was most unjustified. But within the context of its decision, however repulsive it is for us to acknowledge, that reality made it reasonable for justices to accept what "normal" people would have believed: nature had made men of different races different, just as nature had made women different from men, and that difference made reasonable the differences in treatment.

We can understand this case in terms of the matrix I introduced in Chapter 7.

The difference ascribed to African Americans (and the consequent unequal status) was relatively uncontested. Not by everyone, of course—certainly African Americans had a different view—but by the elites within the ranks of society that determined what was "normal" and "reasonable." Indeed, it was the precise point Homer Plessy was trading upon when he insisted the state had taken his property.

That fact, in turn, was a constraint on the Court, in two very different senses. First, it constrained how the "normal" judge on that Court would have seen the legal distinction that Louisiana had drawn. From the perspective of fidelity to meaning, that "normal" judge would not have *seen* such a distinction as discrimination, any more than we see rules banning kids from juries as "discrimination." Indeed, what's striking in the Court's language is its list of examples of perfectly "reasonable" legal distinctions. Invoking Justice Lemuel Shaw writing for the Massachusetts Supreme Judicial Court, the Court notes:

> It was held that the powers of the committee extended to the establishment of separate schools for children of different ages, sexes and colors, and that they might also establish special schools for poor and neglected children, who have become too old to attend the primary school, and yet have not acquired the rudiments of learning, to enable them to enter the ordinary schools.[37]

What is notable about this list of permissible "legal distinctions" for segregated schools—age, sex, skin color, and "poor and neglected children, who have become too old to attend the primary school, and yet have not acquired the rudiments of learning"—is that, but for race, every other distinction is today either completely permissible or at least contested.[38] For the "normal" judge at the time, segregating on the basis of race was as obvious as segregating on the basis of age is to us today.

Again, please don't get me wrong. I certainly do not believe that segregation on the basis of race is the same as segregation on the basis of age. I am an American born in the 1960s and raised in a culture that takes that for granted. But history is only ever the history of *them* then as seen by *us* now. And to know who *they* are, we must work hard to understand how they would have viewed the world. Understanding is not agreement. It is not forgiveness. It is certainly not to assert that the wrong committed was not a wrong. It is a way of coming to see, as much as possible, how they would have seen, so as to come to understand how they would have acted.

It is also a way to understand how they should properly have interpreted a constitutional provision. Because in my view, for a clause like this, interpretation is hopelessly embedded in an existing political and social culture. There is no cognizable claim for equality in the abstract. It is only ever a claim within a particular context. And within any culture, there will be distinctions that fall plainly within the domain of equality (for us, race, sex, sexual orientation), distinctions that are arguably within the domain of equality (for us, teenagers, illegal immigrants), and distinctions plainly outside the domain of equality (for us, dolphins, young children). Culture *always* defines the scope of permissible interpretation. In this sense, "permissible interpretation" is contingent upon culture, and culture is constantly changing.

How, and with what dynamic, is something we will see as we work through the cases. But it is important here to avoid an easy misunderstanding.

To say that the scope of permissible interpretation is contingent upon the culture is not to say that it is contingent upon the whim of the justices. No doubt, a group of five justices has the power to make their view law—for a time, at least. But that power does not define the scope of permissible interpretation, because the decision of that group of five justices could simply be wrong.

Take an extreme case to make the point. Imagine some lawyer taking the view that dolphins (and beluga whales, but let's keep this simple) should be deemed "persons" under the Fourteenth Amendment. She has that view because she has a crude, "lawyer-lite" understanding of the mental and emotional capacity of a dolphin. Given that understanding, this lawyer sees no principled reason to distinguish a creature with the dolphin's capability from any human. It would then follow from this view that the failure of Hawaii to protect dolphins from murder should be actionable under the Fourteenth Amendment as a deprivation of life without due process of law. ("What about a fetus?" I hear you asking. Hold that question until we get to Chapter 19.)

But I take it that this view, however persuasive our lawyer could be, is not the view of Americans generally. It is not the view of the legal elite in particular. It is *understandable*, just as the argument of Roy Batty in *Blade Runner* that Nexus-6 replicants should be considered as "persons" is understandable (and, for saps like me, completely persuasive). But it is neither believable nor believed. And so while it's conceivable that five justices on the Supreme Court would hold that a dolphin is a "person," if they so held in the United States circa 2020, their holding would be a mistake. "A universal feeling," as Lincoln remarked, this time applied to the "feeling" that dolphins are not persons, "whether well or ill-founded, cannot be safely disregarded."[39] One could be hopeful that there will come a time when such a holding would not be a mistake. But today it would be a clear mistake. Frankfurter told his colleagues in connection with the first case to address whether citizens can be compelled to salute the flag, "No duty of judges is more important nor more difficult to discharge than that of guarding against reading their personal and debatable opinions into the case."[40] That is the sense I mean here.

Instead, what is necessary to make that claim about dolphins something more than "personal and debatable"—indeed, one could say, true—is a certain evolution in the attitudes of engaged citizens. For it to be true, it must become *relatively uncontested* among these engaged citizens. That, sad to say, is not going to happen anytime soon.

This way of thinking about the truth of the claim "dolphins are persons" obviously raises a host of questions—How do we know? Who gets to decide? When is it clear? How could a claim that it is true be falsified?—only some of which I address in this book. But bracket those questions for now. My point so far is the simple claim that the truth of the matter is not determined by the vote of five justices on the Supreme Court.

Going back to *Plessy,* then, my claim is, first, that the "normal" judge circa 1896 would have *seen* the legal distinction of race to be the same as a legal distinction of age is for us today. And given that that was how they *saw* things, it would not be true to say that, *for them,* the distinction was a discrimination. So from the perspective of fidelity to meaning, the reading that says that it wasn't discrimination is correct.

That's not to say that the republic was innocent of the history that brought America to this view. The "strange case of Jim Crow," to draw on the title of C. Vann Woodward's book, could have been different. Had the Panic of 1873 been averted, maybe the Republicans could have knit the nation together and avoided the victory of white terrorism. Maybe Thaddeus Stevens would have secured the redistribution of rebel land to former slaves. Maybe a stronger moral commitment to equality in 1876 would have changed what turned out to be the natural view of the elite in 1896. Thus, to say "this is who we were" is not to say "this is who we should have been" or "this is who we had to be." It is simply to report on what a court that is properly reading the legal text against the essential referent, a social context, must say.

But let's imagine that the Supreme Court had been filled with abnormal judges—judges like Harlan, the quintessential outsider, and the only justice of the United States Supreme Court to have graduated from Transylvania University (and not the one in Romania). Let's imagine there were four other justices who agreed with him that Louisiana's law could not be upheld. Harlan doesn't actually engage the Court on its own terms, and therefore it's not clear from his opinion whether if "liberty" entitles an African-American to ride in any railroad car he wishes, it also entitles a fourteen-year-old to sit on a jury. But regardless of the reason, imagine that five justices believe Homer Plessy should have the right to sit wherever he wants to sit.

That view would then implicate the second dimension of fidelity—fidelity to role. Because if those five are enlightened enough to see the injustice being delivered upon Homer Plessy, they are also enlightened enough to recognize just how alien their own view is. That alienness should give them pause to consider what democracy requires. If they recognize that their view conflicts with an uncontested view going the other way, then they should ask themselves, "By what right do I get to declare myself right and everyone else wrong?" And, recognizing the tenuousness of that claim, they should then recognize the costs that making that claim would have for the institution they serve. It is not the job of judges to assert the truth of a moral claim against the uncontested view of the public—at least in a majority opinion, at least with the force of law. In this sense, they are not Dworkin's Hercules.

That claim about the job of a judge is complex. My aim throughout the course of this book is to fill in a rich conception of the job of a judge. This is another installment. And whether you agree with my history or not—whether or not you believe that "normal" people believe this legal distinction is not discrimination—conceptually, my only aim just now is to mark an extreme on the continuum. For a claim like this—which necessarily embeds social understandings in its ontology—it violates fidelity of role *in a democracy* for the Court to insist on a view contrary to a view deemed uncontested.

For other claims, that conflict is not a constraint. Imagine an immensely popular candidate for president, elected with an overwhelming majority of popular and electoral college support, who is then determined to be only thirty-three instead of the minimum of thirty-five required by the Constitution. A decision by the Court that would rule this candidate disqualified (if the Court deemed itself jurisdictionally empowered to so rule) would be immensely unpopular. But that unpopularity is not, on its own, a reason for the Court not to act. If the Court is acting according to role, then so ought the Court to act, whether or not the decision is viewed favorably by the public.

Okay, but what if the five justices who take Harlan's side see their underlying view not as the contradiction of an uncontested view but as itself a contested view? What if they believe that, whether recognized or not, there is a deep conflict about whether such a legal distinction is discrimination? Should they defer then?

Hold that question for now, as it will be essential to understanding how and when the Court ultimately reverses its judgment in *Plessy*. My only point now is that a Court could rule as Justice Brown wrote in 1896 and believe itself justified by fidelity to meaning *and* by fidelity to role.

———

The conclusion so far, then, is both humble and troubling: as I've described the process of fidelity, it reveals both how little the Court *can* do and how little it *should* do. To the extent the Court is articulating meaning, not preference, it is constrained by public meaning, regardless of its private preference. And to the extent propriety will be measured against the background of that public meaning, if the Court deviates from this background understanding, it risks its own institutional standing. The enlightened may know the truths of tomorrow. But my claim is that a Court cannot properly express those truths today. The two-step is thus creating a rule contrary to the rule of the Founding—either because of fidelity-to-meaning reasons (accounting for the shifting meaning of separation) or because of fidelity to role reasons (accounting for the certain reaction if the Court took a more aggressive view).

Against this background, it is clear why Klarman is correct to chastise lawyers who refer to cases like *Plessy* as "mistakes." As he writes:

> Misdescribing the Court's past failures to protect the civil rights and civil liberties that are so valued today as avoidable "mistakes," rather than as inevitable byproducts of very different political and social milieus, enables us to sustain the myth of the Court as "countermajoritarian hero." The myth can survive only if obvious counterexamples are dismissed as contingent mistakes rather than understood, more realistically, as the Court's inevitable capitulations to dominant social norms.[41]

Yet even this way of describing it may smuggle in a normative frame. By imagining the Court as "capitulating," we imagine it giving in to something it sees as wrong, simply because it knows it must. But in the ordinary case, there's nothing to yield to. The judges are humans within a society. They see the society the way the society sees it. To imagine them "capitulating" is to imagine them as better than the society—elevated or enlightened—but yielding because of necessity.

No doubt, there have been enlightened justices (Harlan). And no doubt, there have been justices who knew what the right answer was but yielded to necessity (Jackson in *Wickard*). But in the main, justices see the same world everyone else does. We need to see how the world looked to them, not how we would judge it today. These horrible decisions are, as Klarman remarks elsewhere, "essentially inevitable, given the background social and political context within which the Court necessarily functions."[42]

## POST-*PLESSY*

I've offered a reading of the Court's decision in *Plessy*. Like every reading offered in a theory of constitutional interpretation of this kind, my reading aims to explain and justify. Given the dominant social understanding of the time, reading the legal distinction drawn by Louisiana not as discrimination made sense.

But it is quite clear that after *Plessy*, any subtlety was lost. The principle of "separate but equal" became the mantra for a campaign to embed segregation within society generally. And that campaign itself proved that Justice Brown's central claim—"We consider the underlying fallacy of the plaintiff's argument to consist in the assumption that the enforced separation of the two races stamps the colored race with a badge of inferiority. If this be so, it is not by reason of anything found in the act, but solely because the colored race chooses to put that construction upon it"—was completely wrong.[43]

For the social meaning constructed by *Plessy* went far beyond affirming and enabling a desire by whites and blacks not to associate. Very quickly, *Plessy* became the affirmation of what Harlan had said the Constitution denied—that America indeed did have second-class citizens.

That meaning, in turn, emboldened criminal and terroristic activity. Lynching in America was already climbing dramatically at the time of *Plessy*. It would peak just at the time the justices most firmly looked the other way.[44]

Obviously, no single decision by a court could create such antipathy on its own. Politics had long left African Americans to fend for themselves, and because they had no real right to vote, that in turn had left African Americans in a dire state. The injustice and the hopelessness of the period following *Plessy* through the Second World War are inconceivable to us today. Race relations, as Michael Klarman has described, hit "rock bottom levels of injustice and callousness."[45] No doubt encouraged by the passivity of the judicial response, there was an increasing anarchy throughout the nation, but especially in the South.

Yet surprisingly (for those who think courts simply follow what's popular as opposed to the account I'm offering here), it is at this nadir that the Supreme Court at least begins to draw a line. In a handful of decisions, the Court imposes limits on the lawlessness and on the ongoing effort to erase the Constitution's textual commitments to equality. Two of these cases invalidated laws that coerced labor (presumptively, black labor, despite the Court's emphatic denial).[46] One case invalidated an Oklahoma law that permitted railroads to exclude blacks from first-class travel.[47] Two cases invalidated grandfather clauses in state voting laws—laws that effectively permitted illiterate whites to vote while blocking blacks from voting. And finally, in *Buchanan v. Warley* (1917), the Court invalidated a zoning law that segregated neighborhoods on the basis of race.[48]

These cases need no fancy theory to be understood. As Klarman has argued, however unpopular their results were, some were compelled by a simple textualism: "Where the law is relatively clear, the Court tends to follow it, even in an unsupportive context."[49] Others were bolstered by an importance constraint of consistency: just at the time the Court was advancing an aggressive defense of private liberty and property rights, the Court was also confronted with whether those same principles would be compromised by a hostility based upon race. Allowing that compromise would have weakened the pro-property principle. And thus, without positing any particular affection for African Americans, we can well understand why the Court would not be eager to cave in to these race-based exceptions from principle.

But even these moments of hopeful resistance would not have gone far, or at least fast, without the exogenous shock of World War II. More than anything else, that war forced America to redeem the promise that the Civil War had made. It was Hitler, more than Grant or Lincoln or Du Bois, who enabled America to finally "cash that check," to borrow Martin Luther King Jr.'s words—the check that the Civil War Amendments had written.

## THE WAR THE SOUTH DIDN'T WANT

This much is clear: America at the turn of the nineteenth century was not a nation that embraced a rich sense of social equality. Everyone recognizes the wrongs done to blacks. But we are less likely to remember the wrongs done to Jews, or Native Americans, or Irish, or Chinese. Indeed, even Justice Harlan couldn't imagine granting Chinese equal citizenship. As he wrote in *Plessy:*

> There is a race so different from our own that we do not permit those belonging to it to become citizens of the United States. Persons belonging to it are, with few exceptions, absolutely excluded from our country. I allude to the Chinese race.[50]

America was not a nation that believed in equality applied generally. America was a nation that rationalized all sorts of inequality and racism— just as most nations around the world at that time did.

Indeed, we systematically ignore just how embarrassing white culture was across the world at the turn of the twentieth century. The United States had launched a horrible war of imperial aggression, first against the Spanish in Cuba and then, brutally, against rebels in the Philippines. The war in Cuba began with false pretenses but a defensible purpose—to liberate Cuba from its Spanish oppressors. But with lightning speed, American liberators quickly became imperialist oppressors. Henry Cabot Lodge and Teddy Roosevelt pushed America hard to take up the imperialist cause. And by the time President McKinley fully committed to the war in the Philippines, America had become unrecognizable from the perspective of its past.[51]

Because who was the war in the Philippines against? It was against citizens in the Philippines who wanted to establish a constitutional form of government modeled directly upon America's. This was not the great communist menace. These were wannabe Madisons or Hamiltons or Washingtons who wanted nothing more than to be free to determine their own constitutional future.

We denied them that freedom not because they were a threat to us, but because we did not believe they were capable of self-government. And why was that? Because we believed them lesser humans. America waged the most aggressively brutal war in its history—openly and self-consciously practicing torture against natives—in the name of "the white man's burden."[52]

Of course, America was not the only white nation in the world practicing such incredible injustice. Roosevelt and Lodge wanted us to become colonialists, like Britain, Belgium, France and Germany. Britain would show its mettle in the Boer War, when Lord Kitchener's advance against the Boers torched villages and killed civilians in a scorched-earth campaign to secure its control over South Africa. Belgium would create the racial difference between the Hutus and Tutsis in East Africa—literally, as those were originally social classes, more like the difference between white collar and blue-collar workers than the difference between African Americans and white Americans—and first force the Hutus to obey the minority Tutsis, and then (when Marxism threatened Africa) force the Tutsis to obey the Hutus. That was the seed that grew into the genocide that Rwanda experienced in 1994.

So my point is not about America in particular. It is about racism. And that racism was not limited to the former slaves. "The white man's burden" was the expression of the absurd idea that whites had a natural role to dominate and rule. And as horrible as the racism of *Plessy* is, at least today we've formally rejected it. The consequences of Empire America, however, continue to this day, as expressed in the wars that we are told can never end.

Yet only a few years into the twentieth century, the cultural support for this racism began to wane. Science began to turn its back on its own scientific racism. As Klarman describes:

> Around 1900, the vast majority of scientists believed in natural racial differences and white superiority, but those views came under attack after World War I. Within two decades, they had been almost entirely repudiated in favor of a new paradigm, which attributed racial differences to culture and environment. The changing demography of scientists partially explains this shift in perspective, as many younger researchers came from the ethnic and racial groups purportedly shown to be inferior by the older science.[53]

By the 1930s, the racism taken for granted at the turn of the century became a racism increasingly questioned. The repudiation by the scientists "filtered down to popular opinion."[54]

The Second World War, however, finally forced America to confront its internal contradiction about race. The leverage point was not the defense of African Americans. It was Hitler's attack on German Jews.

Hitler's anti-Semitism was not just German. Anti-Semitism raged across the world. Throughout the early 1940s, Americans viewed Jews as "a greater threat to the welfare of the United States than any other national, religious, or racial group."[55] We were not going to build concentration camps (for Jews at least; the Japanese were a different matter). But we did not enter the twentieth century committed to the equality of Jews any more than to the equality of blacks.

The war forced America to confront its inequalities and to decide finally on which side it stood. Not immediately, but eventually. For World War II, like the Civil War, began for one reason but ended with a very different lesson.

America was drawn into the war to fight "fascism." FDR had succeeded in tricking America into supporting the fight against fascism in Europe long before we formally entered the war. But once the Japanese attacked America directly, we openly and forcefully engaged in the fight against fascism in the Pacific and in Europe.

But the nature of "fascism" was itself a contested idea during the 1930s. When the concept was born as a movement in Italy, many believed it could not reach beyond the particular character of that nation. (Mussolini is reported to have considered it to be strictly "our thing.")[56] Its original ideals were far from the racism that Hitler would bring to it. Mussolini's fascism was really about making the trains run on time—and about making the whole of the Italian economy finally help its people. Italian fascists "reviled" German Nazism "as pagan, anti-Semitic, and alien to the fascism originated by Italians."[57] In 1934, at the Mussolini-organized Montreux Congress, delegates from thirteen European nations tried to tease out a "universal fascism" from the movements it identified in thirty-nine countries across the world. The congress agreed upon "common articles of faith in the monolithic state, economic corporatism, something called the 'national revolution,' and, above all else, the proposition that each nation must solve its problems in its own way."[58] The conference divided on "the Jewish question," leading the conference organizers to give up the universalist project. But a marriage of convenience in 1936 forced German Nazism and Italian fascism into a single movement. Mussolini embraced racism and the "crusade against Bolshevism" and brought those ideas into his movement.[59] Fascism, critically, became a philosophy of racism. As Germany had rendered it, fascism included the idea of racial superiority and the idea that such superiority could be enforced through law—and violence.

This circumstance both increased the desire of Americans to enter the war and decreased the desire of Americans to enter the war. The most striking struggle in America as the war developed was a fight waged by white southern leaders against the idea of us entering the war at all. That struggle was linked directly to racism. If we entered the war to defeat Hitler, wouldn't that also defeat Jim Crow? How could we fight to end the racism practiced against the Jews in Germany without resolving, finally, to end the racism against blacks in America?

This recognition was common among both southern racists and blacks alike. Indeed, it was precisely the reason many blacks cited for declaring that they would not fight in World War II. Why should they risk their lives to secure the civil rights of Jews in Germany when they didn't enjoy those rights in their own home? As historian Jane Dailey writes:

> The sudden rise to power of National Socialism in Germany after 1933 created ideological and rhetorical space for critics of American politics and society, who labored to make fascism synonymous with racism—and vice versa—and to tie democracy to non-discrimination.[60]

Blacks and their supporters increasingly focused the public's attention on the parallels. "America's black press," Dailey observes, "drew attention to three significant markers of degradation propounded by the Nazis during the 1930s: segregated public transportation, segregated schools, and restrictive marriage laws"—all degradations that blacks suffered in America. The *Pittsburgh Courier*, a leading black newspaper, observed a year before Pearl Harbor that "our war is not against Hitler in Europe, but against the Hitlers in America."[61]

These arguments had effect, especially in the South. "According to reports filed in 1942 by field agents for the Bureau of Agricultural Economics," Dailey reports, "Southern whites refused to 'go all out' in the war effort if 'going all out may mean...a revolution in Southern society and Southern societal and racial relationships.'"[62] But Southern society's resistance of that change weakened the war effort abroad. In 1942, Cleo Wright was lynched in Sikeston, Missouri. Within forty-eight hours of the lynching, as Klarman reports, "Axis radio had broadcast the details around the world, warning nonwhite listeners to expect similar treatment should the Allies win the war."[63]

Hitler had done something in America that three centuries of racial egalitarians had failed to do. By the end of a war begun to fight fascism, the war had morphed into a war about the injustice of racism. That fact was not lost on the United States Supreme Court. As Justice Frank Murphy told his colleagues in 1943, statutory racial distinctions are "at variance with the principles for which we are now waging war."[64]

Yet the real punch that would finally dislodge legalized racism came not from Hitler but from Stalin. Because once the wartime alliance between the Soviet Union and the United States ended and the two countries launched their cold war for world domination, America's inconsistency became a powerful weapon for the Soviets. Possibly up to half of Soviet propaganda was tied to race.[65] America was hypocrisy, the Soviets insisted. "Free society" was a lie. As the Soviets vied for influence throughout the world, the embarrassment of the American South became a costly inconsistency for America generally.

And so, slowly, the elite in America recognized as much. After losing more than 400,000 lives in a war against fascism, there was no more ambiguity about the meaning of the legal "distinction" that *Plessy* had drawn: it was discrimination. A social meaning had been shifted—or shoved—by a bloody world war. And the question for the Court would now become how that changed meaning would matter to the rendered meaning of the Fourteenth Amendment.


## *Period 3:* Brown v. Board of Education

From long before *Plessy*, schools had been segregated throughout America, and especially in the American South. So long as those schools were "equal," *Plessy* had implied, that segregation was legal, because it was not "discrimination." And it was not "discrimination" because it made sense of a social reality that every "normal" person embraced.

World War II had changed that meaning, and the two-step needed to take account of that change. If the segregation of Jews was discrimination, then so too was the segregation of blacks. If one racial classification was an expression of racial dominance, so too was the other. Not because, as Justice Brown had written (fantastically) in *Plessy*, "solely because the colored race chooses to put that construction upon it," but because it *was*. The assertion that "because you are black you must go to a different school" was an expression of inequality and discrimination, and any argument that it was not was no longer allowed.

This change finally changed the strategy of the civil rights activists pressing claims for equality. After years of litigating school segregation cases using the framework of *Plessy* by arguing and demonstrating that the separate schools were not in fact equal, the NAACP finally determined to take on *Plessy* directly. Separate schools could not be equal because the meaning of racial segregation had been sealed by the blood of 60 million humans in the Second World War. Separation *because of race* was unequal, and hence segregation had to go.

Or at least, in the framework I've offered for evaluating such a claim, it had to go unless it could be justified. The infamous case of *Korematsu v. United States* (1944) used that framework precisely. In that case, the Court reviewed the decision by Lieutenant General John L. DeWitt of the U.S. Army to segregate both citizens and non-citizens on the basis of ethnic heritage. Japanese Americans were forced into concentration camps as a means, the government insisted, of protecting America against the spies they claimed were embedded in the 110,000 Japanese citizens and non-citizens living on the West Coast.

That line, the Court held, was intrinsically suspect: "It should be noted, to begin with, that all legal restrictions which curtail the civil rights of a single racial group are immediately suspect."[66] It thus placed a burden on the government to justify any discrimination by showing "pressing public necessity."[67] Astonishingly, the Court found that line justified in *Korematsu* because of the imminent threat of violence caused by the war.[68]

That conclusion was not believable when made. History has shown it was also plainly false. But regardless, the case set up the framework that would govern the resolution of segregation: a line drawn on the basis of race was now deemed, uncontestably, to be discrimination. The question, then, was whether the government could justify that discrimination, as it had in *Korematsu*.

This structure interacts directly with the matrix that I first offered in Chapter 7 and referenced earlier in this chapter. For just as we could imagine the claim "Racial segregation is discrimination" being contested or uncontested, we could imagine the claim "This discrimination is justified because of blah blah blah" as contested or uncontested. But here, *because of the structure of a rights claim, the contestedness of the justification does real work.* If the segregation is discrimination, then it must go *unless* it can be justified. But if that justification is contested, then the segregation cannot be justified. The very act of affirming the contested justification would trigger fidelity to role.

Imagine the position the Court would be in when forced to decide whether to accept a justification for what is viewed as discrimination. Once a line is seen as violating equality, the Court must decide whether or not to accept the justification for that inequality. Yet if that justification itself is contested, then for the Court to accept it would be for the Court to take a side in that contest. Depending on the nature of that contest, to take a side could conflict fundamentally with the conception of the Court as a court. Justices on their own could have one view or another. But if the Court engages in that contest, it threatens its own institutional independence.

And this was precisely the tension the Supreme Court faced in *Brown v. Board of Education* (1954). In 1951, thirteen parents (representing twenty children) filed a class-action suit against the Board of Education for Topeka, Kansas. The suit demanded that Topeka end its practice of operating separate (if allegedly equal) schools. The named plaintiff, Oliver Brown, was an assistant pastor and welder at the Santa Fe Railroad. His daughter, third-grader Linda Brown, was bused to a Negro school more than a mile from her house, while a white school was just blocks from her home. When the case arrived at the Supreme Court, it was joined with four other cases brought around the same time, including one in the District of Columbia.

As the case was litigated, the plaintiffs adduced endless evidence of the harm caused by the act of segregation. Segregation, as one expert testified,

> is a symbol of, a perpetrator of, prejudice. It also stigmatizes children who are forced to go there. The forced separation has an effect on personality and one's evaluation of one's self, which is inter-related to one's evaluation of one's group.[69]

When the Court first heard the case in 1953, it seemed strongly inclined to leave segregation jurisprudence settled. That, at least, was the view of the chief justice, Fred Vinson. Then in September 1953, Vinson died of a heart attack at the age of sixty-three. (Justice Frankfurter is reported as having said, upon learning of Vinson's death, that it was "the first indication I have ever had that there is a God.")[70] The case was held over until a new Court could hear it. The new chief justice, Earl Warren, was President Dwight Eisenhower's "biggest mistake"—or so he supposedly said. And Warren resolved that the segregation jurisprudence had to be unsettled. The America that had fought the war against fascism could not sanction fascism within its own borders.

For Warren, the argument was clear. There was no denying anymore that segregation was discrimination—World War II had created that social meaning. And the matter had become so contested that there was no way the Court could accept any justification for that discrimination. These facts together meant *Plessy* could no longer be good law.

We can see the point most directly by focusing upon one question that the lawyer arguing what would become a companion case to *Brown*, *Briggs v. Elliott* (1952), Thurgood Marshall, posed to the Court.[71] In an extraordinary exchange with the justices, Marshall in effect asked the Court what it would have to say about blacks in order to decide the case against his clients. "We submit," Marshall continued, "the only way to arrive at that decision is to find that for some reason Negroes are inferior to all other human beings."[72] Could the Court make such a finding?

The question embeds two assertions: first, that the Court would have to *say something*, and second, that the inequality *Plessy* was premised upon and which had gone without saying in that decision could not go without saying in *Brown*. The social meaning of segregation was no longer contested: racial segregation was discrimination. That judgment was the "situation-sense," as jurisprudential scholar Karl Llewellyn labeled it, of "everybody," as constitutional law specialist Charles Black would later put it, including judges.[73] It was the recognition of humiliation, not an error in legal categorization. The Court (and later Congress) was, as Bruce Ackerman has put it, "translating the Constitution into a commonsense command: *Thou shalt not humiliate.*"[74] Once that translation had been made and segregation was seen as discrimination—as indignity—the burden would be on the government to justify that discrimination.[75]

A justification could conceivably have been made, but in 1954 any such justification would be so contested that it could not overcome the default that the equality claim makes: to strike down rules that embed inequality.

The consequence was profound. Once ideas about the "natural" place for African Americans had become contested, the default of equal protection became the norm. Distinction on the basis of race was discrimination. And no Court could ever accept a justification for that discrimination without rendering its decision "political" in the sense I have described in this book.

Thus both fidelities—to meaning and to role—make *Brown* right. Once attitudes about race had been shaken by the events and allegiances of the Second World War, the social meaning of segregation changed. Once that meaning had changed, it placed the Court in a clear position: either uphold the claims for equality by striking down segregation or accept a now-contested justification for this segregation and thereby threaten its own fidelity to role. Fidelity to meaning and fidelity to role both pointed to the same thing: that the original commitment to equality, translated into a context in which social understandings had radically changed, required a different result. That result further restricted the scope of government power—government could do less after *Brown* than before.

The Court's unanimous decision was a bombshell. While it was supported by a bare majority of the public nationwide, in the South it almost triggered a second civil war.[76] Open resistance to the Court's authority was pressed by southern leaders as well as the public. This first move was clearly not the beginning of a roll downhill. The fight for equality was still at the start.

Yet while *Brown* was certainly just the first word, it was a word that began an extraordinary conversation. As Bruce Ackerman has put it, *Brown* set off "an escalating debate that ultimately penetrated the nation's workplaces, churches, breakfast tables, and barrooms in a way that is rare in America (or any other country, for that matter)."[77] The meaning of apartheid had been spoken aloud. The question for the nation now was what it would do with this truth.


## *BROWN* ON SEX

*Brown* drew a clear line for schools. How far beyond schools it would reach was initially an open question. The Court was quick to extend it broadly—at least as it affected public accommodations such as public beaches, golf courses, city buses, parks, courtrooms, and prisons.[78]

But the Court did hesitate in one critically important domain: sex. Throughout the post-*Plessy* period, the most effective argument on the side of inequality was the argument that white women had to be protected from the "outrage" of interracial sex. That argument would continue for a dozen years after *Brown*.

Of course, there had been plenty of interracial sex in America over the previous four hundred years. The vast majority of that sex had been between white men and black women, and only a tiny portion of that had ever been deemed "outrageous." That white men had routinely used black women for sex was perhaps uncouth (or criminal, if the product of domination), but it wasn't a reason to go to war. Instead, the threat that for many people justified the fight for segregation was the idea of black men having sex with white women. This threatened the whole white race, or so many believed. And that threat was an adequate justification for keeping the races apart.

This battle was in no sense peripheral. Instead, as Dailey's work makes powerfully clear, it was fundamental in the fight about racial equality. For most of the history from the Civil War Amendments through *Brown*, the most effective argument against equality was a *reductio ad absurdum* argument— if you allow this equality, then black men will have sex with white women, leading to "a mongrel breed of citizens," as a Virginia Court would put it in 1955.[79] Dailey reports the recollection of one white northerner, Victor Bernstein, from 1942:

Chatting with the Secretary of the Chamber of Commerce in Birmingham, Bernstein received a lecture on the looming dangers of social equality. "There's one thing you can put in your pipe and smoke," Bernstein was told. "There's no white man down here goin' to let his daughter sleep with a n——, or sit at the same table with a n——, or to walkin' with a n——. The war can go to hell, the world can go to hell, we can all be dead—but he ain't goin' to do it."[80]

This fear had driven legislators to ban "miscegenation" from the start of the republic (though that term only comes to life in the rhetoric of southern states during the Civil War).[81] Maryland passed the first such law in 1661. Virginia's was the second, in 1691. Thirty-eight states had anti-miscegenation laws in the nineteenth century, and so clear was it to the framers of the Fourteenth Amendment that the amendment didn't ban "anti-miscegenation" laws that when repeatedly asked about the question, the sponsors of the amendment expressly denied it. That confidence only grew as scientific racism insisted that mixing the races would weaken both races. Even at the time of *Brown,* it is quite clear that there was no resolve by the Supreme Court to change this inequality. Frankfurter explicitly asked counsel in the oral argument whether striking down segregation laws would threaten anti-miscegenation statutes. He was told it would not.[82] And when the Court was presented with a challenge to an anti-miscegenation statute after *Brown,* it found a way to resist it.[83] The Court knew where the public stood: Klarman reports that 90 percent of whites in the 1950s opposed interracial marriage.[84]

But the courts were not going to be able to avoid the issue forever. And when they finally did begin to consider it, their reasoning precisely tracked the analysis I have offered here.

The most famous case actually predates *Brown v. Board of Education.* In *Perez v. Lippold* (1948), California Supreme Court Chief Justice Roger Traynor struck down California's anti-miscegenation law. Grounded on the U.S. Supreme Court's decision in *Hirabayashi v. U.S* (1943), the California court required the government to show either an "emergency" or a clear justification for the unequal treatment the statute effected between whites and every other race. Whatever clarity there may have been surrounding such discrimination in the 1890s, when *Plessy* was decided, Traynor rejected it in the 1940s. As Justice Carter said in concurrence, though he believed the law had been unconstitutional when enacted, "The rule is that the constitutionality of a statute is not determined once and for all by a decision upholding it. A change in conditions may invalidate a statute which was reasonable and valid when enacted."[85] "Americans of all ranks," Jane Dailey writes, "including several

members of the California Supreme Court, still believed in white racial superiority. . . . But scientific racism had lost the protection of academic credibility
by then and was met with raised eyebrows by those who valued scientific
expertise."[86]

The United State Supreme Court finally ended the fight in 1967. Richard
Perry Loving and Mildred Jeter had fallen in love. Richard was white,
Mildred black. They traveled to Washington, D.C., in June 1958 to get married. They then returned to Virginia—where their marriage was proscribed
by law—and reestablished their residence. In late 1958, they were indicted
for violating Virginia's anti-miscegenation law. In January 1959 they pled
guilty to the charge and were given the choice either to go to jail for one year
or to leave the state for twenty-five years. The trial judge wrapped his decision in these choice words:

> Almighty God created the races white, black, yellow, malay and red,
> and he placed them on separate continents. And but for the interference
> with his arrangement there would be no cause for such marriages. The
> fact that he separated the races shows that he did not intend for the
> races to mix.[87]

The Lovings took the hint and left Virginia. But in 1963, they filed a motion
to vacate the trial court's judgment. When the court refused to rule on the
motion, they filed a class action against the Virginia law. When Virginia's
courts upheld the law, the Lovings appealed to the Supreme Court.

The law was formally equal—just as segregation had been formally equal.
It restricted blacks just as it restricted whites. But the Court rejected the idea
that formal equality meant that the law did not have to withstand strict scrutiny, writing, "There can be no question, but that Virginia's miscegenation
statutes rest solely upon distinctions drawn according to race."[88] That meant
Virginia had to show the law was "necessary to the accomplishment of some
permissible state objective."[89] Try as it might—the state had actually filed a
"Brandeis brief" filled with arguments grounded in eugenics in support of its
racist ban—Virginia had no such argument.[90] At best, the science was contested, and that was not enough to overcome the burden of strict scrutiny.
The *reductio ad absurdum* that had been offered by Democrats in the mid-
1860s while trying to block the passage of the Fourteenth Amendment—
that it would authorize miscegenation—was, a hundred years later, the law
of the land.[91]

Thus contestability does its work here again, even if fidelity to role led the
Court to take its time. Regardless of prejudice, heightened review left the
state with no sufficiently solid ground to stand upon.

## Period 4: Retreat on Affirmative Action

Three hundred and forty-five years after America birthed slavery on its shores, ninety-nine years after it was officially ended, ninety-eight years after the first civil rights act was passed, eighty-one years after the first public accommodations civil rights act was struck down, sixty-eight years after legal apartheid was affirmed by the Supreme Court, and a decade after it was officially ended, the United States Congress, under intense pressure from its former Senate majority leader and new president, Lyndon Baines Johnson, passed the first major equal employment legislation in the history of the nation: the Civil Rights Act of 1964.

That statute was the end product of an extraordinary struggle by African Americans to have the right to participate in the employment market equally. That fight began with a struggle to be allowed to participate in the employment market at all. In the 1930s, unemployed whites from Atlanta organized protests declaring "No Jobs for Niggers Until Every White Man Has a Job!"[92] At the same time, nearly half of blacks in the South could not find employment, and unemployment for blacks nationally was twice that of whites.[93] The presumption among most within the middle-class professions—construction, unionized factory work—was that blacks were not allowed.

Roosevelt was slow to respond to this hopelessness, but black leaders recognized that he could be pushed. Because of their intervention, in 1933 FDR took the first steps to bring African Americans into the American workforce equally, by requiring non-discrimination in hiring at the Public Works Administration.

The principle that animated this simple demand for justice was obvious: if blacks were taxed to pay for public works, they should be able to work in public works. Astonishingly, most Americans did not agree.[94] A 1944 survey of white workers found only 41 percent would find it "all right" if their employer put an African American "next to you," and just 14 percent thought it acceptable that an African American be a supervisor.[95] The same survey found only 44 percent of white Americans believed "Negroes should have as good a chance as white people to get any kind of job." A different survey at roughly the same period found that a

> majority of whites outside of the South believed there should be separate schools, restaurants, and neighborhoods, and that the reason blacks had a lower social status was a result of their own racial shortcomings, rather than the laws passed and traditions practiced by whites.[96]

After World War II, white national leaders became stronger supporters of equality. Yet those leaders were following, not leading. In February 1948, Harry Truman sent a civil rights bill to Congress. The bill would have abolished state poll taxes, strengthened federal anti-lynching and voting rights acts, desegregated the military, and established within the federal government "a permanent Fair Employment Practices Committee, a civil rights division in the Justice Department, and a Commission on Civil Rights."[97] Fifty-six percent of Americans opposed Truman's bill; 6 percent supported it.[98] Two-thirds of Americans supported continued segregation of the military—making Truman's eventual executive order requiring integration all the more amazing.

The 1950s were not much better. Polls found less than a third of Americans supported laws "requiring employers to hire people without regard to color or race."[99] At the turn of the decade, African Americans were trapped in a vicious cycle: "Job discrimination reduced employment opportunity, resulted in low income, and that in turn limited availability of education and training programs, keeping skills low and reducing employment opportunities ties and income."[100]

The protests of the 1960s began to change all this. On February 1, 1960, four black students from North Carolina A&T College started sitting in at a local Woolworth's lunch counter in Greensboro. This began an extraordinary decade of civil rights protests. Those protests started peacefully; the impatience of white supremacists turned them violent. In May 1963, Bull Connor turned fire hoses and attack dogs on protesters (who were actually children) in Birmingham, Alabama. America watched the violence with horror on television. President Kennedy was provoked, and in June he delivered a national address about the need, finally, to pass civil rights legislation. As he told America:

> One hundred years of delay have passed since President Lincoln freed the slaves, yet their heirs, their grandsons, are not fully free.... They are not yet freed from social and economic oppression.... Now the time has come for this nation to fulfill its promise.[101]

A week later, in an address to Congress, Kennedy articulated the principle at stake: "Simple justice requires that public funds, to which all taxpayers of all races contribute, not be spent in any fashion which encourages, entrenches, subsidizes or results in racial discrimination."[102] The protests—and the president's leadership—began to have an effect on public attitudes: 70 percent of Americans—including 56 percent in the South—told pollsters that African Americans were being "discriminated against." Only 43 percent believed blacks had as "good a chance as white people" to get any job for which they were qualified.[103] After the Civil Rights Act of 1964 was passed, a Harris Poll found that 70 percent of Americans supported the legislation.[104]

I rehearse this history because the most striking experience I have as a law professor is recognizing just how little my students know about the long history of discrimination in America. Most limit the wrong of slavery to the nineteenth century; few even know of the continued role the law would play to keep blacks from equal opportunity in America. And fewer still recognize how deeply set attitudes of inequality were within the American public. Law students are slow to recognize that even a law can't change the willingness of white construction workers to include blacks within their union.

What would do that was the simple experience of working with blacks. The most striking truth about racial animus is the extent to which it arises from simple ignorance and inexperience. Before white soldiers served with blacks in World War II, less than a third expressed favorable opinions of them. After fighting with African Americans, more than 80 percent expressed a favorable opinion.[105] A segregated America was a racist America. And while integration was not an elixir, it was a necessary condition for overcoming these attitudes of exclusion.

The Johnson administration discovered this immediately after the president succeeded in getting the Civil Rights Act passed. Title VII had made it an offense for race to be a factor in hiring decisions. But against the background of hundreds of years of inequality, equal opportunity would not happen without some accounting for race.

What is striking initially is the cross-partisan agreement that the starting position should matter. Johnson believed blacks "deserved additional help, more social programs to get them to the starting gate so they could start the race equally with other citizens."[106] Richard Nixon believed much the same. At a speech at Howard University, Nixon promised

> everybody an equal chance at the line and then giving those who haven't had their chance, who've had it denied for a hundred years, that little extra start that they need so that it is in truth an equal chance.[107]

And echoing Kennedy from 1963:

> Nothing is more unfair than that the same Americans who pay taxes should by any pattern of discriminatory practices be deprived of an equal opportunity to work on federal construction contracts.[108]

Both the Johnson and Nixon administrations adopted essentially the same plan for dealing with the radical inequality in opportunity, embracing what today we would call affirmative action plans to establish not quotas but goals and timetables for achieving appropriate diversity.[109]

In a certain pragmatic sense, no one could really question this approach. Without some intervention like this, the extraordinary inequality in employment would only continue. According to one report, if there wasn't fundamental change, then America would not see blacks employed at a rate anywhere close to their proportion in society "in skilled trades until the year 2005, in the professions until 2017, in sales until 2114, and among business managers and owners until 2730."[110] And following riots across the United States, beginning in Watts, American leaders were keenly focused on removing the causes of this frustration. Unequal opportunity was the simplest (and cheapest) cause to remedy. Republicans and Democrats alike fixed on affirmative action as the remedy.

This remedy follows naturally from a very obvious and, I believe, correct interpretation of *Brown v. Board of Education* (1954). If *Brown* stands for a strong anti-subordination principle, then, as Bruce Ackerman has put it, it "requires class-based remedies, most notably affirmative action."[111]

Yet from the very start, these efforts were challenged in the courts and in Congress. The first challenge was directly tied to *Brown*, as the nation increasingly resisted court-ordered busing to address school segregation. The second challenge attacked efforts to remedy unequal employment. In both of these contexts, we can observe a retreat—the second more fundamental than the first.

RETREAT I: BUSING

Throughout the 1960s, the Supreme Court displayed an extraordinarily firm commitment to supporting integration in schools that had been segregated by law—at least *after* Congress stepped up. (After a decade without Congress's help, only 2 percent of black students in the eleven states of the Confederacy were attending integrated schools.)[112] A wide array of statutory and institutional mechanisms was allied to give force to the Court's declaration that school segregation must end. And throughout this period, the Court spoke firmly about the need and appropriateness of aggressive remedies to address the consequences of de jure segregation. Whenever the meaning of racially segmented schools could be tied to acts of the state, the state had to act to correct that meaning. And the most common remedy was court-ordered busing.

But when the fight moved north, the Court's resolve began to wane. Northern schools were segregated as well, but by practice rather than by law.

White neighborhoods were separated from black neighborhoods for many reasons (including reasons the state was responsible for), but state law had never forbidden the mixing of black and white students. Such a law had never been seen as necessary, as de facto school segregation was the (no doubt intended) consequence of a system of neighborhood schools in segregated neighborhoods.

Because of the state's role—not directly, but indirectly—in producing these segregated schools, civil rights activists tried to get the courts to order integration. Many northern cities adopted plans to bus students from one neighborhood to another for the purpose of achieving integration.

Yet from the start, this effort was questioned, and not just by whites. Yes, maybe the state was responsible in some sense, but if the current social meaning of the current pattern of separation did not make that connection, why was integration required? Could black children learn adequately only if white children were present?

These different oppositions began to find their voice in the political process. Overwhelmingly, Americans opposed court-ordered busing. In 1972, Gallup found that 72 percent of all Americans opposed busing, while 18 percent supported it. Even blacks were divided, 47 percent to 45 percent.[113] As voices yelled loudly, politicians began to hear. Congress tried to intervene to block the courts from ordering busing, but liberals in the Senate filibustered. (Bizarrely, a technique that had been used by racist conservatives to block civil rights legislation was now being used by egalitarian liberals to block legislation designed to block a remedy for segregation.)

As public opposition grew, the Court pulled back. In *Milliken v. Bradley* (1974), in an embarrassingly incomplete opinion, the Court refused to recognize any state-based responsibility for segregation in the decisions of neighboring jurisdictions within the same state. Court-ordered busing in the North was effectively over.[114]

Yet this time, the retreat is a mix of fidelity to meaning and fidelity to role. Let's take meaning first. If *Brown* is about the stigma from state-imposed segregation, then not all segregation would trigger that stigma. If neighborhoods were segregated by choice, not by compulsion (as, say, Irish neighborhoods or Italian neighborhoods), then the particular mix of students in a given school in those neighborhoods would not necessarily signal any subordinating stigma. Where there was no stigma, then according to the meaning of *Brown* there was no constitutional wrong and the Court would not insist upon a remedy.[115]

The implication is that courts should determine meaning before imposing an integrating remedy. But that implication raises its own fidelity to role concern. Because while it is appropriate—as I will argue more fully in Chapter 22—for courts to track social meaning, or Llewellyn's "situation-sense," there are obvious limits to the courts' ability to draw fine lines with such a judgment. There may be clear cases at the extremes, but there will be many more unclear cases in the middle. And rather than trying to divine one from the other, fidelity to role would counsel choosing one presumptive meaning over the other.

All things being equal, it would be better, perhaps, to assume stigma and drive districts to integrate where possible. But in the face of overwhelming public opposition, the choice of the opposite presumption is at least understandable.

## RETREAT 2: AFFIRMATIVE ACTION

The legal challenge to affirmative action in employment picks up after the battle against busing. In the states where the earliest challenges were brought, the courts upheld efforts to reset the starting line so long as the state was not applying quotas. In 1967, the Johnson administration adopted what was known as the Philadelphia Plan, a requirement that local contractors bidding on a federal project must "have the result of producing minority group representation in all trades and in all phases of the construction project."[116] Funding was to be withheld until the contractors submitted plans that met that objective. One year into the Nixon administration, the requirements were expanded. Executive Order No. 4 embraced the "goals and timetables" strategy for improving employment opportunities for African Americans. It extended the Philadelphia Plan to include any contractor who received more than $50,000 from the federal government and hired more than fifty employees. The courts accommodated these interventions—and more. The Supreme Court upheld remedies for past discrimination, even if it had been proven with disparate impact only.[117]

But beginning in the 1970s, a growing legal resistance began to brew. In 1978, the Court upheld affirmative action for education in *Regents of the University of California v. Bakke*, at least so long as quotas were avoided. That decision was supported by the public (71 percent to 21 percent among whites), but it fueled opposition as well.[118] Through the 1980s, that opposition found no clear voice in the courts, the legislature, or the presidency. From 1969 through 1980, "all three branches of the federal government lined-up and supported [affirmative action] policy."[119]

That policy began to have important effect as attitudes about race improved substantially. Between 1963 and 1979, fears among whites about blacks moving into a neighborhood fell by half (to 27 percent), and beliefs among whites that blacks were an inferior race fell to 15 percent.[120] Between 1970 and 1980, black union membership doubled, and black officials and managers, professionals, and skilled workers increased by 70 percent—twice the national rate of growth for those positions.[121]

Then the election of Ronald Reagan changed everything. Though Reagan himself was not strongly motivated to resist efforts at equality, his administration gave voice to the most coherent and committed opponents. Reagan was the first president to join with opponents of affirmative action to press for a "return" to "color-blind" standards. And while the administration's direct efforts in the courts to reverse judicial sanctions for failing to meet "goals and timetables" did not succeed, Reagan's judicial appointments seeded the ultimate revolution. By the time he left office, Reagan had appointed more judges than any president ever. And in the first year after he left office, the Supreme Court, with three critical Reagan appointees—O'Connor, Kennedy, and Scalia—began to signal that the law was about to change.

In a series of decisions, the Court would ultimately determine that race-based affirmative action had to be tested with the strictest standard of judicial review. There would be no lesser standard for the federal government over the states, and there would be no different standards for malign and benign discrimination: both would have to pass strict scrutiny, and neither would be allowed unless a state could demonstrate a compelling interest that it pursued in the least restrictive manner.[122]

These judicial developments occurred at the same time that affirmative action itself was becoming more contested. As Reagan Republicans succeeded in framing affirmative action as quotas, support among whites for affirmative action fell. Beginning in the second half of the 1980s, white support for race-based preferences in hiring dropped dramatically. Depending on how the question was framed, support among whites for preferences in hiring was about 20 percent; support for preferences in education was slightly higher.[123] This fact created increased political pressure for Democrats, who both could not afford to back away from support for affirmative action (because of the party's strong African American base) and who paid an increasingly substantial political price for being the "quota party," as Republicans termed them. Senator Robert Dole, a longtime supporter of affirmative action, flipped in his race against Bill Clinton for the presidency, declaring in 1995, "After nearly thirty years of government-sanctioned quotas, time tables, set-asides, and other racial preferences, . . . the American people sense all too clearly that the race-counting game has gone too far."[124] As the Supreme Court would assert in *Adarand v. Pena* (1995), racial preferences in the law—and increasingly in politics—were inherently suspect and "presumptively invalid."[125]

Yet conservatives had still not achieved the abolition of race-based affirmative action. To the contrary, the Court has affirmed the use of race considerations in achieving diversity in education, at least so long as quotas are not used and no fixed formula determines the results. Formally, the Court is applying the same standard of strict scrutiny, but in practice the results are quite different. After three Supreme Court cases affirming a role for race in the context of education, it is clear that it is easier to benefit minorities than it is to harm them, even though the Court insists that it is the same standard being applied.[126]

This difference can be linked directly to the social meanings of these race-conscious interventions. Despite the insistence of jurists such as Justice Clarence Thomas that there is "no difference" between benign and malign race categories,[127] in the public's mind there is an important difference. We can consider it progress that there is relatively little contestation around the notion that lines intended to exclude minorities from employment or education are invalid. But whether lines intended to include—that is, affirmative action—should also be invalid is indeed contested. There are strong views on both sides—for example, Justices Antonin Scalia and Clarence Thomas versus Justices John Paul Stevens and Ruth Bader Ginsburg. This contest points to a parallel contest in views among Americans. In a 2016 poll by PRRI/ Brookings, 49 percent of Americans agreed that "discrimination against whites has become as big a problem today as discrimination against blacks and other minorities." An identical number disagreed.[128]

This difference in attitudes, with the accompanying difference in social meaning, has a consequence for judicial doctrine—at least according to the understanding developed in this book. The difference in the doctrine makes sense given the ambiguity about the wrong. We are resolved about the wrong in race-based categories that burden traditionally harmed groups. That wrong is uncontestably wrong; any justification for such a burden requires overwhelming proof. But we are not resolved about the wrong in affirmative action. The Court has set the questions within the same framework, but its answers prove that in fact it is using different frameworks. As Justice Thomas explained in *Fisher v. University of Texas* (2013), "only those measures the State must take to provide a bulwark against anarchy, or to prevent violence, will constitute a 'pressing public necessity' sufficient to satisfy strict scrutiny" and justify race-based distinctions.[129] In upholding race-based distinctions for admissions, the Court has clearly applied a different standard. It certainly is "obvious," as Thomas put it, that "there is nothing 'pressing' or 'necessary' about obtaining whatever educational benefits may flow from racial diversity."[130] That suggests the Court sees a less demanding barrier to overcome. Justice Stevens had remarked, following Justice Holmes, that even a dog could tell the difference between being kicked and being tripped over. So too does the Court apparently recognize the difference between being excluded because you are black and facing a different opportunity because you are white.

The law is thus clearly not color-blind. And thus, in this sense, it is a retreat from the color-blind conception of equal protection. Yet this retreat tracks complicated understandings of equality itself. Heightened scrutiny for race-based affirmative action allows the Court to frame its doctrine consistent with a color-blind conception of equality. But the actual application of that doctrine permits a wider and more subtle range of applications than that doctrine would suggest.

It is important to note that this retreat is not like the one we saw with federalism. There the retreat was triggered by the limits of judicial capacity, and the retranslations were efforts to respond to that incapacity. Here, though, the retreat is triggered by a change in social meaning. Hidden within the struggle to end racial exclusion was a latent ambiguity about racial inclusion. After legal exclusion was ended, that latency evaporated and the contest over race-based inclusion developed. That contest has not resolved itself in the same way as exclusion has, with a general consensus that race-based inclusion is malign. But neither has it resolved itself in the other direction, with race-based inclusion considered benign. Instead, the practice occupies a contested space that the Court has accommodated by framing its test in the most restrictive way but practicing its test in a more understanding way.

Like every change we've seen regarding the reach of the equality right, this is translation. It is a modification in the reach of the equality right, tracking the dynamic of an evolving social meaning. No doubt that evolution has not ended. But the practice of the Court has always been to track its evolution, despite the changes that might produce in the application of the doctrine.

———

The life of race equality within the context of the Fourteenth Amendment reveals a pattern of interpretation that parallels the other examples I've collected so far.

At first, despite its promise, the footprint of the amendment was small and deformed. Like the feet of women in ancient China, it was bound so as to be beautiful in the eyes of the time, however hideous it is to us today.[131]

Yet crucially, at least in period 1, this foot-binding was not done by the Court primarily. No doubt, the Court kept its head low in the tempest of the period. But its early readings were not unfaithful; they were at least invitations.

The *Slaughterhouse Cases* shut down the industry of unenumerated rights litigation, but it invited Congress to defend the privileges or immunities of citizens and promised to enforce those laws through the force of the Fourteenth Amendment.

The logic of *Cruikshank* (bracket the result for a minute) secured for Congress the clear power to defend the newly crafted rights of African Americans, and it offered the Justice Department a road map for prosecuting the white terrorists who were continuing the war.

And while the *Civil Rights Cases* struck down a critically important law supporting an aspiration of equality, the law it struck was self-consciously crafted to conflict with the framework the Court had already set. Nothing in the opinion indicated that the Court had backed away from that framework, and nothing had stopped Congress from crafting a civil rights act that would have fit.

Yet in each case, the invitation was declined. Congress didn't craft a civil rights law that respected the difference between created and secured rights; administrations after Grant's didn't wage an aggressive war against the terrorists with the road map the Court had offered. The political branches gave up on the South long before the courts did. And as Democrats returned to national power, the fate of blacks in the South was sealed.

Thus, unlike most lawyers looking back at this first period, I don't believe we can say that the Court got the law wrong. I'm not even convinced the Court erred in its fidelity to role. What the pattern of cases through 1896 displays is a clear desire by the Court not to lead. There are a few clear victories for African Americans—though nothing that would stir revolution. There are a few prominent and apparent defeats—though, as I've argued, these were not complete defeats, as each left the political branches a way to go forward. The Court was keen not to be seen as the forward troops in a continued war. As the Illinois Supreme Court remarked when refusing to give Myra Bradwell access to the bar, "Courts of justice were not intended to be made the instruments of pushing forward measures of popular reform."[132] The Supreme Court of Period 1 was not the kind of Supreme Court that would give us *Brown v. Board* (1954).

But is it clear they should have been the same? The Court of period 1, more clearly than we, saw the political support for Reconstruction collapsing. If anything, the justices sought not to accelerate that collapse. Maybe there was a way to affirm the principles in *Cruikshank* without exonerating terrorists. I don't have a clear enough sense of the strictness of nineteenth-century pleading requirements to know whether the harshness was exceptional. But there's no doubt that from the twenty-first-century standpoint the opinion feels bizarrely technical.

But would winning that battle have advanced the war? The nation was on the cusp of a critical election in which the Democrats looked like they could capture the presidency for the first time since Buchanan, after winning the control of the House just two years before. If anything, the decision to affirm Justice Bradley's opinion could have been motivated by the aim not to inflame—and thus further invigorate—Democrats in the South.

The fidelity to role calculation is complicated, here and always. I'm not sure we yet have a clear sense of how a judiciary leads when the political branches refuse to follow. Caution in this context was not crazy. It certainly is not clear evidence of betrayal. The dynamic put serious pressure upon the third assumption of Reconstruction—that law could remake society. Indeed, a strong strand of social theory growing out of the period denied the capacity of law to change norms or society.[133]

Period 2 is a different story. Twenty years after the compromise that ended Reconstruction in the South and three years after the repeal of the last vestige of federal support for voting rights in the South, the political branches—and white America—were resolved in favor of (and a few resigned to) inequality. The Republicans had given up the fight. The Democrats believed the matter settled. Jim Crow had restored a formal inequality throughout America. Though its form was different from slavery, its consequence was the same, and for some, worse.[134]

*Plessy* confirmed that understanding, and though I've defended the opinion on the merits, its most natural analog to the post–New Deal cases is *Wickard v. Filburn*. Recall in that case, the Court articulated the clearest justification for its refusal to second-guess Congress. From the opinion, the Constitution seems clear. From its forcefulness, there seems no way to doubt that Congress can regulate even home-grown wheat.

But behind the opinion, we know from Barry Cushman's work that even its author wasn't sure of its conclusion, though there was nothing he believed could be done. The Court would yield, even though its justices believed Congress had crossed the line.

*Plessy* may well be similar. The opinion speaks with certainty about how inequality is understood. "Reasonableness" elevates the understandings of a society into a justification for the status quo. That reading suggests the distinction was understood then—at least among the elite deciding the case—as same-sex bathrooms might be understood now. On this account, social meaning had rendered the distinction normal, and normal could not yield a ruling against inequality.

Yet is also plausible that other justices besides Harlan saw the infidelity in this result. It is reasonable to believe that other justices thought the rule of *Plessy* betrayed the promise of the Fourteenth Amendment. That understanding was common with respect to the Fifteenth Amendment, and there's no reason to believe it didn't carry over here as well.

Yet if so, then the question becomes one of role: what precisely was the Court to do? The judicial war against segregation was hard enough after *Brown*. Was it even conceivable at a time when no national political leader defended the ideals of Reconstruction anymore? If this was their view, then they were in the same position as the New Deal justices—forced to a conclusion because they knew their institution could do no differently, at least then. A social and political reality constrained the Court. That constraint was real. Fidelity to role reckons that constraint.

But when a war cracked the firmness of that foundation and an enemy exploited the hypocrisy thus displayed, the Court could return to the ideas Harlan had spoken of. Social meaning had changed. And with no uncontested support for a defense of discrimination, it could strike discrimination down. The trigger of race-based classifications gave the Court a simple and clear tool for carrying into effect the ideals of the Civil War Amendments. By the end of the 1960s, those ideals had eradicated even the most sacred of race-based distinctions: the prohibition against mixed-race marriages.

And then, confronting a fundamental ambiguity in the trigger for heightened scrutiny, we can see the Court retreat. The ambiguous complexity of affirmative action leads the Court to feign an identical test but practice a different analysis. As in *Cruikshank*, acoustic separation may well be at play: the Court speaks as if the standard is the same, affirming the public's overwhelming view that the standard should be the same. But it practices a rule that allows more accommodation than would ever be tolerated with race-based exclusion.

Throughout, this has been a constitutional doctrine that hangs upon social understanding or social meaning. As that understanding changes, the doctrine gets translated to track that change.

Such change is never binary. We don't move, as a society, from one view to another overnight. Instead, we move from what seems "natural" to what is contested; once something is contested, a burden of justification emerges.

It might seem odd to imagine a doctrine of constitutional law that is contingent upon social understandings—odd, at least, until we reflect upon the many examples within constitutional law of a doctrine that depends upon something outside the Constitution, even for originalists. Interpreting the Fourth Amendment's requirement that seizures (here, an arrest) be "reasonable," Justice Scalia wrote in dissent:

> [The Court] confuses the…constitutionally permissible reasons for delay, with…the question of an outer time limit. The latter—how much time,

given the functions the officer is permitted to complete beforehand, constitutes "as soon as he reasonably can" or "promptly after arrest"—is obviously a function not of the common law but of helicopters and telephones. But what those delay-legitimating functions are—whether, for example, they include further investigation of the alleged crime or..."mixing" the probable-cause hearing with other proceedings—is assuredly governed by the common law, whose admonition on the point is not at all "vague."[135]

"Reasonable" is a function of "helicopters and telephones"—or technology generally. Thus, the scope of the Constitution changes as technology changes. Likewise with the doctrines reviewed in Section 1—the commerce power and the due process clause. Those too were dependent on facts in the world.

The examples from Section 1, of course, are all external. An originalist might say they are objective in the way that social meanings are not. But again, it is hard to see how the nature of the common law is objective in this sense. And it is not possible, I suggest, to assert that how we see distinctions on the basis of race is how the framers of the Civil War Amendments would have seen distinctions based on race. An originalist committed to what they would have seen can't see the error (for us) in *Plessy*.

We're not finished reviewing the data. And when we account for sex and sexual orientation, this same dynamic will begin to seem second nature.

CHAPTER EIGHTEEN | Sex Equality

THE FOURTEENTH AMENDMENT SECURES to "persons" "equal protection of the law." If you had asked the framers of the Fourteenth Amendment
whether women were "persons," they plainly would have said they were. If
you had asked the framers whether the amendment was meant to invalidate
laws that disabled women relative to men, without a doubt, they would have
said no.[1] And if you had asked them whether it was meant to invalidate laws
that disabled lesbians, gay men, or transgender people relative to straight
people, the universal answer—assuming they even understood the question—
would again have been no.

Yet in different ways, the Fourteenth Amendment today undoubtedly
protects women and LGBT people—two classes that in 1868 would have
been ignored. Most take that fact to mean that either originalism is wrong or
the Court's current interpretation of the Fourteenth Amendment is wrong.
Many in the academy hold the first belief; Justice Scalia openly admitted that
he held the second (the Fourteenth Amendment does not ban sex discrimination, Scalia argued, because "nobody [at the framing] thought it was directed
against sex discrimination").[2]

In my view, neither originalism nor the Court's interpretation is wrong.
The protection of women and LGBT people is perfectly consistent with the
original meaning of the Fourteenth Amendment, properly interpreted. To
see how and why with respect to sex is the purpose of this chapter. We will
return to sexual orientation in Chapter 20.

To telegraph the argument just a bit, equality, as the Court has come to
interpret it, is a function of the social meaning of exclusion or difference for
the relative group. Those social meanings change. As they change, the Court

has, in a complicated way, allowed those changes to change the scope of the equal protection clause's reach—and appropriately so.

## Sex Equality Recognized

Among the many strategies that the Democrats used to try to defeat the Fourteenth Amendment during the Thirty-Ninth Congress (1865–1867), the most interesting for our purposes was an argument related to sex. Equality, the opponents of race equality argued, would reach beyond race and eventually would reach sex. If you can't discriminate on the basis of race under the terms of the equal protection clause, then how could you on the basis of sex? As Ward Farnsworth quotes:

> Sen. Aaron A. Sargent (R-CA): "The fourteenth amendment was not intended merely to say that black men should have rights, but that black and white men and women should have rights. It was a guarantee of equality of right to every person within the jurisdiction of the United States, be he black or white."[3]
> Sen. Augustus S. Merrimon (D-NC): "There is no provision in the Constitution of the United States which protects color any more than sex or age."[4]
> Sen. Oliver Morton (R-IN): "What is meant by 'the equal protection of the laws?' Does it mean simply that every person shall be entitled to protection against an assault and battery or against personal violence, and stop there? It has no such limited meaning as that. The meaning is just the same as if it read 'Every person shall be entitled to the equal benefit and protection of the laws...' Law is made for protection; the protection of person, the protection of property, the definition and protection of civil and political rights. The whole body of the law is for protection in some form—the definition and protection of the rights of person and property; and when the fourteenth amendment declares that every person shall be entitled to the equal protection of the laws, it means to the equal benefit of the laws of the land. It forbids all discriminations of every character against any class of persons, being citizens of the United States."[5]

For us, there is an easy answer to that question: you can't. Yet for the framers of the Fourteenth Amendment, that idea was simply ludicrous. Whatever the framers were trying to do with that amendment, remaking the law of sexual relations was not on that list. To one-step originalists, there was little doubt that sex equality was not a command of the Fourteenth Amendment.

What the Democrats were doing with this argument was the equivalent of what our fourteen-year-old did in Chapter 17: extending the argument from one class of people to another. The words of the amendment, literally taken, applied to women. If they did, then they must protect women. And if they did protect women, then a law library full of statutes and precedent that disabled women relative to men would be rendered unconstitutional by the Fourteenth Amendment.

Of course, the Democrats made this argument not because they wanted a constitutional rule that would protect women against unequal legislation. To the contrary—they made this argument to argue that the Fourteenth Amendment should not be proposed to the states for ratification.

Very few took that argument seriously, just as very few of you took our precocious fourteen-year-old's argument seriously, because however the formal categories might apply, everyone understands the social meaning of the groups involved. Everyone understands (in their proper historical context, at least) that claims of equality would not reach women or children. *Why* they wouldn't is a hard question. *That* they wouldn't is a sanity test.

The Democrats lost their argument in June 1866, and the Fourteenth Amendment was ratified in 1868. Yet soon thereafter, the challenge the Democrats had raised got presented to the Supreme Court directly, by one of America's greatest legal journalists.

Myra Bradwell wanted to be recognized as a lawyer. She was already the author of one of Illinois's most prominent legal publications, the *Chicago Legal News*. Her legal skills plainly outclassed those of many members of the Illinois bar. When she read the text of the Fourteenth Amendment shortly after it was enacted, she believed it was her ticket to law school. (Actually, most lawyers didn't go to law school then, but you get the point.) Being a lawyer, Bradwell believed, was a "common calling." It was just the sort of thing that Justice Bradley had said in the *Slaughterhouse Cases* that the Fourteenth Amendment was meant to secure to all citizens. She was a citizen of the state of Illinois and of the United States. She therefore believed that she had just been given, through the Fourteenth Amendment, the right to become a lawyer.

Bradwell filed her case before the Supreme Court decided the *Slaughterhouse Cases*. As you'll recall, in that case, the Supreme Court, through Justice Miller, radically narrowed the scope of the "privileges or immunities clause." Whether or not it would ultimately be held to incorporate the Bill of Rights, the Court clearly rejected the idea that the privileges-or-immunities clause had embedded an unenumerated right of free labor. Thus, once the Court decided *Slaughterhouse*, the resolution of Bradwell's case was pretty obvious.[6] As the Court observed:

The opinion just delivered in the *Slaughter-House Cases* renders elaborate argument in the present case unnecessary.... It is unnecessary to repeat the argument on which the judgment in those cases is founded. It is sufficient to say they are conclusive of the present case.[7]

In a twenty-two-sentence opinion (shorter than an op-ed in the *New York Times*), Justice Miller (again, the author of the opinion in the *Slaughterhouse Cases*), concluded that

the right to control and regulate the granting of license to practice law in the courts of a State is one of those powers which are not transferred for its protection to the Federal government, and its exercise is in no manner governed or controlled by citizenship of the United States in the party seeking such license.[8]

For our purposes, however, the more interesting opinion was by Justice Bradley. Bradley, remember, had dissented in *Slaughterhouse*. Unlike Justice Miller, he did believe the Fourteenth Amendment protected the right to free labor. But unlike Myra Bradwell, he didn't believe the free labor right secured any protection for women. As he wrote:

It certainly cannot be affirmed, as an historical fact, that this has ever been established as one of the fundamental privileges and immunities of the sex. On the contrary, the civil law, as well as nature herself, has always recognized a wide difference in the respective spheres and destinies of man and woman. Man is, or should be, woman's protector and defender. The natural and proper timidity and delicacy which belongs to the female sex evidently unfits it for many of the occupations of civil life.[9]

Outrage is the easy response to a quote like this. For obviously, anyone uttering such words today would betray an extraordinary ignorance or sexism.

But the better response is to try to understand it—or, more important, to understand the world in which it was uttered. For Bradley was a not crazy man. In the world in which he wrote, what he wrote was normal and accepted—in the words I've used, uncontested. (*The Nation*, in reviewing the opinion, thought the idea that the Supreme Court would recognize the right of a woman to be licensed as a lawyer "crazy.")[10] The lower court had held something similar: "That God designed the sexes to occupy different spheres of action, and that it belonged to men to make, apply, and execute the laws, was regarded as an almost axiomatic truth."[11]

In that world, the presupposition of exclusion on the basis of sex was still baked in. It was no more outrageous to describe the "natural" exclusion of women then than it would be to describe the "natural" exclusion of children today. Of course, we believe in the latter and scorn the former. But for them, both had the same status in social meaning: they were both relatively uncontested truths of the time, whether foregrounded or not.

The story of sex equality in the Supreme Court is the long struggle to render this meaning contested. At the time, it wasn't obviously contested, even to leading progressives: as I described in Chapter 5, Louis Brandeis relied on precisely the same ideas about what many called "the weaker sex" in his first, and most famous, "Brandeis Brief" filed in the Supreme Court. That brief argued that because women were "weaker" and needed the protection of society, it was legitimate for the state to regulate the hours they could work, even if it could not regulate (under *Lochner*, as described in Chapter 5) the same for men. It took strong persuasion from his wife and daughters before Brandeis would even entertain the idea of women's suffrage.

Nor was it obviously contested even to Franklin Delano Roosevelt's appointees to the federal bench. In 1948, Justice Frankfurter wrote an opinion for six justices of the Supreme Court, upholding a Michigan law that forbade a woman from being a bartender "unless she be 'the wife or daughter of the male owner' of a licensed liquor establishment."[12] Why? Well, having women in bars could "give rise to moral and social problems." But having a protective male (her husband or father) in the bar would avoid those problems. Or at least, Frankfurter wrote in *Goesaert v. Cleary*, so a legislature could reasonably believe. And since the "line they have drawn is not without a basis in reason," there was nothing in the equal protection clause that would forbid Michigan from drawing this line.[13]

Thus, despite profound and important insights into the struggles of workers and the safety of consumers, neither progressives nor liberals could even recognize the struggles of women (not to mention African Americans).

But just as World War II had dislodged relatively uncontested views about race, so too did it begin to dislodge uncontested views about sex. The meaning of separate spheres was changing; two-step originalism would increasingly take account of that change. When many of the most productive men in the nation left to go to war, their jobs were performed by women. War proved what women had always said: that they were just as capable, and thus just as entitled to equal benefits within this society as were any, including African Americans.

Through the 1950s and 1960s, the pressure to recognize equality for women grew. It got important political support in the 1964 Civil Rights Act, which included sex among the protected classes addressed by that bill.[14] And then it got critical support from the Supreme Court in a series of decisions beginning in the 1970s, each speaking quite softly about the revolution they would soon effect.

The first of these cases grew out of tragedy. Sally Reed had lost her son to suicide. She linked the boy's depression and subsequent death to her ex-husband, Cecil Reed. When her son's estate was to be administered, she wanted to administer it. Her ex-husband did as well. Because of Idaho law ("As between persons equally entitled to administer a decedent's estate, males must be preferred to females"), the ex-husband got the job.

Idaho's law didn't mean that women were never administrators; a woman could apply alone. It didn't mean a man always displaced a woman; if the woman was more entitled than a man (the statute had a hierarchy of entitled administrators), then she could displace a less entitled man. But if she stood against an equally entitled man, the statute required that the man automatically be selected.

The purpose of Idaho's intestate statute was to ensure the efficient administration of the estates of people who die without a will. No legislator voting for that statute meant it as an insult to anyone. Instead, the presumption of the Idaho legislature was that, *on average*, women were less likely to be experienced in the skills necessary to administer an estate. And if that was true *on average*, then the simplest way to minimize the burden of administration would be to allocate the duty to men rather than women.

That intuition isn't stupid. Lawyers, on average, are more likely to understand how to read a contract than accountants. If you have to pick between a lawyer and an accountant to interpret a contract, it therefore makes perfect sense to pick the lawyer. This is true even though in many cases a particular accountant will be much better at reading a contract than most lawyers. Many lawyers hate contracts. Many have never drafted or studied a contract (at least since their first year in law school). And many accountants spend a great deal of time studying contracts, both their own and others'. In a particular case, then, choosing a lawyer over an accountant might be a bad choice. On average, it isn't. And so, on average, it might make perfect sense to simply adopt a simple rule: pick the lawyer to interpret the contract.

"But why not," you may ask, "try to determine in any particular case who is better, the lawyer or the accountant? Why not give them a test, or ask them some questions about their experience?" No doubt, that more extensive analysis could make sense, depending upon what exactly was at stake. But equally without doubt, sometimes the cost of asking more questions exceeds any possible benefit. Sometimes the more efficient thing to do is to simply make an assumption and run with it.

It's perfectly clear that if Idaho had said, "Between a lawyer and an accountant, the intestate's will shall be administered by the lawyer," there would have been, then or now, absolutely no constitutional concern. As we saw in Chapter 6, the Court would apply a rational-basis test to evaluate that statute. The rational-basis test asks whether there is any conceivable set of facts that makes the regulation make sense. Obviously there is with lawyers and accountants. And so, obviously, a court would conclude that a statute that preferred lawyers raised no constitutional problem. As the Court said in *Goesaert,* "If it is entertainable, as we think it is, [then the state] has not violated its duty to afford equal protection of its laws." It is "entertainable" that lawyers are more skilled at administering the estate of someone who died without a will than accountants. The question is not *"Are* lawyers better on average than accountants?" The question instead is *"Is it possible* that lawyers are better on average than accountants?"

You might well think that's not much of a standard at all. Yet that's exactly the point: in the ordinary case, it is not the job of a court to second-guess the judgments of a legislature. God knows, those judgments are often wrong. But the role of the Court is not to ensure that the legislature never gets it wrong. Under the ordinary rational-basis test, the only job of the Court is to ask, "Has the legislature gone nuts?"

Sally Reed wanted to challenge Idaho's law. With her own money, she hired a Boise attorney, Allen Derr. Derr took the case through three levels of appeal. Then the ACLU volunteered to help in the Supreme Court. A young attorney named Ruth Bader Ginsburg wrote the brief. Derr argued the case in the Supreme Court. The Idaho law, Ginsburg through Derr argued, was "discrimination" and should be disallowed under the equal protection clause of the Constitution.

It's pretty clear that if a court applied the ordinary rational-basis test to this statute, the statute would survive. Who knows whether Sally would be a better administrator than Cecil? The question the court would ask under ordinary rational-basis review is whether it is "entertainable" that, on average, men are better able at administering wills than women. Though no one knows whether that is true or not, the notion was plainly "entertainable."

Yet the Supreme Court disagreed. In a stunning decision written by Chief Justice Burger, the Court first observed that "the Fourteenth Amendment does not deny to States the power to treat different classes of persons in different ways."[15] But, the Court continued, "the Equal Protection Clause... does, however, deny to States the power to legislate that different treatment be accorded to persons placed by a statute into different classes on the basis of criteria wholly unrelated to the objective of that statute."[16] So the question, as the Supreme Court put it, was "whether a difference in the sex of competing applicants for letters of administration bears a rational relationship to a state objective that is sought to be advanced by the operation" of the statute.[17]

Well, what was the objective of the statute? It was, the Court determined, to "reduce the workload of the probate courts" by efficiently eliminating one class of applicants to administer intestate estates.

Did it reduce the workload? It was certainly "entertainable" that it would. And the Court certainly had no evidence that it had not. Yet the Supreme Court concluded nonetheless that the law violated the equal protection clause. "The crucial question," the Court wrote, "is whether [the statute] advances that objective in a manner consistent with the command of the Equal Protection Clause." The Court held it did not.

What the Court did not do is what the ACLU had asked it to do, which was to apply the same system of heightened scrutiny for sex-based claims of inequality as it had applied to race-based claims of inequality. Under heightened scrutiny, the question is not whether it is "entertainable" that the statute makes sense. Under heightened scrutiny, the Court must show that it actually does make sense. The ACLU wanted that standard here. But the Court did not go that far. According to the language of the opinion, all the Court was doing was applying the same old rational-basis test. As the Court wrote:

> To give a mandatory preference to members of either sex over members of the other, merely to accomplish the elimination of hearings on the merits, is to make the very kind of arbitrary legislative choice forbidden by the Equal Protection Clause of the Fourteenth Amendment; and whatever may be said as to the positive values of avoiding intrafamily controversy, the choice in this context may not lawfully be mandated solely on the basis of sex.[18]

Whatever this was, it was not rational basis. (As law professor Gerald Gunther would remark, "It is difficult to understand [the] result without an assumption that some special sensitivity to sex as a classifying factor entered into the analysis.")[19] Consider an alternative statute, one that randomly chose between the two applicants. There is no doubt in the world that flipping a coin would be a permissible way to decide.[20] Though a coin flip is arbitrary, the objective of reducing the costs of deciding is perfectly legitimate. So if random is okay, why isn't a presumption that is at least possibly likely to improve administration also permissible? How can an arguably more efficient system (since better administered) be unconstitutional while a perfectly random system is constitutional?

The answer is unspoken in the case but obvious to everyone. The statute drew a "legal distinction," to remix *Plessy v. Ferguson* a bit. For the whole of

American constitutional law from 1868 through the middle of the twentieth century, that legal distinction was not recognized as discrimination—or, to put it differently, discrimination was not the social meaning of a sex-based distinction. Instead, for the whole of that period, it was a perfectly reasonable standard to draw lines on the basis of sex.

But the struggles for sex equality that took off in the middle of the twentieth century had begun to change the social meaning of such distinctions. As with distinctions on the basis of race, distinctions on the basis of sex were increasingly characterized as, and then seen as, "discrimination." The distinctions were no doubt drawn on the basis of stereotypes, and it may well be that the stereotypes were true. But the critical injunction that flows from the recognition that something is discrimination is that the individual cannot be burdened by the stereotype, true or not. She has the right to be free of the stereotype, even if the stereotype is statistically true, and even if that right imposes costs on others.

This is not a rational basis. But neither was it the heightened scrutiny that the Court had elsewhere applied to race. The case was a weird anomaly, applying a kind of heightened scrutiny, yet calling it nothing more than rational basis.[21]

It was clear to everyone this was only the beginning. Within two years, the Court had another case, grounded on a similar presumption about the difference between men and women. (With this one, the young attorney Ruth Bader Ginsburg made her first Supreme Court argument).[22] The military had a rule that men could automatically claim their wives as dependents and thus secure increased housing allowances and medical and dental benefits. Women in the military could claim their husbands as dependents only if they could prove the husband was actually dependent. This rule made it harder for men to get benefits in the military. Those families were not happy about that inequality. They sued, claiming that difference violated the equal protection clause.

Once again, in *Frontiero v. Richardson* (1973), the Court agreed with them. Three justices joined an opinion by Justice William Brennan, applying heightened scrutiny (specifically, strict scrutiny) to the military regulations. This was sex-based discrimination, for such a distinction "frequently bears no relation to ability to perform or contribute to society. As a result, statutory distinctions between the sexes often have the effect of invidiously relegating the entire class of females to inferior legal status without regard to the actual capabilities of its individual members."[23] To test whether the burden makes sense, these justices would have required the government to meet the same standard it must meet when making race-based categorizations: strict scrutiny.

Four of the other justices agreed that this law had to fall. But none of these four would agree that all sex-based discriminations had to be tested under the strict-scrutiny standard. Justice Stewart thought *Reed* had resolved the case. Justice Lewis F. Powell, Chief Justice Warren Burger, and Justice Harry Blackmun agreed with Justice Stewart but went on to insist that it was not the right time for the Court to impose heightened scrutiny on sex-based claims. For as Justice Brennan had noted, at the same time the Court was considering additional constitutional protections for women under the equal protection clause, the states were considering an amendment to the constitution that would have secured equal rights to women explicitly.

This was a crucially important argument among these eight justices about fidelity to role. It was wrong, Justice Powell was insisting, for the Court to determine judicially what the people were determining constitutionally. It was certainly possible that in 1973 the right reading of the equal protection clause would protect women, but that protection notwithstanding, the people felt it necessary to make the protection explicit. Stepping into the process and securing judicially what the proponents of the amendment wanted to secure constitutionally risked muddying the waters. There would be many who would think, "There's no reason to push for an amendment now that the Court has given us what we want judicially." That would slow support for passing the amendment—which the opponents would interpret as public resistance to the ideal of equality for women. Better to wait the process out, these concurring justices believed, than to risk mucking up an important constitutional process.

This wasn't the first time the Court had intervened in the middle of an amendment process. And no doubt, the argument for restraint was a strong one. But this difference shouldn't obscure a more basic agreement—that eight of the nine justices had recognized again that sex-based distinctions were also discriminations.

Over the next two decades, the fight would continue. And round after round, the Court upped the ante. In *Craig v. Boren* (1976), the Court (Justice Brennan writing) invalidated a statute that made it illegal for men to drink until they were twenty-one while allowing women to drink when they were eighteen.[24] That sex-based distinction, men complained, was an unjust stereotype that was burdening them (even if also saving their lives).[25]

The Court agreed. Once again, it applied the so-called rational basis test, as it had in *Reed*. But unlike any other rational basis analysis, in *Craig* the Court entertained and then evaluated the evidence meant to prove that men were less safe drinkers than women. The Court was not impressed, deciding that the evidence did "not satisfy [the Court] that sex represents a legitimate, accurate proxy for the regulation of drinking and driving." The statute thus fell.

After *Craig*, the Court was more willing to move the bar of the judicial standard. Never to the same level that would govern race, but in *United States v. VMI* (1996) the Court raised the bar pretty close. In an opinion written by Justice Ruth Bader Ginsburg, the Court held the standard high: "Focusing on the differential treatment or denial of opportunity for which relief is sought, the reviewing court must determine whether the proffered justification is 'exceedingly persuasive.'" This was not strict scrutiny. It was not rational basis plus. This was a very heightened form of intermediate scrutiny, certain to make it almost impossible for any government to draw a line that was grounded in sex. As Ginsburg wrote:

> Supposed "inherent differences" are no longer accepted as a ground for race or national origin classifications.... Physical differences between men and women, however, are enduring: "[T]he two sexes are not fungible; a community made up exclusively of one [sex] is different from a community composed of both."[26]

Twenty-five years after writing her first brief for a landmark sex equality case in the Supreme Court, Justice Ginsburg had achieved almost precisely what she had first sought—an extremely strong test to separate out distinctions from discriminations. And it is a test, as law professor Reva Siegel argues convincingly, that is "fundamentally concerned with questions of subordination: Sex-based state action offends the Equal Protection Clause in those circumstances where it perpetuates the status inferiority of women."[27]

We can recognize a pattern in this history that will be a template for equality claims generally. For a range of cases, but in this case in particular, equality claims pass through two stages. First, it takes work to get people to see that a distinction drawn by the law is actually properly seen as discrimination. Sometimes that work succeeds (race, national origin, sex, sexual orientation). Sometimes it fails (youth). If that first step succeeds, that alone doesn't win the argument, of course. Even if something is seen as discrimination, that discrimination can still be justified.

But here's where step two becomes important. As a justification becomes contested, it becomes more and more difficult for an institution such as the Court to defend that justification. For the Court to defend the justification would be for it to take sides on a question that can't help but seem political. Fidelity to role limits the Court's ability to take sides on a contested question. So the Court steps away, leaving the plausible claim for equality standing.

Thus is equality recognized—not so much because justices believe it (maybe they do, maybe they don't), but because the Court can't credibly deny that the claim is an equality claim and also can't credibly affirm any defense for inequality. Contestability has rendered the claim plausible—and has rendered the justification for inequality something the Court can't use.

This argument about the role of contestability renders the alternative argument for equality advanced by Stephen Calabresi and Julia Rickert less convincing. In an important piece of originalist scholarship, they argue that the commitment of the Fourteenth Amendment was against caste legislation, and that once women were given the right to vote, that rendered any disabling legislation invalid. As they put it:

> Once women were given equal political rights by the Nineteenth Amendment, a reading of the general ban on caste systems in the Fourteenth Amendment that did not encompass sex discrimination became implausible.[28]

But while this conclusion may open the door for a sex equality claim, the power of the punch will depend upon an evolving view about women. Calabresi and Rickert write that in the past,

> many members of Congress put forward arguments that the Fourteenth Amendment would not interfere with the legal disabilities of women because women were inherently unequal to men. These are arguments that few, if any, would accept today.[29]

That's certainly true, but it makes clear that the work in the argument is being done by precisely the same social understanding that does the work elsewhere. Contestability is the trigger to reform, since it weakens the justification for the status quo. Social meaning triggers the contestability.

This pattern of contestability reaches beyond equality. Indeed, it is most expressly determinative in the context of the next set of translations on the Left—privacy.

| Privacy II

IS THERE A LIMIT TO HOW MUCH—or how far—the government can regulate? Is there a line beyond which it cannot step?

This was the question that animated the conservatives in Chapter 5. Their answer then was yes: there were regulations that were beyond the legitimate reach of government, because such regulations could not advance any public good. Transfers from A to B, for example, could not benefit the public generally, they believed, and that fact rendered them beyond the legitimate reach of government. Any process that produced such abominations was therefore not "due."

Likewise with the regulation of "common callings": free labor, believed Bradley and Field along with a generation of jurists, was a right protected against regulation. That was a line the government couldn't cross.

These conservatives eventually located the attack on these regulations within the scope of the due process clause. (Remember, Bradley and Field saw it in the privileges-or-immunities clause, but that door was closed quite quickly.) Substantive economic due process was predicated upon the belief that regulation could reach beyond any legitimate end. Many call this idea oxymoronic—how can substance regulate process? But there is nothing incoherent in the idea that there should be a limit to how far the government can regulate. And if there is a limit, there is nothing incoherent in the idea that process crossing that line must be invalid process. Based on this line, throughout the history of the due process clause (most vigorously in the 1920s) conservative courts used the Constitution to strike down laws that went too far.

For liberals, the line has been more personal, or private, or maybe intimate.[1] And it got first drawn in an opinion by one of the Warren Court's most conservative justices, reviewing the struggles over a truly extraordinary regulation from the heart of New England.

## Privacy as Intimacy: Born

In 1958, two Yale law students approached Yale law professor Fowler Harper with an unusual complaint. The two students were married. Because they were enrolled in a fairly intense law school, they were eager to avoid pregnancy for the time being. But Connecticut law made it a crime for the two students to use or procure contraception. Harper was "outraged at this governmental intrusion into the private sector life" of these students. They decided to launch litigation to test the constitutionality of Connecticut's law.[2]

Connecticut had regulated the use of contraceptives since 1879. Regardless of whether a person was married or single, Catholic or not, or capable of bearing children or not, the law prohibited the sale and supply of contraceptive devices. No doubt, the ban on the use of contraception had a strong religious basis. And no doubt, given the power of the Catholic Church in Connecticut, there was little reason for legislators in Connecticut to do anything to revise the rule. The law hung around for generation after generation, largely unnoticed, until the Yale activists began to agitate to get the law struck down.

The Supreme Court was reluctant to take up the challenge—not so much because its views were unclear, but because the statute didn't seem to present any real threat. In the almost eighty years of the statute's existence, there had been one recorded prosecution, in 1940, and that was explicitly a test case. Yet in 1961, the Court agreed to hear arguments in the case, *Poe v. Ullman* (1961). It then changed its mind and dismissed the appeal as not presenting "controversies justifying the adjudication of a constitutional issue."

Dissenting from the dismissal was one of the most influential justices in the history of the Supreme Court, John Marshall Harlan II. Not the Harlan from *Plessy*; he too was influential. This Harlan was that Harlan's grandson. He too would shape the arc of Supreme Court jurisprudence in his own important way.

Harlan's dissent rested upon an uncontroversial fact—that there was a limit to how far the state could regulate. The only question was how that limit was to be drawn. Justice Black saw that limit in the precise terms of the Bill of Rights. He believed the Fourteenth Amendment incorporated those rights against the states. He also believed those were the only rights against the states that could be enforced in a federal court.

Harlan rejected this static view. Instead, in his understanding, there was a core liberty that courts were obligated to protect. That liberty, Harlan insisted, could not be "reduced to any formula" and "its content cannot be determined by reference to any code."[3] Instead, courts were to follow a "rational process," grounded in tradition, but recognizing that "tradition is a living thing." The liberty protected by the due process clause was not "a series of isolated points pricked out," as if by a pin. It was instead

> a rational continuum which, broadly speaking, includes a freedom from all substantial arbitrary impositions and purposeless restraints...and which also recognizes, what a reasonable and sensitive judgment must, that certain interests require particularly careful scrutiny of the state needs asserted to justify their abridgment.[4]

In the case at issue, the interests were as fundamental as any could be: the question was the liberty of intimate relations among married heterosexuals. If ever there was a protected sphere, this was such a beast.

The importance of this liberty was obvious to all. That shifted the question to the justifications for its infringement. Whether or not it would have been seen by one-step originalism, two-step originalism made it salient to all. At base, the only real justification that Connecticut could offer was grounded in morality. In Connecticut's view, contraceptives were immoral, and it was free to advance that moral view through the law.

Harlan didn't doubt that truth in the abstract. As he wrote,

> The laws regarding marriage which provide both when the sexual powers may be used and the legal and societal context in which children are born and brought up, as well as laws forbidding adultery, fornication and homosexual practices which express the negative of the proposition, confining sexuality to lawful marriage, form a pattern so deeply pressed into the substance of our social life that any Constitutional doctrine in this area must build upon that basis.[5]

Connecticut's law was "no more demonstrably correct or incorrect," Harlan noted, than many other such laws. And then, echoing the structure of Justice Holmes's dissent in *Lochner,* he observed:

> If we had a case before us which required us to decide simply, and in abstraction, whether the moral judgment implicit in the application of the present statute to married couples was a sound one, the very controversial nature of these questions would, I think, require us to

hesitate long before concluding that the Constitution precluded Connecticut from choosing as it has among these various views.[6]

Yet the question, as Harlan saw it, was not an abstract question of morality. It was whether the state could use its views about morality to justify penetrating the sacred space of the marital bedroom.

> The statute must pass a more rigorous Constitutional test than that going merely to the plausibility of its underlying rationale....This enactment involves what, by common understanding throughout the English-speaking world, must be granted to be a most fundamental aspect of "liberty," the privacy of the home in its most basic sense, and it is this which requires that the statute be subjected to "strict scrutiny."[7]

This was an extraordinary move. Harlan had recognized a liberty that he deemed fundamental. That meant that the state had to do more to justify infringing that liberty. Harlan wrote at an early stage of the development of the standards of heightened review, so he was stepping into uncharted territory. But in his framing, once a liberty was deemed fundamental, the state's effort to restrict it would be subject to strict scrutiny. And as that standard has come to be known, that means the state must show a compelling state interest and show that it was advancing that interest with the least restriction possible of the fundamental liberty.

This structure creates a dynamic that is parallel to the one we saw for race. Once viewed as fundamental, just as with race, once viewed as discrimination, the burden shifts to the state to justify its infringement. But that means that the contestability of any justification renders the justification insufficient. And that was precisely Harlan's conclusion: that contested justification was not enough to overcome the liberty interest.

Four years later, a challenge to the same law returned, as *Griswold v. Connecticut* (1965), and this time it was more successful, at least from the perspective of the plaintiffs. Again the law was challenged as violating the liberty of married couples. This time, seven justices agreed that the law should be struck down. Yet that was about as far as the agreement reached. For the opinions in the majority ranged widely between the standard set by Justice Harlan and a rule that seemed keen to tie itself to the "pinpricks" of the Bill of Rights. Justice Douglas famously found the right to privacy implicit in the "penumbra and emanations" of the Bill of Rights. Four justices joined Justice Douglas's opinion, though three of them also joined an opinion by Justice Arthur Goldberg, finding the right in the Ninth Amendment. Justice Byron White joined the judgment, but not the Court's opinion. And Justice

Harlan joined the judgment, not the opinion. Instead, Harlan grounded his opinion in the same analysis that he had offered four years before: the liberty was fundamental, and the state's justification was insufficient.

What divided the justices most was the question of stability. Which method was best suited to prevent the justices from roaming the moral universe, using the Constitution as their magic carpet? The dissenters, Justice Black most forcefully, believed that the only way to tie the justices down was to chain them to the words of the Bill of Rights. That was the sole way to avoid the inevitable activism of justices finding justice without any textual constraint.

The Court didn't disagree with Black. Douglas's opinion was careful to ground the analysis upon the actual words of the Bill of Rights. Yes, they seemed to imply a deeper or richer liberty, but the contours of liberty were set by the "pinpricks" of those amendments.

Justice Goldberg went even further, finding in the Ninth Amendment the authority to announce a fundamental right from our tradition. In his view, it was tradition that would bind the justices, rather than the words in the Bill of Rights.

And Harlan too was sanguine about the Court's ability to identify these new rights. His method of reasoned judgment, forcing the Court to identify the liberty at the core of "ordered liberty," would not avoid disagreement. But it was, he believed, the best way of "keeping most judges from roaming at large in the constitutional field."[8]

These opinions thus bounce between the two fidelities at the core of our story. On the one hand, the justices wrestle with fidelity to meaning. The founding value is libertarian, but the essential question is how that value finds voice. That question raises a question about role: How should the justices identify and articulate this libertarian interest? Openly and honestly? Or should the Court forgo this power, for fear of the damage that might be done, through inevitable inconsistencies, to its own institution?

Black feared the activism more than he feared "silly laws" (as Justice Stewart had referred to the Connecticut law). Better to constrain the justices to a fixed text than to trust them to constrain themselves as they wandered the moral field.

Douglas (and, via his opinion, the Court) was willing to recognize rights inherent in the fixed text, even if not expressed in that text.

Harlan was willing to allow the Court to wander beyond the text if it remained committed to the "reasoned judgment" of a careful process.

All the justices saw what was at stake: the standing of the Court. Meaning was subject to this critical constraint, even if there was not yet any consensus about how that constraint would be made real. Yet from the complaint about a forgotten law, a new branch of constitutional law was born.

Fowler Harper never got to see the product of his work: "By the time *Griswold* reached the high court, Harper was incapacitated by illness, which would lead to his death within months."[9] Harper's colleague Thomas Emerson argued the case before the Supreme Court. Though Emerson was perhaps less of an activist than Harper, there have been few among the professoriate whose work on the Constitution has been more significant.

## Privacy: Growing Up

*Griswold* launched the Court on a libertarian project. According to the two-step originalist, it was a project of fidelity. If there was a core protected space of liberty, marital intimacy was a relatively easy case. If anything would be deemed off the regulatory table, consensual sex within a marriage clearly was. The question then was what else.

That there *would* be something else seemed clear. If you're skeptical, consider just one example: Imagine a state got very exercised about its population growth. Its governor ran on a platform promising to limit that growth. As part of her campaign, the governor promoted the "no more than two" program for limiting population. Under this program, no family is permitted more than two children. The child of any birth beyond two is immediately forfeit to the state, to be relocated to a family with fewer than two children. And any woman found to be pregnant who already has two children would be required to abort the fetus, at least within the first trimester of pregnancy.

If you entered this chapter believing that there was no space clearly not subject to government control, I hope you've recognized now that there is at least one. The idea of the government trying to control the decision whether to have a child is, I hope, truly repulsive. Though we can plainly see that the number of children each of us has dramatically affects others, we live in a normative universe in which this kind of effect is not to be reckoned, at least by government. The capacity to give birth is the most fundamental of human capacities, and the idea of the government controlling it is contrary to our most basic traditions.

In the early 1970s, the federal government first entered the debate about procreation not via the Supreme Court's decision in *Roe v. Wade* but through an argument about the nature of a limit on an otherwise uncontroversial (except to Catholics) federal program. The federal government was providing family planning assistance to women. But the law forbids the government from funding abortion "as a method of family planning."[10]

What animated this limit was not so much a view about abortion. It was instead the idea of using "abortion as a method of family planning." And here the bogeyman was Communist China. Throughout the 1960s and 1970s, China had launched an increasingly aggressive policy of population control, including the widespread availability of contraception and abortion as a way to control the size of a family.[11]

This aggressiveness startled people around the world. And in the United States, in our continuing effort to distinguish ourselves from "the communists," it became politically important to celebrate the domain of personal liberty that any free society would respect. In a free society, the state would never purport to regulate whether a woman chose to become pregnant, or whether a woman chose to terminate her pregnancy. Those decisions were private ones, and that privacy was a core value in any free society.

Against this background, we can now consider perhaps the Court's most famous case—*Roe v. Wade* (1973).

Like a majority of states at the time, Texas had a law that made "it a crime to 'procure an abortion,' . . . or to attempt one, except with respect to 'an abortion procured or attempted by medical advice for the purpose of saving the life of the mother.'"[12] That law, in effect, regulated one-half of the liberty that I described above. It didn't purport to tell women they had to get pregnant. But it did purport to tell women that if they were pregnant, for whatever reason, they were required by the state to carry that pregnancy to term.

Justice Blackmun's opinion for the Court (which voted 7–2) was his longest and most personal. Blackmun is said to have spent the summer researching the history behind the regulation of abortion. His opinion is replete with facts drawn from this work.

But his analysis begins where my hypothetical left off. The core question for due process, Blackmun insisted, was whether there was a "fundamental liberty" at stake. If there was, then the government's justification for invading that liberty would have to be very strong. If there was not, then in principle, any reason for invading that liberty would be enough. The was the structure introduced by Justice Harlan in *Poe*.

So, what was the liberty at stake here? In Blackmun's frame, the liberty was not "the right to abortion." The issue instead was the more fundamental question of the liberty of a woman "to choose to terminate her pregnancy."[13] The liberty was therefore the freedom to choose whether or *not* to procreate. And that choice, the Court held, was fundamental. Like the decisions relating to marriage, procreation, contraception, family relationships, and child rearing, this liberty was presumptively beyond the reach of government.[14]

By calling the liberty fundamental, the Court then demanded of the government a compelling reason to restrict it. The state of Texas initially offered the Court three possible reasons, but two of those reasons quickly faded away.[15] That left a single justification that could suffice to overcome the fundamental liberty the Court recognized the woman had: that the fetus was a "person."

If this claim was "true," in the sense that it was relatively uncontested that people believed the fetus a person, then it would suffice to justify the invasion of this privacy. But as Blackmun writes:

> We need not resolve the difficult question of when life begins. When those trained in the respective disciplines of medicine, philosophy, and theology are unable to arrive at any consensus, the judiciary, at this point in the development of man's knowledge, is not in a position to speculate as to the answer.[16]

The Court considered the question contested. And were it to take sides on this contested matter, it would expose itself as taking sides in a contested domain. That partisanship—in this case not political, but normative—would in turn trigger concerns about fidelity to role. Why was the Court in the business of resolving these contested moral questions? What gave the Court that sanction?

The structure of this analysis thus precisely parallels the analysis of discrimination under the equal protection clause. The first question here is whether there is a "fundamental liberty" with due process. If there is, then (as with equal protection) the question shifts to the justification. Is there, with due process, a sufficiently compelling justification for invading the fundamental liberty (just as with equal protection the question is whether there is a sufficiently compelling justification for the discrimination)? In both contexts, if the justification is contestable, the matter resolves to the favor of the protected right. If the justification for the discrimination is contested, the discrimination must end. If the justification for invading the protected liberty is contested, then the liberty must be protected.

Justice Blackmun's opinion traces this logic to a historically startling position. A woman's liberty whether or not to procreate is fundamental. Texas's justification for invading that liberty—that the fetus is a person—was contested. Thus, the liberty prevails—at least where there is no other uncontested justification. The Court recognizes certain justifications as uncontested. In particular, it recognizes protecting the health of the mother as an uncontested justification. But in each case, the Court will ask whether the justification for restricting the protected liberty is enough.

In the first trimester, it is not. As pregnancy itself is risky, forbidding abortion in that first trimester could not promote the health of the woman. As Blackmun writes, it is a "now-established medical fact...[that] until the end of the first trimester mortality in abortion may be less than mortality in normal childbirth."[17] During that first trimester, the only regulations that could survive are those ensuring the safety of the procedure itself. These would include regulations to ensure that the doctor is qualified, the facility is safe, and the procedure is properly monitored. After the end of the second trimester, when the fetus becomes viable, then the state could express an interest in protecting the life of the fetus. At that point, abortion could be banned.

*Roe* is thus erected upon a framework of individual liberty. Having defined the liberty as the Court did—whether or not to procreate—the court, in effect, shifted the burden to the state. If the state couldn't meet that burden, then the liberty was protected.

But why was that the right way to frame the inquiry? Why wasn't the proper liberty the liberty to terminate a pregnancy? No doubt, that question is conceivable. But in the context of the time, to frame it so narrowly missed a social understanding of what was at stake. Characterizing it as the liberty to terminate a pregnancy belied the very nature of the decision that a woman was forced to make. There are no fetus-hunters. No one chooses to terminate a pregnancy because that alone gives her anything she would want.

Instead, in the view of the Court, the decision was about procreation. And that decision was no less personal when choosing to terminate the pregnancy than it was when choosing to proceed with the pregnancy.

## Roe *Contested*

Even if the first question in the *Roe* inquiry—the liberty whether or not to procreate—was not contested, there is no doubt the ultimate judgment of the Court was contested. The public isn't constrained by the structures of what Justice David Souter would call "reasoned judgment."[18] They were not obligated to identify, first, the relevant liberty and, second, the justification for invading that liberty. Instead, the public was free to ask a much simpler question: "Is there, or should there be, a right to abortion?" And depending upon which side of the public asked that question—the side that believed a fetus was a person, or the side that didn't believe the fetus was a person—the answer was quite different. Among those different publics, there was then a deep contest about what the Court had done.

It is important to make understandable just why people of good faith could create this conflict. In the reasoning that I outlined, the question was whether the justification for the state's regulation of abortion was "contested." That question is collective. It asks about a particular community. That collective question is fundamentally different from the view of any particular individual within that community. Indeed, in an important sense, collectively the question could be contested even though every single person within the community was absolutely certain about its resolution.

Abortion is the perfect example of this structure. Though the question whether a fetus is a person may be contested for the community, for any particular individual it need not be contested at all. A devout Catholic, for example, has no doubt about the status of the fetus: the fetus is a person. And so for the devout Catholic the question of whether abortion should be permitted is as simple as the question whether homicide should be permitted. Not that the question about homicide is always easy (there are cases of self-defense, defense of others, etc.), but in the main it is easy—homicide is prohibited.

This gap between what is privately believed and what can be publicly recognized is common, though not commonly acknowledged. Yet it is perfectly familiar to any lawyer. Every lawyer understands the distinction between what is true and what a court can treat as true. Consider, for example, something the law calls "summary judgment." After a plaintiff has filed a civil suit against a defendant, either party is free to move for summary judgment. When that happens, the judge is then called upon to make a very particular kind of decision: has the party making the motion established that "there is no genuine dispute as to any material fact"?[19] This frame does not resolve the factual questions. It isolates them and asks whether, given what is not contested, there is a resolution of the case that favors the party moving for summary judgment. If in such a situation the court rules in favor of the plaintiff, it is not ruling that the facts the plaintiff asserts are true. It is instead saying that, whether or not the allegations are true, the plaintiff wins.

This is precisely the dynamic at play with *Roe*. We can assume there is a truth to the matter of whether a fetus is a person. Contestability, however, means that the Court can't recognize that truth. And given that inability, a kind of summary judgment falls to the favor of liberty.

The collective judgment is thus the perspective from which the Court must act. But it is not the perspective of politics. Politics is fed by individuals. And thus, even if *Roe* rightly expressed the balance *from the perspective of the Court*, it did not express the view of a significant portion of the political landscape. To them, *Roe* sanctioned murder. And thus, for them, the appropriate response was the response appropriate to state-sanctioned murder.

This view drove a political movement. And the Republicans were quick to latch on to this anti-*Roe* movement (even though it was a Republican who wrote the opinion in *Roe,* and five other Republicans joined it). The Supreme Court—a "liberal" court, as the Right framed it—was simply "mak[ing]" rather than "implement[ing] value choices" for a democratic society.[20]

In one sense this was true. The Court was "making up" limits on government power nowhere expressed in the Constitution. But in another sense the complaint is misleading. If the first move of *Roe* was correct—if this liberty to procreate is properly read as fundamental—then this "making it up" was the same sort of translation that both liberals and conservatives had engaged from the very beginning. The Court was translating the principle into a new context. Against the background of totalitarian tinkering, the freedom of a woman to choose whether or not to have a child was properly deemed fundamental.

That fact, of course, didn't stop principled opponents of abortion from rallying against the Court's decision. Indeed, that rally turned into a movement. Conservatives leveraged moral opposition to abortion into a powerful political and legal force. And in case after case, opponents tested the limits of this newly expressed constitutional right.[21]

The aim of anti-abortion activists throughout this period was to get the Court to reverse the judgment it had made before. The hope in each of these cases was that the Court would view the public activism as putting too much pressure on the institution. From 1976 on, every platform of the Republican Party made *Roe* key, and in 1980, the platform included an attack on the Supreme Court's "intrusion into the family structure."[22]

In 1980, the movement helped elect the most consequential conservative president in the twentieth century. Ronald Reagan was "pro-life"—he wanted to appoint justices who would interpret the Constitution to protect life (at least fetal life). Over the course of his presidency, he appointed three new justices— Sandra Day O'Connor, Antonin Scalia, and Anthony Kennedy—and he elevated to chief justice one of the only two dissenters in *Roe,* William Rehnquist. George H. W. Bush followed the same playbook. When Justice Brennan retired, Bush appointed the relatively inscrutable but promised-to-be conservative David Souter. And then when Justice Thurgood Marshall died, the plan was completed with the appointment of Justice Clarence Thomas. By 1991, only Harry Blackmun remained from the majority that had decided *Roe.* Five of the other six had been replaced by justices presumed to be against *Roe.*[23] For those counting noses, the opinion seemed not long for this jurisprudential world. Indeed, quite plausibly, the reversal could have been 7–2 the other way.

And then something extraordinary happened.

## Losing by Winning

Once Justice Thomas replaced Justice Marshall on the Supreme Court, anti-abortion activists were convinced that the time had come to get the Supreme Court to overturn *Roe*. Plausibly, they had five votes, possibly even as many as seven. The twenty-year war had recruited presidents and politicians. The clear understanding of everyone was that two conservative presidents had appointed justices to the Court with at least one distinct purpose—to overturn *Roe v. Wade*.

And then that understanding triggered a recognition of fidelity. Not fidelity to meaning, but fidelity to role.

For at some point, it became unavoidably evident to all, and especially O'Connor, Kennedy, and Souter, that while these new justices had been appointed with an expectation, it was their choice whether they would let that expectation rule. If they had acted as they were expected to act, the practice of appointment-to-amend would have been confirmed. Once they saw that their vote would ratify the strategy of amending the Constitution through judicial appointments, they decided to reject the strategy by refusing to ratify it.

The case was *Planned Parenthood v. Casey* (1992). Pennsylvania had adopted a strict new abortion law. The law required minors to have parental consent in order to get an abortion. It also required a twenty-four-hour waiting period, and that the woman be provided specific information to ensure "informed consent." Abortion opponents believed they finally had what they needed to effect the change the Republican Party had sought since 1980.

But for O'Connor, Kennedy, and Souter, this political reality had just poisoned the game. When the test came, the concern that became central to these judges was not the question "Was *Roe* right?" but the question "Can the Court overturn *Roe*?" And that question was answered not in the traditional way, by invoking traditional understandings of *stare decisis*, but in a way that explicitly considered the social meaning of the Court's bending to a political will. As they put it in a rare joint opinion, overturning *Roe* "would seriously weaken the Court's capacity to exercise the judicial power and to function as the Supreme Court of a Nation dedicated to the rule of law."[24] As the joint opinion explained:

> The Court's power lies . . . in its legitimacy, a product of substance and perception that shows itself in the people's acceptance of the Judiciary as fit to determine what the Nation's law means and to declare what it demands.[25]

Notice the role of "perception." The question is not just what is, but what will be perceived.

Because not every conscientious claim of principled justification will be accepted as such, the justification claimed must be beyond dispute. The Court must take care to speak and act in ways that allow people to accept its decisions on the terms the Court claims for them, as grounded truly in principle, not as compromises with social and political pressures having, as such, no bearing on the principled choices that the Court is obliged to make. Thus, the Court's legitimacy depends on making legally principled decisions under circumstances in which their principled character is sufficiently plausible to be accepted by the Nation.[26]

The obligation is thus more than simply getting it right, the Joint Opinion insists. It is getting it right in circumstances in which the "principled character" of the decision "is sufficiently plausible to be accepted."

And then the political opposition to *Roe* proved self-defeating. For to overrule a constitutional rule in circumstances in which the Court is "under fire"—and without "the most compelling reason to reexamine" the rule—"would subvert the Court's legitimacy beyond any serious question." "Diminished legitimacy may be restored," the Court acknowledged, "but only slowly."[27] To avoid that diminishment, these justices refused to vote as they might well have voted originally—to deny the right recognized by *Roe*.

In as clear an example as we will see, fidelity to role trumped fidelity to meaning—at least for these judges. It is plain that at least some of these three believed *Roe* had been wrongly decided. That is, some believed fidelity to meaning would have meant reaching the opposite result in *Roe*. But reversing *Roe* now would signal something about the institution that would fundamentally weaken that institution.

*Roe* thus stands in a precarious place. For some justices, it is right as a matter of fidelity to meaning: recognizing that the liberty to choose whether or not to procreate is fundamental, and that the state has no relatively uncontested justification for overcoming that liberty. For these justices, the rule is relatively stable—at least subject to the justifications.

But for the justices in the joint opinion, *Roe* stands as a matter of fidelity to role. To reverse the constitutional rule because of politics would change the understanding of the nature of the Constitution itself.

Neither position is immovable. But I suspect the fidelity to role justification for *Roe* is ultimately more vulnerable. If the abortion question could become muted in the political process for appointing judges, reversing is less likely to trigger the perception that the authors of the joint opinion were concerned about. No amount of careful packaging will change the nature of the liberty interest. But institutional appropriateness can be massaged.

| Equality Meets Privacy

C LIVE MICHAEL BOUTILIER, A CANADIAN, ENTERED the United
States in 1955. He was then twenty-one. Eight years later, he applied to
become a citizen. In his application, Boutilier admitted that he had been arrested in 1959 on a charge of sodomy. Immigration officials then asked him
for a full history of his sexual behavior. He provided that history in 1964. By
affidavit, Boutilier admitted to an average of three or four homosexual relations a year during his time in the United States.[1]

I trust that someday the previous paragraph will strike everyone as being
just as bizarre as if I had reported that the government surveyed the number
of sexual encounters straight immigrants had, or the number of extramarital
affairs married immigrants had had. But in 1967, that paragraph was wholly
unremarkable. I've lifted it, with a bit of massaging, from the Supreme
Court opinion that gave Michael Boutilier his fifteen seconds of fame—an
opinion in which the Court upheld the decision of the government to exclude Boutilier because of, as the Court described it, his "psychopathic personality."

For in 1964, immigration law required that anyone deemed to have a
"psychopathic personality" be banned from admission into the United States.
Michael Boutilier was found, without "any serious question," to have such a
personality. The sole basis upon which that judgment was made was the finding, conceded by Boutilier, that he was a homosexual. That fact alone entailed a finding of pathology.

Yet not because the immigration statute said as much. Indeed, the text of
the statute didn't even mention homosexuality. Instead, the Court divined
the meaning of the statute by looking first to its legislative history. (Hey,

textualists—this is a classic case illustrating the absurdity you attack. As the opinion begins: "The legislative history of the Act indicates beyond a shadow of a doubt that the Congress intended the phrase 'psychopathic personality' to include homosexuals such as petitioner.") The legislative history cited a "Public Health Service report" that "recommended that the term 'psychopathic personality' be used to 'specify such types of pathologic behavior as homosexuality or sexual perversion.'"[2]

And why had a Public Health Service report recommended homosexuality be deemed a "pathology"? Because that's how medical science viewed homosexuality. The *Diagnostic and Statistical Manual of Mental Disorders* (1952) defined "sexual deviation" thus:

> The term includes most of the cases formerly classed as "psychopathic personality with pathologic sexuality." The diagnosis will specify the type of the pathologic behavior, such as homosexuality, transvestism, pedophilia, fetishism and sexual sadism (including rape, sexual assault, mutilation).[3]

And so clear was this status that even the Court's most liberal justice described homosexuality as follows:

> Those "who fail to reach sexual maturity (hetero-sexuality), and who remain at a narcissistic or homosexual stage" are the products "of heredity, of glandular dysfunction, (or) of environmental circumstances."

> The homosexual is one who, by some freak occurrence, is the product of an arrested development: "All people have originally bisexual tendencies which are more or less developed and which in the course of time normally deviate either in the direction of male or female. This may indicate that a trace of homosexuality, no matter how weak it may be, exists in every human being. It is present in the adolescent stage, where there is a considerable amount of undifferentiated sexuality."[4]

One-step originalism had nothing to offer gays or lesbians. And given the attitudes of the time, neither would the two-step.

In the early 1970s, this view among professionals began to change. In 1970, the American Psychiatric Association (APA) held its annual meeting in San Francisco. For the first time in its history, gay and lesbian activists organized protests at the meeting. Two years later, the APA organized its first open panel "on the lifestyles of non-patient homosexuals." The following year, it held panels on "the extent to which heterosexual biases had colored the work of psychiatrists." In that same year, 1973, the board and membership of the APA approved a change in the psychiatric status of homosexuality. From that point on, it was no longer classified as a "psychiatric disorder."[5]

This change in classification had both direct and indirect effects. The direct effect happened less than six years later. In 1979, the Surgeon General determined, in light of the APA's change in classification, that "homosexuality per se will no longer be considered a 'mental disease or defect.'"[6]

This, in turn, produced an indirect effect. For this change caused real trouble at the Immigration and Naturalization Service (INS). The INS had drawn on the Public Health Service determination, which in turn rested upon the judgment of the surgeon general that homosexuality was "psychopathic." The surgeon general's new view removed the scientific predicate to the judgment, and so the Public Health Service determined that it could no longer certify homosexuals as "sexual deviates."[7] The INS thus no longer had any predicate to exclude homosexuals. So it decided simply to ignore the matter, and beginning in June 1982, it no longer refused admission to the United States on the grounds of homosexuality alone.

This decision by the INS was not acceptable to the (Carter!) Justice Department. In an opinion of the Justice Department, the INS was ordered to exclude gays under a statute that banned "psychopathic personalities" even though science no longer deemed gays "psychopathic." That decision was then challenged in federal court. In 1982, the Court reversed it. In an opinion by Judge Robert Aguilar, the District Court concluded that the statute was built to rest upon science; as science changed, so too would the scope of the statute have to change.[8] Whatever the specific intent of Congress in 1952 with respect to homosexuals, the scope of the statute would hang upon the current view of science.

This story about the INS regulation is a perfect template for understanding the extraordinary history of equality and liberty claims tied to sexual orientation. When a particular sexual orientation is deemed a disease, it becomes, in the language of *Plessy*, a "legal distinction" the state is unproblematically allowed to draw. Laws regulating "disease" are not "discriminations," any more than laws regulating the quarantine of people with smallpox are "discriminations." Those laws could be excessive. They could be cruel. But they don't trigger an equality analysis because they don't begin with something that's seen as "discrimination."

But once that box is broken—once one cannot without controversy simply frame a particular sexual orientation as a "disease"—the regulation of sexual orientation becomes more complicated. Distinctions become discriminations, and discrimination demands justification. With the INS, once "disease" disappeared as a box around homosexuality, the government had no other basis for exclusion. The law worked, in the sense that it forced the government to justify its behavior, and when the government could not, the law demanded that behavior stop.

The constitutional history of claims affecting sexual orientation is not as clean or as quick, but it is precisely analogous. Here too, the story begins at a moment when it was almost inconceivable to recognize any constitutional claim on behalf of homosexuals. Yet in an incredibly short time, that claim has matured. Against it, the government has not been able to muster a sufficiently uncontested justification for ignoring it.

As we'll see, the constitutional claims here are grounded both in equality and in (substantive) due process. As they ultimately resolve (or at least, resolve for now), they have established a clear right not to be burdened or disadvantaged because of sexual orientation.

In the beginning, the constitutional basis for the claim of equality was obscure. That obscurity can be glimpsed in the very first case to address the constitutional questions raised by the regulation of homosexuality, *Bowers v. Hardwick* (1986). (Boutilier's lawyers apparently didn't think it worth their time to raise a constitutional claim grounded in either equality or privacy.)

Michael Hardwick was arrested by Atlanta police when they discovered him and another man engaged in homosexual sodomy in his home. Though the charges against him were dismissed, he (with the help of the ACLU and Harvard's Laurence Tribe) challenged the Georgia law. But Hardwick didn't challenge it with an equality claim. He grounded his argument instead in due process. It was a simple extension, or so his lawyers believed, of the argument upholding the right of a woman to choose whether to terminate her pregnancy in *Roe v. Wade*: if the choice whether or not to procreate was fundamental, then the choice whether or not and with whom to have sex was also fundamental. And if it was fundamental, then the government needed a compelling interest to justify its regulation.

An extremely impatient Supreme Court disagreed. In one of his worst opinions, Justice Byron White, who had been appointed by John F. Kennedy, ridiculed the very idea that the Constitution protected homosexuals.[9] After reviewing the history of laws regulating homosexual conduct, White wrote, "To claim that a right to engage in such conduct is 'deeply rooted in this Nation's history and tradition' or 'implicit in the concept of ordered liberty' is, at best, facetious."[10] Chief Justice Burger simply piled on.[11]

It fell then to Justice Stevens—in many ways the John Marshall Harlan (the first one) of that Court—to see what was really at stake in this case. The issue for Stevens was not primarily substantive due process. The issue was equality.

As Stevens put the case, Georgia's sodomy laws regulated married and un-married couples, as well as gay and heterosexual couples. Like other similar laws, sodomy laws regulate a certain act, regardless of who engages in that act. Thus, for Stevens, the question was simply whether a state can ban such conduct, regardless of who engages in it, and if not, does the fact that the law is applied only against homosexuals somehow render it constitutional?

It seemed clear to Stevens—and indeed, it is clear—that a sodomy statute applied to married couples would not withstand constitutional scrutiny. Georgia had conceded as much. So how, Stevens asked, did selective enforcement of the blanket prohibition render the law constitutional? In Stevens's view, it could not. Homosexuals have the same liberty interests as straight people do. And selective enforcement of a law must be grounded, Stevens argued, on something more substantial than simple dislike of another group. Equality, in other words, was why the Georgia law was unconstitutional.

Only two justices joined Stevens's opinion. Yet time would show that his understanding was the most insightful of any.

From a political perspective, there was nothing surprising about the Court's decision. In 1986, the Court was on balance conservative. Though White's opinion was more extreme than most would have put the matter, it wasn't out of step with much of what America thought about the matter then. Americans opposed legal protection for same-sex relationships by almost a two-to-one margin in the late 1980s. While that opposition would decline somewhat in the 1990s, it did not decline substantially until the 2000s.[12]

Yet just as *Roe v. Wade* would trigger a political response, so too did *Bowers* excite an extraordinary political response, this time on the Left, as activists used the extreme rhetoric of the opinion to awaken America to just how backward the law was—or rather, how backward it was at this point in time. For a long campaign of public awareness was changing how gays were perceived. With "pathology" no longer predicated of gay people's behavior, the debate about homosexuality (ignoring for a moment the religious component of that debate) shifted to different grounds. Was homosexuality chosen or innate? Either way, why should that matter? Whether homosexuality is chosen or not, what justifies its regulation? And is that justification partial and contested, or not?

As the Court was forced to address these questions, its opinions followed a now familiar pattern. In the beginning, the Court was unwilling to say that it was applying anything other than rational-basis review. But the actual review that it applied was clearly something more than simple rational basis. As with sex discrimination, that was because justices viewing the law being challenged couldn't see the distinctions it made as anything other than discrimination.

The first big surprise was *Romer v. Evans* (1996). A state referendum had made it illegal for local governments in Colorado to

> enact, adopt or enforce any statute, regulation, ordinance or policy whereby homosexual, lesbian or bisexual orientation, conduct, practices or relationships shall constitute or otherwise be the basis of or entitle any person or class of persons to have or claim any minority status, quota preferences, protected status or claim of discrimination.[13]

As Justice Scalia noted in dissent, in the nature of things, this was a small offense. Colorado didn't ban homosexual conduct. It didn't criminalize homosexuality itself. Its "intolerance," as the plaintiffs would frame it, was to deny to homosexuals what Scalia called the "special protection" of the law through the protections of anti-discrimination legislation.

Yet to evaluate this law, we need to understand a bit more fully the history of civil rights legislation. From the beginning of the United States, it had been the view of most jurists that natural law secured to everyone the protection against discrimination. Those natural rights were implemented through particular laws and in different ways. But at base, the view was that the law would protect anyone against discrimination by treating everyone "equally."

That objective, of course, faced precisely the ambiguity that I have described throughout this and the previous chapters: when is a legal distinction "discrimination"? Conceivably, a jurisdiction could leave that judgment up to a court or a jury. Alternatively, it could begin to identify particular kinds of legal distinctions that will be deemed discrimination.

American civil rights law has followed the second path. As I described in Chapter 16, in 1866 Congress passed the first federal Civil Rights Act, which identified certain privileges or immunities that had to be secured to everyone with the same nature or vigor as applied "to white people." Then the strategy of the laws shifted by identifying particular classifications that will be deemed suspect. "Suspect" doesn't mean illegal. But if a penalty or restriction gets triggered by a classification deemed suspect, then the entity applying the penalty or restriction needs a strong justification for its behavior.

What Colorado had said was that gays or lesbians (but not heterosexuals) could not try to secure protection against discrimination by having the classification of sexual orientation included within civil rights statutes—regardless of whether those within that classification were in fact subject to discrimination.

This qualification is important. Imagine Colorado's Amendment 2 had said that handedness cannot be a protected class within Colorado's civil rights legislation. The consequence of the amendment would then be that left-handers could not try to attack the "discrimination" they in fact suffered. As a left-hander myself, I can well attest that there are many burdens left-handers experience because we are left-handed. (Just pick up a pencil with your left hand and try to read what's printed on the barrel. The orientation of the printing is designed for right-handers. Outrageous!) Likewise, we can certainly establish that historically, left-handedness was severely burdened. Left-handers, as one author describes it, "have been subjected to centuries of discrimination and sometimes even persecution."[14] The burden can be traced all the way back to ancient Greece and Rome. The philosopher Pythagoras, for example, saw left-handedness as synonymous with evil. Aristotle described good as "what is on the right, above, and in front, and bad what is on the left, below, and behind." The Romans standardized the right-handed handshake, and in Western countries alphabets favored right-handed individuals.[15] In medieval Europe, left-handers were accused of consorting with the devil and practicing witchcraft.[16] By the eighteenth and nineteenth centuries, there were deliberate attempts to suppress left-handedness. A child's left hand could be tied behind his chair in school, and often children were punished for writing with their left hand.[17] Even today, the world is crafted for the right-hander still. As John Sciortino brilliantly summarizes our world:

> The kitchen typically has a right-hander-designed can opener, soup ladle, frying pans, coffee maker, measuring cups, knives (beveled on the right side), electric food slicer, cheese server, grapefruit sectioning knife, microwave oven, ice cream scoop, and clothes dryer. Schools are no friendlier for the left-hander. The left-to-right writing pattern is set up for right-handers. Also, the spiral notebook, rulers, and most desks are all right-handed. Offices are not much better, containing right-handed adding machines, computers, computer printers, copying machines, telephones (including pay phones), and vending machines. Blue collar southpaws are in even more trouble. Much industrial machinery is right-hander-designed, making things like power saws remarkably dangerous for left-handers. The professions are not immune. Surgical and dental instruments are almost always right-handed in design. The left-hander cannot even find comfort at play. Cameras, rifles (bolts), handguns (ejection chambers), fishing rods, field hockey sticks, polo (patterns of play), television sets, ballroom dancing, and even books and magazines are all designed for right-handers.[18]

But it would be absurd today for a left-hander to insist that his life is burdened by the "discrimination" visited against him. And if, that absurdity notwithstanding, a bunch of Colorado towns and cities had passed ordinances purporting to protect left-handers, I would think it perfectly sensible for the state of Colorado to say, "Oh, come on. This is ridiculous. Stop wasting state resources on such an absurd 'protection.'"

It was precisely because the social meaning of the protection for gays and lesbians in Colorado was not absurd that an ordinance forbidding the inclusion of that category within civil rights laws raised a constitutional question: Was that exclusion discrimination, and if it was, could it be justified? Given how social understanding has evolved, the line based on sexual orientation is different from a line based on handedness. The social meaning of distinctions based on sexual orientation had become discrimination.

Justice Anthony Kennedy wrote the opinion that struck the ordinance down. That fact alone is important because of who Justice Kennedy is. A Republican and a conservative, Kennedy was appointed by Ronald Reagan after the Senate rejected the appointment of Judge Robert Bork. Unlike Justice Ginsburg for the rights of women, few would ever have thought of Kennedy as an activist for gay rights.

Yet even this conservative could see the character of this exclusion. Or maybe more precisely, even this conservative could see that the Court could no longer view such a line as a mere distinction. This was discrimination. The Fourteenth Amendment required the state to remain neutral "where the rights of persons are at stake."[19] But by expressly forbidding protection for persons based on sexual orientation, the state had not remained neutral. "It is not within our constitutional tradition," Justice Kennedy observed, "to enact laws of this sort."[20] At least a "tradition" increasingly sensitive to the discrimination built into its rules.

But what sort of law was this? That was the question Justice Scalia pressed "vigorously," as he put it, in his dissent. Colorado was not being vicious, Scalia insisted. Instead, this was "rather a modest attempt by seemingly tolerant Coloradans to preserve traditional sexual mores against the efforts of a politically powerful minority to revise those mores through use of the laws."[21]

That may well have been the aim of the citizens of Colorado. But the question for the Court was how it could reckon that aim. Scalia said that

> in holding that homosexuality cannot be singled out for disfavorable treatment, the Court...places the prestige of this institution behind the proposition that opposition to homosexuality is as reprehensible as racial or religious bias.[22]

To be fair to the Court, Justice Kennedy wasn't saying anything about *how* reprehensible such opposition is. His opinion only requires that it is reprehensible. Or more precisely, it only requires that the distinction being drawn by the law be recognized legally as discrimination. No doubt, Scalia was right that "whether [such opposition] is or is not [as reprehensible as racial bias] is *precisely* the cultural debate that gave rise to the Colorado constitutional amendment." But the cultural debate is separate from the legal question. At the time of *Brown*, whether segregation was reprehensible was a cultural debate as well. But for the Court, the question was whether there was any way to avoid viewing de jure segregation as anything other than discrimination—and once it was so viewed, whether there was any justification for such discrimination.

So, was the law a manifestation of discrimination?

Importantly, nothing in that question turns on the malice of Coloradans. The question is interpretive, involving a culture that reaches far beyond Colorado. Did Amendment 2 manifest the kind of discrimination that triggered equal protection analysis?

Here, the cultural distance of a decade is astonishing to recognize. In *Bowers v. Hardwick* (1986), the Court took it as obvious that laws aiming to drive people away from homosexual conduct were appropriate.[23] Justice Stevens in that case tried to get the Court to engage an equal protection analysis. But for the justices, equality was not on the table. The only question was whether the Constitution stood against hundreds of years of tradition.

Yet by the time of *Romer*, that way of speaking was no longer costless. Not because a cabal of liberal activists had taken over the Supreme Court, but because of the way even conservative justices understood the social meaning of what Colorado had done. It was, as they saw, a kind of discrimination.

If it was discrimination, the question was whether it could be justified. The state could not meet its burden. "We cannot say," Kennedy wrote, "that Amendment 2 is directed to any identifiable legitimate purpose or discrete objective. It is a status-based enactment divorced from any factual context from which we could discern a relationship to legitimate state interests; it is a classification of persons undertaken for its own sake."[24]

This was discrimination. There was no justification given how the act was now understood. The law was thus struck down.

*Romer* was just the beginning. Over the course of the next twenty years, the Supreme Court would deliver a string of victories for same-sex activists. Those victories would sound in both equality claims and privacy claims.

*Lawrence v. Texas* (2003) was next. Texas punished sodomy criminally. Unlike Georgia in *Bowers*, however, its statute punished homosexual sodomy only. The law was valid, the Supreme Court believed, only if *Bowers* was valid.

On the basis of the due process clause, the Court concluded that *Bowers* was no longer good law.

Yet as Justice Scalia noted in dissent, the Court in *Lawrence* did not reject the core conclusion of *Bowers*—that there was no "fundamental right" to engage in homosexual sodomy. Instead, the decision was grounded in a kind of rational basis test. As with the first decisions in the context of gender equality, however, this was not ordinary rational basis. It was a kind of rational-basis-plus. All agreed that the law infringed the liberty of homosexuals. All should agree that the liberty the law infringed was as personal and intimate as any.

The question was whether there was a legitimate state interest to justify that infringement. The Court identified that interest as the moral interests of Texas. But that interest was not significant enough to overcome the liberty interest in being left alone. No doubt the moral interest of Texas was sincere. But that alone could not resolve the question.

The issue is whether the majority may use the power of the State to enforce these views on the whole society through operation of the criminal law. "Our obligation is to define the liberty of all, not to mandate our own moral code," wrote Justice Kennedy in *Lawrence*.[25]

Justice O'Connor would not agree to overturn *Bowers*. But she did agree that Texas can't punish homosexual sodomy if it did not punish heterosexual sodomy. That it didn't meant it violated an equality norm, O'Connor held, because a law that "exhibits . . . a desire to harm a politically unpopular group" must withstand "a more searching form of rational basis review." This law, O'Connor concluded, failed that review.

But why?

The answer to that question was framed by Scalia. In his view, what animated the Court's decision was that the Court viewed the statute "as 'discrimination' which it is the function of our judgments to deter." Yet Scalia rejected the idea that Texas's law could be "discrimination," for two distinct reasons. First, it was actually contested within contemporary society whether laws targeting homosexuals were discrimination:

> So imbued is the Court with the law profession's anti-anti-homosexual culture, that it is seemingly unaware that the attitudes of that culture are not obviously "mainstream"; that in most States what the Court calls "discrimination" against those who engage in homosexual acts is perfectly legal; that proposals to ban such "discrimination" under Title VII have repeatedly been rejected by Congress, that in some cases such "discrimination" is *mandated* by federal statute, and that in some cases such "discrimination" is a constitutional right.[26]

Second, whether those laws are considered discrimination or not, the "emerging awareness" that they are could not, in Scalia's view, ground a constitutional holding that they are invalid. "Constitutional entitlements do not spring into existence," Scalia insists. We must today be who we were at the Founding—in this respect at least.

Yet that practice of stasis is not the practice of the Court. And no decision affecting same-sex liberty made that point as clearly as the decision in *Obergefell v. Hodges* (2015) to invalidate restrictions on same-sex marriage.

It was, of course, a long time in coming. For years activists had been fighting the state's refusal to grant same-sex partners the right to marry. They had won and lost referenda at the state level for decades. They had won in some state courts. But twenty years after the justice appointed by John F. Kennedy (Justice White) expressed his impatience with the idea that the Constitution might be invoked on behalf of same-sex partners, a justice appointed by Ronald Reagan (Justice Kennedy) penned an opinion that established the constitutional right of same-sex couples to marry.

That right was grounded in both equality and privacy. As in *Lawrence*, Kennedy began with privacy. The Constitution secured to individuals liberty. That liberty included "certain specific rights that allow persons, within a lawful realm, to define and express their identity."[27] The commitment of marriage is part of that identity. Reviewing our tradition and the cases articulating that fundamental interest, Kennedy concluded that the right to marriage was "fundamental." It was not fundamental because it had always been fundamental; it was fundamental because of what we now know. "Rights come not from ancient sources alone," Kennedy wrote. "They rise, too, from a better informed understanding of how constitutional imperatives define a liberty that remains urgent in our own era."[28]

In reaching this conclusion, Kennedy affirmed strongly the tradition that would permit the rights recognized under due process to change. "The identification and protection of fundamental rights is an enduring part of the judicial duty to interpret the Constitution," Kennedy wrote. But "that responsibility . . . has not been reduced to any formula." Or more accurately, it has not been reduced to any static formula. Instead, the duty required "courts to exercise reasoned judgment in identifying interests of the person so fundamental that the State must accord them its respect." History is a part of that process, since "history and tradition guide and discipline" the inquiry. But history and tradition "do not set its outer boundaries." Reasoned judgment thus "respects our history and learns from it without allowing the past alone to rule the present."[29]

The "limitation of marriage to opposite-sex couples may long have seemed natural and just," he went on, but its inconsistency with the central meaning of the fundamental right to marry is now manifest. With that knowledge must come the recognition that laws excluding same-sex couples...impose stigma and injury of the kind prohibited by our basic charter.[30]

There are several critical ideas embedded within these forty-some words. First, equal protection is about meaning—the "central meaning" of the right to marry. Second, meaning becomes "manifest." We didn't see it before; it is now manifest for us to see. Third, what is manifest is "knowledge." It is a truth that has revealed itself, not a political preference. And that truth leads, fourth, to a "recognition" again about meaning—that exclusion "impose[s] stigma." No doubt, not all stigma raises a constitutional problem. The law stigmatizes pedophiles without equality skipping a beat. But the stigma imposed on gay people is "of the kind prohibited by our basic charter."

Kennedy has described an understanding that is fundamentally different from the one described by the dissent—not because the opinion yields a right not previously expressly protected, but because it yields a right that would have been expressly rejected before. In dissent, Chief Justice Roberts rejected the idea that the approach he and the dissenters advanced would result in a static Constitution, or one that would never yield a new right. As he wrote,

[This approach] does not require disavowing the doctrine of implied fundamental rights, and this Court has not done so. But to avoid repeating *Lochner*'s error of converting personal preferences into constitutional mandates, our modern substantive due process cases have stressed the need for "judicial self-restraint."...Our precedents have required that implied fundamental rights be "objectively, deeply rooted in this Nation's history and tradition," and "implicit in the concept of ordered liberty, such that neither liberty nor justice would exist if they were sacrificed."[31]

Thus, a right taken for granted for two hundred years could find expression in an opinion by Roberts. But a right that conflicted with the actual regulations of society for two hundred years could not, by definition.

Both approaches live within due process jurisprudence, as both Kennedy and Roberts acknowledge. *Obergefell* was an instance of reasoned judgment. By contrast, *Washington v. Glucksberg* (1997), asking whether due process secured a right to die, was an instance of what we could call "historical judgment." In declining to find a right to die, the Court merely looked to the long-standing history regulating against it. Kennedy acknowledged that approach "for the asserted right there involved";[32] but, *ipse dixit,* that was not the right approach for the right involved in the same-sex marriage case.

Whether this difference in approach can be sustained is an open question. Only a minority ever felt the restrictions from a rule that mandates opposite-based marriage. Given the nature of medicine, a more significant minority is likely to feel the restriction on terminating life with dignity. But the important point for our purposes is not so much the difference as the dynamic of translation. As the fundamental liberty question gets asked across a range of contexts, reasoned judgment translates the libertarian protection as the social meaning of the liberty at issue changes.

Due process was not the only ground upon which the ban on same-sex marriage was invalidated. After articulating the due process analysis, Kennedy linked that understanding to the equal protection clause as well. Just as with due process, when interpreting equal protection, Kennedy noted, "The Court has recognized that new insights and societal understandings can reveal unjustified inequality within our most fundamental institutions that once passed unnoticed and unchallenged."[33] That is, Kennedy asserts, now true with sexual orientation: "It is now clear that the challenged laws burden the liberty of same-sex couples, and it must be further acknowledged that they abridge central precepts of equality." That abridgment "serves to disrespect and subordinate"—the core actionable harm now recognized under the equal protection clause.

Astonishingly, then, just thirty years after the Court had found it "facetious" to suggest that the Constitution blocked the criminalization of homosexual sex, the Court recognizes that the Constitution guarantees the equal right of gays and lesbians to access the sacred institution of state-sponsored marriage.

———

In spring 2017, the Seventh Circuit Court of Appeals held that the sex discrimination provision of Title VII, America's employment discrimination law, protected gays and lesbians from being discriminated against on the basis of their sexual orientation. Described as a landmark decision, the case confirmed that while that court is in some ways conservative, it is often at the forefront of protecting gay and lesbian rights.

The opinion was written by Chief Judge Diane Wood, a former law professor and frequent name on the list of potential nominees to the Supreme Court (by a Democratic president at least). But concurring in the opinion and judgment was Judge Richard Posner, perhaps the most influential judge and law professor in the history of both professions. Posner is considered a conservative. He's more accurately described as an independent thinker. And he's long defended a more enlightened view about how the law should protect rights regardless of a person's sexual orientation.[34]

But Posner used the opportunity of the case to speak more directly about the need for courts to acknowledge more plainly their constructive role in interpretation. That activity, in the context of statutes at least, comes in three flavors, Posner instructed. "The first and most conventional is the extraction of the original meaning of the statute—the meaning intended by the legislators—and corresponds to interpretation in ordinary discourse." The second "is interpretation by unexpressed intent"—the recognition that "no vehicles in the park" does not mean "no ambulances." And the third—the focus of his concurrence—is an interpretation that "give[s] fresh meaning to a statement...a meaning that infuses the statement with vitality and significance today."

This third form is not translation, though translation also accomplishes a similar infusion of vitality and significance. Posner's analysis does little to distinguish between "fresh meaning" that could be seen as faithful to an original meaning and "fresh meaning" that is inconsistent with original meaning. But his analysis is nonetheless relevant and powerfully instructive for the dynamic I've described in this chapter, because the emphasis that Posner makes in his opinion is upon what we have "learned."

Consider this passage mapping the predicate to the "fresh meaning" Posner intends to imbue Title VII with:

> We now understand that homosexual men and women (and also bisexuals, defined as having both homosexual and heterosexual orientations) are normal in the ways that count, and beyond that have made many outstanding intellectual and cultural contributions to society (think for example of Tchaikovsky, Oscar Wilde, Jane Addams, André Gide, Thomas Mann, Marlene Dietrich, Bayard Rustin, Alan Turing, Alec Guinness, Leonard Bernstein, Van Cliburn, and James Baldwin—a very partial list). We now understand that homosexuals, male and female, play an essential role, in this country at any rate, as adopters of children from foster homes—a point emphasized in our *Baskin* decision.[35]

Posner is describing a process of understanding that pushes the court to read a statute differently. That process is not democratic (in the sense of waiting for a consensus among people polled), but neither is it willful. The social context crafts the space that Posner is able to occupy. "We now understand that" is a clause with a truth value. It is true when appended to "homosexuals, male and female, play an essential role, in this country at any rate, as adopters of children from foster homes." It is not true—as much as I wish it were—when appended to "dolphins are sentient beings deserving of respect and judicial protection."

Yet Posner's real aim in this concurrence was to insist on a kind of judicial integrity. As he closed the opinion:

> I would prefer to see us acknowledge openly that today we, who are judges rather than members of Congress, are imposing on a half-century-old statute a meaning of "sex discrimination" that the Congress that enacted it would not have accepted. . . . We should not leave the impression that we are merely the obedient servants of the 88th Congress (1963–1965), carrying out their wishes. We are not. We are taking advantage of what the last half century has taught.[36]

In the terms that I have developed throughout this book, the point is not that Courts take advantage of what time has taught. It is that they are *constrained* by it. In a world in which the LGBT community is uncontestably marginalized, either because their condition is deemed immoral (as in the nineteenth century) or a disease (as in much of the twentieth), the anti-egalitarian has an easy ride. He can dismiss the claims of right because the social context makes such a dismissal uncontroversial. Indeed, at its most extreme, it is no more seen as discrimination than excluding twelve-year-olds from jury duty is.

But culture works changes. And when the Court finds itself in a place where rules are read as discrimination, that forces it to determine what before it could ignore. If this is discrimination, can it be justified? Is there a relatively uncontested reason that the Court can fall back on, so that it is not forced to dislodge the status quo?

The sexual orientation cases evince this dynamic more clearly than any other. As conservatives have recognized the rights of the LGBT community, they have not been "taking advantage of what the last half century has taught." There is no advantage to be taken. They are, in the main, reluctant reformers, just as O'Connor, Souter, and Kennedy were reluctant defenders of *Roe*. Conservatives have been yielding to what the last half century has taught. Within the structure of reasoning that equality presents, the last fifty years have eroded the grounds upon which the denial of equality claims must rest. And within the space of privacy—as in freedom from regulation—the teachings of the last half century have made it increasingly difficult to exclude same-sex relations from the domain that all believe should be free from the reach of the state. Understanding has constrained the courts; it has not empowered them. But the dynamic of contestability makes these judges reformers nonetheless. And the weakness in the framing that this great judge gives us is that it just taunts the other side. It is not willfulness; it is the unwillingness to spit in the wind of what we all know is true.

Which leads to a second point: If the originalists really do mean for us to ignore what "we now understand," they need to explain how, in fact, we do that. How do we spit in the wind of what everyone believes it true?

Especially, how do we do so in light of the commitment to a fidelity to role? One can agree firmly that such a fidelity requires courts to stay far from "legislative" judgments. But this view denies that all changes in light of "we now understand" are properly considered "legislative." And even more important, the view I am advancing understands that the further out there the Court lives, the easier it is for the political branches to render it meaningless. The credibility and standing of the judicial branch depend critically upon it being seen as "reasonable."

That fact is not morally comfortable, since morally, what has been "reasonable" has also often been wrong. But here's where the judge as philosopher and the judge as Scalia (at least sometimes) stand in the very same place: you can insist on something crazy all you want, but if you insist too loudly or too frequently, the political types will swat you like a gnat, and the people will see very little reason to rally to your defense.

Reality constrains even judges. And reality includes what we now understand to be true.

––––––

In his dissent from the Court's most protective sex equality decision, *United States v. VMI*, Scalia scolds the Court for its self-satisfied smugness vis-à-vis the Framers. As he writes:

> Much of the Court's opinion is devoted to deprecating the closed-mindedness of our forebears with regard to women's education, and even with regard to the treatment of women in areas that have nothing to do with education. Closed-minded they were—*as every age is, including our own, with regard to matters it cannot guess, because it simply does not consider them debatable.* The virtue of a democratic system with a First Amendment is that it readily enables the people, over time, to be persuaded that what they took for granted is not so, and to change their laws accordingly. That system is destroyed if the smug assurances of each age are removed from the democratic process and written into the Constitution. So to counterbalance the Court's criticism of our ancestors, let me say a word in their praise: They left us free to change. The same cannot be said of this most illiberal Court, which has embarked on a course of inscribing one after another of the current preferences of the society (and in some cases only the counter-majoritarian preferences of the society's law-trained elite) into our Basic Law.[37]

Notice the elements in Scalia's diagnosis. Our forebears were "closed-minded" about matters they did not consider "debatable." Yet what they thought not debatable obviously changed. And the question for fidelity is how we respond to that sort of change. How is change in the undebatable to be reckoned? What method do we use to account?

Scalia's framing here makes it seem as if the choice is binary: a matter is either debatable or not. Yet as we've seen, those are not the only options. A matter can move from being undebatable to debatable. It can also move from being debatable to being undebatable in precisely the opposite way. Justice Bradley took for granted the separate status of women. For him it was undebatable. For Justice Brandeis, at least late in his life, the matter became debatable. He was willing to listen. What he heard may well have changed his mind. Once the Court heard advocate Ginsburg, they were destined to agree with Justice Ginsburg that women cannot be placed into a separate sphere and that any pedestal is but a cage.

There is no justice on the Court today who believes the matter of sex equality is debatable anymore. To every justice, and every normal soul within our legal system, the matter is again undebatable. We take for granted the equal status of women. What that means in practice is a hard question, given the (so far) physical differences between men and women that nature gave us. But that difficulty doesn't undermine what we all know is true.

As these things that are seen as not debatable change, a tradition committed to fidelity must decide how that change will get reckoned. The matter can't simply be ignored—it was because of what Bradley took to be not debatable that his decision in *Bradwell* made sense. A Court today must account for the attitudes that he relied upon. It must decide whether Bradley's undebatables will continue to rule, or whether their change will be tracked.

I take it as obvious that a Court couldn't and shouldn't proceed as if things that once were not debatable have not changed today. It would be crazy to imagine the Supreme Court of today deciding questions of equal protection through the eyes of Justice Bradley. He may well have had his "not debatables," but so do we. And no society is going to permit its highest Court to rule through the lenses of nineteenth-century values.

Nor should it. For unlike provisions actually enacted in the Constitution, these things considered not debatable were never ratified as part of the Constitution by anyone. There wasn't a vote about whether women should be inferior. No one thought it even a question. It was assumed, not enacted. Unlike slavery or the bicameral legislature, it was not expressly made part of our highest law.

So, when these undebatables change, prudence and a fidelity to role require at least caution during the uncertain period. As I've described it, a debatable issue is one from which courts rightly retreat if the controlling legal text will permit it. To retreat does not mean to do nothing. Instead, retreat can well mean simply doing what the default requires. If a treatment is viewed as discrimination, and the justification for that discrimination is now viewed as debatable, the proper response for a Court may well be to simply ignore the justification and strike the discrimination.

But when the non-debatable flips and becomes non-debatable in the other way, the Court has no option to simply ignore the change. Even the Supreme Court can't thumb its nose at what we all know is true, not even if that Court recognizes the ultimate or historical relativity of that truth. Fidelity to role compels "normal," "decent" "mainstream" attitudes— even if those attitudes are 180 degrees away from what the Framers believed, and even if we acknowledge how grossly unjust those attitudes have been.

Even Justice Scalia got this—sometimes. Consider again the words of Justice Brandeis in *Erie*: "Law in the sense in which courts speak of it today does not exist without some definite authority behind it." This is Brandeis channeling Posner. He is explaining what "we now understand." Yet Scalia had no hesitation in embracing *this* newly discovered knowledge. Recall again his opinion about customary international law discussed in Chapter 13. In the old days, Scalia reports, judges thought (or at least acted as if) they "found" the law. That was, for them at least, undebatable. *Erie* rejected that undebatable and replaced it with a very different view. In the post-*Erie* world, the undebatable is that law is made by common law judges. That the Framers may have understood differently was just a joke. Like bloodletting, it was something to chuckle at, not something to respect.

Likewise with the understanding of how independent agencies function. Recall again Scalia's words:

> It is not as obvious today as it seemed in the 1930s that there can be such things as genuinely "independent" regulatory agencies, bodies of impartial experts whose independence from the President does not entail correspondingly greater dependence upon the committees of Congress to which they are then immediately accountable; or indeed, that the decisions of such agencies so clearly involve scientific judgment rather than political choice that it is even theoretically desirable to insulate them from the democratic process.[38]

"It is not as obvious today as..." is just a more humble way to say "We now understand that..." Yet Scalia had no problem embracing what "we now understand," even when that meant striking down the laws of Congress.

The point is just this: Our actual tradition of constitutional interpretation has responded repeatedly to what "we now understand." Liberals have done it. Conservatives have done it. Even Scalia did it. The question has never been "whether"; it has always been "when." That's not a simple question, but its answer is very different from "never." "Never" has never been the consistent practice of our Court. Always the Court—including *every* justice—has yielded to what "we now understand."

Scalia shows us—in *Sosa,* and in the unitary executive cases (Chapter 13)—that he has no problem following the evolution of the undebatable. But why then is there a problem when it comes to gender (or any other kind of) equality? Indeed, the flip on gender is more solid and certain than the flip on the nature of the common law. So why must the Court follow one but reject the other?

The general answer offered by the conservatives—Scalia, Roberts, Thomas especially—is democracy. These are the choices that citizens should determine, the skeptics insist. And it is wrong, they say, for judges to "take advantage" of their protected power to displace that democratic judgment.

But the point of this whole book is that democracy operates subject to certain constraints. The Constitution is one constraint. Reality is another. "What we now understand" is a phrase that should only be deployed with humility. No doubt, there are plenty of examples of it having been deployed wrongly. But equally without doubt, it has formed a critical constraint on the evolution of the Supreme Court's doctrine. As ideas get thrown up for grabs, the Court's readings of the Constitution changes. And likewise, when ideas get rendered undebatable, the Court's readings of the Constitution change again. Those changes are not simply politics. They are not simply the political preferences of a legal elite. They are a reality—one that the legal elite processes differently from the public, no doubt. But they are part of a social reality that our Constitution is subject to.

Should it be? Can such a system be defended? Justified? If my account is indeed a fair account of the practice of our tradition, should we change it? Does the truth render that practice unjust? Or unjustified?

PART THREE | Justifications

THERE'S A PARK ACROSS THE STREET from where I live. In that park, there are two baseball fields. Sometimes Commonwealth types (as in the British Commonwealth) play cricket on one of those fields. As I was walking by the field one day when a gaggle of players was playing cricket, I passed a young boy walking with his father. "They're so stupid!" the boy exclaimed. "You can't stand so far away from second base. And what's the batter doing next to third?"

The boy's mistake was not crazy. There was someone standing with something that looked like a bat. The bizarre structure (the wicket) that holds the balls was an anomaly the boy ignored. And it did seem that there were people waiting to catch a ball that it looked like the batsman was waiting to hit. The boy only knew baseball. He interpreted what he saw against the background of what he knew. What he saw, against that background, did look pretty stupid. But as the father, beautifully patient and with endless love, explained, "They're playing a different game, puppy. That's cricket, not baseball."

The American Constitution is a large park, upon whose fields many different games are being played. Some are political, focused on the power of government. Those games keep immigrants out, or invite them in. The players in those games work to protect certain rights to guns or the right of a woman to choose (or not).

Some games are more academic. They include the study of constitutional history—who did what, when and why. Or they include the study of constitutional doctrine: What is the rule of the free speech clause of the First Amendment? Who has standing to test the president's compliance with the emoluments clause? When is a warrant required? When does Congress have to declare war?

The game of this book has been different. I suspect it will strike many in just the way that game of cricket struck the boy I described at the start of this chapter. I have not simply tried to tell the story of our Constitution's history. I'm obviously not just reporting on the current state of constitutional law in a few specific domains. I'm not grading the Supreme Court, separating the "correct" opinions from the "incorrect." I'm not romanticizing the work of the Supreme Court or Supreme Court justices—there is no one remotely Hercules-like anywhere on the stage I've constructed.

Instead, the game I am playing involves a very specific type of interpretation. As I said at the start, its method is essentially anthropological. Indeed, it is motivated by Geertzian or Davidsonian ideas about the very possibility of understanding. It is the game that Ronald Dworkin practiced.[1]

This game has certain framing assumptions. Core among them is an assumption of charity: we must tell a story that makes the most of the practice we're trying to understand. That's not because we're nice, or because we believe the Court is good. We embrace an assumption of charity because, in a critical sense, that's what understanding requires. As Davidson put it:

> Charity is not an option, but a condition of having a workable theory.... [I]t is meaningless to suggest that we might fall into massive error by endorsing it. Until we have successfully established a systematic correlation of sentences held true with sentences held true, there are no mistakes to make. Charity is forced on us; whether we like it or not, if we want to understand others, we must count them right in most matters. If we can produce a theory that reconciles charity and the formal conditions for a theory, we have done all that could be done to ensure communication. Nothing more is possible, and nothing more is needed.[2]

No one need play this game. I'm certainly not interested in persuading others to play, or to insist they are not "doing constitutional law" if they don't. Yet I do believe there is value in approaching the story of our Constitution in this way. For if the account we develop has salience and significance, we can understand better where constitutional doctrine is likely to go.

The most important player of this game in American constitutional law—by far—is Yale law professor Bruce Ackerman. Beginning with his Storrs Lectures in 1984, Ackerman has crafted a beautifully elegant account of American constitutional law. His story is both edifying—as the title of his series *We the People* suggests—and surprising. And while the full reach of his writing over the past four decades is far beyond what I've offered here, the core of my argument covers much the same ground as the core of his. Yet though we look at the same material, our accounts are importantly different.

That difference is an opportunity. For by contrasting the account I've offered here with the much more substantial account of Ackerman's, I can draw together the essential parts of mine, and suggest its advantages over his.

That is my objective in Chapter 21. Others have offered historical accounts of the American constitutional tradition.[3] But beyond Dworkin, no one more than Ackerman has so clearly tried to use the history to derive a theory.

That is Ackerman's aim—and not just for theory's sake, but also and critically to guide constitutional law going forward. My aim in this book has not been to defend my account against all comers. But the contrast with Ackerman's will make mine clearer.

Yet before I attempt this exercise, I should acknowledge what will be clear to anyone who has ever studied Ackerman's work. There is no comparison between the depth and historical significance of the account I have offered and the account that Ackerman provides. Independent of his theory, the history within the volumes of *We the People* alone should be required reading for every citizen, or at least any citizen purporting to account for our constitutional past. I think Ackerman has gone too far in his understanding of the New Deal—or, better, he's gone further than he needs to. But I certainly have not gone far enough in developing a historical account to match his.

| Ackerman's Accounting

**B**RUCE ACKERMAN IS MUCH MORE than a constitutional theorist. His early work on environment law radically changed the field and gave birth to the most important legal techniques for regulating carbon. His work in theory of social justice is an essential part of the philosophical canon, standing next to the work of Rawls and Nozick as an essential framework for understanding what justice requires. He has been a critically important advocate for a more restrained and responsible executive. And his ideas for improving our democracy are at the core the most important reforms now happening in America.

His work on the Constitution was inspired by a puzzle: how could it be that in the name of the Constitution, the actions of a present democratic majority could be stopped? This is the "countermajoritarian difficulty" that Ackerman's teacher Alexander Bickel had described in his classic book *The Least Dangerous Branch* (1962). It is the problem that motivated a whole generation of scholars and jurists, from John Hart Ely to Robert Bork.

The answer for Ackerman begins with a distinction. Constitutions, or constitutional traditions, are either monist or dualist. The monist does not distinguish between the significance of democratic instruction. The dualist distinguishes fundamentally. The dualist believes there is higher law that constrains the actions of normal politics. The challenge for a dualist is to understand the source and meaning of that higher law—and to build a constitutional practice that "distinguish[es] between ordinary decisions made by government and considered judgments made by the People."[4]

So far, that doesn't sound so different from a conventional account of the American Constitution. Everyone in our system recognizes there is a

Constitution that operates to constrain the actions of government. That constraint is ordinarily referred to as higher law. Whether the words of the Constitution, or the words plus Supreme Court authority, the net is a set of rules that in some ways at least limit or empower government.

But Ackerman is not convinced that we have any simple or self-validating set of texts that constitute this higher law. Indeed, not even every bit of the Constitution is higher law in the sense that Ackerman is focused upon. Instead, higher law is the product of a certain kind—a very special kind—of democratic engagement. It is the product of a public focused on fundamental questions and determining the answers to those questions with seriousness and reflection. When that reflection happens—in what Ackerman calls "constitutional moments"—the product deserves special deference within our constitutional and legal tradition. These are promises of the most important sort in the life of a nation, as the promises of marriage (or better, parenting) are in the life of a person.

In the period relevant to this book, there were, in Ackerman's view, three such constitutional moments. The first, and most obvious, was the Founding. The second, and most tragic, was the Civil War. And the third, and most important for modern constitutional jurisprudence, was the New Deal. Each of these was a moment of higher lawmaking, in Ackerman's view. Each has therefore earned a special deference from the democracy.

That deference is both individual and joint. These moments, Ackerman believes, add substance to the Constitution. Yet they must also be interpreted with the other moments, and with the less significant bits of our Constitution as well. Synthesis is an essential tool of constitutional interpretation, reading the parts together to make a sensible whole.[5] But proper synthesis requires recognizing the changes that each moment brings. After each moment, the Constitution is different, because the essence of each moment recognizes a significant decision by "we the people."

That the Founding is such a moment won't surprise anyone. Neither the Civil War, and especially its amendments. The puzzle for most when they first encounter Ackerman's theory is the New Deal. Yes, the New Deal Court seemed to change the doctrine of the Supreme Court fundamentally. But that change was not produced by any amendment of the Constitution's text. Instead, if there was a change at the New Deal, most lawyers view that change as unrelated to any newly expressed democratic will. It was either the product of infidelity (giving up on the Framers' federalism) or the correction of infidelity (ending the aberration of the old Court's limits on federal and state power). Either way, it had nothing to do with "we the people" saying anything. It was just judges rewriting the rules of constitutional law.

And it is here that Ackerman makes his most interesting and important move. For implicit in the conventional account of the changes after the New Deal is the idea that *democratically* authorized amendments require *procedurally* authorized constitutional texts. Or more generally, that amendments require the political process to follow the rules laid down for changing constitutional texts. On that understanding, the New Deal couldn't have amended anything, since of course, no constitutional text came out of that struggle—except the texts of the opinions of the Supreme Court.

Yet as Ackerman argues (persuasively, in my view), that text-based or process-based test for determining whether there was constitutional change cannot account for either the Founding or the Civil War amendments either. Put differently, if following the rules is the rule, then none of the most important moments of constitutional history are part of the Constitution.

The flaw in the first moment we saw in Chapter 1. If the test for a valid constitutional amendment was whether the new text followed the rules laid down, we've already seen in Chapter 1 why our Constitution fails that test. The rules laid down in 1787 required Congress to propose amendments and that those amendments be ratified by all thirteen state legislatures. (They also required that state constitutions be amended in ways the Framing certainly did not follow.) If the rule requires following the rules, then the Constitution fails the rule because the process for adopting the Constitution certainly violated the then existing rules.

Less familiar is the flaw in the second moment, the Civil War Amendments. As Ackerman, following others, has noted, the Radical Republicans certainly violated every normal rule in forcing the Civil War Amendments into the Constitution. They moved the goalposts when needed—there is no consistent way of counting that yields the conclusion that all three amendments were ratified—and, as I described in Chapter 16, the very idea of forcing states to adopt an amendment while under military rule was deeply troubling.

Yet no one doubts that these two moments produced valid and normatively fundamental parts of our constitutional tradition. And so if they did, why did they? Or *how* did they? What was it about those moments that could produce fundamental higher law, despite failing to follow the rules laid down? Or more precisely for the theory, what do we have to assume about the nature, structure, or content of American constitutional law to make it possible to understand these moments as constitutional?

That question is critical because, in Ackerman's view, the same considerations show why the political context surrounding the New Deal should also count as establishing fundamental law. Put most simply: if the Founding and

Civil War count as contributing fundamental parts of our constitutional tradition, then for the same reasons the New Deal must as well.

I rehearse the details why in the notes to this chapter.[6] For now, suffice it to say that Ackerman has established a powerful argument from parity for recognizing each moment as contributing to the normative structure of our constitutional tradition. More important for my account, he has done so using precisely the same interpretive approach that I am following here. We are both playing cricket. Ackerman is trying to fit the history of constitutional law to a theory that can account for the most important moving parts, and which is ultimately justified democratically. And so reading these three moments as effecting legitimate constitutional change justifies, first, that we have a Constitution; second, that that Constitution embraces certain fundamental values surrounding equality; and finally, that it empowers a federal government to regulate far beyond the reach of anything the Framers would have imagined. The story fits the history, Ackerman maintains. And because the moves that craft the amendments that allow the history to be called constitutional are themselves the product of a deep and reflective democratic engagement, the story is also normatively justified. Our history, in Ackerman's account, is the story of "we the people" making a constitutional tradition—actively and reflectively. It is a tradition that any of us should be proud of.

## Anomalies

Yet Ackerman's account has important anomalies. And as we understand these anomalies, we will begin to see the motivation for the differences I've offered here.

The first anomaly points to an incompleteness; the second to a mistake.

### THE FORGOTTEN MOMENT I

The second moment of America's Constitution was the post–Civil War Amendments. As I described in Chapter 16, those amendments effected a fundamental change in the nature of America's Constitution. Gone was slavery; embedded was a fundamental principle of equality; guaranteed was a certain federal protection for the rights now promised to all.

But then these fundamental reforms seemed to just disappear. In 1876, six years after the Fifteenth Amendment was ratified, federal enforcement of Reconstruction ended. In 1883, the Civil Rights Act of 1875 was struck down. A few cases affirm the principles of the amendments, yet more seem to doubt it. And by 1896, the Court could slide to a view that would effectively affirm de jure apartheid. If the Civil War Amendments were a constitutional moment, it was a moment that seemed quickly to be forgotten.

Michael McConnell has used this post–Civil War history to—somewhat mischievously—argue that there was another constitutional moment: one that repealed the Civil War Amendments. In an elaborate argument mimicking Ackerman's own technique, McConnell suggests that the democratic engagement from 1876 on manifested a democratic resolution to reverse the commitments of Reconstruction and to return to a republic that allowed states to treat their citizens unequally.[7]

Ackerman, of course, does not accept McConnell's argument. The election of 1874 did not mark a constitutional moment: an off-year repudiation of the president is the norm, and any meaning to the Democrats' victory was rendered ambiguous by the Panic of 1873. Nor did 1876 signal repudiation of the Civil War Amendments: Samuel Tilden, the Democrat who received the most popular votes, expressly endorsed the Civil War Amendments. Likewise, throughout the balance of the nineteenth century, though the Democrats worked hard to repudiate the Enforcement Act protecting voting rights, their repeal was vetoed repeatedly. Hayes served just a single term and was replaced by another Republican, James Garfield, who was even more committed to equal rights. And though this genius president (Garfield penned an original proof to the Pythagorean theorem while in the White House) was assassinated in his first year as president, his replacement, Chester Arthur, continued the support for civil rights enforcement. "There was no moment," Ackerman writes, "in the late nineteenth century in which a mobilized national majority repudiated the Reconstruction amendments"[8]—which means, on Ackerman's theory, that post-Reconstruction was not a new constitutional moment.

Ackerman is right, yet McConnell has a point. If we imagine constitutional commitments to live by default, then there is something very odd about the roughly hundred years after the Civil War Amendments were ratified: for those commitments were, in important respects, simply ignored. If they were not repealed, then what explains—or justifies—their being ignored? Or more specifically, what in the theory that Ackerman has offered makes sense of this constitutional disobedience? The amendments were not repealed. But given the open conspiracy to ignore them, did they even have to be?

## THE FORGOTTEN MOMENT II

On Ackerman's account, the New Deal effected a non-textual constitutional amendment. Beginning in 1937, the Supreme Court recognized that amendment in a series of "ratifying" opinions, recognizing the power of the state to regulate the economy and the power of Congress to regulate an unprecedented range of commerce.

If these changes were "amendments," it follows at a minimum that they define a new set of baseline rules for the Supreme Court. Decisions by the Court resisting that baseline would, in turn, be mistakes—at least without "a higher lawmaking process comparable to the one led by President Roosevelt in the 1930's."[9] Just as it would be an error for the Court in 1920 to conclude that Congress could not pass an income tax (since in 1913, the Sixteenth Amendment expressly gave Congress the power "to lay and collect taxes on incomes"), it would be an error for the Court in 1950 to conclude that Congress couldn't, for example, regulate home-grown wheat. As Ackerman puts it:

> [The] New Deal opinions have operated as the functional equivalent of formal constitutional amendments, providing a solid foundation for activist intervention in national social and economic life for the past sixty years.[10]

Except that they haven't. The problem for Ackerman's account, as Chapters 9 and 10 make plain, is that the Court has repeatedly tried to reset the balance that was itself reset in 1937–1942. The line of cases from *National League of Cities* through *Garcia*, the line from *Lopez* through *Raich*, and the line begun with the Obamacare case (*Sebelius*): These cases view the New Deal cases not as amendments but as subject to continued judicial revision. Sometimes that revision is more effective than at other times. Sometimes it is stable, sometimes not. But the point is that the Court at least has not treated these "amendments" as amendments—which means on Ackerman's account, these modern federalism cases are, like the post-Reconstruction cases, simply mistakes.

## Resolving Anomalies

Mistakes are important for a theory like Ackerman's—or my own. As the aim is to explain and justify as much of the doctrine as possible, multiplying the numbers that can't be explained weakens the value of the theory. If the conclusion of the theory is that the period from roughly 1876 through 1954 was filled with error, or similarly that the new federalism born in 1976 and continuing through today is likewise in error, that invites an obvious question: is there another account that avoids viewing these cases as errors, and which itself can be justified normatively?

The theory I've sketched does not view these cases as errors. Or more precisely, the theory offers an account of these cases *within* the contours of the theory. In both the post-Reconstruction and New Deal periods, on my account, the Constitution was not amended. Instead, in both periods, fidelity to role forced the Court to suppress the Constitution's actual or proper meaning. Put differently, the question in each period was not just what the Constitution meant. The question was also whether the Court was capable of giving that meaning effect. Did the institution have the capacity to enforce the norms the law imposed?

In both periods, I have argued, the answer was no. In the post-Reconstruction period, the reason was likely existential: had the Court waged an all-out war to enforce a *Brown v. Board* (1954)–like conception of equality from 1876 on, it is almost certain that it would have triggered either a revolt against the Court or an amendment to shut the Court up. And in the New Deal period, the reason was likely existential as well: the Court came to recognize its own incapacity to draw lines that Jackson would call essentially "economic" and "not legal," and saw the imminent threat of either court-packing or a legislative veto of its decisions. Both responses would have weakened the power of the Court—or so the Court reasonably could have believed. Thus, in both periods the excuse for ignoring the Constitution's commitments, if indeed that can be excused, is a kind of *force majeure:* the obligations were not changed, but the ability to carry them out was suspended.

The consequence of this understanding within both periods is important. If indeed the change was a kind of *force majeure,* then it follows that when the force is removed, the obligation to return to the Constitution's (translated) meaning returns as well. Indeed, the point could be made more strongly: throughout the *force majeure* condition, the obligation remains to return if possible. After the crafting of Jim Crow and the cementing of America's racism, it took a war to enable the restoration. After 1937, it took just the careful planning of federalist justices to enable at least a partial restoration. In both cases, the normative implication of this way of accounting for the post-Reconstruction and post-New Deal Constitution is that fidelity to meaning argues for a return to original values, at least when fidelity to role will permit it.

Thus, when Ackerman asks of the New Deal, "Was it merely a strategic retreat or the inauguration of a new vision of constitutional government in America?"[11] the answer is *both*—but we need not view that new vision as effecting non-textual constitutional "amendments." No doubt, there was a change in constitutional doctrine, but that change reflects a fidelity to something beyond meaning. The reality with the current jurisprudence is that the tussle to define the scope of that something continues. My account is not sanguine about the consequence of that tussle—I'm a nationalist, not a federalist, at least on the question of power. But my account does allow us to understand the tussle as something other than constitutional theft, whether democratically justified (as Ackerman believes) or not.

My account leaves open the question of justifying the Founding and Civil War Amendments. And though I've not engaged that argument in this book, I fully agree with Ackerman that in each of the first two moments, the giant, to borrow from Hobbes, woke up.[12] In each of the first two moments, the constituent power (as the French would invent the idea) was summoned to the stage and succeeded in authorizing what otherwise was not authorized.

Ackerman is right, moreover, that our ignorance about these two struggles is a democratic tragedy. Even just knowing this history today would spark a democratic creativity that we have all but lost. The hopelessness that marks our current time is only fed by our ignorance about how we escaped at earlier times. We've fallen, but we've forgotten that we've fallen before and in fact can get up.

The story of the first two of Ackerman's moments celebrates this power. Both triggered (while crafting) a latent understanding for addressing a patent catastrophe.[13] At the Founding, the nation was sinking. Some device had to enable an escape. The device that had just been utilized—the Declaration's "self-evident truth" that it is an "unalienable right" of any people to "alter or abolish" their form of government—was a handy tool to have lying around from the very recent past. The challenge for the federalists was to earn the right to pick it up and use it. And the struggle that Ackerman's writing describes with extraordinary clarity convincingly shows how they earned the right to step above the rules previously laid down.

Likewise with the Civil War Amendments: if our collective understanding of the history of the Founding is small, our collective understanding of the extraordinary history of the Civil War Amendments is tiny. There is no honest way to understand the ratification of the Civil War Amendments as consistent with the plain or original or textual meaning of Article V. Here again, the reformers, the Radical Republicans, had to trigger (while crafting) a recognition of just why their violations should nonetheless be excused. That story in Ackerman's hands is powerful and compelling.

Yet that's not to say that the story doesn't raise questions. In his account of the Founding, Ackerman refers repeatedly to the "illegality" of the framing convention. But it's hard to see the sense in which a convention can be "illegal." No doubt, the Philadelphia convention did not do what Congress expected it would do. Yet that can't possibly be a crime. And while the

Constitution that it drafted certainly contemplated a mode of ratification that deviated from the rules laid down in the Articles of Confederation, in the hands of the convention that deviation was just a proposal. In a free society, how can a proposal be "illegal"?

If there was "illegality" in 1787, it was Congress's. It was Congress that received the proposed Constitution, and Congress that decided to follow the recommendation of the convention to ratify the new Constitution without following the rules of the Articles of Confederation. Maybe we can understand the convention as a co-conspirator in the conspiracy to violate those articles. But it is better to see the convention as a kind of lawyer to Congress: "We tried to do what you asked, but we couldn't; here's an alternative you can consider if you'd like."

This is an important quibble—not so much for the framing history, but for the continuing relevance of the framing history to constitutional struggles today. Ackerman's way of talking about the framing convention is commonplace. It is the common view (among the tiny fraction of Americans who have any view at all) that the convention "ran away" and was therefore "illegal."[14] This understanding of our past produces anxiety about an equivalent today: What if the states, pursuant to Article V, get Congress to convene a convention to propose amendments to the Constitution, and that convention runs away too? What if it recommended that its proposed amendments could be ratified by a national referendum? Would the "precedent" of the Philadelphia Convention justify that change in the rules of Article V?

Here's where it becomes critical to be clear about where the illegality in 1787 was. No doubt, an Article V convention could ignore its instructions, just as the Philadelphia convention could. But in both cases, all that the convention would produce is the recommendation of an amendment to Congress. Our hypothetical runaway Article V convention could no doubt say to Congress, "Hey, this amendment won't pass unless you send it out for a national referendum, so we recommend you do that." But saying that doesn't violate any law; a proposal is not "illegal." The illegality would come only if Congress followed their advice.

So then imagine Congress did, and accepted the recommendation of a convention to ratify a proposed amendment not through the procedure outlined in Article V but through, say, a national referendum. And imagine Congress tried to justify its breach of the rules of Article V by reference to the "precedent" of the framing convention. What would the consequence of that attempted justification be?

Ackerman's work shows us that we can't answer that question in the abstract. In every case, the answer will depend upon the success of the reformers in triggering the recognition that their reform speaks for "we the people." I completely agree with Ackerman's account that it is certainly possible to imagine (or, let's say, dream) that reformers could succeed in rallying "we the people" to authorize Congress to alter the rules previously laid down.

But standing where we do now, that possibility seems incredibly and insanely remote. Much more likely is that if Congress adopted rules for amending the Constitution that were inconsistent with the text of Article V, our Supreme Court—an institution whose power was unimaginable in 1787—would find a way to see to it that no such amendment was law.[15] In our current legal culture, bracketing the possibility of constitutional-moment-like mobilization, Congress could never get away with expressly changing the rules for adopting an amendment to the Constitution.

That's not to say there aren't gray cases. The Twenty-Seventh Amendment—which prevents members of Congress from changing their salaries in the middle of a congressional term, and which was first proposed in 1789 and ratified only in 1992—is a great example. (Ackerman doesn't even consider it an amendment.)[16] Whether an amendment could survive for two hundred years and still remain adoptable is a hard question. When it happened, we constitutional scholars wondered. But the political branches embraced it and no court dared to second-guess that political judgment.

Yet just because there is gray does not mean there is not also black and white. And a Congress that said "The proposed amendment will be considered ratified if 60 percent of Americans vote for it in a national referendum" would be an open and notorious breach of a black-and-white line.

Congress in 1787 broke the rules. The federalists in 1787 succeeded in deploying an understanding that excused that breach. The question going forward is not whether a Congress can or will break the rules again. The question is whether future reformers will succeed in triggering an understanding of any breach that authorizes it as the will of the people. That question does not arise only because of a convention. It is present at every moment Congress acts.

There is a related puzzle about Ackerman's understanding of the Civil War Amendments. Here again, rules were no doubt broken, and the reformers had to bring to the fore (or at least craft) an understanding that would excuse that breaking. The ultimate excuse—deployed both by the Radical Republicans and by the Supreme Court when it finally signaled it was not going to upset the Republicans' applecart—was the republican guarantee clause: "The United States shall guarantee to every State in this Union a Republican Form of Government." Yet in an unusually formalistic way, Ackerman pooh-poohs the idea that the actions of the Reconstruction Congress could find justification or excuse in the republican guarantee clause. As he writes:

These last two Congressional conditions [keeping states out until the Fourteenth Amendment was ratified] cannot conceivably be justified by the Guaranty Clause, however expansively interpreted—for the simple reason that Congress had, by this point, already approved the states' constitutions as republican. Nevertheless it was still asserting its power to keep the states out in the cold until they went along with its demand to ratify the Fourteenth Amendment.[17]

Yet the answer to this skepticism was never better stated than by E. L. Godkin just after President Johnson vetoed the Freedman's Bureau Act in 1866. As Godkin wrote for *The Nation*:

> The President's message, vetoing the Freedmen's bill, is based throughout on the assumption that in the late war we simply suppressed a rebellion. If this were true, there is no doubt that much of what he says of the propriety of at once admitting the revolted States to a full share in the Government would be well founded. The luxury of reigning over a conquered people is one which no republic can enjoy with impunity. No man who has read history to any purpose, or who knows anything of human nature, would deliberately propose to keep eight millions of Southerners in a state of vassalage merely as a punishment for having rebelled....
>
> But the war has not been simply a contest between two sets of men, one maintaining the authority of a government and the other seeking to overthrow it. The fighting of the last four years has not simply, as Mr. Johnson assumes, re-established the jurisdiction of the United States over a certain territorial area, and over a certain number of people. It has wrought a social revolution, which for magnitude, for rapidity, and for the gravity of its consequences has never been equaled in history. That greatest of modern revolutions by which the French church and aristocracy were overthrown—a movement which shook the civilized world to its centre, and whose consequences are still felt in every quarter of the globe—radical as it was—was far from going down so deeply into the social soil as ours has done. In that case some millions of the bravest and most energetic and intelligent men in the world simply reformed their government by destroying the fetters of feudalism. In our case four millions of men have been lifted from a legal condition hardly superior to that of beasts of the field into that of free citizens.
>
> It is therefore a fallacy, and a very gross one, to tell us that when the war which did this thing is over, all is over. All is not over. Northern

men and Southern men are not the only parties to the peace, and therefore, when Mr. Johnson asks us all to be as we were, we find it impossible to comply.

The great question after all, the question which it may be Mr. Johnson seeks as earnestly to have fairly answered as we do, is how to assist the freedmen in passing through the transition state between slavery and freedom and independence without increasing or embittering the hostility between them and the whites, and without creating in their minds the feeling that any aid afforded them is more than temporary. He acknowledges this duty as fully as anybody, but, as we understand him, thinks it can be best discharged by handing the whole black population over at an early period to their old masters, with the least possible aid in educating them or relieving their distress. In short, Mr. Johnson believes it more safe and prudent, and therefore a more honorable discharge of responsibility to the liberated slaves of the South, to trust solely to the sense of duty, the fears of future military punishment, and the enlightened self-interest of their late masters for their being treated justly and mercifully, than to maintain for any but the briefest period a method of protection so uncongenial to the American people as that contemplated by the Freedmen's Bureau bill. And it is upon this point that the question arises between him and Congress.

Now, let us ask ourselves plainly what it is that the blacks of the South need that they may become intelligent and useful members of society in the shortest possible period. Is it not, first of all, the education of civilized life, the means of becoming familiarized with the use of their new rights and the discharge of their new duties? Must we not rouse in them, or encourage in them, a love of industry, a love of accumulation, and a respect for property? Can there be any way of doing this which fails to impress them with the belief that they are sure of having exact justice meted out to them, sure of as complete protection as law and police can give them, both for their persons and for the fruits of their industry? Is not this feeling the very basis of civil society? Has any society ever prospered, ever been anything but a dead and decaying carcase, in which any considerable portion of the people were deprived of this assurance? Look at Ireland, look at the "sick man" of Turkey, look at Jamaica. Is the whole earth not full of the most awful warnings against depriving human beings, of any race or color or creed, of the perfect confidence that what they sow they shall reap, that where they lie down to rest at night there they shall rise unharmed in the morning, that there stands around their houses a power stronger than all their enemies put together? We must, in short, if we mean to regenerate Southern society, take care that no portion of it is left outside the law.[18]

This is the distinction strangely suppressed in Ackerman's account of the argument from the republican guarantee clause. If the Civil War had taught anything, it was that a republican government must guarantee the equality of republican citizens. The war had established presumptive equality—expressed as the end of a racial caste, at a minimum through the end of slavery. The puzzle for them was how to bring that equality about. And against the background of that puzzle, there was an obvious latent ambiguity in the meaning of a guarantee. If equality was a necessary condition, then ensuring a commitment to equality was a completely plausible application of that guarantee—not simply because anyone just said so, but because of the pedigree of the democratic engagement evinced by Ackerman's account. The reformers earned the right to say, "We can be excused for not following the rules precisely. We needed to ensure that the entities within our republic complied with this necessary condition of a republican government, even if we hadn't recognized expressly the necessity before."

Thus, in my view, both moments are exceptional. Both moments evince the constituent power—a power we can only ever recognize retrospectively.[19] In the terms used in Chapter 1, both moments succeeded in bringing to the fore an idea that had been at best latent in the context, and both succeeded in making that idea sufficiently uncontested to have normative force. Ackerman's account shows us the rich political history that earns such ideas their constituent force. Like learning your great-grandmother once wrestled Teddy Roosevelt to the ground, this history should teach us awe and respect.

Yet in both moments, the history also suggests an unambiguous subjective understanding of the people that is not unambiguous during the New Deal change. In both of the first two moments, one could imagine asking the reformers, "Are you changing your Constitution?" In both cases, their response would plainly have been yes. Both were self-conscious efforts at constitutional transformation. Everyone knew what game was being played, and as Ackerman shows us, the reformers succeeded in playing that constitutional-moment game spectacularly.

Yet the same is not clear with the reformers in the New Deal. No doubt they believed they were trying to change the Supreme Court's interpretation of the Constitution. But many—including FDR—believed that such a change was not necessarily an amendment. Specifically, it could also have been error correction. In his defense of the court-packing plan, FDR did indeed articulate a nationalist conception of the federal power. But he also argued that the Court's narrow interpretation of federal and state power was just a mistake. Ackerman is no doubt correct that FDR had succeeded in rallying America to the idea of national power. But Ackerman has not shown that FDR succeeded in convincing America that such power required amending the Constitution.

The Supreme Court had certainly denied Congress the national power that FDR convinced America Congress needed. But Ackerman writes as if the Supreme Court's interpretation of federal and state power was itself obvious or unchallenged. Yet as Chapters 4 and 5 made clear, it was not obvious, and it was certainly challenged. In both cases, the interpretation was a translation. It had a claim of fidelity, but the normative status of a translation is different from the status of accepted constitutional meaning.

Consider a hypothetical to better make the point. Imagine the Supreme Court held that Congress had no power "to lay and collect taxes on incomes" in 1915, two years after the Sixteenth Amendment granting that power precisely was ratified. And imagine the Supreme Court's holding was unanimous. Nine justices asserted that the plain words of the Constitution did not mean what they plainly meant.

Imagine then that in the election of 1916, both the Democrat, Woodrow Wilson, and the Republican, Charles Even Hughes (a future chief justice of the Supreme Court), agreed that the Supreme Court was wrong. Imagine they both pledged that if elected, they would either pack the Court with ten more justices to reverse the Court's holding or adopt an amendment to the Constitution to give Congress the power to reverse Supreme Court decisions. And imagine that when Wilson is elected, he does indeed accomplish this, and either the Court reverses itself by a vote of 10–9 or Congress votes an amendment to reverse the Supreme Court's decision.

Either way, we wouldn't say that Wilson had effected a constitutional "amendment." Even if we believe that 90 percent of voters agreed with the candidates' response to the Court—because both candidates had signaled they agreed the Court was wrong—we wouldn't say that the Constitution was amended. What we'd say was that the president and Congress had acted with extraordinary power to force the Court to abandon a mistaken interpretation of the Constitution. "We the people" may have spoken. But our vocabulary includes the command "fix it."

Now let's modify the example a bit. Imagine the Court holds, again unanimously and again in 1915, that dividends on stock are not "income" for purposes of the Sixteenth Amendment. Income, they say, is not simply the product of ownership. Dividends, they say, are simple liquidations of owner-ship. And imagine again that Wilson and Hughes both agree that the Court is just wrong. They wage the same campaign to reverse the Court's decision. Wilson wins, and again effects that reversal, either through court-packing or through the veto amendment.

In this case, whether we say that "we the people" have amended the Constitution depends upon whether we believe the Court was right in exclud-ing dividends from income. If we believe the Court was right, then we could possibly say that the people had effected an amendment. But if we believe that the Court was wrong, the change is not an amendment but a correction.

Throughout his account of the New Deal struggle, Ackerman simply pre-sumes the correctness of the old Court's doctrine. He doesn't establish it. He argues for many points, but he leaves to one side the question whether the old Court was right—not right in its view about what the Framers expected, but right in its view about how to read the Framers' text.

If the old Court was right, or more precisely, if the understanding of "we the people" was that the old Court was right but that we now wanted that view changed, then Ackerman would have succeeded in establishing a paral-lel between the first two moments and the New Deal. But if "we the people" were uncertain, or if we believed we were simply reforming a misbehaving Court, then there would be a critical failure of the analogy with moments one and two. Those moments would be amendments; the New Deal would be a correction.

Because, of course, there was no ambiguity about whether the new Constitution was an amendment (or abolition) of the old, or whether the Civil War Amendments were amendments of the antebellum Constitution. Everyone understood these changes as *changes* (even if some believed that at least some parts of the Civil War Amendments expressed a value always latent in the original Constitution). In those cases, the people awoke to amend their Constitution—unambiguously. But with the New Deal, to this day we have no clear idea about what anyone really believed.

Nor did the New Dealers try to clear up this ambiguity, at least after it was clear they had won. Once the Supreme Court retreated, Congress and the president withdrew. Roosevelt continued to prosecute his court-packing plan until his floor leader, Senator Joseph Robinson, died of a heart attack. Once that happened, the promises made to Robinson dissolved, and support for the president's plan dissolved as well. The Supreme Court's decision in *Jones & Laughlin* and Justice Van Devanter's retirement removed the need for ex-traordinary action. And the efforts many in Congress had made to amend the Constitution—either by adopting Senator Wheeler's amendment or changing the substantive powers of Congress—died as well. With world war looming, the nation had more pressing issues. It was completely obvious that there was no good *political* reason to continue the fight with the Court.

But that decision left ambiguous what had already happened. And to the extent we are uncertain about whether the extraordinary democratic action that FDR triggered was for amendment or for correction, support for Ackerman's parallel with two clear moments of amendment falters as well.

My point is not to dismiss the complexity, weirdness, and democratic extraordinariness of the New Deal changes. It is certainly not to minimize the sophistication (practically unimaginable today) with which FDR addressed complicated constitutional questions. It is only to suggest that even if, as Ackerman believes, the democratic will behind FDR was stronger than at the first or second moments, it is not obvious that it was a will to amend. (As William Leuchtenburg puts it, "Whatever else the voters might have been doing in 1936, they were not consciously amending the Constitution.")[20] And if that's true, then if there is an alternative account that makes the changes in doctrine understandable without us believing in an unintentional amendment, that alternative should, on a Dworkinian account at least, be compelling.

I say this acknowledging that the Court itself may have been responsible for this ambiguity. As Greg Caldeira argues, court-packing was avoided because of the interventions by the Court. Likewise, we could say that the Wheeler amendment was avoided because of the interventions by the Court. It was the Court, then, that stopped the extraordinary democratic process that was brewing to determine what our Constitution should mean. But for the Court's intervention, we would likely know whether "we the people" were trying to say "amend it" or "fix it."

I share with Ackerman the regret that the people didn't get a clearer chance to speak—though as Barry Cushman has evinced, it is not clear that what the people would have said is what Ackerman believes they would have said.[21] As a nationalist, I am sorry that we don't have a clearer nationalist Constitution. I acknowledge the federalists' continued authority to try to craft limits on the federal power as best they can. I don't think those limits make us a more perfect union, even though I am a strong believer in the benefits that would come from more local control.

But the history is the history. The question for Ackerman's theory is whether Hercules, in the Dworkinian sense, *must* read the third moment as an amendment. In my view, the answer to that question is clearly no. There is an alternative to the amendment account. Offering that alternative has been the purpose of this book.

# Whither Textualism

Ackerman's ultimate purpose in his multivolume work *We the People* is to wean American lawyers away from textualism, or what he calls "hypertextualism"—the view that "all the modern lawyer needs to know about constitutional revision can be found within 'the four corners' of Article Five," and (with respect to law more generally) that the law of the Constitution is to be found in the text of the Constitution alone.[22] The first two volumes of *We the People* are devoted to breaking that presumption regarding Article V. The third volume extends the approach to twentieth-century constitutionalism generally.

The Constitution's text, Ackerman insists, is neither necessary nor sufficient for identifying the most important parts of our higher law tradition. Instead, to identify and understand the democratically significant parts of that tradition, we must track moments of the democratic dance between the people and the institutions of government. At critical moments, that dance has yielded higher law despite the failures of text. Specifically, it has justified the Founding and the Civil War amendments. It explains, in Ackerman's view, why the Constitution was amended at the New Deal, despite the absence of any constitutional text. And it is essential for understanding the most important parts of the American legal canon of the twentieth century. The "civil rights revolution," as Ackerman calls it, is higher law on Ackerman's account, even though that revolution barely expressed itself in any constitutional text.

Ackerman's practice is to use history to reveal the nature of a tradition. It is the use of history to inform a theory. And that theory, once established, is meant to be normative: once you see how the people have spoken, you must read our Constitution differently. Or more precisely, once American lawyers come to see how the people have spoken, American lawyers should read their Constitution differently.

Yet in the end, Ackerman's argument founders on a critical normative question: does history show us that the non-liquidated moments of democratic higher law—those moments when the people have spoken but have failed to reduce our words to constitutional text—survive once the normative power of those moments fades? No doubt, the dynamic that Ackerman displays for us shows us why the taken-for-granted democratic norms of an age dominate the law of that age at any particular moment. But do we see these non-textual bits of our higher law tradition surviving with normative force once the democratic power behind them fades or they are rendered contestable? And once they are contestable, do we see their power disappear like a dream upon wakening, leaving us with only the bits of our constitutional tradition that have been rendered in a constitutional text?

Ackerman's normative claim is that they *should* survive. He thinks we should read the history beyond the *United States Reports,* where Supreme Court opinions are reported, and incorporate the normative force of those moments in our ongoing practice of constitutional law.

But an alternative understanding of that same history denies that normative conclusion. Yes, of course the Constitution gets read against the background of the dominant ideas of any age. But once those ideas are rendered contested, the only bits of the Constitution that survive are those that were rendered in a constitutional text. The failure to memorialize, on this view, is fatal. It leaves the Constitution's ultimate meaning vulnerable to changes in the dominant background understanding of constitutional laws.

We can see this dynamic more plainly using the matrix of contestability from Chapter 7.

The democratic dance that Ackerman describes is always the move from box 1 to box 2. The six steps of higher lawmaking that he tracks throughout our constitutional history—constitutional impasse → electoral mandate → challenge to dissenting institutions → switch in time → consolidating election—are the steps taken to move a set of normative ideas from contested to uncontested, obviously in the foreground.

That nine state conventions could ratify a new Constitution for the United States was contested. After the dance that Ackerman describes, it was not.

That the Republicans in Congress could leverage a war to amend the Constitution was contested. After the dance, it was not.

That the federal government could address the economic problems of the nation was a contested battle through the middle of the 1930s. After the dance and the switch, it was contested no more.

That equal protection embedded an anti-subordination principle was contested through the middle of the twentieth century. After the most engaged democratic dance in the history of the nation, it was not contested anymore.

|  | CONTESTED | UNCONTESTED |
|---|---|---|
| FOREGROUND | (1) | (2) |
| BACKGROUND | (4) | (3) |

FIGURE 6 Matrix original

In each case, extraordinary democratic progress was achieved. Before each achievement, the dissenters were dissenters. After, they would be, as Ackerman calls them, "cranks."[23]

Sometimes the ideas in box 2 have been rendered in text, and sometimes not. The Founding and the Civil War produced constitutional text. The New Deal and the civil rights revolution did not (at least beyond the weird Twenty-Fourth Amendment, which banned the poll tax for federal elections only). The New Deal produced Supreme Court opinions. The civil rights revolution produced a set of framework statutes. Those texts have their effect when the democratic ideals that animate them continue to dominate. Or in terms of the matrix, they have their effect so long as our constitutional culture is in box 2 or box 3 with respect to those ideals.

The question that twenty-first-century constitutionalism raises is what happens to these settlements when we move to box 4, or even back to box 1: do ideas that are rendered uncontested at an earlier time but not ultimately expressed in constitutional text continue to have a normative or constitutional force? Or do those ideas, once rendered contestable, lose their constitutional significance?

Ackerman's work is an earnest and honest effort to convince us that those ideas *should* continue to hold sway. As he puts it, these "constitutional commitments"—including those not rendered in text—must not be erased. His aim is to marshal the arguments against "such acts of erasure from the constitutional canon."[24]

As a nationalist and an egalitarian, I certainly wish they did continue to hold. But if the history of the last quarter century is teaching us anything, it is that once those ideas standing in the background move from the uncontested to the contested, their normative force fades. Nationalism is an argument today, not a premise to an argument. The anti-subordination norm is one view of equality, no longer the presupposition of two generations of politicians from both political parties.

Put more directly, we are at a moment in our history when the ideas that Ackerman tells us our ancestors rendered as higher law, though not in text, have been rendered contestable. Not by "cranks" but by mainstream actors within our constitutional tradition.

If that's right, then what Ackerman's account is showing us is how ideas in box 2 and box 3 can dominate the reading of a constitutional text at some point. Yet once those ideas get rendered contestable again, all that survives is a constitutional text.

"A funny thing happened to Americans on the way to the twenty-first century," Ackerman tells us. "We have lost our ability to write down our new constitutional commitments in the old-fashioned way."[25]

That's true, but it's not funny. Ackerman regrets the failure of the New Deal generation to express its ideals in constitutional text. We can all regret that the civil rights revolution also failed to inscribe their ideals into constitutional text. The lesson of our history, I suggest, is that while such text is not needed when the ideals it would express are dominant, those ideals remain vulnerable so long as they are not expressed in text.

That's not to say that text always survives and has force regardless. The history of the Civil War amendments after Reconstruction shows us that text alone is not enough. But the genius of the American constitutional tradition was in recognizing the time-capsule quality of constitutional text. The text is never a perfect vehicle for carrying normative force across context. And no doubt, text needs special treatment to keep it alive—such as translation. But without text, the higher law of an age remains vulnerable to the deviance of its children. What we all took for granted becomes just an argument for some. And the critical error of our constitutional tradition—at least for us nationalist egalitarians—was the failure to fix the machine that would inscribe constitutional text within our tradition. The failure, in other words, to fix Article V.

"We're all textualists now," Justice Elena Kagan told the Harvard Law School in December 2015.[26] The event was the newly launched Scalia Lecture, and Kagan was the first lecturer. And over the course of an hour's speech, she explained to a rapt audience the dominance of text within the American legal tradition.

We could imagine a different tradition. We could imagine an almost Talmudic or British constitutional practice. We could imagine a culture that did not just focused on text but was trained to identify those special moments when the people speak beyond the text, and to listen when they do.

Ackerman is arguing for this alternative. I fear the facts are consistent with a less ambitious, textualist past. No doubt, the hypertextualist must yield to the uncontesteds of an age. But when those uncontesteds get rendered contested, our tradition suggests that those commitments fade.

That positive account, I suggest, fits more of our history than Ackerman's. Can it also be justified?

| Justifying Fidelities

T HE BULK OF THIS BOOK HAS REVEALED a Court sensitive to two
kinds of fidelities—to the Constitution's meaning and to its own role.
The interaction between those two fidelities explains, or at least tracks, the
changes in the doctrine that I've mapped. As I've said from the start, my account is incomplete. I've not tried to describe the Constitution generally. If
this approach has value, the work to apply it elsewhere is work for others.

These two fidelities trigger different justifications. I begin here with the
more intuitive, justifying fidelity to meaning.

## Fidelity to Meaning

The whole premise of a written constitution is that the words have meaning
and that meaning both enables and constrains. "That those limits may not be
mistaken, or forgotten," Marshall wrote in *Marbury v. Madison* (1803), "the
constitution is written."

That constraint means nothing without an effort to remain faithful to the
meaning so written. The whole project of this book has been to map the elements in that practice of faithfulness.

Translation, I have argued, is a fidelity-enhancing technique within the
scope of that practice. It is an effort to neutralize the changes in context—as
much as possible—in order to preserve an original meaning. The qualification "as much as possible" is critical, as we have seen. There is never a guarantee that a translation is possible, let alone good. Time bends everything,
and the effort to hold some part firm always twists elsewhere.

Within our tradition of constitutional law, significant swaths of doctrine change, even when the constitutional text has not been changed. Facts in the world drive that. The law is contingent upon those facts.

That claim is obvious with respect to some facts—"helicopters and telephones," as Scalia put it when speaking of the Fourth Amendment's "reasonable" time within which to present an arrestee to a magistrate.[1] More generally, it applies to an integrated economy that brings more and more within the reach of Congress.

That claim has not been obvious with respect to certain social meanings. I have argued here that just as it is proper to track changes in economic integration when translating the scope of Congress's power, it is proper—subject at least to fidelity to role concerns—to track changes in social meaning when translating the scope of the equal protection clause. Social meaning is the reality that determines whether the law's treatment is equal or not. And just as Congress's power is relative to economic integration, the reach of the equal protection clause is relative to social meaning.

Should it be? Should a practice of constitutionalism leave itself open to changes in the world? Should it stand vulnerable to evolving social meanings? Or vulnerable to the changing dynamics of economic integration?

That question could mean many things. Here, the "should" is relative to a conception of democracy. More precisely, to a conception of democracy that could be affirmed within our tradition. Or more precisely still, that could be affirmed today. Is a practice of constitutionalism that leaves the doctrine of constitutional law open to evolving changes in the facts—whether economic, or technical, or social—consistent with democracy?

One part of this question is relatively easy—the part evoked by Scalia's "helicopters and telephones." It's inconceivable that constitutional doctrine would be oblivious to changes in facts or technologies. To the contrary, such changes are completely ordinary within the work of any constitutional court.

It is the other half of my claim that triggers anxiety among constitutionalists. Yes, social meanings are facts. Yes, like facts, social meanings change. But the idea that courts should track those changes—as I've argued our Court has—is, to many, troubling.

That anxiety, however, can be divided between two questions, one ontological and the other epistemological. The ontological version of the justification challenge asks: Does it make democratic sense that doctrine evolves as meaning evolves? The epistemological version asks: Could it make sense, democratically, for a court to determine social meaning and apply it?

The ontological question is easier, for the construction of social meaning itself is, in its nature, deeply democratic. Not in the sense that we have elections that decide whether being gay is cool. But in the sense that to the extent there is social meaning, it has been produced by a radically decentralized process of understanding and construction. No doubt, there are big players in this game; social conservatives complain that Hollywood played an outsized role in redefining the meaning of being gay. But so long as the economy of meaning-making is not improperly influenced, the meanings that would affect the scope of constitutional doctrine are not, I argue, democratically unjustified.

To be sure, there is plenty built into the idea of "improperly influenced." But equally surely, to the extent there is a theory of justice for social meaning, it is an incredibly underdeveloped theory.[2] Suffice it here that we don't have any well-developed democratic reason for rejecting as undemocratic the evolving contours of social understanding or meaning. That's not to say that they've always reflected democratic culture well. Just ask the marginalized women or minorities whose very existence was defined out of the norm. But my claim is narrower: that recognizing the evolving contours of social understanding as part of the process for developing constitutional doctrine cannot now be said to be unjustified.

That leaves the epistemological concern—which is real and repeatedly articulated. Whether or not there is a democratic problem with a Constitution that rests upon social meanings, there is an obvious democratic question about who gets to specify what those meanings are.

My positive claim has been that in fact, our tradition has allowed the Supreme Court a jurisdiction to say what the social meaning is. Not without objection, certainly, but the practice has followed Harlan more than Scalia. The Court has come to see things differently, as it has come to understand social meanings differently. That fact has triggered, in response, strongly aggressive (and anti-institutional) criticism from leading justices. The Court is not articulating a social meaning, these justices insist. It is "imposing" the judgment of "the law-profession culture," as Justice Scalia put it in *Lawrence v. Texas* (2003). As Chief Justice Roberts put it in *Obergefell v. Hodges* (2015):

> The majority's decision is an act of will, not legal judgment. The right it announces has no basis in the Constitution or this Court's precedent. The majority expressly disclaims judicial "caution" and omits even a pretense of humility, openly relying on its desire to remake society according to its own "new insight" into the "nature of injustice."[3]

Or again, as he closed his dissent:

> If you are among the many Americans—of whatever sexual orientation— who favor expanding same-sex marriage, by all means celebrate today's

decision. Celebrate the achievement of a desired goal. Celebrate the opportunity for a new expression of commitment to a partner. Celebrate the availability of new benefits. But do not celebrate the Constitution. It had nothing to do with it.[4]

This concern has not only been expressed from the Right. Bruce Ackerman too has worried about modes of justification that seem cut off from democratic authority. In *Harper v. Virginia* (1966), Justice Douglas had declared that the equal protection clause "is not shackled to the political theory of a particular era." Criticizing Douglas, Ackerman writes:

> Why is Douglas so sure that he is speaking for the zeitgeist? Perhaps the Court is talking only for a tiny minority of judicial do-gooders.
>
> Douglas encourages the charge of elitism by blandly declaring that [the Court's earlier] support for the "unequal and discriminatory treatment" imposed by the poll tax "sound[s] strange to a contemporary ear"—as if this were a matter of music appreciation.[5]

Yes, there should be strong concern about unelected justices making judgments like this. To the extent we diversify the Court, so that there are justices from a wider range of perspectives, those concerns might be lessened. But the ultimate justification for this method turns not only upon its strengths and weaknesses. It turns as well upon the strengths and weaknesses of any alternative. And it is in light of that alternative that we can see the (limited) virtues in the Court's current practice.

Imagine resolving these questions more explicitly democratically. Imagine just how that would happen.

As I described in Chapter 20, in his dissent in *VMI*, Justice Scalia rejected the idea of the Court resolving the question of equality based upon undebatables. Instead, Scalia suggested, the question of equality should be decided democratically. As he wrote,

> The virtue of a democratic system with a First Amendment is that it readily enables the people, over time, to be persuaded that what they took for granted is not so, and to change their laws accordingly. That system is destroyed if the smug assurances of each age are removed from the democratic process and written into the Constitution.[6]

What would "the people [being] persuaded that what they took for granted is not so" look like? How would it proceed?

As I've unpacked the question of equality, I've argued that it has turned upon an evolving judgment about the social meaning of a particular distinction.

As Steven Calabresi and Julie Rickert put it with respect to the constitutional status of women, the question is whether the meaning expresses "caste."[7] They believe, and I agree, that in 1868 it did not. Today they believe, and I agree, that it certainly does.

For the sake of clarity, let us stipulate to that belief. We know from the discussion in Chapter 18 how it came to be manifested within the domain of the Supreme Court. A process of "reasoned judgment," as Justice Souter described it, led the Court to recognize the caste-like character of the distinction and, simultaneously, the weakening justifications for its use.

Those conclusions follow from a process of reasoning. If they are reached properly, it is because they are constrained by that process of reasoning. To the extent we imagine disciplined sorts applying that process to those questions, we have reason to have confidence in the truth of their conclusions.

But non-disciplined sorts would not necessarily reach this conclusion. Or better, non-disciplined *processes*. I have little doubt that a properly representative body of citizens could be walked through the reasoned judgment that the Court engages and reach a very similar conclusion. Indeed, if we could trigger such processes—modeled on James Fishkin's notion of "deliberative polling"—easily or regularly, that might be a fair check on the process engaged in by courts.[8]

Yet regardless of whether one believes ordinary people in a properly constituted process could come to a similar result, it's fairly clear that an ordinary democratic process through elections would not. Again, that view does not depend upon believing that people are incapable of answering these questions. It depends instead upon a judgment about what such a process produces. Whatever it produces, it is not the reasoned judgment that the defense of civil rights depends upon. It is not the balance and reasoning that the consistent defense of fundamental ideals relies upon.

The best example of this dynamic is the history of the Equal Rights Amendment. Launched in a principled and moral way, the amendment would have constitutionalized the idea that sex-based distinctions should trigger heightened, maybe strict, judicial scrutiny. And launched roughly a century after the Fourteenth Amendment seemed to many to say as much, the amendment was intended to motivate a political push to bring a women's rights movement to the fore.

Its effect was quite the contrary. Rather than triggering a feminist movement, the amendment actually invigorated an anti-feminist response—led by conservative men (Ronald Reagan) and conservative women, including most prominently Phyllis Schlafly. Schlafly didn't oppose equality. But she opposed the implications of that equality. And very quickly the debate turned not upon whether the undebatables from 1868 were different in 1972, but upon whether women should serve in the military, or whether women should work outside the home. And thus, when the amendment failed, no one really read that failure as negating a presumption of equality. They read it instead as the inevitable confusion of resolving a question of principle through the democratic process. To the very end, the public overwhelmingly supported the ERA. (When the amendment was launched, support was 74 percent to 21 percent; at the end, it was still 62 percent to 23 percent). But what motivated the opposition was the complexity of the implications that this clear principle might entail.[9]

Don't misunderstand the point I am making. I am not arguing that politics is inapt for any matter of principle. My argument here is very specifically tied to the idea of equality in the Fourteenth Amendment. For my own view of the Equal Rights Amendment is that it is unnecessary in 2020. And it is unnecessary precisely because—given the current and, I'd say, undebatable social meaning of sex discrimination—any such discrimination would violate the equal protection clause. I thus don't think explicitly adding sex to the constitutional principle of equality is necessary. And more important, I think it would be harmful. Who knows what other distinctions will come to be seen as discriminations. And when they do, why should we have to pass a constitutional amendment to affirm the equality the Constitution would otherwise seem to demand?

My view would be different if this were 1875 (and I were as enlightened as John Stuart Mill was). To pass the ERA in 1875 would be to explicitly transform a social meaning through a constitutional text—just as the equal protection clause in 1868 was meant to effect a transformation in the social meaning of race through a constitutional text. The specific intent in both cases should have forced a court to treat as equal what most of the society at the time would not. The amendment would be an effort at transformative constitutionalism—using the Constitution to make us different from how we now are.

But once that commitment to equality gets expressed in a constitutional form, the ongoing question is simply how it applies. To whom does it extend? To women? To same-sex couples? To children? To immigrants? To fetuses? To beluga whales?

Scalia is quite colorful in his criticism of the "smug assurances" of the Court. But he offers no account of why we should expect the democratic process to be able to apply a principle of equality any better. And while I would certainly agree that the assurances that the Court relies upon should not be smug—humility is the most important virtue here, too—still, if the Court is confident that the meaning has so evolved, why is it any different from recognizing a change in the reach of the commerce clause?

The epistemological choice thus resolves not just upon whether one believes judges are from an elite or are politically biased. They certainly are both, and that fact is an important concern that must be addressed through proper diversity and humility. The choice resolves as well upon whether one believes that the alternative—the ordinary democratic process, at least as it is now—is capable of fairly evaluating the values at stake at all. Acknowledging the problems with the judges, it's still hard to see those problems as being within the same universe as the problem with the democratic process. The judges will get it wrong sometimes; the people (as currently constituted) will get it wrong mostly. Neither error is good; one seems clearly better.

## Fidelity to Role

The harder fidelity for lawyers to accept is the fidelity to role. I've argued throughout this book that this fidelity has both internal and external aspects. Internally, it points the Court to doctrines that allow it to avoid inevitably conflicting judgments. Administrability is the watchword: how will the rule or any particular doctrine of constitutional law play out over time? Will courts be able to apply it consistently or reliably? Or will their applications come to be seen as undetermined, or worse, political?

The external constraint is more dramatic: how does this case or doctrine enable courts to flourish or to remain relatively stable and capable within a proper conception of the judiciary?

My claim has been that critical moments in the history of the Supreme Court are understood best as instances of this kind of fidelity. My claim in this section is that this kind of fidelity is justified.

The internal constraint is the easier to justify. Indeed, the guide looks like simple judicial craft. Avoid doctrines that are indeterminate, or uncertain in application—especially when there are strong political or social forces on one side or the other. Stay formal where formalism is possible. Avoid balancing where that inevitably reflects badly on the capacity of the Court. There should be nothing controversial in the range of these constraints; they are the stuff of Judicial Craft 101.

The external constraints trigger greater resistance. In a very literal sense, they are instances of infidelity (to meaning) in order to preserve or enable the capacity of the judicial institution more generally. If they can be justified, then the scheme of justification cannot be strictly deontological. Indeed, that is my positive claim—that meaning has not been a primary duty; that another, sometimes conflicting duty (to the institution) has sometimes constrained the capacity to enact meaning.

I do believe that this constraint is justified as well. Every case is important, but much more important is that there be a stable and authoritative institution that can decide cases in the future. Especially at the birth of a court, or at moments of overwhelming political pressure, a court can rightly recognize that there is a limit to what it can do. Necessity is a defense in most legal contexts. It should be a defense here too.

Yet obviously, and always, that defense must be challenged and checked. A court is neither Hercules nor Zeus, but neither should it be Ares (the cowardly son of Zeus and Hera). I've worked hard to make more understandable the fidelity to role reading of the post-Reconstruction Court. I believe, with Brandwein, its decisions are better than we otherwise regard them. But that belief does not disable me from also believing they could have done more. Or that the justices could have better deployed the moral force of dissents. Maybe the decisions of that Court were necessary, but the dissents of Harlan were necessary too if the institution was to retain (or regain) any moral integrity.

There is an inevitability to this practice and thus, I believe, an essential link to the practice of judicial review. Yes, it is to be minimized; yes, it is to be avoided if possible. But yes, it is *always* a part of what any court in any political system must reckon.

How a court practices this type of fidelity is complicated as well. It is in its nature that its nature cannot be announced. Indeed, like Justice Powell's rule in *Bakke* for affirmative action, its motive and dynamic must be fuzzy and uncertain.[10] Recall Justice Jackson suggesting the Court acknowledge openly that it was giving up on commerce power review; recall that the Court in effect did give up commerce power review, but not openly or frankly. The reason was obscured to preserve a different image of the Court.

There is one important implication that follows from the epistemological concern raised in the previous section. There I said that courts were the better institution to track the evolution of social meanings—even though courts are clearly flawed in important ways. But fidelity to role shows why courts should go slow in performing their social meaning tracking role. Even if they're right, their rightness won't, as the joint opinion in *Casey* put it, always be obvious:

> Because not every conscientious claim of principled justification will
> be accepted as such, the justification claimed must be beyond dispute.
> The Court must take care to speak and act in ways that allow people
> to accept its decisions on the terms the Court claims for them, as

grounded truly in principle, not as compromises with social and political pressures having, as such, no bearing on the principled choices that the Court is obliged to make.[11]

If they are right, they should see the trend moving in the direction they believe it should go. Yet they should avoid leading in that trend. Again, not because their view is wrong. But because their view must be both right and seen as right.

The obvious example here is marriage. It was clear after *Brown* that antimiscegenation laws were unconstitutional. There was no way to write an opinion after *Brown* that could have upheld them. But the Court recognized clearly that acting quickly would jeopardize the whole anti-apartheid enterprise. It thus self-consciously allowed the injustice of apartheid marriage rules to remain until it believed it could act without triggering social revolt. And while we don't yet have the sources to know whether the same dynamic operated with the gay marriage cases, I would be incredibly surprised if it did not.

The justification for this hesitation is obvious, at least if you believe that righteousness would be self-defeating. The more interesting implication, however, is for justices dissenting from this evolution. For of course a justice could believe that it was not the job of the Court to recognize the evolution of social meaning. I do not believe such a justice could account for the Court's history consistently with that position. Or put differently, the justice would have to say that for much of the Court's history, the Court just got it wrong. Justices are constitutionally free to determine how they will read the Constitution and its tradition. And it is quite politically correct today to simply condemn rather than understand.

But given the repeated and consistent practice of the Court—given that evolving the application of the Constitution in light of evolving social meaning has been a core project of the Court since at least Harlan's opinion in *Poe*—fidelity to role should also constrain how a dissenter to that practice expresses her dissent. For what's striking about recent dissents is the absolute absence of humility. No doubt, Justice Scalia set the tone for the outraged dissent. But his rhetoric has become more common and, institutionally, more troubling.

It is one thing—and a fair thing—to disagree with a practice. It is quite another to call that practice illegitimate. The practice of evolving the understanding of the social meaning of equality is plainly not illegitimate. It is what the Court in a certain sense has always done. And rather than fueling increased skepticism about the legitimacy of the judicial role, the dissenters should better be expressing a principled dissent to a common practice, with a map of the alternative that they imagine a court could actually follow.

That they have not yet done.

———

At the end of his masterly work about the evolution of civil rights law in America, Michael Klarman writes:

> Whether social and political context *should* play such a large role in constitutional interpretation is beyond the scope of this book. That the justices have behaved a certain way in the past does not make it right, nor does it necessarily suggest that they will continue to behave that way in the future. On the other hand, if the Court's constitutional interpretations have always been influenced by the social and political contexts of the times in which they were rendered, perhaps it is impossible for them not to be. If that is so, then arguing against the inevitable seems pointless.[12]

The argument of this book is that social and political context *inevitably and appropriately* plays a significant role, especially for courts within a democracy. If it didn't, then the work of the courts would become more and more remote from the understanding and intuitions of that democracy. That's not to say the Supreme Court should be free to change the meaning of the Constitution. It is only to affirm that the Court should preserve the meaning through translation, recognizing the complex fidelities triggered through that process.

For here is where fidelity to role begins to speak sharply against the one-step originalist—as described in Chapter 2, the originalist who finds the meaning, and application, in an original context and simply applies that result in the current context. For imagine that Scalia had gotten his way. Imagine the Court had adopted the one-step approach that he affirmed for equal protection claims, denying that equal protection applied to sex discrimination. And imagine the Court explained its approach in exactly the terms Scalia offered.[13]

We've already stipulated that the social meaning of distinctions based on sex has changed. No one would doubt that at one time sex-based distinctions did not express "caste," and that at another time they did. And so when they did, imagine Justice Ginsburg (here in her role as lawyer) appealing to the Court to give effect to this changed understanding.

On the one-step's view, Ginsburg should lose. But imagine a hypothetical exchange that Ginsburg could have had with Scalia:

ANTONIN SCALIA: It's clear the framers of the Fourteenth Amendment didn't view these distinctions as discriminations; therefore, these distinctions do not violate "equal protection of the law."

RUTH BADER GINSBURG: But it's equally clear that we now view these distinctions as discrimination. It is as undebatable for us now as the opposite was for them then.

AS: Maybe, but if that's true, then get the democratic process to reflect it.

RBG: How? What must the democratic process do?

AS: Well, one thing would be to only pass laws that reflected this new and evolved understanding. Or another would be to amend the Constitution to add women to the list of protected groups.

RBG: But there is no list of protected groups within the Constitution. It says "persons," and it ensures those "persons" equality.

AS: Yes, but we all know they meant blacks and they didn't mean to include women.

RBG: Maybe. But that's not what they said, and that's precisely what they expressly rejected. In the end, what you're saying is that for democratic reasons, we have to read the Constitution in a way that most people would not recognize. Most would see that a law against hiring blacks is the same sort of thing as a law against hiring women. Yet the Constitution, on your view, is not allowed to see the same thing.

Ginsburg's point in this hypothetical dialog is a point about fidelity to role. The Court shouldn't get too far out there. (This is the same point Dick Fallon makes about statutory interpretation—that regardless of interpreted meaning, there is a moral constraint to avoid situations in which that meaning veers too far from an ordinary meaning as citizens would recognize it.)[14] Neither can the Court stay too far back. The crazier the Court's opinions seem—because so dissonant with cultural understanding—the weaker the institution becomes. Maybe lawyers would get the point. Maybe. But most in the public would read the resistance as political, not principled. And if political, then it would undermine the character of the Court as a judicial body.

And this is precisely because social and political context matters. As always, social and political context will give the action of the Court a meaning. That meaning is not chosen, nor can the Court fully control it. But if the practice renders the Court vulnerable, fidelity to role should steer the Court away from that practice.

The social and political context is thus a constraint on constitutionalism. It is also a feature of constitutionalism, not a bug. It is an ongoing assurance that the Constitution will not become too remote. The key is to give up on any theory that treats context as compromise or as an error, and instead build a theory that places context right in the middle.

We build a practice of judicial review, interpreting and defending the Constitution, *subject to* social and political contexts. How best to do that is an open question. This book has offered one answer to that open question. But whether you agree with my answer or not, we need a more common recognition that there is no such thing as a healthy and integrated Court that doesn't recognize how context matters—not as compromise or as a corruption, but as the essential tool to making and keeping alive the values that any constitution must embrace.

# Conclusion

A T THE CORE OF OUR constitutional tradition lie two fundamental values—liberty and equality. The history of our Constitution in the hands of the Supreme Court has been the constant struggle to keep those values alive as the world around us has changed.

Justices on the Right did that initially most forcefully with economic liberty. Throughout our tradition, they crafted readings of our Constitution that tried to translate its commitment to liberty, despite the growing practical justifications for increased governmental power. These justices crafted limits on the power to regulate economic liberty and on the power of Congress to regulate, in order to preserve autonomy for the states. The objective throughout was to cabin the government's power, in the name of preserving a space for the individual, or the states.

Justices on the Left did the same for a different liberty—and, more distinctively, for a conception of equality and privacy. They crafted limits on the government's power to protect the liberty beyond economic rights. And they crafted limits on the government's power to protect an evolving understanding of the scope of equality and privacy.

In both cases, these practices of translation—manifested always in made-up limits on what the democratic branches can do—have been constrained. They have been practices animated by two-step originalism, or fidelity to meaning; they have been constrained by a persistent fidelity to role. The history of constitutionalism in the Supreme Court is thus the dynamic between these two fidelities. Context enables both. Context constrains both. The practice of interpretation is the practice of applying these two fidelities, subject to the context—the facts, or social meanings, or a Llewellyian "situation-sense"—of the time.

That history, however, is of an institution, not an idea, and not particular judges. The judges within this institution are humans, not Hercules. The institution is not self-generating. It requires care and feeding; it depends upon a smart institutional politics to sustain itself when context renders the two-step too costly.

The account I have offered builds on these two fidelities. Its aim of describing the two together is to make understandable the twists in the history of that institution that are otherwise suspicious. The readings of our Court constitute a practice; that practice is, ultimately, justifiable—at least given the constraints of an old and entrenched Constitution. If the objective is the two-step, then the dance is always subject to, and sometime enabled by, the constraint of role. "Subject to" when, as with commerce or economic due process, fidelity to role pushes the Court away from fidelity to meaning. "Enabled by" when, as with equality or personal liberty, it helps speed the process of recognizing a social understanding that determines how those rights are read.

I am reluctant to recommend this practice elsewhere. I regret that it seems likely to disappear here. As I write these final words, I can't escape a certain foreboding. There is, I fear, a constitutional climate change as well. And as I reflect on the character of these times, I fear the uncontesteds of our time will no longer support the practice that this book has described.

For so deeply have we allowed partisan norms to infect the institution of the judiciary that we don't even recognize the essentially nonpartisan character of its past. Not that values have been irrelevant or that partisan values have not mattered. But the practice of constitutionalism stood above them, or beyond them, and the effort to keep alive commitments thought fundamental could therefore flourish.

That practice will not survive a Court perceived by us all to be political. If justices are openly appointed to reverse the decisions of an earlier Court— as Democrats promise with cases such as *Citizens United v. FEC* (2010) and Republicans promise with *Roe v. Wade* (1973)—and if the perception that the work of the Court is only and always inherently partisan continues to climb, then this practice will change. There is a fragility to great institutions of justice that we notice only when they are no longer great. That passing seems almost inevitable just now, as the divisions within our political culture grow.

I will, like any from my profession, whether on the Right or Left, lament that passing. Though it has stood watch over many great injustices, the Court is still an extraordinary institution within our constitutional tradition.[1] The justices are anonymous, or relatively so. They do their work carefully and personally. No other institution of the Framers' design works in a way closer to how they imagined it would work—in process, if not in substance. It is hard—as in scary—to conceive of a time when that character would pass.

I do not believe the Supreme Court has been the most important or most vital part of our constitutional tradition. It is the part we see the most, but only because we've allowed the democratic parts of our constitutional tradition to atrophy or fall from sight. As Ackerman has argued, rightly in my view, the eighteenth, nineteenth, and twentieth centuries were filled with constitutionalism that was as good as it gets, with publics rallied to fundamental values, themselves the product of serious and engaged reflection. Yet the legal profession obscures that democratic vitality and democratic pedigree. It only ever allows us to see constitutional change as the act of a noble (or evil) Supreme Court.

When we can no longer locate the pulse of principled constitutional change in a Court, maybe we will again find it in the people. If so, then this passing may ultimately be for the good.

# AFTERWORD

This is the first book that I wrote, back in 1997. I put the book away, and then wrote the first book that I published, *Code and Other Laws of Cyberspace* (New York: Basic Books, 1999). Over the past twenty years, I have returned to this work from time to time. Much as if I were working on a cottage in the country, I've torn down sections and rebuilt them; I've added critical bits and left others in a corner of my hard drive. I've changed my mind about parts; I found other parts to be more fundamental than I had originally seen.

I'm sure I could have tinkered and remodeled for another two decades. Certainly the stack of must-read articles and books would take at least that much time to go through. But last year I determined that it was time to let it go. There is a core framing here that I believe is fundamental and true. My hope is that that structure can be glimpsed despite the incompleteness and any error that surrounds it.

There is no way to thank all those who deserve thanks for a work spanning twenty years. My biggest debt goes to the central figure in this text, Bruce Ackerman. Every thought here was inspired by his, first in a series of extraordinary classes at the Yale Law School and then in a lifetime of interrupted and incomplete conversations.

But perhaps just as consequential was the influence of a man I never really had a chance to thank, Antonin Scalia, even though I had the honor of working for him. I doubt he would like all that I write here, but I believe I could have convinced him of the core of it. There was an integrity to the Scalia I knew, admittedly early in his career. That integrity was an invitation to argument and thinking. It drove me as I tried to understand the puzzle of the American Constitution in the hands of the Supreme Court.

The psychologically adept may well read this work as the product of the struggle to reconcile two dominant fathers. If it is indeed that, then it is certainly time to leave home, and leave to others the thoughts this might inspire.

The work to bring this book to closure has been herculean. I am endlessly grateful to the team of students who checked what I said and checked that what I said was supported. In the most recent round, they have included David Benger, Sam Bookman, Suman Dev, Han Ding, Sarah Joy Dorman, Mohammed El Shafie, Megan Field, Medha Gargeya, Andrei Gribakov, Ross Holley, Ernst-Wesley Laine, Thomas Oskar Marshall, Gregory D. Muren, Patrick O'Bryant, Catherine Padhi, Gareth Thomas Rhodes, Tyler Starr, Thomas Weber, Jenna Welsh, and Daren Zhang. I am especially grateful to Kevin Crenny, Zak Lutz, and Kyle Skinner for their work and leadership, as well as to the hardest-working Harvard undergraduate I've ever known, Abraham Moffat. I am thankful as well for my endlessly thoughtful and careful assistant, Valentina de Portu. And no one not from my law school could begin to understand my debt to the people at the Harvard Law School Library.

I am also grateful to the many who have steered me over the years, directly and indirectly, at critical turns on this path. They include Samantha Barbas, Jack Goldsmith, Sina Kian, John Manning, Alan Meese, Cyrus Mokri, Richard Posner, Darien Shanske, David Strauss, Oren Tamir, Cass Sunstein, and Jon Zittrain, as well as some at the very beginning whose contact I have lost (Cindy). Lawrence Venuti helped me see and accept the limits in this aspiration. Steven Calabresi gave me the core framing of fidelity to role.

In an obvious way, the argument throughout this book is about the place and role of the taken-for-granted. I hope the book teaches a discipline for coming to understand that which we—and they—take for granted, as well as a deep and endless respect for its place in our lives. I am endlessly and joyfully grateful for the love of a partner who is taken for granted in the simple sense that I couldn't imagine living without her or her precious love. This book is dedicated to another woman whose love and influence I have taken for granted, in ways I'm not sure I will ever really understand.

## NOTES

### Introduction

The Internet references cited in this book have been permanently archived using the perma.cc system. All the links referenced in these notes (e.g., as "link #23," "link #4") can be found at http://fidelity.lessig.org. If the originally referenced source is no longer at the original link, perma.cc will provide an archived copy.

1. Tyler Vigen, *Spurious Correlations, available at* link #1.

2. This book draws together work I have done since the beginning of my career. As my thinking has evolved over that period, I have not taken the space here to address the criticism of my earlier work. Instead, I review and respond to that criticism on the website associated with this book, http://fidelity.lessig.org. That earlier work includes primarily *Fidelity in Translation*, 71 Texas L. Rev. 1165 (1993); *Readings by Our Unitary Executive*, 15 Cardozo L. Rev. 175 (1993); *The President and the Administration* (with Cass Sunstein), 94 Colum. L. Rev. 1 (1994); *Understanding Changed Readings: Fidelity and Theory*, 47 Stan. L. Rev. 395 (1995); *The Limits of Lieber*, 16 Cardozo L. Rev. 2249 (1995); *Post-Constitutionalism (Book Review)*, 94 Mich. L. Rev. 1422 (1996); *What Drives Derivability: Response to Responding to Imperfection (Book Review)*, 74 Texas L. Rev. 839 (1996); *Translating Federalism:* United States v. Lopez, 1995 Supreme Court Rev. 125 (1996); *Fidelity and Constraint*, 65 Fordham L. Rev. 1365 (1997); *The Puzzling Persistence of Bellbottom Theory: What a Constitutional Theory Should Be*, 15 Georgetown L.J. 1837 (1997); *The Erie-Effects of Volume 110: An Essay on Context in Interpretive Theory*, 110 Harv. L. Rev. 1785 (1997); *Understanding Federalism's Text*, 66 Geo. Wash. L. Rev. 1218 (1998).

3. The field of originalism is vast. An incomplete sample of recent and important work would include Lawrence B. Solum, *Originalist Methodology*, 84 U. Chi.

L. Rev. 269 (2017); John O. McGinnis & Branden Stein, "Originalism, Hypothesis Testing, and Big Data," *Proceedings of 15th Annual Conference of the International Association of Artificial Intelligence & Law* 201 (2015); John O. McGinnis, *Public Choice Originalism: Bork, Buchanan and the Escape from the Progressive Paradigm*, 10 J.L. & Econ. & Pol'y 669 (2015); Stephen E. Sachs, *Originalism as a Theory of Legal Change*, 38 Harv. J.L. & Pub. Pol'y 817 (2015) (advancing a positive theory of originalism as "our law"); William Baude, *Is Originalism Our Law?*, 115 Colum. L. Rev. 2349 (2015); John O. McGinnis & Michael B. Rappaport, *Originalism and the Good Constitution* (Cambridge, MA: Harvard University Press, 2013); Larry Alexander, *Originalism, the Why and the What*, 82 Fordham L. Rev. 539, 540 (2013); Robert W. Bennett & Lawrence B. Solum, *Constitutional Originalism: A Debate* 181 (Ithaca, NY: Cornell University Press, 2011) (Kindle ed.); *The Challenges of Originalism: Theories of Constitutional Interpretation* (Grant Huscroft & Bradley W. Miller eds., Cambridge, UK: Cambridge University Press, 2011); John O. McGinnis & Michael B. Rappaport, *Originalism and the Good Constitution*, 98 Georgetown L.J. 1693 (2010); John O. McGinnis & Michael B. Rappaport, *Original Methods Originalism: A New Theory of Interpretation and the Case against Construction*, 103 N. W. L. Rev. 751 (2009); Mitchell N. Berman, *Originalism Is Bunk*, 84 N.Y.U. L. Rev. 1 (2009); Richard S. Kay, *Original Intention and Public Meaning in Constitutional Interpretation*, 103 Nw. U. L. Rev. 703, 718–726 (2009); Thomas B. Colby & Peter J. Smith, *Living Originalism*, 59 Duke L.J. 239, 244–245 (2009) (calling originalism a "smorgasbord of distinct constitutional theories"); Stephen M. Griffin, *Rebooting Originalism,* 2008 U. Ill. L. Rev. 1185 (2008); Jack M. Balkin, *Abortion and Original Meaning*, 24 Const. Comment. 291 (2007); Jack M. Balkin, *Original Meaning and Constitutional Redemption*, 24 Const. Comment. 427 (2007); John O. McGinnis & Michael B. Rappaport, *Original Interpretative Principles as the Core of Originalism*, 24 Const. Comment. 371 (2007); John O. McGinnis & Michael B. Rappaport, *Originalism and Supermajoritarianism: Defending the Nexus*, 101 Nw. L. Rev. 1919 (2007); *Originalism: A Quarter-Century of Debate* (Steven G. Calabresi ed., Washington, DC: Regnery, 2007) (includes speeches by Attorney General Edwin Meese and Justice William Brennan and conference presentations by academics); Bernadette Meyler, *Towards a Common Law Originalism*, 59 Stan. L. Rev. 551 (2006); John O. McGinnis & Michael B. Rappaport, *A Pragmatic Defense of Originalism*, 100 Nw. L. Rev. 383 (2006); Johnathan O'Neill, *Originalism in American Law and Politics: A Constitutional History* (Baltimore, MD: Johns Hopkins University Press, 2005); Keith E. Whittington, *The New Originalism*, 2 Geo. J.L. & Pub. Pol'y 599 (2004); Randy E. Barnett, *Restoring the Lost Constitution: The Presumption of Liberty* (Princeton, NJ: Princeton University Press, 2004); Vasan Kesavan & Michael Stokes Paulsen, *The Interpretive Force of the Constitution's Secret Drafting History*, 91 Geo. L.J. 1113 (2003); Randy Barnett & Evan Bernick, *The Letter and the Spirit: A Unified Theory of Originalism* (2018) (working paper), *available at* link #2; Keith E. Whittington, *Constitutional Construction: Divided Powers and Constitutional Meaning* (Cambridge, MA: Harvard University Press, 1999); Mark D. Greenberg & Harry Litman, *The Meaning of Original Meaning*, 86 Geo. L.J. 569, 592 (1998); Antonin Scalia, A *Matter of Interpretation: Federal Courts and the Law* (Princeton, NJ: Princeton University Press, 1997) (includes an essay by Justice Scalia and comments by Amy Gutmann, Gordon S. Wood, Laurence H. Tribe, Mary Ann Glendon, and Ronald Dworkin); Gary Lawson, *On Reading Recipes...and Constitutions*, 85 Geo. L.J. 1823 (1997); John O. McGinnis, *The Original Constitution and Its Decline: A Public Choice Perspective*, 21 Harv. J.L. & Pub. Pol. 195 (1997); John O. McGinnis, *The Original Constitution and Our Origins*, 19 Harv. J.L. & Pub. Pol. 251 (1996); Michael W. McConnell, *Originalism and the Desegregation Decisions*, 81 Va. L. Rev. 947 (1995); Keith E. Whittington, *Constitutional Interpretation: Textual Meaning, Original Intent, and Judicial Review* (Lawrence: University Press of Kansas, 1991); Antonin Scalia, *Originalism: The Lesser Evil*, 57 U. Cinn. L. Rev. 849 (1989); Daniel A. Farber, *The Originalism Debate: A Guide for the Perplexed*, 49 Ohio St. L.J. 1085 (1989); Richard S. Kay, *Adherence to the Original Intentions in Constitutional Adjudication: Three Objections and Responses*, 82 Nw. U. L. Rev. 226 (1988); H. Jefferson Powell, *The Original Understanding of Original Intent*, 98 Harv. L. Rev. 885 (1985); Raoul Berger, *Government by Judiciary: The Transformation of the Fourteenth Amendment* (Cambridge, MA: Harvard University Press, 1977); William H. Rehnquist, *The Notion of a Living Constitution*, 54 Tex. L. Rev. 693 (1976); Robert H. Bork, *Neutral Principles and Some First Amendment Problems*, 47 Ind. L.J. 1 (1971).

The skeptics have been even more numerous. Certainly the most important framing critique, while simultaneously enabling much of the most important originalism that survives, is Jack N. Rakove's *Original Meanings: Politics and Ideas in the Making of the Constitution* (New York: Alfred A. Knopf, 1996). Among the most effective critical critiques have been James E. Fleming, *Fidelity to Our Imperfect Constitution: For Moral Readings and Against Originalism* (New York: Oxford University Press, 2015); David A. Strauss, *The Living Constitution* (New York: Oxford University Press, 2010); Stephen Breyer, *Active Liberty: Interpreting Our Democratic Constitution* (New York: Alfred A. Knopf, 2005); Philip Bobbitt, *Constitutional Fate: Theory of the Constitution* (New York: Oxford University Press, 1982); Paul Brest, *The Misconceived Quest for the Original Understanding*, 60 B.U. L. Rev. 204 (1980).

This book, however, will not engage the intra-originalism debates. Whether an originalist should adopt original meaning, or intent, or purpose and whether an "originalist" can be "living" in the sense Balkin describes are important questions beyond the scope of this book. Whatever you believe "originalism" is, this book documents a practice that evokes a discipline that is within the family of originalist theories, recognizing the essential contextuality of meaning, both original and current. Balkin's description of the evolution of theories originalism is as clear as any. See Jack Balkin, *Living Originalism* 1295–1299 (Cambridge, MA: Harvard University Press 2011) (Kindle ed.). My belief is that we can make progress if we bracket that theoretical debate and immerse more deeply in actual practice.

4. Simon Blackburn, *The Oxford Dictionary of Philosophy* 62 (New York: Oxford University Press 1994), cited in Richard Fallon Jr., *Law and Legitimacy in the Supreme Court* 208 (Cambridge, MA: Belknap Press of Harvard University Press, 2018).

5. This was Ronald Dworkin's metaphor in *Law's Empire* 239 et seq. (Cambridge, MA: Belknap Press of Harvard University Press, 1986). Hercules, in Dworkin's hands, is wise, with full knowledge of legal sources, and with plenty of time to resolve hard legal questions correctly. Dworkin's metaphor is considered in E. W. Thomas, *The Judicial Process: Realism, Pragmatism, Practical Reasoning and Principles* 192–208 (Cambridge, UK: Cambridge University Press, 2005); Cass Sunstein, *Legal Reasoning and Political Conflict* ch. 2 (New York: Oxford University Press, 1996); Jürgen Habermas, *Between Facts and Norms: Contributions to a Discourse Theory of Law and Democracy* ch. 5 (Cambridge, MA: MIT Press, 1996); Edward B. Foley, *Requiem for Hercules*, 18 Const. Comment. 463 (2001) (review of Dworkin's *Sovereign Virtue*); Sanford Levinson, "Hercules, Abraham Lincoln, the United States Constitution, and the Problem of Slavery," in *Ronald Dworkin* (Arthur Ripstein ed., Cambridge, UK: Cambridge University Press, 2007); Frank I. Michelman, *The Supreme Court, 1985 Term—Foreword: Traces of Self-Government*, 100 Harv. L. Rev. 4, 76–77 (1986) (arguing that "Hercules, Dworkin's mythic judge, is a loner. He is much too heroic. His narrative constructions are monologues"); John Finnis, *On Reason and Authority in* Law's Empire, 6 Law & Phil. 357, 376 (1987).

6. For a sample of these legal empiricists, see Lee Epstein, William M. Landes, & Richard A. Posner, *The Behavior of Federal Judges: A Theoretical and Empirical Study of Rational Choice* (Cambridge, MA: Harvard University Press, 2013). Unsurprisingly, this work has evoked considerable debate. See, e.g., Lawrence B. Solum, *The Positive Foundations of Formalism: False Necessity and American Legal Realism*, 127 Harv. L. Rev. 2464, 2498 (2014) (book review); Erwin Chemerinsky, *Measuring Judging*, 99 Judicature 74, 78 (2015) (book review); Ian Ayres, 52 Journal of Economic Literature 866 (2014) (book review); Geoffrey R. Stone, *The Behavior of Supreme Court Justices When Their Behavior Counts the Most: An Informal Study*, 97 Judicature 82, 89 (2013); Linda Greenhouse, *Chief Justice Roberts in His Own Voice: The Chief Justice's Self-Assignment of Majority Opinions*, 97 Judicature 90, 97 (2013); Sebastián Castro, 77 Mod. L. Rev. 151 (2014) (book review); Alison Newman, *Lee Epstein, William M. Landes, Richard A. Posner: The Behavior of Federal Judges*, 159 Public Choice 577 (2014) (book review); David A. Hughes, 76 *Journal of Politics* E10 (book review).

   Richard Fallon also considers the relationship between these skeptics and "the view that the Justices regard themselves as law bound and seek to meet their legal obligations" in Fallon, *Law and Legitimacy* 121. As he reports, there is substantial research supporting the argument that "justices frequently seek to identify and adhere to constitutional norms as an alternative to voting in accordance with their naked ideological preferences." *Id.* 122.

## Chapter One

1. Akhil Reed Amar, *Philadelphia Revisited: Amending the Constitution Outside Article V*, 55 U. Chi. L. Rev. 1043 (1988). The puzzle, as explained in the text, is that the Constitution was enacted according to a procedure that was inconsistent with the text of its predecessor, the Articles of Confederation.

2. Calvin H. Johnson, *Righteous Anger at the Wicked States: The Meaning of the Founders' Constitution* 17 (Cambridge, UK: Cambridge University Press, 2005).

3. Johnson, *Righteous Anger at the Wicked States* 15.

4. Warren L. McFerran, *Birth of the Republic: The Origin of the United States* 149 (Sanford, FL: Southern Liberty Press, 2005).

5. Mervin B. Whealy, *"The Revolution Is Not Over": The Annapolis Convention of 1786*, 81 Maryland Historical Magazine 228 (1986); Jack N. Rakove, *The Gamble at Annapolis*, This Constitution: A Bicentennial Chronicle, Fall 1986, at 4; Shirley Baltz, *Annapolis on the Threshold*, 81 Maryland Historical Magazine 222 (1986).

6. *The Report of the Annapolis Conference* (1786), *available at* link #3.

7. Including its indirect effect on state constitutional law. As Ackerman demonstrates, the adoption of the federal constitution effectively amended state constitutions. Yet the states did not follow their own rules for amending their constitutions. Bruce Ackerman, 2 *We the People: Transformations* 36–38 (Cambridge, MA: Belknap Press of Harvard University Press, 2000).

8. As James Wilson stated at the Pennsylvania ratifying convention: "There necessarily exists, in every government, a power from which there is no appeal, and which, for that reason, may be termed supreme, absolute, and uncontrollable. Where does this power reside? To this question writers on different governments will give different answers.... The truth is, that, in our governments, the supreme, absolute, and uncontrollable power *remains* in the people. As our constitutions are superior to our legislatures, so the people are superior to our constitutions. Indeed, the superiority, in this last instance, is much greater; for the people possess over our constitutions control in *act*, as well as right. The consequence is, that the people may change the constitutions whenever and however they please. This is a right of which no positive institution can ever deprive them." James Wilson, Address at the Convention of the State of Pennsylvania on the Adoption of the Federal Constitution, November 26, 1787, *in* 2 *The Debates in the Several State Conventions on the Adoption of the Federal Constitution as Recommended by the General Convention at Philadelphia in 1787* 432 (Jonathan Elliot ed., 2d ed. Philadelphia: J. B. Lippincott, 1876). See also Akhil Reed Amar, *The Consent of the Governed: Constitutional Amendment Outside Article V*, 94 Colum. L. Rev. 457, 464 n. 18 (1994).

Hamilton made a similar argument in the Federalist Papers: "I trust the friends of the proposed Constitution will never concur with its enemies in questioning that fundamental principle of republican government which admits the right of the people to alter or abolish the established Constitution whenever they find it inconsistent with their happiness." *The Federalist No. 78* 469 (Alexander Hamilton) (Clinton Rossiter ed., New York: New American Library, 1961) (footnote omitted).

Madison also believed the Articles of Confederation had lost their binding force because of repeated breach by the confederate states. As he wrote: "[Under] the doctrine of compacts, that a breach of any of the articles of the confederation by any of the parties to it, absolves the other parties from their respective obligations, and gives them a right, if they chuse to exert it, of dissolving the Union altogether." James Madison, "Vices of the Political System of the United States," April 1787, quoted in Johnson, *Righteous Anger at the Wicked States* 81. As Johnson comments, "On this issue, Madison was more nationalist than Hamilton, who was 'not yet prepared to admit the doctrine that the Confederacy could be dissolved by partial infractions of it.' Indeed, no one but Madison seems to have given much weight to the breach of contract argument."

9. The original rough draft written by Thomas Jefferson contains only slight differences from the final: "We hold these truths to be sacred & undeniable; that all men are created equal & independant, that from that equal creation they derive rights inherent & inalienable, among which are the preservation of life, & liberty, & the pursuit of happiness; that to secure these ends, governments are instituted among men, deriving their just powers from the consent of the governed; that whenever any form of government shall become destructive of these ends, it is the right of the people to alter or to abolish it, & to institute new government, laying its foundation on such principles & organising its powers in such form, as to them shall seem most likely to effect their safety & happiness." Information was obtained from an image of the original rough draft, as well as from the following: 1 *The Papers of Thomas Jefferson* 243–247 (Julian P. Boyd ed., Princeton, NJ: Princeton University Press, 1950).

10. *Extract from Thomas Jefferson to John Cartwright* (June 5, 1824), Jefferson Quotes & Family Letters, *available at* link #4.

11. The argument for non-exclusivity has more behind it than merely logical inference. As Akhil Amar puts it: "The best argument for Article V nonexclusivity came not from what the Constitution *said*, but rather from what it *did*. In 1787, as has been seen, most states had Article V analogues in their state constitutions—that is, clauses or articles setting forth the rules for state constitutional amendment. Often, Article V analogues used explicit language seeming to affirm exclusivity: 'no' amendments could occur except via the specified procedure. Nevertheless, a great many states ratified the federal Constitution in 1787–88—and thereby amended their state constitutions— without complying with the procedures specified in their Article V analogues."

Akhil Reed Amar, *America's Constitution: A Biography* 296–297 (New York: Random House, 2005). Madison too thought apparently exclusive modes of amendment merely "specified only the way ordinary government could amend the constitution." Akhil Reed Amar, "Popular Sovereignty and Constitutional Amendment," in *Responding to Imperfection: The Theory and Practice of Constitutional Amendment* 89, 97 (Sanford Levinson ed., Princeton, NJ: Princeton University Press, 1995).

12. David Ramsay, 1 *The History of the American Revolution* 356–357 (Philadelphia, PA: R. Aitken & Son, 1789), as quoted in Amar, "Popular Sovereignty" 100. James Wilson said the same: the power of the people was "supreme, absolute, and uncontrollable." They "may change the constitutions whenever and however they please." Michael Klarman, *The Framers' Coup: The Making of the United States Constitution* 14069 (New York: Oxford University Press, 2016) (Kindle ed.).

13. "The people of the United States have given their reasons for doing a certain act. Here we propose . . . to let them know that they had a right to exercise a natural and inherent privilege, which they have asserted in the solemn ordination and establishment of the constitution. Now, if this right is indefeasible, and the people have recognized it in practice, the truth is better asserted than it can be by any words whatever." Ackerman, 2 *We the People* 79.

14. Richard Tuck develops the grounding conceptual argument, founded in Hobbes, that supports this understanding at the Founding. See Richard Tuck, *The Sleeping Sovereign: The Invention of Modern Democracy* (Cambridge, UK: Cambridge University Press, 2016). Bruce Ackerman has mapped the understanding in practice: "On sixteen occasions before the Civil War, state legislatures refused to read . . . silence [about whether a mode of amendment was exclusive] to imply exclusivity." Ackerman, 2 *We the People* 80.

15. As I describe in Chapter 20, Bruce Ackerman has brilliantly insisted that no faithful interpretation of our past can conclude that Article V is exclusive. I agree with him, though not necessarily every part of the theory he advances. In particular, as we'll see, I offer a very different way to understand the New Deal. But despite the brilliance and truth in Ackerman's account, I suspect my claim about the views of ordinary lawyers is certainly true.

16. Nor did it for much of the nineteenth century. The core of the argument justifying the state resistance to the Supreme Court, and then the South's resistance to the commands of the Union, was the "state-rights compact theory of the Union" as developed by John C. Calhoun. As Sean Wilentz describes it: "The states, so the argument went, existed before the Union. The Constitution did not alter the states' powers and prerogatives as autonomous governments. By seceding, the states were merely reasserting the total sovereignty they had exerted in creating the Union in the first place." Sean Wilentz, *The Rise of American Democracy: Jefferson to Lincoln* 773 (New York: W. W. Norton, 2005). See also Mark E. Brandon, "The 'Original' Thirteenth Amendment and the Limits to Formal Constitutional Change," *in* Levinson, *Responding to Imperfection*

215, 232: "In nineteenth-century America, popular sovereignty . . . was empirically empty as was the popular founding of the new constitutional order in 1789. In fact, there was a substantial body of opinion in the nineteenth century holding that the national political order was a creature, not of the people-as-sovereign, but of preexisting sovereign states. At the very least, notwithstanding Marshall's attempts to asset national governmental primacy and a version of national popular sovereignty, the Constitution was generally held out to be a document under which states retained a large degree of discretion over their internal affairs and 'domestic institutions.'"

17. Amar, *America's Constitution* 299.

18. Amar, *America's Constitution* 299.

19. All interpretation deals with context, but different schools consider different aspects of context for interpretive authority. Strict textualists claim to derive their interpretations of laws entirely from the language of the law itself, with dictionary meanings of words and internal coherence as context, see John F. Manning, *Textualism and Legislative Intent*, 91 Va. L. Rev. 419 (2005) and William N. Eskridge Jr. & Philip P. Frickey, *Statutory Interpretation as Practical Reasoning*, 42 Stan. L. Rev. 321, 340–345 (1990), though textualists distinguish between two frames of textualism, one less ambitious and serving more as a guide to legislative intent and purpose than as a constraint. See also John F. Manning, *What Divides Textualists from Purposivists?*, 106 Colum. L. Rev. 70, 79 (2006). Simple originalism expands from the words of an original text to words written and ideas expressed by the Framers at the time of the Founding. See Raoul Berger, *Government by Judiciary: The Transformation of the Fourteenth Amendment* 363–372 (Cambridge, MA: Harvard University Press, 1977). Paul Brest first sketched originalism as a kind of translation in *The Misconceived Quest for the Original Understanding*, 60 B.U. L. Rev. 204, 205, 222–224 (1980). Brest's account was the inspiration for my own early work.

I have written elsewhere about the role of context in interpretation: Lawrence Lessig, *Understanding Changed Readings: Fidelity and Theory*, 47 Stan. L. Rev. 395 (1995). There I use a contextualized understanding of meaning that resembles the notion of "pragmatic hermeneutics" discussed in James T. Kloppenberg, *The Theory and Practice of American Legal History*, 106 Harv. L. Rev. 1332, 1336 (1993) (reviewing Morton J. Horwitz, *The Transformation of American Law, 1870–1960: The Crisis of Legal Orthodoxy* (New York: Oxford University Press, 1992)). As Kloppenberg suggests, pragmatic hermeneutics is grounded in the efforts of scholars such as Quentin Skinner. *Id.* at 1335, citing Quentin Skinner, *The Foundations of Modern Political Thought* (Cambridge, UK: Cambridge University Press, 1978). For a recent and comprehensive philosophical account from the perspective of constitutional law, see Fallon, *Law and Legitimacy* 47–51.

Yet, as with the debate among originalists, I do not engage the important and interesting philosophical debate about the nature of meaning. I use philosophy to help understand why not all change is change. But I don't believe the ultimate legal question will be resolved by a more precise conception of the philosophy.

20. Fallon, *Law and Legitimacy* 141.

21. Balkin, *Living Originalism* 193.

## Chapter Two

1. *Marbury v. Madison*, 5 U.S. 137 (1803); *McCulloch v. Maryland*, 17 U.S. 316 (1819); *Gibbons v. Ogden*, 22 U.S. 1 (1824).

2. Ten allocated their electoral votes via the legislature, and six allocated electors by popular vote. See *Election of 1800—Breakdown y State, Method of Choosing Electors, Tally Results, and Electoral Vote Outcome, available at* link #5.

3. See Nancy Isenberg, *Fallen Founder: The Life of Aaron Burr* 208–220 (New York: Viking, 2007).

4. The first use of the term appears to be in the late nineteenth century. See "running mate, n.," OED Online, March 2018, Oxford University Press, *available at* link #6.

5. For many years this conclusion has been suspected but never clearly shown. But recent scholarship affirms the view that the acknowledged scheming by Burr's lieutenant, William P. Van Ness, was most likely at Burr's explicit behest. See Thomas N. Baker, *"An Attack Well Directed": Aaron Burr Intrigues for the Presidency*, 31 Journal of the Early Republic 553 (2011); John S. Pancake, *Aaron Burr: Would-Be Usurper*, 8 Will. & Mary Q. 204 (1951).

6. See James Kent & William Kent, *Memoirs and Letters of James Kent, LL.D.* 36 (Boston: Little, Brown, 1898) (Burr).

7. The story is told well in Willard Sterne Randall, *Thomas Jefferson: A Life* 546–547 (New York: Henry Holt, 1993).

8. Thomas Jefferson to Spencer Roane, September 6, 1819, as quoted in Randall, *Thomas Jefferson* 547.

9. I have not described, though it was a central part of the original political dynamic, the impeachment of Justice Samuel Chase. Chase had been a strongly partisan federalist judge under Adams. The Republicans impeached Chase in a trial that, had it been successful, would have radically reduced the perceived independence of the judiciary—and set up Marshall for his own impeachment. See Bruce Ackerman, *The Failure of the Founding Fathers: Jefferson, Marshall, and the Rise of Presidential Democracy* 209–222 (Cambridge, MA: Belknap Press of Harvard University Press, 2005).

10. See John Copeland Nagle, *The Lame Ducks of* Marbury, 20 Const. Comment. 317, 320, 324–325 (2004).

11. Larry D. Kramer, *The People Themselves: Popular Constitutionalism and Judicial Review* 116 (New York: Oxford University Press, 2004).

12. 1 *Journal of the Executive Proceedings of the Senate of the United States of America* 388, 390 (Washington, DC: Duff Green, 1828), reprinted in *Marbury Versus Madison: Documents and Commentary* 308 (Mark A. Graber & Michael Perhac eds., Washington, DC: CQ Press, 2002).

13. Susan Low Bloch, *The* Marbury *Mystery: Why Did William Marbury Sue in the Supreme Court?*, 18 Const. Comment. 607, 608–609 (2003). See also Sean Wilentz, *The Rise of American Democracy: Jefferson to Lincoln* 100 (New York: W. W. Norton, 2005).

14. Repeal Act of 1802, 2 Stat. 132 (March 8, 1802). See generally Justin Crowe, *Building the Judiciary: Law, Courts, and the Politics of Institutional Development* 71–72 (Princeton, NJ: Princeton University Press, 2012).

15. Crowe, *Building the Judiciary* 72–73. Crowe does note that some believed that this motive was unlikely, since any challenge to the Repeal Act would not reach the Court before its June term. *Id.* at 73 n. 248; *id.* at 63 ("Despite the conventional emphasis on the timing of the infamous 'midnight judges,' the Judiciary Act of 1801 was prompted more by a desire to further an economic policy vision than strengthen a partisan or electoral coalition and intended more as a check upon state officers and judges than upon Jefferson and the incoming Democratic-Republican Congress"). See also Robert Lowry Clinton, Marbury v. Madison *and Judicial Review* 15 (Lawrence: University Press of Kansas, 1989). As Kramer describes it, "Anticipating the possibility of such challenges, the Republican Congress had already passed legislation designed to put off a ruling from the Supreme Court. This was accomplished by legislation adopted in early April that abolished the Supreme Court's June and December terms, thus delaying the Court's next sitting until February 1803, by which time Jefferson hoped that tempers in the capital would have cooled." Kramer, *The People Themselves* 120.

   It is more likely that the real motivation of Congress was not *Marbury* but rather the protection of its Repeal Act of 1802. By virtue of that act, Supreme Court justices were required to once again ride circuit. By canceling the spring term, Congress was, in effect, forcing the justices to acknowledge the legitimacy of the Repeal Act. And indeed, as we'll see, when the Court finally ruled on the act in *Stuart v. Laird* (1803), it noted the fact that the Supreme Court justices' behavior had operated as a "precedent" supporting the act.

16. Next to *Brown v. Board of Education*, 347 U.S. 483 (1954), no case in the Supreme Court is as famous as *Marbury*. The literature on the case is appropriately extensive. See, e.g., Christopher L. Eisgruber, Marbury, *Marshall, and the Politics of Constitutionality Judgment*, 89 Va. L. Rev. 1203 (2003); Jeremy Waldron, "'Despotism in Some Form': *Marbury v. Madison*," in *Great Cases in Constitutional Law*, 55 (Robert P. George ed., Princeton, NJ: Princeton University Press, 2000); Larry D. Kramer, Marbury *and the Retreat from Judicial Supremacy*, 20 Const. Comment. 205, 230 (2003); Mark Tushnet, "*Marbury v. Madison* and the Theory of Judicial Supremacy," *in Great Cases in Constitutional Law* 17 (Robert P. George ed., Princeton, NJ: Princeton University Press, 2000); Michael J. Klarman, *How Great Were the "Great" Marshall Court Decisions?*, 87 Va. L. Rev. 1111 (2001); Michael W. McConnell, "The Story of *Marbury v. Madison*: Making Defeat Look Like Victory," *in Constitutional Law Stories* 13

(Michael C. Dorf ed., New York: Foundation Press, 2004); Paul W. Kahn, *The Reign of Law:* Marbury v. Madison *and the Construction of America* (New Haven, CT: Yale University Press, 1997); Richard H. Fallon Jr., Marbury *and the Constitutional Mind: A Bicentennial Essay on the Wages of Doctrinal Tension*, 91 Cal. L. Rev. 1 (2003); William E. Nelson, Marbury v. Madison: *The Origins and Legacy of Judicial Review* (Lawrence: University Press of Kansas, 2000); Clinton, Marbury v. Madison *and Judicial Review*. The classic work is William W. Van Alstyne, *A Critical Guide to* Marbury v. Madison, 1969 Duke L. J. 1 (1969). For excellent edited works, see Marbury Versus Madison: *Documents and Commentary* (Mark A. Graber & Michael Perhac eds., Washington DC: CQ Press, 2002); *Arguing* Marbury v. Madison (Mark Tushnet ed., Stanford, CA: Stanford Law and Politics, 2005).

17. Valery Zorkin, quoted in Kim Lane Scheppele, *Guardians of the Constitution: Constitutional Court Presidents and the Struggle for the Rule of Law in Post-Soviet Europe*, 154 U. Pa. L. Rev. 1757, 1795–1796 (2006).

18. Scheppele, *Guardians of the Constitution*, 1796.

19. Crowe says Jefferson's reaction at first was "measured," but that "over the course of his first year in office, however, a conglomeration of events gradually converted his stance from conciliatory to bellicose." Crowe, *Building the Judiciary* 68. See also Louis H. Pollak, Marbury v. Madison: *What Did John Marshall Decide and Why?*, 148 Proceedings of the American Philosophical Society 1, 6–8 (2004).

20. Letter from Thomas Jefferson to George Hay (June 2, 1807), *in* 4 *Memoir, Correspondence and Miscellanies from the Papers of Thomas Jefferson* 75, 76 (Thomas Jefferson Randolph ed., Charlottesville, VA: F. Carr, 1829).

21. This view is "departmentalism," which, as Richard Fallon notes, was dominant even if it is no longer. Fallon, *Law and Legitimacy* 115.

22. 1 Stat. 68, 68–69 (1789). It is unclear exactly how or where the obligation to "deliver" the commission is drawn from. Marshall clearly decides that "to withhold the commission [from Marbury] . . . is an act deemed by the Court not warranted by law." *Marbury v. Madison*, 5 U.S. (1 Cranch) 137, 162 (1803). But the obligations of the statute are to affix a seal, not deliver a commission.

23. See, e.g., H. Jefferson Powell, *The Political Grammar of Early Constitutional Law*, 71 N.C. L. Rev. 949, 968–974 (1993). Justin Crowe discounts the significance of *Marbury* because in effect it left things as they were; see Crowe, *Building the Judiciary* 76–77. I share with Powell the view that this discounts too much the importance of the precedent. On the role of precedent generally, see the extraordinary Philip Hamburger, *Law and Judicial Duty* (Cambridge, MA: Harvard University Press 2008).

24. *Ex parte McCardle,* 74 U.S. (7 Wall.) 506, 514 (1869).

25. Kramer argues that the "status of judicial review on the eve of the Federal Convention was . . . uncertain at best." Kramer, *The People Themselves*, 69. It was clear to the delegates, Kramer argues, that there would be "judicial review over state laws," but there was "no similar decision . . . to endorse judicial review of

federal legislation." *Id.* at 75. Indeed, as Kramer argues, "judicial review was, in the context of the times, such a radical departure from experience that even proponents regarded its possibility with what Gordon Wood describes as a 'sense of awe and wonder.'" *Id.* at 65. The more natural mode of enforcing constitutional—e.g., sovereign—limits on the government was presumed to be "by the people rather than in courts." *Id.* at 91. Nonetheless, as Barry Friedman has nicely catalogued, whether the point was explicitly recognized or not, the trend toward judicialization of judicial review was strong in the republic at the time of the Founding. Whether originally conceived of or not, most eventually recognized that it would be necessary—at least (or especially) to control state governments. See Barry Friedman, *The Will of the People: How Public Opinion Has Influenced the Supreme Court and Shaped the Meaning of the Constitution* 5 (New York: Farrar, Straus and Giroux, 2009). Initially, as Friedman writes, there was "remarkably quick acceptance of judicial review, followed by grave threats to the independence of the judiciary as the implications of the practice became evident." *Id.* at 12.

26. In the relevant part, Section 13 of the Judiciary Act of 1789, 1 Stat. 73, provided: "The Supreme Court shall also have appellate jurisdiction from the circuit courts and courts of the several states, in the cases herein after specially provided for; and shall have power to issue writs of prohibition to the district courts, when proceeding as courts of admiralty and maritime jurisdiction, and writs of mandamus, in cases warranted by the principles and usages of law, to any courts appointed, or persons holding office, under the authority of the United States." Marshall conceded that "a mandamus may be directed to courts." But he read the power to issue mandamus against "persons holding office . . . under the authority of the United States," as "in effect the same as to sustain an original action for that paper." If it was an "original action," he concluded, then Congress couldn't do that, since Congress couldn't grant original jurisdiction beyond the grant of the Constitution.

Yet nothing in the language of the act even suggests that reading. The section at issue comes after the act has described the Supreme Court's original jurisdiction. It then continues by explaining its "appellate jurisdiction." The act is saying in effect that when the Court has appellate jurisdiction, it can issue writs of mandamus to "courts" or "persons holding office" under the authority of the United States *"according to the principles and usages of law."* Had Marshall had appellate jurisdiction over Marbury's case, he might have had to answer the question whether, "according to the principles and usages of law," he had the power to issue a mandamus to Madison (or whether that was for another Court, after the Supreme Court completed its appellate review). If he didn't have that power, it would be not because the statute was unconstitutional but because such a writ was beyond the "principles and usages of law." Regardless, given that this was not a case of appellate jurisdiction, what power he might then have was not a proper question for Marshall to answer. It certainly was not a proper question for Marshall to rely upon to strike down a law of Congress.

27. Susan Bloch has indeed established that Marbury had another forum in which he could have filed his suit. Bloch, *The* Marbury *Mystery*, 611–613. Given he did not, she speculates reasonably that the decision to file in the Supreme Court was orchestrated by Marshall to enable him to do precisely what he did. *Id.* 624–627.

28. See also Kramer, quoting Dean Alfange: "It was important to invoke the power of judicial review in order to establish a precedent for its later use and to include in the Reports of the Supreme Court a statement of the reasoning by which the power could be shown to be absolutely necessary. Thus, since judicial review could not safely have been used to invalidate a law that the Republicans cared about, it was necessary to find a law that the Republicans did not care about. And what more perfect law could have been found for this purpose than § 13 of the Judiciary Act of 1789?" Dean Alfange Jr., Marbury v. Madison *and Original Understanding of Judicial Review: In Defense of Traditional Wisdom*, 1993 Sup. Ct. Rev. 329, 367–368 (1993), as quoted in Kramer, *The People Themselves* 124. See also Wilentz, *The Rise of American Democracy* 113, describing political context.

29. Alexander Hamilton, "The Examination Number VI, [2 January 1802]," *Founders Online,* National Archives, last modified April 12, 2018, *available at* link #7. For the original source, see 25 *The Papers of Alexander Hamilton* 484–489 (Harold C. Syrett ed., New York: Columbia University Press, 1977).

30. "From Washington, February 3, 1803," *Columbian Centinel*, February 16, 1803, at 2, quoted in Charles Warren, 1 *The Supreme Court in United States History* 226 (Boston: Little, Brown, 1922).

31. The Repeal Act, 2 Stat. 132 (1802), was then followed a month later by the Judiciary Act of 1802, 2 Stat. 156 (1802).

32. *Stuart v. Laird*, 5 U.S. (1 Cranch) 299, 303 (1803).

33. As Richard Fallon writes, "Over the course of U.S. history, nearly all commentators have agreed that Congress's action in doing so violated the guarantee of Article III that federal judges shall hold their offices during 'good Behaviour.'" Fallon, *Law and Legitimacy* 112.

34. Most commentators believe the Court avoided the issue because it could. The judges whose salary had been canceled were not before the Court. At most, the claim of Stuart was indirect. As Jack Balkin puts it, "[The Court] did not in fact directly address the question whether the abolition of the circuit judgeships violated the life tenure provisions of Article III, perhaps because none of the judges actually affected chose to litigate the issue." Sanford Levinson & Jack M. Balkin, *What Are the Facts of* Marbury v. Madison?, 20 Const. Comment. 255, 260 (2003). Others view the decision as an effort by the Court to avoid further political conflict, as does Charles F. Hobson, *Marshall, the Mandamus Case, and the Judiciary Crisis*, 1801–1803, 72 Geo. Wash. L. Rev.

289, 298 (2003). "The repeal crisis also brought forth Marshall's essential moderation and instinctive caution.... Marshall was acutely aware of the judiciary's weakness and vulnerability.... His overriding concern...was to insure the judiciary's survival by directing a prudent retreat away from 'politics' and into the comfort zone of 'law.' Only in the safety of that refuge could the judiciary consolidate its institutional strength and aspire to elevate its status and authority." *Id.* at 298–299. Importantly, Marshall didn't directly participate in the case, since he had sat on the circuit court that decided the case below. But doubtless, he exercised influence in the case. See Ackerman, *The Failure of the Founding Fathers* 234.

35. Justin Crowe, *Building the Judiciary* 76.

36. Ackerman, *The Failure of the Founding Fathers* 193–194, 221.

37. Kramer, *The People Themselves* 122.

38. Justin Crowe, *Building the Judiciary* 76–77, acknowledges the advisability of Marshall's strategic choices, but claims this establishes that the cases were not about institution building: "As purported episodes of institution building in the aftermath of the repeal of the Judiciary Act of 1801 and the passage of the Judiciary Act of 1802, then, the Marshall Court's decisions in *Marbury* and *Stuart* are hardly noteworthy." *Id.* 77. That's certainly true at the moment of the decisions. But the question is how these decisions enable, not what they created. As Crowe comments about the full range of Marshall opinions, "They altered the strategic environment within which such institution building was already occurring." *Id.* 94. That sense, I suggest, is the right way to understand these first two decisions as well.

39. As described brilliantly by Barry Friedman, the first years of the Court were very hit-and-miss. Powerful political actors from every part of the American republic were open in their contempt or disrespect for the institution. Indeed, the Supreme Court suffered embarrassment after embarrassment at the hands of the states. In case after case, governors and state legislatures insisted that the Supreme Court had no authority to tell them to obey the law. It had no authority to invalidate state law. Thus, the Court could issue its opinions however much it wanted, but in many states (particularly in the South), those opinions would simply be ignored. Indeed, the states routinely failed to even show up at the Court to defend themselves. Georgia even executed a man in the face of a Supreme Court order to the contrary. See Friedman, *The Will of the People* 12.

40. Hamilton's language was almost directly lifted by Chief Justice Marshall in *McCulloch*: "This criterion is the end to which the measure relates as a mean. If the end be clearly comprehended within any of the specified powers, and if the measure have an obvious relation to that end and is not forbidden by any particular provision of the constitution—it may safely be deemed to come within the compass of national authority." Alexander Hamilton, quoted in Randall, *Thomas Jefferson* 506–507.

41. Act of February 25, 1791, Sess. 3, Ch. 10, 1 Stat. 191.

42. Daniel A. Farber, *The Story of* McCulloch: *Banking on National Power*, 20 Const. Comment. 679, 691 (2003).

43. The case was *Osborn v. Bank of the United States,* 22 U.S. 738 (1824). See Mark R. Killenbeck, M'Culloch v. Maryland: *Securing a Nation* 162–166 (Lawrence: University of Kansas Press, 2006).

44. See Hamilton's letter to Washington, February 23, 1791, reprinted in Alexander Hamilton, *Opinion on the Constitutionality of the Bank,* The Founders' Constitution, *available at* link #8.

45. Excerpts from the *OED* for "necessary":

> I. That is needed.
> 1.a. Indispensable, vital, essential; requisite…In the 16th and early 17th centuries the sense frequently approaches "useful" without being "absolutely indispensable."
> [The sample of representative quotes, however, only gives examples of the "Indispensable, vital, essential; requisite" sense, and does not shed any light on the editor's note.]
>
> …
>
> 4. Of an action: that needs to be done; that is done in order to achieve the desired result or effect. if necessary: if required by the circumstances.…1771: "Junius" *Stat Nominis Umbra* (1772) II. lxiv. 298 "In this sense the levy of ship-money…was not necessary." 1819: Shelley *Cenci* III. ii. 51 "Still doubting if that deed Be just which was most necessary."
> III. That must be so; inevitable.
>
> …
>
> 6.a. Inevitably determined or fixed by predestination or the operation of natural laws; happening or existing by an inherent necessity. (In early use also as postmodifier, with plural *necessaries.*) Now chiefly *Philos.* and *Theol.*
> 7. Of an action:
> a. Determined by force of nature or circumstances. *Obs.*

See "necessary, adj. and n.," OED Online, March 2018, Oxford University Press, *available at* link #9.

46. *McCulloch v. the State of Maryland et al.*, 17 U.S. (4 Wheat.) 316, 413–415 (1819).

47. *Stell v. Savannah-Chatham County Bd. of Ed.*, 220 F.Supp 667 (S.D. Ga. 1963), *rev'd* 333 F.2d 55 (5th Cir. 1964), *cert. denied,* 379 U.S. 933 (1964).

48. 220 F.Supp. 667, 684.

49. 318 F.2d 425 (5th Cir. 1963).

50. The modern scholar most attuned to the project of translating constitutional principles into useable doctrine is Richard Fallon. See Richard H. Fallon Jr., *Judicially Manageable Standard and Constitutional Meaning,* 119 Harv. L. Rev. 1274 (2006). As Fallon describes, the crafting of doctrine is the task of rendering constitutional value in usable form. The sensitivity—and creativity—of that project is an expression of fidelity to role.

51. See Robert Nozick, *Anarchy, State, and Utopia* 30–33 (New York: Harper and Row, 1974).

52. Facts drawn from *Ogden v. Gibbons*, 1 N.Y. Ch. Ann. 797 (Ch. Ct. N.Y. 1819).

53. Apparently the bad blood between Ogden and Gibbons went beyond this particular conflict. In 1816, Gibbons challenged Ogden to a duel over his involvement in an unrelated family dispute. See Thomas Cox, *Gibbons v. Ogden, Law, and Society in the Early Republic* 94 (Athens: Ohio University Press, 2009).

54. For early careful work trying to understand what the Framers would have understood "commerce" to mean, see Albert Abel, *The Commerce Clause in the Constitutional Convention and in Contemporary Comment,* 25 Minn. L. Rev. 432, 444 (1941).

55. *United States v. Robertson*, 514 U.S. 669, 671 (1995).

56. *United States v. Coombs*, 37 U.S. (12 Pet.) 72, 79 (1838).

57. For work arguing the Framers did not intend the reach of the commerce power to grow, see Raoul Berger, *Federalism: The Founders' Design* (Norman: University of Oklahoma Press, 1987) (arguing that the Framers intended federal authority to remain limited); Richard A. Epstein, *The Proper Scope of the Commerce Power,* 73 Va. L. Rev. 1387, 1388, 1444 (1987) ("I think that the expansive construction of the clause accepted by the New Deal Supreme Court is wrong.... Congress used a legal fiction to expand federal jurisdiction beyond its original grant"); Randy E. Barnett, *The Original Meaning of the Commerce Clause,* 68 U. Chi. L. Rev. 101, 146 (2001) (arguing that the original meaning of "commerce" was a narrow one that could not support the expansion of power that modern commerce clause interpretations do today); Albert S. Abel, *The Commerce Clause in the Constitutional Convention and in Contemporary Comment,* 25 Minn. L. Rev. 432, 493 (1941) (describing "the restricted field which was deemed at the time [of the Founding] to constitute Commerce"); Gary Lawson & Patricia B. Granger, *The "Proper" Scope of Federal Power: A Jurisdictional Interpretation of the Sweeping Clause,* 43 Duke L.J. 267, 270–271 (1993) (arguing that the Framers did not think of the necessary-and-proper clause as "a grant of general legislative power" but rather as "a jurisdictional limitation on the scope of federal power [and thus a] vital part of the constitutional design"); Charles J. Cooper, *The Demise of Federalism,* 20 Urb. Law. 239 (1988) (chronicling the growth of a national government with "virtually unlimited power...notwithstanding [the] historical evidence of the Framers' original intent").

For work arguing the Framers did intend the reach of the commerce clause power to grow, see Walton H. Hamilton & Douglas Adair, *The Power to Govern* (New York: W. W. Norton, 1937) (arguing that the Framers intended for the commerce clause to support a federal government that could grow alongside the national economy); Herbert Hovenkamp, *Judicial Restraint and Constitutional Federalism: The Supreme Court's* Lopez *and* Seminole Tribe *Decisions,* 96 Colum. L. Rev. 2213 (1996) (describing the *Lopez* and *Seminole Tribe* decisions as "instances where the Court's fervor to intervene forced it to depart from the historical meaning of the Constitution"); William W. Crosskey, *Politics and the Constitution in the History of the United States* (Chicago: University of Chicago

Press, 1953) (arguing that the Framers intended for Congress to have general legislative authority and decrying the 1930s Court's too-narrow understanding of the commerce clause); Charles Fried, *Federalism—Why Should We Care?*, 6 Harv. J.L. & Pub. Pol'y 1, 2 (1982) (noting that when it comes to "the allocation of power between the states and the federal government, . . . the seeds of what we see now may very well have been present then").

For the best accounts of the mixed evidence, see Ernest A. Young, *Making Federalism Doctrine: Fidelity, Institutional Competence, and Compensating Adjustments*, 46 Wm. & Mary L. Rev. 1733, 1767, 1804–1805 (2005); Keith E. Whittington, *Constitutional Construction: Divided Powers and Constitutional Meaning* 75 (Cambridge, MA: Harvard University Press, 1999) ("[Ratification] . . . left many issues regarding the nature of American federalism unresolved and available to future debate"); Gordon S. Wood, *The Creation of the American Republic, 1776–1787* 525–526 (Chapel Hill: University of North Carolina Press, 2009) ("as crucial as the idea of federalism was to the Federalists in explaining the operation of their new system, it seems clear that few of them actually conceived of it in full before the Constitution was written and debated").

## Chapter Three

1. Matthew Weiner, the show's creator, acknowledges that part of his intent in writing to show was to understand his own baby-boomer parents: "Part of the show is trying to figure out—this sounds really ineloquent—trying to figure out what is the deal with my parents. Am I them? Because you know you are. . . . The truth is it's such a trope to sit around and bash your parents. I don't want it to be like that. They are my inspiration, let's not pretend." Alex Witchel, "Smoking, Womanizing, Drinking, Writing: How Matthew Weiner Turned Early-'60s Advertising Culture into the Smartest Show on Television," *New York Times*, June 22, 2008, at A33. Yet the show does heap scorn on his parents' generation, prompting the audience to act as critics of the culture of the 1960s, because of what Caroline Levine calls the "shock of the banal": "We are startled less by sensational plot twists or characters' hidden depths, in other words, than by the recognition that eating raw eggs or smacking a neighbor's child across the face used to be so awfully ordinary." Caroline Levine, "The Shock of the Banal," *in Mad Men, Mad World: Sex, Politics, Style, and the 1960's* 133, 136 (Lauren M. E. Goodlad, Lilya Kaganovsky, & Robert A. Rushing eds., Durham, NC: Duke University Press, 2013).

2. Greg Carvey, "Recalling Clarence Jordan, Radical Disciple," *Huffington Post*, June 3, 2012, 9:02 a.m., updated August 3, 2012, *available at* link #10.

3. Clarence Jordan, *The Cotton Patch Version of Luke and Acts: Jesus' Doings and the Happenings* 46–47 (New York: Koinonia Publications, Association Press, 1969).

4. Clarence Jordan, *The Cotton Patch Version of Paul's Epistles* 7–11 (New York: Koinonia Publications, Association Press, 1968).

5. Antoine Berman, The Experience of the Foreign: Culture and Translation in Romantic Germany 233 (Albany: State University of New York Press, 1992).

6. George Steiner, *After Babel: Aspects of Language and Translation* 245 (New York: Oxford University Press, 1975).

7. That limit was changed in 1988 with a rule that capped attorney's fees at 20 percent of an award. Pub. L. No. 100-687, 102 Stat. 4105, 4108 (1988). In 2006, Congress added that the Department of Veterans Affairs may issue additional regulations limiting attorney fees, with fees not exceeding 20 percent of benefits awarded presumed reasonable. Pub. L. No. 109-461, 120 Stat. 3403, 3406 (2006). See Title 38, § 5904(d).

8. *Walters v. National Association of Radiation Survivors*, 473 U.S. 305 (1985).

9. Another way to understand the oddness of the Court's result is to imagine Congress had changed the currency in 1980 from dollars to schmallers. Then clearly the Court would have faced the question of which exchange rate to use—the one indexed to 1868 or the one indexed to 1986.

10. Francis Lieber describes two similar cases in *Legal and Political Hermeneutics, or Principles of Interpretation and Construction in Law and Politics, with Remarks on Precedents and Authorities* 131 (Boston: Charles C. Little and James Brown, enlarged ed. 1839): "Before a graduate can become a fellow he must take an oath that he has not otherwise an income above a certain amount, expressed in pounds sterling. Yet there are many who have more and nevertheless take the oath. Bishop Fleetwood wrote a whole volume to prove that the oath might be taken, because this condition was prescribed by Henry VI., when, as he shows from the prices of the necessaries of life, that prescribed small amount was worth perhaps twenty times what it is now, when in short a pound sterling has a totally different meaning."

11. Remigio Sabbadini, *Del tradurre i classici antichi in Italia*, Atene e Roma 201–217, July-August 1900; Leonardo Bruni, "On Correct Translation," *in The Humanism of Leonardo Bruni: Selected Texts* 217–228 (Gordon Griffiths, James Hankins, & David Thompson trans., Binghamton, NY: Medieval and Renaissance Texts and Studies, 1987).

12. David Bellos, *Is That a Fish in Your Ear? Translation and the Meaning of Everything* 4383 (New York: Farrar, Straus and Giroux, 2011) (Kindle ed.).

13. See, e.g., *Griswold v. Connecticut,* 381 U.S. 479, 522 (1965) (Black, J., dissenting) ("I realize that many good and able men have eloquently spoken and written, sometimes in rhapsodical strains, about the duty of this Court to keep the Constitution in tune with the times. The idea is that the Constitution must be changed from time to time and that this Court is charged with a duty to make those changes"); *Katz v. United States*, 389 U.S. 347, 373 (1967) (Black, J., dissenting) ("I will not distort the words of the Amendment in order to 'keep the Constitution up to date' or 'to bring it into harmony with the times'"); *Harper v. Virginia Board of Elections*, 383 U.S. 663, 675–676 (1966)

(Black, J., dissenting). See also *West Coast Hotel Co. v. Parrish*, 300 U.S. 379, 402 (1937) (Sutherland, J., dissenting).

14. As Daniel Farber suggests, "Probably the most prevalent argument against originalism is that it is too static, and thereby disregards the need to keep the Constitution up to date with changing times. Originalism is unworkable, then, even if the original intent can be reliably determined, because originalism would make the Constitution itself unworkable." Daniel A. Farber, *The Originalism Debate: A Guide for the Perplexed*, 49 Ohio St. L.J. 1085, 1095 (1989). Compare *Harper v. Virginia Board of Elections*, 383 U.S. 663, 677–678 (1966) (Black J., dissenting): "The Court's justification for consulting its own notions rather than following the original meaning of the Constitution ... apparently is based on the belief of the majority of the Court that for this Court to be bound by the original meaning of the Constitution is an intolerable and debilitating evil; that our Constitution should not be shackled 'to the political theory of a particular era,' and that to save the country from the original Constitution the Court must have the constant power to renew it and keep it abreast of this Court's more enlightened theories of what is best for our society."

15. Charles Reich would disagree about Black's missing the point. Reich, certainly the most ingenious of translators, has found a way of reading Black's opinions as translations, despite their apparent rejection of anything like translation. Charles Reich, "The Living Constitution and the Court's Role," *in Hugo Black and the Supreme Court: A Symposium* 139–149 (Stephen P. Strickland ed., Indianapolis, IN: Bobbs-Merrill, 1967).

16. Terence Ball & J. G. A. Pocock, "Introduction," in *Conceptual Change and the Constitution* 17 (Terence Ball & J. G. A. Pocock eds., Lawrence: University Press of Kansas, 1988).

17. *United States v. Philadelphia National Bank*, 374 U.S. 321, 346 (1963) provides a good example. There the Court held that a stock acquisition provision in § 7 of the Clayton Antitrust Act, though "in haec verba" with an earlier amendment, "must be deemed expanded in its new context." See also *In the Matter of Sinclair*, 870 F.2d 1340, 1342 (7th Cir. 1989) ("What 'clearly' means one thing to a reader unacquainted with the circumstances of the utterance—including social conventions prevailing at the time of the drafting—may mean something else to a reader with a different background"). Cf. Letter from James Madison to H. Lee (June 25, 1824) and letter from James Madison to N. P. Trist (March 2, 1827), *in Letters and Other Writings of James Madison* 442–443, 565 (Philadelphia, PA: J. B. Lippincott, 1865), discussing change in meaning of words as a problem to the constant interpretation of the Constitution.

18. Bellos, *Is That a Fish in Your Ear?* 4383.

19. Bo Hanson, *Application of Rules in New Situations: A Hermeneutical Study* 13 (Lund, Sweden: Liber Läromedel/Gleerup, 1977); Cass R. Sunstein, *Interpreting Statutes in the Regulatory State*, 103 Harv. L. Rev. 405, 493–494 (1989).

20. Hence when the *Wall Street Journal* writes in its New York edition of "Mr. [Richard] Branson, an English public-school dropout" (see Ken Wells, "High Flier: Adventure Capitalist Is Nipping at the Tail of Big British Airways," *Wall Street Journal*, May 22, 1992, at 1, col. 6), only questions are raised.

21. Oliver Wendell Holmes, *The Theory of Legal Interpretation*, 12 Harv. L. Rev. 417, 417–418 (1899). I don't mean that these formulations are equivalent. I mean only that whatever formulation is selected, the same conclusion applies.

22. See, e.g., *McLaughlin v. Richland Shoe Co.*, 486 U.S. 128 (1988); *Goodyear Atomic Corp. v. Miller*, 486 U.S. 174 (1988).

23. As Judge Easterbrook puts it, speaking of statutes: "Legislation speaks across the decades, during which legal institutions and linguistic conventions change. To decode words, one must frequently reconstruct the legal and political culture of the drafters." *In the Matter of Sinclair*, 870 F.2d 1340, 1342 (7th Cir. 1989). Cf. Edward S. Corwin, *Judicial Review in Action*, 74 U. Pa. L. Rev. 639, 658 (1926) ("In the case of the Constitution...the question at once arises whether this is the ordinary meaning of 1789 or the present year of grace. The divergence is, naturally, at times a very broad one").

24. George Steiner, *After Babel* 414.

25. A theory that Steiner, at least, believes is long-standing and quite stable: "Despite [the] rich history, and despite the calibre of those who have written about the art and theory of translation, the number of original, significant ideas in the subject remains very meager.... Over some two thousand years of argument and precept, the beliefs and disagreements voiced about the nature of translation have been almost the same. Identical theses, familiar moves and refutations in debate recur, nearly without exception, from Cicero and Quintilian to the present day." Steiner, *After Babel* 238–239. Or again: "List Seneca, Saint Jerome, Luther, Dryden, Holderlin, Novalis, Schleiermacher, Nietzsche, Ezra Pound, Valery, MacKenna, Franz Rosenzweig, Walter Benjamin, Quine—and you have very nearly the sum total of those who have said anything fundamental or new about translation." *Id.* at 269.

26. Steiner, *After Babel* 249.

27. Steiner, *After Babel* 251.

28. Steiner, *After Babel* 249–250.

29. Renato Poggioli, "The Added Artificer," in *On Translation* 137, 146 (Reuben A. Brower ed., Cambridge, MA: Harvard University Press, 1959).

30. Steiner, *After Babel* 402.

31. Poggioli, "The Added Artificer," 145–146. See also Bayard Quincy Morgan, "Bibliography," in *On Translation* 271, 275 (describing Samuel Johnson's view: "A translator is to be like his author: it is not his business to excel him"); Vladimir Nabokov, "The Art of Translation," *The New Republic*, August 4, 1941, at 160; Steiner, *After Babel* 402, 302 ("Fidelity is ethical, but also in the full sense economic").

32. Benedetto Croce, quoted in Morgan, "Bibliography," in *On Translation* 278.

33. Reuben A. Brower, "Introduction," in *On Translation* 6.

34. Steiner, *After Babel* 296–297.

35. Bruni, *On Correct Translation* 220–221.

36. Steiner, *After Babel* 262–263.

37. Ball & Pocock, "Introduction" 107.

38. Steiner, *After Babel* 375–376.

39. From Thomas Jefferson to William Johnson, June 12, 1823, *Founders Online, National Archives,* last modified April 12, 2018, *available at* link #11.

40. Joseph Story, 1 *Commentaries on the Constitution of the United States: With a Preliminary Review of the Constitutional History of the Colonies and the States, Before the Adoption of the Constitution* 283 (Boston, Charles C. Little and James Brown, 2nd ed. 1851).

41. Paul Brest, "The Misconceived Quest for the Original Understanding," in *Interpreting Law and Literature: A Hermeneutic Reader* 81 (Sanford Levinson & Steven Mailloux eds., Evanston, IL: Northwestern University Press, 1988), originally published as Paul Brest, *The Misconceived Quest for the Original Understanding,* 60 B.U. L. Rev. 204 (1980) ("*The Misconceived Quest*").

42. William Blackstone, 1 *Commentaries on the Laws of England: In Four Books* 59 (William Draper Lewis ed., Philadelphia: Rees Welsh & Company, 1898) (1765).

43. Eugene A. Nida, "Principles of Translation as Exemplified by Bible Translating," in *On Translation* 22–24.

44. Roman Jakobson, "On Linguistic Aspects of Translation," in *On Translation* 232, 236.

45. See *West Virginia Hospitals v. Casey,* 499 U.S. 83 (1991).

46. Richard A. Posner, *The Problems of Jurisprudence* 263 (Cambridge, MA: Harvard University Press, 1990); Paul Freund made a similar point about an air force. Robert C. Post, *Constitutional Domains: Democracy, Community, Management* 33 (Cambridge, MA: Harvard University Press, 1995).

47. Posner, *The Problems of Jurisprudence* 267; Holmes, *The Theory of Legal Interpretation,* 130.

48. James Boyd White, *Justice as Translation: An Essay in Cultural and Legal Criticism* 235 (Chicago: University of Chicago Press, 1990).

49. Gregory Rabassa, "No Two Snowflakes are Alike: Translation as Metaphor," in *The Craft of Translation* 9 (John Biguenet & Rainer Schulte eds., Chicago: University of Chicago Press, 1989).

50. Bellos, *Is That a Fish in Your Ear?* 4428.

51. Brest, *The Misconceived Quest,* 82–83.

52. Cicero, *On Invention: The Best Kind of Orator: Topics* 365 (H. M. Hubbell trans., Cambridge, MA: Harvard University Press, 1949).

53. See Antonin Scalia in *Michael H. v. Gerald D.,* 491 U.S. 110 (1989) and John Marshall Harlan II in *Poe v. Ullman,* 367 U.S. 497 (1961). See also Jack M. Balkin, *Tradition, Betrayal, and the Politics of Deconstruction,* 11 Cardozo L. Rev. 1613,

1614–1629 (1990); Laurence H. Tribe & Michael C. Dorf, *Levels of Generality in the Definition of Rights*, 57 U. Chi. L. Rev. 1057, 1058 (1990).

54. Reuben A. Brower, "Introduction" in *On Translation* 3.

55. Reuben A. Brower, "Seven Agamemnons," in *On Translation* 173.

56. Steiner, *After Babel* 10.

57. Lieber, *Legal and Political Hermeneutics* 126.

58. Lieber, *Legal and Political Hermeneutics* 136.

59. Obviously, I am not the first to suggest a method of interpretation similar to translation. Paul Brest first described the practice as a charitable understanding of originalism in Brest, *The Misconceived Quest*. And as I've already described, Francis Lieber had a practically identical device he calls "construction." So too did Richard A. Posner, at least at times, under the description of "imaginative reconstruction of a legislature's purpose." Posner rejects the skeptics' claim that such reconstruction is not possible: "Some strict constructionists argue that imaginative reconstruction of a legislature's purposes is impossible because there is no such thing as 'collective intent'; there is just the intent of the individual legislators who vote for or against a statute. That is the autistic theory of interpretation. It denies the possibility of meaningful interpersonal communication and agreement, of a 'meeting of minds.' The theory is bad philosophy, bad psychology, and bad law." Richard A. Posner, *How Judges Think* 194 (Cambridge, MA: Harvard University Press, 2008). Likewise, Kermit Roosevelt has mapped a method called "meaning originalism" that is similar to the practice I describe as translation. Kermit Roosevelt III, *The Myth of Judicial Activism: Making Sense of Supreme Court Decisions* 485–488 (New Haven, CT: Yale University Press, 2006).

60. For others reflecting on this approach, see Le Cheng & King Kui Sin, *Terminological Equivalence in Legal Translation: A Semiotic Approach*, Semiotica: J. of the Int. Ass'n for Semiotic Stud., Nov. 10, 2008, at 33; Vincent Crapanzano, "Text, Context, and Fidelity in American Jurisprudence: The Metaphoricity of Translation," in *Translation and Ethnography: The Anthropological Challenge of Intercultural Understanding* 44–62 (Tucson: University of Arizona Press, 2003); Jeanne Gaaker, "Iudex Translator: The Reign of Finitude," in *Methods of Comparative Law* 252–269 (Pier Giuseppe Monateri ed., Cheltenham, UK: Edward Elgar, 2012); Rina Villars, *Same-Sex Marriage and the Spanish Constitution: The Linguistic-Legal Meaning Interface*, 30 Int. J. Semiotics of Law 273 (June 2017).

61. See Antonin Scalia, *Originalism: The Lesser Evil*, 57 U. Cinn. L. Rev. 849 (1989). I describe one-step and two-step originalism more extensively in *Fidelity in Translation*, 71 Tex. L. Rev. 1166, 1183–1184 (1993). In Balkin's terms, the one-step is an "original expected application" originalist; I agree with him that one-step originalism "cannot account for the modern protection of constitutional civil rights and civil liberties"—and much else as well. Balkin, *Living Originalism* 2317.

62. *United States v. Classic*, 313 U.S. 299 (1941).

63. 313 U.S. at 315–316.

64. 313 U.S. at 318–319.

65. See David A. Strauss, *The Living Constitution* (New York: Oxford University Press, 2010). See also David A. Strauss, *Common Law, Common Ground, and Jefferson's Principle*, 112 Yale L.J. 1717 (2003); David A. Strauss, *Common Law Constitutional Interpretation*, 63 U. Chi. L. Rev. 877 (1996).

66. This was the view advanced most famously by Richard Posner. See his *Economic Analysis of Law* 98–99 (Boston: Little, Brown, 1973).

67. The quote is drawn from Brief for the United States as *amicus curiae* at 24, *Thornburgh v. American College of Obstetricians and Gynecologists*, No. 84-495, June 11, 1986, cited by Edwin Meese, Address to the Federalist Society Lawyers Division (November 15, 1985), *available at* link #12.

68. Balkin, *Living Originalism* 332.

69. Balkin, *Living Originalism* 332 (emphasis in the original).

*Chapter Four*

1. *Gibbons v. Ogden*, 22 U.S. 1, 195 (1824).

2. *Gibbons v. Ogden*, 22 U.S. 1, 9–10 (1824).

3. *Gibbons v. Ogden*, 22 U.S. 1, 85 (1824).

4. *Garcia v. San Antonio Metro. Transit Auth.*, 469 U.S. 528, 584 (1985) (O'Connor, J., dissenting).

5. See book III of Adam Smith, *The Wealth of Nations* (1776; repr., New York: Penguin, 1982).

6. Franklin D. Roosevelt, "Press Conference," May 31, 1935, online by Gerhard Peters and John T. Woolley, *The American Presidency Project*, *available at* link #13.

7. *Pensacola Tel. Co. v. Western Union Tel. Co.*, 96 U.S. 1, 9 (1877).

8. *In re Debs*, 158 U.S. 564, 590–591 (1895). See also Maurice M. Feuerlicht Jr., *The Interstate Commerce Clause and NRA*, 9 Ind. L.J. 434, 435–441 (1934).

9. Thomas Reed Powell, *The Child Labor Law, the Tenth Amendment and the Commerce Clause*, 3 So. L.Q .175, 200 (1918). See also David P. Currie, *The Constitution in the Supreme Court: The First Hundred Years, 1789–1888* 429–430 (Chicago: University of Chicago Press, 1985), discussing Waite's view of *Pensacola Telegraph*, 96 U.S. 1.

10. *Stafford v. Wallace*, 258 U.S. 495, 518–519 (1922).

11. William O. Douglas, *Recent Trends in Constitutional Law*, 30 Or. L. Rev. 279, 285 (1951).

12. *Garcia v. San Antonio Metropolitan Transit Authority*, 469 U.S. 528, 584 (1985).

13. Edward Corwin, *Constitutional Revolution, Ltd.* 19 (Claremont, CA: Pomona College, Scripts College, Claremont Colleges, 1941).

14. *United States v. E. C. Knight Co.*, 156 U.S. 1, 16 (1895).

15. See Lawrence Lessig, *Translating Federalism:* United States v. Lopez, 1995 Sup. Ct. Rev. 125 (1995).

16. Augustine L. Humes, *The Power of Congress over Combinations Affecting Interstate Commerce*, 17 Harv. L. Rev. 83, 99 (1903) ("In regard to the regulation of such a monopoly of manufacture, it cannot be doubted that the power of Congress extends further than does that act").

17. As would the Court just a few terms later. See Currie, *The Constitution in the Supreme Court, 1888–1986* at 23, citing *Addyston Pipe & Steel Co. v. United States*, 175 U.S. 211, 240 (1899).

18. What was central to Chief Justice Fuller's opinion was that there was no necessary connection between the monopoly of manufacturing and the interference in interstate commerce. However likely the interference was, it was not shown, nor was the intent to interfere shown. Since the essence of the Sherman Act violation was an intent to obstruct interstate commerce, what the opinion says is simply that this level of intent had not been demonstrated. It could not be presumed, that is, and it certainly had not been shown. See *Knight*, 156 U.S. at 17 ("Nevertheless it does not follow that an attempt to monopolize, or the actual monopoly of, the manufacture was an attempt, whether executory or consummated, to monopolize commerce, even though, in order to dispose of the product, the instrumentality of commerce was necessarily invoked. There was nothing in the proofs to indicate any intention to put a restraint upon trade or commerce, and the fact, as we have seen, that trade or commerce might be indirectly affected was not enough to entitle complainants to a decree").

19. Lessig, *Translating Federalism*.

20. For a collection of how these distinctions get applied, see F. D. G. Ribble, *State and National Power over Commerce* 120–121 n. 72 (New York: Columbia University Press, 1937): "Examples of exclusion in cases of particular activities may prove useful. 'Bookkeeping, it is said, is not interstate commerce. True it is not.' *Interstate Commerce Commission v. Goodrich Transit Co.*, 224 U.S. 194, 216 (1912). The making of contracts for the insertion of advertising matter in *The Saturday Evening Post*, *The Ladies' Home Journal*, and *The Country Gentleman* was declared not to be interstate commerce. *Blumenstock Bros. v. Curtis Publishing Co.*, 252 U.S. 436 (1920). Notable recent cases have presented concepts of certain activities as not being interstate commerce. See *A. L. A. Schechter Poultry Corp. v. United States*, 295 U.S. 495 (1935); *United States v. Butler*, 297 U.S. 1 (1936); *Carter v. Carter Coal Co.*, 298 U.S. 238 (1936). Cf. *Ramsey Co. v. Associated Bill Posters of the United States and Canada*, 260 U.S. 501 (1922); *Indiana Farmer's Guide Publishing Co. v. Prairie Farmer Publishing Co.*, 293 U.S. 268 (1934). An exhibition of baseball, 'although made for money would not be called trade or commerce in the commonly accepted use of those words.' *Federal Baseball Club of Baltimore v. National League of Professional Baseball Clubs*, 259 U.S. 200, 209 (1922). See 19 Mich. L. Rev. 867 (1921). For other instances of activities declared not to be interstate commerce, see *Metropolitan Opera Co. v. Hammerstein*, 147 N.Y. Supp. 535 (1914); *American Baseball Club of Chicago v. Chase*, 149 N.Y. Supp. 6 (1914); *In re Oriental Society*, Bankrupt, 104 Fed. 975

(E.D. Pa. 1900); *National League of Professional Baseball Clubs v. Federal Baseball Club of Baltimore*, 269 Fed. 681 (Ct. of App. D.C. 1920) (affirmed in *Federal Baseball Club of Baltimore v. National League of Professional Baseball Clubs, supra*)." See also Corwin, *Constitutional Revolution, Ltd.* 24 (describing limits on "commerce").

21. William H. Nicholls, *Constitutional Aspects of Public Regulation of Business Price Policies*, 25 J. Farm. Econ. 560, 564–565 (1943); Edward S. Corwin, *Congress's Power to Prohibit Commerce: A Crucial Constitutional Issue*, 18 Cornell L. Q. 477, 503 (1933), quoting *Farmers' Loan & T. Co. v. Minnesota*, 280 U.S. 204, 211 (1930).

22. *Champion v. Ames*, 188 U.S. 321, 356 (1903); *Hipolite Egg Co. v. United States*, 220 U.S. 45, 57–58 (1911); *Caminetti v. United States*, 242 U.S. 470, 491–492 (1917) (White Slave Traffic Act).

23. *Swift & Co. v. United States*, 196 U.S. 375 (1905); Forrest Revere Black, *Commerce Clause and the New Deal*, 20 Cornell L.Q. 169 (1935) (cited in n. 34: "Chief Justice Taft characterized the *Swift* case as 'a milestone in the interpretation of the commerce clause of the Constitution'").

24. *Swift & Co. v. United States*, 196 U.S. 397 (1905); Forrest Revere Black, *Commerce Clause and the New Deal*, 20 Cornell L.Q. 179 (1934–1935).

25. *Southern Railway Company v. United States*, 222 U.S. 20, 26–27 (1911); *Interstate Commerce Commission v. Goodrich Transit Co.*, 224 U.S. 194, 211 (1912); *Houston, E. & W. Texas Ry. Co. v. United States*, 234 U.S. 342, 353–354 (1914); *United States v. Ferger*, 250 U.S. 199, 204 (1919); *Stafford v. Wallace*, 258 U.S. 495, 521 (1922).

26. *Champion v. Ames*, 188 U.S. 321, 371 (1903).

27. *Houston, E. & W. Texas Ry. Co. v. United States*, 234 U.S. 342 (1914).

28. *Houston, E. & W. Texas Ry. Co. v. United States*, 234 U.S. 342, 351 (1914).

29. *Hammer v. Dagenhart*, 247 U.S. 251 (1918).

30. Edward S. Corwin. *The Commerce Power Versus States Rights: "Back to the Constitution"* 164–165 (Princeton, NJ: Princeton University Press, 1936), citing a brief for the appellees in *Hammer*.

31. *Hammer v. Dagenhart*, 247 U.S. 251, 276 (1918).

32. As the Court wrote: "To sustain this statute would not be in our judgment a recognition of the lawful exertion of congressional authority over interstate commerce, but would sanction an invasion by the federal power of the control of a matter purely local in its character, and over which no authority has been delegated to Congress in conferring the power to regulate commerce among the states." *Hammer v. Dagenhart*, 247 U.S. 251, 276 (1918).

33. *Hammer v. Dagenhart*, 247 U.S. 251, 272 (1918).

34. See Henry Wolf Biklé, *The Commerce Power and* Hammer v. Dagenhart, 67 U. Pa. L. Rev. 21, 29 (1919); *Kentucky Whip and Collar Co. v. Illinois Cent. R.R. Co.*, 299 U.S. 334, 350 (1937) ("In the *Hammer* case, the Court concluded that the Act of Congress there under consideration had as its aim the placing of local production under federal control") (citations omitted).

35. *Hammer v. Dagenhart*, 247 U.S. 251, 271–272 (1918).

36. *U.S. v. Doremus*, 249 U.S. 86, 94 (1919). As David Currie writes, "Any hopes that *Hammer* portended an era of increased protection of state prerogatives, however, were chilled by later decisions. In the very next term, for example, in *United States v. Doremus*, the Court permitted Congress effectively to regulate narcotics sales under the cloak of the federal tax power." Currie, *The Constitution in the Supreme Court, 1888–1986* at 98.

37. Horace Kallen, quoted in Alan Brinkley, *The End of Reform: New Deal Liberalism in Recession and War* 155 (New York: Vintage, 1996).

38. Herbert Croly, quoted in Brinkley, *The End of Reform* 155.

39. Donald Richberg, quoted in Brinkley, *The End of Reform* 43.

40. R. G. Tugwell, "The Protagonists: Roosevelt and Hoover," *Antioch Review*, Dec. 1953.

41. P. H. Irons, *The New Deal Lawyers* 19 (Princeton, NJ: Princeton University Press, 1982).

42. Irons, *The New Deal Lawyers* 23.

43. Brinkley, *The End of Reform* 39.

44. Irons, *The New Deal Lawyers* 20.

45. Irons, *The New Deal Lawyers* 20.

46. Thurman W. Arnold, *The Symbols of Government* 118 (New Haven, CT: Yale University Press, 1935; repr., New York: Harcourt, Brace & World, 1962), page numbers refer to the 1962 edition.

47. The three unanimous opinions issued on May 27, 1935, were for *A. L. A. Schechter Poultry Corporation v. U.S.*, 295 U.S. 495 (1935), *Louisville Joint Stock Land Bank v. Radford*, 295 U.S. 555 (1935), and *Humphrey's Ex'r v. U.S.*, 295 U.S. 602 (1935).

48. Irons, *The New Deal Lawyers* 104.

49. *Panama Refining Co. v. Ryan*, 293 U.S. 388, 430 (1935).

50. Justice Cardozo dissented, but not because he did not agree with the principle that a standard had to limit delegated discretion. Instead, he believed, with respect to one key provision, there was sufficient clarity about that standard. *Panama Refining Co. v. Ryan*, 293 U.S. 388, 434 (1935).

51. See, e.g., *Local 167 v. United States*, 291 U.S. 293 (1934) (Sherman Act covers attempts to establish a local monopoly on poultry); *Thornton v. United States*, 271 U.S. 414 (1926) (Congress can require federal employees to dip cattle (within a single state) for the purpose of preventing disease); *Board of Trade of City of Chicago v. Olsen*, 262 U.S. 1 (1923) (Congress can regulate the market in grain futures, even if much trading is confined to Chicago); *Stafford v. Wallace*, 258 U.S. 495 (1922) (Congress could regulate meatpackers and stockyards preemptively, without waiting for monopolies to develop; "streams of commerce from one part of the country to another, which are ever flowing, are in their very essence the commerce among the states and with foreign nations, which historically it was one of the chief purposes of the Constitution to bring under

national protection and control." *Id.* at 519); *United States v. Ferger*, 250 U.S. 199 (1919) (Congress could punish the use of fraudulent bills of lading involving nonexistent interstate commerce); *United States v. Patten*, 226 U.S. 525 (1913) (conspiring in the New York Cotton Exchange to corner the market on cotton was sufficiently direct a restraint on interstate commerce to be covered by the Sherman Act).

52. The government argued firmly that Schechter's chickens moved across state borders. Of all live poultry marketed in New York City, all the freight receipts, and over 96 percent of all receipts (including by freight, by truck, and by express) were from other states, with thirty-five states contributing. New York City consumed, on average, over 175 rail cars' worth of poultry a week, in contrast to Chicago's 30 and Philadelphia's, Boston's, and Newark's 10–12 each; in 1933, over 73 percent of the country's "original carload shipments" of live poultry were unloaded in New York City. Because of this, live poultry markets in some other cities, including Boston and Newark, based their prices on the New York City price. The brief notes that the New York City price was published daily in "representative newspapers" in 23 "Western and Southern states" (and lists these newspapers); two of these newspapers *only* published the New York price. Graphs plotting prices in New York City versus prices in Chicago, Louisville, and Missouri are included. Brief for the United States at 30–37, *A. L. A. Schechter Poultry Corp. v. United States*, 295 U.S. 495 (1935).

53. See *Swift & Co. v. United States*, 196 U.S. 375, 387 (1905) (butchered meat), *Lemke v. Farmers' Grain Co.*, 258 U.S. 50, 55 (1922) (grain), *Stafford v. Wallace*, 258 U.S. 495, 519 (1922) (livestock), *Board of Trade of City of Chicago v. Olsen*, 262 U.S. 1, 35, 43 (1923) (grain futures), *Tagg Bros. & Moorhead v. United States*, 280 U.S. 420, 439 (1930) (livestock).

54. *A. L. A. Schechter Poultry Corporation v. U.S.*, 295 U.S. 495, 546 (1935).

55. *A. L. A. Schechter Poultry Corporation v. U.S.*, 295 U.S. 495, 546 (1935).

56. *A. L. A. Schechter Poultry Corporation v. U.S.*, 295 U.S. 495, 549 (1935).

57. *A. L. A. Schechter Poultry Corporation v. U.S.*, 295 U.S. 495, 554 (1935).

58. *Railroad Retirement Board v. Alton Railroad Co.*, 295 U.S. 330 (1935).

59. *Railroad Retirement Board v. Alton Railroad Co.*, 295 U.S. 330, 368 (1935).

60. 298 U.S. 238 (1936).

61. *Carter v. Carter Coal Co.*, 298 U.S. 238, 308 (1936).

62. *Carter v. Carter Coal Co.*, 298 U.S. 238, 308 (1936).

63. Corwin, *The Commerce Power Versus States Rights* 208 (emphasis added).

64. *U.S. v. Lopez*, 514 U.S. 549, 585 (1995).

65. *Carter v. Carter Coal Co.*, 298 U.S. 238, 317–318 (1936).

66. *Carter v. Carter Coal Co.*, 298 U.S. 238, 327–328 (1936).

67. Irons, *The New Deal Lawyers* 75.

68. Corwin, *The Commerce Power Versus States Rights* 156.

69. See, for example, Lindsay Rogers, *The Postal Power of Congress: A Study in Constitutional Expansion* 180 (Baltimore, MD: Johns Hopkins University Studies

in Historical and Political Science, series XXXIV, no. 2, 1916): "If congressional control may be thus extended, every business and every individual needing to use the mails would become subject to federal regulation on the vague ground of public policy. The reserved powers of the states would then exist only by the sufferance of Congress, and the cardinal theory of the American system—that the federal government is one of enumerated powers—would become a cynical fiction."

70. *United States v. E. C. Knight Co.*, 156 U.S. 1, 16 (1895).

71. Corwin, *The Commerce Power Versus States Rights* 42–43, citing *Dooley v. U.S.*, 183 U.S. 151, 171 (1901): "If that power of regulation is absolutely unrestricted as respects interstate commerce, then the very unity the Constitution was framed to secure can be set at naught by a legislative body created by that instrument."

*Kidd v. Pearson*, 128 U.S. 1, 21 (1888): "If it be held that [the regulation of interstate commerce] includes the regulation of all such manufactures as are intended to be the subject of commercial transactions in the future, it is impossible to deny that it would also include all productive industries that contemplate the same thing. The result would be that Congress would be invested, to the exclusion of the states, with the power to regulate not only manufactures, but also agriculture, horticulture, stock-raising, domestic fisheries, mining—in short, every branch of human industry."

*Hooper v. California*, 155 U.S. 648, 655 (1895) (holding that a state law criminalizing the procuring of insurance for state residents from a company that did not comply with state law was not regulation of interstate commerce): "If the power to regulate interstate commerce applied to all the incidents to which said commerce might give rise and to all contracts which might be made in the course of its transaction, that power would embrace the entire sphere of mercantile activity in any way connected with trade between the States and would exclude state control over many contracts purely domestic in their nature."

*Heisler v. Thomas Colliery Co.*, 260 U.S. 245, 259–260 (1922) (holding that a higher state tax rate on a certain kind of coal, produced almost exclusively within the state but largely consumed elsewhere, was not a regulation of interstate commerce): "If the possibility, or indeed certainty, of exportation of a product or article from a State determines it to be in interstate commerce before the commencement of its movement from the State, it would seem to follow that it is in such commerce from the instant of its growth or production, and, in the case of coals, as they lie in the ground. The result would be curious. It would nationalize all industries, it would nationalize and withdraw from state jurisdiction and deliver to federal commercial control the fruits of California and the South, the wheat of the West and its meats, the cotton of the South, the shoes of Massachusetts and the woolen industries of other States at the very inception of their production or growth—that is, the fruits unpicked, the cotton and wheat ungathered, hides and flesh of cattle yet 'on the hoof,' wool yet unshorn, and coal yet unmined, because they are in varying percentages destined for and surely to be exported to States other than those of their production."

A. L. A. Schechter Poultry Co. v. United States, 295 U.S. 495, 546 (1935): "If the commerce clause were construed to reach all enterprise and transactions which could be said to have an indirect effect upon interstate commerce, the federal authority would embrace practically all the activities of the people, and the authority of the State over its domestic concerns would exist only by sufferance of the federal government. Indeed, on such a theory, even the development of the State's commercial facilities would be subject to federal control."

72. Bruce Ackerman, 1 *We the People: Foundations* 103 (Cambridge, MA: Belknap Press of Harvard University Press, 1991).

73. *Railroad Retirement Board v. Alton R. Co.*, 295 U.S. 330, 368 (1935).

74. Felix Frankfurter, *The Commerce Clause Under Marshall, Taney, and White* 115–116 (Chapel Hill, NC: University of North Carolina Press, 1937).

75. F. D. G. Ribble, *National and State Cooperation Under the Commerce Clause*, 37 Colum. L. Rev. 43, 47 (1937); John T. Ganoe, *The Roosevelt Court and the Commerce Clause*, 24 Or. L. Rev. 71, 74 (1945).

## Chapter Five

1. In this list, each parenthetical describes the violation of procedural due process.

Administrative context: *Londoner v. Denver*, 210 U.S. 373 (1908) (city making individual tax determinations without hearing), *Wong Yang Sung v. McGrath*, 339 U.S. 33 (1950) (deportation proceeding run by single person with combined prosecutorial and adjudicative functions [the constitutional issue is actually avoided by construing this as a violation of the Administrative Procedure Act), *Goldberg v. Kelly*, 397 U.S. 254 (1970) (city authority terminating welfare benefits prior to eligibility hearing).

Criminal context: *Tumey v. Ohio*, 273 U.S. 510 (1927) (trial by city official who is only paid for convictions), *In re Oliver*, 333 U.S. 257 (1948) (state judge, sitting as "one man grand jury," convicting and sentencing a witness for contempt in a secret proceeding), *In re Murchison*, 349 U.S. 133 (1955) (state judge both charging defendant with contempt while sitting as "one man grand jury" and presiding over the separate public contempt hearing mandated by *In re Oliver*), *Griffin v. Illinois*, 351 U.S. 12 (1956) (denial of free transcript of trial to indigent defendant), *Gideon v. Wainwright*, 372 U.S. 335 (1963) (denial of counsel to indigent defendant), *Morrissey v. Brewer*, 408 U.S. 471 (1972) (revocation of parole without hearing), *Hamdi v. Rumsfeld*, 542 U.S. 507 (2004) (detention of citizen classified as "enemy combatant" without notice of the basis for this classification, or an opportunity to challenge it before an impartial authority).

Civil context: *Walker v. City of Hutchinson*, 352 U.S. 112 (1956) (condemnation proceeding with notice to property owner only given by newspaper publication, though address of owner was known), *Schroeder v. City of New York*, 371 U.S. 208 (1962) (condemnation proceeding affecting vacation property, notice of which had only been by newspaper publication, and by signs posted near property in January), *Sniadach v. Family Finance Corp.*, 395 U.S. 337 (1969) (state statute authorizing freezing of unpaid wages in debt collection action before any hearing [possibly limited by *North Georgia Finishing v. Di-Chem*, 419 U.S. 601 (1975) to situations where consequences of freezing would be severe]), *Wisconsin v. Constantineau*, 400 U.S. 433 (1971) (state statutory scheme where people could be classified as "excessive drinkers" and banned from places that sold alcohol, without opportunity for hearing or rebuttal), *Fuentes v. Shevin*, 407 U.S. 67 (1972) (state statute allowing court to issue writs of replevin, allowing summary seizure of goods, in response to any claimant who posts a bond, without notice to defendant), *Robinson v. Hanrahan*, 409 U.S. 38 (1972) (forfeiture of incarcerated man's car in proceeding where notice was given by mail to home address, not jail address), *Greene v. Lindsey*, 456 U.S. 444 (1982) (service of notice of eviction proceeding by posting on door, in housing project where door posts were frequently removed before tenants could see them), *Connecticut v. Doehr*, 501 U.S. 1 (1991) (state statute allowing pre-judgment attachment of real property in suits filed by plaintiffs who submit an affidavit of probable cause, without notice to defendant), *Jones v. Flowers*, 547 U.S. 220 (2006) (tax sale of real property made after certified letter providing notice of sale was returned unclaimed to tax official).

Family context: *Griffin v. Griffin*, 327 U.S. 220 (1946) (court issuing judgment for accrued alimony without notice to defendant), *Armstrong v. Manzo*, 380 U.S. 545 (1965) (failing to give notice of adoption proceedings to a parent), *Little v. Streater*, 452 U.S. 1 (1981) (indigent man denied state-funded paternity test in state-required paternity action).

Cases finding violations of procedural due process are much easier to find than cases that get explicit about what kind of process might be due. *Mullane v. Central Hanover Bank & Trust Co.*, 339 U.S. 306 (1950) has some general discussion of when notice of legal proceedings is "adequate." *Goldberg* (cited earlier in this note) contains some general discussion of the procedure appropriate in hearings involving government benefits; the related *Mathews v. Eldridge*, 424 U.S. 319 (1976) contains even more general discussion, introducing a balancing test (intended to operate context by context, not case by case) to guide the analysis of how much procedure the Constitution requires. Many subsequent procedural due process cases, even outside the administrative setting, make reference to the *Mathews* balancing test.

2. See U.S. Const. amend. V; Randall T. Shepard, *Is Making State Constitutional Law Through Certified Questions a Good Idea or a Bad Idea?*, 38 Val. U. L. Rev. 327, 351 (2004).

3. *Moore v. Illinois*, 55 U.S. 13, 18 (1852).

4. Thomas M. Cooley, *A Treatise on the Constitutional Limitations Which Rest upon the Legislative Power of the States of the American Union* 572 (Boston: Little, Brown, 1868). Among the obsolete meanings of "police" listed in the *OED*: (1) "policy," especially in the term "public police." [Examples: "It was an object of public police, as well as of private curiosity, to examine and describe the countries which composed this great body," from 1777, and "The king ... forbade the University to meddle in any matter of public police," from 1874.] (2) "A department of a government or state concerned with maintaining public order and safety, and enforcing the law." [Example: "The police of Glasgow consists of three bodies; the magistrates with the town council, the merchants house, and the trades house," from 1774.].

See also Justice Taney in the *License Cases*: "But what are the police powers of a State? They are nothing more or less than the powers of government inherent in every sovereignty to the extent of its dominions. And whether a State passes a quarantine law, or a law to punish offenses, or to establish courts of justice, or requiring certain instruments to be recorded, or to regulate commerce within its own limits, in every case it exercises the same powers; that is to say, the power of sovereignty, the power to govern men and things within the limits of its dominion. It is by virtue of this power that it legislates, and its authority to make regulations of commerce is as absolute as its power to pass health laws except insofar as it has been restricted by the Constitution of the United States." 46 U.S. 504, 583 (1847).

Justice Shaw, in the Massachusetts Supreme Court (cited in the *Slaughterhouse Cases*): "The power we allude to is rather the police power, the power vested in the legislature by the constitution, to make, ordain and establish all manner of wholesome and reasonable laws, statutes and ordinances, either with penalties or without, not repugnant to the constitution, as they shall judge to be for the good and welfare of the commonwealth, and of the subjects of the same. It is much easier to perceive and realize the existence and sources of this power, than to mark its boundaries, or prescribe limits to its exercise. There are many cases in which such a power is exercised by all well ordered governments, and where its fitness is so obvious, that all well regulated minds will regard it as reasonable. Such are the laws to prohibit the use of warehouses for the storage of gunpowder near habitations or highways; to restrain the height to which wooden buildings may be erected in populous neighborhoods, and require them to be covered with slate or other incombustible material; to prohibit buildings from being used for hospitals for contagious diseases, or for the carrying on of noxious or offensive trades; to prohibit the raising of a dam, and causing stagnant water to spread over meadows, near inhabited villages, thereby raising noxious exhalations, injurious to health and dangerous to life." *Commonwealth v. Alger*, 61 Mass. 53, 85–86 (1851).

Also, "the power of the State, sometimes termed its police power, to prescribe regulations to promote the health, peace, morals, education, and good order of the people, and to legislate so as to increase the industries of the State, develop its resources, and add to its wealth and prosperity." *Barbier v. Connolly*, 113 U.S. 27, 31 (1885).

"The power of promoting the public welfare by restraining and regulating the use of liberty and property." Ernst Freund, *The Police Power: Public Policy and Constitutional Rights* iii (Chicago: Callaghan, 1904).

Emphasizing that the constitutionality of police power is fact-bound and situation-specific: "[The police] power...embraces regulations designed to promote the public convenience or the general prosperity, as well as regulations designed to promote the public health, the public morals or the public safety. We do not enter, therefore, into the discussion whether the sheep industry is legitimate and not offensive. Nor need we make extended comment on the two-mile limit. The selection of some limit is a legislative power, and it is only against the abuse of the power, if at all, that the courts may interpose. But the abuse must be shown. It is not shown by quoting the provision which expresses the limit. The mere distance expressed shows nothing. It does not display the necessities of a settler upon the public lands. It does not display what protection is needed, not from one sheep or a few sheep, but from large flocks of sheep, or the relation of the sheep industry to other industries. These may be the considerations that induced the statutes, and we cannot pronounce them insufficient on surmise or on the barren letter of the statute." *Bacon v. Walker*, 204 U.S. 311, 317 (1907).

"The police power of a state extends beyond health, morals and safety, and comprehends the duty, within constitutional limitations, to protect the well-being and tranquility of a community. A state or city may prohibit acts or things reasonably thought to bring evil or harm to its people." *Kovacs v. Cooper*, 336 U.S. 77, 83 (1949).

"The power of Congress over the District of Columbia includes all the legislative powers which a state may exercise over its affairs. We deal, in other words, with what traditionally has been known as the police power. An attempt to define its reach or trace its outer limits is fruitless, for each case must turn on its own facts. The definition is essentially the product of legislative determinations addressed to the purposes of government, purposes neither abstractly nor historically capable of complete definition. Subject to specific constitutional limitations, when the legislature has spoken, the public interest has been declared in terms well-nigh conclusive.... Public safety, public health, morality, peace and quiet, law and order—these are some of the more conspicuous examples of the traditional application of the police power to municipal affairs. Yet they merely illustrate the scope of the power and do not delimit it." *Berman v. Parker*, 348 U.S. 26, 31–32 (1954) (citation omitted).

5. *Barbier v. Connolly*, 113 U.S. 27, 31 (1884).

6. In the language of economics, either Pareto efficient (everyone is at least as well off, and at least one is better off) or Kaldor-Hicks efficient (those gaining could

afford to compensate those who lose enough to make the situation Pareto efficient).

7. Cooley, *A Treatise on the Constitutional Limitations* 1223.

8. *Calder v. Bull*, 3 U.S. 386, 388 (1798). The interesting and important exceptions to this strong statement are poor laws. As Barry Cushman describes it, "Constitutional conservatives from Brewer to Cooley concurred that poor relief was 'among the unquestionably legitimate functions of government.' Only public wealth transfers to non-indigents were constitutionally problematic." Barry Cushman, *Mr. Dooley and Mr. Gallup: Public Opinion and Constitutional Change in the 1930s*, 50 Buff. L. Rev. 7, 60 (2002), citing Thomas Grey, *The Malthusian Constitution,* 41 U. Miami L. Rev. 21, 44 (1986). Justice Miller expressed as much explicitly in *Kelly v. City of Pittsburgh,* 104 U.S. 78, 81 (1881): "The support of the poor . . . [is a] public purpose[] in which the . . . community [has] an interest, and for which, by common consent, property owners everywhere in this country are taxed." Indeed, in the struggle to unravel the conservatives' constitutional limits on the scope of government power (described in Chapter 6), the minimum wage was justified as a means to reducing the burden of poor laws on the state. Cushman describing Frankfurter's reasoning: "Frankfurter's argument contained suggestions that the *absence* of minimum wage legislation would effectively result in special legislation. 'A contract for labor below its cost must inevitably rely upon a subsidy from outside or result in human deterioration. To the extent of the subsidy or the deterioration the public is necessarily concerned. The employer has no constitutional right to such an indirect subsidy.'" Barry Cushman, *Rethinking the New Deal Court: The Structure of a Constitutional Revolution* 66 (New York: Oxford University Press, 1998).

9. Michael Les Benedict, *Laissez-Faire and Liberty: A Re-Evaluation of the Meaning and Origins of Laissez-Faire Constitutionalism*, 3 Law & Hist. Rev. 293, 323 (1985), citing the Constitution of Virginia (1776), Bill of Rights, Sec. 4, and the Constitution of North Carolina (1776), Declaration of Rights, Sec. 3.

10. Benedict, *Laissez-Faire and Liberty*, 321, citing the Constitution of New Hampshire (1784), Art. I, Sec. 10.

11. Benedict, *Laissez-Faire and Liberty*, 321.

12. *Calder v. Bull*, 3 U.S. 386, 388 (1798). Note that, despite condemning taking from A and giving to B, the Court held that the rights at issue in this alleged transfer had not yet vested, so were not subject to that principle.

13. Barry Cushman, *Some Varieties and Vicissitudes of Lochnerism*, 85 B.U. L. Rev. 881, 888 (2005), citing *Wilkinson v. Leland*, 27 U.S. 627, 658 (1829).

14. Benedict, *Laissez-Faire and Liberty*, 319, quoting Andrew Jackson, "Veto Message," July 10, 1832, in 2 *A Compilation of the Messages and Papers of the Presidents, 1789–1907* 591 (James D. Richardson ed., Washington, DC: Bureau of National Literature and Art, 1908).

15. Benedict, *Laissez-Faire and Liberty*, 319, citing Alan Jones, *Thomas M. Cooley and "Laissez-Faire Constitutionalism": A Reconsideration*, 53 Journal of American History 751, 755 (1967).

16. Cushman, *Some Varieties and Vicissitudes of Lochnerism* 886, citing Hannis Taylor, *Due Process of Law and the Equal Protection of the Laws* 304 (Chicago: Callaghan, 1917).

17. So, for example, Maryland courts questioned the constitutionality of "an act providing that 'no Black Republican . . . shall be appointed to any office' within the jurisdiction of the Baltimore Board of Police.'" William E. Nelson, *The Roots of American Bureaucracy, 1830–1900* 153 (Cambridge, MA: Harvard University Press, 1982).

18. *Davidson v. New Orleans*, 96 U.S. 97, 102 (1878) (emphasis added).

19. *Davidson v. New Orleans*, 96 U.S. 97, 102 (1877).

20. 113 U.S. 27, 32 (1885).

21. Cushman, *Some Varieties and Vicissitudes of Lochnerism* 934–935, quoting Rodney Mott, *Due Process of Law* 538–539 (Indianapolis, IN: Bobbs-Merrill, 1926).

22. Gordon Wood, *Empire of Liberty: A History of the Early Republic, 1789–1815* 43 (New York: Oxford University Press, 2009).

23. Wood, *Empire of Liberty* 42.

24. Thomas Malthus, quoted in Drew R. McCoy, *The Elusive Republic: Political Economy in Jeffersonian America* 190–191 (Chapel Hill, NC: University of North Carolina Press, 1980).

25. McCoy, *The Elusive Republic* 118–119.

26. McCoy, *The Elusive Republic* 131.

27. McCoy, *The Elusive Republic* 91.

28. McCoy, *The Elusive Republic* 160–161.

29. McCoy, *The Elusive Republic* 105.

30. McCoy, *The Elusive Republic* 126.

31. McCoy, *The Elusive Republic* 185.

32. McCoy, *The Elusive Republic* 186.

33. McCoy, *The Elusive Republic* 231–232.

34. The embargo was challenged on constitutional grounds, unsuccessfully. See *United States v. The William*, 28 F. Cas. 614 (D. Mass. 1808).

35. McCoy, *The Elusive Republic* 227.

36. McCoy, *The Elusive Republic* 219.

37. As McCoy describes it: "If America were forced to become a 'world within itself' on any kind of permanent basis, either its agricultural surplus would be seriously diminished for want of adequate markets, which raised the problem of how to sustain active, industrious, and prosperous republican farmers in an isolated and undeveloped America, or a vast domestic market would have to be created to absorb this large surplus, which implied the need to develop large-scale, urban manufacturing most Jeffersonians could not accept. Both versions of this alternative political economy were incompatible with the traditional

Jeffersonian conception of a republican political economy, and both were implicitly rejected in the decision for war in 1812. It is interesting to note, in this regard, that in April 1812 Jefferson was reminded through personal experience of just how dependent American farmers were on foreign markets to sustain them. A sixty-day general embargo, generally recognized as the necessary prelude to a declaration of war, caught Virginia farmers, including Jefferson, with a large part of their spring harvest unmarketed. The ex-president noted to several correspondents, including President Madison, that a vent for this surplus was so absolutely necessary that even trade with 'our enemies' would be desirable." McCoy, *The Elusive Republic* 234.

38. I've drawn heavily on McCoy's work. Historical academic literatures discussing the work are generally positive. See, e.g., Robert E. Shalhope, *Republicanism and Early American Historiography*, 39 Wm. & Mary Q. 334 (1982) ("the most cogent analysis of American attempts reduce the tension between the economic 'liberalism' of Smith and 'classical' American republicanism"). Some have criticized him for underplaying the classical liberalism in Jefferson's thought. See, e.g., Thomas L. Pangle, *The Spirit of Modern Republicanism: The Moral Vision of the American Founders and the Philosophy of Locke* 35, 285–286 (Chicago: University of Chicago Press, 1988), and Joyce Appleby, *What Is Still American in the Political Philosophy of Thomas Jefferson?*, 39 Wm. & Mary Q. 287 (1982). Joyce Appleby also criticizes the suggestion that Jefferson embraced Malthus. *Id.* at 304. McCoy has been defended against these critics. See, e.g., Lance Banning, *Founding Visions: The Ideas, Individuals, and Intersections That Created America* 39–40 (Lexington: University Press of Kentucky, 2014).

39. In 1800, agricultural employment was 74 percent of total employment. Agricultural production was the dominant source of economic growth throughout the country. See Stanley Lebergott, "Labor Force and Employment, 1800–1960," *in Output, Employment, and Productivity in the United States After 1800* 117–204 (Dorothy Brady ed., New York: National Bureau of Economic Research, 1966); *Historical Statistics of the United States 1789–1945*, Bureau of the Census, 97 (1949); *Consumer Price Index (Estimate) 1800–*, Fed. Reserve Bank of Minneapolis, *available at* link #14.

40. R. Douglas Hurt, *American Agriculture: A Brief History* 119–120, 123 (rev. ed., West Lafayette, IN: Purdue University Press, 2002).

41. Hurt, *American Agriculture* 123.

42. The "free labor" literature is vast. For a selection, see William E. Forbath, *Law and the Shaping of the American Labor Movement* (Cambridge, MA: Harvard University Press, 1991); William E. Forbath, *The Ambiguities of Free Labor: Labor and the Law in the Gilded Age*, 1985 Wisc. L. Rev. 767 (1985); *Perspectives on American Labor History: The Problem of Synthesis* (J. Carroll Moody & Alice Kessler-Harris eds., DeKalb: Northern Illinois University Press, 1989); Mark A. Lause, *Free Labor: The Civil War and the Making of an American Working Class* (Urbana: University of Illinois Press, 2015); *The Labor Movement: The*

*Problem of Today* (George E. McNeill ed., New York: M.W. Hazen, 1887); Leon Fink, *Workingmen's Democracy: The Knights of Labor and American Politics* (Urbana: University of Illinois Press, 1983); E. L. Godkin, *The Labor Crisis*, 105 North American Rev. 177 (1867); David Montgomery, *Beyond Equality: Labor and the Radical Republicans* (Urbana: University of Illinois Press, 1981); Bernard Mandel, *Labor, Free and Slave: Workingmen and the Anti-Slavery Movement in the United States* (Urbana: University of Illinois Press, 2007); Robert J. Steinfeld, *The Invention of Free Labor: The Employment Relation in English and American Law and Culture, 1350–1870* (Chapel Hill: University of North Carolina Press, 1991); John Godard, *The Exceptional Decline of the American Labor Movement*, 63 Indus. & Lab. Rel. Rev. 82 (2009).

One rich and distinctive line of work is by Lee VanderVelde. See Lee VanderVelde, *The Labor Vision of the Thirteenth Amendment*, 138 U. Pa. L. Rev. 437 (1989); Lee VanderVelde, *The Thirteenth Amendment of Our Aspirations*, 38 U. Tol. L. Rev. 855 (2007); Lee VanderVelde, *Henry Wilson: Cobbler of the Frayed Constitution, Strategist of the Thirteenth Amendment,* 15 Geo. J.L. & Pub. Pol'y 173 (2017).

43. See Steinfeld, *The Invention of Free Labor*.

44. Forbath, *The Ambiguities of Free Labor* 774.

45. Forbath, *The Ambiguities of Free Labor* 776.

46. Jedediah Purdy, *A Tolerable Anarchy: Rebels, Reactionaries, and the Making of American Freedom* 177 (New York: Alfred A. Knopf, 2009).

47. Jack Beatty, *Age of Betrayal: The Triumph of Money in America, 1865–1900* 970–971 (New York: Alfred A. Knopf, 2007) (Kindle ed.).

48. Abraham Lincoln, "Speech at Kalamazoo, Michigan," August 27, 1856, in 2 *The Collected Works of Abraham Lincoln* 364 (Roy T. Basler ed., New Brunswick, NJ: Rutgers University Press, 1953), *available at* link #15, quoted in Forbath, *The Ambiguities of Free Labor* 776.

49. Abraham Lincoln, "First Annual Message," December 3, 1861. Online by Gerhard Peters and John T. Woolley, *The American Presidency Project, available at* link #16.

50. Robin Blackburn, "Lincoln and Marx," *Jacobin*, August 28, 2012, *available at* link #17.

51. Cass R. Sunstein & Richard H. Thaler, *Libertarian Paternalism Is Not an Oxymoron*, 70 U. Chi. L. Rev. 1159 (2003).

52. Forbath, *The Ambiguities of Free Labor* 774–775.

53. Eric Foner, *Free Soil, Free Labor, Free Men: The Ideology of the Republican Party Before the Civil War* xii (New York: Oxford University Press, 1995).

54. Amy Dru Stanley, *From Bondage to Contract: Wage Labor, Marriage, and the Market in the Age of Slave Emancipation* 9 (Cambridge: Cambridge University Press, 2011).

55. Foner, *Free Soil, Free Labor, Free Men* xii.

56. Foner, *Free Soil, Free Labor, Free Men* xii.

57. And for many, not even because they cared about blacks. As Sean Wilentz describes, "Steeped in the Jacksonian tradition of protecting the rights of free

labor, the antislavery Democrats made it clear that in trying to halt slavery's spread, they were chiefly interested in preventing the degradation and dishonor of white workingmen. 'If slavery is not excluded by law,' Preston King proclaimed when he reintroduced the Proviso in January 1847, 'the presence of the slave will exclude the laboring white man.' Unlike antislavery Whigs— who took more liberal stances on black rights and more conservative stances on economic policies—antislavery Democrats, radicals on economic matters, were primarily concerned with the future of white workers." Sean Wilentz, *The Rise of American Democracy: Jefferson to Lincoln* 598 (New York: W. W. Norton, 2005).

58. Akhil Reed Amar, *America's Constitution: A Biography* 388 (New York: Random House, 2005).

59. As Fergus M. Bordewich writes, "Year after year, the House . . . adopted a 'gag rule,' in the process originating the term, stating that all petitions that related to slavery must be tabled[.] . . . Abolitionists knew this would be the outcome, but they kept the petitions coming. By March 1838 Congress had received so many petitions that they filled to the ceiling a room twenty feet wide by thirty feet square. . . . [T]he refusal of Congress to even consider them helped to radicalize Northern public opinion by vividly illustrating the grip that proslavery interests held upon the national government. Abolitionist rhetoric would henceforth be stippled with evocative descriptions of the nation 'fettered and gagged' like a slave." Fergus Bordewich, *Bound for Canaan: The Underground Railroad and the War for the Soul of America* 155 (New York: Amistad, 2005).

60. Wilentz, *The Rise of American Democracy* 627.

61. Abraham Lincoln, quoted in Eric Foner, *Reconstruction: America's Unfinished Revolution, 1863–1877* 29 (New York: Harper & Row, 1988).

62. This is the story told most powerfully in Chandra Manning's extraordinary book, *What This Cruel War Was Over: Soldiers, Slavery and the Civil War* (New York: Alfred A. Knopf, 2007).

63. Foner, *Reconstruction* 235.

64. Thadeus Stevens, quoted in Foner, *Reconstruction* 236.

65. Foner, *Reconstruction* 246.

66. Foner, *Reconstruction* 132.

67. Foner, *Reconstruction* 143–144.

68. It is Bruce Ackerman whose work has influenced legal academics to organize American constitutional history around moments, and among the peaks of those moments, the Civil War is certainly among the highest. The separate question whether "moment-hood" creates some special constitutional authority is addressed in Chapter 20.

69. *Slaughterhouse Cases*, 83 U.S. 36 (1873).

70. Beatty, *Age of Betrayal* 984–986.

71. Forbath, *The Ambiguities of Free Labor* 779 n. 28.

72. Stanley, *From Bondage to Contract* 62.

73. Forbath, *The Ambiguities of Free Labor* 776.

74. Forbath, *The Ambiguities of Free Labor* 787.

75. Foner, *Free Soil, Free Labor, Free Men* xvii.

76. Forbath, *The Ambiguities of Free Labor* 787.

77. Foner, *Free Soil, Free Labor, Free Men* xviii. See also Ganesh Sitaraman, *The Crisis of the Middle-Class Constitution: Why Economic Inequality Threatens Our Republic* 161 (New York: Alfred A. Knopf, 2017).

78. Beatty, *Age of Betrayal* 1657–1659.

79. Stanley, *From Bondage to Contract* 86.

80. Foner, *Free Soil, Free Labor, Free Men* xiii.

81. Stanley, *From Bondage to Contract* 71.

82. Michael A. Ross, *Justice of Shattered Dreams: Samuel Freeman Miller and the Supreme Court During the Civil War Era* 244 (Baton Rouge: Louisiana State University Press, 2003).

83. Stanley, *From Bondage to Contract* 158.

84. Stanley, *From Bondage to Contract* 153.

85. Stanley, *From Bondage to Contract* 152.

86. Foner, *Free Soil, Free Labor, Free Men* xx.

87. Beatty, *Age of Betrayal* 995–996; Forbath, *The Ambiguities of Free Labor* 811.

88. Forbath, *The Ambiguities of Free Labor* 810.

89. Stanley, *From Bondage to Contract* 156.

90. Forbath, *The Ambiguities of Free Labor* 802.

91. Forbath, *The Ambiguities of Free Labor* 769.

92. Forbath, *The Ambiguities of Free Labor* 801.

93. Benedict, *Laissez-Faire and Liberty*, 311–312.

94. Benedict, *Laissez-Faire and Liberty*, 312.

95. Forbath, *The Ambiguities of Free Labor* 769.

96. Steven Siegel and Michael Les Benedict make similar points. See Steven Siegel, *The Revision Thickens*, 20 Law and Hist. Rev. 631 (2002); Benedict, *Laissez-Faire and Liberty* 293.

97. See Herbert Hovenkamp, *Enterprise and American Law, 1836–1937* 119–121 (Cambridge, MA: Harvard University Press, 1991). For the original text of the act, see "An Act to Protect the Health of the City of New Orleans, to Locate the Stock Landings and Slaughter houses, and to Incorporate 'The Crescent City Live Stock Landing and SlaughtervHouse [*sic*] Company,'" No. 118, in *Acts Passed by the General Assembly of the State of Louisiana at the Second Session of the First Legislature, Begun and Held in the City of New Orleans, January 4, 1869* (New Orleans, LA: A. L. Lee State Printer, 1869).

98. *Slaughterhouse Cases*, 77 U.S. 273, 285 (1870).

99. Roscoe Pound, *Liberty of Contract*, 18 Yale L. J. 454, 470 (1909).

100. Beatty, *Age of Betrayal* 3143–3148. As the Court would later make clear in *Bradwell v. Illinois*, 83 U.S. 130 (1873), this right to pursue "lawful callings" was indeed meant to apply to men only, not women.

101. As Field wrote in dissent, "The abolition of slavery and involuntary servitude was intended to make everyone born in this country a freeman, and, as such, to give to him the right to pursue the ordinary avocations of life without other restraint than such as affects all others, and to enjoy equally with them the fruits of his labor." 83 U.S. at 90 (Field, dissenting).

102. 83 U.S. at 116 (Bradley, dissenting).

103. 83 U.S. at 120 (Bradley, dissenting).

104. 83 U.S. at 128. As Justice Swayne wrote in dissent: "Property is everything which has an exchangeable value, and the right of property includes the power to dispose of it according to the will of the owner. Labor is property, and as such merits protection. The right to make it available is next in importance to the rights of life and liberty. It lies to a large extent at the foundation of most other forms of property, and of all solid individual and national prosperity." 83 U.S. at 127.

105. The contrast was drawn sharply the next year in a case upholding a monopolist's right to preserve its monopoly despite the same change in the Louisiana constitution. In *New Orleans Gas-light Co. v. Louisiana Light & Heat*, 115 U.S. 650 (1885), the Court held that while *Butchers' Union* had established the principle that "one legislature cannot so limit the discretion of its successors that they may not enact such laws as are necessary to protect the public health or the public morals" (*Id.*, at 669), that limit did not extend to all aspects of the police power.

106. *Butcher's Union Slaughter-House & Live-Stock Landing Co. v. Crescent City Live-Stock Landing & Slaughter-House Co.*, 111 U.S. 746, 762 (1884) (Bradley, concurring, emphasis in original).

107. *Butcher's Union Slaughter-House & Live-Stock Landing Co. v. Crescent City Live-Stock Landing & Slaughter-House Co.*, 111 U.S. 746, 763 (1884).

108. *Butcher's Union Slaughter-House & Live-Stock Landing Co. v. Crescent City Live-Stock Landing & Slaughter-House Co.*, 111 U.S. 746, 755 (1884) (Field, concurring).

109. *Butcher's Union Slaughter-House & Live-Stock Landing Co. v. Crescent City Live-Stock Landing & Slaughter-House Co.*, 111 U.S. 746, 756–757 (1884) (Field, dissenting).

110. *Butcher's Union Slaughter-House & Live-Stock Landing Co. v. Crescent City Live-Stock Landing & Slaughter-House Co.*, 111 U.S. 746, 764–766 (1884) (Bradley, concurring).

111. *Butcher's Union Slaughter-House & Live-Stock Landing Co. v. Crescent City Live-Stock Landing & Slaughter-House Co.*, 111 U.S. 746, 766 (1884) (Bradley, concurring).

112. The rise is told most powerfully by Christian Wolmer, *The Great Railroad Revolution: The History of Trains in the America* (New York: Public Affairs, 2012).

113. Stephen A. Siegel, *Understanding the* Lochner *Era: Lessons from the Controversy over Railroad and Utility Rate Regulation*, 70 Va. L. Rev. 187, 197 (1984).

114. *Munn v. People of State of Illinois*, 94 U.S. 113, 132 (1876) (emphasis added).

115. Justice Morrison Waite, quoted in Siegel, *Understanding the* Lochner *Era* 197.

116. Justice Morrison Waite, quoted in Siegel, *Understanding the* Lochner *Era* 212. This quote originally appears in the *Railroad Commission Cases,* 116 U.S. 307, 331 (1886).

117. Frederick F. Blachly, *The Role of* Smyth v. Ames *in Federal Rate Regulation,* 33 Va. L. Rev. 141, 142 (1947).

118. Justice Morrison Waite, quoted in Barry Cushman, *Rethinking the New Deal Court: The Structure of a Constitutional Revolution* 49 (New York: Oxford University Press, 1998).

119. Chief Justice Waite followed Salmon P. Chase. Chase died in 1873. President Grant first offered the seat to New York senator Roscoe Conkling. Conkling declined. Grant then offered the seat to Senator Oliver Morton of Indiana. He declined. Then to Timothy Howe of Wisconsin. He too declined. Then to Secretary of State Hamilton Fish, who also declined. Attorney General George H. Williams at first agreed to be nominated and then withdrew. Democrat and former attorney general Caleb Cushing agreed to be nominated, but then Grant withdrew the nomination. Finally, Grant nominated the little-known Waite, who as I noted in the text stood, *The Nation* reported, "in the front-rank of second-rank lawyers." Nonetheless, the nomination was unanimously confirmed. See Bruce R. Trimble, *Chief Justice Waite, Defender of the Public Interest* (Princeton, NJ: Princeton University Press, 1938); Donald Grier Stephenson Jr., *The Waite Court: Justices, Rulings, and Legacy* (Santa Barbara, CA: ABC-CLIO Supreme Court Handbooks, 2003).

120. Pamela Brandwein, *Rethinking the Judicial Settlement of Reconstruction* 107 n. 109 (Cambridge, UK: Cambridge University Press, 2011).

121. Barry Cushman, *Rethinking the New Deal Court: The Structure of a Constitutional Revolution* 90 (New York: Oxford University Press, 1998).

122. Cushman, *Rethinking the New Deal Court* 144.

123. "Excluding the civil liberties cases, there were 159 decisions under the due process and equal protection clauses in which state statutes were held to be unconstitutional, plus 16 in which both the due process and commerce clauses were involved, plus 9 more involving due process and some other clause or clauses." Benjamin Wright, *The Growth of American Constitutional Law* 154 (New York: Reynal & Hitchcock, 1942).

124. *Allgeyer v. State of La.,* 165 U.S. 578, 589–590 (1897).

125. *Powell v. Com. of Pennsylvania,* 127 U.S. 678, 684 (1888).

126. *Allgeyer v. State of La.,* 165 U.S. 578, 590 (1897).

127. *Allgeyer v. State of La.,* 165 U.S. 578, 589 (1897).

128. Brief of the Attorney General of the State of New York on Behalf of the State of New York on Behalf of the Defendants in Error, The People of the State of New York at 8, *Lochner v. New York,* 198 U.S. 45 (1905) (No. 292). For a powerful account of the doctrine embodied in the case, see Howard Gillman, *The Constitution Besieged: The Rise and Demise of Lochner Era Police Powers Jurisprudence* (Durham, NC: Duke University Press, 1993).

129. Brief of the Attorney General of the State of New York at 15–16, *Lochner v. New York*, 198 U.S. 45 (1905) (No. 292).

130. *People v. Lochner*, 15 Bedell 145, 149 (1904).

131. *Lochner v. New York*, 198 U.S. 45, 53 (1905).

132. *Lochner*, 198 U.S. at 64.

133. *Lochner v. New York*, 198 U.S. 45, 75 (Holmes dissenting).

134. *Giles v. Harris*, 189 U.S. 475 (1903).

135. *Lochner*, 198 U.S. at 73.

136. This framing famously appears first in the Supreme Court's opinion *Calder v. Bull*, 3 U.S. 386 (1798), though the Court did not strike the law said to take from A and give to B.

137. Oliver H. Dean, *The Law of the Land*, 48 Am. L. Rev. 641, 654, 672 (1914), quoted with slight variation in Cushman, *Some Varieties and Vicissitudes of Lochnerism* 892.

138. Early references in the *Harvard Law Review* were initially supportive of the decision. See Victor Morawetz, *The Power of Congress to Regulate Railway Rates*, 18 Harv. L. Rev. 572, 574 (1905); Adelbert Moot, *Railway Rate Regulation*, 19 Harv. L. Rev. 487, 504 (1906); Frank M. Cobb, *Reasonableness of Maximum Rates as a Constitutional Limitation upon Rate Regulation*, 21 Harv. L. Rev. 175, 179–180 (1908). But then in the first article to address the case directly, written just before he became a district court judge, Learned Hand attacked the opinion strongly. As he wrote, "If the measure may possibly promote the 'welfare' of the public, then it is valid. There would seem to be so direct a relation between the welfare of a worker and the hours of his work that no doubt could be raised about it, yet in *Lochner v. People* it was held that it did not exist." Learned Hand, *Due Process of Law and the Eight-Hour Day,* 21 Harv. L. Rev. 495, 503 (1908). In the press, the *New York Times* noted that the case would prove significant, as the power of the legislatures would be "sharply checked by [the] decision." "The Ten-Hour Decision," *New York Times*, April 28, 1905, at 8. Five years later, the *Times* was defending the decision against attacks by Theodore Roosevelt. "Mr. Roosevelt's Attack on the Courts," *New York Times*, August 31, 1910, at 8.

The pattern is similar with *Allgeyer*. Immediate reactions were more surprised than with *Lochner*. *Recent Cases*, 11 Harv. L. Rev. 60, 62 (1897) (a "notable decision" because willing to accept a "vague and comprehensive interpretation of the term 'liberty'"). While the case was not remarked upon in the *New York Times* or *Chicago Tribune*, an extensive consideration published without byline in the *Central Law Journal* considered the decision "sound in principle and eminently proper and just." 44 Central Law Journal 299, 300 (April 4, 1897).

139. *Adair v. U.S.*, 208 U.S. 161 (1908).

140. *Adair v. U.S.*, 208 U.S. 161, 174–175.

141. *Coppage v. Kansas,* 235 U.S. 1, 17 (1915).

142. Cushman, *Some Varieties and Vicissitudes of Lochnerism* 926.

143. Robert C. Post, *Due Process in the Taft Court Era*, 78 B.U. L. Rev. 1489 (1998).

144. Post, *Due Process in the Taft Court Era* 1490.

145. Post, *Due Process in the Taft Court Era* 1506.

146. Post, *Due Process in the Taft Court Era* 1491.

147. *Wolff Packing Co. v. Court of Ind. Relations*, 262 U.S. 522 (1923). The Court distinguished in this case between regulations of "rates" the business charges the public and "wages" that it offers its employees. Conceptually, the public's ability to regulate the one does not necessarily entail the ability to regulate the other. "A business may be of such character that only the first is permissible, while another may involve such a possible danger of monopoly on the one hand, and such disaster from stoppage on the other, that both come within the public concern and power of regulation." 262 U.S. at 539.

148. Cushman, *Some Varieties and Vicissitudes of Lochnerism* 960.

149. Cushman, *Some Varieties and Vicissitudes of Lochnerism* 899.

150. Post, *Due Process in the Taft Court Era* 1518.

151. Post, *Due Process in the Taft Court Era* 1518.

152. Robert C. Post, *Defending the Lifeworld: Substantive Due Process in the Taft Court Era*, 78 B.U. L. Rev. 1489, 1535 (1998).

153. Post, *Defending the Lifeworld* 1535–1536.

154. *Bailey v. Alabama*, 219 U.S. 219 (1911).

155. Robert Post, *Federalism in the Taft Court Era: Can It Be Revived?*, 51 Duke L.J. 1513, 1573 (2002).

156. *Adkins v. Children's Hospital*, 261 U.S. 525 (1923).

157. 261 U.S. at 545.

158. Barry Cushman, *Lost Fidelities*, 41 Wm. & Mary L. Rev. 95, 100–101 (1999).

159. Forbath, *The Ambiguities of Free Labor* 790.

160. Forbath, *The Ambiguities of Free Labor* 799–800.

161. Daniel R. Ernst, *Free Labor, the Consumer Interest, and the Law of Industrial Disputes, 1885–1900*, 36 Am. J. Legal Hist. 19, 30 (1992), citing *State v. Stewart*, 59 Vt. 273, 289, 9 A. 559, 568 (1887).

162. Forbath, *The Ambiguities of Free Labor* 798.

163. Forbath, *The Ambiguities of Free Labor* 800.

164. Purdy, *A Tolerable Anarchy* 63.

165. Purdy, *A Tolerable Anarchy* 64.

166. Purdy, *A Tolerable Anarchy* 64.

167. Purdy, *A Tolerable Anarchy* 65.

168. Cushman, *Rethinking the New Deal Court* 175.

## Chapter Six

1. Marian C. McKenna, *Franklin Roosevelt and the Great Constitutional War: The Court-Packing Crisis of 1937* 263 (New York: Fordham University Press, 2002).

2. Since the essentially uncontested election of 1820, 8 is the smallest number of electoral votes ever received by a second-place presidential candidate (Mondale

got 13 in) and 523 is the second-highest number of electoral votes ever received by a winner (Reagan got 525 in 1984, when there were more electoral votes to be gotten), and FDR's 60.8 percent of the popular vote is second only to Lyndon Johnson's 61.1 percent in 1964.

3. *N.L.R.B. v. Jones & Laughlin Steel Corp.*, 301 U.S. 1, 37 (1937).

4. Bruce Ackerman sees *N.L.R.B. v. Jones & Laughlin Steel Corp.,* 301 U.S. 1 (1937) as less significant a shift, since steel was obviously national in a way that the sick chickens in *A.L.A. Schechter Poultry Corp. v. United States* 295 U.S. 495 (1935) were not. That allowed the Court to distinguish *Schechter.* But the real comparison is *Carter Coal,* which involved an industry every bit as national as steel. In any case, as Ackerman rightly argues, a companion case not as well known, *N.L.R.B. v. Friedman-Harry Marks Clothing Co.*, 301 U.S. 58 (1937), reveals the lie: though *Jones* involved the national steel industry, *Friedman-Harry Marks Clothing* involved a small clothing manufacturing company. As Justice McReynolds wrote in dissent, "The Clothing Company is a typical small manufacturing concern which produces less than one-half of one per cent of the men's clothing produced in the United States and employs 800 of the 150,000 workmen engaged therein. If closed today, the ultimate effect on commerce in clothing obviously would be negligible." Id. at 87. See Bruce Ackerman, 2 *We the People: Transformations* 363 (Cambridge, MA: Harvard University Press, 2015).

5. *United States v. Darby*, 312 U.S. 100 (1941).

6. *Wickard v. Filburn*, 317 U.S. 111 (1942).

7. *Nebbia v. People of New York*, 291 U.S. 502, 536 (1934).

8. *West Coast Hotel Co. v. Parrish*, 300 U.S. 379, 391 (1937).

9. *West Coast Hotel Co. v. Parrish*, 300 U.S. 379, 391 (1937).

10. *West Coast Hotel Co. v. Parrish*, 300 U.S. 379, 399–400 (1937).

11. "Court 'Vacillation' Charged in Senate," *New York Times,* April 1, 1937, at 10.

12. "The Federal Power Broadens," *Wall Street Journal*, April 13, 1937, at 4.

## Chapter Seven

1. For a related philosophical discussion of reasonable disagreement and its relevance to constitutional and political theory, see, for example, Amy Gutmann & Dennis Thompson, *Democracy and Disagreement* 1 (Cambridge, MA: The Belknap Press of Harvard University Press, 1996); Christopher McMahon, *Reasonable Disagreement: A Theory of Political Morality* (Cambridge, UK: Cambridge University Press, 2009); John Rawls, *Political Liberalism* 54–58 (New York: Columbia University Press, 1993); Cass R. Sunstein, *Legal Reasoning and Political Conflict* 39 (New York: Oxford University Press, 1996); Jeremy Waldron, *Law and Disagreement* (Oxford, UK: Clarendon Press of Oxford University Press, 1999).

2. I introduce my sense of the idea of "social meaning" in Lawrence Lessig, *The Regulation of Social Meaning,* 62 U. Chi. L. Rev. 943 (1995).

3. At least within a normal context of discourse. Bruce Ackerman's *Social Justice and the Liberal State* (New Haven, CT: Yale University Press, 1981) reasons from his principle about what entitles a human to protection (their dialogic capacity) to the conclusion that abortion and infanticide both cannot be regulated. That's a fine argument to make in a fine philosophy text. It's not the stuff of polite dinner conversation.

4. Catharine A. MacKinnon, *Sexual Harassment of Working Women: A Case of Sex Discrimination* 116–118, 174–192, 233–238 (New Haven, CT: Yale University Press, 1979).

5. Thomas Kuhn, *The Structure of Scientific Revolutions* (Chicago: University of Chicago Press, 1962).

6. For other views of Hovenkamp's book, see Gerald Spindler, *Reshaping Legal and Economic History in the 19th Century*, 42 Am. J. Comp. L. 811 (1994) (largely positive review critical of evidence that economic theory drove doctrine in some areas); Geoffrey P. Miller, *The Rise and Fall of the Classical Corporation*, 59 U. Chi. L. Rev. 1677 (1992) (critical of Hovenkamp's understanding of the "classical corporation"); Morton Keller, *Law, Enterprise, and the Marketplace of Ideas: Hovenkamp's View*, 18 Law & Soc. Inquiry 337 (1993) (praising focus on "belief" rather than "interest"). Richard Epstein is strongly critical of Hovenkamp's view, unsurprisingly, as his interpretation of constitutional doctrine depends upon the ideals of classical liberalism being constant across constitutional history. See Richard A. Epstein, *Rediscovering the Classical Liberal Constitution: A Reply to Professor Hovenkamp*, 101 Iowa L. Rev. 55 (2015). Hovenkamp has the better argument about the historical contingency of those views.

7. Herbert Hovenkamp, *Enterprise and American Law, 1836–1937* 204 (Cambridge, MA: Harvard University Press, 1991).

8. Hovenkamp, *Enterprise and American Law* 182.

9. *Tyson & Brother-United Theatre Ticket Offices v. Banton*, 273 U.S. 418, 451 (1927) (Justice Stone, dissenting) cited by Hovenkamp, *Enterprise and American Law* 201.

10. Hovenkamp, *Enterprise and American Law* 18.

11. Herbert Hovenkamp, *Regulatory Conflict in the Gilded Age: Federalism and the Railroad Problem*, 97 Yale L.J. 1017, 1030 (1988). The case referred to is *Charles River Bridge v. Warren Bridge*, 36 U.S. 420 (1837).

12. Hovenkamp, *Enterprise and American Law* 197.

13. Hovenkamp, *Enterprise and American Law* 195. See also Michael Les Benedict, *Laissez-Faire and Liberty: A Re-Evaluation of the Meaning and Origins of Laissez-Faire Constitutionalism* 299, 3 Law & Hist. Rev. 293 (1985).

14. Hovenkamp, *Enterprise and American Law* 195.

15. Herbert Hovenkamp, *The Marginalist Revolution in Legal Thought*, 46 Vand. L. Rev. 305, 314 (1993).

16. Oliver Wendell Holmes, *The Common Law* 1 (New York: Little, Brown, 1881).

17. Deborah Hellman cleared a whole forest of confusion with her *The Importance of Appearing Principled*, 37 Ariz. L. Rev. 1107 (1995), which develops a theory for

how and when what "seems" needs to matter. The joint opinion in *Planned Parenthood v. Casey* 505 U.S. 833, 865–866 (1992) expressed a similar sensitivity: "The Court's power lies, rather, in its legitimacy, a product of substance and perception that shows itself in the people's acceptance of the Judiciary as fit to determine what the Nation's law means and to declare what it demands.... [E]ven when justification is furnished by apposite legal principle, something more is required. Because not every conscientious claim of principled justification will be accepted as such, the justification claimed must be beyond dispute. The Court must take care to speak and act in ways that allow people to accept its decisions on the terms the Court claims for them, as grounded truly in principle, not as compromises with social and political pressures having, as such, no bearing on the principled choices that the Court is obliged to make."

18. I develop this analysis more extensively in Lawrence Lessig, *America, Compromised* (Chicago: University of Chicago Press, 2018).

## Chapter Eight

1. Marian McKenna argues the blunder began before the election, as FDR was silent about the Court in the lead-up to the 1936 election. That prevented him, she argues, from explicitly claiming a post-election mandate to act against the judiciary. Marian McKenna, *Franklin Roosevelt and the Great Constitutional War: The Court-Packing Crisis of 1937* 263 (New York: Fordham University Press, 2002).

2. In 1935, Roosevelt had asked Attorney General Homer S. Cummings to investigate the possible responses to a recalcitrant Court. Over the next two years, Cummings and his assistants worked on the plan in secret. Harold Ickes's diary reports a discussion at a cabinet meeting on December 27, 1935, at which FDR expressed his belief that the Court would strike down every piece of major New Deal legislation. The president outlined three responses— court-packing (which the diary entry reports as "distasteful," not indicating whether distasteful to the president or to Ickes), constitutional amendments, or an amendment that would give Congress the power to overrule Supreme Court opinions through express legislation. See William E. Leuchtenburg, *The Supreme Court Reborn: The Constitutional Revolution in the Age of Roosevelt* 95 (New York: Oxford University Press, 1996), citing Harold L. Ickes, Diary (December 27, 1935). But though history has looked back skeptically at Roosevelt's plan, the expectation, especially after the 1936 landslide, was that he would certainly succeed in passing it.

3. Jean Edward Smith, *FDR* 382 (New York: Random House, 2007), citing *Annual Report of the Attorney General, 1913* 5 (Washington, DC: U.S. Government Printing Office, 1913).

4. Gregory Caldeira has modeled public support for court-packing over the eighteen-week history of the plan. He finds the most significant events weakening support to be the interventions by the Court itself. Specifically, the Court's

reversal in *Jones & Laughlin* and the resignation of Justice Willis Van Devanter were the most impactful on overall public support. The president's speeches in support were the most significant factors enhancing support. See Gregory Caldeira, *Public Opinion and the U.S. Supreme Court: FDR's Court-Packing Plan,* 81 American Pol. Sci. Rev. 1139, 1148 (1987).

5. Turner Catledge, "Denies Bench Lags: Chief Justice's Letter Is a Surprise to Forces Backing Roosevelt," *New York Times,* March 23, 1937, at 1.

6. *Morehead v. New York ex rel. Tipaldo,* 298 U.S. 587 (1936).

7. There is some controversy about the source of the phrase. As Burt Solomon describes: "The best guess, according to scholars, was Edward Corwin of Princeton. Six weeks after the Court's reversal on the minimum wage, the eminent political scientist joked in a letter to Homer Cummings that 'a switch in time saved nine.' Three weeks later, the *New York Times* quoted a Yale Law School professor, Abe Fortas, at a meeting of labor activists in New Jersey. They applauded the future justice when he cracked, 'Mr. Justice Roberts's theory must be a switch in time serves nine.' Others credited the jest to Harvard's legal heavyweight Thomas Reed Powell." Burt Solomon, *FDR v. the Constitution: The Court-Packing Fight and the Triumph of Democracy* 162 (New York: Bloomsbury, 2009).

8. McKenna, *Franklin Roosevelt and the Great Constitutional War* 417–418.

9. As he wrote to Charles Wyzanski the day after the opinion, "To me it is all painful beyond words, the poignant grief of one whose life has been dedicated to faith in the disinterestedness of a tribunal and its freedom from responsiveness to the most obvious immediacies of politics....It all...gives one a sickening feeling which is aroused when moral standards are adulterated in a convent." Quoted in Barry Cushman, *Lost Fidelities,* 41 Wm. & Mary L. Rev. 95, 97 (1999). As noted, Frankfurter came to regret his letter, and he wrote an essay that vindicated Roberts of the charge of political judging. Felix Frankfurter, *Mr. Justice Roberts,* 104 U. Pa. L. Rev. 311 (1955–1956).

10. See, e.g., "The *Jones & Laughlin* Decision," *Chicago Daily Tribune,* April 14, 1937, at 12; James Morgan, "F.D.R. Has Remade the Court After All," *Daily Boston Globe,* January 23, 1938, at C4; "High Court Assailed at Labor Institute," *New York Times,* June 15, 1937, at 19 (quoting Abe Fortas: "Mr. Justice Roberts's theory must be a switch in time serves nine"). See also Dean Dinwoodey, "Surprise Decisions Widen the Commerce Clause: Limits of Federal Government Power Left for Future Rulings," *New York Times,* April 18, 1937, at E8 (rejecting the link).

11. See, e.g., Frank R. Kent, "The Great Game of Politics: His Case Shot to Pieces," *Wall Street Journal,* April 15, 1937 at 4.

12. See Smith, *FDR* 387, citing Charles A. Leonard, *A Search for a Judicial Philosophy: Mr. Justice Roberts and the Constitutional Revolution of 1937* (Port Washington, NY: Kennikat Press, 1971). Michael Ariens argues nonetheless that it was reasonable that Roberts and Chief Justice Hughes knew of the plan before it

was announced. See, e.g., Michael Ariens, *A Thrice-Told Tale, or Felix the Cat,* 107 Harv. L. Rev. 620 (1994).

13. See John W. Chambers, *The Big Switch: Justice Roberts and the Minimum-Wage Cases,* 10 Labor History 44, 73 (1969) (Roberts acknowledged in 1954 that at the time he was "fully conscious of the tremendous strain and threat to the existing Court inherent in the reorganization plan").

14. See Laurence Tribe, *God Save This Honorable Court* 66–67 (New York: Random House, 1985).

15. Frankfurter, *Mr. Justice Roberts* 311.

16. Robert C. Post, *Due Process in the Taft Court Era,* 78 B.U. L. Rev. 1489, 1495 (1998).

17. Sam Rosenfeld, *The Polarizers: Postwar Architects of Our Partisan Era* (Chicago: University of Chicago Press, 2018).

18. "Control," *Time,* November 7, 1932, at 13.

19. Franklin D. Roosevelt, "Address at the Democratic Victory Dinner. Washington, D.C.," March 4, 1937, *available at* link #18.

20. Franklin D. Roosevelt, "Fireside Chat," March 9, 1937, *available at* link #19.

21. Roosevelt, "Fireside Chat," March 9, 1937.

22. Franklin D. Roosevelt, "Excerpts from the Press Conference," July 23, 1937, *available at* link #20.

23. While we have no adequate polling data on public attitudes about whether the court was behaving politically during the time, one Boston University master's student noticed a significant rise in the use of the phrases "legislating from the bench" and "sociological jurisprudence" during the period of the conflict between FDR and the Court. See Matthew Pastore, *The Story of Supreme Court Politicization: The Mass Public v. Elite Divide,* OpenBU, 33–38 (2017), *available at* link #21. As Pastore writes, "The President's attempts to pack the court represented an effort to dilute the Court's authority in order to prevent the New Deal policies from being declared unconstitutional. Controlling the court became a priority of the Roosevelt administration, creating a greater incentive to politicize the court so that its decisions would be more predictable and would see the New Deal policies in a more favorable light." *Id.* 37–38.

Barry Cushman finds the public generally supportive of the Court during the period. Before the court-packing fight, in April 1936, Gallup found that 21.7 percent of Americans thought the Court had "stood in the way of the people's will," while 39.2 percent thought the Court had "protected the people." In July the next year, five months after the court-packing plan was announced, those numbers were if anything more supportive of the court—23.1 percent versus 43.1 percent. Barry Cushman, *Mr. Dooley and Mr. Gallup: Public Opinion and Constitutional Change in the 1930s,* 50 Buffalo Law Rev. 7, 67–70 (2002).

24. *West Coast Hotel Co. v. Parrish,* 300 U.S. 379 (1937).

25. Herbert Hovenkamp, *Enterprise and American Law, 1836–1937* 198 (Cambridge, MA: Harvard University Press, 1991).

26. Thurman Wesley Arnold, *The Symbols of Government* 106 (New York: Harcourt, 1962).

27. Lester Chandler, *America's Greatest Depression: 1929–1941* 9 (New York: Harper & Row, 1970).

28. Arnold, *The Symbols of Government* 231.

29. Arnold, *The Symbols of Government* 105.

30. Roosevelt, "Fireside Chat," March 9, 1937.

31. Bruce Ackerman, 2 *We the People: Transformations*, 319–323 (Cambridge, MA: Belknap Press of Harvard University Press, 2000) (Kindle ed.).

32. John W. Chambers, *The Big Switch: Justice Roberts and the Minimum-Wage Cases*, 10 Labor History 44, 70 (1969).

33. Burt Solomon, *The Original Justice Roberts*, 34 J. Sup. Ct. Hist. 196, 202 (2009).

34. Solomon, *The Original Justice Roberts* 196, 202.

35. Caldeira, *Public Opinion* 1150.

36. Cushman's work has not been without critics. See especially William Lasser, *Justice Roberts and the Constitutional Revolution of 1937—Was There a "Switch in Time"?*, 78 Texas L. Rev. 1347 (1999). Mark Tushnet argues Cushman's is essentially an externalist account of the change; see Mark Tushnet, *The New Deal Constitutional Revolution: Law, Politics, or What?*, 66 U. Chi. L. Rev. 1061 (1999). Keith Whittington argues the account is weakened by the failure to consider political science literature from the period; Keith E. Whittington, *Rethinking the New Deal Court: The Structure of a Constitutional Revolution*, 73 Business History Rev. 306, 308 (1999). Andrew Rutten reads Cushman as arguing there is no politics within law. See Andrew Rutten, *Rethinking the New Deal Court: The Structure of a Constitutional Revolution*, 6 Independent Rev. 144 (2001). I don't share Rutten's understanding of Cushman's work. His aim is to emphasize the law, not deny the politics.

37. "*Wickard v. Filburn* has been regarded as the most expansive assertion of the commerce power in our history." *National Federation of Independent Business v. Sebelius*, 567, 657 U.S. 519 (2012).

38. Barry Cushman, *Rethinking the New Deal Court: The Structure of a Constitutional Revolution* 212 (New York: Oxford University Press, 1998).

39. Cushman, *Rethinking the New Deal Court* 212–213.

40. Cushman, *Rethinking the New Deal Court* 214.

41. Cushman, *Rethinking the New Deal Court* 216.

42. Cushman, *Rethinking the New Deal Court* 216.

43. Cushman, *Rethinking the New Deal Court* 217.

44. Cushman, *Rethinking the New Deal Court* 217.

45. Cushman, *Rethinking the New Deal Court* 217.

46. Cushman, *Rethinking the New Deal Court* 217.

47. Cushman, *Rethinking the New Deal Court* 217.

48. Cushman, *Rethinking the New Deal Court* 217.

49. Cushman, *Rethinking the New Deal Court* 217.

50. Cushman, *Rethinking the New Deal Court* 217.

51. Cushman, *Rethinking the New Deal Court* 218.

52. Roosevelt, "Address at the Democratic Victory Dinner."

## Chapter Nine

1. *Osborn v. Bank of U.S.*, 22 U.S. 738 (1824) (from the opinion: "The amended bill charges, that, subsequent to the service of the subpoena and injunction, to-wit, on the 17th of September, 1819, J. L. Harper, who was employed by Osborn to collect the tax, and well knew that an injunction had been allowed, proceeded by violence to the office of the Bank at Chillicothe, and took therefrom 100,000 dollars, in specie and bank notes, belonging to, or in deposit with, the plaintiffs").

2. *McCulloch v. the State of Maryland et al.*, 17 U.S. (4 Wheat.) 431 (1819).

3. *Collector v. Day*, 78 U.S. 113 (1870), in which a Massachusetts probate court judge successfully recovered a federal tax that had been assessed on his salary. The majority emphasizes the importance of symmetry, noting that "the two governments are upon an equality," *id.* at 126, and "if the means and instrumentalities employed by [the federal government] to carry into operation the powers granted to it are necessarily . . . exempt from taxation by the States, why are not those of the States . . . for like reasons, equally exempt from Federal taxation? Their unimpaired existence in the one case is as essential as in the other." *Id.* at 127. The case is, in some sense, a mirror image of *Dobbins v. Commissioners of Erie County*, 41 U.S. 435 (1842), which held that Pennsylvania could not apply a tax on "all offices and posts of profit" to the captain of a United States revenue cutter.

4. This was, practically speaking, Justice Douglas's practice by the end of his tenure. While in his first years on the bench, Douglas favored the government even more than the majority of the Court (75 of 91 cases), he subsequently switched to the taxpayer for the rest of his tenure on the bench. In the first sixteen years after the switch, he found for the taxpayer in 54 of 116 cases (the Court decision favored the taxpayer in only 33 cases); in the next six, he found for the taxpayer in 24 of 33 cases (the Court decision favored the taxpayer in 6 cases). His rebellion was tempered only slightly during his last nine years on the bench, when he found for the taxpayer in 23 of 38 cases (the Court decision favored the taxpayer in 10 cases). After switching, he was the lone dissenter 26 times in 187 cases. See Bernard Wolfman et al., *The Behavior of Justice Douglas in Federal Tax Cases*, 122 U. Pa. L. Rev. 235 (1973).

5. *State of New York v. U.S.*, 326 U.S. 572, 579 (1946).

6. *Ohio v. Helvering*, 292 U.S. 360, 369 (1934).

7. *State of New York v. U.S.*, 326 U.S. 572, 580 (1946).

8. *State of New York v. U.S.*, 326 U.S. 572, 581 (1946).

9. *National League of Cities v. Usery*, 426 U.S. 833 (1976).

10. *Usery*, 426 U.S. 833, 860 (Brennan, J., dissenting).

11. Those cases were *United Transportation Union v. Long Island Railroad Co.*, 455 U.S. 678 (1982) (finding that ownership of a railroad was not a traditional state function); *Hodel v. Va. Surface Mining & Reclamation Ass'n*, 452 U.S. 264 (1981) (establishing conditions for the application of the National League of Cities standard); *Bell v. New Jersey*, 461 U.S. 773 (1983) (finding that forcing states to repay misused funds allotted under Title I of the Elementary and Secondary Education Act was not a violation of the Tenth Amendment); *EEOC v. Wyoming*, 460 U.S. 226 (1983) (finding that the Age Discrimination in Employment Act did not impair the performance of traditional state functions in violation of the Tenth Amendment); *Molina-Estrada v. Puerto Rico Highway Authority*, 680 F.2d 841 (1st Cir. 1982) (finding that operation of the Highway Authority was a traditional government function); *Alamo v. Autoridad de Comunicaciones de Puerto Rico*, 569 F. Supp. 1434 (D.P.R. 1983) (finding that the FLSA did not apply to the Puerto Rico Communications Authority, as this was a traditional state function); *Friends of Earth v. Carey*, 552 F.2d 25 (2nd Cir. 1977) (finding that the Clean Air Act did not violate the Tenth Amendment); *Kramer v. New Castle Area Transit Auth.*, 677 F.2d 308, 310 (3d Cir. 1982) (finding that public bus operations are not a traditional state function); *Virginia Surface Mining & Reclamation Ass'n v. Andrus*, 483 F. Supp. 425 (W.D. Va. 1980) (finding that the Surface Mining and Reclamation Act violated state authority under the Tenth Amendment); *Texas v. United States*, 730 F.2d 339, 353–354 (5th Cir. 1984) (finding that a federal railway act did not regulate "states as states"); *Crawford v. Pittman*, 708 F.2d 1028 (5th Cir. 1983) (finding that placing conditions upon receipt of federal funding for disabled children did not regulate states as states); *Bryson v. De Ridder*, 707 F. Supp. 245 (W.D. La. 1987) (finding that the FLSA did not apply to a city ambulance service prior to the *Garcia* decision); *San Antonio Metropolitan Transit Authority v. Donovan*, 557 F. Supp. 445 (W.D. Tx. 1983) (finding that the FLSA did not apply to state transit workers); *Young v. Texas*, 511 F. Supp. 169 (S.D. Tx. 1981) (finding that the state could set its own wage and hour standards for non-academic employees of a university); *Amersbach v. Cleveland*, 598 F.2d 1033 (6th Cir. 1979) (finding that operation of an airport was an integral government function); *Dove v. Chattanooga Area Regional Transp. Authority*, 539 F. Supp. 36 (E.D. Tenn. 1981) (finding that operation of a transit system is an integral government function); and *Usery v. Owensboro-Daviess County Hospital*, 423 F. Supp. 843 (W.D. Ky. 1976) (finding that equal pay provisions of federal law did not apply to state employees).

12. *I.N.S. v. Chadha*, 462 U.S. 919, 967 (1982).

13. *Garcia v. San Antonio Metropolitan Transit Authority*, 469 U.S. 528, 538–539 (1985) (citations excluded).

14. *Garcia v. San Antonio Metropolitan Transit Authority*, 539 U.S. 528, 539 (1985).

15. *Garcia v. San Antonio Metropolitan Transit Authority*, 544 U.S. 528, 544 (1985).

16. *Garcia v. San Antonio Metropolitan Transit Authority*, 469 U.S. 528, 546 (1985).

17. *Garcia v. San Antonio Metropolitan Transit Authority*, 469 U.S. 528, 580 (1985).

18. *Garcia v. San Antonio Metropolitan Transit Authority*, 469 U.S. 528, 581, 587 (1985).

19. *Garcia v. San Antonio Metropolitan Transit Authority*, 469 U.S. 528, 588 (1985).

20. *Garcia v. San Antonio Metropolitan Transit Authority*, 469 U.S. 528, 589 (1985).

21. *Garcia v. San Antonio Metropolitan Transit Authority*, 469 U.S. 528, 589 (1985).

22. Kevin Fedarko, "A Gun Ban Is Shot Down," *Time* 85 (May 8, 1995).

23. *U.S. v. Lopez*, 115 S.Ct. 1624, 1629–1630 (1995).

24. *U.S. v. Lopez*, 115 S.Ct. 1624, 1630–1631(1995).

25. *U.S. v. Lopez*, 514 U.S. 549, 564 (1995).

26. *U.S. v. Lopez*, 115 S.Ct. 1624, 1632 (1995).

27. This is how David Currie had referred to *Lopez*'s parallel from the early twentieth century, *Hammer v. Dagenhart*, 247 U.S. 251 (1918). David P. Currie, *The Constitution in the Supreme Court: The Second Century, 1888–1986* 101 (Chicago: University of Chicago Press, 1990).

28. *U.S. v. Morrison*, 529 U.S. 598 (2000).

29. Congress received evidence for, among other things, the findings that violence is "the leading cause of injuries to American women ages 15–44," S. Rep. No. 103-138 at 38 (1993); that since 1974, "the assault rate against women has outstripped the rate for men by at least twice for some age groups and far more for others," S. Rep. No. 101-545 at 30 (1990); that battering "is the single largest cause of injury to women in the United States," *id.* at 37; that "over 1 million women in the United States seek medical assistance each year for injuries sustained [from] their husbands or other partners," *id.*; that "partial estimates show that violent crime against women costs this country at least 3 billion...dollars a year," *id.* at 33; that "estimates suggest that we spend \$5 to \$10 billion a year on health care, criminal justice, and other social costs of domestic violence," S. Rep. No. 103-138 at 41 (1993); that "three-quarters of women never go to the movies alone after dark because of the fear of rape and nearly 50 percent do not use public transit alone after dark for the same reason," S. Rep. No. 102-197 at 38 (1991); and that "almost 50 percent of rape victims lose their jobs or are forced to quit because of the crime's severity," S. Rep. No. 103-138 at 38 (1993). All quotes and citations taken from *United States v. Morrison*, 529 U.S. 598, 631–636 (2000) (Souter, J., dissenting). Souter notes that this "mountain of data" is much larger than what was in the record when the Civil Rights Act was undergoing commerce clause scrutiny. *Id.* at 628, 635.

30. S. Rep. No. 103-138 at 54 (1993).

31. While criticized and, by some, vilified, the Supreme Court's *Civil Rights Cases* (1883) were still the law of the land. Though many in the Justice Department believed the government should challenge that authority, the safer path was deemed to be defending the law under the commerce authority. Jack Balkin has revived the call to correct the error of the *Civil Rights Cases,* resting his claim on the view that the Fourteenth Amendment embodied a new federal

right to equality (and therefore not limited by the state action doctrine). See Jack M. Balkin, *The Reconstruction Power*, 85 N.Y.U. L. Rev. 1801 (2010).

32. *Heart of Atlanta Motel, Inc. v. United States*, 379 U.S. 241 (1964).

33. *Heart of Atlanta Motel, Inc. v. United States*, 379 U.S. 241, 252–253 (1964).

34. H.R. Conf. Rep. No. 103-711, at 385, U.S. Code Cong. & Admin. News 1994, pp. 1803, 1853.

35. *U.S. v. Morrison*, 529 U.S. 598, 615–616 (2000).

36. *U.S. v. Morrison*, 529 U.S. 598, 616 (2000).

37. Brandon P. Denning & Glenn H. Reynolds, *Rulings and Resistance: The New Commerce Clause Jurisprudence Encounters the Lower Courts*, 55 Ark. L. Rev. 1253, 1254 (2003).

38. Brief for Petitioners, *Eldred v. Ashcroft*, 537 U.S. 186 (2003), 11.

39. *Gonzales v. Raich*, 545 U.S. 1 (2005).

40. Brief of Constitutional Law Scholars as *Amici Curiae* in Support of Respondents at 8, *Gonzales v. Raich*, 545 U.S. 1 (2005) (No. 03-1454).

41. *Gonzales v. Raich*, 545 U.S. 1, 17 (2005) (emphasis added).

42. *Gonzales v. Raich*, 545 U.S. 1, 35 (2005).

43. *Gonzales v. Raich*, 545 U.S. 1, 37 (2005).

44. *Gonzales v. Raich*, 545 U.S. 1, 37 n.2 (2005).

45. *Gonzales v. Raich*, 545 U.S. 1, 47 (2005).

46. *Gonzales v. Raich*, 545 U.S. 1, 39 (2005).

47. *Printz v. U.S.*, 521 U.S. 898 (1997).

48. *Gonzales v. Raich*, 545 U.S. 1, 42 (2005).

49. *Gonzales v. Raich*, 545 U.S. 1, 49–50 (2005).

50. *Gonzales v. Raich*, 545 U.S. 1, 43 (2005).

51. See, e.g., Jonathan Adler, *Federalism After* Gonzales v. Raich*: Is Morrison *Dead? Assessing a Supreme Drug (Law) Overdose*, 9 Lewis & Clark L. Rev. 751 (2005); Simon Lazarus, *Federalism R.I.P.? Did the Roberts Hearings Junk the Rehnquist Court's Federalism Revolution?* 56 DePaul L. Rev. 1, 7–8 (2006); Gerard N. Magliocca, *A New Approach to Congressional Power: Revisiting the Legal Tender Cases*, 95 Geo. L.J. 119, 120–121 (2006).

52. *National Federation of Independent Business v. Sebelius*, 567 U.S. 519, 547 (2012).

53. *Reagan's Solicitor General Promises to "Eat a Hat Made of Kangaroo Skin" if Courts Repeal Health Law*, ThinkProgress, *available at* link #22. For an account by the architect of the litigation, see Randy E. Barnett, *Our Republican Constitution: Securing the Liberty and Sovereignty of We the People* (New York: Broadside Books, 2016).

54. *National Federation of Independent Business v. Sebelius*, 567 U.S. 519, 551 (2012).

55. *National Federation of Independent Business v. Sebelius*, 567 U.S. 519, 552 (2012).

56. Einer Elhauge, *Obamacare on Trial* 30–37 (n.p.: Einer Elhauge, 2012) (Kindle ed.).

57. Elhauge, *Obamacare on Trial* 30.

58. Bruce Ackerman, 3 *We the People: The Civil Rights Revolution* 514 (Cambridge, MA: The Belknap Press of Harvard University Press, 2014) (Kindle ed.).

## Chapter Ten

1. The debate on constitutional immunity is endless. For a beginning, see, e.g., Martha A. Field, *The Eleventh Amendment and Other Sovereign Immunity Doctrines: Part One*, 126 U. Pa. L. Rev. 515 (1978) (arguing that sovereign immunity is a common law doctrine and not constitutionally compelled); William A. Fletcher, *A Historical Interpretation of the Eleventh Amendment: A Narrow Construction of an Affirmative Grant of Jurisdiction Rather than a Prohibition Against Jurisdiction*, 35 Stan. L. Rev. 1033 (1983) (arguing that the amendment does not cover federal question or admiralty jurisdiction); John J. Gibbons, *The Eleventh Amendment and State Sovereign Immunity: A Reinterpretation*, 83 Colum. L. Rev. 1889 (1983) (arguing from a historical standpoint that the amendment's passage was primarily secured as part of a bargain to enforce the peace treaty); Vicki C. Jackson, *Principle and Compromise in Constitutional Adjudication: The Eleventh Amendment and State Sovereign Immunity*, 75 Notre Dame L. Rev. 1010 (2000) (arguing that "sovereign immunity is in some respects unjust" and "the Eleventh Amendment need not be understood to have endorsed that injustice as a general proposition"); James E. Pfander, *History and State Suability: An "Explanatory" Account of the Eleventh Amendment*, 83 Cornell L. Rev. 1269 (1998) (arguing that the amendment represented a compromise on fiscal policy between the states and the federal government).

2. So why would we ever permit such a choice? The answer is familiar to theologians defending free will: if the right thing to do is to subject oneself to a process, then we give an entity the ability to do right, and display right, by choosing to submit to that process. I'm not a charitable person if the government takes 10 percent of my income and gives it to the poor. But I am a charitable person if, under no legal compulsion to do so, I give 10 percent of my income to the poor. Good comes from doing good when the opportunity for not doing good remains. And decent people give others the freedom to do good.

3. I am eternally grateful to the members of a seminar I taught at Stanford in 2005 for this insight. I can't precisely remember from whom it emerged, but I am quite certain it was not I.

4. Federal Tort Claims Act, 28 U.S.C. § 1346(b); Tucker Act, 28 U.S.C. § 1491.

5. Or at least changed. The relevant "people" before were juries. Today, it may be the legislative process that is authorizing the governmental action.

6. Jed S. Rakoff, *Why Innocent People Plead Guilty*, The New York Review of Books, Nov. 20, 2014, *available at* link #23. See also Daniel S. McConkie, *Judges as Framers of Plea Bargaining*, 26 Stan. L. & Pol'y Rev. 61, 62–63 (2015).

7. *Chisholm v. Georgia*, 2 U.S. 419 (1793).

8. Bradford R. Clark, *The Eleventh Amendment and the Nature of the Union*, 123 Harv. L. Rev. 1817, 1904 (2010).

9. Clark, *The Eleventh Amendment and the Nature of the Union* 1908.

10. *Hans v. Louisiana*, 134 U.S. 1 (1890) at 10–11 (even if "it is true, the amendment does so read").

11. *Hans v. Louisiana*, 134 U.S. at 16.

12. Sina Kian makes a similar point in *Pleading Sovereign Immunity: The Doctrinal Underpinnings of Hans v. Louisiana and Ex Parte Young,* 61 Stan. Law Rev. 1233, 1278 (2009).

13. Clark, *The Eleventh Amendment and the Nature of the Union* 1829.

14. *Parden v. Terminal Ry. of Alabama State Docks Dept.*, 377 U.S. 184, 198 (1964).

15. *Green v. Mansour,* 474 U.S. 64, 68 (1985).

16. *Seminole Tribe of Florida v. Florida,* 517 U.S. 44 (1996).

17. *Alden v. Maine,* 527 U.S. 706 (1999).

18. *Alden,* 527 U.S. at 729, quoting *Blatchford v. Native Village of Noatak,* 501 U.S. 775, 779 (1991).

19. *Alden,* 527 U.S. at 756.

## Chapter Eleven

1. This is the contribution of Stewart Baker. See his *Federalism and the Eleventh Amendment*, 48 U. Colo. L. Rev. 139, 179–180 (1977) (arguing that the Eleventh Amendment "preserves…a formal federalism" and acts as "an independent limit on the federal government only when Congress has acted within its delegated powers"). But while Baker says that the courts can use the Eleventh Amendment as a mechanism for "balanc[ing] federal and state interests," he also says that its "primary effect is to pay homage to the formal sovereignty of state governments." *Id.* at 140, 180. See also *id.* at 169 ("When primary aspects of state sovereignty are implicated, the Court demands a very clear waiver of eleventh amendment immunity"). It is a point made by others as well. See, e.g., George D. Brown, *State Sovereignty Under the Burger Court— How the Eleventh Amendment Survived the Death of the Tenth: Some Broader Implications* of Atascadero State Hospital v. Scanlon, 74 Geo. L.J. 363, 365, 394 (1985) (arguing that Eleventh Amendment doctrine is a form of "process federalism that grants the states meaningful protection").

2. *Gregory v. Ashcroft,* 501 U.S. 452 (1991).

3. Subject, at least, to the limitations later imposed by *New York v. U.S.*, 505 U.S. 144 (1992), discussed later in this chapter.

4. *Gregory v. Ashcroft,* 501 U.S. at 460 (1991). This language notwithstanding, the focus is not field preemption, but rather clear statement.

5. *Gregory v. Ashcroft,* 501 U.S. 452 (1991), citing *Atascadero State Hosp. v. Scanlon,* 473 U.S. 234, 243 (1985).

6. *Gregory v. Ashcroft,* 501 U.S. 452, 460 (1991), citing *Atascadero State Hospital v. Scanlon,* 473 U.S. 234, 242 (1985).

7. Individual rights: see, for example, *Kent v. Dulles,* 357 U.S. 116, 129 (1958). Eleventh Amendment: see, for example, *Atascadero State Hosp. v. Scanlon,* 473 U.S. 242 (1985). Invasion of traditional state functions: *Gregory v. Ashcroft,* 501 U.S. at 464.

8. *Gregory v. Ashcroft,* 501 U.S. at 460.

9. *National Federation of Independent Business v. Sebelius*, 567 U.S. 519 (2012).

10. *New York v. U.S.*, 505 U.S. 144 (1992) (NYII); *Printz v. United States*, 521 U.S. 898 (1997).

11. *State of New York v. U.S.*, 326 U.S. 575–576 (1946) (NYI).

12. *New York v. U.S.*, 505 U.S. 144 (1992), citing *Hodel v. Virginia Surface Mining & Reclamation Assn., Inc.*, 452 U.S. 264, 288 (1981).

13. See especially Richard H. Fallon Jr., *Implementing the Constitution* 111–26 (Cambridge, MA: Harvard University Press, 2001); Richard H. Fallon Jr., *The Meaning of Legal "Meaning" and Its Implications for Theories of Legal Interpretation*, 82 U. Chi. L. Rev. 1235 (2015); Richard H. Fallon, *Strict Judicial Scrutiny*, 54 UCLA L. Rev. 1267 (2007).

## Chapter Twelve

1. The Supreme Court has concluded differently, finding adequate support for an individual right of self-defense in the amendment. See *District of Columbia v. Heller*, 554 U.S. 570 (2008). Chief Justice Warren Burger thought that right "one of the greatest pieces of fraud—I repeat the word 'fraud'—on the American public by special interest groups that ever seen in my lifetime." Balkin, *Living Originalism* 4129. By contrast, a federalist view of the Second Amendment— reading the clause as ensuring to states the unbridled authority to regulate guns as they deem proper, free of federal interference—could survive, changing contexts notwithstanding. See David Weisberg, *A Unique, Stand-Alone Second Amendment Implies That Both Heller and McDonald Were Wrongly Decided* (February 8, 2018), *available at* link #24.

## Chapter Thirteen

1. *Erie Railroad Co. v. Tompkins*, 304 U.S. 64 (1938). The case is usefully (and accessibly) described by Wikipedia (Apr. 25, 2018), *available at* link #25.

2. Ernest A. Young, *A General Defense of* Erie Railroad Co. v. Tompkins, 10 J.L. Econ. & Pol'y 17, 21–23 (2013); Tony Freyer, *Harmony and Dissonance: The* Swift *and* Erie *Cases in American Federalism* 122–123 (New York: New York University Press, 1981).

3. Edward A. Purcell Jr., *Brandeis and the Progressive Constitution:* Erie, *the Judicial Power, and the Politics of the Federal Courts in Twentieth-Century America* 96 (New Haven, CT: Yale University Press, 2000).

4. Judiciary Act of 1789, ch. 20, § 34, 1 Stat 73, 92 (codified as amended at 28 U.S.C. § 1652 (1994)).

5. *Swift v. Tyson*, 41 U.S. 1, 18 (1842).

6. *Swift v. Tyson*, 41 U.S. 1, 18–19 (1842).

7. Holmes uses the phrase in *Southern Pac. Co. v. Jensen*, 244 U.S. 205, 222 (1917).

8. Herbert Hovenkamp, *Federalism Revised*, 34 Hastings L.J. 201, 214 (1982) (reviewing Tony Freyer, *Harmony and Dissonance* (1981)).

9. There are whole schools of jurisprudence and economics that try to collapse this top-down/bottom-up distinction. Criminal law, on this account, isn't really top-down. Criminal law is the law we all would agree to in advance of entering into a society governed by that law. Or alternatively, commercial law isn't really bottom-up. Commercial law is a set of rules imposed by judges, in light of which commerce happens. I don't deny the utility of these different collapsing structures. But they miss something important in their understanding of actual law and actual judges. The framework of bottom-up law is to facilitate. The framework of top-down law is to direct or control. Those two frameworks might bleed into each other at the margin. But they are still different.

10. Young, *A General Defense of* Erie Railroad Co. v. Tompkins 31.

11. For a general view of customary law, see David J. Bederman, *Custom as a Source of Law* (New York: Cambridge University Press, 2010).

12. Young, *A General Defense of* Erie Railroad Co. v. Tompkins 32.

13. Hovenkamp, *Federalism Revised* 201, 208.

14. *Watson v. Tarpley*, 59 U.S. 517 (1855).

15. Freyer, *Harmony and Dissonance* 45.

16. Freyer, *Harmony and Dissonance* 58.

17. Defending Story by remarking on the growth, Ed Purcell writes, "Whatever the First Congress intended with Section 34, it surely did not intend the large-scale social practice that had evolved under *Swift* by the end of the nineteenth century." Edward A. Purcell Jr., *Brandeis and the Progressive Constitution:* Erie, *the Judicial Power, and the Politics of the Federal Courts in Twentieth Century America* 306 (New Haven, CT: Yale University Press, 2000).

18. Young, *A General Defense of* Erie Railroad Co. v. Tompkins 31.

19. Young, *A General Defense of* Erie Railroad Co. v. Tompkins 63.

20. Hovenkamp, *Federalism Revised* 225.

21. Justin Zaremby, *Legal Realism and American Law* xv (New York: Bloomsbury, 2014).

22. *Gelpcke v. City of Dubuque*, 68 U.S. 175, 206–207 (1863). To highlight *Gelpcke's* language is not to doubt the correctness of its result. In that case, the Iowa legislature changed the law as it applied to the enforceability of public bonds after the bonds had been issued. The court accepted the lower court's interpretation of Iowa law. But for the same reasons Justice Story rejected improperly applied local law generally, it rejected the application of this local law against the general principle that the enforceability of a contract is determined at the time the contract was made.

23. In the nineteenth century, the English court system was highly fragmented and underwent significant reorganization. Theodore Plucknett, *A Concise History of the Common Law* 211–212 (5th ed., Boston: Little, Brown, 1956). In 1873, the Court of Appeal was the highest court, while appeal to Parliament was eliminated. The number of judges fluctuated: three in 1875, six in 1876, and five in 1881. Sir John Sainty, *The Judges of England 1272–1990*, 10 Selden Soc'y Supp. Series 1 (London: Selden Society, 1992). In 1875, appeal to Parliament

was reinstated and a higher court was reformed in 1876 to consist of "Lords of Appeal in Ordinary" (consisting of House Lords). Their number also fluctuated: two in 1876, three in 1882, and four in 1891. *Id.* at 229.

24. Erwin C. Surrency documents the explosion in reported cases, noting the shift from a period when the law was articulated from general principles to the period when it was drawn from particular cases. Erwin C. Surrency, *Law Reports in the United States*, 25 Am. J. Legal Hist. 48, 66 (1981). Whether "the increased production of decisions coupled with the exclusive reliance upon this source of law result in a lasting transformation of common law reasoning" is a question he leaves unanswered. *Id.*

25. Robert Stevens, *Law School: Legal Education in America from the 1850s to the 1980s* 132 G. Edward White ed., Chapel Hill: University of North Carolina Press, 1983).

26. William R. Casto, *The* Erie *Doctrine and the Structure of Constitutional Revolutions,* 62 Tul. L. Rev. 907, 908 (1988).

27. See Ernest A. Young, *A General Defense of* Erie Railroad Co. v. Tompkins, 10 J.L. Econ. & Pol'y 17, 18 (2013).

28. *Erie R. Co. v. Tompkins*, 304 U.S. 64, 78 (1938).

29. *Erie R. Co. v. Tompkins*, 304 U.S. 64, 79 (1938).

30. See, e.g., Jack Goldsmith and Steven Walt, Erie *and the Irrelevance of Legal Positivism*, 84 Va. L. Rev. 673 (1998); Michael Steven Green, Erie*'s Suppressed Premise*, 95 Minn. L. Rev. 1111, 1127–1135 (2011) (emphasizing logical independence); Young, *A General Defense of* Erie Railroad Co. v. Tompkins. Craig Green goes even further, claiming "judicial lawmaking does not violate legal positivism. On the contrary, many positivists have acknowledged that, when judges decide cases, that is positive law." Craig Green, *Repressing* Erie*'s Myth*, 96 Calif. L. Rev. 595, 605 (2008). I share Ernest Young's view of the significance of this claim: "That is true so far as it goes, but it conflates an external perspective with the internal perspective of the judge deciding cases. From the external perspective, one can readily construct a positivist account of judge-made law: judicial decisions are social facts, and they derive their legal force from the community's acceptance of them as law. But the question is more difficult from the internal perspective of the judge, who typically must ground her own decision in some other source—either a delegation of authority to make law or some *other* positive law...that she interprets and applies. The interesting question about *Swift* is how the judges thought about what they were doing in diversity cases." Young, *A General Defense of* Erie Railroad Co. v. Tompkins 31, 59 n. 239.

31. Goldsmith and Walt's essay Erie *and the Irrelevance of Legal Positivism* is illuminatingly incomplete in a number of ways beyond the cultural. When denying any historical link between the rise of positivism and *Erie*, they emphasize that positivism had achieved its prominence in American jurisprudence by the late nineteenth century, long before *Erie*. They are certainly right that *Swift* does not depend upon the opposite of positivism—as I've already argued. But they both overstate the dominance of positivism in the late nineteenth century and have an unstated and

unconvincing account about how ideas have their effect within a legal culture. It is certainly true that the elite within the legal culture were predominantly positivists by the end of the nineteenth century—just as leading economists were neoclassical by the early part of the twentieth century. But in both cases, it takes time for ideas to seep into their respective cultures. Indeed, it takes the death of a generation before the teachings of a new generation become truth. How much time this takes, or at what rate it occurs, are hard questions. They are not answered by a logic sheet demonstrating what is or is not logically compelled. It is certainly also true that while positivism is increasingly dominant, it was not either conceptually or politically uncontested. This is a perfect application of the matrix that I described in Chapter 7. While Holmes and the like were advancing the positivism, James Carter and many from the school of laissez-faire were advancing something very different. It was, at least initially, contested. What the view of "the practicing bar" was is not clear and certainly not established by anything Goldsmith and Walt rely upon. But we can see in the evolution of the writing how that contest resolves itself, until the moves become not arguments, but truths. In the end, the "relevance" of positivism and realism is not about a logical proof. It is about a cultural affordance. My view is not that positivism entails *Erie*. It is that the legal culture of the time—in which the truth of positivism and realism had achieved a certain dominance—made *Erie* easier, and made the opposite of *Erie* much harder. We don't have a good method for measuring cultural affordance. We certainly don't have logical proofs. But we do have ways of understanding cultures. Those ways are not exhausted by arguments grounded in historical causation, logic, or morality alone.

32. *Erie R. Co. v. Tompkins*, 304 U.S. 64, 79 (1938).

33. For an outstanding piece putting *Sosa* in its jurisprudential context, see Curtis A. Bradley, Jack L. Goldsmith, & David H. Moore, Sosa, *Customary International Law, and the Continuing Relevance of* Erie, 120 Harv. L. Rev. (2006), *available at* link #26.

34. *Sosa v. Alvarez-Machain*, 542 U.S. 692, 746 (2004) (citations omitted).

35. *James B. Beam Distilling Co. v. Georgia*, 501 U.S. 529, 549 (1991) (emphasis in original).

36. Bradford R. Clark, *Separation of Powers as a Safeguard of Federalism*, 79 Tex. L. Rev. 1321, 1414 (2001).

37. *Erie R. Co. v. Tompkins*, 304 U.S. 64, 79 (1938).

38. Michael Green reads some courts—specifically Georgia's—as continuing to follow the *Swift*ian view. Green, Erie's Suppressed Premise 1123–1127. I share Young's skepticism about this reading. Young, *A General Defense of* Erie Railroad Co. v. Tompkins 108–111.

## Chapter Fourteen

1. 12 U.S.C. § 225a (2000).

2. Michael McConnell, *Logical Construction of Article II* (2016) (unpublished draft), *available at* link #27.

3. McConnell, *Logical Construction of Article II.*

4. U.S. Const. art. 1, § 8.

5. *Kendall v. U.S.*, 37 U.S. 524 (1838).

6. *Kendall v. U.S.*, 37 U.S. 524, 610 (1838).

7. *Kendall v. U.S.*, 37 U.S. 524, 610 (1838).

8. *Kendall v. U.S.*, 37 U.S. 524, 610 (1838).

9. Kimberly Amadeo, *The Balance: U.S. Debt by President by Dollar and Percent* (2018), *available at* link #28

10. There is an important dispute about the extent of independence the Framers expected the comptroller to have. All agree that the president had limited supervisory authority over the comptroller. Not all agree he did not have the power of removal. Madison noted that the nature of the office suggested why there would "be strong reasons why an officer of this kind should not hold his office at the pleasure of the executive branch of the government" (1 Annals of Cong. 636 (1789) (Joseph Gales ed., Washington, DC, 1834)), but Madison's original proposal for the office would have made him appointed for a (renewable) term, but removable by the president (1 Annals of Cong. 636 (1789)). That structure would have made him dependent upon both the president (since he could be removed by the president) and the Senate (since he was subject to its consent for reappointment). See *Free Enterprise Fund v. Public Company Account Oversight Board* 561 U.S. 477, 517–518, 530, 500 n. 6 (2010).

11. 15 U.S.C. § 41–58 (2015).

12. *Synar v. United States*, 626 F. Supp. 1374, 1398 (D.D.C.) (per curiam), aff'd sub nom. *Bowsher v. Synar*, 478 U.S. 714 (1986).

13. *Morrison v. Olson*, 487 U.S. 654, 660 (1988).

14. *Morrison v. Olson*, 487 U.S. 654, 663 (1988).

15. *Morrison v. Olson*, 487 U.S. 654, 699 (1988) (citations omitted).

16. Lawrence Lessig & Cass R. Sunstein, *The President and the Administration*, 94 Colum. L. Rev. 1 (1994).

17. *Morrison v. Olson*, 487 U.S. 654, 727 (1988) (Scalia, J., dissenting).

18. *Morrison v. Olson*, 487 U.S. 654, 729 (1988) (Scalia, J., dissenting).

19. *Morrison v. Olson*, 487 U.S. 654, 729–731 (1988).

20. I am completing this book in the middle of special prosecutor Robert Mueller's investigation of alleged crimes relating to the Trump administration. Though that investigation will no doubt affect these conclusions, the effect cannot be properly characterized until after that investigation is completed.

21. This conclusion is strongly supported by the Supreme Court's most recent removal jurisprudence, *Free Enterprise Fund v. Public Company Oversight Board,* 561 U.S. 477 (2010). In that case, the Court struck a for-cause removal clause for its effect in limiting the president's ability to determine whether cause for removal existed. The norm animating the opinion of Chief Justice Roberts was democratic accountability.

## Chapter Fifteen

1. See Akhil Reed Amar, *Fourth Amendment First Principles*, 107 Harv. L. Rev. 757, 786 (1994).
2. See Thomas Y. Davies, *Recovering the Original Fourth Amendment*, 98 Mich. L. Rev. 547, 563–565 (1999); Telford Taylor, *Two Studies in Constitutional Interpretation* 44 (Columbus, OH: Ohio State University Press, 1969).
3. 277 U.S. 438 (1928).
4. Brief for The Pacific Telephone and Telegraph Co. et al. as Amici Curiae Supporting Petitioners, *Olmstead v. United States*, 277 U.S. 438, 453 (1928).
5. *Olmstead v. United States*, 277 U.S. 438, 464 (1928).
6. *Olmstead v. United States*, 277 U.S. 438, 476 (1928).
7. *Olmstead v. United States,* 277 U.S. 438, 472 (1928).
8. *Weems v. United States,* 217 U.S. 349, 373 (1910).
9. *Olmstead v. United States,* 277 U.S. 438, 473, 478 (1928).
10. *Katz v. United States,* 389 U.S. 347 (1967).
11. The organized public police force emerged in the first half of the nineteenth century—beginning with London's (1829), followed by Boston's (1838) and New York's (1844). Edward R. Maguire, *Organizational Structure in American Police Agencies* 117 (Austin T. Turk ed., Albany: State University of New York Press, 2003). By the 1880s, all major U.S. cities had police forces. William Briggs, *Police Oversight: Civilian Oversight Boards and Lessons Learned from Our Neighbors to the North*, 40 Suffolk Transnat'l L. Rev. 139, 141–142 (2017). Before then, law enforcement consisted of "a loose system of sheriffs, constables, and night watchmen." Carol S. Steiker, *Second Thoughts About First Principles,* 107 Harv. L. Rev. 820, 830 (1994).
12. The most extensive work linking trespass actions and Fourth Amendment jurisprudence is Laurent Sacharoff, *Constitutional Trespass*, 81 Tenn. L. Rev. 877 (2014). Sacharoff finds the two doctrines closely linked until *Boyd, id.* at 886, and then reunited after *Olmstead*. After *Katz*, they separate. Orin S. Kerr argues the Court intentionally avoided bringing important trespass principles and remedies into Fourth Amendment jurisprudence; see Orin S. Kerr, *The Curious History of Fourth Amendment Searches*, 2012 Sup. Ct. Rev. 67 (2012). Yet even if kept separate, the incentive effect produced by the former would help define the protection of the latter.
13. Ronald A. Cass, *Damage Suits Against Public Officers*, 129 U. Penn. L. Rev. 1110, 1111 (1981).
14. *Weeks v. United States,* 232 U.S. 383, 391–392 (1914).
15. *People v. Cahan*, 282 P.2d 905, 907 (Cal. 1955).
16. *People v. Cahan*, 282 P.2d 905, 913 (Cal. 1955).
17. *In re Lance W.*, 694 P.2d 744 (Cal. 1985).
18. *New York Times Co. v. Sullivan*, 376 U.S. 254 (1964).
19. *Mapp v. Ohio,* 367 U.S. 643, 659 (1961) (citations omitted).
20. See Richard A. Posner, *The Cost of Rights: Implications for Central and Eastern Europe—and for the United States*, 32 Tulsa L.J. 1, 7–9 (1996). A similar point

is made in William J. Stuntz, *The Uneasy Relationship Between Criminal Procedure and Criminal Justice*, 107 Yale L.J. 1, 4 (1997).

21. *Olmstead v. United States*, 277 U.S. 438, 470 (1928) (Holmes, J., dissenting).

22. *Katz v. United States*, 389 U.S. 347, 357 (1967).

23. Yale Kamisar, *The Warren Court and Criminal Justice: A Quarter-Century Retrospective*, 31 Tulsa L.J. 1, 40 (1995).

24. Thomas N. McInnis, *The Evolution of the Fourth Amendment* 45 (Lanham, MD: Lexington Books, 2009).

25. George Steiner, *After Babel: Aspects of Language and Translation* 249 (New York: Oxford University Press, 1975).

26. *Miranda v. Arizona*, 384 U.S. 436, 467–469, 71, 73 (1966).

27. *Miranda v. Arizona*, 384 U.S. 436, 442 (1966).

28. *Miranda v. Arizona*, 384 U.S. 436, 443–444 (1966).

29. *Miranda v. Arizona*, 384 U.S. 436, 467 (1966).

30. Akhil Amar makes a similar point in *The Constitution Today: Timeless Lessons for the Issues of our Era* 187–188 (New York: Basic Books, 2016).

31. See Paul G. Cassell, Miranda*'s Social Costs: An Empirical Reassessment*, 90 Nw. U. L. Rev. 387, 498 (1996). See also Michael C. Dorf & Charles F. Sabel, *A Constitution of Democratic Experimentalism*, 98 Colum. L. Rev. 267, 460 (1998) ("Although *Miranda* was initially met with hostility by law enforcement agencies, this hostility was not matched by exertions to devise alternative procedures for safeguarding the right to silence.... Nor have the states been especially eager to experiment in this area"). Phillip E. Johnson did propose a statutory solution to *Miranda*. See Phillip E. Johnson, *A Statutory Replacement for the Miranda Doctrine*, 24 Am. Crim. L. Rev. 303 (1986). No state adopted it.

Cassel's characterization is accurate still, though he himself had been a vocal opponent of *Miranda* and became lead attorney in an effort to read a federal statute as supplanting *Miranda*. In *Dickerson v. United States*, 530 U.S. 428 (2000), the Court rejected the federal statute, viewing it as an effort to overrule the Supreme Court. The Court left open the opportunity for legislatures to encourage regimes more protective than the *Miranda* baseline. See *Dickerson v. United States*, 530 U.S. 428, 440 (2000).

## Chapter Sixteen

1. Charles Lane, *The Day Freedom Died: The Colfax Massacre, the Supreme Court, and the Betrayal of Reconstruction* 90–91 (New York: Henry Holt, 2008).

2. See Michael W. McConnell, *The Forgotten Constitutional Moment*, 11 Const. Comment. 115, 134–135 (1994).

3. See William J. Stuntz, *The Collapse of American Justice* 106 (Cambridge, MA: The Belknap Press of Harvard University Press, 2011), citing Lane, *The Day Freedom Died*.

4. *Giles v. Harris*, 189 U.S. 475, 486–488 (1903).

5. Those are not directly the words of scholars, though it is a fair impression of the writing. See, e.g., Damon Keith, *One Hundred Years After* Plessy v. Ferguson, 65 U. Cin. L. Rev. 853, 856 (1997); Judith A. Baer, *Equality Under the Constitution: Reclaiming the Fourteenth Amendment* 112 (Ithaca, NY: Cornell University Press, 1983); Paul Oberst, *The Strange Career of* Plessy v. Ferguson, 15 Ariz. L. Rev. 389, 417 (1973); Michael J. Perry, *The Constitution in the Courts: Law or Politics?* 145 (New York: Oxford University Press, 1994); Richard Kreitner, "This Long-Lost Constitutional Clause Could Save the Fight to Vote," *The Nation*, Jan. 21 2015, *available at* link #29; Erwin Chemerinsky, *The Supreme Court and the Fourteenth Amendment: The Unfulfilled Promise*, 25 Loy. L. A. L. Rev. 1143, 1149 (1992). Edward A. Purcell notes the tendency in legal scholarship to avoid strong criticism of the Waite and Fuller Courts and contests that tendency; see *The Particularly Dubious Case of* Hans v. Louisiana: *An Essay on Law, Race, History, and Federal Courts*, 81 N.C. L. Rev. 1927, 1950–1952 (2008). See also Edward A. Purcell Jr., *On the Complexity of Ideas in America: Origins and Achievements of the Classical Age of Pragmatism*, 27 Law & Soc. Inquiry 967, 977 (2002); J. Morgan Kousser, "The Voting Rights Act and the Two Reconstructions," in *Controversies in Minority Voting: The Voting Rights Act in Perspective* 135, 163 (Bernard Grofman & Chandler Davidson, eds. Washington, DC: Brookings Institution, 1992); Rosemarie Unite, *The Perrymander, Polarization, and Peyote v. Section 2 of the Voting Rights Act*, 46 Loy. L. A. L. Rev. 1075, 1092 (2013). The classic statement is found in Benno C. Schmidt Jr., *Juries, Jurisdiction, and Race Discrimination: The Lost Promise of* Strauder v. West Virginia, 61 Tex. L. Rev. 1401, 1412 (1983) ("Those of us who came of age during or after the Warren Court's great achievements in the law of race relations tend to dismiss the period from Reconstruction to the New Deal as one of Bankruptcy for racial justice. It is taken for granted that the Supreme Court simply turned a deaf ear to the promises of the Reconstruction amendments. The times were racist, and the Court was in tune with the times").

6. The first version provided as follows:

Sec. 1. No discrimination shall be made by any state, nor by the United States, as to the civil rights of persons because of race, color, or previous condition of servitude.

Sec. 2. From and after the fourth day of July, in the year one thousand eight hundred and seventy-six, no discrimination shall be made by any state, nor by the United States, as to the enjoyment by classes of persons of the right of suffrage, because of race, color, or previous condition of servitude.

Sec. 3. Until the fourth day of July, one thousand eight hundred and seventy-six, no class of persons, as to the right of any of whom to suffrage discrimination shall be made by any state, because of race, color, or previous condition of servitude, shall be included in the basis of representation.

Benj. B. Kendrick, *The Journal of the Joint Committee of Fifteen on Reconstruction* 83–84 (New York: n.p., 1914).

7. Richard L. Aynes, *Constricting the Law of Freedom: Justice Miller, the Fourteenth Amendment, and the* Slaughter-House Cases, 70 Chi.-Kent L. Rev. 627, 686 (1994).

8. *Civil Rights Cases*, 109 U.S. 3, 25 (1883).

9. *Plessy v. Ferguson*, 163 U.S. 537 (1896).

10. Bruce Ackerman, 1 *We the People: Foundations* 51–52 (Cambridge, MA: Belknap Press of Harvard University Press, 1991) ("While the Reconstruction Republicans broke new ground in their use of the separation of powers as the principal engine of constitutional revision, they nonetheless managed to codify their reforms in legal instruments that bore the surface appearance of 'constitutional amendments.' These Reconstruction texts are only amendment-simulacra, since they were not generated in accordance with the principles laid down by the Federalist Constitution. Nonetheless, at least the Republicans managed to pour their new constitutional wine into old legal bottles. In contrast, the New Dealers rejected the traditional form of an amendment; instead they relied on the New Deal Court to elaborate their new activist vision through a series of transformative opinions").

11. The clearest exposition is by Howard Jay Graham, in *Our "Declaratory" Fourteenth Amendment,* 7 Stan. L. Rev. 3 (1954). See also Pamela Brandwein, *Rethinking the Judicial Settlement of Reconstruction* 94–97 (Cambridge, UK: Cambridge University Press, 2011); Balkin, *Living Originalism* 2481 ("The rights enumerated in the Constitution—like *habeas corpus* and the rights contained in the Bill of Rights—were declaratory; they stated the basic kinds of liberties that all republican governments should protect.").

12. Especially Brandwein, *Rethinking the Judicial Settlement of Reconstruction.*

13. "'Radicalism" of the Common Law," *Oregonian*, January 6, 1861.

14. *United States v. Rhodes*, 27 F. Cas. 785, 793 (C.C.D. Ky. 1866) (No. 16,151).

15. *United States v. Rhodes*, 27 F. Cas. 785, 794 (C.C.D. Ky. 1866) (No. 16,151).

16. *United States v. Hall*, 26 F. Cas. 79, 81 (C.C.S.D. Ala. 1871) (No. 15,282).

17. *United States v. Hall*, 26 F. Cas. 79, 81 (C.C.S.D. Ala. 1871) (No. 15,282).

18. Brandwein, *Rethinking the Judicial Settlement of Reconstruction* 47–48.

19. *United States v. Hall*, 26 F. Cas. 79, 82 (C.C.S.D. Ala. 1871) (No. 15,282).

20. *United States v. Given*, 25 F. Cas. 1324, 1327 (C.C.D. Del. 1873) (No. 15,210).

21. Civil Rights Act of 1866, ch. 31, 14 Stat. 27. See also *State v. Strauder*, 11 W. Va. 745, 747–749, *rev'd*, 100 U.S. 303 (1880).

22. *Strauder v. West Virginia*, 100 U.S. 303, 308 (1880). Or at least the clarity continues on issues of race. The opinion is quite narrow in its view of equality beyond race. See *Strauder v. West Virginia*, 100 U.S. 303, 310 (1880) (denying equality would reach sex).

23. *Strauder v. West Virginia*, 100 U.S. 303, 308 (1880).

24. Justice Alito surveys the history of the debate about whether the Bill of Rights were to be incorporated against the states via the Fourteenth Amendment in *McDonald v. City of Chicago*, 561 U.S. 742, 759–766 (2010). See also Akhil Reed Amar, *The Bill of Rights and the Fourteenth Amendment* (1992), Faculty Scholarship Series Paper 1040, *available at* link #30.

25. For a similar effort at understanding the limited initial effect of *Slaughterhouse*, see Leslie Friedman Goldstein, *The Specter of the Second Amendment: Rereading*

*Slaughterhouse and Cruikshank*, 21 Studies in American Political Development 131–148 (2007).

26. Blacks had been elected to northern legislatures before—Vermont in 1836 elected Alexander Twilight, and Massachusetts in 1866 elected Edward G. Walker and Charles L. Mitchell (*Black America: A State-by-State Historical Encyclopedia* 385, 868 (Alton Hornsby Jr. ed., Santa Barbara, CA: Greenwood Press, 2011))—but Louisiana opened the way to more than tokenism, at least initially. As Michael Klarman writes, "At times during Reconstruction, blacks were nearly half of the lower-house delegates in Mississippi and Louisiana and a majority in South Carolina. Sixteen southern blacks served in Congress; many held state executive offices; and a black justice sat on the South Carolina Supreme Court. Hundreds of blacks held local offices as sheriffs, magistrates, county councillors, and school board members." Michael J. Klarman, *From Jim Crow to Civil Rights: The Supreme Court and the Struggle for Equality* 29 (New York: Oxford University Press, 2004).

27. Despite the events that occurred there in April 1873, Colfax, Louisiana, was perhaps one of those few places. A former plantation owner and Republican, Willie Calhoun, formed the parish out of his own property on the day U.S. Grant was sworn into office in 1869. The parish was named after the Speaker of the House, Schuyler Colfax, among the most radical of the Radical Republicans. Calhoun leased the small village a building for its courthouse and helped establish the original black/Republican government. Lane, *The Day Freedom Died* 866–872 (Kindle ed.).

28. See Balkin, *Living Originalism* 2477 ("Congressional debates over the Fourteenth Amendment resolve this ambiguity in original meaning").

29. See John Harrison, *Reconstructing the Privileges or Immunities Clause*, 101 Yale L. J. 1385, 1413 (Durham, NC: Duke University Press, 1992). See also the powerful account offered by Michael Kent Curtis, *No State Shall Abridge: The Fourteenth Amendment and the Bill of Rights* (1990). Justice Thomas's opinion in *McDonald v. City of Chicago,* 561 U.S. 742, 805 (2010) (concurring in part and concurring in the judgment) is the most elaborate originalist opinion arguing for the revival of the privileges-or-immunities clause as a central part of Fourteenth Amendment jurisprudence. Harrison's view that the Equal Protection Clause does not regulate legislation is rejected by Balkin. See *Living Originalism* 2819.

30. *Bradwell v. Illinois*, 83 U.S. 130 (1873).

31. *Bartemeyer v. Iowa*, 85 U.S. 129 (1873).

32. Michael A. Ross, *Justice of Shattered Dreams* 18 (Baton Rouge: Louisiana State University Press, 2003).

33. Ross, *Justice of Shattered Dreams* 203.

34. Aynes, *Constricting the Law of Freedom* 663 ("In a private letter to his brother-in-law, Miller complained about the 'vast increase' in the Court's docket").

35. This point is suggested as well by Aynes, *Constricting the Law of Freedom* 652; Kevin Christopher Newsom, *Setting Incorporationism Straight: A Reinterpretation of the Slaughter-House Cases*, 109 Yale L.J. 643, 693 (2000); Bryan H. Wildenthal, *The Lost*

*Compromise: Reassessing the Early Understanding in Court and Congress on Incorporation of the Bill of Rights in the Fourteenth Amendment*, 61 Ohio St. L.J. 1051 (2000).

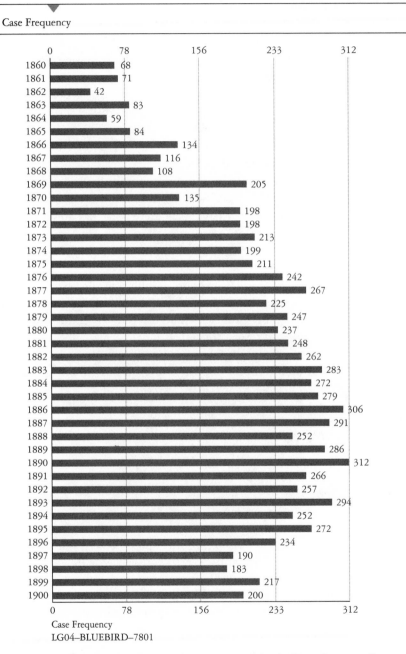

Case Frequency

| Year | Case Frequency |
|------|----------------|
| 1860 | 68 |
| 1861 | 71 |
| 1862 | 42 |
| 1863 | 83 |
| 1864 | 59 |
| 1865 | 84 |
| 1866 | 134 |
| 1867 | 116 |
| 1868 | 108 |
| 1869 | 205 |
| 1870 | 135 |
| 1871 | 198 |
| 1872 | 198 |
| 1873 | 213 |
| 1874 | 199 |
| 1875 | 211 |
| 1876 | 242 |
| 1877 | 267 |
| 1878 | 225 |
| 1879 | 247 |
| 1880 | 237 |
| 1881 | 248 |
| 1882 | 262 |
| 1883 | 283 |
| 1884 | 272 |
| 1885 | 279 |
| 1886 | 306 |
| 1887 | 291 |
| 1888 | 252 |
| 1889 | 286 |
| 1890 | 312 |
| 1891 | 266 |
| 1892 | 257 |
| 1893 | 294 |
| 1894 | 252 |
| 1895 | 272 |
| 1896 | 234 |
| 1897 | 190 |
| 1898 | 183 |
| 1899 | 217 |
| 1900 | 200 |

Case Frequency
LG04–BLUEBIRD–7801

**FIGURE 5** Docket image, Washington University School of Law Supreme Court database, available at link #47.

36. The explosion of the United States Supreme Court docket is apparent from this graph, produced with the Washington University School of Law Supreme Court database (see above).

See also Newsom, *Setting Incorporationism Straight* 703; Charles Fairman, 4 *Reconstruction and Reunion, 1864–8, Part One* 8 at 420 (New York: Macmillan, 1987).

37. As Howard Graham points out, the framers of the Fourteenth Amendment certainly didn't intend this very significant distinction. The citizenship clause was added to the draft amendment long after the privileges-or-immunities clause. That addition thus rendered ambiguous what before would have been clear. Graham, *Our "Declaratory" Fourteenth Amendment* 23–24.

38. *Slaughterhouse Cases*, 83 U.S. 36, 77 (1873) (emphasis added).

39. *Slaughterhouse Cases*, 83 U.S. 36, 79, 80 (1873).

40. Not all of the framers of the Fourteenth Amendment realized this. See Graham, *Our "Declaratory" Fourteenth Amendment* 13 (discussing Rep. James Wilson of Iowa, chairman of the Judiciary Committee). Nor was this universally understood even judicially. See *Rhinehart v. Schuyler*, 7 Ill. 375 (1845), discussed in Howard Jay Graham, *Procedure to Substance*, 40 Calif. L. Rev. 483, 499 (1952).

41. Aynes, *Constricting the Law of Freedom* 632. See also David Bogen, *Slaughterhouse Five: Views of the Case*, 55 Hastings L.J. 333 (2003); Fairman, *Reconstruction and Reunion* (Holmes Devise); Walter Murphy, Slaughterhouse, *Civil Rights, and Limits on Constitutional Change*, 32 Am. J. Juris. 1 (1987); Michael A. Ross, *Justice Miller's Reconstruction: The* Slaughter-House Cases, *Health Codes, and Civil Rights in New Orleans, 1861–1873*, 64 J. of Southern Hist. No. 4, 649–676 (1998); Michael Ross, *Justice of Shattered Dreams*.

42. James W. Fox Jr., *Re-Readings and Misreadings:* Slaughter-House, *Privileges or Immunities, and Section Five Enforcement Powers*, 91 Ky. L.J. 67 (2002).

43. Civil Rights Act of 1866, ch. 31, 14 Stat. 27.

44. *Davidson v. New Orleans*, 96 U.S. 97, 104 (1877).

45. *Slaughterhouse Cases*, 83 U.S. 36, 77 (1873).

46. *Slaughterhouse Cases*, 83 U.S. 36, 78 (1873).

47. *Davidson v. New Orleans*, 96 U.S. 97, 104 (1877).

48. There's one final puzzle in Miller's opinion that we need to explain. In the portion of his opinion in which he distinguished between federal and state "privileges or immunities," Miller quoted the language of the sister clause in the Constitution, Article IV, section 2, clause 1—the "Privileges and Immunities Clause." Here are Miller's words from the opinion:

> In the Constitution of the United States . . . the corresponding provision is found in section two of the fourth article, in the following words: "The citizens of each State shall be entitled to all [the] privileges and immunities of citizens [of] the several States."

Here is the actual language of the Constitution's "Privileges and Immunities Clause":

> The Citizens of each State shall be entitled to all Privileges and Immunities of Citizens in the several States.

Pay attention to where I bracketed the language from Miller's opinion. Justice Miller has plainly misquoted the language of the Constitution, and in a way that seemed plainly intended to support the idea that the Framers were speaking of two bundles of rights. And even more astonishingly, he does so even though Justice Bradley in dissent calls him on the error. See *Slaughterhouse Cases*, 83 U.S. 36, 117 (1873) (Bradley, J., dissenting) ("It is pertinent to observe that both the clause of the Constitution referred to, and Justice Washington in his comment on it, speak of the privileges and immunities of citizens in a state; not of citizens of a state").

How is it possible for a Supreme Court opinion to base its reasoning on the misquotation of the Constitution—and, when called on it, simply ignore the objection? We don't actually know. It wasn't the practice of justices to circulate written drafts of opinions prior to issuing them during the Chase Court. According to Justice Ginsburg, the justice would simply read the opinion out loud to the court, and the justices would vote. But that makes the Miller misquotation even more bizarre because it is clear Bradley noticed it and his opinion responding to it must have been known by Miller. See Newsom, *Setting Incorporationism Straight* 649; Louis Lusky, *By What Right?: A Commentary on the Supreme Court's Power to Revise the Constitution* 194–195 (Charlottesville, VA: Michie, 1975).

49. James Gray Pope, *Snubbed Landmark: Why* United States v. Cruikshank *(1876) Belongs at the Heart of the American Constitutional Canon*, 49 Harv. C.R.-C.L. L. Rev. 385, 388 (2014). See also Chux Onyenyeonwu, *The Sixth Finger* 3274–3282 (Xlibris, 2015) (Kindle ed.) ("The *Cruikshank* ruling did not only kill the spirit of the black man in the journey toward his total emancipation in America, it also took away the fight from the northern white who stood relentlessly for the oppressed black minority"); Stephen P. Halbrook, *Freedmen, the Fourteenth Amendment, and the Right to Bear Arms, 1866–1876* 175 (Westport, CT: Praeger, 1998) (*Cruikshank* "heralded the end of Reconstruction"); William E. Forbath, *Caste, Class, and Equal Citizenship*, 98 Mich. L. Rev. 1, 51 (1999).

50. The dates, not uncontested, are drawn from Halbrook, *Freedmen, the Fourteenth Amendment, and the Right to Bear Arms*.

51. Bradley was already well known by the New Orleans press, and already well liked. Just after he had been confirmed by the Senate, the Louisiana Supreme Court had upheld the legislation at issue in the *Slaughterhouse Cases*. As Charles Lane describes, that decision triggered something of a riot in New Orleans, as the militia tried to enforce the statute. Bradley was asked to stay the application of the state decision while it was pending in the Supreme Court. At first, while

in New Orleans, he indicated he was not able to. Then after a night of protest and potential riots, he changed his mind and indicated the decision would be stayed. This led the *Daily Picayune* to call his decision "one of the ablest that has ever been delivered from the bench." Lane, *The Day Freedom Died* 6350–6380 (Kindle ed.), citing Ronald Labbé & Jonathan Lurie, *The Slaughterhouse Cases: Regulation, Reconstruction, and the Fourteenth Amendment* 148 (Lawrence: University of Kansas Press, 2005).

52. Pope, *Snubbed Landmark* 412–413.

53. Pope, *Snubbed Landmark* 413–414.

54. Pope, *Snubbed Landmark* 414.

55. Pope, *Snubbed Landmark* 415.

56. William Pitt Kellogg, quoted in Pope, *Snubbed Landmark* 415.

57. Robert J. Kaczorowski, *The Politics of Judicial Interpretation: The Federal Courts, Department of Justice, and Civil Rights, 1866–1876* 150–151 (New York: Fordham University Press, 2005).

58. LeeAnna Keith, *The Colfax Massacre: The Untold Story of Black Power, White Terror, and the Death of Reconstruction* 148 (New York: Oxford University Press, 2008).

59. James K. Hogue, *Uncivil War: Five New Orleans Street Battles and the Rise and Fall of Radical Reconstruction* 124, 198–199 (Baton Rouge: Louisiana State University Press, 2006).

60. Frederick Douglass, quoted in Pope, *Snubbed Landmark* 405.

61. See Everette Swinney, *Enforcing the Fifteenth Amendment, 1870–1877,* 28 J. of So. Hist. 202, 211–213 (1962).

62. John R. Lynch, *The Facts of Reconstruction* 115–116 (New York: Neale, 1913).

63. Lynch, *The Facts of Reconstruction* 116.

64. *United States v. Cruikshank,* 25 F. Cas. 707, 711 (C.C.D. La. 1874) (No. 14,897).

65. *United States v. Cruikshank,* 25 F. Cas. 707, 712 (C.C.D. La. 1874) (No. 14,897).

66. *United States v. Cruikshank,* 25 F. Cas. 707, 712 (C.C.D. La. 1874) (No. 14,897).

67. *United States v. Cruikshank,* 25 F. Cas. 707, 712 (C.C.D. La. 1874) (No. 14,897).

68. *Hirabayashi v. United States,* 320 U.S. 81 (1943).

69. Steven G. Calabresi & Julia T. Rickert, *Originalism and Sex Discrimination,* 90 Tex. L. Rev. 1, 35 (2011).

70. *United States v. Cruikshank,* 25 F. Cas. 707, 712 (C.C.D. La. 1874) (No. 14,897).

71. *United States v. Cruikshank,* 25 F. Cas. 707, 712 (C.C.D. La. 1874) (No. 14,897).

72. *United States v. Cruikshank,* 25 F. Cas. 707, 714 (C.C.D. La. 1874) (No. 14,897).

73. *United States v. Cruikshank,* 25 F. Cas. 707, 714 (C.C.D. La. 1874) (No. 14,897).

74. *United States v. Cruikshank,* 25 F. Cas. 707, 714 (C.C.D. La. 1874) (No. 14,897) (emphasis added).

75. It is this distinction that throws into relief one potential weakness in the analysis of Robert J. Kaczorowski in *The Supreme Court and Congress's Power to Enforce Constitutional Rights: An Overlooked Moral Anomaly,* 73 Fordham L. Rev. 153 (2004). Kaczorowski draws his understanding of the enforcement power

from the enforcement clause of the Thirteenth Amendment. But if there's a difference between the nature of the Thirteenth and (some of) the Fourteenth Amendment rights, then the analysis of the enforcement power of the Thirteenth Amendment does necessarily carry over to the Fourteenth.

76. Letter from Justice Joseph P. Bradley to Judge William B. Woods (Mar. 12, 1871) (on file with the New Jersey Historical Society), cited in *Bell v. Maryland*, 378 U.S. 226, 286 (1964) (opinion of Goldberg, J.). The case Woods was deciding was *United States v. Hall*, 26 F. Cas. 79, 81 (C.C.S.D. Ala. 1871) (No. 15,282). See Ruth Ann Whiteside, *Justice Joseph Bradley and the Reconstruction Amendments* 174–182 (April 1981), *available at* link #31.

77. *United States v. Cruikshank*, 25 F. Cas. 707, 714 (C.C.D. La. 1874) (No. 14,897). To be fair, James Pope does not miss this point. Pope, *Snubbed Landmark* 412 (2014).

78. And indeed, neither did the statute, which seemed to indicate that Bradley thought this section unconstitutional. Yet as we'll see, the Supreme Court, while affirming Bradley's result, did not strike the provision down. *United States v. Cruikshank*, 25 F. Cas. 707, 714 (C.C.D. La. 1874) (No. 14,897).

79. *United States v. Cruikshank*, 25 F. Cas. 707, 715 (C.C.D. La. 1874) (No. 14,897). This conclusion would certainly be different today. While the law might be overly broad, today the Court would ask whether, as applied, it violated the Constitution. As applied, it interfered with the right of blacks to vote because they were black, so the Court would have no problem under Bradley's scheme. But the "as applied" analysis was not yet part of the Supreme Court's tools for evaluating a statute. It was thus not available to Bradley as a way to uphold the Court, even while flagging a problem with the statute.

80. *United States v. Cruikshank*, 25 F. Cas. 707, 708, 715 (C.C.D. La. 1874) (No. 14,897).

81. Brandwein, *Rethinking the Judicial Settlement of Reconstruction* 93.

82. *Slaughterhouse Cases*, 83 U.S. 36, 111–124 (1873) (Bradley, J., dissenting).

83. A survey of the top five leading casebooks indicates that two refer to the case only for its rejection of the Second Amendment as incorporated against the states: Kathleen Sullivan and Gerald Gunther, *Constitutional Law* (17th ed., 2010); Russell L. Weaver et al., *Constitutional Law: Cases, Materials, and Problems* (2nd ed., 2011). Two others consider the case as relevant to incorporation more generally. See Paul Brest et al., *Processes of Constitutional Decision-Making: Cases and Materials* (5th ed., 2006); Randy E. Barnett, *Constitutional Law: Cases in Context* (1st ed., 2008). And one focuses on the case's narrowing of the scope of Enforcement Act prosecution. See Geoffrey R. Stone et al., *Constitutional Law* (6th ed., 2009).

84. Lane, *The Day Freedom Died* 231.

85. Brandwein, *Rethinking the Judicial Settlement of Reconstruction* 153.

86. Or maybe not to anyone schooled in the law. Robert Kaczorowski suggests the "nuances of Bradley's constitutional analysis were not clearly understood by

contemporaries, but the end result certainly was." Kaczorowski, *The Politics of Judicial Interpretation* 150.

87. Meir Dan-Cohen, *Decision Rules and Conduct Rules: On Acoustic Separation in Criminal Law*, 97 Harv. L. Rev. 625 (1984).

88. For the most compelling counter view, see Kaczorowski, *The Politics of Judicial Interpretation* 140–160.

89. Lane, *The Day Freedom Died* 252–253.

90. J. R. Beckwith, quoted in Lane, *The Day Freedom Died* 137.

91. George Henry Williams, quoted in Lane, *The Day Freedom Died* 141.

92. Lane, *The Day Freedom Died* 145.

93. Lane, *The Day Freedom Died* 156–157.

94. Lane, *The Day Freedom Died* 204.

95. The most important turncoats here include Edward Godkin, founder of *The Nation*, initially a prominent abolitionist and then skeptic about Reconstruction and black equality, and other liberal republicans who grew increasingly skeptical of government (because of corruption) and more keen to push civil service reform than black equality. See Andrew L. Slap, *The Doom of Reconstruction* 93 (New York: Fordham University Press, 2007). See also Eric Foner, *Reconstruction* 488 (New York: Harper & Row, 1988) (listing "E. L. Godkin, Horace White, and Samuel Bowles, academic economists Francis Amasa Atkinson and Isaac Sherman, and reform-minded politicians Carl Schurz and James A. Garfield").

96. The best historical account of this argument that I have seen is Mark Walgren Summers, *The Era of Good Stealings* (New York: Oxford University Press, 1993). As Summers argued, the period is likely no more corrupt than any other, but the coverage in the press was certainly greater. More relevant is that the corruption itself was less important than "the corruption issue," as Summers puts it. That issue led onetime reformers to turn against the South. For a smattering of material from the period, see *Money in Politics*, Harper's Weekly, January 30, 1869; "Young Men in South Carolina," *New York Times*, May 26, 1874 (describing a call to a convention to "put down the enormous frauds and every species of corruption which exist in the State").

97. Bruce Ackerman, 2 *We the People: Transformations* 207–211 (Cambridge, MA: The Belknap Press of Harvard University Press, 1998).

98. *Ex parte Milligan,* 71 U.S. 2 (1866).

99. Cynthia Nicolette, "Strategic Litigation & Reconstruction," in *Signposts: New Directions in Southern Legal History* 265, 275 (Sally E. Hadden & Patricia Hagler Minter eds., Athens: University of Georgia Press, 2013).

100. *Mississippi v. Johnson*, 71 U.S. 475, 482–485 (1866).

101. *Georgia v. Stanton*, 73 U.S. 50, 77 (1867).

102. *Georgia v. Stanton*, 73 U.S. 50, 76–77 (1867).

103. Nicolette, "Strategic Litigation & Reconstruction," 285.

104. Lane, *The Day Freedom Died* 246.

105. Bruce Ackerman is skeptical that even this would have been enough. What was necessary was a massive intervention, beginning with Thaddeus Stevens's demand for compensation, and complemented by a much more extensive bureaucratic infrastructure. See Bruce Ackerman, *3 We the People: The Civil Rights Revolution* (Kindle ed.) at 3058 (Cambridge, MA: The Belknap Press of Harvard University Press, 2014).

106. *Civil Rights Cases*, 109 U.S. 3, 25 (1883).

107. *Civil Rights Cases*, 109 U.S. 3, 14 (1883).

108. *Civil Rights Cases*, 109 U.S. 3, 20–21, 24–25 (1883).

109. *Civil Rights Cases*, 109 U.S. 3, 40 (1883) (Harlan, J., dissenting).

110. *Civil Rights Cases*, 109 U.S. 3, 40 (1883) (Harlan, J., dissenting).

111. Brandwein, *Rethinking the Judicial Settlement of Reconstruction* 2648 (Kindle ed.).

112. *Civil Rights Cases*, 109 U.S. 3, 25 (1883).

113. Jack M. Balkin, *The Reconstruction Power*, 85 N.Y.U. L. Rev. 1801 (2010).

114. Brandwein, *Rethinking the Judicial Settlement of Reconstruction* 188 (emphasis added).

115. *United States v. Reese,* 92 U.S. 214 (1876).

116. Goldstein's comment is cited in Brandwein, *Rethinking the Judicial Settlement of Reconstruction* 123.

117. *Blyew v. United States*, 80 U.S. 581, 599 (1871) (Bradley, J., dissenting).

## Chapter Seventeen

1. *Schenck v. United States*, 249 U.S. 47, 52 (1919).

2. *Frohwerk v. United States*, 249 U.S. 204, 209 (1919).

3. *Debs v. United States*, 249 U.S. 211 (1919).

4. *Gitlow v. New York*, 268 U.S. 652, 672 (1925).

5. *Whitney v. California*, 274 U.S. 357, 373 (1927).

6. *Giles v. Harris*, 189 U.S. 475 (1903).

7. Klarman, *From Jim Crow to Civil Rights* 24–35.

8. C. Vann Woodward, *The Strange Career of Jim Crow* (New York: Oxford University Press, 2002).

9. Marianne H. Wanamaker, *150 Years of Economic Progress for African American Men: Measuring Outcomes and Sizing Up Roadblocks*, 32 Economic History of Developing Regions 211–220 (2017).

10. Wanamaker, *150 Years of Progress for African American Men* fig. 2.

11. W. E. B. Du Bois, "Introduction" to *NAACP, An Appeal to the World!* 2 (W. E. B. Du Bois ed., New York: NAACP, 1947).

12. George M. Fredrickson, *The Arrogance of Race* 203 (Middletown, CT: Wesleyan University Press, 1988).

13. Nancy Stepan, *The Idea of Race in Science: Great Britain 1800–1960* ix (Hamden, CT: Archon Books, 1982).

14. Stepan, *The Idea of Race in Science* xii–xiii.

15. Fredrickson, *The Arrogance of Race* 204.

16. Elazar Barkan, *The Retreat of Scientific Racism* 2 (New York: Cambridge University Press, 1992).

17. Herbert Hovenkamp, *Social Science and Segregation Before* Brown, 1985 Duke L.J. 624, 664.

18. Hovenkamp, *Social Science and Segregation Before* Brown 627.

19. Stepan, *The Idea of Race in Science* xvi.

20. Stepan, *The Idea of Race in Science* xvi.

21. Richard Hofstadter, *Social Darwinism in American Thought* 192–193 (Boston: Beacon Press, 1992). For work describing these skeptics, see John P. Jackson & Nadine M. Weidman, *Race, Racism, and Science: Social Impact and Interaction* 137–161 (Santa Barbara, CA: ABC-CLIO, 2004); Hubert B. Ross et al., "Pioneer Black Physical Anthropologist," in *African-American Pioneers in Anthropology* 37–49 (Ira E. Harrison and Faye V. Harrison eds., Urbana: University of Illinois Press, 1995); Lesley M. Rankin-Hill & Michael L. Blakey, *W. Montague Cobb (1904–1990): Physical Anthropologist, Anatomist, and Activist*, 96 American Anthropologist 74, 79–80 (1994); Thomas F. Gossett, *Race: The History of an Idea in America* 244–252 (1997); Carol M. Taylor, *W. E. B. Du Bois's Challenge to Scientific Racism*, 11 Journal of Black Studies 449 (1981); Edward H. Beardsley, *The American Scientist as Social Activist: Franz Boas, Burt G. Wilder, and the Cause of Racial Justice, 1900–1915,* 64 Isis 50 (1973).

22. Barkan, *The Retreat of Scientific Racism* 5.

23. See, e.g., Mary Beckman, *Crime, Culpability, and the Adolescent Brain*, 305 Science 596 (2004) (surveying research).

24. Elizabeth Cauffman & Laurence Steinberg, *(Im)maturity of Judgment in Adolescence: Why Adolescents May Be Less Culpable Than Adults*, 18 Behav. Sci. & L. 741 (2000).

25. Wallace J. Mlyniec, *A Judge's Ethical Dilemma: Assessing a Child's Capacity to Choose*, 64 Fordham L. Rev. 1873 (1996).

26. C. Antoinette Clark, *Bridging the Gap: An Interdisciplinary Approach to Juvenile Justice Policy*, 56 DePaul L. Rev. 927 (2007).

27. For work criticizing the inherent difference position, see Richard Farson, *Birthrights* 1–16 (New York: Macmillan, 1974); John Holt, "Why Not a Bill of Rights for Children," in *The Children's Rights Movement: Overcoming the Oppression of Young People* 319 (Beatrice Gross & Ronald Gross eds., Garden City, NY: Anchor Books, 1977); Howard Cohen, *Equal Rights for Children* 42–55 (Totowa, NJ: Littlefield, Adams, 1980); John Harris, "The Political Status of Children," in *Contemporary Political Philosophy: Radical Studies* 35 (Keith Graham ed., Cambridge, UK: Cambridge University Press, 1982); Christopher Phillips, "Why Aren't Kids Part of 'All Men Are Created Equal'?," *Huffington Post* (Dec. 9, 2014), *available at* link #32.

28. Lawrence Lessig, *The Regulation of Social Meaning*, 62 U. Chi. L. Rev. 943 (1995).

29. Cases finding that the government had met the burden under strict scrutiny are rare and infamous. See, e.g., *Korematsu v. United States*, 323 U.S. 214 (1944) (compelling interest justifying race-based exclusion in time of war); *United Jewish Organizations, Inc. v. Carey*, 430 U.S. 144 (1977) (race could be considered under Voting Rights Act); *Sheet Metal Workers v. EEOC*, 478 U.S. 421 (1986) (race could be used to remedy past discrimination); *Grutter v. Bollinger*, 539 U.S. 306 (2003) (race could be used as a factor in admissions); *Fisher v. Univ. of Texas*, 136 S. Ct. 2198 (2016) (same).

30. *Plessy v. Ferguson*, 163 U.S. 537, 551 (1896).

31. Hovenkamp, *Social Science and Segregation Before* Brown 664.

32. *Strauder v. West Virginia*, 100 U.S. 303 (1880).

33. *Plessy v. Ferguson*, 163 U.S. 537, 550 (1896).

34. *Yick Wo v. Hopkins*, 118 U.S. 356, 373–374 (1886).

35. Klarman, *From Jim Crow to Civil Rights* 58.

36. Though it is evident this example will become less and less clear, as awareness about transgender equality becomes more pronounced. I bracket those questions here, though note that eliminating gendered bathrooms is only one remedy to the discriminatory effect from denying gender choice. See Vincent J. Samar, *The Right to Privacy and the Right to Use the Bathroom Consistent with One's Gender Identity*, 24 Duke J. Gender L. & Pol'y 33 (2016); Diana Elkind, Comment, *The Constitutionalism Implications of Bathroom Access Based on Gender Identity*, 9 U. Pa. J. Const. L. 895 (2007); Jennifer Levi & Daniel Redman, *The Cross-Dressing Case for Bathroom Equality*, 34 Seattle U. L. Rev. 133 (2010).

37. *Plessy v. Ferguson*, 163 U.S. 537, 544–545 (1896); *see also Roberts v. City of Boston*, 59 Mass. (5 Cush.) 198, 208 (1850).

38. Federal law explicitly permits same sex schools for elementary and high school education. 20 U.S.C. § 1681; 34 C.F.R. § 106.34(c). That rule has been upheld. *Doe v. Wood Cty. Bd. of Educ.*, 888 F. Supp. 2d 771 (S.D. W. Va. 2012); *A.N.A. v. Breckinridge Cty. Bd. of Educ.*, 833 F. Supp. 2d 673 (W.D. Ky. 2011).

39. Abraham Lincoln, "Speech on the Kansas-Nebraska Act at Peoria, Illinois" (Oct. 16, 1854), in *Abraham Lincoln: Speeches and Writings 1832–1858*, 316 (Don E. Fehrenbacher ed., Washington, DC: Library of America, 1989). But note this was Lincoln's view in 1854 about the idea of making blacks "politically and socially our equals."

40. Klarman, *From Jim Crow to Civil Rights* 303.

41. Michael J. Klarman, Brown, *Originalism, and Constitutional Theory: A Response to Professor McConnell*, 81 Va. L. Rev. 1881, 1933–1934 (1995).

42. Klarman, Brown, *Originalism, and Constitutional Theory* 1932.

43. *Plessy v. Ferguson*, 163 U.S. 537, 551 (1896).

44. Stewart E. Tolnay & E. M. Beck, *A Festival of Violence* 30–31 (Urbana: University of Illinois Press, 1995).

45. Klarman, *From Jim Crow to Civil Rights* 62.

46. *Bailey v. Alabama*, 219 U.S. 219 (1911); *United States v. Reynolds*, 250 U.S. 104 (1919).

47. *McCabe v. Atchison, T. & S.F. R. Co.*, 235 U.S. 151 (1914).

48. *Buchanan v. Warley*, 245 U.S. 60 (1917).

49. Klarman, *From Jim Crow to Civil Rights* 62.

50. *Plessy v. Ferguson*, 163 U.S. 537, 561 (1896) (Harlan, J., dissenting).

51. Stephen Kinzer, *The True Flag: Theodore Roosevelt, Mark Twain, and the Birth of American Empire* 49–158 (New York: Henry Holt, 2017).

52. See Kinzer, *The True Flag* 120 (referring to Rudyard Kipling's famous poem "The White Man's Burden: The United States and the Philippine Islands").

53. Klarman, *From Jim Crow to Civil Rights* 113.

54. Klarman, *From Jim Crow to Civil Rights* 188.

55. Mark J. Penn & E. Kinney Zalesne, *Microtrends* 58 (New York: Twelve, 2007). In November 1938, Gallup asked, "Should we allow a larger number of Jewish exiles from Germany to come to the United States to live?" and 69 percent indicated "no." Susan Welch, *American Opinion Toward Jews During the Nazi Era: Results from Quota Sample Polling During the 1930s and 1940s*, 95 Social Science Quarterly 615, 622 (Table 1) (2014). Six months later, *Fortune* polled American attitudes toward Jews and the explanations for anti-Semitism. Among the responses they found were: "Jews control and monopolize enterprise, hoard money, have too much power," "Jews are unfair and dishonest in business," and "Jews are clannish, nonmixers, not good citizens, interested only in race." For the *Fortune* poll, see Jewish Telegraphic Agency, *Poll Reveals Majority Here Would Bar Doors to Refugees; View on Jews Held Static*, V.J.T.A. News 1, 6–7 (Mar. 27, 1939). Four months after the Fortune study, a Roper Center poll revealed that 10 percent of the respondents believed that "Jews are in some ways distinct from other Americans" and 53 percent expressed that "Jews are different and should be restricted." In addition, 31 percent maintained that "Jews have somewhat different business methods and therefore some measures should be taken to prevent Jews from getting too much power in the business world." Welch, *American Opinion Toward Jews During the Nazi Era* 622 (Table 1); see also Glen Yeadon & John Hawkins, *The Nazi Hydra in America: Suppressed History of a Century* 135 (Joshua Tree, CA: Progressive Press, 2008).

56. Gilbert Allardyce, *What Fascism Is Not*, 84 Am. Hist. Rev. 367, 381 (1979).

57. Allardyce, *What Fascism Is Not* 381.

58. Allardyce, *What Fascism Is Not* 382.

59. Allardyce, *What Fascism Is Not* 382.

60. Jane Dailey, *Sex and Civil Rights* 62 (forthcoming).

61. Klarman, *From Jim Crow to Civil Rights* 175.

62. Dailey, *Sex and Civil Rights* 86.

63. Klarman, *From Jim Crow to Civil Rights* 177.

64. Klarman, *From Jim Crow to Civil Rights* 175.

65. Klarman, *From Jim Crow to Civil Rights* 182.

66. *Korematsu v. United States*, 323 U.S. 214, 216 (1944).

67. *Korematsu v. United States*, 323 U.S. 214, 216 (1944).

68. Susan Kiyomi Serrano & Dale Minami, Korematsu v. United States: *A Constant Caution in a Time of Crisis*, 10 Asian Am. L.J. 37, 42–43 (2003) ("Peter Irons and Aiko Yoshinaga-Herzig uncovered a clear trail of reports, notes, and memoranda penned by government lawyers and high civilian leaders which showed that the Department of Justice and War Department suppressed, altered, and destroyed important evidence during the prosecution of these three cases in order to win them at any cost. This evidence demonstrated that: (1) government prosecutors suppressed authoritative intelligence reports showing that Japanese Americans, as a whole, were loyal; (2) General DeWitt's original Final Report was altered, the original Final Report was destroyed, and an altered report was submitted to the Supreme Court to support the government's position; 31 and (3) General DeWitt's allegations of espionage and sabotage by Japanese Americans were false and known to be false by government attorneys who failed to inform the Supreme Court of this deception"). See also Eric K. Yamamoto, Korematsu *Revisited—Correcting the Injustice of Extraordinary Government Excess and Lax Judicial Review: Time for a Better Accommodation of National Security Concerns and Civil Liberties*, 26 Santa Clara L. Rev. 1, 2 (1986) ("Those now declassified government documents, many of which were discovered through Freedom of Information Act requests, revealed two extraordinary facts: first, government intelligence services unequivocally informed the highest officials of the military and of the War and Justice Departments that the West Coast Japanese as a group posed *no* serious danger to the war effort and that *no need* for mass evacuation existed; and second, that the Supreme Court was deliberately misled about the 'military necessity' which formed the basis of the *Korematsu* decision").

69. *Testimony of Expert Witness David Krech*, May 29, 1951, part II, page 10, *Briggs v. Elliott*, 342 U.S. 350 (1952), *available at* link #33.

70. Klarman, *From Jim Crow to Civil Rights* 302.

71. 342 U.S. 350 (1952).

72. *Thurgood Marshall: His Speeches, Writings, Arguments, Opinions, and Reminiscences* 43 (Mark V. Tushnet ed., Chicago: Lawrence Hill Books, 2001) (quoting from rebuttal argument in *Briggs v. Elliott*, December 7, 1953).

73. See Karl Llewellyn, *The Common Law Tradition: Deciding Appeals* 121–157 (Boston: Little, Brown, 1960); Charles L. Black Jr., *The Lawfulness of the Segregation Decisions*, 69 Yale L.J. 421, 427 (1959).

74. Ackerman, 3 *We the People: The Civil Rights Revolution* 3002 (Kindle ed.).

75. Hubert Humphrey would later embrace this understanding to argue that the "freedom from indignity" should be ranked among FDR's "four freedoms." See his speech on the floor of the Senate, 110 Cong. Rec. 6091 (March 24 1964).

76. Jack Ludwig, *Race and Education: The 50th Anniversary of* Brown v. Board of Education 2 (April 27, 2004), *available at* link #34.

77. Ackerman, 3 *We the People: The Civil Rights Revolution* 970 (Kindle ed.).

78. See *Mayor of Baltimore v. Dawson*, 350 U.S. 877 (1955) (beaches); *Holmes v. City of Atlanta*, 350 U.S. 879 (1955) (golf courses); *Gayle v. Browder*, 352 U.S. 903 (1956) (buses); *New Orleans City Park Improvement Ass'n v. Detiege*, 358 U.S. 54 (1958) (parks); *Johnson v. Virginia*, 373 U.S. 61 (1963) (court rooms); *Lee v. Washington*, 390 U.S. 333 (1968) (prisons).

79. *Naim v. Naim*, 197 Va. 80, 90 (1955).

80. Dailey, *Sex and Civil Rights* 87.

81. Ron Chernow, *Grant* 452 (New York, Penguin Press, 2017).

82. Klarman, *From Jim Crow to Civil Rights* 321.

83. The case was *Naim v. Naim*, 87 S.E.2d 749 (Va. 1955), and it presented a real problem for the post-*Brown* Supreme Court. See *id.*, *vacated and remanded*, 350 U.S. 891 (1955), *aff'd*, 90 S.E.2d 849 (Va. 1955), *motion to recall mandate denied and appeal dismissed*, 350 U.S. 985 (1956). The Supreme Court's jurisdiction is divided between cases the Court has discretion to take (certiorari) and cases it is supposed to take so long as the issue is not insubstantial. In 1955, that distinction placed much more in the appeals category than it does today. *Naim* was an appeal, and the justices believed they had a real obligation to hear it. But they also believed hearing it would be a disaster. As Justice Frankfurter wrote, "To thrust the miscegenation issue into 'the vortex of the present disquietude' would risk 'thwarting or seriously handicapping the enforcement of [*Brown*].'" Klarman, *From Jim Crow to Civil Rights* 322. As Klarman describes, the Court at first ducked the case by returning it to Virginia with instructions to flesh out better the relationship of their parties to the state. The Virginia Supreme Court essentially refused. When the case was appealed to the Court again, the Court had to "swallow[] their collective pride and vote[] to dismiss the appeal on the ground that the Virginia court's response 'leaves the case devoid of a properly presented federal question.'" As Klarman writes, "A majority of the justices apparently preferred to be humiliated at the hands of truculent state jurists rather than to stoke further the fires of racial controversy." Klarman, *From Jim Crow to Civil Rights* 323.

84. Klarman, *From Jim Crow to Civil Rights* 321.

85. *Perez v. Lippold*, 198 P.2d 17, 32 (Cal. 1948) (Carter, J., concurring).

86. Dailey, *Sex and Civil Rights* 196.

87. *Loving v. Virginia*, 388 U.S. 1, 3 (1967).

88. *Loving v. Virginia*, 388 U.S. 1, 11 (1967).

89. *Loving v. Virginia*, 388 U.S. 1, 11 (1967).

90. Ackerman, 3 *We the People: The Civil Rights Revolution* 6034 (Kindle ed.).

91. As Alfred Avins writes in a 1966 article defending anti-miscegenation laws on originalist grounds:

> The spectre of miscegenation was then, as it is at times today, a bugaboo which the southerners in Congress and their northern sympathizers overworked at every opportunity. It became the *reductio ad absurdum* of the congressional

debates. Whenever anyone proposed measures for the protection of Negro rights, the cry "Do you want your daughter to marry a Negro?" was raised. In context these posturings must be read for what they were: political smokescreens, which everyone discounted at the time, and which are merely indicative of what the Congress clearly thought it was not doing.

Alfred Avins, *Anti-Miscegenation Laws and the Fourteenth Amendment: The Original Intent*, 52 Va. L. Rev. 1224, 1227 (1966). These quotes are drawn from Avins's article:

At 1228: "Senator Willard Saulsbury, a Delaware Democrat,... mentioned that a colored soldier was punished in Delaware for having the 'insolence' to tell a respectable white storekeeper, without provocation, that the soldier expected to have a white wife in three years" (citing, at n. 11, Cong. Globe, 38th Cong., 1st Sess., pt. 1, at 841 (1864)).

At 1229: "Senator Reverdy Johnson, a Maryland Democrat, brought the point up again during a debate on the use of Washington, D.C., streetcars by Negroes. He argued that since all were agreed that the marriage of white women to Negro men was undesirable, they should not have to sit next to each other on the streetcar" (citing, at n. 13, supra n. 11, pt. 2, at 1157).

At 1230–1231: "Congressman Andrew J. Rogers...asserted that Negro voting would lead to miscegenation, and that it was hypocritical for New England representatives to advocate Negro suffrage, since the Rhode Island statutes of 1822 and 1844 made miscegenation criminal" (citing, at n. 22, Cong. Globe, 39th Cong., 1st Sess., pt. 1, at 200 (1866)).

At 1232–1234: "Senator Garrett Davis, the unreconstructed Kentucky Democrat...defied the Republicans to force his state to change its law which punished a Negro who raped a white woman with death, but merely imprisoned a white man found guilty of the same offense" (citing, at n. 31, supra n. 22, at 397, 418); "Davis also decried the bill for overriding state anti-miscegenation statutes" (citing, at n. 32, supra n. 22, at 418); "Davis returned to the fray with a long harangue attacking the civil rights bill for, *inter alia,* overruling state anti-miscegenation laws" (citing, at n. 37, supra n. 22, at 598).

At 1235: "When the first drafts of what was later to become the fourteenth amendment were considered by the House, Rogers, the long-winded New Jersey Democrat, engaged in another lengthy harangue, addressed more to political sympathizers in the galleries than to members on the floor" (citing, at n. 46, supra n. 22, at 135–40); "Once again, Republicans sat back and baited him" (citing, at n. 47, *id.*); "His onslaught included a familiar charge that the privileges-and-immunities clause would ban state anti-miscegenation laws" (citing, at n. 48, *id.* at 134) "but the majority treated the charge with scorn."

At 1237: "During consideration of Negro suffrage in the District of Columbia, Senator Davis of Kentucky delivered an extended harangue on Negro inferiority, including a dire warning on the evils to be anticipated from miscegenation as illustrated by the Latin American experience, and accusing northern Radicals of hypocrisy for not marrying colored women" (citing, at n. 59, Cong. Globe., 39th Cong, 2d Sess., pt. 1, at 78–81 (1866)).

At 1238: "Congressman James P. Knott of Kentucky, in the course of a long speech attacking Negro suffrage, read from a portion of *Kent's Commentaries* which condemned miscegenation" (citing, at n. 65, Cong. Globe, 40th Cong., 2d Sess., pt. 2, at 1963 (1867)); "A Michigan Republican promptly declared that this had nothing to do with the right to vote" (citing, at n. 65, *id.*, at 1970).

At 1239: "Senator James R. Doolittle, a 'lame-duck' Wisconsin conservative and ardent opponent of the Republican policy of Reconstruction, likewise made a speech discussing the racial theories of 'ethnologists,' and the physical characteristics of Negroes. He claimed that mulattoes could not propagate their species indefinitely, and concluded: 'It is the fiat of the Almighty which is stamped upon this very idea of forcing an amalgamation of the races against nature and against the laws of God'" (citing, at n. 72, Cong. Globe, 40th Cong., 3d Sess., pt. 2, at 1010 (1869)).

At 1239–40: "Saulsbury of Delaware added his own warning about racial hybrids and the resulting national degeneracy, exemplified by Mexico, to be apprehended from allowing Negroes to vote" (citing, at n. 74, *id.*, app. at 163); "He made a humorous speech suggesting that a constitutional amendment be passed eliminating all distinctions of color" (citing, at n. 75, *id.*, pt. 2, at 1310–11), "and Davis chimed in to suggest that Congress require all races 'to enter into universal miscegenation'" (citing, at 76, *id.*, pt. 2, at 1311).

92. Terry H. Anderson, *The Pursuit of Fairness: A History of Affirmative Action* 10 (New York: Oxford University Press, 2004).
93. Anderson, *The Pursuit of Fairness* 11.
94. Anderson, *The Pursuit of Fairness* 23.
95. Anderson, *The Pursuit of Fairness* 26–27.
96. Anderson, *The Pursuit of Fairness* 31–32.
97. Anderson, *The Pursuit of Fairness* 40.
98. Anderson, *The Pursuit of Fairness* 40.
99. Anderson, *The Pursuit of Fairness* 50.
100. Anderson, *The Pursuit of Fairness* 56.
101. Anderson, *The Pursuit of Fairness* 71.
102. Anderson, *The Pursuit of Fairness* 71.
103. Anderson, *The Pursuit of Fairness* 73.
104. Anderson, *The Pursuit of Fairness* 73.
105. Anderson, *The Pursuit of Fairness* 33.
106. Anderson, *The Pursuit of Fairness* 89.
107. Anderson, *The Pursuit of Fairness* 119.
108. Anderson, *The Pursuit of Fairness* 123.
109. The debate about "affirmative action" is wide-ranging and extensive, and in the main, it has framed an attack against originalists for being inconsistent. See, e.g., Cass R. Sunstein, *Radicals in Robes: Why Extreme Right-Wing Courts Are Wrong for America* 131 (New York: Basic Books, 2005); Jed Rubenfeld, *Affirmative Action,* 107 Yale L.J. 427, 431–432 (1997); Eric Schnapper,

*Affirmative Action and the Legislative History of the Fourteenth Amendment*, 71 Va. L. Rev. 753 (1985); Reva Siegel, *The Supreme Court, 2012 Term—Foreword: Equality Divided*, 127 Harv. L. Rev. 1, 73 n. 371 (2013) (remarking "Justice Scalia's failure to offer any nominally originalist justification in striking down affirmative action"); Stephen A. Siegel, *The Federal Government's Power to Enact Color-Conscious Laws: An Originalist Inquiry*, 92 Nw. U. L. Rev. 477, 481 (1998). For a defense of the originalists, see Michael B. Rappaport, *Originalism and the Colorblind Constitution*, 89 Notre Dame L. Rev. 71, 73 (2013).

110. Anderson, *The Pursuit of Fairness* 56–57.

111. Ackerman, 3 *We the People: The Civil Rights Revolution* 2481 (Kindle ed.).

112. U.S. Commission on Civil Rights, Survey of School Desegregation in the Southern and Border States 1965–1966 1–2 (Feb. 1966).

113. See George Gallup, 3 *The Gallup Poll* 2328 (1972), *cited in* Ackerman, 3 *We the People: The Civil Rights Revolution* 5177 (Kindle ed.).

114. 418 U.S. 717 (1974).

115. Bruce Ackerman describes such a practice in 3 *We the People: The Civil Rights Revolution* 5667 (Kindle ed.).

116. Anderson, *The Pursuit of Fairness* 105.

117. *Griggs v. Duke Power*, 401 U.S. 424 (1971).

118. Anderson, *The Pursuit of Fairness* 158.

119. Anderson, *The Pursuit of Fairness* 157.

120. Anderson, *The Pursuit of Fairness* 158.

121. Anderson, *The Pursuit of Fairness* 159.

122. Anderson, *The Pursuit of Fairness* 502 (Kindle ed.).

123. Anderson, *The Pursuit of Fairness* 2900 (Kindle ed.).

124. Anderson, *The Pursuit of Fairness* 235.

125. *Adarand v. Pena*, 515 U.S. 200 (1995).

126. *Gratz v. Bollinger*, 539 U.S. 244 (2003); *Grutter v. Bollinger*, 539 U.S. 306 (2003); *Fisher v. Univ. of Texas*, 136 S. Ct. 2198 (2016).

127. *Adarand v. Pena*, 515 U.S. 200, 241 (1995) (Thomas, J., concurring in part and concurring in the judgment).

128. Robert P. Jones, Daniel Cox, et al., *How Immigration and Concerns About Cultural Changes Are Shaping the 2016 Election*, PRRI/Brookings, Jun. 23, 2016, *available at* link #35. It is worth noting, however, that there is a pronounced view among many whites that the government has gone too far. See Kathleen Cramer, *The Politics of Resentment: Rural Consciousness in Wisconsin and the Rise of Scott Walker* (Chicago: University of Chicago Press, 2016).

129. *Fisher v. University of Texas at Austin*, 570 U.S. 297, 318 (2013) (Thomas, J., concurring).

130. *Fisher v. University of Texas at Austin*, 570 U.S. 297, 319 (2013) (Thomas, J., concurring).

131. See generally Dorothy Ko, *Cinderella's Sisters: A Revisionist History of Footbinding* (Los Angeles: University of California Press, 2005).

132. *In re Bradwell*, 55 Ill. 535, 540 (1869).

133. See Lewis A. Grossman, *James Coolidge Carter and Mugwump Jurisprudence*, 20 Law & Hist. Rev. 577, 579 (2002) ("legislation contrary to custom...not only futile, but promoted grave mischief").

134. For some, only. Many have a relatively rosy view about slavery. Not that it was good, or just, or fulfilling, or decent, but that it was not perpetual misery. No doubt, the conditions of slaves differed. But as Edward Baptist's *The Half Has Never Been Told* (New York: Basic Books, 2014) makes unavoidably clear, for most slaves, slavery was literally torture.

135. *Cty. of Riverside v. McLaughlin*, 500 U.S. 44, 62 n.1 (1991) (Scalia, J., dissenting) (emphases omitted).

## Chapter Eighteen

1. This position is advanced most forcefully by Ward Farnsworth, *Women Under Reconstruction: The Congressional Understanding*, 94 Nw. U. L. Rev. 1229 (2000). Farnsworth's work is incredibly comprehensive, but, unsurprisingly, it has been resisted. See, e.g., Steven G. Calabresi & Julia T. Rickert, *Originalism and Sex Discrimination*, 90 Tex. L. Rev. 1 (2011); Nina Morais, *Sex Discrimination and the Fourteenth Amendment: Lost History*, 97 Yale L.J. 1153, 1157–1158 (1988) ("Comments made during the debates indicate that some of the framers were not averse to women claiming rights under the Fourteenth Amendment's first section.... Congressmen restricted their negative comments on women's rights to the question of the vote....When all the framers' comments on women are read together, they suggest that women's rights, short of suffrage, were thought to be within the reach of the Fourteenth Amendment"); Jill Elaine Hasday, *Federalism and the Family Reconstructed*, 45 UCLA L. Rev. 1297, 1350 (1998) (concluding from the debates over the application of the Fourteenth Amendment to marriage laws that "the Reconstruction consensus that the federal government had jurisdiction over family law was profound and widespread"); Sandra L. Rierson, *Race and Gender Discrimination: A Historical Case for Equal Treatment Under the Fourteenth Amendment*, 1 Duke J. Gender L. & Pol'y 89, 106 (1994) ("in light of the contemporaneous advances in women's common law property rights through state legislation, it appears likely that, had Congress wanted to exclude women from coverage under Section One and thus deny women the civil rights of citizenship, it would have done so explicitly, as it did in crafting Section Two's denial to women of the right to vote"). For work agreeing with the conclusion Farnsworth reaches, see Reva B. Siegel, *She the People: The Nineteenth Amendment, Sex Equality, Federalism, and the Family*, 115 Harv. L. Rev. 947 (2002); Adam Winkler, *A Revolution Too Soon: Woman Suffragists and the Living Constitution*, 76 NYU L. Rev. 1456 (2001); Ruth Bader Ginsburg, *Sexual Equality Under the Fourteenth and Equal Rights Amendments*, 1979 Wash. U. L.Q. 161, 161 (1979) (arguing that "boldly dynamic

interpretation, departing radically from the original understanding, is required to tie to the fourteenth amendment's equal protection clause a command that government treat men and women as individuals equal in rights, responsibilities, and opportunities"); David H. Gans, *The Unitary Fourteenth Amendment*, 56 Emory L.J. 907, 915 (2007) (citing Farnsworth to conclude that "the Amendment's framers did not intend Section 1 to nullify the plethora of existing state laws that sharply limited the rights and freedoms of married women"); Michael C. Dorf, *Equal Protection Incorporation*, 88 Va. L. Rev. 951 (2002).

2. Calabresi & Rickert, *Originalism and Sex Discrimination* 2 (alteration in original).

3. 43 Cong. Rec. 4174 (1874); Ward Farnsworth, *Women Under Reconstruction: The Congressional Understanding*, 94 Nw. U. L. Rev. 1229, 1235 (2000).

4. 43 Cong. Rec. app. 313 (1874); Farnsworth, *Women Under Reconstruction* 1235.

5. 43 Cong. Rec. app. 358 (1874); Farnsworth, *Women Under Reconstruction* 1236.

6. Bradwell had raised an equality claim in the court below (Point VII), but Judge Lawrence for the Illinois Supreme Court found it had "no pertinency." *In re Bradwell*, 55 Ill. 535, 541 (1869).

7. *Bradwell v. Illinois*, 83 U.S. 130, 139 (1873).

8. *Bradwell v. Illinois*, 83 U.S. 130, 139 (1873).

9. *Bradwell v. Illinois*, 83 U.S. 130, 141 (1873) (Bradley, J., concurring).

10. "The Supreme Court Righting Itself," 16 *The Nation* 280, 281 (Apr. 24, 1873).

11. *Bradwell v. Illinois*, 83 U.S. 130, 132 (1873) (quoting *In re Bradwell*, 55 Ill.535, 539 (1869)).

12. *Goesaert v. Cleary*, 335 U.S. 464, 465 (1948).

13. *Goesaert v. Cleary*, 335 U.S. 464, 467 (1948).

14. The term was added to the bill by Representative Howard Smith (D-VA), apparently as a way to sink the bill. Smith was an opponent of integration; as he commented when he added women to the list of protected classes, "What harm can this do to the condition of the bill?" 110 Cong. Rec. 2577 (1964). The harm was obvious, as there were many (including the many who laughed at Smith as he made the proposed amendment) who were not ready to grant that the law should protect women too. But it is possible that Smith, having resigned himself to the coming passage of the Civil Rights Act, aimed to protect white women who were competing against black women. Smith offered a hypothetical case: "[The employer] will say, 'Well, now, if I hire the colored woman I will not be in any trouble, but if I do not hire the colored woman . . . then the Commission is going to be looking down my throat and want to know why I did not. I may be in a lawsuit.'" 110 Cong. Rec. 2583 (1964).

15. *Reed v. Reed*, 404 U.S. 71, 75 (1971).

16. *Reed v. Reed*, 404 U.S. 71, 75–76 (1971).

17. *Reed v. Reed*, 404 U.S. 71, 76 (1971).

18. *Reed v. Reed*, 404 U.S. 71, 76–77 (1971).

19. Gerald Gunther, *Foreword: In Search of Evolving Doctrine on a Changing Court: A Model for a Newer Equal Protection*, 86 Harv. L. Rev. 1, 34 (1972).

20. This is the rule in Virginia when the election is tied; Va. Code. § 24.2-674. It is the rule in Canada when bids for government contracts are the same amount; Kirsten Smith, "Heads or Tails? Federal Government Contract Awarded by Tossing a Coin," *National Post* (Mar. 7, 2013). Likewise, when a new state is added to the Union, the seniority of senators is determined by a coin flip; United States Senate, *Frequently Asked Questions About a New Congress*, visited Aug. 3, 2017, *available at* link #36. Relatedly, randomness in the selection of jurors was one justification for Akhil Reed Amar's suggestion of random selection of representatives. Akhil Reed Amar, *Note, Choosing Representatives by Lottery Voting*, 93 Yale L.J. 1283, 1287 n. 25 (1984) ("the right to grand and petit juries selected at random from a fair cross section of the community") (quoting 28 U.S.C. § 1861).

21. *Reed* was not the only rational-basis anomaly of the 1971 Supreme Court term. In addition, the Supreme Court struck down a contraceptive regulation from Massachusetts that required a doctor's advice before distributing contraceptives. There too, the Court surprised the bar with its aggressive evaluation of the defense of the statute. Calling this "intensified rationality scrutiny," Professor Gunther speculated that the cases might be the beginning of a new trend, as "the standards the Court applied in these cases seem on their face applicable to a wide range of statutory schemes." Gunther, *Foreword: In Search of Evolving Doctrine on A Changing Court* 33. Later cases confirmed, however, that this was no new trend.

22. Ruth Bader Ginsburg, Gillian Metzger, & Abbe Gluck, *A Conversation with Justice Ruth Bader Ginsburg,* 25 Colum. J. Gender & L. 6, 10–11 (2013).

23. *Frontiero v. Richardson*, 411 U.S. 677, 686–687 (1973) (plurality).

24. *Craig v. Boren*, 429 U.S. 190 (1976).

25. See *Walker v. Hall,* 399 F. Supp. 1304, 1314–1321 (W.D. Okla. 1975) (District Court); Brief for Petitioner at 19–24, *Craig v. Boren*, 429 U.S. 190 (1976) (No. 75-628), 1976 WL 194244.

26. *United States v. Virginia*, 518 U.S. 515, 533 (1996) (citations omitted) (alterations in original).

27. Reva B. Siegel, "Gender and the United States Constitution: Equal Protection, Privacy, and Federalism," in *The Gender of Constitutional Jurisprudence* 317 (Beverley Baines & Ruth Rubio-Marin eds., Cambridge: Cambridge University Press, 2004).

28. Calabresi & Rickert, *Originalism and Sex Discrimination* 11.

29. Calabresi & Rickert, *Originalism and Sex Discrimination* 52.

## Chapter Nineteen

1. For an argument rejecting the ability to "translate" due process to protect intimate liberty without protecting economic liberty, see Alan J. Meese, *Will, Judgment, and Economic Liberty: Mr. Justice Souter and the Mistranslation of the Due Process Clause*, 41 Wm. & Mary L. Rev. 3 (1999), *available at* link #37.

2. Thomas I. Emerson, *Fowler Vincent Harper*, 74 Yale L.J. 601, 602 (1965).

3. *Poe v. Ullman*, 367 U.S. 497, 542 (1961) (Harlan, J., dissenting).

4. *Poe v. Ullman*, 367 U.S. 497, 543 (1961) (Harlan, J., dissenting).

5. *Poe v. Ullman*, 367 U.S. 497, 546 (1961) (Harlan, J., dissenting).

6. *Poe v. Ullman*, 367 U.S. 497, 547 (1961) (Harlan, J., dissenting).

7. *Poe v. Ullman*, 367 U.S. 497, 548 (1961) (Harlan, J., dissenting).

8. *Griswold v. Connecticut*, 381 U.S. 479, 502 (1965) (Harlan, J., concurring in the judgment).

9. Jonathan T. Weisberg, *In Control of Her Own Destiny: Catharine G. Roraback and the Privacy Principle*, 51 Yale L. Rep. 39, 42–43 (2004).

10. *Rust v. Sullivan*, 500 U.S. 173, 173 (1991).

11. See Judith Banister, *China's Changing Population* 147–152 (Stanford, CA: Stanford University Press, 1987); William Lavely & Ronald Freedman, *The Origins of the Chinese Fertility Decline*, 27 Demography 357, 357, 362–365 (1990); Judith Banister and Christina Wu Harbaugh, U.S. Census Bureau, U.S. Dep't of Commerce, *China's Family Planning Program: Inputs and Outcomes* 9–10 (1994).

12. *Roe v. Wade*, 410 U.S. 113, 117–118 (1973).

13. *Roe v. Wade*, 410 U.S. 113, 129 (1973).

14. *Roe v. Wade*, 410 U.S. 113, 152–153 (1973).

15. No one defended an interest related to a "Victorian social concern to discourage illicit sexual conduct." *Roe v. Wade*, 410 U.S. 113, 148 (1973). Likewise, the Court did not credit an absolute interest in regulating abortion at any point in a pregnancy based on an interest in regulating medical procedures. *Roe v. Wade*, 410 U.S. 113, 148–149 (1973).

16. *Roe v. Wade*, 410 U.S. 113, 159 (1973).

17. *Roe v. Wade*, 410 U.S. 113, 163 (1973).

18. See, e.g., *Washington v. Glucksberg*, 521 U.S. 702, 738 (1997) (Souter, J., concurring).

19. Fed. R. Civ. P. 56.

20. Robert H. Bork, *Neutral Principles and Some First Amendment Problems*, 47 Ind. L.J. 1, 6 (1971).

21. See *Doe v. Bolton*, 410 U.S. 179 (1973) (holding that three procedural conditions the state's abortion statutes imposed on women seeking abortion, including requiring that all abortion be performed in a hospital, violated the Fourteenth Amendment); *Planned Parenthood v. Danforth*, 428 U.S. 52 (1976) (striking down certain provisions of the state abortion law that required spousal consent prior to an abortion, imposed a blanket parental consent requirement for minors, and proscribed abortions by saline amniocentesis); *Maher v. Roe*, 432 U.S. 464 (1977) (upholding state regulation limiting state Medicaid benefits for first-trimester abortions to those that are "medically necessary" as applied to indigent women); *Colautti v. Franklin*, 439 U.S. 379 (1979) (holding that provisions of the state's abortion statute directing the physician performing an abortion to determine whether the fetus may be viable and imposing a standard of care to preserve the fetus's life in case of viability are void for vagueness); *Bellotti v. Baird*, 443 U.S. 622 (1979) (striking down state statute requiring parental or judicial consent before an abortion can be performed on an

unmarried minor woman); *Harris v. McRae*, 448 U.S. 297 (1980) (upholding federal statute severely limiting the use of federal funds to reimburse the cost of abortions); *H. L. v. Matheson*, 450 U.S. 398 (1981) (upholding provision requiring parental notification of a minor seeking abortion, as applied to an unemancipated minor girl living with her parents, and making no claim or showing as to maturity or relations with her parents); *Akron v. Akron Ctr. for Reprod. Health*, 462 U.S. 416 (1983) (striking down the provisions of the city ordinance that required all abortions after the first trimester to be performed in hospitals, parental or judicial consent for unmarried minors under the age of fifteen, physicians to counsel patients with respect to their pregnancy and risks associated with abortion, a twenty-four-hour waiting period, and that fetal remains be disposed of in a "humane and sanitary manner"); *Planned Parenthood Assn. v. Ashcroft*, 462 U.S. 476 (1983) (striking down second-trimester hospitalization requirement, while upholding requirements of second physician during abortions performed after viability, pathology report, and parental consent for minors, providing for a judicial bypass); *Thornburgh v. Amer. Coll. of Obstetricians*, 476 U.S. 747 (1986) (invalidating state statute imposing restrictions on abortion, including "informed consent" of the woman, reporting procedures, requirement that a physician performing a post-viability abortion exercise the degree of care needed to preserve the life and health of any unborn child, and the presence of a second physician during an abortion performed when viability is possible without providing for a "medical emergency exception," for impermissibly intimidating women into continuing pregnancies); *Webster v. Reproductive Health Svcs.*, 492 U.S. 490 (1989) (upholding restrictions of the state statute on employees and facilities for the performance or assistance of nontherapeutic abortions); *Rust v. Sullivan*, 500 U.S. 173 (1991) (upholding federal regulations prohibiting the use federal funds appropriated under Title X for family-planning services in programs where abortion is a method of family planning).

22. Republican Nat'l Convention, Republican Party Platform of 1980, *available at* link #38.

23. Justices Scalia and Thomas were fairly obvious, given the nature of their jurisprudential commitments. The uncertainty was about Justices Kennedy, O'Connor, and Souter.

Justice Kennedy indicated directly that he had no "undisclosed intention, or fixed view" on *Roe*. Nomination of Anthony M. Kennedy to be Associate Justice of the Supreme Court of the United States: Hearings Before the Comm. on the Judiciary, 100th Cong. 90 (1987). But the president of the National Organization for Women, Molly Yard, argued that the record suggested he had. Nomination of Anthony M. Kennedy to be Associate Justice of the Supreme Court of the United States: Hearings Before the Comm. on the Judiciary, 100th Cong. 374 (1987) (testimony of Molly Yard, Pres., National Organization for Women) ("In light of his opinion in *Beller v. Middendorf*, the support of his confirmation by anti-abortion leader Helms and the now wide acceptance by right-to-life leaders that he is one of 'theirs,' we have serious question whether Kennedy would uphold a woman's right to privacy in birth control and abortion"). Kennedy had certainly joined earlier opinions that signaled *Roe* would be revised. See, e.g., *Webster v. Reproductive Health Servs.*, 492 U.S. 490, 518–521 (1989) (Rehnquist, joined by White and Kennedy) ("To the extent indicated in our opinion, we would modify and narrow *Roe* and succeeding cases").

Justice O'Connor had indicated that to her, as a personal matter, abortion was "offensive [and] repugnant." Nomination of Sandra Day O'Connor of Arizona to serve as an Associate Justice of the Supreme Court of the United States: Hearings Before the Comm. on the Judiciary, 97th Cong., 125 (1981) (statement of Justice O'Connor in response to question of Senator Denton on how she feels about the offensiveness of abortion), but she refused to signal her position on *Roe* in her hearings. Nomination of Sandra Day O'Connor of Arizona to serve as an Associate Justice of the Supreme Court of the United States: Hearings Before the Comm. on the Judiciary, 97th Cong., 107–108 (1981). She too, however, had signaled a willingness to "reexamine *Roe*." *Webster v. Reproductive Health Servs.*, 492 U.S. 490, 525–526 (1989) (O'Connor, J., concurring in part and concurring in the judgment).

Justice Souter had, through his writings, "reveal[ed] real empathy for those who are morally opposed to abortion," Senator Metzenbaum noted. Moreover, as Attorney General of New Hampshire, Souter had filed a brief that had argued, "It is not accurate to say that the moral feelings of other individuals and groups, both public and private, may not constitutionally interfere with a woman's otherwise unrestricted right to decide to have an abortion." Nomination of David H. Souter to be Associate Justice of the Supreme Court of the United States: Hearings Before the Comm. on the Judiciary, 101st Cong. 115–116 (1990) (statement of Senator Metzenbaum). These facts, and others, led at least Kate Michelman, the executive director of the National Abortion Rights Action League, to conclude, "Nothing in Judge Souter's record or his testimony has convinced us that he, indeed, recognizes a fundamental right to privacy, including the right to choose." Nomination of David H. Souter to be Associate Justice of the Supreme Court of the United States: Hearings Before the Comm. on the Judiciary, 101st Cong. 363 (1990).

24. *Planned Parenthood v. Casey*, 505 U.S. 833, 836 (1992).
25. *Planned Parenthood v. Casey*, 505 U.S. 833, 865 (1992).
26. *Planned Parenthood v. Casey*, 505 U.S. 833, 865 (1992).
27. *Planned Parenthood v. Casey*, 505 U.S. 833, 868 (1992).

## Chapter Twenty

1. *Boutilier v. INS.*, 387 U.S. 118, 120 (1967).
2. *Boutilier v. INS.*, 387 U.S. 118, 122 (1967).

3. Am. Psychiatric Ass'n, *Diagnostic and Statistical Manual of Mental Disorders* 39 (Washington, DC: APA, 1952).

4. *Boutilier v. INS.*, 387 U.S. 118, 127 (1967) (Douglas, J., dissenting) (citations omitted).

5. See Ronald Bayer, *Homosexuality and American Psychiatry* 136–137 (Princeton, NJ: Princeton University Press, 1981).

6. Lawrence Lessig, *Understanding Changed Readings: Fidelity and Theory*, 47 Stan. L. Rev. 395, 418 (1995) (quoting 56 Interpreter Releases 387, 398 (1979)).

7. Lessig, *Understanding Changed* Readings 418.

8. See *Lesbian/Gay Freedom Day Comm., Inc. v. United States Immigration & Naturalization Serv.*, 541 F. Supp. 569 (N.D. Cal. 1982).

9. Justice White is reported to have had a very bad practice of racing his clerks to complete opinions—between him and his clerk, the one who finished first got his or her opinion published. See Jeffrey Rosen, *The Next Justice: How Not to Replace Byron White*, New Republic 24 (Apr. 12, 1993). *Bowers* is said to be one of those opinions.

10. *Bowers v. Hardwick*, 478 U.S. 186, 194 (1986).

11. "To hold that the act of homosexual sodomy is somehow protected as a fundamental right would be to cast aside millennia of moral teaching." *Bowers v. Hardwick*, 478 U.S. 186, 197 (1986) (Burger, C.J., concurring).

12. Gallup, Inc., Gay and Lesbian Rights, *available at* link #39.

13. *Romer v. Evans*, 517 U.S. 620, 624 (1996).

14. Lee Ellis, "Left- and Mixed-Handedness and Criminality: Explanations for a Probable Relationship," in 67 *Left-Handedness: Behavioral Implications and Anomalies* 489 (Stanley Coren ed., New York: Elsevier, 1990).

15. Warren J. Blumenfeld, *Treatment of Left-Handedness Offers a Window into LGBTQ Discrimination*, LGBTQ Nation (Aug. 7, 2016), *available at* link #40.

16. "Characteristics: Left in a Right-Handed World," 93 *Time* 1 (Jan. 10, 1969), *available at* link #41.

17. See Luke Mastin, *History of Handedness*, Right Left, Right Wrong, *available at* link #42; see also Elaine Fowler Costas, *The Left-Handed: "Their Sinister" History*, Education Resources Information Center, Paper No. 399519 (1996), *available at* link #43.

18. John J. Sciortino, *Sinistral Legal Studies*, 44 Syracuse L. Rev. 1103, 1117–1118 (1993). See also Adrian E. Flatt, *Is Being Left-Handed a Handicap? The Short and Useless Answer is "Yes and No,"* 21 Baylor Univ. Med. Ctr. Proceedings 304 (2008).

19. *Romer v. Evans*, 517 U.S. 620, 623 (1996).

20. *Romer v. Evans*, 517 U.S. 620, 633 (1996).

21. *Romer v. Evans*, 517 U.S. 620, 636 (1996).

22. *Romer v. Evans*, 517 U.S. 620, 636 (1996) (Scalia, J., dissenting).

23. *Bowers v. Hardwick,* 478 U.S. 186 (1986).

24. *Romer v. Evans*, 517 U.S. 620, 635 (1996).

25. *Lawrence v. Texas*, 539 U.S. 558, 571 (2003).

26. *Lawrence v. Texas*, 539 U.S. 558, 602–603 (2003) (Scalia, J., dissenting) (citations omitted).

27. *Obergefell v. Hodges*, 135 S. Ct. 2584, 2593 (2015).

28. *Obergefell v. Hodges*, 135 S. Ct. 2584, 2602 (2015).

29. *Obergefell v. Hodges*, 135 S. Ct. 2584, 2598 (2015).

30. *Obergefell v. Hodges*, 135 S. Ct. 2584, 2602 (2015).

31. *Obergefell v. Hodges*, 135 S. Ct. 2584, 2618 (2015) (Roberts, C.J., dissenting).

32. *Obergefell v. Hodges*, 135 S. Ct. 2584, 2602 (2015).

33. *Obergefell v. Hodges*, 135 S. Ct. 2584, 2603 (2015).

34. Richard A. Posner, *Sex and Reason* (Cambridge, MA: Harvard University Press, 1992).

35. *Hively v. Ivy Tech Cmty. Coll. of Indiana*, 853 F.3d 339, 355 (7th Cir. 2017) (emphasis added).

36. *Hively v. Ivy Tech. Cmty. Coll. of Indiana*, 853 F.3d 339, 357 (7th Cir. 2017).

37. *United States v. Virginia*, 518 U.S. 515, 566–567 (1996) (Scalia, J., dissenting) (emphasis added).

38. *Synar v. United States*, 626 F. Supp. 1374, 1398 (D.D.C.).

## Chapter Twenty-One

1. Beginning with Hercules in *Hard Cases,* 88 Harv. L. Rev. 1057, 1083 (1975), and continuing throughout his work.

2. Donald Davidson, *On the Very Idea of a Conceptual Scheme*, 47 Proceedings and Addresses of the American Philosophical Association 5, 19 (1973).

3. See, e.g., Jack M. Balkin, *Living Originalism* (Cambridge, MA: The Belknap Press of Harvard University Press, 2011); Randy Barnett, *Restoring the Lost Constitution: The Presumption of Liberty* (Princeton, NJ: Princeton University Press, 2003); David P. Currie, *The Constitution in the Supreme Court: The First Hundred Years, 1789–1888* 429 (Chicago: University of Chicago Press, 1985); David P. Currie, *The Constitution in the Supreme Court: The Second Century, 1888–1986* 101 (Chicago: University of Chicago Press, 1990); Richard A. Epstein, *The Classical Liberal Constitution: The Uncertain Quest for Limited Government* (Cambridge, MA: Harvard University Press, 2014); Barry Friedman, *The Will of the People: How Public Opinion Has Influenced the Supreme Court and Shaped the Meaning of the Constitution* 5 (New York: Farrar, Straus and Giroux, 2009); Keith E. Whittington, *Constitutional Construction: Divided Powers and Constitutional Meaning* (Cambridge, MA: Harvard University Press, 1999).

4. Bruce Ackerman, 2 *We the People: Transformations* 5 (Cambridge, MA: The Belknap Press of Harvard University Press, 1998). See also Bruce Ackerman, 1 *We the People: Foundations* ch. 2 (Cambridge, MA: The Belknap Press of Harvard University Press, 1991).

5. Ackerman, 1 *We the People: Foundations* 1622–1679 (Kindle ed.).

6. Ackerman identifies three constitutional moments, each of which suffers from a fundamental process-flaw. None of them, he argues, were ratified consistent

with the rules then laid down. All of them innovated on the process of adoption, gaining democratic legitimacy from the sustained attention each struggle drew from a democratic public.

The Founding failed according to the then-existing rules, because, as described in Chapter 1, the then-existing federal Constitution required unanimous consent by state legislatures, but instead the Constitution was ratified by three-fourths of state conventions. Likewise, the state constitutions themselves—which were effectively amended by the Constitution—had many different modes for their own amendment. Those modes were not followed.

The Civil War Amendments failed the then-existing rules, both because of the inconsistent manner that Congress used for recognizing which "states" counted for purposes of proposing amendments and because of Congress's essentially forcing southern states to adopt the Fourteenth Amendment before they could be readmitted to Congress.

The New Deal, Ackerman believes, amended the Constitution outside the rules of Article V as well—obviously so, if it was an amendment, since it produced no text added to the Constitution and never passed through ratification by the states.

While Ackerman has elaborated this account in many contexts, the most comprehensive is in volume 2 of *We the People: Transformations*.

7. Michael McConnell, *The Forgotten Constitutional Moment*, 11 Constitutional Commentary 115 (1994).

8. Ackerman, 2 *We the People: Transformations* 474 n. 126.

9. Ackerman, 2 *We the People: Transformations* 26.

10. Ackerman, 2 *We the People: Transformations* 26.

11. Bruce Ackerman, 3 *We the People: The Civil Rights Revolution* 158 (Cambridge, MA: Belknap Press of Harvard University Press, 2014) (Kindle ed.).

12. The idea is brought to life in Richard Tuck, *The Sleeping Sovereign: The Invention of Modern Democracy* (Cambridge, UK: Cambridge University Press, 2016).

13. Ackerman wants to formalize this crafting into a five-step process— "constitutional impasse → electoral mandate → challenge to dissenting institutions → switch in time → consolidating election." This is helpful for structuring the story, but I don't read it as ontological to our tradition. The simpler understanding involves just the conditions necessary to convince the public that there needs to be a constitutional "time-out": a moment to reset the field and begin again. Or alternatively, the conditions necessary to summon Carl Schmitt's sovereign—the entity that "decides on the exception." See Ackerman, 2 *We the People: Transformations* 20. On Schmitt, see Carl Schmitt, *Political Theology: Four Chapters on the Concept of Sovereignty*, trans. George Schwab. (Chicago and London: The University of Chicago Press, 2005).

14. See Paul J. Weber & Barbara A. Perry, *Unfounded Fears* (Santa Barbara, CA: Praeger, 1989), 56–60; Sanford Levinson, *Our Undemocratic Constitution: Where the Constitution Goes Wrong (And How We the People Can Correct It)* 174 (New

York: Oxford University Press, 2008) ("Most liberals these days appear to be fully Madisonian in being close to terrified of the passions of their fellow citizens. They envision a runaway convention that would tear up the most admirable parts of the Constitution").

15. Ackerman insists that *Coleman v. Miller,* 307 U.S. 433 (1939), precludes the Court from reviewing the amendment process. Ackerman, 2 *We the People: Transformations* 117. I agree with Michael Stern that this reads *Coleman* too broadly. While *Coleman* applied the political question doctrine to the facts of that case, only four justices suggested the doctrine would apply in all cases. See Michael Stern, Coleman v. Miller *and the Political Question Doctrine,* Point of Order (Sept. 16, 2016), *available at* link #44. Deference to Congress, as Stern argues, quoting Walter Dellinger, is particularly inapt for questions involving a convention. *Id.,* citing *The Legitimacy of Constitutional Change: Rethinking the Amendment Process,* 97 Harv. L. Rev. 386, 399 (1983) (applying the political question doctrine "squarely contrary to the deliberate conferral of amendment-proposing power on a national convention provided as an *alternative* to Congress"). In my view, nothing in *Coleman* would preclude the Court from finding a referral expressly contrary to the express terms of Article V invalid, even if it refused to opine on implicit terms within Article V.

16. Ackerman, 2 *We the People: Transformations* 490–491 n. 1.

17. Ackerman, 2 *We the People: Transformations* 111.

18. E. L. Godkin, "The Fallacy of the Veto," *The Nation* (March 1, 1866).

19. This is Ulrich Preuss's powerful point: the "retroactive ascription is the core of the juristic construction of the relationship between the constituent power and the constitution." Ulrich Preuss, *The Implications of "Eternity Clauses": The German Experience,* 44 Isr. L. Rev. 429, 444 (2011). See also Mark V. Tushnet, *Peasants with Pitchforks, and Toilers with Twitter,* 13 iCon 639, 647 (2015).

20. William E. Leuchtenburg, *When the People Spoke, What Did They Say?: The Election of 1936 and the Ackerman Thesis,* 108 Yale L.J. 2077, 2111 (1999). Leuchtenburg's article surveys a wide range of sources to understand the public's opinion.

21. Cushman's review of public opinion polls taken at the birth of scientific polling reveals a much more conservative public, both constitutionally and politically. There was no overwhelming support for amending the Constitution—reinforcing Leuchtenburg's conclusion that the people did not think they were amending the Constitution—even though there was support for Congress having more regulatory power than it did at the time (March 1937). Barry Cushman, *Mr. Dooley and Mr. Gallup: Public Opinion and Constitutional Change in the 1930s,* 50 Buffalo Law Rev. 7, 37 (2002) (58 to 42 percent). Even that support was fleeting—by August of the same year, 48 percent of people with an opinion supported "centralizing power in Washington." *Id.* 39. As Cushman notes, though the public supported much of what the New Deal did, the things it supported most did not need much or any constitutional revision. The greatest support was for pensions, though the Court

found no constitutional problem in the government providing pensions. The public did support "the modification of some discrete areas" of constitutional law, but "the data would not appear to support the claim that they demanded a revolution in constitutional law." *Id.* at 66. Maybe even more surprising is that while 50 percent of respondents in March 1937 called themselves "Democrats," 52 percent of respondents called themselves "conservatives," while 46 percent called themselves "liberal." *Id.* at 74. This reflects the non-ideological character of political parties during much of the twentieth century (and earlier). It weakens support for the conclusion that the public was demanding fundamental constitutional change in the elections of 1932, 1934, and 1936.

22. Ackerman, 2 *We the People: Transformations* 72 (Kindle ed.).
23. Ackerman, 3 *We the People: The Civil Rights Revolution* 183 (Kindle ed.).
24. Ackerman, 3 *We the People: The Civil Rights Revolution* 6647 (Kindle ed.).
25. Ackerman, 3 *We the People: The Civil Rights Revolution* 507 (Kindle ed.).
26. *Justice Kagan on Textualism's Success,* Prawfs Blog (Dec. 7, 2015), *available at* link #45.

## Chapter Twenty-Two

1. *County of Riverside v. McLaughlin,* 500 U.S. 44, 62 n.1 (1991) (Scalia, J., dissenting).
2. Lawrence Lessig, *The Regulation of Social Meaning,* 62 U. Chi. L. Rev. 943 (1995). Work on social meaning has been developed by many, Cass Sunstein most prominently. See Cass R. Sunstein, *Social Norms and Social Roles,* 96 Colum. L. Rev. 903 (1996). See also Eric A. Posner, *Law, Economics, and Inefficient Norms,* 144 U. Pa. L. Rev. 1697 (1996), Eric A. Posner, *Standards, Rules, and Social Norms,* 21 Harv. J. L. & Pub. Pol'y 101 (1997), and Eric A. Posner, *Symbols, Signals, and Social Norms in Politics and the Law,* 27 J. Legal Stud. 765 (1998); Richard H. McAdams, *The Origin, Development, and Regulation of Norms,* 96 Mich. L. Rev. 338 (1997); Robert E. Scott, *The Limits of Behavioral Theories of Law and Social Norms,* 86 Va. L. Rev. 1603 (2000); Ann E. Carlson, *Recycling Norms,* 89 Calif. L. Rev. 1231 (2001).

   "Expressive theories" of the law more generally are discussed by Cass R. Sunstein, *On the Expressive Function of Law,* 144 U. Pa. L. Rev. 2021 (1996); William Stuntz, *The Pathological Politics of Criminal Law,* 100 Mich. L. Rev. 505 (2001); Dan M. Kahan, *The Secret Ambition of Deterrence,* 113 Harv. L. Rev. 413 (1999); Dan M. Kahan, *Social Influence, Social Meaning, and Deterrence,* 83 Va. L. Rev. 349 (1997); Dan M. Kahan, *What Do Alternative Sanctions Mean?,* 63 U. Chi. L. Rev. 591 (1996); Bernard E. Harcourt, *After the "Social Meaning Turn": Implications for Research Design and Methods of Proof in Contemporary Criminal Law Policy Analysis,* 34 Law & Soc'y Rev. 179 (2000).

   For particular applications, see as follows:

   Criminal law: Kahan, *Social Influence, Social Meaning, and Deterrence*; Kahan, *What Do Alternative Sanctions Mean?*; Tracey Meares, *The Coming Crisis of Criminal Procedure,* 27 Ann. Rev. Crim. Proc. 1153 (1998).

Expert testimony: Scott Brewer, *Scientific Expert Testimony and Intellectual Due Process*, 107 Yale L.J. 1535 (1998).

Institutional racism: Ian F. Haney López, *Institutional Racism: Judicial Conduct and a New Theory of Racial Discrimination*, 109 Yale L. J. 1717 (2000).

Marriage: Elizabeth S. Scott, *Social Norms and the Legal Regulation of Marriage*, 86 Va. L. Rev. 1901 (2000); Katharine B. Silbaugh, *Marriage Contracts and the Family Economy*, 93 Nw. U. L. Rev. 65 (1998–1999).

Nonprofit accountability: James J. Fishman, *Improving Charitable Accountability*, 62 Md. L. Rev. 218 (2003).

Internet law: Julie E. Cohen, *Copyright and the Jurisprudence of Self-Help*, 13 Berkeley Tech. L.J. 1089 (1998); Julie E. Cohen, *Lochner in Cyberspace: The New Economic Orthodoxy of Rights Management*, 97 Mich. L. Rev. 462 (1998); Michael J. Madison, *Legal-Ware: Contract and Copyright in the Digital Age*, 67 Fordham L. Rev. 1025 (1998).

Sex crimes: Katharine K. Baker, *Sex, Rape, and Shame*, 79 B.U. L. Rev. 663 (1999).
Public health law: Mark A. Hall, *Law, Medicine, and Trust*, 55 Stan. L. Rev. 463 (2002); Lawrence O. Gostin, Scott Burris, & Zita Lazzarini, *The Law and the Public's Health: A Study of Infectious Disease Law in the United States*, 99 Colum. L. Rev. 59 (1999).

3. *Obergefell v. Hodges*, 135 S.Ct. 2584, 2612 (2015).
4. *Obergefell v. Hodges*, 135 S.Ct. 2584, 2626 (2015).
5. Bruce Ackerman, 3 *We the People: The Civil Rights Revolution* 2253–2254 (Cambridge, MA: Belknap Press of Harvard University Press, 2014) (Kindle ed.).
6. *U.S. v. Virginia*, 518 U.S. 515, 567 (1996) (Scalia, J., dissenting). Justice Black had expressed a similar sentiment in *Harper v. Virginia*, 383 U.S. 663, 678 (1966) (Black, J., dissenting):

> When a "political theory" embodied in our Constitution becomes outdated, it seems to me that a majority of the nine members of this Court are not only without constitutional power but are far less qualified to choose a new constitutional political theory than the people of this country proceeding in the manner provided by Article V.

7. Steven G. Calabresi & Julia T. Rickert, *Originalism and Sex Discrimination,* 90 Tex. L. Rev. 1 (2011).
8. See, e.g., James Fishkin, *Democracy When the People Are Thinking: Revitalizing Our Politics Through Public Deliberation* (Oxford: Oxford University Press, 2018).
9. Mark R. Daniels, Robert Darcy, & Joseph W. Westphal, *The ERA Won. At Least in the Opinion Polls,* 15 American Political Science Association 578, 579 (Autumn 1982), *available at* link #46.
10. *Regents of the University of California v. Bakke*, 438 U.S. 265 (1978).
11. *Planned Parenthood v. Casey*, 505 U.S. 833, 865–866 (1992).
12. Michael J. Klarman, *From Jim Crow to Civil Rights: The Supreme Court and the Struggle for Racial Equality* 449 (New York: Oxford University Press, 2004).
13. Calabresi & Rickert, *Originalism and Sex Discrimination* 1.

14. See Richard Fallon, *Law and Legitimacy in the Supreme Court* (Cambridge, MA: Harvard University Press, 2018), Richard Fallon, *The Statutory Interpretation Muddle* (working paper, Harvard Law School, 2018).

## Conclusion

1. The injustices are cataloged with emphasis by Ian Millhiser in *Injustices: The Supreme Court's History of Comforting the Comfortable and Afflicting the Afflicted* (New York: Nation Books, 2015).

# INDEX

*Figures and notes are indicated by "f" and "n" following page numbers.*

interracial sex, prohibition against,
361–363, 375, 453, 538n83,
538–540n91
interstate commerce. *See* commerce clause
Interstate Commerce Commission, 83
*Interstate Commerce Commission v. Goodrich
Transit Co.* (1912), 82, 486n20
intertextuality of constitutional
interpretation, 46
intrastate commerce, 82
    federal government without power to
        regulate unless substantial
        relationship to interstate
        commerce, 182–191
Iredell, James, 198, 199
Irons, Peter, 86–88

Jackson, Andrew, 100, 290
Jackson, Robert H., 169–171,
    172, 279, 280, 351,
    431, 452
Japanese Americans, internment of,
    358, 537n68
Jaworski, Leon, 247
Jefferson, Thomas
    banking power and, 37
    construing Constitution in spirit of
        the Framers, 60
    Declaration of Independence and, 13
    election (1800) and Burr as running
        mate, 20–24
    liberalism and, 497n38
    *Marbury* (1803) and, 27, 28, 33,
        472n15, 473n19
    *Notes on the State of Virginia*, 108
    in opposition to Federalist Marshall,
        35
    as president, 20
    on right of people to alter or abolish
        the constitution, 14, 229
    on social decline as danger to United
        States, 103

as vice president, 21
    on yeoman farmer as essential
        component of democracy,
        104–106, 108
Jeffersonian Republicans, 103–105,
    108, 112
Jews. *See* anti-Semitism
Jim Crow laws, 349, 374, 431. *See also*
    segregation
Johnson, Andrew, 321, 324, 435
Johnson, Calvin, 11
Johnson, Lyndon Baines, 185, 364,
    366, 369
*Jones & Laughlin Steel Co.; NLRB v.*
    (1937), 138–139, *139*, 162–163,
    439, 505n4, 508n4
Jordan, Clarence: *Cotton Patch Version of
    Luke and Acts*, 51–52, 53
judge's role. *See also* fidelity to role
    in keeping with ordinary person
        standard, 270
    prominence in Anglo-American legal
        tradition, 67
    similarity to linguistic translator,
        57–63
judicial activism, 153, 163, 267, 278,
    393
judicial branch, 25–26, 33
judicial review, 473–474n25
    *Marbury* (1803) and, 25–27, 30–31,
        33, 475n28
Judiciary Act of 1789, 30–34, 474n26,
    475n28
Judiciary Act of 1801, 22–23, 24, 34,
    472n15, 476n38
Judiciary Act of 1802, 24, 476n38
jurisdiction, 29–32, 474n26, 478n57,
    538n83
    Alien Tort Statute and, 229
    Fugitive Slave Law and, 282
    *habeas corpus* and, 322
jury duty, 288–289